D0026693

SECOND EDITION

Marketing Research

Alvin C. Burns
Louisiana State University

Ronald F. Bush
University of West Florida

PRENTICE HALL
Upper Saddle River, New Jersey 07458

I dedicate this book to all my former students who taught me something new every day we shared, and to all my present students who continue to teach me new things daily.

A.C.B.
Baton Rouge, Louisiana

I dedicate this book to the memory of my lifelong friend, John B. Strubel III. A student of marketing and a successful practitioner, John lived his life in a way that serves as a model for us all.

R.F.B.
Pensacola, Florida

Acquisitions Editor: Whitney Blake
Assistant Editor: John Larkin
Editorial Assistant: Rachel Falk
Vice President/Editorial Director: James Boyd
Marketing Manager: John Chillingworth
Marketing Director: Brian Kibby
Production Editor: Aileen Mason
Production Coordinator: Carol Samet
Managing Editor: Dee Josephson
Associate Managing Editor: Linda DeLorenzo
Manufacturing Supervisor: Arnold Vila
Manufacturing Manager: Vincent Scelta
Manufacturing Buyer: Kenneth J. Clinton
Design Manager: Pat Smythe
Interior Design: Robert Freese
Cover Design: Jill Little
Illustrator (Interior): Andrew Barnes/Rainbow Graphics, LLC
Composition: Rainbow Graphics, Inc.
Cover Digital Art: Fumio Kurosaki/IMA USA, Inc.

Credits and acknowledgments for materials borrowed from other sources and reproduced, with permission, in this textbook appear on page C1.

Library of Congress Cataloging-in-Publication Data
Burns, Alvin C.
Marketing research / Alvin C. Burns and Ronald F. Bush. — 2nd ed.
p. cm.
Includes bibliographical references (p.) and index.

ISBN 0-13-896606-0

1. Marketing research. I. Bush, Ronald F.
HF5415.2.B779 1998
658.8′3—dc21 97-36415
CIP

Prentice-Hall International (UK) Limited, London
Prentice-Hall of Australia Pty. Limited, Sydney
Prentice-Hall Canada, Inc., Toronto
Prentice-Hall Hispanoamericana, S.A., Mexico
Prentice-Hall of India Private Limited, New Delhi
Prentice-Hall of Japan, Inc., Tokyo
Simon & Schuster Asia Pte. Ltd., Singapore
Editora Prentice-Hall do Brasil, Ltda., Rio de Janeiro

Printed in the United States of America

10 9 8 7 6 5 4 3 2 1

Contents

CHAPTER 8 Observation, Focus Groups, and Other Qualitative Methods 206

CHAPTER 9 Survey Data Collection Methods 242

CHAPTER 10 Measurement in Marketing Research 282

CHAPTER 13 Determining the Size of a Sample 390

CHAPTER 14 Data Collection in the Field, Nonresponse Error, and Questionnaire Screening 420

Preface

We are pleased to release the second edition of *Marketing Research.* We were very encouraged with the reception of the first edition of our book in the marketplace. We received many positive comments as well as good reviews from professors of marketing research, both adopters and nonadopters. Furthermore, we have the advantage of having input from many practitioners in the marketing research industry. Many of their suggestions are identified throughout the book. A formal review, sponsored by Prentice Hall, indicated that the first edition had many strengths, and we have wisely chosen to bolster these strengths and, at the same time, bring the book up to date and to provide even more new insights that we believe will enhance student learning of marketing research.

PURPOSE AND INTENDED AUDIENCE

Of the many positive comments we received about the first edition, we were constantly reminded that our product met its intended purpose and audience. Our purpose, once again, is for *Marketing Research* to serve as an *introduction* to the field of marketing research. It is designed for professors whose major objectives are to educate students on the purposes, procedures, and applications of marketing research as well as to introduce them to the various types of firms in the marketing research industry. The book places much emphasis on learning fundamental marketing research concepts. It is written at a basic level and is not intended for professors who wish to emphasize advanced data analysis.

PHILOSOPHY

For many years, authors of marketing research texts proclaimed that their intent was to help students become "users," as opposed to "doers," of marketing research. We broke from this tradition with our first edition by stating that in addition to emphasizing how a "user" should evaluate a research project, we believe a research course today should also help students become "doers" of research. Why? Because the age of information has brought about a significant change in the ability of managers to access information. A few years ago, even secondary information gathering was the domain of specialists. Today, given the Internet and the myriad of online and CD-ROM-based information services (e.g., Lexis-Nexis™, Dow Jones News/Retrieval Service™, DataStar™, DataTimes EyeQ™, Dialog™, FirstSearch™, NewsNet™, etc.), everyone has the ability to search millions of records for pertinent research information.

Primary data collection and analysis have likewise experienced dramatic change. Data collection firms and sampling firms make the collection of data fast and reasonably simple. CATI programs make in-house data collection much easier. New-generation software, such as SPSS® for Windows®, make data analysis and report writing available to managers with the time and inclination to learn them. In short, marketing research is no longer just for specialists. As these developments continue, we expect to see more in-house research. More people will become "doers" as well as "users."

What have we done to make this a book for "users" and "doers"? We keep our process approach; our 11-step marketing research process we used in the first edition. Beginning in chapter 3, we discuss marketing research as a step-by-step process, and we refer to this process continually as students make their way through the text. With each new chapter, we highlight the appropriate section of the research process so that students always know where they are in terms of the overall research process. Students are reminded that each section of the research process is linked to some previous section.

What else have we done to make this a book for "doers"? We devote two chapters, 6 and 7, to information acquisition. We point out some of the innovations taking place in today's research environment. Chapter 6 introduces students to many of the changes taking place in the availability of secondary data. The Internet and other information services are updated. Chapter 7 illustrates many of the syndicated information services available. The latest developments in this competitive area are highlighted. Second, we devote a complete chapter to one of the fastest growing areas of research, qualitative research. Third, we give students special applications ideas by providing marketing research insights throughout the book. Many of these give students practical insights and provide example "how tos" on many of the steps of the research process. Fourth, we provide students with insights on international and ethical issues in research. Finally, but important, we teach students how to use SPSS. Our CD-ROM-based SPSS Student Assistant provides much of the instructional support needed to master SPSS. Students completing a course using our book should know the basics of data analysis and reporting. In the hands of a good marketing research professor, we believe we have developed a powerful teaching tool with *Marketing Research*—and its instructional support ancillaries.

STRENGTHS RETAINED FROM THE FIRST EDITION

Of course, as always, we listen to our students as they are the true consumers that we must satisfy. All of our improvements have been geared to making *Marketing Research* an enjoyable and insightful educational experience. Accordingly, this edition retains many of the features that made the first edition successful. You will not find a dramatic departure from the first edition. We strongly believe the old adage: "If it ain't broke, don't fix it!" In *Marketing Research* you will find the following.

A Managerial Orientation. We wrote *Marketing Research* using a managerial orientation. We devote an entire chapter, chapter 4, to the importance of management's properly defining the research problem. We present marketing research as a useful source of information but one that has its own costs. Students are taught that managers must weigh the benefits of more information with the costs of obtaining that information. Throughout the text, a decision-making approach is used. Students are also taught the many trade-offs involved in research that managers constantly make; the use of a probability sample versus a nonprobability sample; the effects of under-sampling, and so on.

Real-World Input. Again, we have relied on our many friends in the research industry. These individuals, many leaders of large research firms and industry leaders in their own right, have given us special insight, which we have included in this edition. Almost every chapter has been reviewed by a research professional. *Marketing Research* passes their up-to-date knowledge and special insights along to students of marketing research.

Global Applications. We noted in the first edition that the "business world" has become the "world's business." Global business has impacted the marketing research industry. Revenues from global research have increased dramatically as firms use more and more research to help them make decisions for distant markets. Our globe icon is used throughout the text to note specific attention to the international aspects of marketing research.

Ethical Issues. This book points out where ethical issues occur in the conduct of marketing research. Our ethics icon is used throughout the text to call the student's attention to an ethical issue. Several cases are also devoted to ethical issues.

Marginal Comments. Students will find comments in the margins. We do this to repeat important points and to serve as effective study guides.

Bold Key Terms. We set key terms in bold print and define them at that point. We list all key terms at the end of the chapters in order to serve as a review and study guide.

Review Questions, Applications, Exercises, and Cases. Each chapter contains a section devoted to review questions and applications and short cases. These materials are provided to enrich the student's learning of marketing research. Some of the questions require answers that may be taken directly from the text material. Such questions serve to organize and reinforce what the student has just read. Other questions or applications require the students to synthesize the chapter material with other business course material. Finally, there are applications that require extensive work outside of class; for instance, talking with local business firms, looking up additional library material, or working with SPSS. Professors can assign different questions/applications to suit their particular course objectives. For example, if a class project is not used in the course, there is adequate supplementary material at the end of the chapters.

Data Sets. We provide four real-world data sets that are written onto students' hard disk drives when they install the SPSS Student Assistant using the CD-ROM that accompanies the textbook. These data sets are provided to aid the students in running various analyses using SPSS.

We use the SPSS icon to alert students to SPSS-related material in the textbook.

NEW STRENGTHS OF THE SECOND EDITION

SPSS Student Assistant. A separate Windows program on a CD-ROM has been provided with this textbook. The program is a stand-alone tutorial for SPSS for Windows. Students are instructed to use the SPSS Student Assistant by side notes in the textbook. The SPSS Student Assistant shows the cursor movements and resulting SPSS operations captured as movies by Lotus ScreenCam™ software. At the end of their review of each SPSS Student Assistant movie, there is an accompanying test of the basic concepts involved with that menu item.

SPSS Student Version. Through a special arrangement with SPSS, we are pleased to provide with each purchase of *Marketing Research,* 2e, SPSS Student Version. SPSS Student Version is a very powerful software package. It allows for the analysis of up to 50 variables and 1,500 cases. It contains all of the statistical techniques covered in this textbook plus many more. Prentice Hall has an exclusive agreement with SPSS to provide this service.

SPSS for Windows. The integration of SPSS for Windows is an important part of our book. With this edition, we use SPSS Version 7.5. The improvements in SPSS have made our package stronger because the output and graphing aspects of SPSS are much better. *Note:* The text is compatible with earlier versions of SPSS. However, keystroke instructions (see next section) may vary between versions.

SPSS Keystroke Instructions. *Marketing Research* goes a step beyond the first edition by providing SPSS keystroke instructions for students on critical applications. With all the statistical analyses covered in the textbook, we indicate the cursor actions and keystrokes necessary to execute them with SPSS. This "shorthand" approach complements our SPSS Student Assistant movies as it may not always be convenient for students to review the movies when they are using SPSS. In addition, SPSS 7.5 provides not only the traditional SPSS "state-of-the-art" data analysis, but features vastly improved abilities necessary for reporting data analysis output. We take this one step further by providing keystroke instructions on how to incorporate SPSS 7.5 output into a word processing program for the purposes of report writing. The report writing chapter, chapter 19, now contains keystroke instructions on making graphs and charts and importing this output into word processing programs.

New, Relevant Examples. *Marketing Research* contains current, relevant examples including General Motors' research on the electric car, the EV1. When we introduce students to geodemography, we worked on a page-by-page example with the firm Claritas to provide a real example of the use of their geodemography program, MarketReporter™. We also provide an example of database marketing due to our close relationship with Claritas. In short, we endeavored to find in-depth examples illustrating the issue being discussed in the text. You will find these examples strategically placed in the text to provide relevant and current illustrations of a concept just introduced to the reader.

Current Industry Changes. As information sources and delivery change, so does the marketing research industry. We provide a description of many of these recent changes. For example, the Standard Industrial Classification (SIC) is changing to the new system referred to as the North American Industrial Classification System (NAICS). We provide a complete discussion of NAICS, which will become commonplace in the next few years and, no doubt, will become a necessity for anyone conducting secondary research. Changes in the legal environment that impact marketing research are also included. The same is true for many of the technological changes in the industry. We provide, for example, a much more thorough discussion of computer-assisted questionnaire design and data collection. We worked closely with Mercator Corporation to illustrate some of these developments. Finally, the Internet is changing the research industry and textbooks, and we have utilized Internet examples and noted homepage sites at various places in *Marketing Research.*

To conclude, *Marketing Research,* 2e, is an improvement over its forerunner, but we did not abandon the basic approach, style, and presentation format that made the first edition popular. Rather, we attempted to build on these strengths and provide you with a current, updated text. We hope you'll enjoy learning from *Marketing Research* as much as we enjoyed writing it.

INSTRUCTIONAL SUPPORT

Adopters of this textbook will receive the following ancillary materials to help them prepare their course and teach it effectively.

Instructor's Manual. A comprehensive *Instructor's Manual* accompanies the textbook. The manual includes sample syllabi; chapter summaries; chapter outlines; answers to end-of-chapter questions; hints on material coverage; SPSS for Windows and SPSS Student Assistant information; and a set of transparency masters.

PowerPoint® Presentations. A complete set of chapter-by-chapter presentations have been created using Microsoft's PowerPoint. Files will be available to adopters.

Test Bank. A test bank using Prentice Hall's new and improved test bank software is available to adopters. All test questions were rewritten by the authors for this edition of *Marketing Research.* Both print and electronic versions are available.

SPSS Student Assistant. As previously noted, a separate Windows program on a CD-ROM has been provided with this textbook. The program is a stand-alone tutorial for SPSS for Windows. Students are instructed to use the SPSS Student Assistant by side notes in the textbook. At the end of their review of each SPSS Student Assistant menu item, there is a set of written exercises to test their comprehension of the basics. The SPSS Student Assistant shows the cursor movements and resulting SPSS operations captured as movies by Lotus ScreenCam software.

SPSS Student Version. As previously noted, through a special arrangement with SPSS, we are pleased to provide with each purchase of *Marketing Research,* 2e, SPSS Student Version. SPSS Student Version is a very powerful software package. It allows for the analysis of up to 50 variables and 1,500 cases. It contains all of the statistical techniques covered in the textbook plus many more. Prentice Hall has an exclusive agreement with SPSS to provide this service.

ACKNOWLEDGMENTS

Some may think that writing the second, or subsequent, editions to a book is an easy task. Not true! Once again, we have many people to thank for their support and involvement during the years we have been working on the second edition of *Marketing Research.* First, we want to thank the professional staff at Prentice Hall. Sandra Steiner was instrumental in getting the first edition of *Marketing Research* published. Just to prove that Sandra always makes great decisions, she is now President of the Business Division of Prentice Hall. Our editors, David Borkowsky, Whitney Blake, and Aileen Mason have been very professional in handling all the issues that arise in publishing a book. We also thank Rachel Falk, Editorial Assistant; Pat Smythe, Design Manager; Dee Josephson, Managing Editor; Kenneth J. Clinton, Manufacturing Buyer; Joanne Jay, Director of Production and Manufacturing, as well as Jennifer Ballentine for her thorough editing, Kathy Ringrose for her photographic research skills, and the staff at Rainbow Graphics, LLC. Thanks to Andrea Hall of SPSS who expedited the software that accompanies this book.

We are thankful for our colleagues at our universities. They provide us with support, comments, and constructive criticism. We thank our Deans, Dean Thomas Clark of Louisiana State University (LSU) and Dean William Carper of the University of West Florida (UWF), for providing us with an environment conducive to pursuing knowledge in our discipline. We thank the members of our support staff who help us with the myriad of detail necessary to write a book. Thank you Marianne Baker, Barbara Dinsmore, and Marja Cooper of UWF and Barbara Ross, Rene Lebreton, and Jed Yaggi of LSU. We wish to again acknowledge the input of Assistant Dean, Dr. Marcia Howard, UWF, for her input on the report writing chapter. Kevin Weseman, MBA student at UWF, helped with many tasks and added many insights as well. Michelle Steward, a wonderfully creative former student, is recognized for her enduring work on this project.

There are always a few special people who make special contributions to any project. Pushkala Raman, now on the marketing staff at Florida State University, played a major role in this edition of *Marketing Research.* Pushkala provided many insights on the organization of material and did a tremendous job of researching new information. Peggy Toifel is the Business Reference Librarian at UWF. We thank Peggy for being the professional that she is; always keeping up with the fast-changing world of information technology. Peggy's contributions are especially noted in our chapter on secondary data.

Without our friends in the marketing research industry, *Marketing Research,* 2e would have been an impossible task. We thank these individuals for giving us information on new products and services, reviewing our manuscripts, and providing us with many practitioner insights you will find in the book. Specifically, we wish to thank Richard A. Spitzer, NFO Research; Karen Kratz, Nielsen Media Research; Donna E. O'Neil, Mercator Corporation; Vincent P. Barabba, General Motors Corporation; Jack Honomichl, Marketing Aid Center, Inc.; Ronald L. Tatham and Nancy Bunn, Burke, Inc.; Edna Hedblad, Gale Research; Bill Jameson, Polaris Marketing Research; William H. Neal, Sophisticated Data Research, Inc.; Nancy G. Deck, Brent Roderick, and John Behler, Claritas, Inc.; Jan DeVita, ACNielsen; Tracy Bacon, SPAR/Burgoyne Retail Services, Inc.; Jill Axelrod, Simmons Market Research; Thomas Mocarsky, The Arbitron Company; Robert J. Bregenzer, Information Resources, Inc.; Dee Beck, Bridgestone/Firestone Tire Sales; Linda Keairns, Decisive Technology; Kip Knight, PepsiCo Restaurants International; and Diane K. Bowers, CASRO. All of these dedicated professionals in the research industry gave us their time, opinions, and much valuable information.

We thank the many individuals who served as reviewers for this book. We thank those who reviewed the several drafts of this second edition: Siva Balasubramanian, Southern Illinois University; Thomas Cossee, University of Richmond; Ashok Gupta, Ohio University; James Leigh, Texas A&M University; Joann Lindrud, Mankato State University; Don Sciglimpaglia, San Diego State University; Terri Shaffer, Southeastern Louisiana University; and Steve Vitucci, University of Central Texas. Also, the suggestions of those who reviewed the first edition are still a part of *Marketing Research,* 2e. We thank Linda Anglin, Mankato State University; Ron Beall, San Francisco State University; Jacqueline J. Brown, University of Nevada, Las Vegas; Joseph D. Brown, Ball State University; Corbett Gaulden, Jr., University of Texas of the Permian Basin; Diane Parente, State University of New York, Fredonia; Bruce L. Stern, Portland State University; John H. Summey, Southern Illinois University; Nicolaos E. Synodinos, University of Hawaii; Peter K. Tat, The University of Memphis; Jeff W. Totten, University of Wisconsin, Oshkosh; Gary McCain, Boise State University; and V. Padmanabhan, Stanford University.

Finally, we always owe the most to our wives, Jeanne and Libbo. Both of them have busy, professional lives themselves. But they are both always supportive of us, and they smile a lot!

Al Burns,
Louisiana State University

Ron Bush,
University of West Florida

CHAPTER 1

The Nature of Marketing Research

Learning Objectives

- *To know what is meant by the terms "marketing" and "marketing research"*
- *To understand the role of marketing research, its uses, and its characteristics*
- *To describe a marketing information system, and explain how marketing research and marketing information systems differ*

GM's EV1, the world's most energy-efficient car platform.

PRACTITIONER VIEWPOINT

The key determinant to the quality of decision making is critical thinking about the decision prior to the collection and analysis of information. Or, as the old saying goes, "A problem well defined is half-solved."

— Vincent P. Barabba
General Motors Corporation

The GM Electric Car[1]

General Motors (GM) chairman John F. Smith, Jr., said GM was the first major automaker to market an electric vehicle, the EV1, to the public. The two-seat EV1 was introduced to the market in the Fall of 1996. GM believes this car will define the GM of the future, and they believe auto historians will see this as the first of a new generation of automobiles. The vehicle comes with dual airbags, antilock brakes, a CD player, and cruise control. Smith says the car is "quiet, peppy, and fun to drive." The EV1 is the world's most aerodynamic automobile, with a drag coefficient equivalent to that of an F-16 fighter aircraft. In designing the car, GM used marketing research and studied the responses of more than 500 consumers who tested the vehicle prototype. The research project, called "PrEView," provided the EV1 to consumers in 11 different cities. Consumers were given the car to use for several weeks and were asked to record their responses to the car in a diary. GM recorded vital statistics on the cars' use in a "black box." They were then able to read diary entries and compare consumer responses to actual car operating statistics. According to Shawn McNamara, GM marketing researcher, the "black box" let them know whether or not the car was operating up to its specification levels. If it was operating normally and consumers didn't like the performance, GM realized it had to go back and redesign the car to improve the operating performance. Visit the EV1 at http://av.yahoo.com/bin/search?p+GM+Electric+Car.

We are pleased that Vincent Barabba has had some influence on the chapter you are about to read. Mr. Barabba's 30-plus years' experience with Eastman Kodak, Xerox, government, and General Motors (GM) has enabled him to write two books that are having a major impact on marketing philosophy and practice. Both these books, *Hearing the Voice of the Market* and *Meeting of the Minds*,[2] focus on the need to have the proper information to understand consumers' wants and needs. Much of GM's strategy relating to the development, design, and marketing of their electric car has been based on information from consumers. Marketing research is the function that allows the firm to "hear the voice" of the consumer; it brings consumer information to decision makers. In this chapter, we introduce you to marketing research by showing how marketing research is related to marketing, the marketing concept, and marketing strategy. We define marketing research, and discuss its role in marketing management, its uses, and its characteristics. To further aid your understanding of marketing research, we take a look at the different types of marketing research studies. Finally, we explain how marketing research is related to marketing information systems (MIS).

MARKETING

The AMA defines marketing as the performance of all activities necessary for the conception, pricing, promotion, and distribution of ideas, goods, and services to create exchanges that satisfy individual and organizational objectives.

The American Marketing Association defines **marketing** as the performance of all activities necessary for the conception, pricing, promotion, and distribution of ideas, goods, and services to create exchanges that satisfy individual and organizational objectives.[3] Marketers such as GM, McDonald's, Wal-Mart, Paramount, and Procter & Gamble typically have had long, successful marketing histories. Why are these companies so successful? In each case, it is because the marketers have correctly "heard" the consumers' wants and needs and conceived a product (or service), price, promotion, and distribution method that satisfied those wants and needs.

Marketing managers should practice the marketing concept by developing strategies using information from the market.

Although this may sound simple, don't be deceived. Many companies go out of business or experience product failures each year. So how do businesses achieve success? Their marketing managers access and then apply the right information. No easy task—otherwise every product ever introduced would have been successful. So how should marketing managers do it? They follow two basic steps: (1) they endorse a philosophy called the marketing concept, and (2) they develop marketing strategies that satisfy consumers. But, as we will see in the following discussion, marketers cannot be successful without having information about the market and the competition.

The Marketing Concept

The philosophy called the marketing concept emphasizes that the key to achieving goals consists of determining the needs and wants of target markets and delivering the desired satisfactions more effectively than competitors.

The **marketing concept** is a business philosophy that holds that the key to achieving organizational goals consists in determining the needs and wants of target markets and delivering the desired satisfactions more effectively and efficiently than competitors.[4] The bottom line is that the focus of the entire firm is on satisfying consumers' wants and needs. Time has proven that such a philosophy is superior to one in which company management focuses on production, the product itself, or some promotional gimmick. If you satisfy consumers, they will seek to do business with your company. But how does a company know what consumers' wants and needs are? Obviously, marketers must have information about consumers' wants and needs if they are to truly endorse the marketing concept. Second, having the right philosophy is only part of the battle. Marketers must implement plans, called marketing strategies, that actually satisfy consumers' wants and needs.

Marketing Strategy

Marketing strategy consists of selecting a target market and designing the "mix" (product/service, price, distribution, and promotion) necessary to satisfy the wants and needs of that target market.

A **marketing strategy** consists of selecting a segment of the market as the company's target market and designing the proper "mix" of product/service, price, promotion, and distribution system to meet the wants and needs of the consumers within the target market. Again, this may sound simple, but consider some of the questions that confront marketing managers as they design marketing strategies:

- What is the market?
- How do we segment the market?
- What are the wants and needs of each segment?
- How do we measure the size of each market segment?

- Who are our competitors, and how are they meeting the wants and needs of each segment?
- Which segment(s) should we target?
- Which model of a proposed product will best suit the target market?
- What is the best price?
- Which promotional method will be the most efficient?
- How should we distribute the product/service?

Marketers need information in order to develop, implement, and evaluate strategies.

These questions must be answered. Therefore, marketing managers need objective, accurate, and current information in order to develop marketing strategies that will work. Even when marketers have the right information to implement an effective marketing strategy, they must be constantly aware of changing environments. A change in the environment may alter the appeal of a marketing strategy to consumers. So because the environments are constantly changing, marketers' needs for information are never ending.

Marketers must monitor the social and cultural environments as well as the economic environment.

Consider changes taking place in the *social and cultural environment.* As the population grows older, companies are developing products and services for the elderly. In the service sector, there has been a startling growth in geriatric care services. Several companies are also redesigning their products for the elderly. For instance, computer keyboards have been developed with large type, making them easier for older people to use. Marketing strategy is also highly dependent upon the *economic environment.* Many firms watch Federal Reserve statements very closely, knowing that a change in the interest rate can have a significant impact on their business. Companies also closely monitor other economic variables such as the level of consumer debt, level of business inventories, and indexes of consumer sentiment and expectations, because they know these are indicators of consumer and business spending and business activity.[5]

Marketers must also keep tabs on the political and legal environment as well as the technological environment.

The current restrictions on cigarette advertisements have caused significant changes in the *political and legal environment* of the tobacco industry. Cigarette manufacturers have to rethink their entire marketing strategy in view of these changes. The signing of the Telecommunications Act in February 1996 has caused sweeping changes in the political and legal environment of the communications industry. As a result of the deregulation, broadcasters, cable TV operators, and local and long-distance phone companies are free to enter one another's markets. As carriers begin to market bundles of communication services, they will require information to tailor their products to meet consumer needs. Deregulation is also occurring in the electric utilities industry. Consumers will soon be allowed to buy their electricity from a choice of several utility firms. The electric car example at the beginning of this chapter is a good example of how change in the political and legal environment affects business. The impetus for the development of the electric car has come from laws passed by various states' legislatures. California started the trend by mandating to the auto industry that by May 13, 1998, 2 percent of the vehicles sold by the high-volume automakers must be electric cars.[6] The rate of change in the *technological environment* is unprecedented in the history of the world. The popularity of the World Wide Web has spurred demand for digital cameras, particularly for on-line images. To be competitive, all firms must keep abreast of information about technological changes that may impact their productivity and, in some instances, their ability to survive.

Environments are forever changing, and this means marketers constantly need updated information about those environments.

The point here is not to discuss all of the forms of environmental change; rather, it is to note that marketers must develop and implement strategies, and those strategies must constantly be revised as required by changing environments. This means marketers *constantly* need information—they need information provided by marketing research.

MARKETING RESEARCH DEFINED

Marketing research is the process of designing, gathering, analyzing, and reporting information that may be used to solve a specific marketing problem.

The AMA has defined marketing research as the function that links the consumer, customer, and public to the marketer through information—information used to identify and define marketing opportunities and problems; generate, refine, and evaluate marketing performance; and improve understanding of marketing as a process.

We define **marketing research** as the process of designing, gathering, analyzing, and reporting information that may be used to solve a specific marketing problem. The American Marketing Association (AMA) has defined marketing research as the function that links the consumer, customer, and public to the marketer through information—information used to identify and define marketing opportunities and problems; generate, refine, and evaluate marketing actions; monitor marketing performance; and improve understanding of marketing as a process.[7] Both definitions are correct; ours is short and focuses on the steps involved in the process of marketing research; that is, gathering, analyzing, and reporting information. The AMA definition is longer and spells out both the basic function as well as the uses of marketing research.

Because the marketing concept implies that the consumer's needs should be fulfilled, the consumer's voice must be heard within the company. As the AMA definition states, marketing research provides this important link; the consumer is "heard" through marketing research. Of course, marketing research information is also collected on entities other than the consumer. Information is routinely gathered on members of distribution channels, and, of course, competitors.[8] As the AMA definition states, there are many *uses* of marketing research information. We discuss these uses in the following section, which introduces you to the role of marketing research.

THE ROLE OF MARKETING RESEARCH: INFORMATION TO AID IN DECISION MAKING

The role of marketing research is to provide information that facilitates marketing decisions.

The main **role of marketing research** is to provide information that facilitates marketing decisions. The importance of this role cannot be overstated; it is the *raison d'etre* for marketing research. Without marketing research information, it is hard—if not impossible—for management to make sound marketing decisions or to properly implement the marketing concept. As a result, costly failures may occur, as evidenced by the examples presented in Marketing Research Insight 1.1 and Marketing Research Insight 1.2 (page 6) illustrates how failures may be avoided.

The role of marketing research in marketing management is so important that the American Marketing Association's definition of marketing research specifies the ways that the information provided by marketing research may be used. For example, such information can be "used to identify and define marketing opportunities and problems; generate, refine, and evaluate marketing actions; monitor marketing performance; and improve understanding of marketing as a process."[9] Lets take a closer look at these uses.

MARKETING RESEARCH INSIGHT 1.1

Costly Failures

The value of having the right information at the right time and place in the right form cannot be overstated. Could marketing research information have prevented these costly mistakes?

Marketing Intelligence Service, Ltd. stated that the rate of new product failure is getting worse. Companies are too prone to introduce "me too" products that really are no better at satisfying consumers' needs than are existing brands.

Several years ago, Planters marketed peanuts in a vacuum-packed "brick" that resembled a coffee package. The product was called **Planters Fresh Roast.** *Unfortunately, customers thought the product was coffee. Supermarket managers from all over the country complained that customers were putting peanuts in their coffee grinders.*

Heinz Salsa Ketchup *was a tasty product. However, it failed because ketchup and salsa usually sit in different supermarket aisles and shoppers did not know whether to dip nachos in it or pour it onto a hamburger.*

Kids "R" Us, *a subsidiary of Toys "R" Us, suffered a setback in Puerto Rico because of insufficient market knowledge. The fast-growing retailer of children's clothing opened three stores in Puerto Rico in late 1992. The opening of these stores was timed for the back-to-school sales. What the retailer did not know was that Puerto Rican children wear uniforms to school! In this case, at least, marketing research information certainly could have prevented a costly mistake.*

Sometimes the failure of one product may lead to the success of another. 3M adhesive technicians were dismayed at one glue formulation that was not very sticky. Fortunately, an alert 3M employee saw the value in a glue that did not stick permanently and developed the successful product **Post-It Notes.**

Visit The New Products Showcase & Learning Center's homepage at http://www.showlearn.com/

The New Products Showcase and Learning Center in Ithaca, New York, houses famous and failed new products. Corporations and developers pay hundreds of dollars to visit the center and learn from past mistakes.

Source: *Ted Anthony, "Where's Farrah Shampoo?,"* Marketing News *1 (May 6, 1996): 13; "FLOPS,"* Business Week *(August 16, 1993): 76–80, 82; and* Business Week *(February 28, 1994), 8.*

To identify and define marketing opportunities means to define those wants and needs in the market that are not being met by the competition. Many food processing firms such as Campbell's Soup, Nabisco, General Mills, and General Foods have discovered opportunities in consumers' increasing concerns about health, weight, and diet. These firms are frequently introducing new foods to the market that are low in cholesterol, fat, sodium, and sugar.[10] A New York–based consulting firm has estimated that a record 1,236 new "light" products were introduced in 1996, 28 percent more than in 1995. There are market opportunities not only for healthy foods but for foods that are convenient to eat. Campbell's has test marketed a line of what it calls "clinically proven" meals designed to combat high blood pressure, high cholesterol, and diabetes. It worked in secret with the American Heart Association and The American Diabetes Association to develop the products and offered consumers 41 varieties of meals called "Intelligent Cuisine." The meals are frozen

MARKETING RESEARCH INSIGHT 1.2

The CASE for Marketing Research

http://www.casecorp.com/corporate/index.html

CASE CORPORATION LISTENS TO "THE VOICE OF THE CONSUMER"

Case Corporation is a manufacturer of construction and farm equipment. Operating losses for 1991 and 1992 reached $900,000. In 1994 Case hired a new CEO, Jean-Pierre Rosso. He learned that since the 1980s, Case had not included customers in its product design decisions. Instead, products were developed that could optimize factory production capability. This resulted in products that wouldn't sell such as a new tractor that had horsepower too low to suit consumers. When dealers found themselves overstocked with Case products, dealer relations soured, which further hurt sales.

CEO Rosso knew that the company had to become market-driven. In the words of Vincent Barabba, there had to be a "meeting of the minds" of corporate departments with those of the consumer. Consumers were flown in to compare Case equipment, item by item, with equipment of the major competitors, John Deere and Caterpillar. Case engineers and marketing personnel interviewed potential customers, as well as customers of competitors products, asking about features, benefits, and problems. The data collected from the customers was then incorporated into new product prototypes. Rosso's marketing research information led to improved decision making. Case's net income more than tripled in 1994 and sales increased by 14 percent. In 1995 revenues reached $4.2 billion. During the first half of 1996, Case reported revenues and profits up by 20 percent over 1995. Obviously, Case's decision to "hear the voice of the consumer" through marketing research was the right strategy.

Source: *Norton Paley, "The Case for Market Research,"* Sales & Marketing Management *(October 1996), 38–40.*

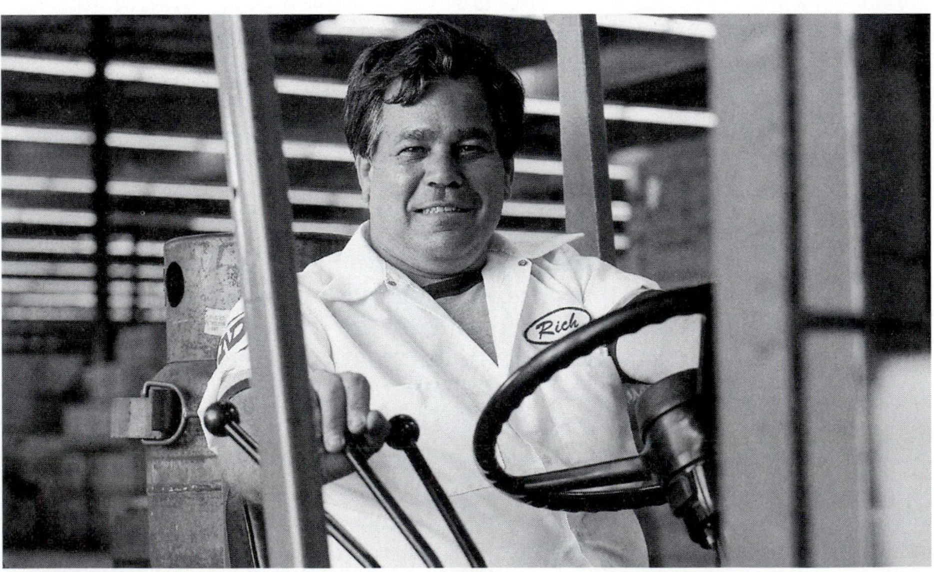

and shipped in the mail to consumers.[11] Campbell's research has told them that there is an opportunity in the market for "intelligent cuisine."

Marketers need information to help them identify market opportunities.

Many companies today are searching for opportunities along the "information highway" in health care, energy, transportation, and so on. Opportunities, and problems, are everywhere but decision makers need information to help them identify and define them adequately. As the nation has become more concerned about environmental hazards and the problem with hazardous waste in landfills, Green Paint Co. took advantage of this opportunity by developing a paint that could be recycled. Almost every home has several gallons of used paint in the garage, basement, or storeroom. Eventually, this hazardous product ends up in a landfill or incinerator. Green Paint has experienced increased sales by collecting waste paint and producing Green Paint, a line of 90 percent recycled paint in cans that are themselves recyclable.[12] Many companies today are searching for such opportunities, but they need information to identify and define them adequately.

Marketers need information to help them determine which strategy will best take advantage of a market opportunity.

To generate and refine marketing actions means to determine which plan, or marketing strategy, will best meet market opportunities. What combination of the four Ps (product, price, promotion, and place) will best take advantage of an existing marketing opportunity? Sears, the nation's No. 2 retailer, has been running a $40 million-a-year, "Softer Side of Sears" campaign since 1993 to woo middle-income women. This opportunity in the women's market was identified through a nationwide research study conducted in 1992. The company discovered that its best customers for Craftsman tools and Kenmore appliances were women, aged 25 to 50, who do almost all the family shopping. However, when it came to their own needs, women went elsewhere because Sears did not carry much brand name apparel. Cashing in on the campaign to target women, Sears is now launching its "Circle of Beauty" line of makeup, skin care products, and fragrances. Sears has spent heavily on consumer re-

search, testing everything from names to products and packaging. The result of this turnaround is that Sears went from a $2.9 billion loss in 1992 to a $1.6 billion operating profit during 1993 and 1994.[13]

Both Sears and Fingerhut rely heavily on marketing research information to make marketing decisions.

A company that relies heavily on information is Fingerhut, the second largest consumer catalog marketer in the country. The company maintains an extensive database of consumers that includes demographic details such as age, marital status, and number of children. It tracks hobbies and birthdays and uses that knowledge to hit customers with personalized catalogs when they are most likely to buy. Fingerhut has made knowledge of their customers a core competency.[14]

Another company that has used market research data to *refine its marketing strategy* is Parmalat, the makers of long-life, shelf-stable milk available in aseptic packages. Research conducted before the launch showed that consumers believed fresh milk could only come from refrigerated containers. To overcome these reservations, the company delivered coupons for a free quart of milk to millions of prospective purchasers. Consumer use was tracked through store intercepts, mail from consumers, and analysis of sales data from IRI Infoscan in every market after each promotion and schedule of ads. Parmalat adjusted its advertising based on the analysis after the initial launch. Follow-up ads addressed consumers' questions and concerns. At the end of the first year, Parmalat generated $66 million in sales in the $9 billion U.S. retail milk market.[15]

Marketing research is used for services as well as for products.

Many of the examples used thus far involve products. However, *marketing research is also used for services.* American Express Financial Advisors, Inc. conducts client satisfaction surveys using a random list of clients. This information helps financial planners better serve their customers, which in turn brings more business to the company.[16]

Monitoring marketing strategies once they are implemented is a way of maintaining control over the success of a new product or service. Any control system requires feedback of information to management. Marketing research brings that information to management personnel, allowing them to compare actual performance with desired performance standards.

Marketers need information to help them monitor their performance.

To improve our understanding of the marketing process means that some marketing research is conducted to expand our basic knowledge of marketing. Typical of such research would be attempts to define and classify marketing phenomena and to determine optimum methods for carrying out marketing activities. For example, this includes studies to determine optimum returns on promotional expenditures or studies to determine the operating characteristics of the most profitable firms within an industry. Much of this research is conducted by marketing professors at colleges and universities and by other organizations, such as the Marketing Science Institute.

We have defined the role and illustrated some of the uses of marketing research. In the following section, we discuss some of the characteristics of marketing research.

CHARACTERISTICS OF MARKETING RESEARCH

There are so many characteristics of marketing research that we cannot discuss all of them here. In the following paragraphs, we describe marketing research in terms of its being basic or applied research, as being sometimes inaccurate, and as being affected by budget and time constraints.

Applied or Basic Research?

Research may be characterized as either applied or basic. By **applied research,** we mean that the research is undertaken to solve a specific problem. By **basic research,** we mean that research is undertaken for the sake of extending knowledge. This does not mean that basic research is not valuable. In fact, basic research often leads to major scientific breakthroughs that may then be used to solve specific problems. For example, laser technology was discovered through basic research on photons, which are particles of light. Understanding photons allowed scientists to create lasers, which are used today in many applications, including eye surgery. In any event, marketing research is almost always applied research—it is conducted to solve specific problems: Which entertainment group will attract the largest crowd and revenue to the local civic center? Will a frozen meal shipped to the home for persons on special diets prove profitable?

Applied research is undertaken to solve a specific problem. Basic research is undertaken to extend knowledge. Marketing research is almost always applied research.

Sometimes Inaccurate

Unfortunately marketing research results are sometimes inaccurate. This, however, is not so surprising when we consider that most marketing research seeks to predict human behavior. Humans are neither stable nor constant in their attitudes, beliefs, or behaviors. Consumers are in a constant state of flux—changing brands, store preferences, fashions, attitudes toward companies, and so on. This means that it is very difficult to predict consumers' behavior with any high degree of accuracy. We find many instances of companies that, even after conducting extensive marketing research, experienced failure in the marketplace. For example, Beecham introduced a cold water wash product, Delicare, to compete with the market leader, Woolite. The product failed even though a marketing research firm, Yankelovich, Skelly and White, had predicted that Delicare would surpass Woolite's market share.[17] Of course, everyone is familiar with the now famous attempt by Coca-Cola to abandon their "classic" Coke in favor of "New" Coke. Even though "New" Coke's formulation was preferred by consumers in marketing research involving more than 190,000 people, Coke's research did not provide a clue that the public would be upset with their decision to replace the old Coke product with the "New" Coke. They scurried to put "Classic Coke" back on the shelves.[18]

Because marketing research attempts to predict human behavior, it is not foolproof in its predictions.

The marketing research conducted on hair styling mousse in the United States indicated the product would be a flop. Marketing research on telephone answering machines predicted they would flop.[19] Although we can look at these examples of marketing research being inaccurate, most companies agree that the information they receive from marketing studies is invaluable. Often, such studies do accurately predict the success of a company's new product or service.

Shaped by Budget and Time Constraints

Marketing research can be very expensive. It is not uncommon for researchers to design studies for clients only to have top management ask for the same study at half the proposed cost. Time constraints arise because companies often seek marketing input after their product is already performing poorly in the market. Such companies want immediate results.

Operating under budget and time constraints, marketing researchers realize there must be trade-offs if the project is to be completed using the money and time available. How is this accomplished? What, if anything, is compro-

Marketing research studies are typically conducted under time and budget constraints.

mised? Obviously, it is easier to make budget and time decisions regarding projects that fall at either end of the "importance" spectrum—those that are very unimportant or those that are extremely important. But what about the projects that fall in the middle? In such cases, the company's philosophy regarding the value and use of marketing research plays a role in deciding whether to use marketing research and how much money and time to allocate to it. In other words, if the company places a high value on marketing information, then they will pursue it; if they do not, they will not pursue it.

TYPES OF MARKETING RESEARCH STUDIES

Today there are thousands of marketing research studies being conducted around the world. Is there any way we can "group" these studies into different types? Yes, they can be grouped on the basis of their area of application or by management function. The AMA groups marketing research studies on the basis of the area to which they are applied. For example, studies conducted on cost analyses, demand analyses, and profitability are all classified under the area of "pricing" studies. Research studies conducted to determine the proper number and location of warehouses or the types of retail distributors to use are classified under the area of "distribution." Other types of marketing research studies, as defined by the AMA, include "promotion," "buyer behavior," "product," and "business, economic, and corporate research."[20]

Marketing research studies can be classified by the functions of management; analysis/planning, implementing, and controlling.

Consistent with the AMA definition of marketing research, marketing research studies can be classified by management function. Categories of **management functions** include analysis/planning, implementing, and control-

TABLE 1.1

Research Studies May Be Categorized According to Management Function

MANAGEMENT FUNCTION	ISSUES ADDRESSED BY RESEARCH
Analysis/Planning	Are there demands in the market not being met?
	Does our firm have the marketing resources necessary to satisfy this demand?
	What are the future growth potentials for markets we are currently serving?
	What are the future growth potentials for markets we are not serving?
Implementing	What features, styling, and options should be offered on our new product?
	Should the product be offered at the market price, at a premium price, or at a discount price?
	Should "network marketing" be used to augment our current distribution system?
	What impact will there be on sales and profits if we reduce network TV advertising and increase sales promotions?
Controlling	What is our image in the community in terms of social responsibility?
	What is our profitability by sku number by customer account?
	What is our sales volume by geographic territory?

ling. To see how management functions classify marketing research studies, let us consider three marketing studies. For example, one study conducted to determine the demand in the market for a new type of product is an example of an *analysis/planning study.* We discussed this earlier using the phrase "identifying and defining market opportunities." Such a study allows the firm to analyze the size of the demand and to plan whether to market such a product. Another research study devoted to determining the best methods of distributing a new product is an *implementing study.* These studies are conducted to help management determine how to best implement the four Ps, or what we have referred to as the "mix." These are studies that are designed to "generate, refine, and evaluate" marketing mixes. After the product has been on the market for some time, another study is devoted to studying market shares achieved by the product relative to competitive brands. This is a *controlling study,* used to "monitor marketing performance." Controlling studies are designed to determine how well a firm's strategy is working in the marketplace. See Table 1.1 for examples of additional issues that are addressed by each management function.

So far we have presented marketing research as if it were the *only* source of information. This is not the case, as we discuss in the following section on marketing information systems.

THE MARKETING INFORMATION SYSTEM

Marketing research is not the only source of information that may be available to decision makers. Information is also supplied by various components of the **marketing information system (MIS).** An MIS is a structure consisting of people, equipment, and procedures to gather, sort, analyze, evaluate, and distribute needed, timely, and accurate information to marketing decision makers.[21] The role of the MIS is to determine decision makers' information needs, acquire the needed information, and distribute that information to the decision makers in a form and at a time when they can use it for decision making. But, wait a moment! Isn't this about the same role we gave to marketing research—providing information to aid in decision making? The distinction may be found by understanding the components of an MIS.

An MIS is a structure consisting of people, equipment, and procedures to gather, sort, analyze, evaluate, and distribute needed, timely, and accurate information to marketing decision makers.

Components of an MIS

The components of an MIS are illustrated in Figure 1.1 on page 12. Managers need to carry out the managerial functions of analysis/planning, implementing, and controlling (first component, far left). Of course, managers cannot operate in a vacuum—they must keep abreast of changes occurring in the marketing environment (last component, far right). That is, they must be aware of changes occurring among their own targeted customers, their channel members, competitors, and other publics such as legislative, governmental agency, and other groups. As we noted before, these managers must also be cognizant of change occurring in the other (macro) environments such as the social and cultural environment, technological environment, and so on. As previously noted, the MIS is designed to assess managers' information needs, to gather this information, and to distribute the information to the marketing managers who need to make decisions. Information from these environments

The four subsystems of an MIS are the internal reports system, marketing intelligence system, marketing research system, and the marketing decision support system (DSS).

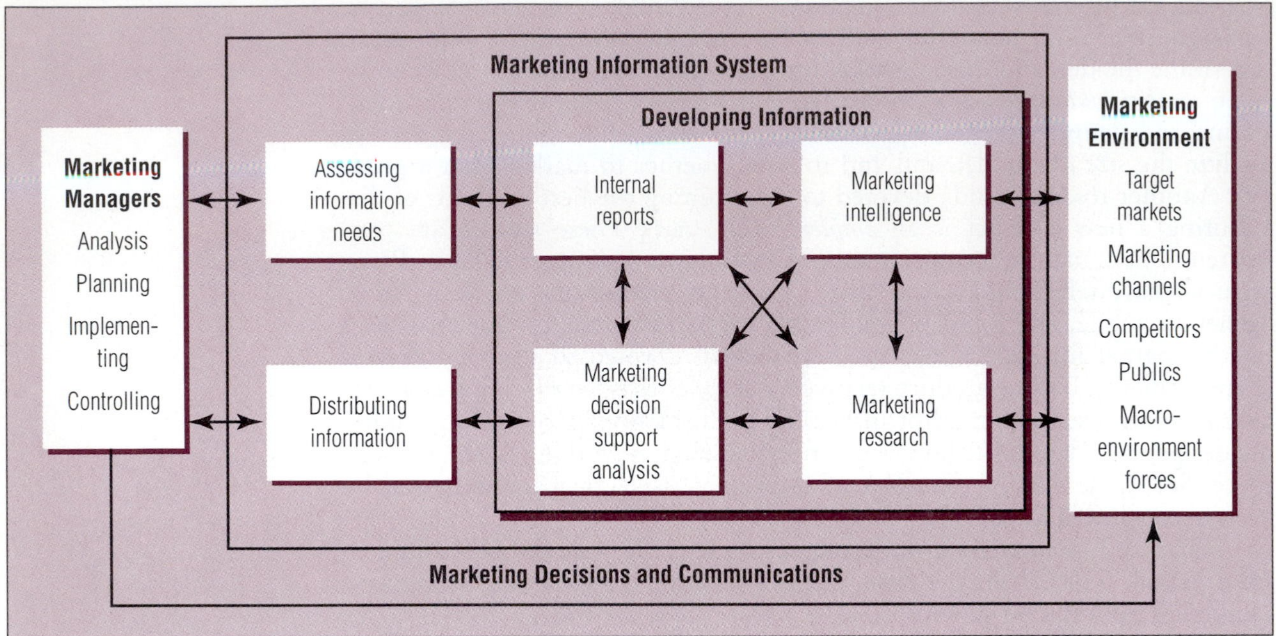

Figure 1.1

The Marketing Information System

is gathered and analyzed by the four subsystems of the MIS: internal reports, marketing intelligence, marketing decision support system, and marketing research. Each of these subsystems is discussed next.

Internal Reports System

The internal reports system gathers information generated by internal reports, which include orders, billing, receivables, inventory levels, stockouts, and so on.

The **internal reports system** gathers information generated by internal reports, which include orders, billing, receivables, inventory levels, stockouts, and so on. Salespeople record orders on their laptops and this information is sent via modem to the company headquarters, which notifies the warehouse to put the desired goods into delivery. The information recorded during this process—customer name, location, goods ordered, prices, delivery location, method of delivery, date, and so on—becomes the information ingredients in the internal reports system. Note in addition that inventory records are updated and this, too, becomes part of the recorded information. The internal reports system does not generate any information that was not available before the MIS was put in place. It does, however, ensure that this information is recorded, stored, and made available for retrieval by managers.

Many innovations have been made recently that enhance the salesperson's ability to provide and receive information to and from the internal reports system. Many companies are using new software that allows the salespersons themselves to interact with the internal reports system. The salesperson can quickly determine past orders for a customer he or she is about to call on, examine promised and actual delivery dates for the last order, and gain access to any correspondence between the customer and any other entity within the company since the last sales call. Salespersons today typically receive a laptop on their first

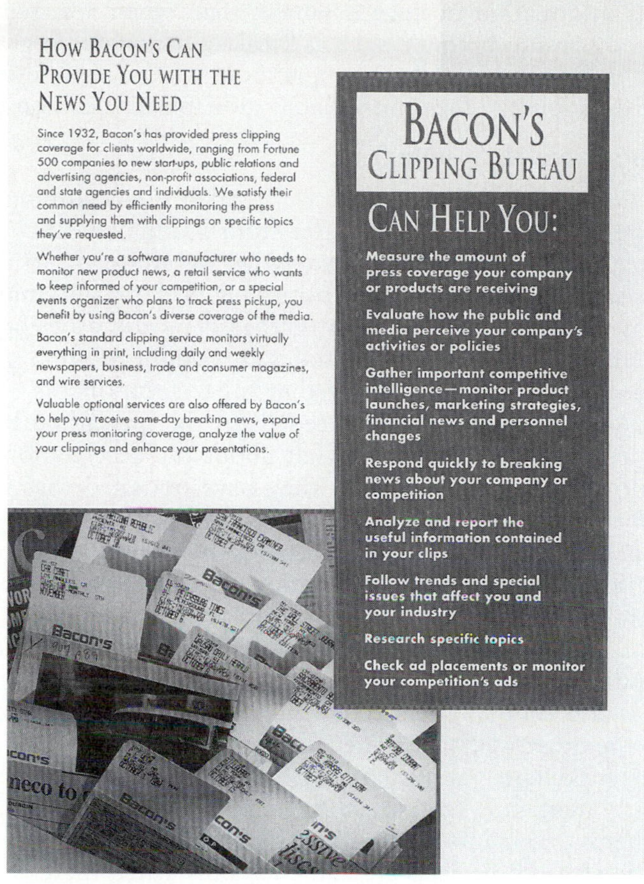

day on the job. An ad in a magazine targeting marketing managers, sales managers, and salespersons, *Sales & Marketing Management Magazine,* reads, "In 1953, the pay phone was a salesperson's lifeline. Today, it's Lotus Notes™."[22]

Explore Notes@Work at www.lotus.com

Marketing Intelligence System

The marketing intelligence system is defined as a set of procedures and sources used by managers to obtain everyday information about pertinent developments in the environment.

The **marketing intelligence system** is defined as a set of procedures and sources used by managers to obtain everyday information about pertinent developments in the environment. Professor Philip Kotler writes that an internal reports system focuses on *results,* and the intelligence system focuses on *happenings* in the environment. Such systems include both informal and formal information-gathering procedures. Informal information-gathering procedures involve such activities as scanning newspapers, magazines, and trade publications. Formal information-gathering activities may be conducted by staff members who are assigned the specific task of looking for anything that seems pertinent to the company or industry. They then edit and disseminate this information to the appropriate members or company departments. There are companies, such as Bacon's, who specialize in intelligence gathering.

Marketing Decision Support System (DSS)

A **marketing decision support system (DSS)** is defined as collected data that may be accessed and analyzed using tools and techniques that assist managers in decision making. Once companies collect large amounts of information, they store this information in huge databases that, when accessed with decision-making tools and techniques (such as break-even analysis, regression models, and linear programming), allow companies to ask "what if" questions. Answers to these questions are then immediately available for decision making.

Marketing Research System

Marketing research studies are for specific problems and are referred to as "ad hoc studies." They are also conducted on an "as needed" basis. Hence, they are also referred to as marketing research "projects."

We still have not answered the question we asked at the beginning of this section. How does marketing research differ from MIS? Now that you understand the three other components of an MIS, we are ready to discuss how marketing research differs from these components. First, the **marketing research system** gathers information not gathered by the other MIS component subsystems: Marketing research studies are conducted for a *specific situation* facing the company. It is unlikely that other components of MIS have generated the *particular* information needed for the *specific* situation. When GM wanted to know how consumers felt about the acceleration and speed available to drivers of the EV1, could they have obtained that information from internal reports? From the intelligence system or the DSS? No. This then is how marketing research plays a unique role in the total information system of the firm. By providing information for a specific problem at hand, it provides information not provided by other components of the MIS. This is why persons in the industry sometimes refer to marketing research studies as "*ad hoc* studies." *Ad hoc* is Latin meaning "with respect to a specific purpose." There is also another characteristic of marketing research that differentiates it from the other MIS components. Marketing research projects, unlike the previous components, are *not* continuous—they have a beginning and an end. This is why marketing research studies are sometimes referred to as "projects." The other components are available for use on an ongoing basis. However, marketing research projects are launched only when there is a justifiable need for information that is not available from internal reports, intelligence, or the DSS. GM tested consumer reactions to EV1 prototypes for several months. Once they felt they had an answer to their questions, they were able to solve their problem of trying to determine how much battery capacity and power to build into the vehicle to have the desired acceleration and speed.

THE FUTURE OF MARKETING RESEARCH

Some experts in the industry believe that marketing research, as we know it today, is due to undergo vast changes in the near future. They base this belief on the notion that technological advances in information processing have greatly increased the availability and applicability of information to the point that managers will find less need to conduct traditional "projects" or "*ad hoc* studies." David J. Curry's excellent book, *The New Marketing Research Systems*,[23] portrays the future (indeed, the present!) world of information technology as one that allows managers access to a continuous flow of real-world data (i.e., scanning data), augmented by embedded "experiments" illustrating consumer reactions to price changes, TV ads, and in-store point-of-purchase materials (i.e., single-source data). In addition, new technology allows managers to determine the characteristics of those purchasing their products/services and to then target individuals or small "microtargets" of consumers, with marketing strategies; for instance, by using databases and geodemographic programs. (We realize we're mentioning some terms here with which you may not be familiar. We explain them later in the book.) As decision makers are armed with such information, it is Curry's belief that traditional marketing research studies will become passé. Others argue that there are pitfalls in the "new" information systems and that there is room for traditional marketing research studies and these new systems to coexist as the two are complementary.[24] So, our conclusion is that technology is having a tremendous impact on marketing research and the types of marketing research studies will change as technological improvements occur. Furthermore, we still see a world full of managers who need a lot of information to help them make their decisions. The future for marketing research is bright!

SUMMARY

The marketing concept is a philosophy that states that the key to business success lies in determining and fulfilling consumers' wants and needs. Marketers attempting to practice the marketing concept need information in order to determine wants and needs and to design marketing strategies that will satisfy customers in selected target markets. Environmental changes mean that marketers must constantly collect information to monitor customers, markets, and competition.

We defined marketing research as the design, gathering, analyzing, and reporting of information that may be used to solve a specific problem. The uses of marketing research are to (1) identify and define marketing opportunities and problems; (2) generate, refine, and evaluate marketing actions; (3) monitor marketing performance; and (4) improve our understanding of marketing. Some characteristics of marketing research are that it is generally applied research, it is sometimes inaccurate, and it is shaped by budget and time constraints. There are many ways of classifying types of marketing research studies, including by management function: analysis/planning, implementing, and controlling. Marketing research is one of four subsystems making up a marketing information system (MIS). Other subsystems include internal information, marketing intelligence, and decision support systems. Marketing research gathers information not available through the other subsystems and is conducted on a project basis as opposed to on an ongoing basis.

KEY TERMS

Marketing (p. 2)
Marketing concept (p. 2)
Marketing strategy (p. 2)
Marketing research (p. 4)
Role of marketing research (p. 4)
Applied research (p. 9)
Basic research (p. 9)
Management functions (p. 10)
Marketing information system (MIS) (p. 11)
Internal reports system (p. 12)
Marketing intelligence system (p. 13)
Marketing decision support system (DSS) (p. 13)
Marketing research system (p. 14)

REVIEW QUESTIONS/APPLICATIONS

1. Define marketing research.
2. What is marketing? Explain the role of marketing research in the process of marketing management.
3. Distinguish among MIS, marketing research, and a DSS (decision support system).
4. Describe the characteristics of marketing research.
5. In this chapter, we gave you two definitions of marketing research and we discussed basic versus applied research. Is all marketing research applied? Does either definition recognize that marketing research can be both basic and applied?
6. How would you classify marketing research studies? How does this classification relate to the AMA's definition of marketing research?
7. Go to your library and look through several business periodicals such as *Advertising Age, Business Week, Fortune,* and *Forbes.* Find three examples of companies using marketing research.
8. Select a company in a field in which you have a career interest and look up information in your library or the Internet on this firm. After gaining some knowledge of this company, its products and services, customers, and competitors, list five different types of decisions that you believe this company's management may have made within the last two years. For each decision, list the information the company's executives would have needed to make these decisions.
9. Kevin Weseman is finishing his M.B.A. degree. He has a B.S. in marketing and has had a few years' work experience with a firm in the health care industry. Kevin took advantage of his school's marketing club and attended the meetings every week. Different speakers from industries including communications, packaged foods, industrial supply firms, and financial services presented weekly programs. The presentations allowed Kevin to develop insights into career opportunities and expectations within each industry. However, Kevin had an entrepreneurial spirit as well. He was interested in looking into acquiring his own business. Realizing he was lacking in experience, he became interested in franchising. What should Kevin do to satisfy his interest in franchising?

CASE 1.1

Pensacola Civic Center[25]

Kat Colley graduated from Arizona State University's College of Business in 1986. While a student, she interned with the ASU department responsible for the campus's entertainment complex. This includes a stadium, indoor sports arena, and a large performing arts auditorium. The intern experience enabled Kat to get a job with an international arena management firm in San Diego, California. She was soon transferred to Michigan where she opened the Detroit Pistons' coliseum. Recently, she became the marketing director of the Pensacola Civic Center in Pensacola, Florida. Kat has a choice of dozens of types of entertainment she can book at the Center. Examples include ice skating, wrestling, rodeos, magicians, and recording artists representing many types of music such as country & western, rock, jazz, classical, and so on. Within any one of these categories, she has anywhere from a few to several hundred entertainment groups from which to base her booking selections. The Pensacola Civic Center is a for-profit business. Civic Center owners are interested in maximizing revenues generated by the center. Of course, revenues are a function of the size of the audience and the price it is willing to pay to see a particular form of entertainment. Kat has learned from her experience in three different markets in Arizona, California, and Michigan that audience size and ticket prices vary both for types of entertainment as well as for different entertainers.

1. What should Colley do first?
2. What kind of information should she seek?
3. Where should she get this information?

CASE 1.2

CHELCO Electric Utility[26]

Visit Chelco's homepage at http://www.chelco.com/

CHELCO is an electric utility cooperative serving counties in Northwest Florida. Mike Richards and Bryan Gilbert, executives with CHELCO, have been concerned about what has become known as "retail wheeling" in the utility industry. What this means is that consumers will have a choice from among several utility companies to select their supplier of electricity. Previously, electrical utilities, such as CHELCO, have operated in an environment that substantially guaranteed no significant threats from other providers of electricity. In 1994, the California Public Utilities Commission, regulator of the state's utilities, announced that it was restructuring the electric utility industry to allow customers a choice in purchasing electric utilities. Retail wheeling allows a consumer to choose a company to provide his or her electricity. For example, if a company in Texas had excess capacity and wished to offer its service to California residents, Californians could choose to buy their electricity from the Texas company. Of course, fees would have to be paid to the local California company for use of their lines to carry the electricity to the homes.

Deregulation of industry is not new to utilities. In the early 1980s, AT&T was broken up into the "Baby Bells." Long-distance services such as MCI and SPRINT compete with AT&T. Telecommunications today is very different from the world of regulated monopoly prior to deregulation.

Being astute businessmen, Mike Richards and Bryan Gilbert realize that their customers will, one day, be able to choose from whom they purchase their electricity. Mike recently stated, "We know that customers buy products and services from suppliers that meet and exceed their expectations. We must be customer focused and market driven."

1. Assume you are a CHELCO executive. How do you become customer focused and market driven when you market a homogeneous service that, in use, is indistinguishable from that of competitors?
2. Given your answer to the above question, would you need marketing research to help you implement a customer-focused, market-driven program?

CHAPTER 2

The Industry: Structure, Evaluation, and Ethics

Learning Objectives

- *To know the history of marketing research*
- *To know how to classify marketing research firms*
- *To evaluate how the marketing research industry has performed*
- *To understand how a researcher's philosophy might dictate behavior*
- *To learn which key ethical issues face the marketing research industry today*

Deidre Beck-Guertin, manager of Marketing Research, Bridgestone/Firestone.

PRACTITIONER VIEWPOINT

The marketing research industry's surge toward maturity and recognition stepped up in the 1990s. There are 13 marketing/advertising/public opinion research firms that are public companies—listed on exchanges in Amsterdam and London as well as the NYSE, NASDAQ, and Amex in the U.S. There has also been an increase in concentration of power. The world's 25 largest research conglomerates now control 61 percent of the total world spending for marketing research services and they'll probably control more than 65+ percent by the year 2000. The balance is distributed among about 1,400 smaller firms.

There are two other indications of maturity. One firm—Custom Research Inc., a survey firm based in Minneapolis—won the Malcolm Baldrige National Quality Award. Also, Forbes *magazine updated its annual listing of "200 Best Small Companies" for the first time, a research firm—NFO Research Inc., Greenwich, Connecticut—was listed.*

These are all signs of a rapidly maturing industry.

— Jack Honomichl[1]
Marketing Aid Center, Inc.

A Career Is Born

Deidre Beck-Guertin was a marketing major at the University of West Florida in Pensacola, Florida. She took the course in marketing research and excelled in learning SPSS®, the statistical software package. She enjoyed working with analysis techniques to determine which techniques were most useful for communicating the meanings hidden in the raw data. Upon graduation she decided to get her MBA and continued her work with SPSS in other coursework. Through networking she met one of the members of the College of Business' Dean's Advisory Council, Mr. William Neal, who is president and CEO of Sophisticated Data Research (SDR). SDR is a large marketing research firm specializing in data analysis. Impressed with Deidre's knowledge of SPSS, Mr. Neal offered her an opportunity to interview with SDR at their headquarters in Atlanta. Deidre accepted the position with SDR where she fine-tuned her data analysis skills by working on many marketing research projects. She began as a project manager and was promoted to account manager. She was later offered a job as research analyst with the marketing research department of Fruit of the Loom. She continued to excel at her job and learn more about marketing research. Today Deidre is the manager of marketing research for Bridgestone/Firestone Tire Sales Company in Nashville, Tennessee. She is responsible for five divisions and ten brands including Bridgestone, Firestone, and Dayton Tires. Her work includes projects in the United States, Canada, and Latin America.

You may also have an interest in knowing more about the marketing research industry and career opportunities in the industry. In this chapter, we acquaint you with the history of marketing research and the structure of the industry. First we give a brief history of how the marketing research business has evolved to its present position. We then describe the various types and sizes of marketing research firms. The chapter will also familiarize you with some of the industry's representative firms. Next, you will learn something about evaluations of the industry's past performance. Several important ethical challenges face the industry today, and you will find that the industry is concerned about maintaining high ethical standards. Finally, we have included an appendix titled "A Career in the Marketing Research Industry."

HISTORICAL PERSPECTIVES OF MARKETING RESEARCH

The Pre-Marketing Research Era

To give you a better appreciation of the evolution of marketing research, let's examine the practice of marketing research during different time periods of our country's history. The time period from colonization until the industrial revolution, we could refer to as the *pre-marketing research era*. The economy

The significance of the pre-marketing research era is that business owners knew their customers so that there was little need for formal marketing research.

was primarily made up of artisans and craftsmen bartering one good for another. Towns and villages were small and the businesses that served them were also small. Everyone knew what each craftsman or artisan made. The significance of this time period is that the craftsmen or small business owners knew their customers personally. When these conditions exist, even today, there is little need for formal marketing research studies.

The Early Development Era

The significance of the early development era is that customers were separated from business managers, and marketing research was needed to understand the distant markets.

A second period of significance occurred between the industrial revolution and about 1920 that we refer to as the *early development era.* Several important events had taken place by this time. First, the industrial revolution made an everlasting impact on mankind. For the first time in the history of the world, we had the ability to mass produce goods. Second, transportation systems were developed to move the large quantities of goods streaming forth from the new factories. The St. Lawrence seaway was opened, which facilitated water transportation along an East–West route and connected the Great Lakes with the Atlantic. Settlements in the Far West developed and grew, and transportation to these markets was aided by the completion of the transcontinental railroad in 1869. Third, means of communication also improved with the introduction of the telegraph in 1895 and the wireless radio in 1906, and literacy levels increased. Both of these developments, communications and increases in literacy, were important if companies with factories located in one part of the country were going to advertise their products in distant markets. For the first time, companies could mass produce products and advertise and distribute them to *distant* markets. This meant that business managers were no longer near or acquainted with their customers; they needed marketing research to tell them about these distant consumers.

The Questionnaire Era

Questionnaires, still an important tool of marketing research, became prominent in marketing research during the time period from about 1920 to 1940.

We call the third era the *questionnaire era* (1920–1940). Although the questionnaire survey is said to have first been used in 1824 by some newspapers, and N. W. Ayres and Company is said to have surveyed grain production in each of the states in 1879, questionnaire surveys were in limited use until the 1920s. During World War I, the military used questionnaires for personnel screening. This increased familiarity with this research tool led to its use in opinion polls conducted by magazine publishers.[2] Severe changes in the economy led to increased use of questionnaires. When the "boom" during the 1920s gave way to the severe Depression, beginning in 1929, there was increased interest in the use of the questionnaire as a survey tool.

The Quantitative Era

Many quantitative techniques were applied to studying consumers and markets for the first time during the quantitative era—1940 to 1960.

We call the time period from 1940 to 1960 the *quantitative era.* Census data and, in particular, the taking of the censuses of business, led to an interest in statistical analysis. Marketing research was used to set sales quotas and to determine equitable sales territories. It was applied to managerial accounting techniques, such as cost analyses, to determine the costs of distribution. Also, marketing researchers began to borrow methodological techniques from the social sciences. Sampling theory, hypothesis testing, and the application of statistical techniques to hypotheses involving consumers' behavior, intentions, and attitudes became part of the marketing research industry's toolkit.[3] The study of "why people buy," or motivational research, started during this time period. For the first time, the marketing researcher was aided in his or her task of analysis by a new invention—the computer.[4]

The Organizational Acceptance Era

During the organizational acceptance era, management began to realize that, in order to survive, marketing research was needed to implement the marketing concept.

It wasn't until about 1960 that marketing research gained real acceptance in business organizations. We call the period from 1960 to 1980 the *organizational acceptance era.* As the marketing concept was accepted, the marketing research function was established as a formal part of the organization of the firm. The number of firms having their own research departments grew rapidly during this time period. During this era, other changes were taking place. More firms became involved in international marketing activities requiring management to make decisions about consumers and competition with which they had little, if any, firsthand experience. Worldwide communications and innovations in product and service technologies created a smaller world, but one that was filled with greater diversity and changing environments. To keep up, firms embraced the concept of the marketing information system (MIS), of which marketing research is a key component. Marketing research had not only gained acceptance in the organization but was recognized as being a key to understanding distant and fast-changing markets. It was needed for survival.

The Technological Era

The technological era has brought many new products and services to the research industry that have impacted the way business is conducted.

From 1980 to the present, we call the *technological era.* Technology has greatly impacted marketing research. A key catalyst to this change was the development of the personal computer (PC) during the late 1970s and the many technological applications that evolved as a result of the PC. Computer-assisted questionnaire programs were developed that allow researchers to design questionnaires that can be administered using the computer; touchscreen entries automatically record data during the interview process. Sophisticated, yet user-friendly software, such as SPSS, evolved during this period. By now, technological applications to the marketing research industry are appearing at a rapid rate and will no doubt significantly impact the industry by the end of the 1990s. Socratic Software's Visual Q illustrates how technological advancements affect the research industry (see Figure 2.1 on page 22). Visual Q is a Windows-based, computer-aided research design (CARD) program. It allows a manager to design a questionnaire using libraries of questions and response scales including multi-item constructs, such as customer satisfaction. Visual Q–designed questionnaires are then displayed on interviewers' computer screens and, therefore, serve as a method of achieving computer-aided telephone interviewing (CATI). If interviews are personally conducted, the program serves as a method of achieving computer-aided personal interviewing (CAPI). If the disk is sent to respondents by mail, the program serves as a method for achieving disk-by-mail (DBM) interviews. Once the data is obtained, the program's DataManager function automatically records data entry for export to a variety of spreadsheet programs or statistical analysis programs such as SPSS. For Visual Q users, Socratic maintains its own field service should managers not want to conduct the interviews themselves. Visual Q is one of the many advanced, "off-the-shelf" packages that allow today's managers to come closer to being a researcher, as opposed to a user, by designing their own research projects.

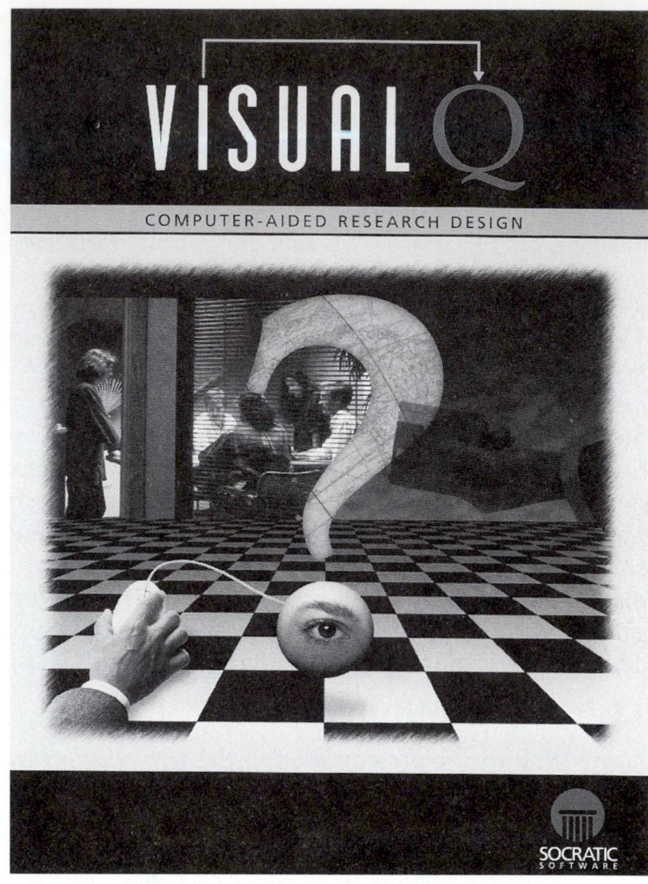

Figure 2.1

Visual Q is one of many high-tech products in the marketing research industry.

THE STRUCTURE OF THE MARKETING RESEARCH INDUSTRY

Part of developing an appreciation of any industry is to understand the structure of the industry. By structure, we mean the types and characteristics of the firms making up the industry. In the marketing research industry we refer to providers of marketing research information as research *suppliers.* There are several ways we can classify suppliers. We use a classification developed by Naresh Malholtra,[5] slightly modified for our purposes here. This classification system is shown in Figure 2.2. As shown in this figure, suppliers may be classified as either internal or external. An **internal supplier** means an entity within the firm supplies marketing research. These firms spend roughly about 1 percent of sales on marketing research, whether it is supplied internally or externally.[6] Johnson & Johnson, Kodak, Ford, and Chrysler have research departments of their own. AT&T has an in-house research department that constantly monitors consumer satisfaction and environmental trends. They also provide research support to AT&T's advertising agencies.

An internal supplier means an entity within the firm supplies marketing research information.

Hewlett-Packard organizes its research around the many divisions of the company. Although they have centralized the functions of marketing intelli-

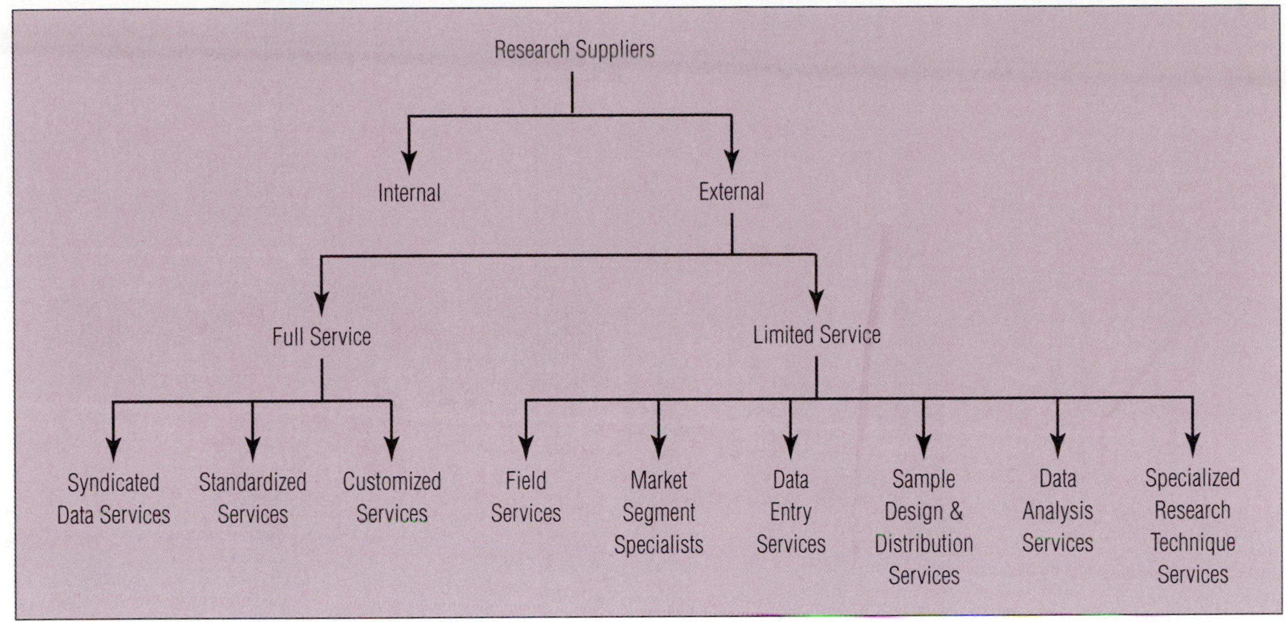

Figure 2.2

A Classification of Marketing Research Suppliers

gence, much marketing research is carried out by research teams that are assigned to the divisions needing research studies. Research is housed not only at company headquarters but at satellite locations as well.[7]

Internal Suppliers: How Do They Organize the Research Function?

A firm having its own internal supply of marketing research can elect several organizing methods to provide the research function. They may (a) have their own formal departments, (b) have no formal department but at least a single individual responsible for marketing research, or they may (c) assign no one responsibility for conducting marketing research. Most large firms, like those we just named, have the resources to staff their own formal marketing research departments. Firms with higher sales volumes (over $500 million) tend to have their own formal marketing research departments. Also, with the exception of financial services firms, the number of firms having their own formal departments has increased in recent years (see Figure 2.3 on page 24).[8] Many large advertising agencies have their own formal research departments.[9] The key to whether a company has its own research department lies in justifying the large fixed costs of supporting the personnel and facilities of the department day in and day out. A major advantage of having your own department is that the staff is fully cognizant of the firm's operations and the changes in the industry. This may give them better insights into identifying problems suitable for marketing research action.

Internal suppliers may (a) have their own formal departments, (b) have no formal department but at least a single individual responsible for marketing research, or they may (c) assign no one responsibility for conducting marketing research.

Marketing research departments are usually organized according to one, or a combination, of the following functions: area of application, marketing function, or the research process. Some firms organize the research function

Marketing research departments are usually organized according to one, or a combination, of the following functions: area of application, marketing function, or the research process.

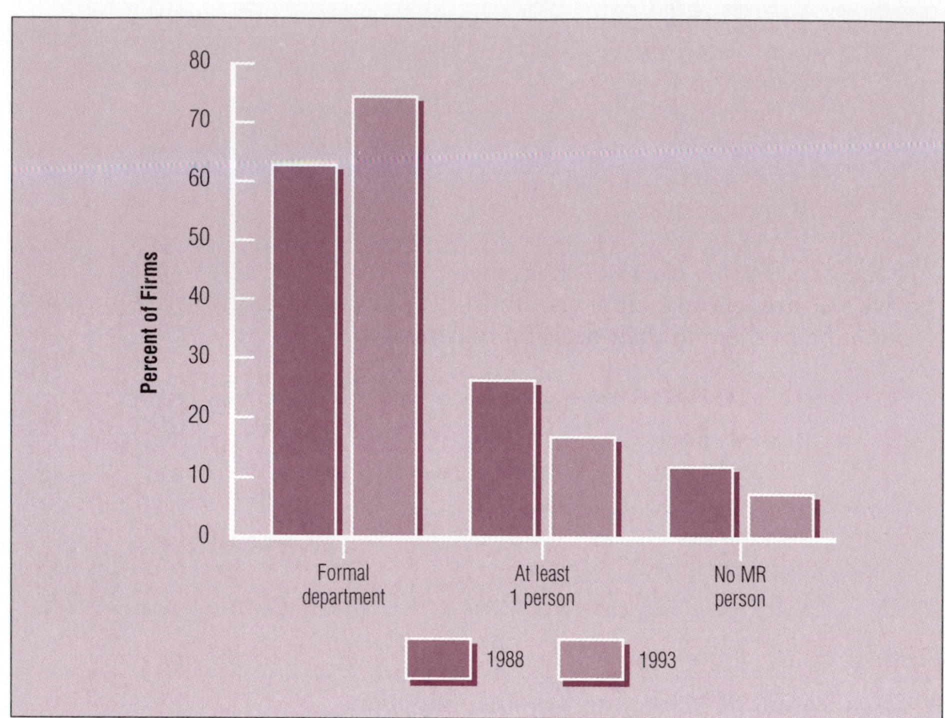

Figure 2.3

Organization for Marketing Research

around the "areas" to which the research is being applied. For example, some firms serve both ultimate consumers as well as industrial consumers. Therefore, the marketing research department may be organized into two divisions: consumer and industrial. Some firms organize their research department around brands or lines of products or services. Marketing research may be organized around functional areas such as advertising research, product research, distribution research, and so on. Finally, the research function may be organized around stages in the research process such as data analysis, data collection, or field data collection.

It is rare to find no one responsible for marketing research in large organizations; small companies who see their customers daily conduct their own "informal" research constantly.

If firms elect not to have a formal marketing research department, there are many other organizational possibilities. Assignment for marketing research may be made across company departments or divisions. That is, although there is no formal research department, responsibility for research rests within existing organizational units. One problem with this method is that research activities are not coordinated; a division conducts its own research, and other units of the firm may be unaware of useful information. One way to remedy this is to have a committee whose primary function is to coordinate research activities to ensure that all units of the firm have input into and benefit from any research activity undertaken. In some cases, committees or individuals assigned to marketing research may actually conduct some limited research but typically their primary role is that of helping other managers recognize the need for research and coordinating the purchase of research from external research suppliers. Obviously, the advantage here is limiting fixed costs incurred by maintaining the full-time staff required for an ongoing department. No one may be assigned to marketing research in some organizations. This is rare in large companies and, as shown in Figure 2.3, the percentage of firms electing this option is decreasing. It is equally rare to find someone in charge of marketing research in small firms where specialization simply is not affordable. In very small firms, the owner/manager plays many roles, ranging from strategic planning to salesperson to security staff. He or she must also be responsible for marketing research, making certain to have the right information before making decisions. Fortunately, small business owner/managers can more easily gather certain types of information than can CEOs of large, multinational corporations. This is because small business owner/managers have daily contact with customers and suppliers. In this way, they constantly gather information that helps them in their decision making.

External Suppliers

External suppliers are outside firms hired to fulfill a firm's marketing research needs.

External suppliers can be classified as either full-service or limited-service supplier firms.

External suppliers are outside firms hired to fulfill a firm's marketing research needs. Marketing Research Insight 2.1 (pages 26–28) provides a list of directories useful for finding research firms. Over one-half of firms' spending on marketing research goes to pay for the services of external suppliers.[10] In 1995, the top 50 marketing research firms in the United States had combined revenues of $4.6 billion, up 9.4 percent from 1994.[11] Interestingly, 39 percent of these revenues came from work done abroad. This is a definite indication of the globalization of the marketing research industry. These research firms range in size from one-person proprietorships to large, international corporations. Table 2.1 (pages 29–30) lists the top 50 marketing research firms. This list is updated annually in *Marketing News* by Jack Honomichl. External suppliers can be classified as either *full-service* or *limited-service* supplier firms. A discussion of these types of firms follows.

Full-Service Supplier Firms

Full-service supplier firms have the ability to conduct the entire marketing research project for the buyer firms. Full-service firms can be further broken down into syndicated services, standardized services, and customized services.

Full-service supplier firms have the ability to conduct the entire marketing research project for the buyer firms. Full-service firms will often define the problem, specify the research design, collect and analyze the data, and prepare the final written report. Typically, these are larger firms that have the expertise as well as the necessary facilities to conduct research studies in their entirety. Firms such as Burke Marketing Research, Market Facts, Inc., ACNielsen, and The M/A/R/C Group are full-service firms. Full-service firms can be further broken down into syndicated services, standardized services, and customized services.

Syndicated data service firms collect information that is made available to multiple subscribers.

Syndicated data service firms collect information that is made available to multiple subscribers. The information, or data, is provided in standardized form (information may not be tailored to meet the needs of any one company) to a large number of companies, known as a syndicate. By forming a syndicate of companies who agree to subscribe to the service, the firms share the cost of gathering this information. Therefore, syndicated data service firms offer valuable standardized marketing research information at relatively low cost to any one subscribing firm in the syndicate. A potential disadvantage to the client is that the same information will be available to a competitor as well. You may have already heard of or participated in the syndicated work done by some of the research firms in the top 50 list. Take, for instance, the Arbitron Company (http://www.arbitron.com). Arbitron measures the size and characteristics of radio audiences for radio stations in radio markets around the United States. This information is syndicated to more than 800

Visit Arbitron at http://www.arbitron.com

MARKETING RESEARCH INSIGHT 2.1

Where to Find Marketing Research Firms

There are a number of sources of marketing research firms. Many of these sources, like Quirk's Marketing Research Review *and* The Greenbook® International Directory of Marketing Research Companies and Services, *list firms alphabetically, by geographic region served, and by types of services offered.*

Advertising Research Foundation
641 Lexington Ave., 11th fl.
New York, NY 10022
Ph. 212-751-5656
Michael Naples, President

American Association for Public Opinion Research
P.O. Box 1248
Ann Arbor, MI 48106
Ph. 313-764-1555
Fax 313-764-3341
Marlene Bednar, Administrator

American Association of Advertising Agencies
405 Lexington Ave., 18th fl.
New York, NY 10174
Ph. 212-682-2500
Fax 212-953-5665
O. Butch Drake, President

American Economic Association
2014 Broadway, Ste. 305
Nashville, TN 37203
Ph. 615-322-2595
Fax 615-343-7590
C. Hilton Hinshaw, Secretary/Treasurer

American Marketing Association
250 S. Wacker Dr.
Chicago, IL 60606
Ph. 312-648-0536
Fax 312-993-7542

American Public Relations Association
33 Irving Pl., 3rd fl.
New York, NY 10003
Ph. 212-995-2230
Fax 212-995-0757
Ray Gaulke, COO

American Statistical Association
1429 Duke St.
Alexandria, VA 22314
Ph. 703-684-1221
Fax 703-684-2037
Ray Wallace, Executive Director

Center of Statistical and Economic Studies
29 Ave. Hoche
F-75008 Paris
France
Ph. 1-43590456
Fax 1-45638679

The Council for Marketing and Opinion Research (CMOR)
170 North Country Rd.
Port Jefferson, NY 11777
Ph. 516-928-6206
Fax 516-928-6041

Council of American Survey Research Organizations (CASRO)
3 Upper Devon
Port Jefferson, NY 11777
Ph. 516-928-6954
Fax 516-928-6041
Diane K. Bowers, Executive Director

European Confederation of Public Relations
51 rue de Verdun
F-92158 Suresnes Cedex
France
Ph. 1-46972000
Fax 1-46972010

European Society for Opinion and Marketing Research (ESOMAR)
Central Secretariat
J.J. Viottastraat 29
1071 JP Amsterdam, The Netherlands
Ph. 31-20-664-2141
Fax 31-20-664-2922

FEMRA (Industrial Market Research)
Studio 38, Wimbledon Business Center
Riverside Road
London SW17 OBA
England

International Research Institutes (IRiS)
98 Ave. de Floreal
B-1180 Brussels, Belgium
Ph. 32-2-344-3581
Fax 32-2-343-9828
E-mail: 100517.3211@compuserve.com

Marketing Research Association
2189 Silas Deane Highway, Suite 5
Rocky Hill, CT 06067
Ph. 860-257-4008
Fax 860-257-3990

Marketing Research Association-Great Lakes Chapter
599 Industrial Dr., Ste. 310
Carmel, IN 46032
Ph. 606-655-6072

New York AMA - GreenBook® Directories
60 East 42nd St., Ste. 1765
New York, NY 10165
Ph. 212-687-3280
Fax 212-557-9242
E-mail: NewYorkAMA@aol.com
WWW: http://www.greenbook.org
Mary Lee Keane, Executive Director

The GreenBook® International Directory of Marketing Research Companies and Services, and its companion Focus Group Directory´ are one-stop resources for instant access to thousands of marketing research firms and offices in the United States, Canada, and 80 other countries. Both the print and Internet versions are completely cross-referenced by 169 company service categories, 130 market and industry specialties, 60 computer program specialties, trademarks, geographic location, and principal personnel.

Population Association of America
1722 N. St. NW
Washington, DC 20036
Ph. 202-429-0891
Fax 202-785-0146
Ina Young, Administrator

Population Reference Bureau
1875 Connecticut Ave. NW, Ste. 520
Washington, DC 20009
Ph. 202-483-1100
Fax 202-328-3937
Peter Donaldson, President

Qualitative Research Consultants Association (QRCA)
P.O. Box 6767, FDR Station
New York, NY 10022
Ph. 888-674-7722
Fax 607-699-3269
E-mail: qrcapros@qrca.org
WWW: http://www.qrca.org
Patricia Sabena, President

Founded in 1983, QRCA is the worldwide association of more than 575 independent qualitative research professionals committed to the highest professional standards and the advancement of the discipline.

Quirk's Marketing Research Review
Quirk Enterprises
P.O. Box 23536
Minneapolis, MN 55423
Ph. 612-854-5101
Fax 612-854-8191
E-mail: Quirk19@skypoint.com
WWW: http://www.quirks.com
Tom Quirk, Publisher

Quirk's publishes an annual directory that lists research firms by geographic area covered, research specialty, and industry specialty. Personnel are also cross-referenced by company.

subscribers to Arbitron's ratings, including firms such as newspapers, radio and TV stations, cable systems, agencies, and advertisers.

Nielsen Media Research (http://www.nielsen.com/home/yahoo.cgi) provides the Nielsen National Television Index (NTI). The NTI provides information on the demographics and size of the audience for specific television programs. The index is based on a sample of 5,000 households equipped with people meters for reporting TV, cable, and home video viewing. This information is sold to a large number of subscribing organizations who use the ratings primarily to set advertising rates. The networks themselves subscribe to the information as it is used as a basis for making decisions about television programming. InfoScan is a syndicated market tracking service that provides weekly sales, price, and store condition information on products sold in a sample of food, drug, and mass merchandise stores. We discuss syndicated data service firms in greater detail in chapter 7.

Standardized service firms provide syndicated services as opposed to syndicated data. Each client gets different data, but the service used to collect the data is standardized so that it may be offered to many clients at a cost less than that of a custom-designed project.

Standardized service firms provide syndicated *services* as opposed to syndicated *data.* Each client gets different data, but the service used to collect the data is standardized so that it may be offered to many clients at a cost less than that of a custom-designed project. Audits & Surveys provides a standardized service for test marketing. If a firm decides to test market on their own, they must spend resources in order to find distributors who will carry the test product and to make arrangements with various media firms to promote the product. Audits & Surveys has *preestablished* relationships with these firms so that they can offer a standardized test market package to firms wishing to use their service. Note that, unlike syndicated data services, the standardized services provide data unique to the client. The service itself is what is being sold by standardized services firms. NFO (National Family Opinion) Research, Inc. provides a standardized service called the "NFO Multicard," shown in Figure 2.4 (page 31). NFO maintains large panels of households who have agreed to provide NFO with information on request. Many times companies would like to know how the public would respond to specific questions. Knowing what percentage of the population is brand loyal to toothpaste brands, for example, may help a company make a decision to continue development of a new toothpaste formulation. NFO allows client firms to ask several questions, which are then mailed out to their thousands of panel members. Client firms receive responses to their questions in a matter of days. NFO requires that client firms submit their questions on certain dates of the year. Here again, the *data* is unique to the client; the *service* is standardized for all clients.

Customized service firms offer a variety of research services that are tailored to meet the client's specific needs.

Customized service firms offer a variety of research services that are tailored to meet the client's specific needs. Each client's problem is treated as a

TABLE 2.1

Top 50 U.S. Research Organizations

Rank 1996	Rank 1995	Organization	Headquarters	Phone	Total Research Revenues* (millions)	Percent Change from 1995**	Percent and Revenues from outside U.S. ($ in millions)	
1	–	ACNielsen Corp.	*Stamford, CT*	(203) 961-3330	$1,358.6	6.0%	78.9	$1,072.1
2	–	Cognizant Corp.	*Westport, CT*	(203) 222-4200	1,223.8	10.2	57.0	697.5
3	2	Information Resources Inc.	*Chicago, IL*	(312) 726-1221	405.6	12.8	15.0	61.0
4	3	The Arbitron Co.	*New York, NY*	(212) 887-1300	153.1	11.6		
5	6	PMSI/Source Informatics	*Phoenix, AZ*	(602) 381-9500	152.2	8.9	28.6	43.6
6	4	Westat Inc.	*Rockville, MD*	(301) 251-1500	146.5	18.1		
7	5	Maritz Marketing Research Inc.	*St. Louis, MO*	(314) 827-1610	133.6	8.0	23.0	30.7
8	9	NFO Research Inc.	*Greenwich, CT*	(203) 629-8888	109.2	10.5	4.0	4.8
9	7	The Kantar Group	*London, UK*	(44-171) 656-5599	103.3	12.3	15.2	15.7
10	8	The NPD Group	*Port Washington, NY*	(516) 625-0700	99.6	16.1	16.0	15.9
11	10	Market Facts Inc.	*Arlington Heights, IL*	(708) 590-7000	83.8	29.7	7.5	6.3
12	11	Audits & Surveys Worldwide Inc.	*New York, NY*	(212) 627-9700	60.4	10.5	32.9	19.9
13	12	The M/A/R/C Group Inc.	*Irving, TX*	(214) 506-3400	55.7	6.7	1.8	1.0
14	15	The BASES Group	*Covington, KY*	(606) 655-6000	53.3	28.1	15.4	8.2
15	13	Opinion Research Corp.	*Princeton, NJ*	(908) 281-5100	47.3	5.7	24.1	11.4
16	16	Intersearch Corp.	*Horsham, PA*	(215) 442-9000	45.4	10.5	15.4	7.0
17	14	Abt Associates Inc.	*Cambridge, MA*	(617) 492-7100	44.3	3.3		
18	17	NOP Information Group	*New York, NY*	(212) 599-0444	44.0	15.8		
19	18	Macro International Inc.	*Calverton, MD*	(301) 572-0200	42.4	6.6	42.7	18.1
20	22	J.D. Power and Associates	*Agoura Hills, CA*	(818) 889-6330	40.3	33.0		
21	20	Elrick & Lavidge	*Tucker, GA*	(770) 938-3233	38.9	24.4	2.8	1.1
22	23	Burke Inc.	*Cincinnati, OH*	(513) 241-5663	36.8	15.0	13.9	5.1
23	21	Roper Starch Worldwide Inc.	*Mamaroneck, NY*	(914) 698-0800	35.3	12.1	11.9	4.2
24	19	Walker Information	*Indianapolis, IN*	(317) 843-3939	35.1	6.9	26.7	9.4
25	28	M.O.R.-PACE Inc.	*Farmington, MI*	(810) 737-5300	32.7	45.3	16.3	5.3
26	29	Wirthlin Worldwide	*McLean, VA*	(703) 556-0001	31.7	35.9	12.9	4.1
27	24	C&R Research Services Inc.	*Chicago, IL*	(312) 828-9200	28.9	6.6		
28	31	Total Research Corp.	*Princeton, NJ*	(609) 520-9100	26.0	13.0	26.9	7.0
29	25	Lieberman Research Worldwide	*Los Angeles, CA*	(310) 553-0550	25.7	9.8	15.2	3.9
30	27	Yankelovich Partners Inc.	*Norwalk, CT*	(203) 846-0100	23.6	1.7	1.8	.4
31	34	Custom Research Inc.	*Minneapolis, MN*	(612) 542-0800	22.8	23.2		
32	32	Market Strategies Inc.	*Southfield, MI*	(810) 350-3020	22.3	15.5		
33	30	ASI Market Research Inc.	*Stamford, CT*	(203) 328-7000	22.3	27.3		
34	–	Diagnostic Research International Inc.	*Los Angeles, CA*	(213) 254-4326	22.2	4.0	3.6	.8

(continued)

TABLE 2.1 (continued)

RANK 1996	1995	ORGANIZATION	HEADQUARTERS	PHONE	TOTAL RESEARCH REVENUES* (MILLIONS)	PERCENT CHANGE FROM 1995**	PERCENT AND REVENUES FROM OUTSIDE U.S. ($ IN MILLIONS)	
35	26	**Chilton Research Services**	*Radnor, PA*	(610) 964-4600	20.8	10.7		
36	33	**Data Development Corp.**	*New York, NY*	(212) 633-1100	20.2	8.6	7.1	1.4
37	35	**ICR-Survey Research Group**	*Media, PA*	(610) 565-9280	19.4	8.3		
38	37	**IntelliQuest Inc.**	*Austin, TX*	(512) 329-0808	19.1	22.1	30.0	5.7
39	44	**Harris Black International**	*Rochester, NY*	(716) 272-8400	18.9	9.8	5.8	1.1
40	38	**Market Decisions**	*Cincinnati, OH*	(513) 721-8100	17.4	15.2		
41	39	**RDA Group Inc.**	*Bloomfield Hills, MI*	(810) 332-5000	17.0	18.1	29.2	5.0
42	42	**National Analysts Inc.**	*Philadelphia, PA*	(215) 496-6800	14.9	24.2	4.	.7
43	36	**Response Analysis Corp.**	*Princeton, NJ*	(609) 921-3333	14.3	−16.9		
44	41	**Conway/Milliken & Associates**	*Chicago, IL*	(312) 787-4060	12.8	3.2		
45	43	**Guideline Research Corp.**	*New York, NY*	(212) 947-5140	12.5	6.8		
46	40	**MATRIXX Marketing Research**	*Cincinnati, OH*	(513) 841-1199	11.8	−16.3	44.1	5.2
47	45	**Ross-Cooper-Lund Inc.**	*Teaneck, NJ*	(201) 836-0040	11.7	13.5	3.	4
48	–	**Directions Research Inc.**	*Cincinnati, OH*	(513) 651-2990	10.8	31.7		
49	48	**TVG Inc.**	*Fort Washington, PA*	(215) 646-7200	10.5	22.1		
50	–	**The PreTesting Co. Inc.**	*Tenafly, NJ*	(201) 569-4800	10.0	8		
				Subtotal, Top 50	**$5,048.8**	**12.0%**	**41.1%**	**$2,074**
All other (119 CASRO member companies not included in Top 50)*					**457.7**	**7.4**		
				Total (169 organizations)	**$5,506.5**	**11.7%**		

*Total revenues that include nonresearch activities for some companies are significantly higher. This information is given in the individual company profiles in the main article (see reference below).

**Rate of growth from year to year has been adjusted so as not to include revenue gains or losses from acquisitions. See company profiles for explanation.

***Total revenues of 119 survey research firms, beyond those listed in Top 50, that provide financial information on a confidential basis to the Council of American Survey Research Organizations (CASRO).

Source: *"The Honomichl 50,"* Marketing News, *31, 12 (June 9, 1997), H-4. American Marketing Association, by permission.*

distinct research project. For example, a research firm, such as Burke, spends considerable time with a client firm to determine the problem and then designs a research project specifically to address that particular client's problem. Other such firms include Market Facts, Inc., Elrick & Lavidge, Inc., Burke Marketing Research, and Custom Research, Inc. Market Facts, for instance, provides custom marketing research services through a range of research methodologies including test marketing, focus groups, and consumer and industrial surveys. Also, keep in mind that many of the large research firms fit

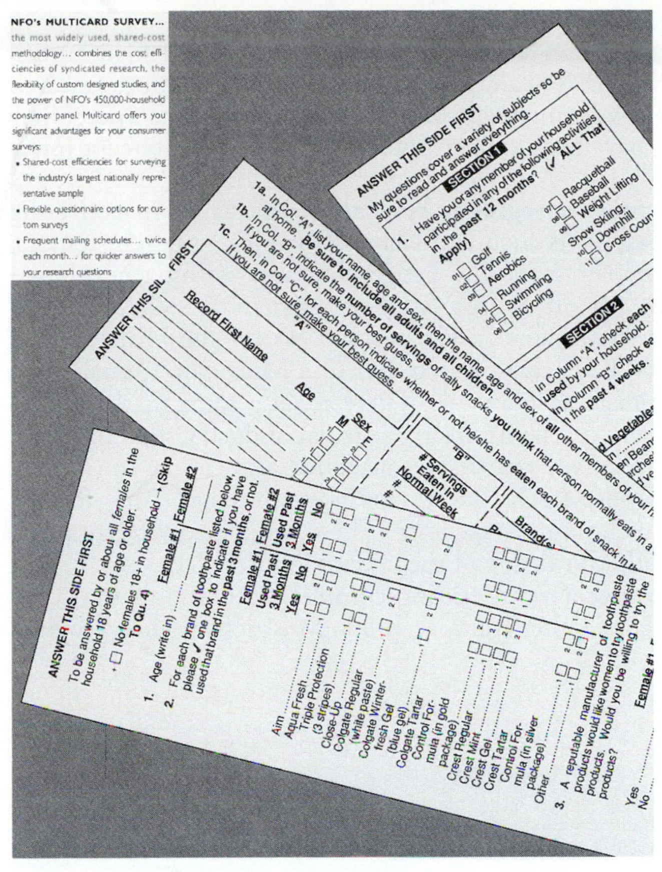

Figure 2.4

NFO's Multicard is a syndicated surveying service.

into several of the classifications shown in Figure 2.2. NFO Research Inc., previously cited as a supplier of standardized services, also provides customized services.

Limited-Service Supplier Firms

Limited-service supplier firms typically specialize in one or, at most, a few marketing research activities. Firms can specialize in types of marketing research techniques such as eye-testing and mystery shopping, or specific market segments such as senior citizens or certain sports segments such as golf or tennis. The limited-service suppliers can be further classified on the basis of their specialization. These include field services, market segment specialists, data entry services, sample design and distribution services, data analysis, and specialized research technique service suppliers.

Limited-service supplier firms typically specialize in one or, at most, a few marketing research activities.

Field service firms specialize in collecting data. These firms typically operate in a particular territory conducting telephone surveys, focus group interviews, mall intercept surveys, or door-to-door surveys. Because it is expensive and difficult to maintain interviewers all over the country, other firms will use the services of field service firms in order to quickly and efficiently gather data. There is specialization even within firms that specialize in field services. Some firms, for example, conduct only in-depth personal interviews; others conduct only mall intercept surveys. Some firms, known as "phone banks," limit their

Field service firms specialize in collecting data.

practice to telephone surveying. Nancy Levine Research Services, based in California, offers expertise in on-site supervision, briefings, and field audits. The New York–based Meyers Research Center specializes in in-store research using consumer point-of-sale intercept interviews. Quick Test, Inc. offers clients interviewers who have been trained specifically for mall intercept interviews (Figure 2.5).

Market segment specialists collect data for special market segments such as Blacks, Hispanics, children, seniors, gays, industrial customers, or a specific geographic area within the United States or internationally.

Other firms, called **market segment specialists,** specialize in collecting data for special market segments such as Blacks, Hispanics, children, seniors, gays, industrial customers, or a specific geographic area within the United States or internationally. Abbott Wool's Market Segment Resource Locator (http://www.amic.com/awool) offers specialized surveys for the Hispanic and Asian-American segments. Kidfacts Research, based in Michigan, specializes in research on children of all ages (Figure 2.6). There are also some marketing research companies who service clients in a particular industry. For instance, Westat, Inc. specializes in survey research projects for agencies of the federal government. Richard Day Research, Inc. (http://www.mcs.net/~rdr/) focuses on marketing research for nonprofit agencies. These limited-service suppliers capitalize on their in-depth knowledge of the client's industry.

Data entry services specialize in editing completed questionnaires, coding, and entering the data.

Data entry services specialize in editing completed questionnaires, coding, and entering the data. Pulse Train Technology is a firm that provides

Figure 2.5

Quick Test is a limited-service firm specializing in the collection of data in shopping malls.

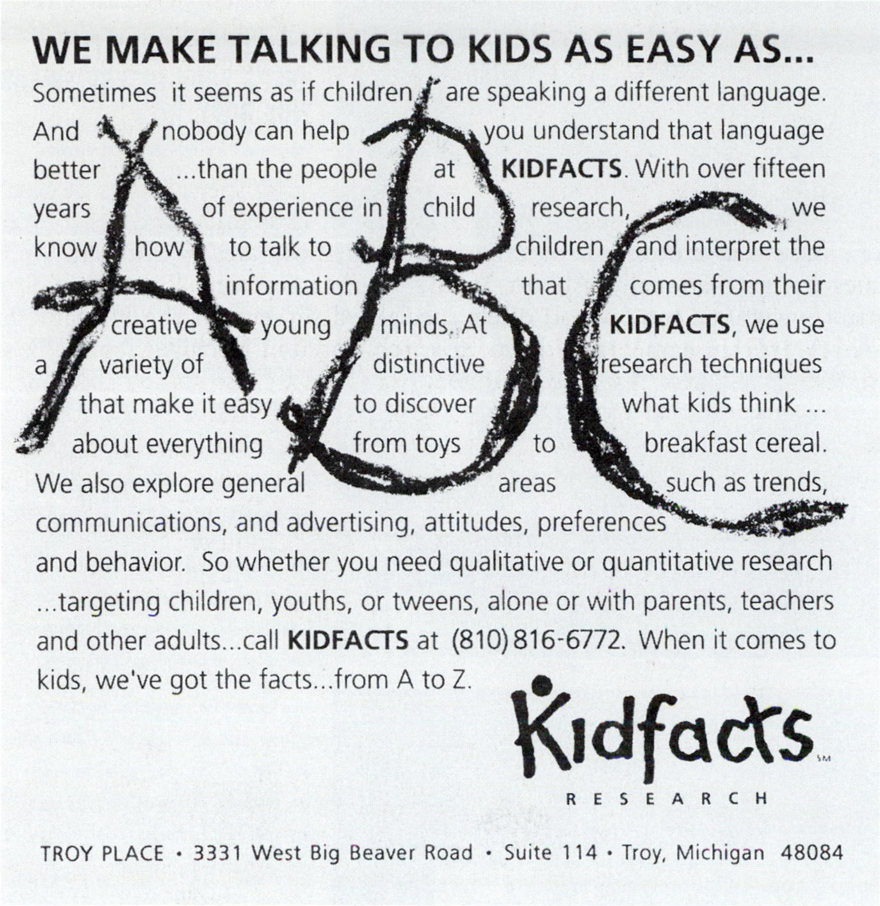

WE MAKE TALKING TO KIDS AS EASY AS...

Sometimes it seems as if children are speaking a different language. And nobody can help you understand that language better ...than the people at **KIDFACTS**. With over fifteen years of experience in child research, we know how to talk to children and interpret the information that comes from their creative young minds. At **KIDFACTS**, we use a variety of distinctive research techniques that make it easy to discover what kids think ... about everything from toys to breakfast cereal. We also explore general areas such as trends, communications, and advertising, attitudes, preferences and behavior. So whether you need qualitative or quantitative research ...targeting children, youths, or tweens, alone or with parents, teachers and other adults...call **KIDFACTS** at (810) 816-6772. When it comes to kids, we've got the facts...from A to Z.

Kidfacts℠
RESEARCH

TROY PLACE • 3331 West Big Beaver Road • Suite 114 • Troy, Michigan 48084

Figure 2.6

Kidfacts specializes in marketing research on children.

high-quality software systems and services for data entry firms (Figure 2.7, page 34). Computers have enabled researchers to increase efficiency by allowing interviewers to collect the data and simultaneously enter it into software programs for analysis.

Survey Sampling Inc. and Scientific Telephone Samples (STS) are examples of limited-service firms that specialize in **sample design and distribution.** It is not uncommon, for example, for a company with an internal marketing research department to buy its sample from a firm specializing in sampling and then send the samples and a survey questionnaire to a phone bank for completion of the survey. In this way, a firm may quickly and efficiently conduct telephone surveys using a probability sample plan in markets all over the country. Another research firm that specializes in sample design and selection is GENESYS Sampling Systems. They have listed household and business samples, congressional district samples, and special programs to purge nonoperating numbers (Figure 2.8, on page 35).

Sample design and distribution firms specialize in providing samples to firms that are conducting research studies.

There are limited-service marketing research firms that specialize strictly in **data analysis.** Their contribution to the research process is to provide the technical assistance necessary to analyze and interpret data using the more so-

There are limited-service marketing research firms that specialize strictly in data analysis.

ONLY BELLVIEW CATI KEEPS YOUR INTERVIEWERS THIS BUSY.

Imagine all the people you could interview using Bellview CATI.

Bellview's powerful sample management quickly selects and presents calls to your interviewers.

With its unique queuing system, it ensures the most important sample groups, appointments and other callbacks are handled promptly and efficiently.

Add an optional predictive dialer and our Bellview TCI (Telephony Computer Interface) module and your productivity goes even higher.

When one interview ends, the Bellview TCI module ensures another call from your sample is automatically connected. (Mrs Robinson won't even know she's been dialed electronically.)

With Bellview and a predictive dialer working together, your people won't have to dial numbers which are busy, not in service or unanswered. In fact, combining Bellview CATI with TCI and a dialer can raise the time spent interviewing to as much as 50 minutes in the hour.

Sounds like music to your ears? To find out more about Bellview, and predictive dialing, call us for details of the world's leading CATI system.

Pulse Train Technology Ltd,
618 U.S. Hwy 1, N. Palm Beach, FL 33408
Tel: (407) 842-4000
Fax: (407) 842-7280
Email: PTTSystems@AOL.COM
Internet: http://www.ws.pipex.com/ptt

PULSE·TRAIN TECHNOLOGY·LTD

Figure 2.7

Pulse Train Technology specializes in CATI software.

phisticated data analysis techniques such as conjoint analysis. Sophisticated Data Research (SDR) is an example of one such firm.

Specialized research technique firms address very specific needs such as eye-tracking, package design, or brand name testing.

Specialized research technique firms have developed to address very specific needs of the industry. One such firm is NameQuest Inc. This is a name-development and name-testing company that tests brand names, corporate

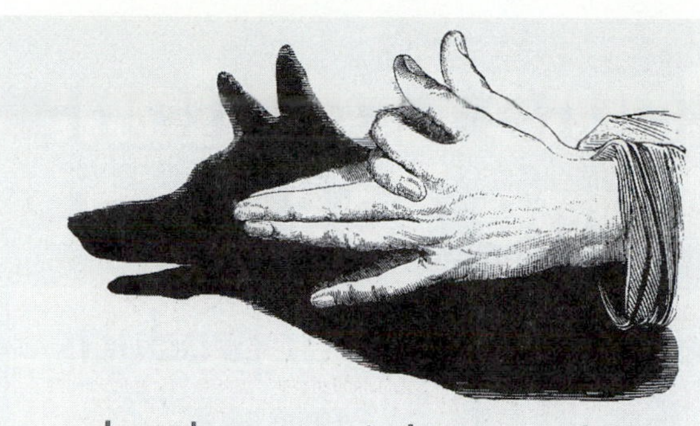

Figure 2.8

GENESYS Sampling Systems specializes in providing sample plans, estimating sizes, and providing sample frames.

names, and so on (Figure 2.9, on page 36). Micromeasurements, Inc. uses computer graphics to test, evaluate, modify, and retest designs for packaging, shelf configurations, logos, etc. They specialize in using eye-tracking to test these communication media.

We should not leave this section without saying that our categorization of reasearch suppliers does not fit every situation. There are other entities supplying research information which do not fit neatly into one of our categories. For example, universities and institutes supply research information. Universities sponsor a great deal of research that could be classified as marketing research. This work is typically conducted by marketing professors and is published in scholarly journals such as the *Journal of Marketing Research*, the *Journal of Advertising Research*, and the *Journal of the Market Research Society.* Universities and research institutes, both public and private, also publish a great deal of marketing research in monographs and newsletters. Because Total Quality Management (TQM) has brought about an interest in consumer satisfaction and benchmarking, some marketing professors at the University of Michigan recently developed a national customer satisfaction index.[12] Academic researchers have also investigated sensitive issues such as the effects of cigarette advertising on adolescents.[13]

There are other entities supplying research information that do not fit neatly into one of our categories.

Name Creation:
Name Testing.

Are you giving your products
Smart Names™?

Smart Names are names that have distinction, value and believability. NameQuest has merged the **art** of name creation with the **science** of name testing. NameQuest will help your products produce more profits.

For Information Contact:
John P. Hoeppner
Phone: (602) 488-9660
Fax: (602) 530-2289
e-mail: namequest @ aol.com
U.S. Mail: P.O. Box 5587
Express: 7440 E. Ridgecrest Road
Santa Fe Suite 101
Carefree, AZ USA 85377

EDISON Best New Products Awards, American Marketing Association
Best New Product Branding

NameQuest®
The Science of Name Creation

Companies that have recently used our advanced methodology include:

American Cyanamid
Ameritech
Anheuser-Busch
Bayer, Inc.
B.C. Hydro & Gas
Campbell Soup
Fuji Photo Film
Good Humor-Breyers
Hunt-Wesson
Jim Beam Brands
Johnson & Johnson
Kellogg USA
MCI
Okidata
Osram Syvania
RJR Nabisco Foods
S.C. Johnson Wax
Thomas J. Lipton
Unilever
W.L. Gore

Figure 2.9
An Advertisement for NameQuest Inc.

HOW HAS THE MARKETING RESEARCH INDUSTRY PERFORMED?

In evaluations of the research industry, the basic conclusion is that the industry has performed well but there is room for improvement.

Periodically, evaluations are made of the marketing research industry. These studies have asked buyers of marketing research studies whether the value of the research performed by the suppliers in the industry is worthwhile. In three separate evaluations, the basic conclusion is that the industry has performed well but there is room for improvement. The criticism has focused on the following areas of concern: there is a lack of creativity, the industry is too survey oriented, the industry does not understand the real problems that need studying, market researchers show a lack of concern for respondents, the industry has a cavalier attitude regarding nonresponse error, and the price of the research is high relative to its value.[14]

Suggested Remedy for the Future: Certification

Many of the problems in the research industry are created by a very small minority of firms, most of which simply are not qualified to deliver quality marketing research services.

Although the evaluations of the industry are "good," few would argue that they are "excellent." Many suggest that the problems are created by a very small minority of firms, most of which simply are not qualified to deliver quality marketing research services. There is obviously a concern among buyers and suppliers with the lack of uniformity in the industry as well. In a 1994 study of buyers' and suppliers' perceptions of the research industry, Dawson, Bush, and Stern found that the key issue in the industry is a lack of uniform quality; there are good suppliers and there are poor suppliers.[15] To remedy this, some have recommended either a **certification** program or a system for **auditing** marketing research firms.

Some have argued that marketing research attracts practitioners who are not fully qualified to provide adequate service to buyer firms. There are no formal requirements; no education level, no degrees, no certificates, no licenses, and no tests of any kind required to open up a marketing research business. Certainly, the vast majority of research firms have staffs thoroughly trained in research methods and have years of excellent performance. However, some say, it is those few firms with unqualified personnel and management that tarnish the industry's image.

Professor Bruce Stern has argued that all practitioners should be certified by being required to pass a four-part exam on each of the following areas: secondary data, research methods, data analysis, and the fundamentals of marketing. As other professions, such as accounting, real estate, and financial analysis have learned, certification programs can raise the overall level of competence within an industry.[16] Alvin Achenbaum[17] as well as Patrick Murphy and Gene Laczniak[18] have proposed a professional designation of Certified Public Researchers (CPRs), analogous to CPAs or CFAs. Those arguing against certification point out that it would be difficult, if not impossible, to agree on defining certification standards, particularly for the creative aspect of the research process.[19]

The marketing research industry is discussing certification and auditing programs. It has also recently developed new professional development programs for members of the industry.

An alternative to certification is auditing. Steve Bernstein, market research manager for Consolidated Freightways, has proposed auditing as a means of providing the industry with some professional oversight. Bernstein suggests that the audit include assessments of, for example, research methods and data integrity. An audit would involve procedures such as retabulation from raw data of a random sample of descriptive surveys, validation of a sample of questionnaires, and even checking questionnaires for evidence of selling under the guise of marketing research.[20] The key issue is that the industry recognizes it has certain problems, and efforts are being made to remedy them. The AMA now sponsors two programs designed to increase skills in the industry. One, the AMA School of Marketing Research, is a program conducted at Notre Dame University designed to benefit the analyst, project supervisor, or manager of marketing research. The other is an annual conference on advanced analytical techniques. Also, the Marketing Research Association has started an introductory program on marketing research. Coordinated at the University of Georgia, this program is designed to develop research skills of those being transferred into marketing research or those who want to enter the profession. All in all, we must conclude that the marketing research industry is healthy and is responsive to its many challenges.

ETHICAL ISSUES FACING THE MARKETING RESEARCH INDUSTRY

We think these ethical issues are so important that we call your attention to them throughout this book using the ethical issue icon that you see above.

Like most areas of business activity, there exist many opportunities for unethical (and ethical) behavior in the marketing research industry.[21] For example, Marketing Research Insight 2.2 raises the ethical issue of truthfulness of research information. Our purpose here is to introduce you to the areas where unethical behavior has existed in the past and to hopefully give you some framework for thinking about how you will conduct yourself in the future when confronted with these situations. We think these ethical issues are so important that we call your attention to them throughout this book using the ethical issue icon that you see at the beginning of this section.

Ethics may be defined as a field of inquiry into determining what behaviors are deemed appropriate. One's philosophy usually determines appropriate, ethical behavior.

Ethics may be defined as a field of inquiry into determining what behaviors are deemed appropriate under certain circumstances as prescribed by codes of behavior that are set by society. Society determines what is ethical and what is not ethical. In some cases, this is formalized by our institutions. Some behavior, for example, is so wrongful that it is deemed illegal by statute. In many ways, behavior that is illegal is unethical, by definition. However, there are many other behaviors that are considered by some to be unethical but are not illegal. When these types of behaviors are not spelled out by some societal institution (such as the justice system, legislature, congress, regulatory agencies such as the FTC, and so on), then the determination of whether the behaviors are ethical or unethical is open to debate.

Systems of Philosophical Belief: Deontology versus Teleology

One philosophy is called deontology, which focuses on the rights of the individual. If an individual's rights are violated, then the behavior is not ethical.

Although there are many philosophies that may be applied to explain one's determination of appropriate behavior given certain circumstances, we use the two philosophies of deontology and teleology. **Deontology** is concerned with the rights of the individual. Is the behavior fair and just for each individual? If an individual's rights are violated, then the behavior is not ethical.[22] For example, consider the marketing research firm that has been hired to study how consumers are attracted to and react to a new form of in-store display. Researchers, hidden from view, record the behavior of unsuspecting shoppers as they walk through the supermarket. A deontologist considers this form of research activity unethical because it violates the individual shopper's right to privacy. The deontologist would likely agree to the research provided the shoppers were informed *beforehand* that their behavior would be recorded, giving them the option to participate or not to participate.

Teleology is a philosophy that focuses on the trade-off between individual costs and group benefits. If benefits outweigh costs, the behavior is judged to be ethical.

On the other hand, **teleology** analyzes a given behavior in terms of its benefits and costs to society. If there are individual costs but group benefits, then there are net gains and the behavior is judged to be ethical.[23] In our example of the shopper being observed in the supermarket, the teleologist might conclude that, although there is a violation of the right to privacy among

MARKETING RESEARCH INSIGHT 2.2

What's True about Truthful Research Information?

Cynthia Crossen, a reporter and editor with The Wall Street Journal, *wrote a book about the truthfulness of research information. Her conclusions were interesting and led her to title the book,* Tainted Truth: The Manipulation of Fact in America. *The following information is excerpted, with permission, from her book.*

> *Americans have a fascination with research information. We give more weight to information if it comes from surveys, studies, experiments, and the polls as reported in the* New England Journal of Medicine, Time, New York Times, *the network news shows, or* The Wall Street Journal. *Yet, more and more of the research information we use to buy, elect, advise, acquit, and heal has been created not to expand our knowledge but to sell a product or advance a cause. If the research results contradict a sponsor's agenda, the results are routinely suppressed.*
>
> *The sheer volume of "truth" being reported to us via research is staggering and growing. Every day's news teems with references to research: about health (does coffee raise cholesterol?, should young women have mammograms?); presidential popularity polls; "lifestyle" surveys on how people work, eat, play, relax; policy studies showing environmental or political effects of a course of action; pharmaceutical studies promising another breakthrough in a dread disease; and advocacy studies showing the worsening plight of a group that needs help. But, behind all the facts and truths that we see everyday, we learn that the study that found that 62% of Americans want to keep the penny in circulation was sponsored by the zinc industry. That 70% of cellular telephone users reported that the cellular phones made them more successful in business was sponsored by Motorola. Efficacy studies on most of today's drugs were sponsored by . . . you guessed it . . . the pharmaceutical company selling the drug! Crossen believes that the explosion of "tainted truth" has come from money. Money is used to "sponsor" (buy) research studies and that even once independent and objective institutions such as universities have given in to the monetary pressures. Few researchers escape the pressures of financial support and they are influenced, whether knowingly or not, by trying to please their financial sponsors. Results can be manipulated by subtle means known to researchers. Consider the different responses you may expect to different wording in a survey question: taxes or revenues? MX missile or Peacekeeper? Pro-choice or pro-abortion? Department of War or Department of Defense?*

Crossen has raised an important ethical issue for the research industry. Are research results totally independent and objective?

---

those shoppers observed (the cost), there is a benefit if the company learns how to market goods more efficiently, thus reducing long-term marketing costs. Because this benefit ultimately is shared by many more individuals than those whose privacy was invaded during the original study, the teleologist would likely declare this research practice to be ethical.

Several organizations in the marketing research industry have established codes of ethical behavior.

As noted previously, there are many ways a society may prescribe wanted and unwanted behaviors. In business, if there are practices that are not illegal but are nevertheless thought to be wrong, trade associations or professional organizations will often prescribe a code of ethical behavior. This has been the case in marketing and, more specifically, marketing research. The American Marketing Association has adopted a Research Code of Ethics, as has the

Figure 2.10

Code of Ethics for the Marketing Research Association

Council of American Survey Research Organizations (CASRO), and the Marketing Research Association (MRA). The MRA's code is shown in Figure 2.10. ESOMAR, the European research group, has issued its own set of guidelines to promote ethical behavior.[24]

The Ethical Issues Confronting the Marketing Research Industry

A number of ethical issues confronts the marketing research industry.

Many instances arise in the marketing research process where ethical decisions must be made. Opportunities for ethical problems occur between research suppliers and research buyers and between research suppliers and research subjects. We have provided some examples to help you gain a better appreciation of these issues.

Ethical Issues between Research Suppliers and Research Buyers

The ethical issues that crop up between research suppliers and research buyers include the integrity of the research, the fairness with which buyers and sup-

I RESPONSIBILITIES TO RESPONDENTS

Data Collection Companies...

1. will make factually correct statements to secure cooperation and will honor promises to respondents, whether verbal or written;
2. will not use information to identify respondents without the permission of the respondent, except to those who check the data or are involved in processing the data. If such permission is given, it must be recorded by the interviewer at the time the permission is secured;
3. will respect the respondent's right to withdraw or to refuse to cooperate at any stage of the study and not use any procedure or technique to coerce or imply that cooperation is obligatory;
4. will obtain and document respondent consent when it is known that the name and address or identity of the respondent may be passed to a third party for legal or other purposes, such as audio or video recordings;
5. will obtain permission and document consent of a parent, legal guardian or responsible guardian before interviewing children 12 years old or younger;
6. will give respondents the opportunity to refuse to participate in the research when there is a possibility they may be identifiable even without the use of their name or address (e.g., because of the size of the population being sampled).

Interviewers...

1. will treat the respondent with respect and not influence him or her through direct or indirect attempts, including the framing of questions and/or a respondent's opinion or attitudes on any issue;
2. will obtain and document permission from a parent, legal guardian or responsible guardian before interviewing children 12 years old or younger. Prior to obtaining permission, the interviewer should divulge the subject matter, length of the interview and other special tasks that will be required.

II RESPONSIBILITIES TO CLIENTS

Data Collection Companies...

1. will ensure that each study is conducted according to the client's exact specifications;
2. will observe confidentiality with all research techniques or methodologies and with information considered confidential or proprietary. Information will not be revealed that could be used to identify clients or respondents without proper authorization;
3. will ensure that companies, their employees and subcontractors involved in data collection take all reasonable precautions so that more than one survey is not conducted in one interview without explicit permission from the sponsoring company or companies;
4. will report research results accurately and honestly;
5. will not misrepresent themselves as having qualifications, experience, skills or facilities that they do not possess;
6. will refrain from referring to membership in the Marketing Research Association as proof of competence, since the Association does not certify any person's or organization's competency or skill level.

III RESPONSIBILITIES TO DATA COLLECTORS

Clients...

1. will be responsible for providing products and services that are safe and fit for their intended use and disclose/label all product contents;
2. will provide verbal or written instructions;
3. will not ask our members who subcontract research to engage in any activity that is not acceptable as defined in this Code or that is prohibited under any applicable federal, state, local laws, regulations and/or ordinances.

IV RESPONSIBILITIES TO THE GENERAL PUBLIC AND BUSINESS COMMUNITY

Data Collection Companies...

1. will not intentionally abuse public confidence in marketing and opinion research;
2. will not represent a non-research activity to be marketing and opinion research, such as:
   - questions whose sole objective is to obtain personal information about respondents, whether for legal, political, private or other purposes,
   - the compilation of lists, registers or data banks of names and addresses for any non-research purposes (e.g., canvassing or fund-raising),
   - industrial, commercial or any other form of espionage,
   - the acquisition of information for use by credit rating services or similar organizations,
   - sales or promotional approaches to the respondent,
   - the collection of debts;
3. will make interviewers aware of any special conditions that may be applicable to any minor (18 years old or younger).

Figure 2.10 *(continued)*

pliers are treated, the confidentiality of the research, and whether society's welfare is being jeopardized by the new product or promotion of the product.

Sometimes research is not totally objective. Information is withheld, falsified, or altered to protect vested interests.

Research Integrity. Often, marketing research information is used in making decisions of significant magnitude. The outcome of the decision may impact future company strategy, budgets, jobs, organization, and so forth. With so much at stake, the opportunity exists for a lack of total objectivity in the research process. This may take the form of withholding information, falsifying data, altering research results, or misinterpreting the research findings in a way that makes them more consistent with predetermined points of view. As one researcher stated, "I refused to alter research results and as a result I was fired for failure to think strategically."[25]

The impetus for a breach in research integrity may come from either the supplier or buyer. If a research supplier knows that a buyer will want marketing research services in the future, the supplier may alter a study's results or withhold information, so that the study will support the buyer's wishes. The buyer may not be aware of any departure from total objectivity but is very pleased with the study results and, according to the thinking of the supplier firm, is more likely to use the supplier company again in the future.

Breeches of research integrity need not be isolated to those managing the research project. Interviewers have been known to make up interviews and to take shortcuts in completing surveys. In fact, there is some evidence that this is more of a problem than was once thought.[26]

Maintaining research integrity is regarded as one of the most significant ethical issues in the research industry. In a study of 460 marketing researchers, Hunt, Chonko, and Wilcox found that maintenance of research integrity posed the *most* significant problem for one-third of those sampled.[27]

Sometimes firms buying marketing research are treated unethically. For example, they are sold unnecessary research or supplier firms subcontract the work to other firms for less money and, therefore, take profits without doing the research themselves.

Treating Buyers and Suppliers Fairly. In the Hunt, Chonko, and Wilcox study cited previously, the second most frequently stated ethical problem facing marketing researchers was fair treatment of buyer firms. A little over one-tenth of the respondents claimed this was the most important ethical problem they faced. Unfair treatment of buyers can take many forms. Passing hidden charges to buyers, overlooking study requirements when subcontracting work out to other supplier firms, and selling unnecessary research are examples of unfair treatment of buyer firms. By overlooking study requirements, such as qualifying respondents on specified characteristics or verifying that respondents were interviewed, the supplier firm may lower its cost of using the services of a subcontracting field service firm. A supplier firm may oversell research services to naive buyers by convincing them to use a more expensive research design such as a causal design in lieu of a descriptive design, or using more subjects than is necessary.

Buyers also treat supplier firms unethically. Agreements are not honored, payments are delayed, and buyers sometimes ask supplier firms to provide them with research designs without ever intending on contracting with an external supplier.

Note that the examples thus far are for situations in which suppliers treat buyers unethically. There are also situations in the industry where buyers abuse suppliers. A major problem exists, for example, when a firm having internal research capabilities issues a request for proposals from external supplier firms. External firms then spend time and money developing research designs to solve the stated problem, estimating costs of the project, and so on. Now, having collected several detailed proposals outlining research designs and costs, the abusing firm decides to do the job internally. There may be cases where this is justifiable, but certainly issuing a call for proposals from external firms with no intention of doing the job outside is unethical behavior. Closely related to this practice is that of issuing proposal requests from external firms when another external firm has been awarded the contract. The proposals are used, once again, as a check on costs and procedures. Other abuses include failure to honor agreements on such items as timetables for work due and schedules of payments.

Sharing of "background knowledge" among firms raises ethical questions.

Research Confidentiality. Virtually all work conducted by marketing research firms is confidential and proprietary. Researchers build up a storehouse of this information as they conduct research studies. Most ethical issues involving confidentiality revolve around how this storehouse of information, or "background knowledge," is treated. One researcher stated, "Where does 'background knowledge' stop and conflict exist (as a result of work with a previous client)?"[28]

The AMA's Code of Ethics specifically states that a researcher cannot use data from one project in a related project for a competitive firm. Let us assume that a marketing research firm conducts a number of market surveys for buyer Firm A. Information collected in the survey reveals important customer perceptions of Firm B, one of Firm A's major competitors. After completing the project for Firm A, the research firm recognizes the value of the survey information to Firm B and approaches the management of Firm B to sell them a survey that is "guaranteed" to identify important consumer perceptions about their firm. Is this ethical? Such a situation illustrates how "background knowledge" may be used but violates the confidentiality trust that must be maintained between research suppliers and buyers.

Involving Society's Welfare. Ethical issues arise as researchers balance marketing requirements with social issues. This is particularly true in the areas of product development and advertising. For example, marketing researchers have expressed concern over conducting research on advertising to children and conducting research on products they felt were dangerous to the public such as certain chemicals and cigarettes.

Ethical concerns arise when marketing researchers are asked to conduct research on advertising to children or on products they feel are dangerous to the public such as certain chemicals and cigarettes.

Ethical Issues between Research Suppliers and Research Subjects

The industry is obviously concerned about fair treatment of subjects. There are a number of ethical issues that appear in the relationship between marketing research suppliers and subjects or respondents used in research, such as disclosure, falsely promising anonymity, and right to privacy.

Disclosure. Research subjects are often not told the true intent of a study in which they are asked to participate.[29] The primary reason for this is the belief that if the subjects knew the true goal of a survey they would not respond in an unbiased fashion. For example, one of the authors recently conducted a marketing research study for a financial institution that was interested in knowing what its image, as well as the images of its major competitors, was in a given market area. Once researchers identify themselves to potential respondents, they normally give the respondent an explanation of what the study is about. It is at this point that subjects rarely receive full disclosure about the intent, procedure, and sponsor of the research project. Prevailing wisdom in the research industry holds that, by telling the respondent the name of the financial institution sponsoring the project, the respondent will not be completely candid or unbiased in his or her opinions about that firm. Consequently, researchers often develop what is known as "cover stories," which serve to generally inform the potential respondent as to the nature of the study, allowing them to make the decision as to whether they will participate or not. For example, to cover the real intent of researching a specific financial institution's image, the researcher identifies the general intent of the study and only names the research company (the client's name is not mentioned) by using a "cover story" such as, "This is a study of consumer attitudes toward financial institutions in Des Moines and is being conducted by the Sharp Marketing Research Company." Such cover stories are often accepted in the marketing research industry. It is generally recognized that full disclosure is not always required in marketing research studies.

Sometimes researchers do not disclose all aspects of the survey—such as the sponsor—to respondents so their answers will be completely candid.

MARKETING RESEARCH INSIGHT 2.3

Sugging: A Federal Offense

With the 1994 passage of the Telemarketing and Consumer Fraud and Abuse Prevention Act, the FTC was given the power to prescribe the rules prohibiting deceptive and abusive telemarketing practices. This law also prohibits sugging by requiring any person engaged in telemarketing for the sale of goods or services to promptly and clearly disclose to the person receiving the call that the purpose of the call is to sell goods and services, and to make other disclosures deemed appropriate by the FTC such as the price of the goods/services.

Sugging occurs in the following way. "You've got something that's worth $1,500 to me . . . Your opinion is valuable. You've always given it away freely. But I'll reward you for it. I'll give you up to $1,500 worth of FREE gifts in exchange for your opinion of the TV programs that you watch." This is an excerpt taken from a direct mail letter soliciting "TV Raters" sent by John Westcott, V. P. of American Media Research Corporation (AMRC). Sounds wonderful, doesn't it? Westcott's letter went on to tell potential "survey respondents" that all they had to do to receive their $1,500 in FREE gifts was to fill out a "TV Survey" form every month for 36 months. They were told that this information would then be delivered to top executives in the TV, entertainment, and consumer goods industries. Also, in order to get the FREE gifts the respondents had to pay a modest "enrollment fee" of $20 and a shipping charge of $2.00 per month. And, if they enrolled within the next 11 days, they would get a "Promptness Gift" worth $95!

This scheme worked. People enrolled as "TV Raters" by the thousands. AMRC claimed a continuing enrollment of more than 50,000 households per month. But, do you see anything wrong with this scheme? Fortunately, this was investigated by CASRO, The Council of American Survey Research Organizations, a trade association representing approximately 130 full-service survey research organizations. CASRO was established in 1975 to promote and preserve professional standards in the survey research industry. CASRO wrote complaints about AMRC to the Wisconsin Better Business Bureau as well as to the Attorney General's office. The Attorney General's office filed a complaint against AMRC charging that:

> *The $95 FREE gift was a misrepresentation. Respondents did not receive it free, they had to pay an enrollment fee and secondly, the "gift" was cheap costume jewelry worth substantially less than $95.*
>
> *Respondents were told that they had been "specially selected," and this was a misrepresentation. Their names were selected from a mailing list and the selection bore no connection to a scientific sample.*
>
> *AMRC wrongly told respondents they were conducting a survey when, in fact, the objective was to make a sale of memberships or identify sales prospects for direct mail activities.*

Sugging refers to "selling under the guise of a survey." It is now illegal for telemarketers to engage in sugging. Frugging refers to "fund raising under the guise of a survey." Frugging is unethical.

There are situations, however, where deception is abused. **Sugging** refers to "selling under the guise of a survey." Typically, sugging occurs when a "researcher" gains a respondent's cooperation to participate in a research study and then uses the opportunity to attempt to sell the respondent a good or service. Marketing Research Insight 2.3 fully explains sugging. The Telemarketing and Consumer Fraud and Abuse Prevention Act of 1994 seeks to put an end to sugging by telemarketers. Under this act, telemarketers will not be allowed to call someone and say they are conducting a survey, and try to sell a

AMRC was permanently enjoined from operations in Wisconsin. They moved to New York. CASRO attempted to call the principals of the company listed on the direct mail letters that continued to be mailed out. CASRO was told that none of these people were in and that there was no way to determine when they would return to the AMRC office. CASRO wrote a letter of complaint to AMRC and was later contacted by Donald Pickman, president and CEO of AMRC. Pickman did say that Westcott and other officers' names were all fictitious. He went on to say that he did not feel he was in violation of any of CASRO's codes of standards, that he was in marketing, and he was just trying to come up with new approaches to gathering data. When asked why he did not call his firm "American Marketing Corporation" he agreed that he could be more forthright but stated that using the name "Media Research" in the company title made consumers believe they were participating in survey research and this made AMRC more successful in its marketing efforts. Importantly, but not suprisingly, Mr. Pickman stated that AMRC had no clients purchasing the results of its surveys at the present time.

CASRO was asked to participate in an investigation of AMRC by the U.S. Postal Service. CASRO provided information on legitimate survey methods and stated that the survey research industry is finding it increasingly difficult to find cooperative respondents and that anything that cast a bad light on the industry should be stopped. AMRC falsely led consumers to think they were participating in a legitimate survey when there were no clients for the survey information. AMRC simply used the survey as a guise in order to "sell" cheap merchandise to these consumers by charging them fees for products whose value was far less than that indicated to the consumers. Futhermore, AMRC violated respondents' anonymity by putting their names on a mailing list to be used for further solicitations. Legitimate research firms, on the other hand, assure respondents that their participation will not result in any future sales contact.

When this case occurred, the research industry had to rely on remedies such as a Cease and Desist Order that was signed by the U.S. Postal Service. This is exactly what happened, and included in the order was the provision that the officers, directors, owners, and employees could not turn around, come up with a new name for their business, and open up the same operation someplace else. Today, however, thanks primarily to the intense lobbying effort of the Council for Marketing and Opinion Research (CMOR), the industry has a law making sugging a federal offense!

What should you do if you are sugged (or frugged)? CMOR has set up a toll free number, (800) 887-CMOR, for you to report the incidence.

Sources: *Diane K. Bowers, "Sugging: A Federal Offense,"* Marketing Research, *vol. 6, no. 4 (Fall 1994), 54–5; Diane K. Bowers, "Saga of a Sugger—Part 1,"* Marketing Research, *vol. 2, no. 1 (March 1990), 68–72; and Diane K. Bowers, "Saga of a Sugger—Part 2,"* Marketing Research, *vol. 2, no. 2 (June 1990), 64–67; and Diane K. Bowers, "CMOR: A Status Report,"* Marketing Research, *vol. 6, no. 3 (Summer 1994) 42–3.*

product or service. Although telemarketers will not be able to legally practice sugging, the act does not prohibit sugging via the mails.[30] **Frugging** is closely related to sugging and stands for "fund raising under the guise of a survey." Because frugging does not involve the sale of a product or service, it is not covered in the Telemarketing and Consumer Fraud and Abuse Prevention Act of 1994, but it is widely considered to be unethical.

Marketing researchers must honor promises made to respondents that the respondent's identity will remain confidential or anonymous if they expect respondents to cooperate in requests for information in the future.

Falsely Promising Anonymity. Legitimate research firms promise prospective research participants anonymity. The assurance of confidentiality to survey research respondents is essential for two reasons. First, many individuals will not participate in a study if they believe that the information given by them is used for other purposes. Even though some individuals might be induced to participate without assurances of confidentiality, the researcher cannot be certain that those who agree to participate are representative of the population. The second reason to ensure confidentiality is to prevent biases in information given. Individuals who are not confident of their anonymity may alter their responses.[31] It is against industry codes of ethics to promise anonymity and then to violate that promise. In fact, it is unethical to use a subject's identification for any purpose outside the objectives of the research itself. Certainly, it is wrong to identify consumers' names as a result of a research project and then to use their names to develop a sales prospect list. Many times, research users are unaware that this is unethical, and it is the researcher's place to inform them of this. A research project, for example, may ask a respondent the likelihood that they will purchase the client's product that has been previously described by the interviewer. Naive clients will often ask the researcher to give them a list of all of the names of the respondents who replied that were likely to purchase the product; the list could then be used as a sales prospect list. The researcher must inform the user/client that this is unethical; respondents will refuse to cooperate in legitimate surveys asking only for their opinions if they learn they will later be contacted by a salesperson. Anonymity *must* be protected by marketing researchers.

The very nature of marketing research requires an invasion, to some degree, of individual privacy. The majority of the United States public is concerned about threats to personal privacy.

Right to Privacy. The issue of respondent privacy poses a major dilemma to the marketing research industry. Technological advances have made it easier for marketers to obtain and compile information on people. Privacy is a basic right that we as individuals would never willingly give up. However, the very nature of marketing research requires us to invade individual privacy. The constant threat to privacy has caused a decline in research response rates. The Harris/Equifax Consumer Privacy Survey of 1992 stated that 78 percent of the United States public is concerned about threats to personal privacy.[32]

CMOR is attempting to address the growing problem of declining respondent cooperation in the face of privacy invasion.

In response to this growing invasion of privacy, there have been at least a dozen legislative bills introduced in recent years at the federal level on privacy issues. The Telephone Consumer Protection Act of 1991 requires the Federal Communications Commission to establish procedures to avoid unwanted telephone solicitations to residences and regulate the use of automatic telephone dialing systems. The marketing research industry has also been proactive in protecting the privacy of individuals. The Council for Marketing and Opinion Research (CMOR), a federation of associations, research suppliers, and research users, has worked with the federal government on bills protecting the privacy of individuals. The council also monitors legislation that could affect marketing and opinion research. The industry believes that the goals of respecting privacy of individuals and increasing response rate are not necessarily incompatible. CMOR addresses the growing problem of declining respondent cooperation in the face of privacy invasion in three ways:

1. Informing the public by preparing educational brochures, respondent thank you cards, a statement of research principles, and a respondent bill of rights. Constant monitoring of the research industry has also been instituted.

2. Improving the interview by reviewing the length and convenience of interviews, modifying interview introductions, and questionnaire construction.
3. Perfecting the interview by improving the selection and training of interviewers and enhancing their skills via an "Excellence in Interviewing" program.[33]

In addition to monitoring groups, research suppliers should be constantly aware of how their actions might affect the privacy of the individual. Suggested actions that could be taken by the industry include the following:

Here are some suggestions on how the marketing research industry can address respondents' rights to privacy.

1. ***Self-evaluation.*** Is each survey firm doing its best to consider the consumer's rights?
2. ***Adoption of universal industry standards.*** This would allow research firms around the world to adopt similar codes of conduct.
3. ***Common industry identifier.*** Some unique identification should be developed to allow the potential respondent to differentiate between legitimate marketing research requests and other direct marketing methods.
4. ***Public relations and education.*** This is needed to inform the public as to the value and legitimacy of any marketing research.
5. ***Respondent advisory board.*** A board of this type would allow input to the industry on its practices from the respondents' viewpoint.[34]

Ethical Issues between Research Suppliers and the Public

Any perception of unethical or false reporting can undermine the credibility of the entire marketing research industry. Inaccurate or untrue market research findings can result from incomplete reporting, misleading reporting, and nonobjective research.

Marketing research information, such as polling data, is often disseminated to the general public. The industry is obviously concerned about accurate reporting of findings. Any perception of unethical or false reporting can undermine the credibility of the entire marketing research industry. Inaccurate or untrue market research findings can result from incomplete reporting, misleading reporting, and nonobjective research. Parts of the following section have been adapted from Tull and Hawkins and Murphy and Laczniak.[35]

Incomplete Reporting. A problem can occur when relevant information is left out of a report that is circulated to the general public. For example, when polls for the presidential race are made public, there seems to be a great disparity among the poll numbers.[36] What is commonly omitted is the composition of the sample and the types of questions asked. Similarly, some companies conduct test markets and report the results in the trade press. They might fail to mention that test markets were conducted in areas where the reputation of the firm is strong. Therefore, the results of the test market may be skewed in the favorable direction. Some publications like *The Wall Street Journal* have now started reporting details of how the sample was drawn and the method of contacting the respondents. This enables the reader to judge the validity of the reported information.

Misleading Reporting. The practice of misleading reporting involves presenting research results in such a way that the intended audience will draw conclusions that are not entirely justified. This can be done by reporting one part of the findings alone. For instance, a comparative cigarette ad claimed that "an amazing 60%" of a sample of consumers said Triumph cigarettes tasted "as good as or better than" Merit. The real results showed that 36 percent preferred Triumph, 24 percent said they were equal, and 40 percent preferred Merit over Triumph. Such partial representation of the results with an intent to mislead has to be avoided.

Nonobjective Research. The general public is not in a position to judge the objectivity of the research. Thus, the use of leading questions can skew the results so as to mislead the public. For example, Burger King used the question "Do you prefer your hamburgers flame-broiled or fried?" to find out customer preference over McDonald's. The results showed that customers preferred Burger King's flame-broiled burger. The results were completely reversed when the question was rephrased as "Do you prefer a hamburger that is grilled on a hot stainless steel grill or cooked by passing the raw meat through an open gas flame?"[37] Because the audience has no way of assessing the objectivity of research findings, it is the researcher's responsibility to stipulate any effects of research bias.

SUMMARY

This chapter covered four introductory topics. First, it reviewed the history of the use of marketing research. In the pre–marketing research era, marketing research was not needed because businesses had many face-to-face contacts with their customers. But, as marketing became a "long-distance" business, questionnaires were used, quantitative techniques were adopted, and marketing research departments emerged. Currently, we are in the midst of expanding applications of technology to research.

The marketing research industry has a number of unique players, and we described them as internal suppliers and external suppliers of marketing research information. The external suppliers may be further categorized as either full-service or limited-service firms. Syndicated data services, standardized services, and customized services firms are all full-service firms. Limited-service firms include field services, market segment specialists, data entry services, sample design and distribution services, data analysis services, and specialized research technique firms. We also described how companies organize the marketing research function.

We reviewed some performance ratings of the marketing research industry as a whole, and we found that it performs adequately but that it can improve. Some authors have called for a formal certification program for marketing research professionals or even an auditing system to ensure consistency of performance across the industry. The research industry has started several professional development programs for its members in recent years.

Our last topic introduced you to very important ethical issues such as integrity, fairness, confidentiality, social welfare, disclosure, anonymity, and the right to privacy. All of these issues concern ethical researchers because the actions of unethical individuals can severely damage the image of the marketing research industry.

KEY TERMS

Internal supplier (p. 22)
External suppliers (p. 25)
Full-service supplier firms (p. 25)
Syndicated data service firms (p. 25)
Standardized service firms (p. 28)
Customized service firms (p. 28)
Limited-service supplier firms (p. 31)
Field service firms (p. 31)
Market segment specialists (p. 32)
Data entry services (p. 32)
Sample design and distribution (p. 33)
Data analysis (p. 33)
Specialized research technique firms (p. 34)
Certification (p. 37)
Auditing (p. 37)
Ethics (p. 38)
Deontology (p. 38)
Teleology (p. 38)
Sugging (p. 44)
Frugging (p. 45)

REVIEW QUESTIONS/APPLICATIONS

1. Explain the significance of marketing research during each of the following periods of history: Industrial Revolution to 1920; 1920 to 1940; 1940 to 1960; 1960 to 1980; and 1980 to the present.
2. We categorized firms as internal and external suppliers of marketing research information. Explain what is meant by each and give an example of each type of firm.
3. Distinguish among full-service, limited-service, syndicated data services, standardized services, and customized services firms.
4. What is the advantage in a firm's having its own formal marketing research department? Explain three different ways such a department may be internally organized.
5. On evaluating the marketing research industry, what has been the general conclusion on how it is doing? What have been the major criticisms of the industry? Given your experiences, how would you rate the industry?
6. Explain the pros and cons of how a certification program, an auditing program, or a professional development program may work to improve the marketing research industry.
7. What are the two fundamental philosophies that can be used as a basis for making ethical decisions? Give an example of how you would use each in your daily life. Then give an example of the use of each as it could be applied to an ethical issue in the marketing research industry.
8. Discuss the basic issues you would include in a code of ethics for the marketing research industry. What practical value do you believe such codes have for those who are internal suppliers? External suppliers? Respondents? The public?
9. Select any three companies from Table 2.1, "The Top 50 Marketing Research Firms." Go to your library or the Internet and find out where you can get additional information on these firms. List the sources and the types of information provided.
10. Look up "marketing research" in your Yellow Pages directory. Given the information provided in the Yellow Pages, can you classify the research firms in your area according to the classification system of research firms we used in this chapter?

11. Comment on each practice itemized below. Is it ethical? Indicate your reasoning in each case.
    a. A research company conducts a telephone survey and gathers information that they use later to send a salesperson to the home of potential buyers for the purpose of selling a product. They make no attempt to sell the product over the telephone.
    b. Would your answer to (a) change if you found out that the information gathered during the telephone survey was used as part of a "legitimate" marketing research report?
    c. A door-to-door salesperson finds that, by telling people that he is conducting a survey, they are more likely to listen to his sales pitch.
    d. The cover letter of a mail questionnaire says that it will "only take a few minutes to fill out." But pretests have shown that at least 15 minutes are needed to fill it out.
    e. Telephone interviewers are instructed to assure the respondent of confidentiality only if the respondent asks about it.
    f. A client insists on inspecting completed questionnaires ostensibly to assess their validity, but the researcher suspects that the client is really interested in finding out what specific comments the respondents had about the client.
    g. In the appendix of the final report, the researcher lists the names of all respondents who took part in the survey, and places an asterisk beside the names of those who indicated a willingness to be contacted by the client's sales personnel.

CASE 2.1

"Burns & Bush Rated the Best Marketing Research Text . . . According to Survey!"[38]

The research industry conducts a great deal of research for firms with the intention of using the results in advertising claims. In 1988, Diet Coke and Diet Pepsi both conducted taste tests, and the results appeared at the same time. According to Coca-Cola's objective results, Diet Coke was the "winner and still champion." Pepsi's objective results showed Diet Pepsi was the "undisputed champion." These results led to an investigation by the Massachusetts Consumer Affairs Office. "If both were done scientifically and were based upon valid research data, how could the outcomes be opposite?" asked staff member Edgar Dworsky. An investigation led to a report that came out several months after both taste test advertising campaigns had long run their course. Dworsky's office was criticized for challenging such a claim. "The feeling was, everyone knows that advertising lies, so why waste precious resources on it?"

Everyone knows advertisers are advocating their products and services in their ads. But, do advertising's subtle deceptions become intolerable when consumers are presented data supposedly representing objective testing and research? Advertisers have learned that surveys and product tests result in statistical data that works. Tylenol's claims that more doctors and hospitals preferred its product helped increase market share in the very competitive analgesic market. Volvo's claim that its cars were safer helped bring record sales in the United States. The problem arises when the research that is used as a basis for these claims is actually contrived so as to ensure that the claims may be stated. In late 1990, Volvo began airing a commercial showing a very large truck driving over the top of several cars including a Volvo. Only the Volvo was not crushed. Consumers were led to believe that Volvos are stronger and safer than other vehicles. What consumers did not know was that the Volvo had extra reinforcement in the form of steel rods placed across its roof and the other cars had their roof supports cut. This was revealed because an onlooker photographed the work and called the Texas state attorney general's office.

Other research results in advertising include the following. Levi's reported that 90 percent of college students in a survey say Levi's 501 jeans are "in" on campus. An examination of the actual survey showed that students were given a choice of different types of clothing such as t-shirts, overalls, and so on. Levi's 501s were the only alternative for voting for jeans. A Litton microwave ad claimed "76% of independent microwave oven technicians surveyed recommend Litton." But, the survey included only Litton-authorized technicians who serviced Litton and at least one other brand. Those who serviced other brands but not Litton were not included in the survey.

1. Estimates are that each day, American consumers collectively are exposed to 12 billion display ads, 2.5 million radio commercials, and more than 300,000 television commercials. If even a small percentage of these messages are half-truths and deceptions, what is the effect on the public?
2. No one wants more government regulation and intervention, right? Before the government required all companies to report fuel economy using the same standard, EPA mileage statistics, one company advertised one of its cars got an incredible 200 miles per gallon. What consumers weren't told was that the car had been driven over a long, mostly downhill, route at 50 mph. Should we have standards, such as EPA statistics, for reporting other advertised criteria such as car size or safety?

Case 2.2

DowBrands[39]

Dow Chemical Company had experienced cyclical earnings, which is normal in the chemical business. Management wanted to expand its consumer goods division as a means of offsetting down-cycles in the chemicals division. Dow purchased the Texize Division of Morton Thiokol in 1985 and Lamaur, maker of hair care products, in 1987. Dow was already making some consumer products such as Saran Wrap and Ziploc bags. When Texize and Lamaur were purchased, these consumer products firms became a wholly owned subsidiary of Dow Chemical called DowBrands.

The question of organizing the marketing research function arose. Dow Chemical had its own research department. The department conducted research for the chemical company and had personnel very knowledgeable about the industry. However, DowBrands managers needed information from various consumer markets. Specifically, managers were interested in tracking studies—

studies comparing unit sales of its products and those of competitors within the same products category over time. Although the consumer products firms had some limited internal capabilities, they had mainly relied on external suppliers for much of their research information in the past. Now, however, they were a part of a much larger firm, having the resources necessary to fund an independent research department for DowBrands.

Dow management had several alternatives to consider. Should they expect the Dow Chemical research department to serve the new companies as well as Dow Chemical? Should the DowBrands group have its own separate, independent marketing research department? To what extent should the company work with external suppliers of marketing research?

1. What considerations should be made by management in making the above decision?
2. Specifically address the issue of using outside supplier firms. What arguments may be made for maintaining, expanding, or deleting contractual arrangements with external firms?
3. Assume that Dow decides to use external suppliers. On what dimensions should Dow evaluate proposals from these external firms to do business with Dow?

APPENDIX 2

A Career in the Marketing Research Industry

As you begin reading about marketing research, you might find yourself wondering, "Is this for me?" Career opportunities exist in the larger companies that have their own marketing research departments or in the external supplier firms. Do not forget that ad agencies, media firms, the government, and trade associations also seek individuals to conduct marketing research.

DO YOU HAVE WHAT IT TAKES?

The traits associated with the most successful and effective marketing researchers include the following: curiosity, high intelligence, creativity, self-discipline, good interpersonal and communication skills, the ability to work under strict time constraints, and feeling comfortable working with numbers. The field is becoming gender neutral. About half of all new researchers are women.[40]

Information Resources, Inc. (IRI) state they prefer a degree in marketing or a related area. Although an undergraduate degree is required, there has been a trend toward requiring postgraduate degrees in some firms. Most universities do not offer a degree in "marketing research."[41] Thus, an M.B.A. with a marketing major is one of the more common combinations for people employed in marketing research. Other possibilities are degrees in quantitative methods, sociology, or economics. Undergraduate training in mathematics or the physical sciences is a very suitable (and employable) background for anyone considering a career in marketing research.

JOB LEVELS AND DESCRIPTIONS

Position titles and the positions themselves vary, depending on whether you work for a full-service firm ("Account Executive/Director" or "Project Manager"), limited-service firm ("Focus Group Moderator" or "Field Supervisor") or within a supplier/buyer firm ("Director of Marketing Research" or "Research Analyst"). Recognizing that position

TABLE 2.1A

MRA Career Guide

POSSIBLE CAREER AREAS*	PRIMARY DUTIES	POSSIBLE DEGREES	HELPFUL SKILLS
Account Executive, Director of Marketing	Direct servicing of the client account to solicit business and oversee its completion.	Marketing Research; Business Administration; Liberal Arts; Statistics and/or Quantitative Analysis.	Previous work experience in business, possible by internship. Analytical, selling, interpersonal.
Data Processor, Tabulation Specialist, Programmer	Responsible for programming, developing and reviewing data, interpreting codes, data entry layout, and tabulation specifications as well as preparing the final data tables.	Computer Sciences; Marketing Research; Statistics; Math.	Recommend design, math, and statistical skills as well as basic business knowledge. Interpersonal skills. Identify problem research designs.
Moderator, Qualitative Consultant	Facilitate focus group discussions to discern consumer interests, opinions, ideas, etc. Analyze the synthesis. Identify issues.	Social Sciences (Sociology & Psychology); Communications.	Exposure to different facets of the business world. Writing and interpersonal skills.
Project Manager, Project Director, Field Manager, Field Director, Project Supervisor, Field Supervisor	Defines the study as received from the Account Executive, creating the specifications and detailed instructions for executing the research for the client.	Marketing Research; Business Administration; Liberal Arts.	Business work experience and attention to detail.
Research Analyst, Supervisor, Manager	Design and analysis of marketing research studies.	Math; Statistics; Liberal Arts; Social Sciences (Sociology & Psychology).	A degree is usually a prerequisite for this area. Conceptual writing and presentation skills.
Sampling Specialist	Develop the sample for a proposed study with attention to meeting client demographic requirements.	Statistics; Computer Sciences.	Math and statistical skills are helpful as well as basic computer skills.

*Not all companies will have all positions

Management opportunities exist in all of the above areas, usually requiring a degree in Marketing or Business Administration.

Marketing Research Association, by permission.

titles vary by company, you could expect entry-level positions to include titles such as "Marketing Research Assistant" or "Junior Project Director." After a year or more, you might advance to "Assistant Marketing Research Manager" or "Project Director." The job titles are not nearly as important as the responsibilities. As you grow in your marketing research career, your assignments will move from problem management to problem definition and project design.[42] See Table 2.1A for additional information on job descriptions supplied by the Marketing Research Association.

SALARY

Salaries may range from a low of less than $20,000 to six-figure salaries. Figure 2.1A shows salary figures taken from the 1994 AMA survey of the marketing research industry. In almost all positions, salaries increased from 1988 to 1993. Also, there are many opportunities for women in marketing research and the gap between male/female compensation has been narrowing.[43]

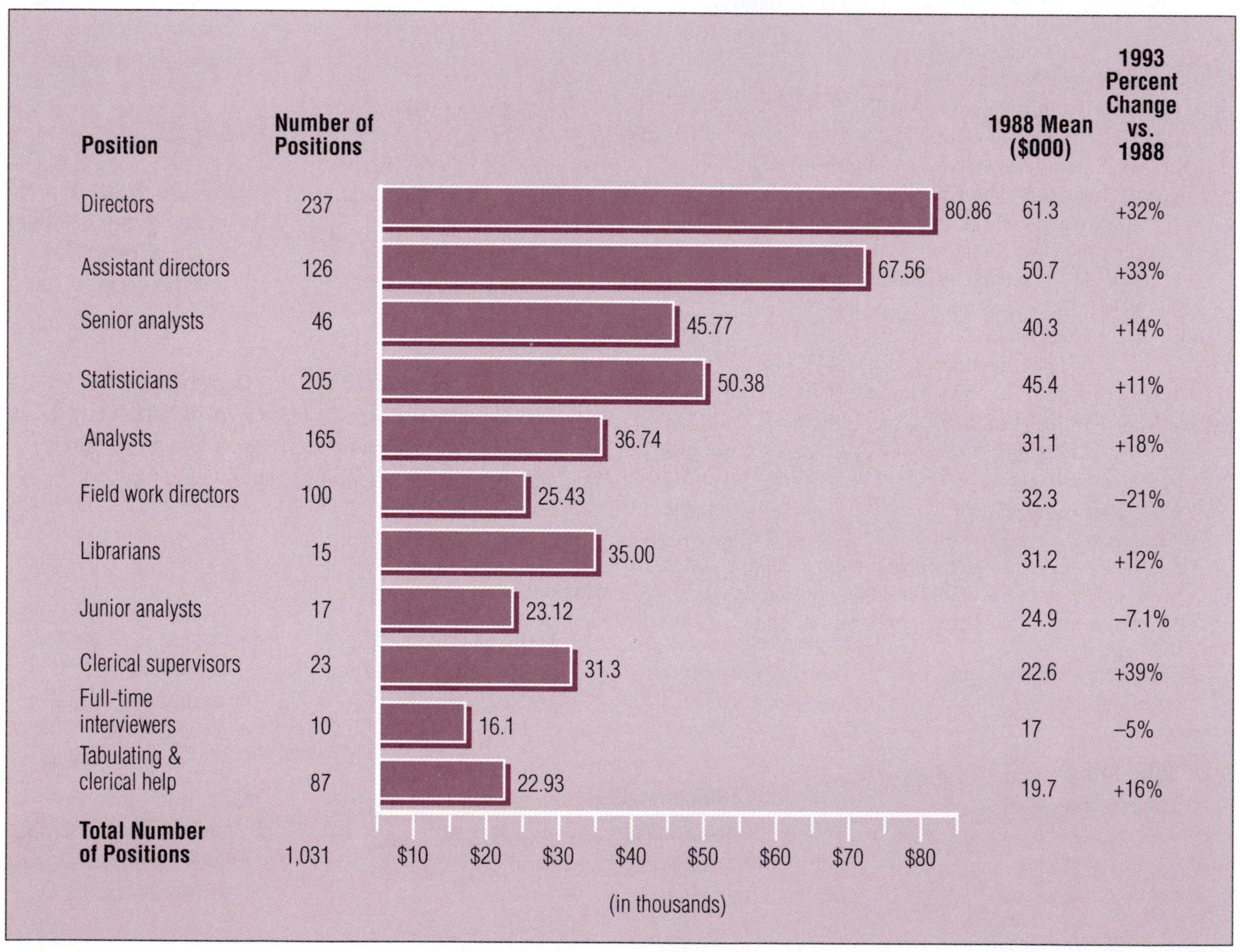

Figure 2.1A

Mean Compensation for All Marketing Research Positions

JOB SEARCH

So, how does one find a job in marketing research? A good way to begin is to write for the following career guide, published by the Marketing Research Association:

Career Guide: Your Future in Marketing Research
Marketing Research Association
2189 Silas Deane Highway, Suite 5
Rocky Hill, CT 06067
Email: MRAH@aol.com

Also, we recommend you go to your library and look at the career guides. We suggest you get the current directory of:

Marketing and Sales Career Directory
published by Gale Research Inc.
835 Penobscot Building
Detroit, MI 48226-4094
(313) 961-2242 or 1 (800) 347-4253

You can find listings of marketing research firms to contact by referring to the directories shown in Marketing Research Insight 2.1.

A large percentage of jobs are filled by networking. You should start building a group of people who can act as mentors and contacts. These people will prove to be invaluable when you begin your job search. While you are in school, become a member of the local American Marketing Association. Most AMA chapters have monthly meetings with presentations from people involved in marketing. As a member of AMA, you will learn about the field and will make contacts with people working in marketing.

Try to keep up with the literature in marketing research by reading publications such as *Marketing Research: A Magazine of Management & Applications, The Journal of Marketing, Marketing News,* and *Sales and Marketing Management.* When you begin interviewing with companies, they will expect you to be knowledgeable about what is happening *today* in marketing.

Internships are extremely useful learning experiences. Directories such as the *Marketing and Sales Career Directory* list companies involved in marketing research and whether they provide internships.

Begin looking in the classified sections of trade magazines and publications such as the *National Business Employment Weekly* to get an idea of what jobs are currently being offered. Not only will this give you an idea of the frequency of jobs in the area, but it will also familiarize you with job titles and starting salaries.

Starting a job search begins while you are in college. It is a constant process. Reviewing current literature, joining marketing associations, making contacts, and interning will increase your possibilities for finding a job suited for your talents.

CHAPTER 3

The Marketing Research Process

Learning Objectives

- To learn the steps in the marketing research process
- To understand how the steps in the marketing research process are interrelated and that the steps may not proceed in order
- To be able to know when marketing research may be needed and when it may not be needed
- To know which step is the most important in the marketing research process

PRACTITIONER VIEWPOINT

One of the key aspects of the market research project is in determining the need for a market research. This one step should be taken before any project is started and, if done properly, will save significant amounts of time and effort for marketers. Too often this one key step in a marketing research project is left out until after the research has already been completed, at which time the need for marketing research is asked in terms of, "Why did you do this study in the first place?"

In this chapter, you will learn about construction and execution of a marketing research project. As a practitioner of marketing research, these are the steps I use. Because this chapter gives you an overview of the marketing research process it, like an Executive Summary in a marketing research report, sets the tone of the remainder of the text.

— Erik Glitman[1]
The Fletcher Mountain Group

How Do You Do Marketing Research?

The Animal Control Center of Tucson (ACCT) had a problem that concerned the increasing numbers of stray and unwanted dogs the center handled each year. By its policy, if a stray was not adopted within 10 days of its arrival at the ACCT, it was destroyed. Without the physical space to house these animals nor the funding to feed and care for them, the ACCT was forced to destroy over 100,000 such animals annually. The ACCT commissioned marketing research to find out what Tucson residents thought about dog overpopulation as well as their reactions to adoption programs.

To help the ACCT understand the problem, a research firm conducted two group discussions called focus groups with 10 Tucson residents in each group. This effort revealed that most people were unaware of the magnitude of the dog overpopulation nor were they aware of the spaying/neutering that was mandatory for each dog adoption from the ACCT. This exploratory research guided the next phase in which the research company designed a telephone interview questionnaire and hired a local service to call 500 households selected at random from all those listed in the Tucson telephone book. A total of 350 respondents took part in the survey, with the remainder either unavailable or unwilling to take part in the survey. Tabulations of the raw responses revealed that a majority (63%) of the respondents would be willing to adopt a male, mixed-breed dog in the next year, mainly for the purpose of personal companionship (46%) or as a family pet (31%), but only one-half of these people saw a need to have the dog spayed or neutered. Less than one-quarter (22%) of the respondents believed that Tucson suffered from a dog overpopulation problem.

Armed with this information, the ACCT launched a public service announcement campaign to educate Tucson residents on the serious overpopulation problem and to promote its pet adoption program. The importance of ensuring that adopted dogs do not make unwanted puppies was also stressed. By the end of the campaign, monthly adoptions had increased by 500 percent. The effects on the dog population will be seen in the next two to five years as most dogs are adopted as puppies, and they take 18 months to reach maturity.

This chapter introduces you to the steps involved in the marketing research process. It also provides you with a brief preview of each of the steps necessary to conduct a marketing research effort. Finally, it serves as an overview of the remainder of the text; the topics it presents are described in detail in subsequent chapters.

STEPS IN THE MARKETING RESEARCH PROCESS

Marketing research is not always a "step-by-step" process.

As depicted in Figure 3.1, we have identified eleven basic **steps in the marketing research process.** These steps include: (1) establishing the need for marketing research, (2) defining the problem, (3) establishing research objectives, (4) determining research design, (5) identifying information types and sources, (6) determining methods of accessing data, (7) designing data collection forms, (8) determining sample plan and size, (9) collecting data, (10) analyzing data, and (11) preparing and presenting the final research report.

Before we discuss these eleven steps in the marketing research process, it is important for us to make a few comments about this "list" of steps. First, although the list does strongly imply an orderly, step-by-step process, it is rare that a research project follows these steps in the exact order that they are presented in the diagram. Actually, marketing research practice is more of an interactive process whereby a researcher, by discovering something in a given step, may move backward in the process and begin again at another step. Finding some new information while collecting data, for example, may cause the researcher to establish different research objectives. Second, any given re-

1. Establish the need for marketing research

2. Define the problem

3. Establish research objectives

4. Determine research design

5. Identify information types and sources

6. Determine methods of accessing data

7. Design data collection forms

8. Determine sample plan and size

9. Collect data

10. Analyze data

11. Prepare and present the final research report

Figure 3.1

Eleven Steps in the Marketing Research Process

search project may not involve each and every step shown here. The research problem could be resolved, for example, by a review of secondary data, thereby eliminating the need to determine a sample plan or size. What is important for you to know is that, although almost every research project is different, there are enough commonalities among the various procedures and activities to enable us to specify the eleven basic steps of the marketing research process. A discussion of these steps follows.

Step 1: Establish the Need for Marketing Research

A good monitoring system will alert the marketing manager to a problem that can be attacked with marketing research.

To establish the need for marketing research, all organizations should monitor their surrounding environments on a continuous basis using a **monitoring system.** The primary objective of a monitoring system is to bring operating information to management. Such information allows management to evaluate whether their current operating results are meeting performance objectives, if proposed legislation has an impact on consumer spending or other industry interests, whether changes in consumer values and lifestyles are occurring, or if new strategies are being implemented by competitors. Monitoring may be accomplished either formally or informally and in a variety of ways. One firm may have a sophisticated formal marketing information system (MIS). Another firm may have a more traditional control system that primarily relies on financial statements as feedback. A small business owner/manager may diligently observe the environments that affect his or her firm.

A good monitoring system constantly searches for hints that the company's marketing mix may be out of "sync" with the marketplace.

Regardless of the type of monitoring system used, a good monitoring system constantly searches for hints that the company's marketing mix may be out of "sync" with the marketplace. To illustrate this point, we provide two examples: one from Millstone Coffee and the other from McDonald's. Millstone is a relatively young company based in Washington, and it has a monitoring system that tracks the freshness of its products in grocery stores. Read Marketing Research Insight 3.1 (page 60) to find out how Millstone uses marketing research in this way.

McDonald's Corporation has been a giant in the restaurant business since 1955 when Ray Kroc, a former Multimixer milkshake machine salesman, opened the first restaurant in Des Plaines, Illinois. McDonald's became an industry leader following a strategy in which they rapidly served hamburgers, french fries, and milkshakes at very low prices.

When McDonald's sales plateaued, management sensed that the cause was a shift in environments. McDonald's management began to conduct research to identify the nature and cause of these shifts. As a result of this research, McDonald's identified three recent trends. First, consumers have become more health conscious and beef consumption has decreased, resulting in fewer hamburgers sold. Second, the fast food industry has reached a saturation level and industry sales are stagnant, just keeping pace with inflation.[2] Third, year after year, new competitors have taken one consumer market segment after another away from the once-standard fast food fare of the burger, fries, and shake. Such competitors include Taco Bell, which has spirited away some of the price-sensitive market segments by serving meals for what was once half the price of a McDonald's meal; pizza chains, which have, by offering free home delivery, taken away much of the convenience-oriented market; and moderately priced restaurant chains, such as Chili's and the Olive Garden,

MARKETING RESEARCH INSIGHT 3.1

Millstone Coffee Monitors Its Products Daily for Freshness

One of the fastest growing categories of coffee in the mid-1990s is gourmet whole-bean coffee. Industry analysts identify the annual growth rate to be between 15 percent and 50 percent. Millstone Coffee is participating in this rapid growth, and its sales grew by more than 40 percent in 1993.

The growth of gourmet whole-bean coffee has not been automatic. It has been a carefully cultivated and orchestrated marketing strategy on the part of coffee companies such as Millstone. Phil Johnson, president of Millstone Coffee, says:

> *It is critical that we introduce consumers to the product. Sampling the product with a wet demo at the point of purchase is the best way to get consumers to try the product and use it. But the sampling needs to be done by a person who is very knowledgeable about coffee. Usually consumers have a lot of questions about this product. Questions like: How do you flavor your coffees? How do you decaffeinate your product?*

To accomplish this introduction successfully, Millstone had 300 employees around the country trained specifically for retail demonstrations.

Another tactic used by retailers is to place whole beans in the store's coffee aisle. Johnson says there is a "bakery phenomenon" when the product is in the aisle because gourmet coffee has a rich aromatic aroma that triggers an "Oh, I need coffee" in shoppers. The trigger is for the darker, roasted straight coffees and blended coffees that are vastly different from what is available in a can. Johnson continues by saying, "From a manufacturer's standpoint, we have to stay up with consumers' palates."

Millstone Coffee constantly monitors its coffee in retail stores with a computerized information system that keeps track of every coffee bin in each of the 4,500 supermarkets that carry Millstone gourmet coffees. The delivery date is noted, and how long the coffee has been in the store is tracked. The slow-seller blends are removed after three weeks, which is when the coffee loses its freshness. Either less of that blend is placed in the bin or another variety with a better selling record is substituted. Phil Johnson knows this is a vital system because, "The consumer's taste bud in this category is constantly changing."

How much success has Millstone Coffee experienced? Johnson says, "Today, virtually every supermarket has the product. What we've seen happen is the product go from virtually being nonexistent to where approximately half of all coffee consumed in the home in this part of the country is a whole-bean gourmet coffee."

Source: *Lisa Saxton, "Wake Up and Smell the Coffee,"* Supermarket News *(November 8, 1993), 6A(1).*

which have lured away dinner customers who want atmosphere, a variety of food choices, and waiters. Recognizing these trends in the fast food industry, McDonald's introduced healthier food and tested a new type of outlet, "The Golden Arch Cafe," to compete for the dinner business. However, not all fluctuations in the market require that businesses automatically conduct marketing research studies as did McDonald's. There are instances in which marketing research may not be needed.

Marketing Research May Not Be Needed

Management should not automatically commission a marketing research study each and every time a decision must be made. There are several situations in which management should not consider a marketing research project. Here are four situations in which marketing research may be inappropriate.[3]

When information is readily available, there is no need to do marketing research.

Information Is Already Available. If management knows its markets, competition, and the products/services, they may have the necessary information to make an informed decision without commissioning a market research study.[4] Contemporary managers have access to much information about their business. One of the problems in the past was that this information was not readily available, and a marketing research project would have to be undertaken just to find the information and produce it in the proper form. Today, computer technology has provided management with the ability to record, store, and retrieve much information about the routine operation of a business. It is possible to have information on sales, costs, and profitability available by product, customer, region, salesperson, and so on, at the touch of a key. This situation is likely to increase as more and more businesses invest in information processing technology that makes more of the right information available to the right decision makers at the right time.[5] In the past, many marketing research studies were undertaken simply to correct inadequacies in information processing capabilities.

Sometimes a tight deadline precludes the application of marketing research to a problem.

There Is Insufficient Time for Marketing Research. Sometimes there simply is not enough time for marketing research. Occasionally, a problem is discovered that requires an immediate response on the part of management. Unfortunately, although some research can be performed in a relatively short time frame, much of it, such as custom-designed surveys, requires weeks or months to complete. When competitive pressures or customer shifts demand quick marketing management action, there may not be enough time to carry out a *properly* conducted marketing research project. Competitive actions may be swift and so damaging that prompt reaction is deemed imperative, and although research would be helpful, circumstances argue strongly against performing it.

If there is insufficient funding, research cannot be undertaken.

Resources Are Not Available. Oftentimes, resources are not available for marketing research. If conducted in-house, marketing research requires a commitment of personnel, facilities, and budget. If conducted by an outside research firm, money as well as some personnel time is needed. If there is not enough money to devote to the market research, management must simply make the decision that those resources are better spent elsewhere. Of course, management always runs the risk of discovering that it invested resources in a strategy that marketing research would have identified as being inferior to alternative strategies. This is one of the "catch-22s" for business management: The firms that are strapped for cash, and thus feel they cannot afford to spend dollars on marketing research, are usually the firms that could probably benefit the most by performing the research to help them make the best decisions.[6] Nevertheless, resources may simply not be available for research.

Doing marketing research when the costs outweigh the benefits is unwise.

Costs Outweigh the Value of the Research. Even when funds and other resources are available to conduct marketing research, management must always weigh the costs of conducting the research with the potential value of conducting the research. Some decisions have relatively little impact on company sales, profits, consumer loyalty, dealer goodwill, and so on, and, as a result, they simply do not justify the expenditure. Other decisions, however, may be very important, thereby justifying research. For example, how a product's packaging is designed for shipment to trade shows may seem relatively unimportant. However, the packaging design used to ship products to dealers could be very important in terms of reducing spillage and spoilage and enhancing dealer loyalty.

The purpose of marketing research is to reduce the uncertainty in marketing decisions.

Another aspect to consider when weighing the value to be gained against the cost of the research has to do with the confidence that the manager has in the outcome of a proposed decision. The purpose of marketing research is to serve as an aid in decision making; in effect, to reduce the uncertainty in the outcomes of alternative decisions. If the manager feels that he or she knows the possible outcomes, then marketing research should not be used.

As management monitors the environments, it receives information from many sources such as stockholders, who may be complaining of poor bottom-line performance; or dealers, who are complaining about losing sales to competition. It is important to note that management may or may not hear about the real problem. That is, they may not discover what is *causing* poor earnings or sales declines. More often, management learns of *symptoms.* It is part of the researcher's job to determine what problem(s) are causing the symptoms. Defining the problem, then, is the next step in the marketing research process.

Step 2: Define the Problem

The most important step in the marketing research process is properly defining the marketing manager's problem.

Defining the problem is the single most important step in the marketing research process. A clear, concise statement of the problem is a key to good marketing research. There is much truth to the saying, "A problem well defined is half solved." Unfortunately, this is much easier to say than to do. Often, clients themselves do not know what the problem is. They know that sales are falling and that market share is shrinking, but they do not know the cause of these symptoms.

Part of the marketing researcher's job is to work closely with the client to correctly determine the problem. All too often, marketing research studies are commissioned without a clear understanding of the problem the research should address. Take the following situation facing Yankee Factory Outlets, a regional discount clothing retail chain. The president was concerned about declining profits during five consecutive quarters of business activity. He hired a consultant who, after one visit to the firm, returned with a proposal to conduct tests of several advertising copy alternatives to be used in the firm's radio advertising program. Do you see anything wrong with this situation? How does Yankee know that profits are declining as a result of problems with ad copy? They do not know, and neither does the consulting firm.

This is a classic situation where marketing research is proposed that does not address the real problem. A firm may spend literally hundreds of thousands of dollars doing market research but, if they have not correctly identified the problem, those dollars will have been wasted. To avoid this scenario, care must be taken to explore all possible causes of the symptom. This requires time and a great deal of communication between the researcher and the client.

Exploratory research helps to clearly define the problem.

Often, a form of research, called **exploratory research,** is needed to clearly define the problem so that the proper research may be conducted. We discuss exploratory research under step 4. The process of defining the problem is discussed in detail in chapter 4.

By way of introduction, however, you should know that problem definition involves: (1) specifying the symptoms, (2) itemizing the possible causes of the symptoms, and (3) listing the reasonable alternative courses of action that the marketing manager can undertake to solve the problem.

Step 3: Establish Research Objectives

Research objectives, although related to and determined by the problem definition, are set so that, when achieved, they provide the necessary information to solve the problem. Let us consider the following example. Independent insurance agents typically belong to a state association called, for instance, the Independent Insurance Agents of Iowa. The association is responsible for educational programs, lobbying with state insurance boards, and technical advice. If the association were concerned with responding to the needs of its members, reasonable research objectives would include (a) to determine how important each of the association's services are to its members, and (b) to assess how satisfied members of the association are with the association's performance of each service.

Research objectives identify what specific pieces of information are necessary to solve the problem at hand.

A good way of setting research objectives is to ask, "What information is needed in order to solve the problem?" Because the association's services are in place, the research objectives would translate as follows:

- Determine the average importance level of each service
- Determine the average level of satisfaction for each service

You should notice that these research objectives are different from the defined problem. Yet, when the information is gathered as a result of carrying out these research objectives, the problem is solved. By collecting the information requested by the first two research objectives, the association is in a position to rank its services based on how important they are to members, and it can identify which highly important services are low in satisfaction. That is, it can identify critical problem areas. Alternatively, it can identify significant strengths indicated by high satisfaction with highly important services, if they exist.

As you can see, a key aspect of the research objectives step is the specification of the specific types of information useful to the managers as they grapple for a solution to the marketing management problem at hand.

Step 4: Determine Research Design

As stated earlier, almost every research project is different. Still, there are enough commonalities among research projects to enable us to categorize them by the research methods and procedures used to collect and analyze data. There are three types of research design: (1) exploratory research, (2) descriptive research, and (3) causal research. A description of these research designs follows.

There are three types of research design: exploratory, descriptive, and causal.

Exploratory Research Design

Exploratory research is defined as collecting information in an unstructured and informal manner. A manager reading periodicals about the status of his or her industry, for example, could be viewed as conducting exploratory research.

Pete and Helen Nichols, owners of Nichols Seafood, a successful restaurant, often eat out at competitor's restaurants in order to gather information about menu selections, prices, and service quality.

Exploratory research is often used to define the problem. This might involve examining not only company sales and profits but industry sales and profits as well. It may be determined that, whereas company sales had been declining, industry sales had fallen even more and the company's own market share had actually increased. This observation would certainly have an impact on defining the problem or even on the decision as to whether or not to conduct any further research.

Exploratory research, while intuitive and second nature to researchers, can be applied with formal procedures.

Exploratory research is very intuitive, and it is practiced as second nature by marketing managers who constantly watch the many factors that influence their markets. However, exploratory research can be applied formally by marketing researchers. That is, marketers can use procedures that help marketing managers define the problem or perhaps make symptoms more visible. With Yankee Factory Outlets, for example, exploratory research could take the form of plotting total retail sales for the region over the same five quarters of decline noted for Yankee. If total retail sales had declined in a parallel fashion, economic conditions such as a recession might be the underlying cause. On the other hand, if total retail sales held level or increased while Yankee's sales declined, the nature of the problem is different, and competition or perhaps some marketing mix change adopted by Yankee might be the problem.

Another example of exploratory research is the ongoing research some companies conduct in order to spot opportunities in the marketplace. For example, some companies employ clipping services whose employees scour the printed news media and other periodicals, and when they encounter an article or comment dealing with the client's markets, they copy it and send it to the client. With this system, the client may become aware of a competitor's problems with inventory, for instance, or dissatisfaction with some aspect of customer service, and the client company may sense and seize a competitive opportunity based on this early warning system. We introduce you to the various methods used to conduct exploratory research in chapter 5.

Descriptive Research Design

Descriptive research is used to describe marketing phenomena.

Descriptive research designs refer to a set of methods and procedures that describe marketing variables. Descriptive studies portray these variables by answering who, what, why, and how questions. These types of research studies may describe such things as consumers' attitudes, intentions, and behaviors, or the number of competitors and their strategies. For instance, several banking firms conduct annual studies wherein consumers' attitudes toward their own banks, as well as competitors' banks, are described. These studies, called "image analysis surveys," essentially describe how consumers rate banks' services, availability of loans, convenience of locations, and so on.

Observation studies are part of the marketing researcher's tool kit.

Occasionally, a firm will use an **observation study,** during which the consumer's behavior is observed and described in such a way as to answer the research problem. General Motors' development of their new electric car relied heavily on descriptive research to provide information on how consumers use their own cars. GM researchers observed, and then described, the daily driving habits of drivers in southern California. At first, GM was considering leaving off many "amenities" on the electric car, which would conserve electricity and thus extend the range the car could travel before recharging. However, their marketing research studies discovered that air conditioning, a radio/tape player, and other "gadgets" are very important to American drivers. The company has concluded that the electric car will have very limited appeal if it does not provide these amenities and still have a range of at least 100 miles before recharging.[7]

Descriptive studies are very common in marketing research and make up a large part of the studies that are conducted by either in-house research departments or commissioned to outside marketing research companies. They are the mainstay of marketing research because they generally allow the marketing manager to draw inferences about his or her customers, target markets, competitors, or other areas of concern. Therefore, it is important that the marketer have some underlying logic by which marketing variables should be included in a descriptive study. Little may be gained by a simple description of whimsically selected variables. For example, if you were going to conduct a survey for Yankee Factory Outlets and you suspected that consumers were buying more clothing by mail catalog, you would want information describing the extent of this type of shopping. If you found that 40 percent of Yankee's customers had made catalog purchases of clothing last year, whereas only 20 percent did so the year before, this pattern would *suggest* that Yankee's sales were being eroded by the strategies of direct market competition.

Descriptive studies are quite common in marketing research.

Causal Research Design

Causal research designs allow us to isolate causes and effects. For example, continuing with our Yankee Factory Outlets example, even if we find that its customers increased their catalog clothing purchases, this does not constitute *proof* that they were buying less at Yankee because of their catalog use. True, it could be argued that this is one reason, but other factors might also explain why Yankee's sales have slumped. Such factors could range from price increases to merchandising changes.

Causal research seeks to find causes and their effects.

Causal research is conducted by controlling various factors to determine which factor is causing the problem. By changing one factor, say price, we can monitor its effects on a key consequence, such as sales. In other words, causal designs allow us to determine *causality*, or which variable is causing another variable to change. We refer to the variables causing the change as *independent* variables, and the variables that are affected by these factors are referred to as the *dependent* variables. Causal research allows for the highest level of understanding that you can achieve regarding any type of phenomenon. It gives the manager the ability to make *if/then statements.* For example, Yankee Factory Outlets' owner might be able to say, "If I increase my advertising by 10 percent, then our sales will increase by 20 percent." Essentially, causal designs involve **experiments** that allow the observer to measure the change in one variable, say sales (dependent), that is ascribed to a change in another variable, say advertising (independent), while holding all other variables constant.

Although causal research designs give you a high level of understanding of the variables you are studying, the designs often require experiments that are complex and expensive. Even with inexpensive experiments, ability to control or at least measure all of the factors that might be causing the phenomenon under study may be uncertain. For this reason, causal research designs are relatively few in the marketing research industry.

Causal research designs typically rely on experiments.

Step 5: Identify Information Types and Sources

Two types of information are available to marketing researchers: secondary data and primary data.

Basically, two types of information are available to a marketing researcher: secondary data and primary data. **Secondary data,** as its name implies, refers to information that has been collected for some other purpose. That is, it is being used for a purpose that is *secondary* to its original function. Sources of secondary data can be *external,* such as census data, *Sales & Marketing Management's Survey of Buying Power,* and countless other publications. Or sources can be *internal,* arising from sources inside the firm, such as Pizza Hut's use of a list of all of the customers to which it delivers pizza for direct mail sales promotion.[8]

Many marketing problems may be resolved with the use of secondary data. A marketer, for example, could easily allocate regional TV advertising budgets based on information contained in *Sales & Marketing Management's Survey of Buying Power.* Secondary data should almost always be used in any research project because it may be collected quickly and it is relatively inexpensive. Secondary data is typically used to carry out exploratory research which, as we stated earlier, is used in many cases to define the problem.

Some problems arise, however, with the use of secondary data. For example, it may be outdated, the information may not be in a form that is usable for the problem at hand, and questions about the integrity of the organization that collected and reported the data may come into play. The sources of secondary data are discussed in detail in chapter 6.

Primary data is information gathered specifically for the research objectives at hand.

The second type of information, **primary data,** refers to information that has been gathered specifically to serve the research objectives at hand. For many types of problems, secondary data simply will not suffice. For example, we mentioned that many banks conduct image analysis studies. Although a bank may have its image analysis studies from years gone by, there simply is no secondary information that will provide the bank with current information. Therefore, if a bank wants this information, it must collect primary data.

Step 6: Determine Methods of Accessing Data

Once the researcher has determined which type or types of information are needed, he or she must determine methods of accessing data. How does he or she accomplish this? It depends on the type of data needed. Compared to primary data, accessing secondary data is relatively easy. If the data are internal, the manager may gather the information from company records, salespersons, other company executives, marketing information systems, or even scanning systems, which offer a wealth of information.

Methods of accessing external secondary data have greatly improved over the last few years. Not only has the quantity of information available increased but, perhaps more significantly, information processing technology (on-line computerized search, CD-ROM databases, and so on) has vastly improved our ability to easily and quickly retrieve the information. Most libraries offer these services at nominal fees, and there are many commercial sources of industry- and even brand-specific data.

There are several alternative methods of accessing the data in marketing research studies.

There are several different methods of collecting primary data. These methods include telephone surveys, mail surveys, door-to-door personal interviews, and mall intercept studies. The advantages and disadvantages of these methods are discussed in chapter 9.

Technology has also impacted access to primary data. New companies are being developed that apply new data collection technologies in unique ways. For example, there are systems that survey TV viewers and radio listeners using computer-generated questionnaires to record respondents' *audio* responses. The computerized questionnaire program customizes each question depending on the respondent's verbal response to the previous question. Some companies are developing virtual reality programs that let consumers "walk" through supermarkets and select their items for purchase. Computers record their purchases and measure their reactions to marketing mix variables such as pricing, packaging shape and color, and in-store promotional displays.

A number of new data collection methods are emerging.

Step 7: Design Data Collection Forms

Because marketing research projects gather information, the actual design of the data collection form that is used to ask and record this information is critical to the success of the project. Even when the correct problem has been defined and the most appropriate research design planned, asking the wrong questions, or asking the right questions in the wrong order, will destroy the usefulness of the research effort.

There are two basic methods by which marketing researchers collect information: by asking questions or by observing. Both information collecting formats use standardized forms, called **questionnaires,** which record the information communicated by respondents or the respondents' behavior as observed by the researcher. There are two types of forms: structured and unstructured. **Structured questionnaires** list questions that have prespecified answer choices. **Unstructured questionnaires** have open-ended questions and/or questions that are asked based on a prior response. Both forms can be **disguised,** which means that the true object of the study is not identified, or **undisguised,** in which case the respondent is made fully aware of the purpose and/or sponsor of the survey.

A questionnaire's apparent simplicity (writing a list of questions) is very deceptive. Care must be taken to design a questionnaire that will cooperatively elicit objective information from the respondents. This means avoiding both ambiguous and leading questions. Additional considerations must be made for observation studies. There are many "dos" and "don'ts" involved with questionnaire or observation form design, and we cover a number of them in chapter 11.

Questionnaires and observation forms must be designed with great care.

Step 8: Determine Sample Plan and Size

It is important to determine a sample plan and its size. Yet, how is this done? Typically, it begins when a marketer wants to know something about a "group," such as the brand manager may want to know the brand preferences among teenagers, aged 13 to 16, for five brands of snacks. Or, a marketing manager may want to know sales of his or her company's products through different types of retail stores by region in the country. The group that the marketer is interested in knowing something about is referred to as the **population.** On occasion, a population is small enough that a manager may study all of the members of the population in order to learn whatever it is they are interested in knowing. However, this is extremely rare. Imagine trying to study *all* teenagers aged 13 through 16! Consequently, marketing researchers study subsets of the population, called **samples,** in order to gather the necessary information in an efficient manner.

Care must be taken in designing and drawing the sample. It is important to note that, because a sample represents something less than the population being studied, the characteristics of the sample will not likely exactly match the characteristics of the population. The difference between sample data and the true, although unknown, population data, is referred to as **sampling error.** Fortunately, as you will see, you can measure the amount of sampling error that exists in a given sample's estimate of some variable of the population (parameter).

A sample plan identifies who is to be sampled and how to select them for study.

There are basically three different issues regarding sampling. The first is that you must determine who, or perhaps what, to sample by defining the problem. Continental Cellular Corporation wanted to estimate the projected demand for cellular telephone usage in Phoenix, Arizona. They felt that cellular telephones would be purchased by business firms as well as individuals for personal use. The decision was made, therefore, to sample "the person in your firm who makes decisions regarding communications equipment" and "heads of households" in order to survey both markets. As an example of a company that did a poor job of specifying *who* to sample, consider an unnamed dog food company that decided to design and market a new type of dog food. The company conducted a great deal of research to choose the best package size, the best package design, and the best advertising program. The product was introduced to the market with a large campaign and the distributors enjoyed excellent sales—for a few weeks. Then, sales dropped to virtually zero. It seemed that, with all of the research that had been undertaken, no one had checked the proper population—the dogs—who did not like the dog food!

A second issue to be included in the final sample is the **sample element,** which refers to a unit of the entity being studied. The sample element could be a supermarket shopper, a head of household, or a retail store, and so on. Also important is the **sample frame,** a list from which sample elements are drawn for the sample, which contains all of the elements in the population being studied. Certainly, Continental Cellular would not want to omit a certain part of the households in Phoenix from its study. If they did, how representative would the study be of the population of Arizona? Continental would not have a very representative study if they selected only business firms from the top of the alphabetical listing of businesses in a specific city. AAAA Barber Shop, AAAA Travel, and AAA Autos simply would not give you a representative sampling of all business firms. In chapter 12, we introduce you to various **sampling plans,** which specify how to draw the sample elements from the sample frame.

A sample frame is a list from which the sample elements are drawn for the sample.

Methods are available to help the researcher determine the sample size required for a research study.

Finally, the third issue to deal with is **sample size,** which determines how many sample elements will be studied. Most people believe that sample size is primarily determined by the size of the population; therefore, the required sample size for a study of Phoenix, Arizona would be much smaller than the required sample size for a study of the United States. You will learn that this is not necessarily true. In fact, only rarely does the size of the population being studied have an impact on the required sample size. A number of alternative methods of sample size determination exist, and we introduce you to them in chapter 13.

Step 9: Collect Data

Data collection is usually done by trained interviewers who are employed by field data collection companies to collect primary data. Many possible errors, called **nonsampling errors** because they are attributable to factors other than sampling errors, may occur during data collection. Such errors include selecting the wrong sample elements to interview, securing subjects who refuse to participate or are simply not at home when the interviewer calls, interviewing subjects who intentionally give out the wrong information, or hiring interviewers who cheat and fill out fictitious survey questionnaires. Even interviewers who honestly complete their interviews may make inadvertent nonsampling errors by copying down the wrong information on their survey form.

Needless to say, good marketing researchers must be aware of the errors that may occur during data collection and should implement plans to reduce these errors. Unlike sampling error, you cannot measure the amount of nonsampling error that may exist in a study. Therefore, it is important to know the possible causes of nonsampling error so that appropriate steps can be taken to limit its occurrence. Data collection in international markets presents new problems for researchers as Marketing Research Insight 3.2 illustrates.

Because nonsampling error cannot be measured, researchers must be aware of the sources of this type of error so that appropriate steps can be taken to limit its occurrence.

Step 10: Analyze Data

Some type of **data analysis** is needed to give the raw data any meaning. Data analysis involves entering data into computer files, inspecting it for errors, and running tabulations and various statistical tests. The first step in data analysis is **data cleaning,** which is the process by which the raw data is checked to verify it is correct and entered where it should be on the data collection form. Typically, data analysis is conducted with the assistance of a computerized data

Data analysis involves entering data into computer files, inspecting it for errors, and running tabulations and various statistical tests.

MARKETING RESEARCH INSIGHT 3.2

Marketing Research in the People's Republic of China

Collecting data has become an international concern. For example, marketing research firms have recently moved into China where marketing research information had previously been nonexistent. The confectionery industry hired Gallup, Inc. of Princeton, New Jersey to gather information about the Chinese market. Among other things, the research revealed that most people in southern China preferred sweet tastes, whereas those in the north showed a preference for sour tastes. The confectionery industry learned they should not expect candy sales to be uniform throughout the country.

Both Gallup and Survey Research Group (Guanzhou), Ltd. (SRG) have learned some interesting things concerning data collection. First, cooperation among Chinese consumers is quite high. SRG cited a study in which they had to interview medical doctors. "In the United States, researchers would have to fork over $200 or $300 to do interviews in the physician's office—and that's if you can get them to cooperate." In China, the doctors agreed to come to SRG offices on weekends to be interviewed in exchange for some household cleaning supplies. Also, consumers in China expect you to educate them as to what marketing research is before they answer your questions, and they are sensitive to personal questions that Americans freely answer, such as questions dealing with one's personal hygiene.[9]

analysis program that, in most cases, allows only numerical entries. **Coding** is the process of assigning all response categories a numerical value; that is, males = 1, females = 2, and so on.

Data analysis involves tabulation, cross-tabulation, and statistical tests.

An important step in data analysis is performed by **tabulation,** which refers to the actual counting of the number of observations that fall into each possible response category. For example, one tabulation of the soft drink brand bought most by the respondents in a study may yield 120 Pepsi buyers and 133 Dr Pepper buyers. As you will see, there are several uses of tabulation, some devoted to data cleaning, and others allow the researcher to understand what the collected data means. Examining two or more response categories at the same time, called **cross-tabulation,** is another form of data analysis. Finally, a variety of **statistical tests,** which include means, frequencies, correlations, trend analysis, and regression, are also used to analyze data.

MARKETING RESEARCH INSIGHT 3.3

Marketing Research May Be Used to Address Ethical Issues

Discriminatory practices exist in many forms, but the most common ones involve equal access to goods and services, equal credit opportunity, and equal employment opportunity. Recent discriminatory cases have resulted in millions of dollars of payments. For example, Denny's paid over $50 million in settlement claims that it discriminated against black customers, and Texaco agreed to pay almost $200 million to African-American employees who claimed race discrimination. Both of these examples pertain to overt discrimination where minorities are denied the same opportunities that are made available to whites. There are, however, subtle discrimination practices that are less obvious, but they nevertheless involve biased business practices.

Marketing research can be applied by companies to investigate their business practices to determine if prejudicial policies are in place. Each company is unique, and the type of marketing research must be suited to the company's operations. One approach is to identify pairs of employees or customers who are matched in gender, age, and along other factors such as disability, and to compare the treatments of these matched pairs. Subtle discrimination may be detected by comparing experiences such as products offered, waiting time, friendliness of service, and prices paid. A different approach is to survey credit applicants to see if those denied credit tend to be minorities. A third method is file audits where a financial services company inspects all of its denied credit applications to assess the degree of discrimination. Finally, the huge data warehouses of some companies allow for statistical modeling techniques that may uncover discriminatory practices of which top executives may be unaware.

Given that minorities constitute about one-quarter of the U.S. population, and minorities are the fastest growing consumer segment, it is important for companies to apply various marketing research techniques as an early warning system. This system will help companies to avoid costly lawsuits, and it will facilitate the company's responses to the inquiries of government investigators who are concerned with discriminatory business practices.

Source: *Paul C. Lubin, "Using Marketing Research to Detect Discrimination,"* Marketing News *(August 14, 1997), vol. 31, no. 8, 11.*

Step 11: Prepare and Present the Final Research Report

Our last step in the marketing research process is to prepare and present the final **research report**—one of the most important phases of marketing research. Its importance cannot be overstated because it is the report, or its presentation, that properly communicates the study results to the client.

Every researcher should confer with the client to determine exactly what is wanted in the research report. However, there are widely accepted standardized sections of a marketing research report, such as the introduction, the methodology, the results, and so on. Computer graphics may be included to present information visually. Graphs are invaluable as communication vehicles when researchers want to summarize meaningful patterns or notable findings for the marketing managers who will be making decisions on the research results. For instance, for our Yankee Factory Outlets example, a bar graph that compares the catalog purchases over two years would be a very effective means of displaying the change in purchases from 20 percent to 40 percent. Such a graph would make Yankee's management take note of this shift in the purchasing behavior of its target market.

Preparing the marketing research report involves describing the process used, building meaningful tables, and using presentation graphics for clarity.

Sometimes researchers not only turn in a written research report but they also make an **oral presentation** of the research methods used to conduct the study as well as the research findings to their client. Typically, the presentation entails overhead transparencies or even color slides with outlines, bulleted lists, and graphs. Additional suggestions on how to give oral presentations are provided in chapter 19.

MARKETING RESEARCH IN ACTION: KFC'S "FAMILY FEAST" INTRODUCTION IN THE UNITED KINGDOM

To illustrate the steps in an actual marketing research process, we describe the steps and findings involved with how Kentucky Fried Chicken (KFC) researched the market for its successful "Family Feast" introduction in the United Kingdom (U.K.). Because the information is proprietary, we have disguised some of the facts.[10] However, the topic that the research involves and the role of this research in the decision to launch the new menu item is real, and we have gained the permission of KFC to use this example as an overview to help you understand how the marketing research process works. We have chosen a U.K. example because marketing research can be applied to any business environment, and it often must be applied by U.S. companies when they are attempting to penetrate markets in other countries.

Establish the Need for Marketing Research

By the early 1990s, KFC had been in the United Kingdom for 30 years, and it had grown to over 300 units. It originally started out as a "takeaway concept" with little or no seating competing directly with the locally popular fish-and-chip shops. With the growth of "Competitor M" in the United Kingdom (now with over 500 units) and the growing popularity of other U.S. "fast food," KFC faced the challenge of trying to find a competitive advantage.

KFC's traditional base of customers in the United Kingdom had evolved to be young males who typically liked to go to KFC late at night after meeting with their friends at the local pub, and this position was not consistent with a restaurant chain that has a strong family appeal as a core strength. In marketing terms, KFC felt it needed to reposition its image away from being a male hangout to a family dining alternative. Clearly, KFC needed to identify and research a family-value strategy that appealed to the U.K. market.

Define the Problem

In 1993, John Shuker, marketing director for KFC-UK, met with his marketing team and advertising agency to decide the best way to broaden their user base from young males to families. Shuker faced several daunting tasks that he discussed with the team. First, in the United Kingdom the KFC brand over the years had become strongly associated as a "takeaway" restaurant and only for young males. Trying to reposition KFC as a "family-friendly" concept could potentially take years because of the entrenched "takeaway" image. Second, the young male KFC customer group, although extremely loyal buyers, had created a negative image for the KFC brand among women because moms ("mums") felt uncomfortable bringing their children to the same place frequented by groups of young, and sometimes intoxicated, men. Finally, even though "Competitor M" had come to the United Kingdom 10 years after KFC was established there, "Competitor M" was making up for the lost time in a hurry and was now spending more on children's advertising alone than KFC spent on all advertising. Figure 3.2 illustrates how "Competitor M" was attracting families more than KFC in the United Kingdom.

Shuker and the ad agency recognized that repositioning KFC's image was critical to its long-term viability because families represent the largest and fastest growing segment of quick-service restaurant users.

The immediate marketing management problem facing the KFC team was to determine what it would take to get U.K. "mums" interested enough to visit and use KFC on a regular basis as a place to buy meals for their families.

Establish Research Objectives

One of the primary advantages of being part of an international business system such as KFC Worldwide is to be able to leverage what is working in other markets. Although KFC-UK had one of the lowest percentages of sales in family meals (also called "high-end" meals given their relatively higher price compared to individual meals), KFC-Australia had recently been successful in growing its high-end business with the introduction of what was called a "Family Feast"—enough food, including dessert, to feed a family of four for a reasonable price.

The proportion of family meals in Australia had grown to 30 percent of KFC-Australia sales compared to only 10 percent of sales in KFC-UK. In fact, as Figure 3.3 (page 74) shows, the KFC "high-end" or family meal volume in the United Kingdom was the lowest in all of the countries where KFC had significant presence. However, it is risky to assume that menu items that are successful in one country can be dropped into another country's environment and be equally successful. Rather, the concept needed careful research and investigation to assess the market's reactions.

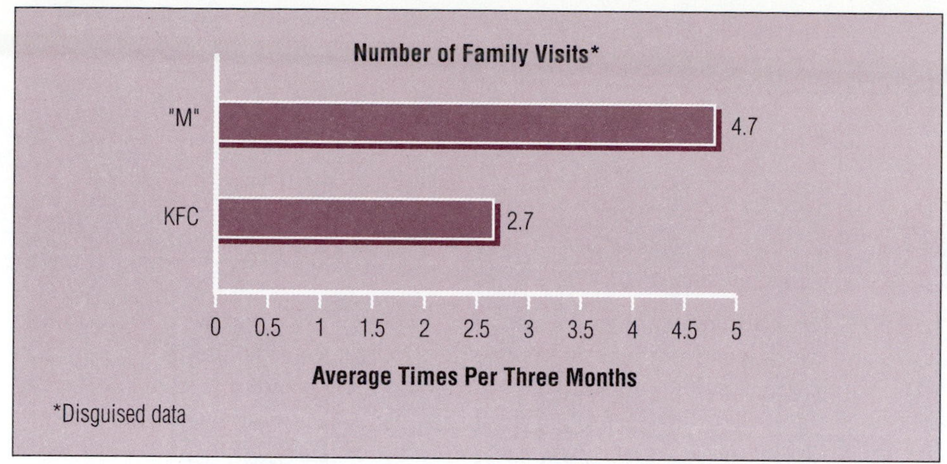

Figure 3.2

"Competitor M" has been more successful than KFC in attracting and retaining families.

So the two key research questions for the KFC-UK team were: (1) would a similar "Family Feast" offering appeal to U.K. mums, and (2) would the introduction of a "Family Feast" help improve the overall image and awareness of the KFC brand in the U.K.?

Determine Research Design

In determining how to go about answering these two questions, it was decided that a "Family Feast" concept study among mums would help determine how viable the idea was in the United Kingdom. If the concept was found to be attractive to mums, the "KFC Family Feast" would be launched nationally and research gathered on its business and consumer performance. The research design was mapped out. It included secondary data analysis, focus group studies, a cross-sectional survey of U.K. mums, and, ultimately, sales and consumer tracking studies when and if the "Family Feast" was launched.

Identify Information Types and Sources

Secondary, or published, information is very limited in analyzing this type of quick-service restaurant issue because most of the data gathered is jealously guarded by the competition. Industry magazines such as *Advertising Age* and *Restaurant News* sometimes provide insights as to what is going on with the competition, but it is typically of limited value. There was, however, substantial case study data in the forms of KFC's family meal experiences in other countries such as Australia. The KFC-UK team studied the Australian experience extensively, but they found that KFC-Australia had not undergone the young male take-out niche transformation that KFC-UK was attempting.

Primary data is much more powerful, and for KFC-UK, it came from two different sources, qualitative and quantitative. Focus groups can be initially helpful in understanding how the target customers feel about certain issues, but the key questions are typically best answered via well-developed quantitative research tools. In both cases, U.K. mums were the primary data sources.

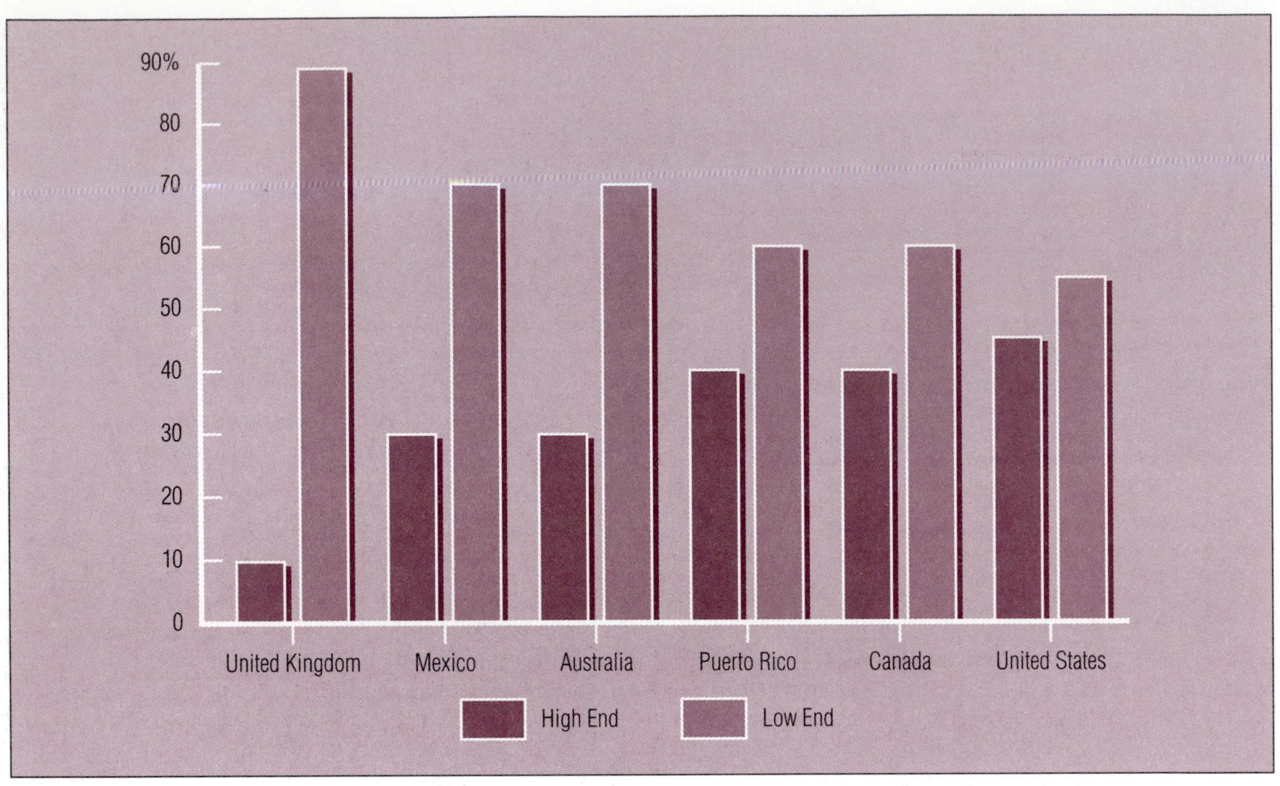

Figure 3.3

KFC High/Low End Menu Mix by Country

Determine Methods of Accessing Data

Once all of the relevant research and business data were collected and analyzed from the KFC-Australia experience, a series of focus groups was set up with U.K. mums with children under 12 to discuss their eating habits and how they provide meals for their families. Additionally, a specialized form of analysis comparing the number of "Family Feast" options was designed to better understand the "ideal" family bundle of food at various price points. If a launch of the "Family Feast" was to take place, regular quantitative brand tracking was already in place for KFC-UK and could be used to measure the impact of the "Family Feast" on various measures such as advertising awareness and brand attributes for a nominal incremental cost.

Design Data Collection Forms

With the focus group phase, the KFC team traveled to the north and south of England to listen to groups of women with children under 12 talk about a variety of topics such as their favorite restaurants and which quick-service restaurants their families liked to visit. Because the KFC team did not want the women to be biased for or against KFC, the sponsor of the research was not identified. The focus groups were recorded on videotape, and the comments were converted to word processing files and hard copy for analysis.

The special-purpose analysis involved a number of comparisons between different variables such as price, amount of food, inclusion of a dessert or drink, and so forth. To capture this data, a structured questionnaire was designed and pretested for ease of administration. The market tracking questionnaire was a standardized, structured, quantitative questionnaire that had the additional advantage of being compared to previous tracking studies.

Determine Sample Plan and Size

With the qualitative component of the study, the focus group, three cities were selected as representative areas to recruit women: Birmingham, Leeds, and London. For each focus group 10 to 12 women who had used a quick-service restaurant in the past 3 months were selected. The quantitative phase of the study utilized a base of 200 women from 10 different mall locations across the United Kingdom. The market tracking study sample was of a similar base size, conducted each month as part of a regular national tracking study. It was conducted utilizing street intercept interviews completed on an ongoing basis in representative parts of the United Kingdom. Specific questions on awareness and usage of the "Family Feast" were added to the end of the regular tracking questionnaire so the data could be compared to previous data gathered without biasing the respondent.

Collect Data

Data collection took place over time. The focus group data were collected over a period of two weeks and required members of the team to visit the three cities and listen to the participants in two-hour sessions per group. In addition, the team spent time at the end of the focus group sessions with the moderator summarizing their impressions.

The 200-respondent survey and tracking study were conducted by a field data collection company whose employees were trained and experienced in these types of interviews. The survey took about two weeks to complete. Once the decision to launch the "Family Feast" nationally was made, the additional "Family Feast" questions were added to the regular tracking study and collected over a period of six months.

Analyze the Data and Prepare the Final Research Report

The first research objective (whether a "Family Feast" offering similar to the one in Australia would appeal to U.K. mums) was addressed with the use of the focus groups and survey analysis. The focus group mums were very interested in the "Family Feast" concept and thought it would motivate them to begin using KFC as a convenient, economical way to provide dinner for their families.

With the survey, the "Family Feast" was compared to the current KFC-UK family meal offering, which was called a "Bargain Bucket." The "Bargain Bucket" included eight pieces of chicken and four regular french fries and sold for around $12. The analysis indicated a "Family Feast" meal selling for under £10 (around $16) that would feed four people (i.e., eight pieces of chicken, four regular french fries, two large side orders such as beans and cole slaw, and a family-size apple pie) would be more popular than the "Bargain Bucket." As illustrated in Figure 3.4 on page 76, the "Family Feast" was perceived to be a better

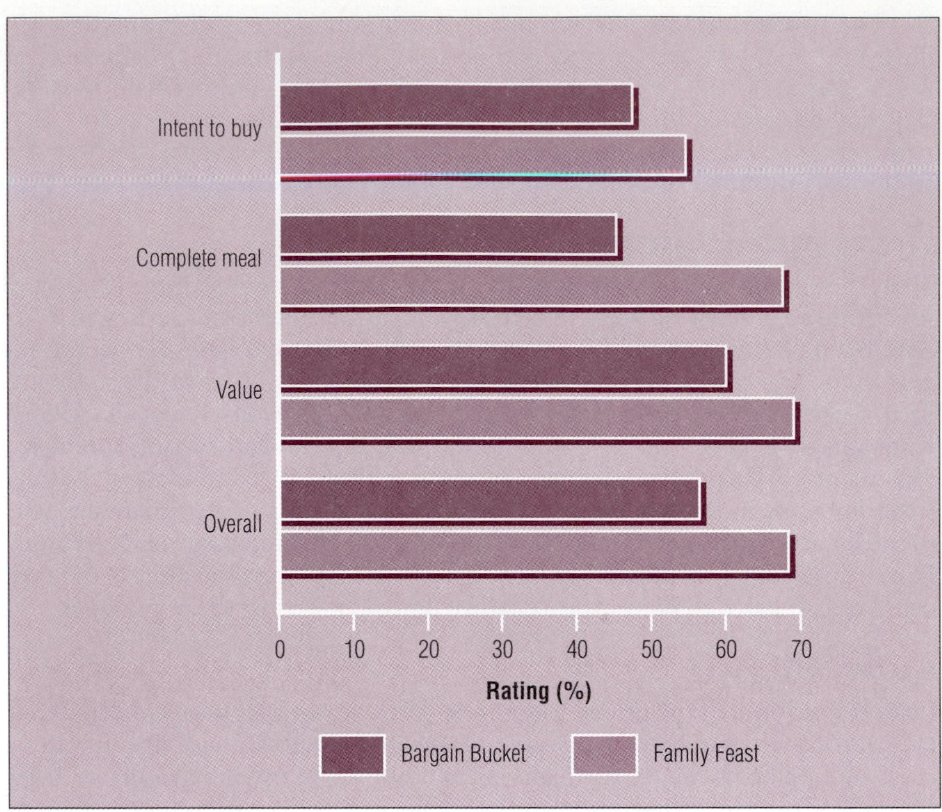

Figure 3.4

Consumer Ratings: Family Feast versus Bargain Bucket

value, a more complete meal, preferred more, and associated with stronger intentions to buy. Based on these findings, KFC-UK launched the "Family Feast."

The second objective (whether the introduction of a "Family Feast" could help improve the overall image of the KFC brand in the U.K.) was answered by the brand tracking study. Overall value was tracked, and for KFC-UK at the launch of the "Family Feast," these ratings were at times 10 points behind "Competitor M." As can be seen in Figure 3.5, by the end of the tracking period, KFC-UK value was neck-and-neck with "Competitor M's" rating. Also, at the end of the launch year, KFC-UK's high-end sales had doubled from 10 percent to 20 percent.

Other tracking factors included restaurant chain awareness, "Family Feast" awareness, and "Family Feast" trial. Although "Competitor M" was spending about four times as much on television advertising in the United Kingdom, the "Family Feast" advertising generated an all-time high advertising awareness for the brand, and as can be seen in Figure 3.6 (page 78), it dramatically helped close the gap in advertising awareness levels between "Competitor M" and KFC.

Continual advertising of the "Family Feast" was also effective in generating new trial and interest in the KFC brand. After only three months of advertising, awareness of KFC's "Family Feast" reached around 50 percent of quick-service restaurant users, and over 10 percent of all these users had purchased a "Family Feast" meal. The tracking information is displayed in Figure 3.7 on page 79.

From a financial perspective, even though the "Family Feast" had a lower gross profit margin than the previous "Bargain Bucket," it proved to be more

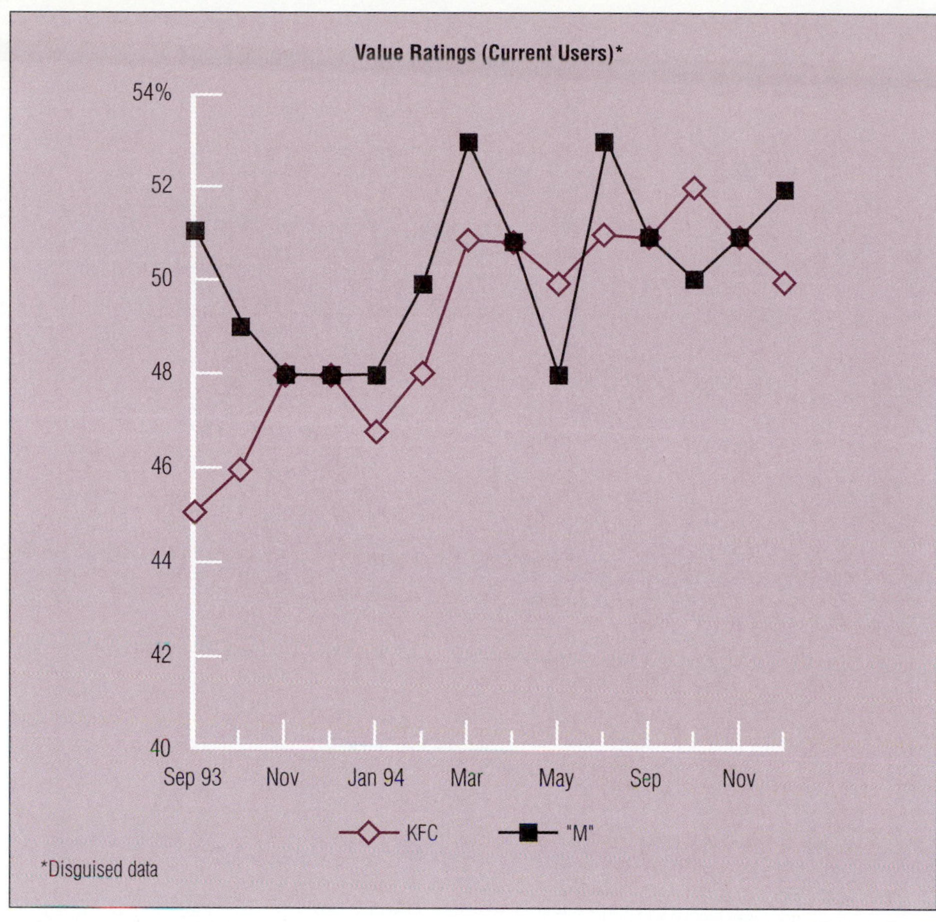

Figure 3.5

Value ratings show steady KFC gains after Family Feast.

popular and therefore generated a greater total profit than the "Bargain Bucket" did because of its larger volume of sales. What surprised the KFC team was that instead of cannibalizing "Bargain Bucket" sales, "Family Feast" sales were incremental. That is, subsequent research among "Family Feast" buyers indicated it appealed to a different type of customer, namely ones with larger families, whereas the "Bargain Bucket" appealed to smaller families who continued to purchase it.

From a positioning perspective, "Family Feast" was very effective in competing against other quick-service restaurants because it played on KFC's natural strenths. Despite the young male patron element, KFC was associated with providing families with a wholesome, home-style dinner a mum would prefer over hamburgers and french fries. This strength was difficult for the burger chain, "Competitor M," to match given their sandwich-based, and less wholesome, menu.

The "Family Feast" eventually became the number one selling item at KFC-UK. In terms of annual sales, it grew to be larger than a number of other well-known brands in the United Kingdom including Nintendo video games, 7-Up, Obsession perfume, and Persil liquid (a popular dishwashing detergent).

In summary, the research and launch of the "Family Feast" played an important role in helping to reposition the KFC brand in the United King-

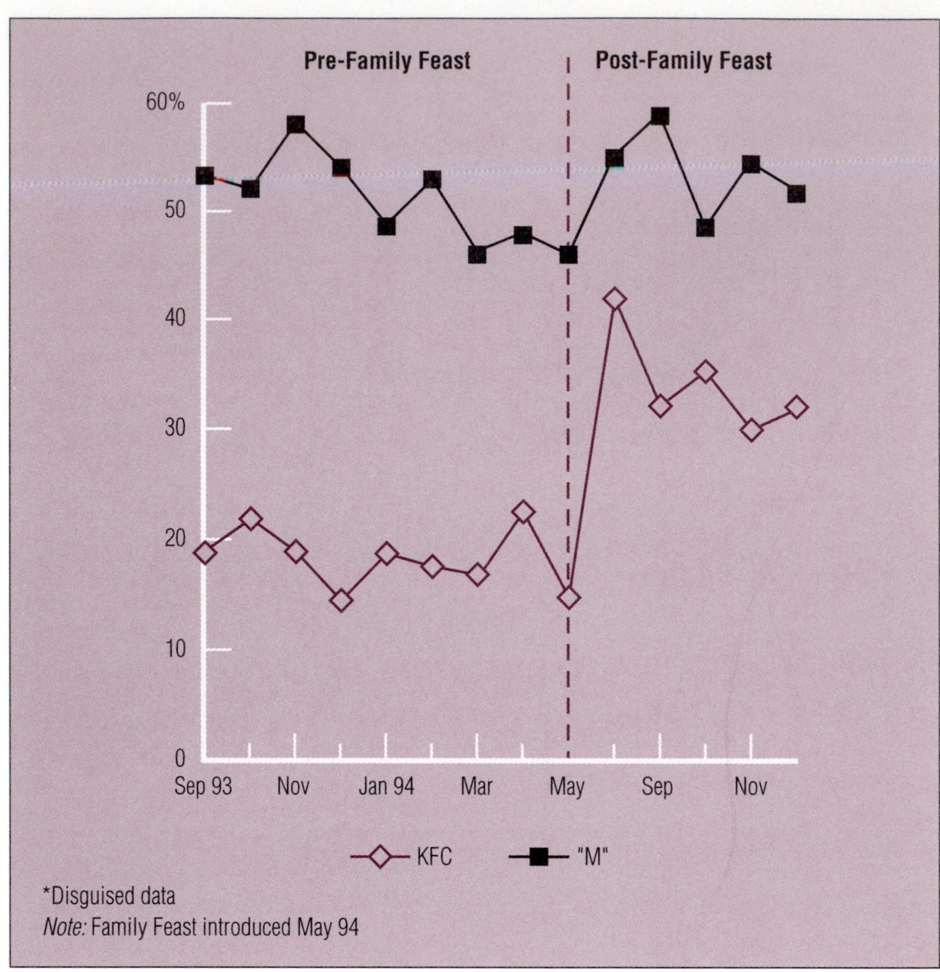

Figure 3.6
Advertising Awareness

dom—one preferred by families. KFC Worldwide continues to invest heavily in marketing research as it constantly seeks to reposition itself and compete aggressively against its many quick-service restaurant opponents.

Install your SPSS Student Assistant. View: "How To Use ScreenCam"

SUMMARY

Virtually all marketing research projects are different. Some studies are limited to a review of secondary data; others require complex designs involving large-scale collection of primary data. While recognizing the diversity of research projects, there are enough commonalities among these projects to enable us to characterize them in terms of "steps of the research process." These steps are: (1) establishing the need for marketing research, (2) defining the problem, (3) establishing research objectives, (4) determining research design, (5) identifying information types and sources, (6) determining methods of accessing data, (7) designing data collection forms, (8) determining sample plan and size, (9) collecting data, (10) analyzing data, and (11) preparing and presenting the final research report.

There is value in characterizing research projects in terms of successive steps. First, the steps give researchers, and nonresearchers, an overview of the entire research process. Second, they provide a procedure in the sense that a

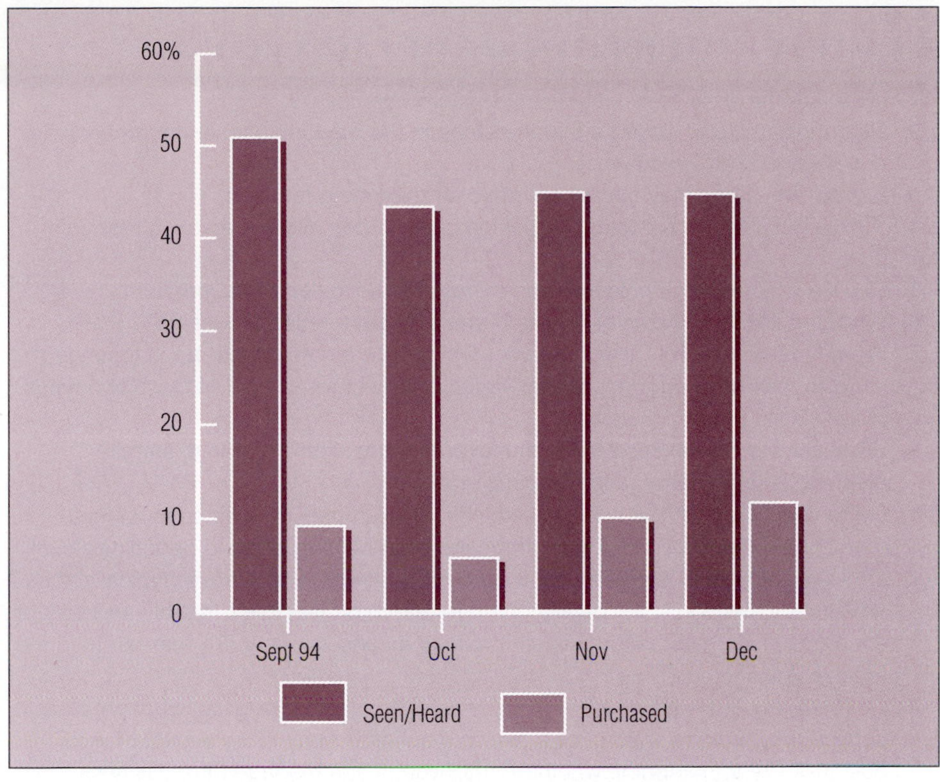

Figure 3.7

Awareness, Trial of Family Feast among U.K. Quick-Service Restaurant Users

researcher, by referring to the steps, knows what tasks to consider and in what order. However, an informed researcher and client should know there are caveats in such a step-by-step procedure. Only by being thoroughly familiar with the research process is a researcher or client in a position to understand some of the problems associated with following a cookbook, step-by-step procedure. Many problems may not require, for example, the collection of primary data, data analysis, and so on. Furthermore, the steps shown in this chapter are interactive. That is, after collecting some data, the researcher may decide that the problem needs to be redefined, and the process may start over.

KEY TERMS

Steps in the marketing research process (p. 58)
Monitoring system (p. 59)
Exploratory research (p. 63)
Descriptive research (p. 64)
Observation study (p. 64)
Causal research (p. 65)
Experiments (p. 65)
Secondary data (p. 66)
Primary data (p. 66)
Questionnaires (p. 67)
Structured/unstructured questionnaires (p. 67)
Disguised/undisguised questionnaires (p. 67)
Population (p. 67)
Samples (p. 68)
Sampling error (p. 68)
Sample element (p. 68)
Sample frame (p. 68)
Sampling plans (p. 68)
Sample size (p. 68)
Nonsampling errors (p. 69)
Data analysis (p. 69)
Data cleaning (p. 69)
Coding (p. 70)
Tabulation (p. 70)
Cross-tabulation (p. 70)
Statistical tests (p. 70)
Research report (p. 71)
Oral presentation (p. 71)

REVIEW QUESTIONS/APPLICATIONS

1. What are the steps in the marketing research process?
2. Use an example to illustrate that the steps in the marketing research process are not always taken in sequence.
3. Explain why firms may not have a need for marketing research.
4. Why is defining the problem the most important step in the marketing research process?
5. Explain why research objectives differ from the definition of the problem.
6. What are the three types of research that constitute research design?
7. What type of research design allows us to isolate the effect that an independent variable may have on a dependent variable? Give an example of these two types of variables.
8. What are the differences among the following: population, sample, sample element, sample frame, and sampling error?
9. Go to your library or the Internet and look for examples of firms conducting a marketing research study. There are many examples reported in periodicals such as *Advertising Age, Marketing News, Business Week,* and *Forbes.* Typically, these articles will mention a few details of the research project itself. Identify as many of the steps in the marketing research process as possible that are referred to in the articles you find.
10. Observe any business in your community. Examine what they do, what products or service they provide, their prices, their promotion, or any other aspect of their business. Try to determine whether or not you, if you managed the business, would have conducted research to determine the firm's products, their design, features, prices, promotion, etc. If you decide that you would not have conducted marketing research on a given area, explain why.

CASE 3.1

Crystal Pepsi

In the early 1990s, Pepsi considered a product extension strategy in the form of a clear formulation called Crystal Pepsi. Pepsi enjoyed great top-of-mind awareness with its mainstay brands, Pepsi and Diet Pepsi, and it considered the new formulation to be a good answer to the need to expand the line without cannibalizing its two winner brands. Crystal Pepsi was a colorless version of the Pepsi taste, and it was positioned to compete with ginger ale, cream soda, or even soda water. Pepsi's initial market tests recorded a 6 percent share, which was three times the minimum required share of 2 percent, but to some degree the initial market test share was inflated by the fad aspect of Crystal Pepsi.

Two types of consumers showed interest in Crystal Pepsi. One type was young soft drink drinkers who were attracted to the new and unique aspects of the drink, and the other type was older consumers who gravitated to Crystal Pepsi's clear and wholesome image. In actuality, Crystal Pepsi did not taste like a cola.

1. Should Pepsi management go ahead with full-scale marketing of Crystal Pepsi? Why? Why not?

2. Assuming Pepsi decided to conduct marketing research, what type of research should they conduct?

Source: *Chet Kane, "New Product Killer: The Research Gap,"* Brandweek, *vol. 35, no. 35 (November 28, 1994), 12.*

Case 3.2

PC Rebuilders, Inc.

PC Rebuilders, Inc. was launched when its founder and owner, Tom Owens, began rebuilding IBM-compatible personal computers as a hobby. Tom soon found that he could easily upgrade a personal computer by purchasing discounted and refurbished components at a low cost and installing them himself. By working out of his basement workshop over the past three years, Tom has rebuilt about 100 PCs and sold all of them to people in his hometown at a considerable profit. In fact, Tom's reputation has spread by word-of-mouth, and he averages two calls per week from people who either want their PC upgraded or are seeking to buy a rebuilt PC. Tom thinks that if he rents 5,000 square feet of floor space in an old factory complex that is now being partitioned and rented out to individual companies and employs and trains three technicians, he can produce 1,000 rebuilt PCs per year. Tom's brother-in-law, who works at the local bank, believes Tom can obtain a short-term business start-up loan of $35,000 if Tom uses the equity in his home mortgage as security.

1. Do you think any marketing research is warranted at this time? Why or why not?
2. If a marketing research study were performed, what do you believe should be the primary objectives?

CHAPTER 4

Defining the Problem and Determining Research Objectives

Learning Objectives

- *To understand basic differences between marketing managers and researchers*
- *To learn how to dissect a marketing management problem*
- *To know what constructs are and how they are used by marketing researchers*
- *To learn how to itemize the objectives of a research project*

Marketing researchers must work closely with managers to properly define the problem.

PRACTITIONER VIEWPOINT

The most important stage in the marketing research process is problem definition. Invariably, marketing problems are imbued with a multitude of conditions, forces, and contigencies. When a marketing manager senses something has gone wrong, it usually triggers a soul-searching investigation of possible causes. Because the marketing researcher has been trained to be objective above all else, you usually find the researcher playing the role of a police detective. That is, it is his or her job to interrogate the marketing manager as to what happened, who was involved, when events occurred, what factors were at play, and what alternatives are open to resolve the problem. Every now and then, I think criminal justice should be a mandatory minor for anyone studying to be a marketing researcher.

— Al Muller, President
Metromarket Trends, Inc.

Jell-O Wonders about What Profiles "Pudding People" and How to Target "Nonpudding People"

1. Establish the need for marketing research
2. Define the problem
3. Establish research objectives
4. Determine research design
5. Identify information types and sources
6. Determine methods of accessing data
7. Design data collection forms
8. Determine sample plan and size
9. Collect data
10. Analyze data
11. Prepare and present the final research report

For many years, Jell-O has enjoyed a commanding lead in the $200 million pudding market, but it had little understanding of what types of consumers were pudding people. What kinds of people eat pudding; what kinds do not, and why not? These questions plagued Jell-O executives in the mid-1990s as they watched sales plateau despite efforts to convert more pudding eaters to Jell-O products. Marketing research was applied to these questions. A study revealed the answer to this question: there are two distinct groups of pudding eaters. One group is the old, retired couples; the other group is the young children between the ages of 6 and 17. Regardless of age, pudding eaters are located in small towns and rural areas, and they enjoy hunting, fishing, and baking from scratch. They embrace traditional values such as prayer in school and support conservative political views. Jell-O's marketing problem became evident with the nonpudding eaters, who are over 60 percent of all Americans and who are profiled as young, college-educated, apartment-dwelling singles and young couples who live in urban and suburban areas. These consumers consider pudding to be a boring and dangerously sugar-saturated dessert that does not compete with yogurt or gourmet foods, so Jell-O executives now knew that pudding had an "image problem" with these consumers. With the knowledge gained by this research, Jell-O's marketing answer was to develop fat-free and sugar-free varieties, which have been successful.[1]

The previous chapters introduced you to the world of marketing research. This chapter addresses what some marketing researchers claim is the most important phase in the marketing research process—defining the nature of the problem confronting the marketing manager, specifying constructs, and determining research objectives. This chapter also discusses the differences between marketing managers and marketing researchers, describing their different orientations so you will understand why a continuous dialogue must take place between these two roles during the problem-formulation and objectives-setting steps. Finally, the components of a decision problem are described, so you will understand how the marketing researcher goes about dissecting it into manageable parts.

DEFINE THE MARKETING MANAGER'S PROBLEM

Defining the problem is critical to setting the direction for all subsequent phases of the marketing research process. This is particularly true for custom-designed research, as opposed to standardized research. The *standardized,* also called *syndicated,* research is generic research that is provided in identical fashion to all buyers by the marketing research supplier. *Custom-designed* research is research that is fashioned to address a unique marketing management problem confronting a client manager. Custom-designed research requires that the marketing researcher fully understand the circumstances of the marketing manager's problem.

Custom-designed marketing research should begin with a thorough problem definition.

It is not unusual for the manager and researcher to conduct many discussions to define the problem as well as the precise nature of the research needed to resolve the problem. For example, the Marriott hotel chain may call in a marketing researcher because it thinks there is a problem with its reservation system. When it contacts the researcher, Marriott may state that it feels that its telephone lines are often tied up, and that it loses business travelers who wait on hold too long when they call its 800 number. If this is the issue to be researched, then a research study could be launched to find out the experience of prospective Marriott hotel patrons when they call the toll-free number. A nationwide telephone study could be undertaken to determine how often business travelers call the number, why they must wait, and what amount of time they do wait before a Marriott reservations representative comes on the line.

However, although this survey would gather much information on this facet of Marriott's reservation system, it might not solve the real problem, which stems from the fact that many business travelers delegate making hotel reservations to their secretaries or company travel agencies, and a competitor has developed an incentive system to reward those employees who make reservations with their hotel chain. Without considering who the "purchasing agents" are, the problem definition is incomplete. So, until all dimensions of the issue are explored the problem has not been defined satisfactorily. If the problem is not defined correctly, satisfactory performance at the other stages in the marketing research process will not remedy the situation.

Differences between Managers and Researchers

Managers' and researchers' backgrounds differ markedly.

Marketing managers and marketing researchers see the world differently because they have different jobs to perform and their backgrounds differ markedly. As illustrated in Table 4.1, managers and researchers actually operate in different worlds. However, during the problem definition phase, their worlds overlap, and they are forced into a discussion of the symptoms perceived by the manager. They also discuss the types of research the researcher envisions will be necessary to generate answers to the question of why the symptoms have arisen and what the manager can do to resolve the problem.

Guidelines to Resolve Differences between Managers and Researchers

Despite their differences, managers and researchers must form a working relationship.

Obviously, despite their divergent orientations, marketing managers and marketing researchers must work together to survive. Although understanding the differences presented in Table 4.1 goes a long way toward helping managers and researchers forge a working relationship, much more is required. Alreck and Settle[2] have formulated six questions that managers and nine questions that researchers should ask themselves to avoid potential misunderstandings as they discuss the problem and determine the objectives of the research involved.

Table 4.1

Eight Fundamental Differences between Managers and Researchers

Area of Difference	Managers	Researchers
Organizational position	Line	Staff
Responsibility	To make profits	To generate information
Training	General decision making	Technique applications
Disposition toward knowledge	Wants answers to questions	Wants to ask questions
Orientation	Pragmatic	Scholarly
Brand involvement	Highly involved; emotional	Detached; unemotional
Use of the research	Political	Nonpolitical
Research motivation	To make symptoms disappear	To find the truth

Six questions help guide the marketing manager.

The *six questions for the marketing manager* include the following:

1. What is the background of the problem?
2. What issues or questions prompted management to consider undertaking research?
3. What types of information could clarify or solve the problem?
4. What decisions, choices, or actions will be based on the research results or findings?
5. How much is the information worth; that is, what risks might be reduced or what opportunities might be gained?
6. What is the time horizon and level of resources available to perform the research?

Nine questions help guide the marketing researcher.

The *nine questions for the marketing researcher* include the following:

1. What are the capabilities and limitations of the research being considered?
2. What is the history of the operations, policies, and procedures of the client?
3. What problems or issues appear to be the focus of the research, and what is uncertain or unknown about them?
4. What decisions, choices, or actions are to be based on the results of the proposed research?
5. What is a preliminary assessment of the worth of the research information to the client?
6. What are the time requirements for the research and what resources can be devoted to it?
7. What degrees of cooperation and participation will be expected of the clients?
8. What ethical issues are associated with the research?
9. How can I gain the client's confidence and trust in a professional and ethical manner?

Ultimately, the problem definition stage of enlightened marketing research must be viewed as a partnership.

The proper way to consider these questions is in the context of what is to be gained or lost. When managers do their homework and thoroughly describe the problem's dimensions, and when they identify reasonable alternatives, noting the resources that can be applied or other pressures operating on the research effort, the communication process is enhanced. At the same time, it is necessary that researchers obtain as complete a preliminary picture as possible by asking pointed questions, reviewing salient materials, or even probing the managers' true motives. Recent research has demonstrated that the quality of interactions that take place between managers and researchers, plus the level of involvement on the part of researchers, directly affect the managers' utilization of the research.[3] Ultimately, the problem definition stage of enlightened marketing research must be viewed as a partnership, and partnerships can survive only with mutual respect, trust, and open communication.

DECIDE WHEN MARKETING RESEARCH IS WARRANTED

Marketing managers are responsible for initiating the marketing research process. This means that they must first determine when to embark on a custom-designed marketing research project. Unfortunately, it is all too easy to commission marketing research without a sober evaluation of whether or not research should be undertaken in the first place.

There are four instances in which research should be undertaken.

As explained in chapter 3, there are at least four instances in which marketing research may *not* help. It is probably wise to forego the expense of research when any one of these is present. Of course, marketing research is performed every day, so there must be general instances when the manager *should* go ahead with marketing research.[4] In general, there are four instances in which research should be undertaken:

1. If it clarifies problems or investigates changes in the marketplace that can directly impact your product responsibility
2. If it resolves your selection of alternative courses of marketing action to achieve key marketing objectives
3. If it helps you gain a meaningful competitive advantage
4. If it allows you to stay abreast of your market(s)

Another way to decide when to do marketing research is to perform a cost–benefit analysis. To do this, the marketing manager estimates how much will be lost if the problem (or opportunity) is not addressed. If the anticipated cost of the research does not exceed this estimate, then the manager should proceed with the research. Some managers fail to compare research cost with its benefits, which is a mistake.[5]

DEFINE THE MARKETING MANAGEMENT AND RESEARCH PROBLEMS

The marketing research problem differs from the marketing management problem.

There are two types of problems with which a marketing researcher must contend: the **marketing management problem** and the **marketing research problem.** A marketing management problem is defined in one of two ways:

(1) if the symptoms of failure to achieve an objective are present, the marketing manager must select a course of action to regain the objective, and (2) if the symptoms of the likelihood of achieving an objective are present, the manager must decide on how best to seize the opportunity. Some researchers refer to the second way as **opportunity identification.**

Once the marketing management problem is fully defined, the marketing researcher must wrestle with the marketing research problem, which is defined as providing relevant, accurate, and unbiased information that managers can use to solve their marketing management problems. Obviously, the marketing management problem is critical, for its improper definition will invalidate the researcher's identification of the research problem. Poor problem definition can expose research to a range of undesirable consequences, including incorrect research designs and inappropriate or needlessly expensive data collection, assembly of incorrect or irrelevant data, and poor choice of the sample selection.[6] It is critical, therefore, that the marketing management problem be defined accurately and fully.

There are eight components to a marketing management problem.

There are eight assessment areas that help the marketing researcher properly define the marketing management problem (Figure 4.1). They are: (1) assess the background of the company, product, and market; (2) understand the decision maker's circumstances, objectives, and resources; (3) clarify the symptoms of the problem; (4) pinpoint suspected causes of the problem; (5) specify actions that may alleviate the problem; (6) speculate on anticipated consequences of these actions; (7) identify the manager's assumptions about the consequences; and (8) assess the adequacy of information on hand. A discussion of each area follows.

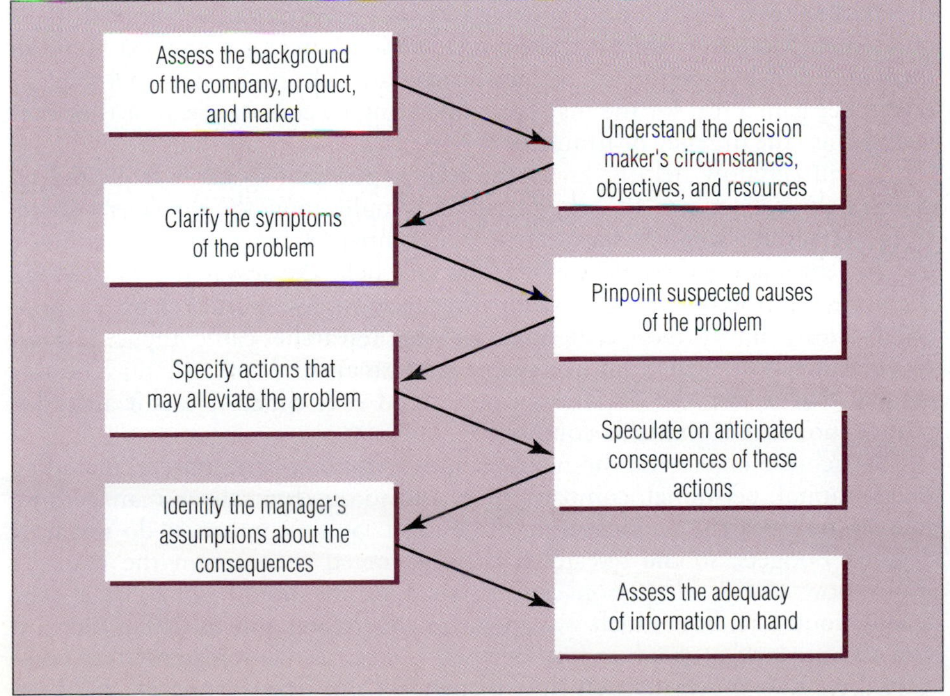

Figure 4.1

The Problem Definition Process

Assess the Background of the Company, Product, and Market

Full sharing of background information between manager and researcher is necessary during problem definition.

It is during the initial meeting between the marketing researcher and the marketing manager that the researcher is informed regarding the **background** of the product or service under investigation, including its performance history and any recent marketing strategy changes. At this meeting, the manager also informs the researcher regarding the company's history, its organizational structure, ownership situation, and overall mission. Additionally, the manager will need to describe the product, including how it works, its composition or production, its various features or benefits, and other aspects of the physical product. The researcher should also be informed about the marketing program, including pricing, distribution, and promotional activities. Some information summarizing key consumer behavior associated with the product will undoubtedly be provided, and the manager will want to describe major competitive players, current trends in the market, and any factors in the environment that are impacting the market. If appropriate, the manager may make a copy of the product's marketing plan along with quarterly or monthly financial documents that track the product's performance. It is also possible that the manager will identify some key news or trade articles that have appeared recently summarizing the industry or otherwise detailing what is going on in the target market. As a result of this initial meeting, the researcher may come away from this meeting with a considerable amount of "homework."

Understand the Decision Maker's Circumstances, Objectives, and Resources

Assessing the background will require the researcher to do much "homework."

Managers are employed for the purpose of achieving company or organizational objectives, and they are provided various resources to accomplish these objectives. Moreover, they operate under various pressures and expectations dictated by their superiors or, perhaps, corporate culture. So it is vital that the researcher gain a feel for the manager's operating **circumstances,** for they may well dictate the urgency or timing of the research.

It will certainly help to know the reasons the manager has requested research help. This means that the researcher should know the manager's **objectives,** which are tangible statements of a company's expectations. Gaining a feel for the manager's specific objectives will help the researcher understand the gravity of the problem. By comparing recent sales, market share, or profitability level, for instance, with objectives, the researcher can compare how far the brand has strayed from acceptable performance. A pattern may be discerned; that is, was the deviation a slow trend over time, or was it a sudden plunge into an unacceptable condition?

Managers work toward specific objectives utilizing a set of resources allocated to them.

To achieve objectives, the manager uses a number of resources, including assets, capital, personnel, company time, and so on. Typically, a manager's resources are apparent by inspecting the budget. Some companies do not have detailed budgets, so the researcher may be forced to question the manager about how many salespersons are assigned to the brand, what their sales records look like, how much was spent on advertising and to which media it was allocated, what product improvements have been implemented or committed to, how much division time is spent on this brand, and who has been performing what tasks. Understanding the level of resources and how they have been utilized may shed light on the real problem.

Clarify the Symptoms of the Problem

During the problem definition phase, the manager and researcher must distinguish between **symptoms,** which are changes in the level of some key monitor that measures the achievement of an objective, and their causes. A symptom may also be a perceived change in the behavior of some market factor that suggests adverse consequences or, perhaps, implies an emerging opportunity.

Symptoms are changes in the level of some key monitor that measures the achievement of an objective.

Marketing managers should continually monitor their situations for changes in market behavior. A sampling of commonly used monitors is provided in Table 4.2. Often, these monitors are formal, which means that they are included in the business plan or they are part of the company's monitoring systems. Sometimes, they are informal and much more subjective. With informal monitors, the problem definition phase is necessarily more protracted because the researcher must construct the activity monitors and track them back in time to gain a feel for when the symptoms moved away from the company's acceptable levels and how much they have wandered into dangerous territory.

Even if formal monitors are in place, they may not present a sufficiently detailed or complete picture of what has happened. This is sometimes referred to as the **"iceberg" phenomenon,** a situation in which you must look beneath the surface to see the complete picture. The researcher may request a breakdown by sales territory, for example, to see if market share has fallen in all areas. Or he or she may want to look at sales for the industry as a whole to see if the phenomenon is industry wide. An astute researcher will ask questions that sometimes tax the manager's patience, but they are necessary to gain an understanding of all of the facets of the problem.

Pinpoint Suspected Causes of the Problem

Problems do not arise out of the blue—there always is an underlying **cause.** For example, sales do not drop without buyers doing something different

For every problem, an underlying cause can be found.

TABLE 4.2

Formal Monitors That Are Helpful in Alerting Managers to Possible Problems

TYPE OF MONITOR	DESCRIPTION
Sales volume	The total units or dollar value of units sold in a given time period
Market share	The percent of total industry sales accounted for by the company's brand
Profit	The total profit generated by a brand
Dealer orders	The amount of goods ordered by the company's dealers
Complaints	The level of consumer complaints registered
Competitors	Actions of the competition such as price reduction, introduction of new products, style changes, expansion into new territories, etc.

from what they have been doing in the past, customer complaints do not increase unless some dissatisfaction has occurred, and dealers do not report returns unless there is a flaw in the product. In other words, changes in market behavior do not occur randomly.

Often, a manager suspects or even has strong opinions concerning the cause of a bothersome symptom. In fact, he or she may even begin the conversation by telling the researcher what to research. However, it is important that the researcher list all possible causes in as objective a manner as possible, because if a possible cause is overlooked, and that cause turns out to be the *real* cause, all research will have been wasted.

A probable cause differs from a possible cause of a problem.

To illustrate the importance of pursuing all *possible causes of a problem,* we present an example involving Delta Business College, a small, private two-year college that specializes in business education curricula. Delta Business College suddenly experienced a decline in its enrollment. The researcher and the director of the college's enrollment office met and began discussing this symptom, asking themselves why enrollment was declining. Over the course of their discussion, they identified four general areas of possible causes: (1) competitors' actions, which had drawn prospective students away; (2) changes in the consumers (student target population); (3) something about the business college itself; and (4) general environmental factors. The results of their brainstorming session are presented in Table 4.3. Given this long list, it was necessary to narrow down the possible causes to a small set of probable causes.

Probable causes are those possible causes that are highly likely to be culprits.

An informal situation analysis was used to determine which of the several factors were likely culprits. Common sense suggests that if a possible cause had not changed over the course of the symptom's change, it is *unlikely* that it was a *probable cause of the problem.* For instance, Delta Business College had not increased its tuition nor had it made any changes in its scheduling of courses, so these two possible causes were crossed off the list. On the other hand, if a possible cause had changed prior to or at about the time of the symptom's appearance, it should remain on the "likely culprit" or probable cause list. That is, any factor that changed prior to or concurrent with the symptoms was a probable cause of the problem. It turned out that, during the past year, Delta had changed advertising agencies. The new agency had changed the advertising theme and the advertising time in an effort to increase advertising exposure by buying less expensive television spots. As a result, the changes in advertising became prime suspects as to the causes because no other probable causes could be identified.

Specify Actions That May Alleviate the Problem

Solutions include any marketing action that may resolve the problem.

As you learned earlier, managers have at their disposal certain resources, and these resources constitute the solutions they may attempt to employ to resolve the decision problem at hand. Essentially, possible **solutions** include any marketing action that the marketing manager thinks may resolve the problem, such as price changes, product modification or improvement, promotion of any kind, or even adjustments in channels of distribution. It is during this phase that the researcher's marketing education and knowledge fully come into play; often, both the manager and the researcher brainstorm possible solutions. Sometimes, this phase is moderated by the marketing researcher. At other times, the manager may independently generate several tactics that might resolve the problem once the probable causes are identified.

TABLE 4.3

Possible Causes for Delta's Enrollment Decline

1. COMPETITOR'S ACTIONS	
a. Reduced tuition	e. Better advertising
b. New, more competitors	f. Financial aid
c. New programs of study	g. Job contacts
d. New facilities, equipment	
2. CONSUMERS (CURRENT AND PROSPECTIVE STUDENTS)	
a. Loss of base numbers	e. Going to four-year schools
b. Change in financial circumstances	f. Cannot afford tuition, fees
c. High employment opportunities elsewhere	g. Negative word-of-mouth from graduates
d. Loss of faith in education	
3. THE BUSINESS COLLEGE ITSELF	
a. Increased tuition	f. New instructors
b. Changes in schedules	g. New administration
c. Curtailment of services	h. Changed location
d. Reduced financial aid	
e. Advertising cutback, change	
4. THE ENVIRONMENT	
a. Less federal financial aid	e. Cost of commuting increased
b. Interest rates on loans too high	f. Other educational alternatives
c. Job market oversupply	
d. Employers' loss of faith in the school	

Speculate on Anticipated Consequences of the Actions

Research on anticipated **consequences** of each action under consideration will help determine whether the solution is correct or not. For example, a solution might resolve the problem; on the other hand, it might intensify the problem if the solution is not the correct action. To avoid resolving the problem incorrectly, the manager asks "what if" questions regarding possible consequences of each marketing action being considered. These questions include:

To help resolve problems, managers ask "what if" questions.

- What will be the impact not only on the problem at hand, but throughout the marketing program, if a specific marketing action is implemented?
- What additional problems will be created if a proposed solution to the current problem is implemented?

Typically, the range of consequences of possible marketing actions is readily apparent. For example, if your advertising medium is changed from *People* magazine to *USA Today,* customers will either see less, see more, or see the same amount of advertising. If a nonsudsing chemical is added to your swimming pool treatment, customers will either like it more, less, or have no change in their opinions about it. Most marketing research investigates consumer consequences of marketing solutions, but it is also possible to research dealers' reactions or even suppliers' reactions, depending on the nature of the problem.

Identify the Manager's Assumptions about the Consequences

As they define the problem, the manager and the researcher make certain **assumptions,** which are assertions that certain conditions exist or that certain reactions will take place if the considered actions are implemented. For example, the manager may say, "I am positive that our lost customers will come back if we drop the price to $500," or "Our sales should go up if we gain more awareness by using advertising inserts in the Sunday paper." However, if a researcher questions a manager about his or her beliefs regarding the consequences of certain proposed actions, it may turn out that the manager is not really as certain as he or she sounds. Conversely, the manager may be quite certain and cite several reasons why his or her assumption is valid. It is imperative, therefore, that the manager's assumptions be analyzed for accuracy.

Assumptions bear researcher attention because they are the glue that holds the decision problem together.

Assumptions bear researcher attention because they are the glue that holds the decision problem together. Given a symptom, the manager assumes that certain causes are at fault. She or he assumes that, by taking corrective actions, the problem will be resolved and that the symptoms will disappear. If the manager is completely certain of all of these things, there is no need for research. But typically uncertainty prevails, and critical assumptions about which the manager is uncertain will ultimately factor in heavily when the researcher addresses the marketing research problem. Research will help eliminate this uncertainty. At the same time, there may be disagreement on key assumptions within the manager's company, and research is needed to determine which competing assumption is true.

Assess the Adequacy of Information on Hand

Information gaps are areas where the manager's information state is one of uncertainty or doubt.

As the manager attempts to formulate a decision problem, available information varies in both quantity and quality. As just noted, the manager may have information that greatly reinforces his or her beliefs, or he or she may not have anything more than a "gut feeling." You should recall that it is the researcher's responsibility to provide information to the manager that will help resolve the marketing manager's problem. Obviously, if the manager knows something with a high degree of certainty, it is of little value for the researcher to conduct research to reiterate that knowledge. It is vital, therefore, that the researcher assess the existing **information state,** which is the quantity and quality of evidence a manager possesses for each of his or her assumptions. During this assessment, the researcher should ask questions about the current information state and determine what the desired information state is. Conceptually, the researcher seeks to identify **information gaps,** which are discrepancies between the current information level and the desired level of information at which the manager feels comfortable resolving the problem at hand. Ultimately, information gaps are the basis for marketing research objectives.

Research objectives are specific bits of knowledge that need to be gathered and that serve to close information gaps. These objectives become the basis for the marketing researcher's work. In order to formulate the research objectives, the marketing researcher considers all the current information surrounding the marketing management problem. The following example illustrates how the marketing management problem is organized around the eight assessment areas we have previously discussed.

The researcher's objectives are based on identifying the manager's information gaps.

PUTTING IT ALL TOGETHER: WHAT THE RESEARCHER NEEDS TO DEFINE THE MARKETING MANAGEMENT PROBLEM

How does the researcher obtain all of this information from the marketing researcher? Actually, it can occur during a fairly systematic question-and-answer session that addresses each of the eight problem definition areas shown in Table 4.4. These areas include symptoms, background, decision maker's situation, information, suspected causes, possible solutions, anticipated consequences, and assumptions. To illustrate how this process works, we provide you with the following example.

There are eight marketing management problem definition areas.

The placement director of a university notices that *Fortune* 500 companies are not sending as many recruiters to the campus as they did in the past (*symptom*). Further, the decline in college recruiting is being experienced by all of the

TABLE 4.4

Questions the Researcher Should Ask the Marketing Manager to Define the Problem

PROBLEM DEFINITION AREAS	SAMPLE QUESTION(S)
Symptoms	What has changed that is causing you concern?
Background	What is the recent history of the brand, service, company, or market involved?
Decision maker's situation	How are these changes impacting your objectives? What resources do you have at your disposal? What is the time frame for required action?
Information	What do you know about the circumstances of these changes?
Suspected causes	Why do you think these changes have come about?
Possible solutions	What is in your power to do about these changes?
Anticipated consequences	If you do the things in your power, what are the most likely results?
Assumptions	Why do you anticipate these responses to your actions to resolve the problem?

Here is an example of a marketing management problem definition.

college placement offices as far as the director knows (*background*). The director is frustrated because there are more and more graduates who cannot find jobs through the placement office, and that is her assigned mission. Her current budget is limited, and she can use only her present staff of two secretaries and four student workers to alleviate the problem over the next year (*decision maker's circumstances, objectives, and resources*). The director meets with a marketing professor who requires his students to do team projects. During the meeting, it becomes apparent that the trend can be traced back to the late 1980s when major companies downsized by eliminating many middle-management positions (*background*). Also, the director is convinced that her university is still graduating very good job prospects and the reason for the hiring decline is companies seeking to reduce their administrative costs (*suspected causes*).

One of the student team members asks the director what she might be able to do to continue finding jobs for graduating seniors, and she responds that she has thought of two strategies. First, she thinks that small businesses in a 100-mile radius of the university might be interested in these potential employees. Second, she hopes that parents of university students might serve as a referral network for job openings in their companies or in the companies of friends and business associates (*actions that may alleviate the problem*). Perhaps the placement office could appeal to students' parents and they would be willing to supply job opening information whenever one became known to them. Or, small businesses might be more inclined to use the university placement office if they were made aware that the *Fortune* 500 companies were not competing with them for the best graduates (*anticipated consequences*). In either case, parents and/or businesses might be willing to respond to quarterly inquiry letters (*assumptions*). No research has been undertaken on either alternative, but there have been some success stories in the *Placement Center Quarterly* about college placement centers that have attracted medium and small businesses to their campuses (*adequacy*).

The problem facing the university placement director can be summarized in the following problem statement: To what extent are small business owners and parents of currently enrolled students likely to make use of the university placement office quarterly inquiry letters when they are informed of the hiring situation on that campus (*marketing management problem statement*).

View: "SPSS Quick Tour Part I"

FORMULATE THE MARKETING RESEARCH PROBLEM

To formulate the research problem, the researcher specifies constructs and operational definitions, identifies relationships, and decides on a model.

You should notice that we have not specified the research objectives in our placement office example. This omission is because in order to state research objectives, the marketing researcher must formulate the marketing research problem. That is, the marketing researcher's first task is to talk to the marketing manager and to develop as complete a picture of the marketing management problem as possible. The researcher develops a tentative set of information needs of the manager to solve the problem. Once this work is accomplished, the researcher formulates the marketing research problem. In doing this, the researcher goes through three steps: (1) specify constructs and operational definitions, (2) identify relationships, and (3) decide on a model. A discussion of each step follows.

Specify Constructs and Operational Definitions

A marketing researcher generally thinks in terms of constructs when he or she listens to the marketing manager articulate the problem. A **construct** is a marketing term or concept that is somehow involved in the marketing management problem that will be researched. Examples of constructs that are often investigated in marketing research studies are listed in Table 4.5. You should recognize some of them from your previous marketing courses. This is not a complete list; other constructs include life-style or psychographics, which are descriptions of how consumers think and behave. A good example of the use of constructs to understand consumer market segments in a foreign country is the system developed by SRI International for Japan. We describe the Japan VALS system in Marketing Research Insight 4.1 (pages 96–97).

The way a marketing researcher thinks of marketing constructs is different from the way the manager thinks of them.

Although managers and researchers share the language of constructs, the researcher translates the construct into an **operational definition,** which describes how a marketing researcher measures the construct. That is, an operational definition implies a specific question format that will be used in a survey to gather information about the construct at hand. You can see by examining the operational definitions in Table 4.5 how the researcher measures each construct. In actuality, there are several alternative operational definitions

TABLE 4.5

A Representative List of Constructs Often Investigated by Marketing Researchers

CONSTRUCT	OPERATIONAL DEFINITION
Brand awareness	Percent of respondents having heard of brand
Recall, recognition of advertising	The number who remember seeing a specific ad
Knowledge of product, features	What they can tell about the product
Brand familiarity	Those who have seen the brand or tried it
Comprehension of product benefits	What respondents think the product does for them
Attitudes, feelings toward brand	The number who feel positive, negative, or neutral
Intentions to purchase	The number that are planning to buy it
Past purchase or use	The percent that bought it
Satisfaction	How they evaluate its performance
Importance of some factor	What factors determined their purchase choice
Demographics	How old, what gender, and so on
Disposal of product and package	What they did with the box, wrapping, or product
Brand loyalty	How many times they bought the brand in the last six months

MARKETING RESEARCH INSIGHT 4.1

How VALS Helps Marketers Segment the Japanese Market

The development of VALS, a value system that describes the central orientations of consumers, by SRI International, has led to the identification of major consumer segments in industrialized countries. Japan, although very different from Western countries, has been analyzed with Japan VALS. SRI claims that Japan VALS is the most reliable and powerful market analysis available for Japan.

Japan VALS operates on the basis of two constructs: One construct is life orientation, *defined as those interests that best describe how a consumer lives his or her life. There are four life orientations in the Japan VALS system: Traditional Ways, Occupations, Innovation, and Self-Expression. Each orientation is a central life theme that characterizes most of a person's activities, interests, and personal goals. The other construct involves* change attitudes, *or how the person views and handles social changes. Change attitudes range from* change leading, *where the person embraces social changes, to* change resisting, *where the person rejects changes.*

The application of Japan VALS has led to the identification of the following Japanese consumer segments. Some of their consumption characteristics are described as well.

NAME	SIZE	VALS ORIENTATION AND CONSUMER BEHAVIOR
Integrators	4% of population	Most innovative. Active, inquisitive, trend-leading, informed, and affluent. Travel frequently and use a wide range of media—print and broadcast, niche and foreign.
Self-Innovators and Self-Adapters	7% and 11% of population	High on self-expression. Desire personal experience, fashionable display, social activities, daring ideas, and exciting, graphic entertainment.
Ryoshiki Innovators and Ryoshiki Adapters	6% and 10% of population	Highest on occupations. Education, career achievement, and professional knowledge are their personal focus, but home, family, and social status are their guiding concerns.
Tradition Innovators and Tradition Adapters	6% and 10% of population	Highest on traditional ways. Adhere to traditional religions and customs, prefer long-familiar home furnishings and dress, and hold conservative social opinions.
High Pragmatics and Low Pragmatics	14% and 17% of population	Score low on all life orientations. Not very active and not well informed; they have few interests, and seem flexible or even uncommitted in their life-style choices.
Sustainers	15% of population	Lowest on innovation and self-expression. Lacking money, youth, and high education, they dislike innovation and are typically oriented to sustaining the past.

SRI International claims that its Japan VALS system is useful to companies in several ways including: (1) monitoring and forecasting life-style trends, (2) identifying new product and service opportunities, (3) market segmentation of the Japanese consumer market, (4) brand positioning, (5) developing effective merchandising and promotional strategies, and (6) creating advertising geared to the interests and life-styles of target audiences.

Source: *http://future.sri.com/VALS/jvals.html (11/13/96).*

---

possible for any construct, and there are important considerations that must be determined before the operational definition is finalized. It is premature to delve into these factors at this time; we develop them in detail in chapter 10. Whereas the marketing manager thinks of constructs as ways to better understand or better respond to this market, the marketing researcher usually envisions them as questions or sets of questions on a questionnaire.

Identify Relationships

Marketing researchers must consider relationships that connect the various constructs. A **relationship** is a meaningful link believed to exist between two constructs. For instance, one such relationship might be that customers will buy more of a product when the price is lowered, and that they will buy less of it when the price is increased. Another relationship might be that a particular advertising campaign will generate more positive attitudes toward your brand. You should note that these relationships typically link the marketing manager's decision factors with their anticipated outcomes.

A relationship is a meaningful link believed to exist between two constructs.

There are two basic sources for the relationships the marketing researcher identifies. The first source is beliefs and assumptions provided by the marketing manager. Granted, there may be some uncertainty involved, but usually the marketing manager is familiar with the basic driving forces in his or her marketing management problem. The second source is the researcher's general marketing knowledge. Where great uncertainty exists or where the marketing manager has not indicated a belief or suspicion, the researcher is likely to fall back on universally accepted relationships.

Decide on a Model

Once you take a set of constructs and order their relationships with some understandable logic, you have created a **model.** Occasionally, the marketing manager can provide a model that ties together the various constraints and their relationships. Often, managers do not have these models in mind so it is up to the researcher to create one. Fortunately, a number of models exist that can serve as frameworks for marketing research objectives. One such model, called the "hierarchy of effects," is provided in Table 4.6 on page 98. The hierarchy of effects traces the steps a consumer goes through in learning about, forming an opinion regarding, trying, and then adopting a brand. The steps constitute constructs, and the progression from unawareness to brand loyalty is the model that ties the constructs together.

A model connects constructs in ordered relationships.

The amount of effort that the researcher expends in gaining a feel for the marketing management problem pays off in model specification. By studying

TABLE 4.6

How the "Hierarchy of Effects" Model Can Frame Research

HIERARCHY STAGE	DESCRIPTION	RESEARCH QUESTION
Unawareness	Not aware of your brand	What percent of the market is unaware of your brand?
Awareness	Aware of your brand	What percent of the market has heard of your brand?
Knowledge	Know something about your brand	What percent of the market can tell your brand's price, features, style, etc.?
Liking	Have a positive feeling about your brand	What percents of the market have positive, negative, or neutral attitudes toward your brand?
Intention	Intends to buy your brand with next purchase	What percent of the market intends to buy your brand the next time they purchase the product?
Purchase	Has purchased your brand in the past	What percent of the market purchased (tried) your brand in the past?
Repurchase/Loyalty	Purchases your brand regularly	What percent of the market has purchased your brand more than other brands in the last (e.g.) five purchases?

the manager's circumstances and resources, pondering the competitive environment, factoring in consumer behavior considerations, and otherwise reflecting on everything he or she has learned during their conversation, the marketing researcher has the opportunity to develop a custom model of possible problem causes, solutions, and consequences. Sometimes these models are elaborate, but often they are simple. For instance, Grolier may want a demographic profile of the buyers of its CD-ROM Multimedia Encyclopedia, and the model may be simply that buyers should have IBM-compatible computers with Pentium processors equipped with a CD-ROM drive, whereas nonbuyers do not.

Specify Marketing Research Objectives

Each research objective must be precise, detailed, clear, and operational.

As we indicated earlier, research objectives address information gaps that must be closed in order for the manager to go about resolving the current problem. Generally, the researcher prepares an itemized listing of the information objections agreed upon by the manager as essential for this purpose. In creating this list, the researcher must keep in mind four important qualities. Each research objective must be precise, detailed, clear, and operational.

We illustrate these qualities using the following example of research objectives. A researcher has formulated the marketing research problem with a model that specifies that AT&T buyers will differ along demographic factors from AT&T nonbuyers. The research objective: "Compare the demographic profiles of AT&T buyers to nonbuyers using age, sex, education, and annual family income." To be *precise* means that the terminology is understandable to the marketing manager and that it accurately captures the essence of each construct to be researched. In the objective just stated, the use of the term "demographic" indicates what type of profile will be investigated. *Detail* is provided by including the four demographic measures of age, sex, education, and annual family income. The objective is *clear* in that there is no doubt as to what will be researched and how the information will be presented to the manager. That is, the age, sex, education level, and income of buyers will be determined and compared to those of nonbuyers. Finally, the objective is *operational.* In other words, it implies specific measurement scales and statistical analyses. These do not need to be in the list of research objectives; however, the manager and researcher will have discussed these in general, and the researcher should have specific operational plans in mind, as described earlier when the researcher's view of constructs was discussed. The operational factor is especially useful to the staff members who will probably perform much of the mechanical aspects such as questionnaire design or data analysis.

AN EXAMPLE OF THE FORMULATION OF A MARKETING RESEARCH PROBLEM

Earlier, we provided an example of the college placement director's marketing management problem where companies were cutting back on their recruiting visits to campuses. Now, we can provide the marketing research problem formulation component of that example. For simplicity, we discuss only the small business strategy.

Here is an example of a marketing research problem definition.

The *marketing research problem* is to provide accurate and useful information on the likelihood of small business owners to use the university placement office quarterly inquiry letters both now and when they are informed of the college recruiting slowdown by major companies. The key *constructs* in this problem are: (1) small businesses, operationally defined as owners of business employing 10 or fewer full-time people and located within 100 miles of campus; (2) awareness, defined as knowing that the university placement office exists; and (3) intentions, defined as the degree of willingness of small business owners to provide job openings to the university placement office by responding to quarterly inquiry letters. A simple *relationship* is implicit in the marketing management definition we formulated earlier: small business owners who know that *Fortune* 500 companies are not competing with them for the best graduates will be more willing to use the placement office. The hierarchy of effects *model* can be applied as small business owners who are unaware of the placement office are unlikely to use it, whereas those with more knowledge of the university placement office and its services are more likely to use it.

Here is an example of research objectives.

Finally, the *research objectives* can be stated: (1) to what extent are small business owners aware of the existence of the university placement office? (2) to what extent are they currently intending to use the university placement center to identify qualified new hires? (3) to what extent do they intend to use the placement office when they are informed that *Fortune* 500 companies will not be competing with them for the best graduates? and (4) to what extent do they intend to respond to the quarterly inquiry letters that the university placement office is considering as its primary solicitation system?

To make sure that you are well versed on research objectives, we have included Marketing Research Insight 4.2 (page 100), which gives a problem statement and list of research objectives for Uniden Radar Detectors when it encountered a sales slump.

MARKETING RESEARCH INSIGHT 4.2

Examples of a Problem Statement and Research Objectives

MARKETING MANAGEMENT PROBLEM

Uniden America Corporation of Fort Worth, Texas, which markets a line of radar detectors, experienced great sales success in the 1980s and early 1990s. However, sales in the past three years have fallen by 20 percent, and the trend suggests another 10 percent decline over the next year. Management believes the decline is attributable to either: (1) competitors' actions, or (2) increased sophistication of police radar devices and tactics leading to a belief in prospective radar detector buyers that detectors will not provide sufficient warning.

MARKETING RESEARCH PROBLEM

Research is necessary to identify what, if any, competitor actions have taken place over the past three years that may have had an adverse effect on Uniden radar detector sales. In addition, research is needed to determine if prospective radar detector buyers are hesitating due to concerns that police radar can be sufficiently detected in general or specifically by Uniden products.

SPECIFIC RESEARCH OBJECTIVES

1. *Track market shares of major radar detector marketers over the past three years.*
2. *Determine competitor changes over the past three years in product design, prices, promotional strategy, and distribution.*
3. *Assess prospective buyers' opinions of:*
   - **a.** *Police radar equipment capabilities and tactics;*
   - **b.** *Ability of radar detectors, in general, to provide early warning of active radar; and*
   - **c.** *Ability of Uniden detectors, specifically, to provide early warning of active radar.*

THE FORMAL RESEARCH PROPOSAL

Once the model is outlined, the marketing researcher must summarize what he or she has discovered and then communicate this information to the marketing manager for agreement on the research to be performed. This is done in the formal research proposal. There are three important functions of the research proposal.[7] (1) It defines the marketing management problem, (2) it specifies the research objectives, and (3) it details the research method proposed by the researcher to accomplish the research objectives.[8]

Define the Marketing Management Problem

The first step in a research proposal is to define the marketing management problem.

The first step in a research proposal is to define the marketing management problem. This is normally accomplished with a single statement, rarely more than a few sentences long, called the **problem statement.** The problem statement typically identifies four factors: (1) the company, division, or principals involved; (2) the symptoms; and (3) the possible causes of these symptoms; and (4) the anticipated uses of the research information.

Identifying the company, division, and principals is important for several reasons. First, if the researcher is external to the company requesting the work, it is common courtesy to reference the company. Second, if the proposal will be reviewed internally, identification of the division involved helps the reviewers understand the need for the research because they should be intimately knowledgeable about the division's circumstances. Finally, it is essential to note which manager (or set of managers) has approached the researcher because it is the manager's perceptions that have served to formulate the marketing management problem. Also, managers sometimes change positions in a company, and noting who initiated the work is helpful for the replacement.

The symptoms and causes are noted to verify that the researcher "sees" the decision problem with the manager's eyes. Again, if internal review occurs, there may be some disagreement about these aspects of the problem, and explicitly stating them in an early stage serves to bring these differences of opinion out into a forum for discussion. Finally, noting in general how the information will be used by the decision maker helps clarify the range of alternatives being considered to remedy the situation.

Specify the Research Objectives

After describing the marketing management problem, the marketing researcher must identify the specific research objectives. You should recall that research objectives address information gaps that must be closed in order for the manager to go about resolving the marketing management problem. Normally, these are listed or itemized in the proposal. Again, the best research objectives are precise, detailed, clear, and operational, as was illustrated in the AT&T example earlier.

The second step in a research proposal is to identify specific research objectives.

Detail the Proposed Research Method

Finally, the research proposal will detail the proposed research method. That is, it will describe the data collection method, questionnaire design, sampling plan, and all other aspects of the proposed marketing research in as much detail as the researcher thinks is necessary for the manager to grasp the plan. It will also include a tentative timetable and specify the cost of the research undertaking. Proposals vary greatly in format and detail, but most share the basic components we have described: problem statement; research objectives; and proposed research method, including timetable and cost.

A research proposal describes the proposed research methods in general terms.

We have included an abbreviated proposal in appendix 4 of this chapter. As you read it, note the problem definition, and the specification of research objectives, and then try to pick out the constructs that the researchers have identified in this proposed research project. Note also how the proposal describes the more technical aspects of the proposal such as "focus groups" so they are understandable to the managers.

SELECT A MARKETING RESEARCH COMPANY

By now it should be evident that any marketing manager must be willing to work closely with his or her marketing research company in order to obtain the best possible assistance. To do so, a manager should have a list of criteria or qualifying questions in order to make judgments on which company to use (see Marketing Research Insight 4.3). However, there is a preliminary consideration to be addressed. It is best to approach this problem just as one would consider buying the services of any supplier company. That is, first get to know the company by reviewing some of its previous work, perhaps checking with prior clients as to their experiences, and discussing the company's expertise and resources with one of its representatives.

The relationship between a marketing research provider and the manager client is critical. In fact, some research companies have formal satisfaction measurement systems to evaluate their client relationships.[9]

An invitation to bid (ITB) is a formal request for research proposals.

Sometimes, the marketing manager can formalize his or her need for marketing research into an **invitation to bid** (ITB), a formal research request that outlines the scope and important details of the work to be performed by the marketing research company. It may even contain important restrictions, or at least spell out details on how the work will progress, what the reporting format will be, and the obligations of the research company during and after the work. Obviously, the preparation of an ITB necessitates that the manager define the problem comprehensively before the researcher is called in. Once the problem is defined, it is communicated to the researcher in the ITB.

If the marketing researcher represents an independent, custom marketing research company, or even if he or she is a company member, it is entirely possible that he or she has no knowledge of the product, market, competition, and other salient factors surrounding the problem. In either case, the marketing researcher must become familiar with the marketing manager's world by taking the time to develop a thorough orientation to the manager's situation and/or specific problem. This is accomplished by defining both the marketing man-

MARKETING RESEARCH INSIGHT 4.3

How Do Companies Decide Who Will Do Their Research?

Just how do firms decide which marketing research company will do the research for a project at hand? This general question was addressed recently in a study of 173 buyers of marketing research conducted by Simon Godfrey Associates located in the United Kingdom. It was found that these factors weigh heavily:

1. *Pleasant or nice people/have a good relationship*
2. *Understands my business/wants to know background*
3. *Thinks about project/suggest ideas*
4. *Meets deadlines/prompt/speedy*
5. *Experienced and knowledgeable/well-trained staff*
6. *Statistical ability*
7. *Good clear presentation*

The research concludes that it is important for a marketing research firm to have a marketing orientation to impress the client that it understands its unique problems, and that it will deliver impartial and creative advice.

Source: *Ken Gofton, "Updated data,"* Marketing *(November 23, 1995), III(2).*

agement and research problems. The formal research proposal goes a long way in communicating to the marketing manager just how well a prospective marketing research provider understands the manager's problem and how competently the research company will execute the procedures it has proposed.

SUMMARY

This chapter began by describing important differences between marketing managers and researchers. Because they have different orientations and work in different worlds, it is essential that an open dialogue be established. Only in this way can the manager's problem be translated into a meaningful marketing research endeavor. The marketing management problem is often complex. It is important that the researcher gain background on the company, product, and market involved. The manager's circumstances, objectives, and resources must be identified as well as any other salient factors in the environment. Symptoms such as slipping market share compel the manager to action, but the researcher and manager must enumerate the possible causes and reasonable courses of action to resolve the problem. During the dialogue, the researcher will become aware of any assumptions or beliefs about the problem or possible solutions held by the manager, and will determine where information gaps exist and the needs that must be addressed with a research effort.

The marketing researcher thinks in terms of constructs or basic marketing concepts such as brand loyalty or demographic descriptors of buyers. These constructs are arranged in logical relationships and sometimes there are models of how they fit together. Ultimately, the marketing researcher must create a research proposal that states the problem, specifies the research objectives, and suggests a research plan that indicates how the marketing researcher will address the marketing management problem at hand.

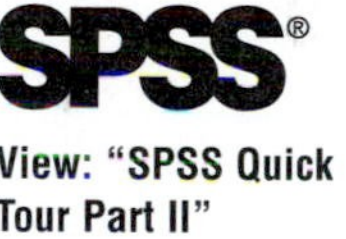

View: "SPSS Quick Tour Part II"

KEY TERMS

Marketing management problem (p. 86)
Marketing research problem (p. 86)
Opportunity identification (p. 87)
Background (p. 88)
Circumstances (p. 88)
Objectives (p. 88)
Symptoms (p. 89)
Iceberg phenomenon (p. 89)
Cause (p. 89)
Solutions (p. 90)
Consequences (p. 91)
Assumptions (p. 92)
Information state (p. 92)
Information gaps (p. 92)
Research objectives (p. 93)
Construct (p. 95)
Operational definition (p. 95)
Relationship (p. 97)
Model (p. 97)
Problem statement (p. 100)
Invitation to bid (p. 102)

REVIEW QUESTIONS/APPLICATIONS

1. List five basic differences between marketing managers and marketing researchers.
2. When a marketing manager and a researcher meet, what should the marketing manager be prepared to do in order to properly brief the researcher on his or her

problem? What should the researcher be prepared to do in order to ensure that the manager understands the role and limitations of research?

3. List and describe the eight elements in a marketing management problem.
4. How does a symptom differ from a cause? How does a cause differ from a potential solution?
5. How do assumptions lead to research objectives?
6. What are constructs, who uses them, and how are they envisioned by the marketing researcher?
7. List the four criteria of a research information objective.
8. How do the marketing management problem and the marketing research problem differ?
9. Sony is contemplating expanding its line of three-inch and six-inch portable televisions. It thinks there are three situations in which this line would be purchased: (1) as a gift, (2) as a set to be used by children in their own rooms, and (3) for use at sporting events. How might the information objective be stated if Sony is primarily interested in whether prospective buyers want color, black and white, or have no preference in each of the three situations?
10. Take the construct of channel (that is, "brand") loyalty in the case of college students viewing MTV. Write out at least three different definitions that indicate how a researcher might form a question in a survey to assess the degree of MTV loyalty. One example is "Channel loyalty is determined by a stated preference to view a given channel for a certain type of entertainment."
11. You are the staff trainer at General Mills, which markets food products such as Betty Crocker cake mix. A new researcher with a degree in applied statistics, but no marketing whatsoever, has just been hired. List and describe five different marketing management concepts that he should understand before interacting with any brand manager at General Mills to discuss undertaking research.
12. The local Lexus dealer thinks that the four-door sedan with a list price in excess of $40,000 should appeal to Cadillac Seville owners who are thinking about buying a new automobile. He is considering a direct mail campaign with personalized packages to be sent to owners whose Cadillac Sevilles are over two years old. Each package would contain a professional video of all the Lexus sedan's features and end with an invitation to visit the Lexus dealership. This tactic has never been tried in this market. State the marketing management problem and indicate what research objectives would help the Lexus dealer understand the possible reactions of Cadillac Seville owners to this campaign.

CASE 4.1

Florida Life Styles Magazine

Florida Life Styles Magazine is positioned as an upscale, life-style magazine targeting affluent residents of Florida living mainly in large metropolitan areas such as Miami, Tampa, and Orlando. It positions itself with: (1) high-quality color photography; (2) a focus on people, places, and current fads; (3) an emphasis on youthful, active, and energetic life-styles; (4) affluent appeals; (5) Florida themes; and (6) highly complementary advertising. Current subscription ranges between 20,000 and 25,000, and some copies are sold in newsstands. Multiple and "pass-along" readership is believed to be high, particularly with professionals, such as doctors, who make the magazine available in waiting rooms.

Recently, magazine advertising salespeople have voiced frustration in targeting and perfecting sales representations to prospective advertising clients. They are uncertain of precisely which companies to approach, and when they do make presentations, they have difficulty answering prospective advertisers' questions about *Florida Life Styles Magazine*'s readers. During the intial conversation, the market researcher learns that informaiton exists on demographic characteristics of subscribers, but little exists in company files on life-style or other relevant buying behavior aspects of subscribers.

1. Specify the marketing management problem and the marketing research problem.

CASE 4.2

Tandem Computers

The vast majority of ATM machines are connected in networks with Tandem computers at their hearts. IBM and NCR computers do not connect these ATM networks, because Tandem scooped the market in the 1980s by inventing a system that allowed for computer processors to link up and share memory so if one processor stops working or becomes overloaded, others step in to pick up the work, and the user never knows the difference. Tandem has been so successful that its sales and earnings grew 18-fold in the 1980s. But by the middle of the 1990s, Tandem's sales became flat even though they were around the $2 billion figure annually.

In the late 1980s, Tandem began looking at the huge mainframe market dominated by IBM, and it wanted to lever its strong ATM processor presence in bank market circles. It introduced its mainframe computer, the Cyclone, with its revolutionary multiprocessor, multimemory system that had many advantages over conventional mainframe computers. The banks did not respond, and because of the huge investment to develop and market the Cyclone, profits fell dramatically. Tandem management is pondering new directions. Included in their thinking are cable video systems and telecommunications systems, such as paging and cellular telephones. Internet banking systems are also under consideration.

1. Specify the marketing management problem and the marketing research problem.

Source: *Stephen Kindel, "The Machine Behind the Curtain,"* Financial World, *vol. 62, no. 15 (July 20, 1993), 30(3).*

APPENDIX 4

A Marketing Research Proposal for Surgi-Center of New Haven

The relevant sections of a marketing research proposal submitted to an ambulatory surgery center attempting to reposition itself in its market are included in this appendix. The actual names of the companies involved have been changed.

PROPOSAL TO DETERMINE THE APPROPRIATE MARKET POSITIONING STRATEGY FOR THE SURGI-CENTER OF NEW HAVEN

INTRODUCTION

This proposal responds to a request on the part of principals of the Surgi-Center of New Haven located at 2525 Bright Drive, New Haven, Connecticut, to provide assistance in the Surgi-Center's pending market positioning strategy decision. The proposal is submitted by Marketing Consultants, Inc.

BACKGROUND

The Surgi-Center of New Haven is currently experiencing success as a same-day surgery center, and it perceives that an opportunity exists in broadening its focus to include "healthy" patients in need of prescribed or elective surgical procedures that require stays of typically one to three nights and up to five nights. Such overnight stays are primarily necessary to allow observation of patients who are experiencing postoperative pain or who require special postoperation medication and/or treatment unavailable in at-home settings. Construction plans are drafted, and the expansion will take place under a timetable that will effect opening in the coming summer, barring any unforeseen delays.

QUESTIONS OF CONCERN

Discussion with Surgi-Center principals suggests that answers are desired to the following three questions:

1. What is the reaction of the market to the building/opening of another hospital in the New Haven area?
2. How is the Surgi-Center currently perceived?
3. What positioning strategy is appropriate given the Surgi-Center's expanded services?

These three questions are related in that reactions to the opening of another hospital, regardless of size, have implications for the Surgi-Center's ultimate positioning strategy. That is, if reactions are negative, it should position itself away from the image of a hospital; whereas, if they are positive, it may behoove the Surgi-Center to move toward the hospital image. Similarly, if the Surgi-Center has a strong, positive image as a same-day surgical center, it may wish to capitalize on this goodwill in its new position. If not, it must seek a competitively advantageous position.

NECESSARY TASKS IN SURGI-CENTER'S POSITIONING DECISION

The purpose of this proposal is to outline possible consulting work for the Surgi-Center of New Haven as it identifies a positioning strategy appropriate to its planned expansion into short-stay surgery. The tasks recommended to accomplish this endeavor are as noted next. Descriptions of these tasks follow.

1. *Identify relevant publics.* Discussions with Surgi-Center principals have identified four relevant publics: (a) current and past patients, (b) the general public, (c) business and industry, and (d) medical professionals.
2. *Determine attitudes harbored by each public toward another hospital in New Haven.* With each relevant public, it is necessary to understand predispositions, opinions, and feelings regarding the prospect of another hospital, albeit small, in the New Haven area.
3. *Identify competitors' images.* Positioning requires an understanding of the positioning strategies of competitors. It is essential to understand how the

market perceives the competition so that Surgi-Center can make an enlightened decision about its own positioning strategy.

4. *Determine Surgi-Center's image.* As a provider of same-day surgical procedures over a number of years, the Surgi-Center represents certain values to the market. These perceptions constitute the Surgi-Center's current image, be it orchestrated or incidental. In either case, knowledge of the Surgi-Center's current image will reveal strengths and weaknesses that should be taken into consideration in its repositioning deliberations.
5. *Identify alternative positioning strategy orientations.* Adroit position strategy selection necessitates evaluating alternatives, and these alternative strategic orientations should be distinguished, based on an understanding of market needs, competitors' images, and the sustainable long-term marketing capabilities of the company.
6. *Evaluate alternative positioning orientations and select position.* Evaluation of the positioning alternatives requires a combination of competitive analysis, target market, and relevant publics' reactions, and an understanding of the unique competencies of the organization. Simultaneous examination of all of these factors is essential in deciding the best positioning strategy.

Proposed Consultation Work

There are three different types of consulting work that can assist the Surgi-Center in resolving the three questions noted earlier. These are: (1) focus group research, (2) market surveys, and (3) positioning strategy identification, evaluation, and consultation.

1. *Focus group research.* Focus groups are small-group discussions conducted under the guidance of a trained moderator and typically tape-recorded for subsequent analysis. Typically, from eight to twelve participants representing a particular group or public are brought to a central facility for a one and one-half hour focused discussion. This qualitative research is invaluable in identifying major issues, gaining initial reactions to concepts, and essentially "hearing" the market. Although focus groups are sometimes used in isolation, their most common application is in gaining a basic understanding of the topic(s) under consideration and in serving as a basis for subsequent survey research. Marketing Consultants, Inc. has extensive experience in the operation, moderating, and interpretation of focus groups.
2. *Market surveys.* Market surveys are essential to gaining a quantitative understanding of the perceptions and reactions of the market(s) or public(s) of concern. Large samples are accessed with structured questionnaires, and results are tabulated. The analyses are interpreted for the client so as to clarify issues and concerns. Also, gaining responses from large groups provides for known estimates of the statistical accuracy of the results. Marketing Consultants, Inc. has executed local, regional, and national surveys over the past decade.
3. *Positioning strategy identification, evaluation, and consultation.* Although the Surgi-Center has notions about its repositioning as a result of its overnight stay expansion, it can benefit from the assistance of a consultant who understands and has had experience with positioning strategy creation and implementation. For instance, the Surgi-Center should be aware of the several generic approaches to positioning, and it should be schooled on the positions claimed by the competition. It can profit from the services of a consultant in the evaluation and selection phases as well. Marketing Consultants, Inc. has abundant experience in strategic marketing consultation.

[*The document continues on to specify time frames and costs.*]

CHAPTER 5

Research Design

LEARNING OBJECTIVES

- To understand what research design is and why it is significant
- To learn how exploratory research design helps the researcher gain a feel for the problem by providing background information, suggesting hypotheses, and prioritizing research objectives
- To know the fundamental questions addressed by descriptive research and the different types of descriptive research
- To explain what is meant by causal research and to describe four types of experimental research designs
- To know the different types of test marketing and how to select test market cities

Debbie Tucker works for MarkSearch Consulting Group, Inc.

PRACTITIONER VIEWPOINT

Research design is the foundation of effective marketing research. In fact, it may be considered analogous to an architect's blueprint, wherein the architectural design clearly describes the overall structure of the project, detailing the specifications and methods needed for completing the project. So it is with the research design, which provides a blueprint for obtaining the desired information using the most effective data collection and analytical techniques.

— Richard A. Spitzer
Executive Vice President
NFO Research, Inc.

MarkSearch Consulting Group, Inc.

1. Establish the need for marketing research
2. Define the problem
3. Establish research objectives
4. Determine research design
5. Identify information types and sources
6. Determine methods of accessing data
7. Design data collection forms
8. Determine sample plan and size
9. Collect data
10. Analyze data
11. Prepare and present the final research report

Debbie Tucker is an experienced project director for MarkSearch Consulting Group, Inc. She had made three client visits during the week and on Friday afternoon she sat down to review her notes.

> Wednesday/A.M. Marianne Baker—new vice president, Marketing, Security & Trust National Bank. Bank only five years old. President suggested to Baker to measure image of the bank in the community. President felt that image was important in the decision-making process that led to deposits and new accounts. No one in management had ever measured bank image. Baker wants to hire us to give her ideas about how to go about measuring bank image. Next meeting set for one week.
>
> Wednesday/1:30 P.M. Appointment with Jeffrey Dean, brand manager for Pooch Plus dog treats. Dog treats market very competitive with constant swings in market shares due to active promotional and pricing activities of competitors. Dean responsible for increasing Pooch Plus market share. Has several promotional campaigns produced by his staff and three ad agencies. Dean wants some ideas as to which types of past competitive promotional campaigns produced the greatest swings in market shares. This information will help him select the best promotional campaign. Wants our independent evaluation. Call him Tuesday A.M.
>
> Friday/8:30 A.M. Met with Laurie Fulkerson, director of Store Operations, Basha's Supermarkets—46-store chain. Fulkerson making decision on new in-store sound systems and question of in-store music has come up. Knows of some limited research on effects of music on customers. Copy of study—conducted in New England—shows type of music (easy-listening, soft-rock, country, and so on) played had affected the average number of sales, time shopped, and overall attitude of consumers. Fulkerson wants to know if we should do study on Basha's own customers. Wants ideas for study in one week.

Debbie Tucker packed her briefcase and started her commute to her home in the suburbs. By the time she arrived, she had determined the basic research design she would propose for each of her three clients. On Monday, she would begin preparing her presentations for the week.

Debbie Tucker's client visits illustrate that research problems take many different forms. No one research approach will satisfy all types of research problems. However, we can design a research plan for each type of research problem that contains the research approaches most suitable to that problem. In this chapter, we introduce you to the concept of research design. An overview is provided of the various types of research design: exploratory, descriptive, and causal. The chapter concludes with a discussion of test marketing. After you have read this chapter, you should be able to correctly identify each of the research designs Debbie Tucker came up with on her commute home and will present to each prospective client next week.

RESEARCH DESIGN

Research design is a set of decisions that make up the master plan specifying the methods and procedures for collecting and analyzing the needed information.

Marketing research methods vary from focus groups to simulated test markets to large, nationally representative sample surveys. Some research problems require only library research, whereas others may require thousands of personal interviews. Each method has certain advantages and disadvantages, and one method may be more appropriate for a given research problem than another. How do marketing researchers decide which method is the most appropriate? After thoroughly considering the research problem, researchers select a **research design,** which is a set of advance decisions that make up the master plan specifying the methods and procedures for collecting and analyzing the needed information.

The Significance of Research Design

Every research problem is unique. In fact, one could argue that, given each problem's unique customer set, area of geographical application, and other situational variables, there are so few similarities among research projects that each study should be completely designed as a new and independent project. In a sense this is true; almost every research problem is unique in some way or another, and care must be taken to select the most appropriate set of approaches for the unique problem at hand. However, there are reasons to justify the significance placed upon research design.

First, although every research problem may seem totally unique, there are usually enough similarities among research problems to allow us to make some decisions, in advance, as to the best plan to use to resolve the problem. Second, there are some basic marketing research designs that can be successfully matched to given research problems. In this way, they serve the researcher much like the blueprint serves the builder.

THREE TYPES OF RESEARCH DESIGNS

There are three basic research objectives that underlie the choice of a research design.

Research designs are classified into three traditional categories: exploratory, descriptive, and causal. The choice of the most appropriate design depends largely upon the objectives of the research. It has been said that research has three objectives: to *develop hypotheses,* to *measure the state* of a variable of interest (that is, level of brand loyalty), or to *test hypotheses* that specify the relationships between two or more variables (that is, level of advertising and brand loyalty). We shall see how these basic research objectives are best handled by the various research designs. Table 5.1 shows the three types of research designs and the basic research objective that would prescribe a given design.

TABLE 5.1

The Basic Research Objective and Research Design

RESEARCH OBJECTIVE	APPROPRIATE DESIGN
To gain background information, to define terms, to clarify problems and hypotheses, to establish research priorities	Exploratory
To describe and measure marketing phenomena at a point in time	Descriptive
To determine causality, to make "if-then" statements	Causal

Research Design: A Caution

We pause here, before discussing the three types of research design, to warn you about thinking of research design solely in a step-by-step fashion. Some may think that it is implied in this discussion that the order in which the designs are presented—that is, exploratory, descriptive, and causal—is the order in which these designs should be carried out. This is incorrect. Three points should be made relative to the interdependency of research designs. First, in some cases, it may be perfectly legitimate to begin with any one of the three designs and to use only that one design. Second, research is an "iterative" process; by conducting one research project, we learn that we may need additional research, and so on. This may mean that we need to utilize multiple research designs. We could very well find, for example, that after conducting descriptive research, we need to go back and conduct exploratory research. Third, if multiple designs are used in any particular order (if there is an *order*), it makes sense to first conduct exploratory research, then descriptive research, and finally causal research. The only reason for this order pattern is that each subsequent design requires greater knowledge about the research problem on the part of the researcher. Therefore, exploratory may give one the information needed to conduct a descriptive study which, in turn, may provide the information necessary to design a causal experiment. Now that you have been cautioned regarding thinking of research design solely in a step-by-step fashion, we begin our discussion of the three types of research design.

Research does not necessarily follow the order of (1) exploratory, (2) descriptive, and (3) causal designs.

Exploratory Research

Exploratory research is most commonly unstructured, informal research that is undertaken to gain background information about the general nature of the research problem. By unstructured, we mean that exploratory research does not have a formalized set of objectives, sample plan, or questionnaire. It is usually conducted when the researcher does not know much about the problem and needs additional information or desires new or more recent information. Often, exploratory research is conducted at the outset of research projects. Because exploratory research is aimed at gaining additional information about a topic and generating possible hypotheses to test, it is described as informal. Such research may consist of going to the library and reading published secondary data; of asking customers, salespersons, and acquaintances for their opinions about a company, its products, services, and prices; or of simply

Exploratory research is unstructured, informal research undertaken to gain background information about the general nature of the research problem.

observing everyday company practices. Exploratory research is systematic, but it is very flexible in that it allows the researcher to investigate whatever sources he or she desires and to the extent he or she feels is necessary in order to gain a good feel for the problem at hand. In the following sections, we discuss the specific uses of exploratory research as well as the different methods of conducting exploratory research.

Uses of Exploratory Research

Exploratory research has a number of issues.

Exploratory research is used in a number of situations: to gain background information, to define terms, to clarify problems and hypotheses, and to establish research priorities.

Gain Background Information. When very little is known about the problem or when the problem has not been clearly formulated, exploratory research may be used to gain much-needed background information. This is easily accomplished in firms having a marketing information system in which a review of internal information tracked over time can provide useful insights into the background of the firm, brand, sales territories, and so on. Even for very experienced researchers it is rare that some exploratory research is not undertaken to gain current, relevant background information. There is far too much to be gained to ignore exploratory information.

Define Terms. Exploratory research helps to define terms and concepts. By conducting exploratory research to define a question such as, "What is bank image?," the researcher quickly learns that "image" is composed of several components—perceived convenience of location, loan availability, friendliness of employees, and so on. Not only would exploratory research identify the components of bank image but it could also demonstrate how these components may be measured.

Exploratory research is helpful for more clearly defining the research problem and hypotheses.

Clarify Problems and Hypotheses. Exploratory research allows the researcher to define the problem more precisely and to generate hypotheses for the upcoming study. For example, exploratory research on measuring bank image reveals the issue of different groups of bank customers. Banks have three types of customers: retail customers, commercial customers, and other banks for which services are performed for fees. This information is useful in clarifying the problem of the measurement of bank image because it raises the issue of which customer group bank image should be measured on.

Hypotheses are speculations on the relationships among two or more variables.

Exploratory research can also be beneficial in the formulation of **hypotheses,** which are statements describing the speculated relationships among two or more variables. Formally stating hypotheses prior to conducting a research study is very important to ensure that the proper variables are measured. Once a study has been completed, it may be too late to state which hypotheses are desirable to test.

Establish Research Priorities. Exploratory research can help a firm prioritize research topics in order of importance, especially when it is faced with conducting several research studies. A review of customer complaint letters, for example, may indicate which product or services are most in need of management's attention. For example, one furniture store chain owner decided to conduct research on the feasibility of carrying office furniture after some exploratory interviews with salespeople revealed that their customers often asked for directions to stores carrying office furniture.

Methods of Conducting Exploratory Research

A variety of methods are available to conduct exploratory research. These include secondary data analysis, experience surveys, case analysis, focus groups, and projective techniques.

Secondary data analysis relies on previously gathered information.

Secondary Data Analysis. By **secondary data analysis,** we refer to the process of searching for and interpreting existing information relevant to the research problem. Secondary data are data that have been collected for some other purpose. Your library and the Internet are full of secondary data, which includes information found in books, journals, magazines, special reports, bulletins, newsletters, and so on. An analysis of secondary data is often the "core" of exploratory research.[1] This is because there are many benefits to examining secondary data and the costs are typically minimal. Furthermore, the costs for search time of such data are being reduced every day as more and more computerized databases become available. Knowledge of and ability to use these databases are already mandatory for marketing researchers. (Additional information on these databases is offered in chapter 6.)

Experience surveys refer to gathering information from those thought to be knowledgeable on the issues relevant to the research problem.

Experience Surveys. **Experience surveys** refer to gathering information from those thought to be knowledgeable on the issues relevant to the research problem. If the research problem deals with difficulties encountered when buying infant clothing, then surveys of mothers or fathers with infants may be in order. If the research problem deals with forecasting the demand for sulphuric acid over the next two years, researchers may begin by making a few calls to some "experts" on this issue. Experience surveys differ from surveys conducted as part of descriptive research in that there is usually no formal attempt to ensure that the survey results are representative of any defined group of subjects. Nevertheless, useful information can be gathered by this method of exploratory research.

Case analysis uses past situations that are similar to the present research problem.

Case Analysis. By **case analysis,** we refer to a review of available information about a former situation(s) that has some similarities to the present research problem. Usually, there are few research problems that do not have some similarities to some situation in the past.[2] Even when the research problem deals with a radically new product, there are often some similar past experiences that may be observed. For example, when cellular telephones were invented but not yet on the market, many companies attempted to forecast how many cellular telephones would be sold. Part of the forecasting process was to determine the rate of adoption. 21st Century Telesis, a wireless communications company, came up with a strategy to market wireless services to those who had never used them. Its research included extensive investigation of a low-power, neighborhood phone system that was very successful in Japan. 21st Century is targeting a mass market of young people who desire a personal phone they can carry around conveniently.[3]

Is this valid? Yes, but researchers must be aware of the caveats in using former case examples for current problems. They should ask themselves questions to determine the relevancy of prior cases. How similar is the phenomenon in the past to the phenomenon in the present? (For example, would adoption rates of *Japanese* have any relationship with adoption rates of *Americans?*) What situational factors have changed that may invalidate using the case to predict a future outcome? To the extent that the researcher can adequately answer these questions, the greater should be his or her confidence in using a case analysis as part of exploratory research.

Focus groups are a popular form of exploratory research.

Focus Groups. An increasingly popular method of conducting exploratory research is through **focus groups,** which are small groups of people brought together and guided by a moderator through an unstructured, spontaneous discussion for the purpose of gaining information relevant to the research problem.[4] Although focus groups should encourage openness on the part of the participants, the moderator's task is to ensure the discussion is "focused" on some general area of interest. For example, the Piccadilly Cafeteria chain periodically conducts focus groups all around the country. The conversation may seem "free-wheeling," but the purpose of the focus group may be to learn what people think about some specific aspect of the cafeteria business such as the perceived quality of cafeteria versus traditional restaurant food. This is a useful technique for gathering some information from a limited sample of respondents. The information can be used to generate ideas, to learn the respondent's "vocabulary" when relating to a certain type of product, or to gain some insights into basic needs and attitudes.[5] Focus groups are discussed extensively in chapter 8.

Projective techniques are techniques marketing researchers have borrowed from clinical psychology.

Projective Techniques. **Projective techniques,** borrowed from the field of clinical psychology, seek to explore hidden consumer motives for buying goods and services by asking participants to project themselves into a situation and then to respond to specific questions regarding the situation. One example of such a technique is the sentence completion test. A respondent is given an incomplete sentence such as, "Andrea Livingston never buys frozen dinners for her family because . . . " By completing the sentence, ostensibly to represent the feelings of the fictitious Ms. Livingston, the respondent *projects* himself or herself into the situation. These techniques are explored in greater detail in chapter 8.

Descriptive Research

Descriptive research provides answers to the questions of who, what, where, when, and how.

When we wish to know how many customers we have, what brands they buy and in what quantities, which advertisements they recall, and what their attitudes are toward our company and our competitors, we turn to **descriptive research,** which provides answers to questions such as who, what, where, when, and how, as they are related to the research problem. Typically, answers to these questions are found in secondary data or by conducting surveys.

Marketing decision makers often need answers to these basic questions before they can formulate effective marketing strategies. Consider the following examples. *Who* may be defined as the firm's (competitor's) customers. *What* may be defined as the products, brands, sizes, and so on that are being purchased. *Where* may be defined as the places the customers are buying these products. *When* refers to the time or the frequency with which purchases are made. *How* may mean the ways in which customers are using the products. Note that we cannot *conclusively* answer the question of *why* using descriptive research. Conclusive answers to questions such as why sales increase or decrease if we increase or decrease advertising or why one ad garners greater attention than another are questions that must be answered through causal research designs.

Classification of Descriptive Research Studies

There are two basic descriptive research studies available to the marketing researcher: cross-sectional and longitudinal (Table 5.2). **Cross-sectional studies** measure a population at only one point in time. Cross-sectional studies are very prevalent in marketing research, outnumbering longitudinal studies and causal studies. Because cross-sectional studies are one-time measurements, they are often described as "snapshots" of the population. As an example, many magazines survey a sample of their subscribers and ask them questions such as their age, occupation, income, educational level, and so on. This sample data, taken at *one point in time*, is used to *describe* the readership of the magazine in terms of demographics. Cross-sectional studies normally employ fairly large sample sizes, so many cross-sectional studies are referred to as sample surveys.

Cross-sectional studies measure the population at only one point in time.

Sample surveys are cross-sectional studies whose samples are drawn in such a way as to be representative of a specific population. ABC often conducts surveys on some topic of interest to report on the evening news. The surveys' samples are drawn such that ABC may report that the results are representative of the population of the United States. Nabisco may want to conduct a survey whose results are representative of chain-owned supermarkets in the northeastern United States. Sample surveys require that their samples be drawn according to a prescribed plan and to a predetermined number. Later on, you will learn about these sampling plans (chapter 12) and sample size techniques (chapter 13). Cross-sectional surveys are often invaluable in helping a marketer understand the pecularities of buying behavior in a foreign country. Marketing Research Insight 5.1 (page 116) describes how Sleep Comfort learned how Japanese consumers are unique in their buying of beds and crafted its marketing strategy accordingly.

Longitudinal studies repeatedly measure the same population over a period of time. Because longitudinal studies involve multiple measurements, they are often described as "movies" of the population. Longitudinal studies are employed by almost 50 percent of businesses using marketing research.[6] To ensure the success of the longitudinal study, researchers must have access to the same members of the sample, called a **panel,** so as to take repeated measurements. Maintaining a representative panel of respondents is a major undertaking.

Longitudinal studies repeatedly measure the same population over a period of time.

TABLE 5.2

Classification of Descriptive Research Studies

TYPE OF STUDY	FEATURES OF STUDY
Cross-sectional	One-time measurement, including a sample survey where the emphasis is placed on a large, representative sample
Longitudinal	Repeated measurements on the same sample, including a traditional panel (questions remain the same) and an omnibus panel (questions differ)

Source: *Adapted from Gilbert A. Churchill, Jr.,* Basic Marketing Research, *2nd ed. (Fort Worth, Tex.: The Dryden Press, 1992), 133.*

MARKETING RESEARCH INSIGHT 5.1

How Marketing Research Helps Japanese Consumers Sleep Better

Select Comfort, located in Minneapolis, Minnesota, sells Select Comfort *sleep systems, which is an air-supported, adjustable-firmness mattress. This system is an innovation that supports the body with a cushion of air rather than innersprings, which are used in conventional beds, or water, which is used in waterbeds. The patented* Select Comfort *system is designed for maximum comfort and optimum spinal support, and it is touted to be the most advanced sleep surface technology available in the United States.*

Select Comfort *has formed a partnership with Bridgestone Corporation, which is a leading Japanese industrial manufacturer and marketer. Marketing research led to the following marketing strategy elements for the following reasons:*

- *Bridgestone's logo and name is associated with* Select Comfort *because Japanese often make purchases with the maker's reputation as important as the product features, and Bridgestone is widely known and respected in Japan.*
- *The selling approach includes telemarketing that answers inquiries generated by advertisements, and when the customer comes to the store, the same employee will serve him or her because retailer–customer relationships are vital to business success in Japan.*
- *Retail locations for Bridgestone/*Select Comfort *are near the largest train and subway stations in Japan, because a number of Japanese commute on these systems.*
- Sleep Comfort *systems manufacturing is altered to dimensions measured in centimeters, not inches, as Japan uses the metric system.*
- *Marketing efforts are focused on comparing* Sleep Comfort *to futons because 50 percent of new mattress purchases in Japan are futons; plus, innerspring mattresses are not the traditional form of bed in Japan.*
- *Advertising will appeal primarily to women because Japanese women typically make the decisions for household furniture.*

Source: *PR Newswire, "Select Comfort Introduces Air Sleep Systems in Tokyo Through Test Market Partnership with Bridgestone" (August 15, 1996), p815NYTH123.*

Several commercial marketing research firms develop and maintain consumer panels for use in longitudinal studies. Typically, these firms attempt to select a sample that is representative of some population. One such company, NFO Research, Inc. (National Family Opinion), maintains a panel of 425,000 households representing one in every 218 households and over one million individuals. NFO's panel is carefully selected so that it is balanced with respect to U.S. demographics (as reported from Census Bureau statistics). Table 5.3 shows how NFO's panel is balanced not only to the United States in total but also within each of nine different geographical regions. NFO also maintains complete demographic information and ownership information (that is, number or households owning dogs, cats, VCRs, and so on) on their panel households. Of course, panels are not limited to consumer

Table 5.3

NFO's Panel Is Demographically Balanced with the Total U.S. and Nine Geographical Regions

Geographic Division	100% Total U.S.	5.3% New England	14.9% Middle Atlantic	17.2% E. North Central	7.4% W. North Central	18.1% South Atlantic	6.2% E. South Central	10.5% W. South Central	5.5% Mountain	14.9% Pacific
Market Size										
Non-MSA/CMSA or MSA under 100,000	22.0	14.9	9.3	23.1	45.1	25.3	45.3	26.6	29.4	6.5
Metropolitan Areas										
100,000–499,999	16.4	12.7	9.6	19.0	17.5	18.9	24.8	19.1	18.9	11.9
500,000–1,999,999	20.6	35.4	15.3	19.6	12.6	21.2	29.9	25.1	35.6	12.6
2,000,000 and over	41.0	37.0	65.8	38.3	24.8	34.6	—	29.2	16.1	69.0
	100.0%	100.0%	100.0%	100.0%	100.0%	100.0%	100.0%	100.0%	100.0%	100.0%
Age of Household Head[1]										
Family										
Under 30 years	10.9	8.8	9.0	10.7	10.9	11.0	12.9	12.7	11.5	11.2
30–39 years	19.2	19.5	18.5	18.6	18.8	18.9	19.9	19.6	20.8	19.9
40–49 years	16.0	16.7	17.1	16.1	14.8	15.3	15.3	16.0	14.8	16.4
50–59 years	9.9	9.3	10.4	10.1	9.6	10.2	11.0	10.9	8.6	8.6
60 years and over	13.7	14.3	14.7	14.1	12.3	14.9	14.3	12.1	13.6	12.4
Nonfamily										
Male under 35 years	5.0	5.6	4.0	5.2	6.0	4.5	3.9	5.2	5.3	5.7
Male 35 years and over	8.2	8.3	8.4	8.2	7.5	8.0	7.4	6.8	9.5	9.4
Female under 35 years	3.3	3.7	2.8	3.3	4.3	3.4	2.3	3.5	3.6	3.0
Female 35 years and over	13.8	13.8	15.1	13.7	15.8	13.8	13.0	13.2	12.3	13.4
	100.0%	100.0%	100.0%	100.0%	100.0%	100.0%	100.0%	100.0%	100.0%	100.0%
Annual Household Income										
Under $12,500	18.3	15.0	18.0	17.6	18.8	18.7	25.5	21.7	17.5	14.4
$12,500–$24,999	20.9	17.6	17.6	20.5	22.1	21.7	24.8	23.7	23.1	20.1
$25,000–$39,999	21.8	18.3	20.1	22.1	23.9	22.5	21.2	22.3	23.6	21.6
$40,000–$59,999	19.3	21.4	20.2	20.6	19.7	19.0	16.8	16.7	18.9	19.4
$60,000 and over	19.7	27.7	24.1	19.2	15.5	18.1	11.7	15.6	16.9	24.5
	100.0%	100.0%	100.0%	100.0%	100.0%	100.0%	100.0%	100.0%	100.0%	100.0%
Size of Household										
1 member	25.5	25.3	26.2	25.8	28.7	25.0	23.7	25.0	25.2	24.7
2 members	32.2	32.6	30.1	32.7	31.9	34.1	33.2	30.6	34.2	31.2
3 members	16.8	17.6	16.9	16.3	15.0	17.7	19.4	18.1	15.3	15.3
4 members	15.3	15.8	15.6	15.5	15.0	14.7	16.2	16.1	13.6	15.5
5 or more members	10.2	8.7	11.2	9.7	9.4	8.5	7.5	10.2	11.7	13.3
	100.0%	100.0%	100.0%	100.0%	100.0%	100.0%	100.0%	100.0%	100.0%	100.0%

[1]Female head of household, if present.

Source: NFO Research, Inc.

households. Panels may consist of supermarkets, law firms, universities, or some other entity. There is currently a trend for retailers, such as supermarket chains, to adopt the use of panels.[7]

Traditional panels ask panel members the same questions on each panel measurement, whereas omnibus panels vary questions from one panel measurement to the next.

There are two types of panels: traditional panels and omnibus panels. **Traditional panels** ask panel members the *same* questions on each panel measurement. **Omnibus panels** vary questions from one panel measurement to the next. Unlike the traditional panel, omnibus panels may be used for a variety of purposes, and the information collected by an omnibus panel varies from one panel measurement to the next. How longitudinal data is applied depends on the type of panel used to collect the data. Essentially, the omnibus panel's primary usefulness is that it represents a large group—people, stores, or some other entity—that is agreeable to providing marketing research information. Omnibus panels, like traditional panels, are also demographically matched to some larger entity, implying representativeness as well. Therefore, a marketer wanting to know how a large number of consumers, matched demographically to the total U.S. population, feel about two different product concepts, may elect to utilize the services of an omnibus panel. In this way, then, omnibus panels represent existing sources of information that may be quickly accessed for a wide variety of purposes.

Traditional panels allow researchers to see changes in consumers.

The traditional panel is used quite differently. Usually, firms are interested in using data from traditional panels because they can gain insights into *changes* in consumers' purchases, attitudes, and so on. For example, data from traditional panels can show how members of the panel switched brands from one time period to the next. Studies examining how many consumers switched brands are known as **brand-switching studies.**

To illustrate the importance of using traditional panel data to gain insights into how consumers change brands, we compare longitudinal data taken from a traditional panel with data collected from two cross-sectional sample surveys. Table 5.4 shows data collected from two separate cross-sectional studies, each having a household sample size of 500. Examination of the two cross-sectional studies would lead us to conclude that (1) Pooch Plus has lost market share because only 75 families indicated that they purchased Pooch Plus in the second survey as opposed to 100 Pooch Plus families in the first survey; and (2) apparently, Pooch Plus has lost out to Milk Bone dog treat brand, which increased from 200 to 225 families. Note that Beggar's Bits remained the same. This analysis would lead most brand managers to focus on the strategies that had been used by Milk Bone to increase market share.

Traditional panels can be used to analyze brand-switching by consumers.

When we examine the longitudinal data, we reach quite a different conclusion from the one we reached by looking at the two cross-sectional studies. Looking at the panel 1 and panel 2 totals, we see the same data that we saw in the two cross-sectional surveys. Panel 1 totals, which are read across, show us that Pooch Plus had 50+50 families for a total of 100 families, Beggar's Bits had 25+150+25 families for a total of 200, and Milk Bone had a total of 200. But, the real value of the traditional panel, longitudinal data, is found in the changes that occur between panel 1 and panel 2 measurements. Here, we must look at both row and column headings. What we find under the Pooch Plus column is that only 50 of the 100 panel 1 Pooch Plus families bought Pooch Plus during panel 2. However, we also see that during panel 2 Pooch Plus picked up 25 families that had bought Beggar's Bits during panel 1. (This gives us our total of 75 families that bought the Pooch Plus brand during

TABLE 5.4

The Advantage of Longitudinal Studies versus Cross-Sectional Studies

RESULTS OF TWO CROSS-SECTIONAL STUDIES

DOG TREAT BRAND	SURVEY 1	SURVEY 2
Pooch Plus	100	75
Beggar's Bits	200	200
Milk Bone	200	225
Total	500	500

RESULTS OF TWO LONGITUDINAL STUDIES

	POOCH PLUS	BEGGAR'S BITS	MILK BONE	PANEL 1 TOTALS
Pooch Plus	50	50	0	100
Beggar's Bits	25	150	25	200
Milk Bone	0	0	200	200
Panel 2 Totals	75	200	225	500

SPSS®

View: "Milk Bone Dog Biscuits I."

panel 2.) Next, looking under the Beggar's Bits column, we find that 50 families switched from Pooch Plus to Beggar's Bits from panel 1 to panel 2. Second, we see that Beggar's Bits retained 150 of its own 200 families. By further examining the data in Table 5.4, we can conclude that Beggar's Bits lost an equal number of families (25) to both Pooch Plus and to Milk Bone. Finally, Milk Bone's total shares increased but at the expense of Beggar's Bits, not Pooch Plus. This, then, is quite different from the conclusion reached by examining cross-sectional data. The key point being made here is that, because longitudinal data allows us to measure the change being made by each sample unit between time periods, we gain much richer information for analysis purposes. It is important to note, at this point, that this type of brand-switching data may be obtained only by using the traditional panel.

Another use of longitudinal data is that of market tracking. **Market tracking studies** are those that measure some variable(s) of interest, that is, market share or unit sales over time. By having representative data on brand market shares, for example, a marketing manager can "track" how his or her brand is doing relative to a competitive brand's performance.

Causal Research

Causality may be thought of as understanding a phenomenon in terms of conditional statements of the form "If *x*, then *y*." These "if–then" statements become our way of manipulating variables of interest. For example, if the thermostat is lowered, then the air will get cooler. If I drive my automobile at lower speeds, then my gasoline mileage will increase. If I spend more on advertising, then sales will rise. As humans, we are constantly trying to under-

Causality may be thought of as understanding a phenomenon in terms of conditional statements of the form "If x, then y."

TABLE 5.5

Formal Conditions for Causality

CONDITION	DESCRIPTION
Covariation	It must be demonstrated that the causal variable occurs with the caused variable and that the two variables have an orderly relationship (for example, as price goes down, sales go up).
Time sequence	It must be demonstrated that the causal variable changed prior to or simultaneous with observed changes in the caused variable (for example, prices were lowered on Monday, and sales go up for Monday and all other days when prices were lower).
Systematic elimination	It must be demonstrated that all other possible causal variables are eliminated from candidacy (for example, if an advertising campaign began on the day we lowered prices, we could not eliminate the ad campaign as a cause of sales going up).
Experimental design	It must be demonstrated that a valid experiment has been conducted in order to state that the variable is unequivocally causal (for example, a formal market test would be designed and conducted in order to determine the effect of a price reduction on sales).

There are four conditions for causality.

stand the world in which we live. Fortunately for mankind, there is an inborn tendency to determine causal relationships. This tendency is ever present in our thinking and our actions. Likewise, marketing managers are always trying to determine what will cause a change in consumer satisfaction, a gain in market share, or an increase in sales. Unfortunately, our desire to understand our world in terms of causal, if–then statements is very difficult, if not impossible, because there are formal conditions that must be in place before a researcher can attest to causality. Table 5.5 describes the formal requirements for causality. Consumers are bombarded on a daily and sometimes even hourly basis by a vast multitude of factors, all of which could cause them to act in one way or another. Nevertheless, there is a high "reward" in the marketplace for even partially understanding causal relationships. How are causal relationships determined? As Table 5.5 indicates, they are determined through the use of experiments.

EXPERIMENTS

Independent variables are those variables over which the researcher has some control and wishes to manipulate. Dependent variables are those that we have little or no direct control over but that we are interested in.

An **experiment** is defined as manipulating an independent variable to see how it affects a dependent variable, while also controlling the effects of additional extraneous variables. **Independent variables** are those variables over which the researcher has some control and wishes to manipulate. Some independent variables include level of advertising expenditure, type of advertising appeal (humorous, prestige), display location, method of compensating salespersons, price, and type of product. **Dependent variables,** on the other hand, are those variables that we have little or no direct control over, yet we have a strong interest in. We cannot change these variables in the same way that we can change independent variables. A marketing manager, for example, can easily change the level of advertising expenditure or the location of the display of a product in a supermarket, but he or she cannot easily change sales, market share, or level of customer satisfaction. These variables are typically dependent variables. Certainly, marketers are interested in changing these variables. But, because they cannot change them directly, they attempt to change them through the manipulation of independent variables. To the extent that marketers can establish causal relationships between independent and dependent variables, they enjoy some success in influencing the dependent variables.

Dependent variables may be influenced by independent variables.

Extraneous variables are those that may have some effect upon a dependent variable but yet are not independent variables. As noted earlier, our world is complex. Consumer behavior, for example, is a function of many, many variables. When we attempt to make causal relationships between an independent variable and a dependent variable, we must understand that extraneous variables may have caused the change in our dependent variable.

An experiment is manipulating an independent variable to see how it affects a dependent variable while controlling the effects of extraneous variables.

Let us illustrate with an example. Imagine that a supermarket chain conducts an experiment to determine the effect of type of display (independent variable) on sales of apples (dependent variable). Management records sales of the apples in their regular produce bins position and then changes (manipulates the independent variable) the position of the apples to end-aisle displays and measures sales once again. Assume sales increased. Does this mean that if we change display position of apples from the produce bins to end-aisle displays, then sales will increase? Could there be other extraneous variables that could have affected the sales of the apples? What would happen to apple sales if the weather changed from rainy to fair? If the apple industry began running ads on TV? If the season changed from summer vacation to fall? Yes, weather, industry advertising, and apples packed in school lunch boxes are viewed in this example as extraneous variables, having an effect on the dependent variable, yet themselves not defined as independent variables. As this example illustrates, it would be difficult to isolate the effects of independent variables on dependent variables without controlling for the effects of the extraneous variables. This task is accomplished through experimental design.

Experimental Design

An **experimental design** is a procedure for devising an experimental setting such that a change in a dependent variable may be attributed solely to the change in an independent variable. In other words, experimental designs are procedures that allow experimenters to control for the effects on a dependent variable by an extraneous variable. In this way, the experimenter is assured that any change in the dependent variable was due only to the change in the independent variable.

An experimental design is a procedure for devising an experimental setting such that a change in a dependent variable may be attributed solely to the change in an independent variable.

Let us look at how experimental designs work. First, we list the symbols of experimental design:

O = The measurement of a dependent variable.

X = The manipulation, or change, of an independent variable.

R = Random assignment of subjects (consumers, stores, and so on) to experimental and control groups.

E = Experimental effect; that is, the change in the dependent variable due to the independent variable.

Time is assumed to be represented horizontally, on a continuum.

Subscripts, such as O_1, or O_2, refer to different measurements made of the dependent variable.

When a measurement of the dependent variable is taken *prior to* changing the independent variable, the measurement is sometimes called a **pretest.** When a measurement of the dependent variable is taken *after* changing the independent variable, the measurement is sometimes called a **posttest.**

There are many research designs available to experimenters. In fact, entire college courses are devoted to this one topic. But, our purpose here is to illustrate the logic of experimental design and we can do this by reviewing four designs of which two are true experimental designs. A **"true" experimental design** is one that truly isolates the effects of the independent variable on the dependent variable while controlling for effects of any extraneous variables. However, we introduce you to the first two designs to help you understand the real benefits of using a true experimental design. The four designs we discuss are: after-only; one-group, before–after; before–after with control group; and after-only with control group.

A "true" experimental design is one that truly isolates the effects of the independent variable on the dependent variable while controlling for effects of any extraneous variables.

After-Only Design

The **after-only design** is achieved by changing the independent variable and, after some period of time, measuring the dependent variable. It is diagrammed as follows:

$$X\ O_1$$

where the X represents the change in the independent variable (putting all of the apples in end-aisle displays) and the distance between the X and the O represents the passage of some time period. The O_1 represents the measurement, a posttest, of the dependent variable (recording the sales of the apples). Now, what have you learned about causality? Not very much! Have sales gone up or down? We do not know because we neglected to measure sales prior to changing the display location. And, regardless of what our sales are, there may have been other, extraneous variables that may have had an effect on apple sales. Managers are constantly changing things "just to see what happens" without taking any necessary precautions to properly evaluate the effects of the change. Hence, the after-only design does not really measure up to our requirement for a true experimental design.

Designs that do not properly control for the effects of extraneous variables on our dependent variable are known as **quasi-experimental designs.** Note that in the after-only design diagram there is no measure of E, the "experimental effect" on our dependent variable due solely to our independent variable. This is true in all quasi-experimental designs. Our next design, the one-group, before–after design, is also a quasi-experimental design, although it is an improvement over the after-only design.

Quasi-experimental designs, unlike true experimental designs, do not properly control for the effects of extraneous variables on dependent variables.

One-Group, Before–After Design

In a before–after design there is a pretest and a posttest.

The **one-group, before–after design** is achieved by first measuring the dependent variable, then changing the independent variable, and finally, taking a second measurement of the dependent variable. We diagram this design as follows:

$$O_1 \; X \; O_2$$

The obvious difference between this design and the after-only design is that we have a measurement of the dependent variable prior to *and* following the change in the independent variable. Also, as the name implies, we have only *one* group (a group of consumers in one store) on which we are conducting our study.

A one-group design does not control for extraneous variable effects.

As an illustration of this design, let us go back to our previous example. In this design, our supermarket manager measured the dependent variable, apple sales, *prior to* changing the display location. Now, what do we know about causality? We know a little more than we learned from the after-only design. We know the change in our dependent variable from time period 1 to time period 2. We at least know if sales went up, down, or stayed the same. But what if sales did go up? Can we attribute the change in our dependent variable solely to the change in our independent variable? The answer is "no"—numerous extraneous variables, such as weather, advertising, or time of year, could have caused an increase in apple sales. With the one-group, before–after design, we still cannot measure E, the "experimental effect," because this design does not control for the effects of extraneous variables on the dependent variable. Hence, the one-group, before–after design is also not a true experimental design; it is a quasi-experimental design.

A true experimental design requires the use of a control group.

Control of extraneous variables is typically achieved by the use of a second group of subjects, known as a control group. By **control group,** we mean a group whose subjects have not been exposed to the change in the independent variable. The **experimental group,** on the other hand, is the group that *has* been exposed to a change in the independent variable. By having these two groups as part of our experimental design, we can overcome many of the problems associated with the quasi-experimental designs presented thus far. We shall use the following true experimental design to illustrate the importance of the control group.

Before–After with Control Group

The **before–after with control group** design may be achieved by randomly dividing subjects of the experiment (in this case, supermarkets) into two groups: the control group and the experimental group. A pretest measurement of the dependent variable is then taken on both groups. Next, the independent variable is changed only in the experimental group. Finally, after some time period, posttest measurements are taken of the dependent variable in both groups. This design may be diagrammed as follows:

Experimental group (R) $\quad O_1 \; X \; O_2$

Control group (R) $\quad O_3 \; X \; O_4$

where $E = (O_2 - O_1) - (O_4 - O_3)$.

In a true experimental design the experimental group must be equivalent to the control group.

In this true experimental design, we have two groups. Let us assume we have 20 supermarkets in our supermarket chain. Theoretically, if we randomly divide these stores into two groups—10 in the experimental group and 10 in the control group—then the groups should be equivalent. That is, both groups should be as similar as possible, each group having an equal number of large stores and small stores, an equal number of new stores and old stores, an equal number of stores in upper income neighborhoods and lower income neighborhoods, and so on. Note that this design *assumes* that the two groups are equivalent in all aspects. An experimenter should take whatever steps are necessary to meet this condition if he or she uses this design. There are other methods for gaining equivalency besides randomization. Matching on criteria thought to be important, for example, would aid in establishing equivalent groups. When randomization or matching on relevant criteria does not achieve equivalent groups, other, more complex, experimental designs should be used.[8]

Looking back at our design, the *R* indicates that we have randomly divided our supermarkets into two equal groups—one a control group, the other an experimental group. We also see that pretest measurements of our dependent variable, apple sales, were recorded at the same time for both groups of stores as noted by O_1 and O_3. Next, we see by the *X* symbol that only in the experimental group of stores were the apples moved from the regular produce bins to end-aisle displays. Finally, posttest measurements of the dependent variable were taken at the same time in both groups of stores as noted by O_2 and O_4.

Now, what information can we gather from this experiment? First, we know that $(O_2 - O_1)$ tells us how much change occurred in our dependent variable during the time of the experiment. But, was this difference due *solely* to our independent variable, *X*? No, $(O_2 - O_1)$ tells us how many dollars in apple sales may be attributed to (1) the change in display location *and* (2) other extraneous variables, such as the weather, apple industry advertising, and so on. This does not help us very much, but what does $(O_4 - O_3)$ measure? Because it cannot account for changes in apple sales due to a change in display location (the display was not changed), then any differences in sales as measured by $(O_4 - O_3)$ must be due to the influence of other, extraneous variables on apple sales. Therefore, the difference between the experimental group and the control group, $(O_2 - O_1) - (O_4 - O_3)$, results in a measure of *E*, the "experimental effect." We now know that *if* we change apple display locations, *then* apple sales will change by an amount equal to *E*. We have, through experimentation using a proper experimental design, made some progress at arriving at causality.

Changes in the control group are due to all extraneous variables but not the independent variable(s).

After-Only with Control Group

The previous design is useful when a researcher wants to explicitly measure the net change in the experimental group and to measure the changes due to extraneous factors, which are then subtracted out of the net change in the experimental group. An alternative design may be used when a precise measure of the effects of extraneous factors is not desired, but the researcher wants to know the experimental effect. This design is called the **after-only with control group** design, and its diagram is as follows:

Experimental group (*R*)	*X*	O_1
Control group (*R*)		O_2

where $E = O_1 - O_2$

Applied to our supermarket example, notice that the after-only with control group design requires that we randomly select experimental stores and randomly select control group stores. This random selection process should result in two sets of stores that are identical in the average number of apple sales with the apples in the produce bins. Note that we do not measure these sales levels. Rather, we trust in the random selection process to give us equivalent groups, so it is very important that a truly random selection process is used. Or an alternative system that ensures two equivalent groups of supermarkets must be used. With the experimental stores, the apples are then placed in end-aisle displays, whereas they are left in the produce bins for the control stores. The sales of apples in both groups of stores are measured over some time period while the experiment is in place. The measure of sales, O_1, equates to the effect of the end-aisle display placement plus extraneous factors, and the measure, O_2, equates to regular bin placement apple sales plus extraneous factors. If the groups are equivalent, the extraneous variables' effects will be identical. By subtracting O_2 from O_1, the extraneous variables' effects cancel out, and we find the difference, which is the net effect of the end-aisle display placement in the experimental stores group.

With an after-only design, there is no pretest.

As we noted earlier, there are many other experimental designs and, of course, there are almost limitless applications of experimental designs to marketing problems. An experimenter, for example, could use the before–after with control group design to measure the effects of different types of music (independent variable) on total purchases made by supermarket customers (dependent variable). Although we have demonstrated how valuable experimentation can be in providing us with knowledge, we should not accept all experiments as being valid. How we assess the validity of experiments is the subject of our next section.

How Valid Are Experiments?

How can we assess the validity of an experiment? An experiment is valid if (1) the observed change in the dependent variable is, in fact, due to the independent variable, and (2) if the results of the experiment apply to the "real world" outside the experimental setting.[9] Two forms of validity are used to assess the validity of an experiment: internal and external.

An experiment is valid if the observed change in the dependent variable is, in fact, due to the independent variable, and if the results of the experiment apply to the "real world" outside the experimental setting.

Internal validity is concerned with the extent to which the change in the dependent variable was actually due to the independent variable. This is another way of asking if the proper experimental design was used and if it was implemented correctly. To illustrate an experiment that lacks internal validity, let us return to our apple example. In the experimental design, before–after with control group, we made the point that the design assumes that the experimental group and the control group are, in fact, equivalent. What would happen if the researcher did not check the equivalency of the groups? Let us suppose that, by chance, the two groups of supermarkets had customers who were distinctly different regarding a number of factors such as age and income. This difference in the groups, then, would represent an extraneous variable that had been left uncontrolled. Such an experiment would lack internal validity because it could not be said that the change in the dependent variable was due solely to the change in the independent variable.

Internal validity is concerned with the extent to which the change in the dependent variable was actually due to the independent variable.

Experiments lacking internal validity have little value. Table 5.6 lists some factors that an experimenter should be concerned with in terms of the validity of his or her experiment. Note that the internal validity concerns are all situations that could cause a change in the dependent variable other than, or in addition to, the independent variable.

External validity refers to the extent that the relationship observed between the independent and dependent variable during the experiment is generalizable to the "real world."

External validity refers to the extent that the relationship observed between the independent and dependent variables during the experiment is generalizable to the "real world."[10] In other words, can the results of the experiment be applied to units (consumers, stores, and so on) other than those directly involved in the experiment? There are several threats to external validity. How representative is the sample of test units? Is this sample really representative of the population? Additionally, there exist many examples of the incorrect selection of sample units for testing purposes. For example, executives, headquartered in large cities in cold winter climates, have been known to conduct "experiments" in warmer, tropical climes during the winter. Although the experiments they conduct may be internally valid, it is doubtful that the results will be generalizable to the total population.

Another threat to external validity is the artificiality of the experimental setting itself. In order to control as many variables as possible, some experi-

TABLE 5.6

Validity Concerns in Marketing Experimentation

INTERNAL VALIDITY CONCERNS	EXTERNAL VALIDITY CONCERNS
Extraneous Factors Have extraneous events or influences affected the outcome of the experiment?	**Representative Sample** Was the sample used representative of the population to which the results were generalized?
Changes in Subjects Have natural, biological, physiological, or psychological changes occurred in subjects during the course of the experiment?	**Realism** Were the experiment's context and conduct so artificial or unusual as to question how realistically subjects behaved?
Measure Error Was the measuring instrument uniform in its sensitivity and accuracy throughout the experiment?	**Generalizability** Is there any other factor that casts doubt on the generalization of the experiment's results to the actual marketing entity for which it was designed?
Subjects Guessing Were subjects "tipped off" as to the experiment's objectives before or during the experiment?	
Equivalent Groups If groups were compared, were the group's components identical across all relevant characteristics?	
Drop-Out If groups were compared, did one group have a different "drop-out" rate than the other(s)?	

mental settings are far removed from real-world conditions. Several experiments have been conducted, for example, wherein consumers were invited to a theater and asked to view a "pilot" TV show in which test commercials (containing copy A or B), the real subject of the experiment, were spliced into the "pilot." After viewing the film, consumers were given vouchers and were told they could spend the voucher in the "store" next door to the theater. The "store," of course, was set up for the experiment and contained displays of the products advertised in the test ads. It is arguable that the shopping data results from an experiment like this do not represent the true shopping behaviors of consumers. Consumers may act differently in a "real" supermarket. Look again at Table 5.6; it presents the various issues that should be of concern to the experimenter in terms of assessing external validity.[11] Note that the external validity concerns all raise questions as to the experimental setting being "real" and, therefore, more generalizable to the real world.

An unrealistic experimental setting hinders external validity.

Types of Experiments

We can classify experiments into two broad classes: laboratory and field. **Laboratory experiments** are those in which the independent variable is manipulated and measures of the dependent variable are taken in a contrived, artificial setting for the purpose of controlling the many possible extraneous variables that may affect the dependent variable.

Laboratory experiments are those in which the independent variable is manipulated and measures of the dependent variable are taken in an artificial setting contrived to control extraneous variables.

To illustrate, let us consider the study we previously mentioned whereby subjects were invited to a theater and shown test ads, copy A or B, spliced into a TV "pilot" program. Why would a marketer want to use such an artificial, laboratory setting? Such a setting is used to control for variables that could affect the purchase of products other than those in the test ads. By bringing consumers into a contrived laboratory setting, the experimenter is able to control many extraneous variables. For example, you have learned why it is important to have equivalent groups (the same kind of people watching copy A as those watching copy B commercials) in an experiment. By inviting preselected consumers to the TV "pilot" showing in a theater, the experimenter can match (on selected demographics) the consumers who view copy A with those who view copy B, thus ensuring that the two groups are equal. By having the consumers walk into an adjoining "store," the experimenter easily controls other factors such as the time between exposure to the ad copy and shopping and the consumers' being exposed to other advertising by competitive brands. As you have already learned, any one of these factors, left uncontrolled, could have an impact on the dependent variable. By controlling for these and other variables, the experimenter can be assured that any changes in the dependent variable were due solely to differences in the independent variable, ad copy A and B. Laboratory experiments, then, are desirable when the intent of the experiment is to achieve high levels of internal validity.

The primary advantages of laboratory experiments are that they do allow the researcher to control for the effects of extraneous variables. And, compared to field experiments, lab experiments may be conducted quickly and with less expense. Obviously, the disadvantage is the lack of a natural setting and, therefore, the concern for generalizability of the findings to the real world. For instance, blind taste tests of beer have found that a majority of beer drinkers favor the older beers such as Pabst, Michelob, or Coors, yet new beer brands are

Laboratory experiments are desirable when the intent of the experiment is to achieve high levels of internal validity.

introduced regularly and become quite popular,[12] so the generalizability of blind taste tests is questionable.

Field experiments are those in which the independent variables are manipulated and the measurements of the dependent variable are made on test units in their natural setting.

Field experiments are those in which the independent variables are manipulated and the measurements of the dependent variable are made on test units in their *natural setting*. Many marketing experiments are conducted in natural settings, such as in supermarkets, malls, retail stores, and consumers' homes. Let us assume that a marketing manager conducts a laboratory experiment to test the differences between ad copy A, the company's existing ad copy, and a new ad copy, copy B. The results of the laboratory experiment indicate that copy B is far superior to the company's present ad copy, A. But, before spending the money to use the new copy, the manager wants to know if ad copy B will really create increased sales in the real world. She elects to actually run the new ad copy in Erie, Pennsylvania, a city noted as being representative of the average characteristics of the United States. By conducting this study in the field, the marketing manager will have greater confidence that the results of the study will actually hold up in other real-world settings. Note, however, that even if an experiment is conducted in a naturalistic field setting in order to enhance external validity, the experiment is *invalid* if it does not also have internal validity.

Field experiments are desirable when the intent of the experiment is to achieve high levels of external validity.

The primary advantage of the field experiment is that of conducting the study in a naturalistic setting, thus increasing the likelihood that the study's findings will also hold true in the real world. Field experiments, however, are expensive and time consuming. Also, the experimenter must always be alert to the impact of extraneous variables, which are very difficult to control in the natural settings of field experimentation.

The example we just cited of using Erie, Pennsylvania, for a field experiment would be called a "test market." Much of the experimentation in marketing, conducted as field experiments, is known as test marketing. For this reason, test marketing is discussed in the following section.

TEST MARKETING

Test marketing is the phrase commonly used to indicate an experiment, study, or test that is conducted in a field setting.

Test marketing is the phrase commonly used to indicate an experiment, study, or test that is conducted in a field setting. Companies may use one or several **test market cities,** which are geographical areas selected in which to conduct the test. There are two broad classes of uses of test markets: (1) to test the sales potential for a new product or service, and (2) to test variations in the marketing mix for a product or service.[13]

Although test markets are very expensive and time consuming, the costs of introducing a new product on a national or regional basis routinely amount to millions of dollars. The costs of the test market are then justified if the results of the test market can improve a product's chances of success. Test markets are not only conducted to measure sales potential for a new product but to measure consumer and dealer reactions to other marketing mix variables as well. A firm may use only department stores to distribute the product in one test market and only specialty stores in another test market city to gain some information on the best way to distribute the product. Companies can also test media usage, pricing, sales promotions, and so on through test markets.

Types of Test Markets

Gilbert Churchill has classified test markets into four types: standard, controlled, electronic, and simulated.[14] The **standard test market** is one in which the firm tests the product and/or marketing mix variables through the company's normal distribution channels. When McDonald's Corporation used Auburn University's new process for processing a beef patty with very low fat, they tested this product through their own McDonald's restaurants. The test market was successful and the product was sold as the McLean burger. Standard test markets are time consuming, often taking a year or more, and are very expensive, often requiring several hundred thousand dollars. Standard test markets are not confidential; as soon as the test begins, competitors know about the product and can surmise a great deal about the intended marketing strategy for the product. Even with these limitations, however, standard test markets are perhaps the best indicators as to how the product will actually fare in the marketplace. This is because very little is contrived in the standard test market.

The standard test market is one in which the firm tests the product and/or marketing mix variables through the company's normal distribution channels.

Controlled test markets are conducted by outside research firms who guarantee distribution of the product through prespecified types and numbers of distributors. Companies specializing in providing this service, such as Audits & Surveys and ACNielsen, provide dollar incentives for distributors to provide them with guaranteed shelf space. Controlled test markets offer an alternative to the company that wishes to gain fast access to a distribution system set up for test market purposes. The disadvantage is that this distribution network may or may not properly represent the firm's actual distribution system.

Controlled test markets are conducted by outside research firms who guarantee distribution of the product through prespecified types and numbers of distributors.

Electronic test markets are those in which a panel of consumers have agreed to carry an identification card that they present when buying goods and services. These tests are conducted only in a small number of cities wherein local retailers have agreed to participate. The advantage of the card is that as consumers buy (or do not buy) the test product, demographic information on the consumer is automatically recorded. In some cases, firms offering electronic test markets may also have the ability to link media viewing habits to panel members as well. In this way, firms using the electronic test market also know how different elements of the promotional mix affect purchases of the new product. Firms offering this service include Information Resources, Inc. and ACNielsen (we discuss their services more thoroughly in chapter 7). Obviously, the electronic test market offers speed, greater confidentiality, and less cost than standard or controlled test markets. However, the disadvantage is that the test market is not the real market. By virtue of having agreed to serve as members of the electronic panel, consumers in electronic test markets may be atypical. A user firm must evaluate the issue of representativeness. Also, electronic test markets are typically situated in small cities such as Eau Claire, Wisconsin,[15] which is another representativeness consideration.

Electronic test markets are those in which a panel of consumers have agreed to carry an identification card that they present when buying goods and services.

Simulated test markets (STMs) are those in which a limited amount of data on consumer response to a new product is fed into a model containing certain assumptions regarding planned marketing programs, which generates likely product sales volume. It is claimed that IBM has suffered business failures such as the ill-fated Aptiva line of PCs because it failed to use STM research.[16]

Simulated test markets (STMs) are those in which a limited amount of data on consumer response to a new product is fed into a model containing certain assumptions regarding planned marketing programs, which generates likely product sales volume.

Typical STMs share the following characteristics:

- Respondents are selected to provide a sample of consumers who satisfy predetermined demographic characteristics.

- Consumers are shown commercials or print ads for the test product as well as ads for competitive products.
- Consumers are then given the opportunity to purchase, or not to purchase, the test product either in a real or simulated store environment.
- Consumers are then recontacted after they have had an opportunity to use the product in an effort to determine likelihood of repurchase, as well as other information relative to use of the product.
- Information from the preceding process is fed into a computer program that is calibrated by assumptions of the marketing mix and other elements of the environment. The program then generates output such as estimated sales volume, market share, and so on.[17]

STMs are fast, inexpensive, and confidential.

There are many advantages to STMs. They are fast relative to standard test markets. STMs typically take only 18 to 24 weeks compared to as many as 12 to 18 months for standard test markets. STMs cost only 5 percent to 10 percent of the cost of a standard test market. STMs are confidential; competitors are less likely to know about the test. Different marketing mixes may be tested and results of STMs have shown that they can be accurate predictors of actual market response. The primary disadvantage is that STMs are not as accurate as full-scale test markets. They are very dependent on the assumptions built into the models. These assumptions must include estimates as to how the distributors will react to the product and the likelihood that consumers will repurchase the product. Standard test markets do not need to *assume* the impact of these important market factors.[18]

Consumer versus Industrial Test Markets

When we think of test marketing we normally think of tests of consumer products. Test marketing, however, has been growing in the industrial market. Although the techniques are somewhat different between consumer and industrial test markets, the same results are sought—the timely release of profitable products.

With industrial test markets, prototype products are tested, revised, and retested under actual conditions.

In **consumer test markets,** multiple versions of a more-or-less finished product are tested by consumers. In **industrial test markets,** the key technology is presented to selected industrial users who offer feedback on desired features and product performance levels. Given this information, product prototypes are then developed and are placed with a select number of users for actual use. Users again provide feedback to iron out design problems. In this way, the new product is tried and tested under actual conditions before the final product is designed and produced for the total market. The negative side of this process is the time it takes to test the product from the beginning stages to the final, commercialized stages. During this time period, information on the new product is leaked to competitors, and the longer the product is being tested, the more investment costs increase without any revenues being generated. U.S. automakers, for example, take 48 to 60 months to design, refine, and begin production of a new car model. Japanese companies are able to do it in 30 months by having a development team made up of a combination of marketing and production people. Chrysler and 3M are now experimenting with this concept. If adopted by many firms, future industrial test marketing will be fully integrated with the new product development process.[19]

So far, our discussion of test marketing has not mentioned the likelihood of having different results between tests conducted in one country versus another. Markets that differ dramatically in terms of demographics and culture should not be expected to respond equally to any single marketing mix. For this reason, some companies are experimenting with "lead country" test marketing.

"Lead Country" Test Markets

A **lead country test market** is test marketing conducted in specific foreign countries that seem to be good predictors for an entire continent. This is a fairly new concept in test marketing. As markets have become more global, firms are no longer interested in limiting marketing of new products and services to their domestic market.

A lead country test market is test marketing conducted in specific foreign countries that seem to be good predictors for an entire continent.

Colgate-Palmolive used lead country test marketing when they launched their Palmolive Optims shampoo and conditioner. The company tested the product in the Philippines, Australia, Mexico, and Hong Kong. A year later, distribution was expanded to other countries in Europe, Asia, Latin America, and Africa.[20]

Selecting Test Market Cities

There are three criteria that are useful for selecting test market cities: representativeness, degree of isolation, and ability to control distribution and promotion.

There are three criteria that are useful for selecting test market cities: representativeness, degree of isolation, and ability to control distribution and promotion. Because one of the major reasons for conducting a test market is to achieve external validity, the test market city should be *representative* of the marketing territory in which the product will ultimately be distributed. Consequently, a great deal of effort is expended to locate the "ideal" city in terms of comparability with characteristics of the total U.S. (or other country) population. The "ideal" city being, of course, the city whose demographic characteristics most closely match the desired total market. For instance, R. J. Reynolds chose Chattanooga, Tennessee, to test market its Eclipse "smokeless" cigarette because Chattanooga has a higher proportion of smokers than most cities, and R. J. Reynolds needed to test Eclipse with smokers.[21]

It is desirable to have test cities that are geographically isolated.

When a firm test markets a product, distribution of the product and promotion of the product are *isolated to a limited geographical area*, such as Tulsa, Oklahoma. If the firm advertises in the *Tulsa World* newspaper, the newspaper not only covers Tulsa but also has very little "spillover" into other sizeable markets. Therefore, the company, along with its dealers, competitors, and so on, are not likely to get many calls from a nearby city wanting to know why they cannot buy the product. Distribution has been restricted to the test market, Tulsa. Some markets are not so isolated. If you were to run promotions for a product test in the *Los Angeles Times*, you would have very large "spillover" of newspaper readership outside the Los Angeles geographical area. Note that this would not necessarily be a problem as long as you wanted to run the test in the geographical area covered by the *Times* and you also had arranged for the new product to be distributed in this area.

The ability to *control distribution and promotion* depends on a number of factors. Are the distributors in the city being considered available and willing to cooperate? If not, is a controlled test market service company available for the city? Will the media in the city have the facilities to accommodate your test market needs? At what costs? All of these factors must be considered before selecting the test city. Fortunately, because it is desirable to have test markets conducted in a city because it brings in additional revenues, city governments as well as the media typically provide a great deal of information about their city to prospective test marketers.

McDonald's has used Atlanta and Savannah as test market cities representing the Southeastern United States.

A good example of the application of these three criteria is McDonald's test market of its all-you-can-eat breakfast bar. The test was conducted in Atlanta and Savannah, Georgia, which are representative Southeastern cities where McDonald's has control over its outlets and where the promotional media are specific to those markets. The buffet was found to increase weekend family breakfast sales.[22]

Pros and Cons of Test Marketing

Test markets are considered by some to be the "ultimate" way to test a new product.

The advantages of test marketing are straightforward. Testing product acceptability and marketing mix variables in a field setting provides the best information possible to the decision maker prior to actually going into full-scale marketing of the product. Because of this, Philip Kotler has referred to test markets as the "ultimate" way to test a new product.[23] Test marketing allows for the most accurate method of forecasting future sales, and it allows firms the opportunity to pretest marketing mix variables.

There are, however, several negatives to test marketing. First, test markets do not yield infallible results. There have been many instances in which test market results have led to decisions that proved wrong in the marketplace. No doubt, there have probably been many "would-be successful" products withheld from the marketplace due to poor performances in test markets. Much of this problem, however, is not due to anything inherent in test marketing; rather, it is a reflection of the complexity and changeability of consumer behavior. Accurately forecasting consumer behavior is a formidable task. Also, competitors intentionally try to sabotage test markets. Firms will often flood a test market with sales promotions if they know a competitor is test marketing a product. When PepsiCo tested Mountain Dew Sport drink in Minneapolis in 1990, Quaker Oats Company's Gatorade counterattacked with a deluge of coupons and ads. Mountain Dew Sport was yanked from the market although Pepsi says Gatorade had nothing to do with the decision.[24] These activities make it even more difficult to forecast the normal market's response to a product.

Test markets are costly and subject to competitive sabotage.

Another problem with test markets is their cost. Estimates are that the costs exceed several hundred thousand dollars even for limited test markets. Test markets involving several test cities and various forms of promotion can easily reach six figures. Finally, test markets bring about exposure of the product to the competition. Competitors get the opportunity to examine product prototypes and to see the planned marketing strategy for the new product via the test market. If a company spends too much time testing a product, it runs the risk of allowing enough time for a competitor to bring out a similar product and to gain the advantage of being first in the market. In spite of these problems, the value of the information from test marketing makes test marketing a worthwhile endeavor. Finally, as we see in Marketing Research Insight 5.2, ethical issues arise in terms of how test markets are selected as well as how test market results are reported.

MARKETING RESEARCH INSIGHT 5.2

Ethical Issues in Test Marketing

Yes, ethical issues arise as company executives make test market decisions. Some companies conduct test markets and publicize the results in the trade press. There is nothing unethical about this practice. However, sometimes it's the information that is not *reported that causes an ethical problem. Knowing that their test market results will get publicized, some companies have intentionally selected test markets where their distribution and reputation were particularly strong. The test market results, then, are skewed from the outset to make the company's "new product" sound favorable.*

Fortunately, the problem of incomplete reporting (whether of a test market or some other marketing practice) has been addressed by The Wall Street Journal. *In an effort to provide complete information regarding their surveys, the* Journal *has begun publishing a boxed insert containing the details of how their sample was drawn and other facts allowing readers to understand their methodology. Some readers will regard this information as superfluous, but it does allow a basis for judging the quality and meaning of the survey results. Also, the Public Affairs Council of the Advertising Research Foundation (ARF) has published "Guidelines for the Public Use of Market and Opinion Research." This document covers the origin, design, execution, and candor of the research being reported.*

Source: *Patrick E. Murphy and Gene R. Laczniak, "Emerging Ethical Issues Facing Marketing Researchers,"* Marketing Research *(June 1992), 6.*

SUMMARY

Research design refers to a set of advance decisions made to develop the master plan to be used in the conduct of the research project. There are generally thought to be three sets of such designs: exploratory, descriptive, and causal. Each one of these designs has its own inherent approaches. The significance of studying research design is that, by matching the research problem with the appropriate research design, a host of research decisions may be predetermined.

Selecting the appropriate research design depends, to a large extent, on how much information is already known about the research issue. If very little is known, exploratory research is appropriate. Exploratory research is unstructured and informal research that is undertaken to gain background information; it is helpful for more clearly defining the research problem. Reviewing existing literature, surveying individuals knowledgeable in the area to be investigated, and relying on former "like" case situations are methods of conducting exploratory research. If concepts, terms, and so on are already known and the research objective is to describe and measure phenomena, then descriptive research is appropriate. Descriptive research measures marketing phenomena and answers the questions of who, what, where, when, and how. Descriptive studies may be conducted at one point in time (cross-sectional) or several measurements may be made on the same sample at different points in time (longitudinal). Traditional panels and omnibus panels are used in longitudinal studies.

If we know quite a bit about our research issue but wish to know causal relationships of the type "If *x*, then *y*," causal research is appropriate. Causal relationships may be discovered through experiments. Experiments allow us to determine the effects of a variable, known as an independent variable, on another variable, known as a dependent variable. Experimental designs are necessary to ensure that the effect we observe in our dependent variable is due, in fact, to our independent variable and not to other variables known as extraneous variables. The validity of experiments may be assessed by internal validity and external validity.

Laboratory experiments are particularly useful for achieving internal validity while field experiments are better suited for achieving external validity. Test marketing is a form of field experimentation. Test market cities are selected on the basis of their representativeness, isolation, and the degree to which market variables such as distribution and promotion may be controlled.

Various types of test markets exist (standard, controlled, electronic, simulated, consumer, industrial, and lead country), and although test markets garner much useful information, they are expensive and not infallible.

View: "Milk Bone Dog Biscuits II"

KEY TERMS

Research design (p. 110)
Exploratory research (p. 111)
Hypotheses (p. 112)
Secondary data analysis (p. 113)
Experience surveys (p. 113)
Case analysis (p. 113)
Focus groups (p. 114)
Projective techniques (p. 114)
Descriptive research (p. 114)
Cross-sectional studies (p. 115)
Sample surveys (p. 115)
Longitudinal studies (p. 115)
Panel (p. 115)
Traditional panels (p. 118)
Omnibus panels (p. 118)
Brand switching studies (p. 118)
Market tracking studies (p.119)
Causality (p. 119)
Experiment (p. 120)
Independent variables (p. 120)
Dependent variables (p. 121)
Extraneous variables (p. 121)
Experimental design (p. 121)
Pretest (p. 122)
Posttest (p. 122)
"True" experimental design (p. 122)
After-only design (p. 122)
Quasi-experimental designs (p. 122)
One-group, before–after design (p. 123)
Control group (p. 123)
Experimental group (p. 123)
Before–after with control group (p. 123)
After-only with control group (p. 124)
Internal validity (p. 125)
External validity (p. 126)
Laboratory experiments (p. 127)
Field experiments (p. 128)
Test marketing (p. 128)
Test market cities (p. 128)
Standard test market (p. 129)
Controlled test markets (p. 129)
Electronic test markets (p. 129)
Simulated test markets (p. 129)
Consumer test markets (p. 130)
Industrial test markets (p. 130)
Lead country test market (p. 131)

REVIEW QUESTIONS/APPLICATIONS

1. How would you "match" research designs with various research objectives?
2. Give some examples illustrating the uses of exploratory research.
3. What type of research design answers the questions of who, what, where, when, and how?
4. What are the differences between longitudinal studies and cross-sectional studies?
5. In what situation would a traditional panel be more suitable than an omnibus panel? In what situation would an omnibus panel be more suitable than a traditional panel?
6. Explain why studies of the "if–then" variety are considered to be "causal" studies.
7. What is the objective of good experimental design? Explain why certain designs are given the name "quasi-experimental" design.
8. Explain the two types of validity in experimentation and also explain why different types of experiments are better suited for addressing one type of validity versus another.
9. Distinguish among the various types of test marketing.
10. Think of a past job that you have held. List three areas in which you, or some other person in the organization, could have benefited from having information generated by research. What would be the most appropriate research design for each of the three areas of research you have listed?
11. At the beginning of the chapter we introduced you to Debbie Tucker's three client problems. We told you that Ms. Tucker had chosen a research design by the time she commuted to her home for the weekend. From the three types of research designs, match the appropriate design for each one of Ms. Tucker's clients. Explain your choice of design.
12. Design an experiment. Select an independent variable and a dependent variable. What are some possible extraneous variables that may cause problems? Explain how you would control for the effects these variables may have on your dependent variable. Is your experiment a valid experiment?
13. The Maximum Company has invented an extra-strength, instant coffee brand to be called "Max-Caff," and positioned to be stronger tasting than any competing brands. Design a taste test experiment that compares Max-Caff to the two leading instant coffee brands to determine which brand consumers consider to taste the strongest. Identify and diagram your experiment. Indicate how the experiment is to be conducted, and assess the internal and external validity of your experiment.
14. Coca-Cola markets PowerAde as a sports drink that competes with Gatorade. Competition for sports drinks is fierce where they are sold in the coolers of convenience stores. Coca-Cola is thinking about using a special holder that fits in a standard cooler, but moves PowerAde to eye level and makes it more conspicuous than Gatorade. Design an experiment that determines whether the special holder increases the sales of PowerAde in convenience stores. Identify and diagram your experiment. Indicate how the experiment is to be conducted and assess the internal and external validity of your experiment.
15. SplitScreen is a marketing research company that tests television advertisements. SplitScreen has an agreement with a cable television company in a medium-sized city in Iowa. The cable company can send up to four different television ads simultaneously to different households. SplitScreen also has agreements with the

three largest grocery store chains who will provide scanner data to SplitScreen. About 25 percent of the residents have SplitScreen scan cards that are scanned when items are bought at the grocery store and that allow SplitScreen to identify who bought which grocery products. For allowing SplitScreen access to their television hook-ups and their grocery purchases information, residents receive bonus points that can be used to buy products in a special points catalog. Identify and diagram the true experimental designs possible using the SplitScreen system. Assess the internal and external validity of SplitScreen's system.

CASE 5.1

Kmart

Kmart at one time led the retail industry, but its market share eroded steadily in the late 1980s and early 1990s due to aggressive marketing by Sears, Wal-Mart, and Target. In fact, in mid-1996, Kmart suffered its 13th consecutive quarter of losses or less-than-previous-year earnings. However, Kmart management resolved to turn the business around rather than to bury their heads in the sand and wait for its competitors to go away. Kmart executives conceived of a number of strategies that might bring customers back to Kmart. Among these were: (1) a new store layout designed for more convenient shopping, (2) deep discounts on high-turning items such as snacks, beverages, and paper goods, and (3) dividing the business into the three categories of consumables such as snacks, kids' world of games and toys, and home fashion items. If Kmart goes ahead with this approach, it will require approximately $400,000 to remodel each store. About 450 conversions could be made per year, and it will take approximately three years for all Kmart stores to be remodeled.

As can be seen, this strategy will be costly, and it will take some time for the entire Kmart system to convert over to the new approach. Kmart executives need information to help them decide on the appropriateness of this strategy.[25]

1. State what research design or designs you would recommend and why. Would you consider using more than one type of research design? Propose these designs and also speculate on what may be learned from carrying out this research.
2. How does the information you speculate will be gained impact the need for even additional research?

CASE 5.2

Sheehan Brothers Vending Services

The vending machine business has witnessed tremendous technological advances recently. Specifically, where traditional vending machines dispensed candy, snacks, and cold or hot drinks, it is now possible for vending machines to do some amazing things. For example, today's vending machines can dispense hot french fries, hamburgers, and pizza by heating them from a frozen state to piping hot in a few minutes. Up to 30 flavors of ice cream can be stored in a single vending machine. Coffee machines have evolved to a level capable of grinding coffee beans in sight of the consumer and offering selections such as cappuccino or café mocha. Soda dispensers have grown into machines that offer bottled water, juices, and a larger variety of canned beverages.

"Vendaterias" have sprung up in office buildings, schools, and hospitals. With the wide variety of choices available and the ability to serve hot as well as cold foods, vending machines are attractive alternatives to manual-serve cafeterias because they are acceptable to consumers and they are much more cost effective.

Sheehan Brothers of Springfield, Ohio, operates 1,500 vending machines in 12 counties in southwest Ohio. The company experiments regularly with various prepared foods—such as barbecue roast beef sandwiches, chicken cordon bleu, or vegetable trays—which account for about 30 percent of its sales. All foods are prepared daily in Sheehan Brothers' commissary, and every vending machine is restocked daily. A problem is that unless the items in the vending machine are changed, patrons think they are seeing the same items they saw in the vending machine yesterday—this is not true, but it is their perception. So Sheehan Brothers must rotate its 100 different food items. This is an industry problem. As one vending company owner puts it, "When patrons see food in a cafeteria, they know that it is freshly prepared, but when they see it in a machine, they may not buy it solely because they don't know when it was put there." Industry statistics indicate that as much as one-third of all fresh food items stocked in vending machines is thrown out in the restocking process.[26]

1. Should Sheehan Brothers consider using a test market approach for its freshly prepared foods that could be added to its standard line?
2. If so, what type of test market should be considered and why?
3. What specific marketing mix variables can be tested with a test market using products purchased in vending machines?

CHAPTER 6

Secondary Data Sources

LEARNING OBJECTIVES

- *To learn how to distinguish between secondary and primary data*
- *To find out some of the uses marketers make of secondary data*
- *To understand the advantages and disadvantages of secondary data*
- *To acquire the ability to evaluate secondary data sources*
- *To learn how to find secondary data using indices, directories, and computerized databases*

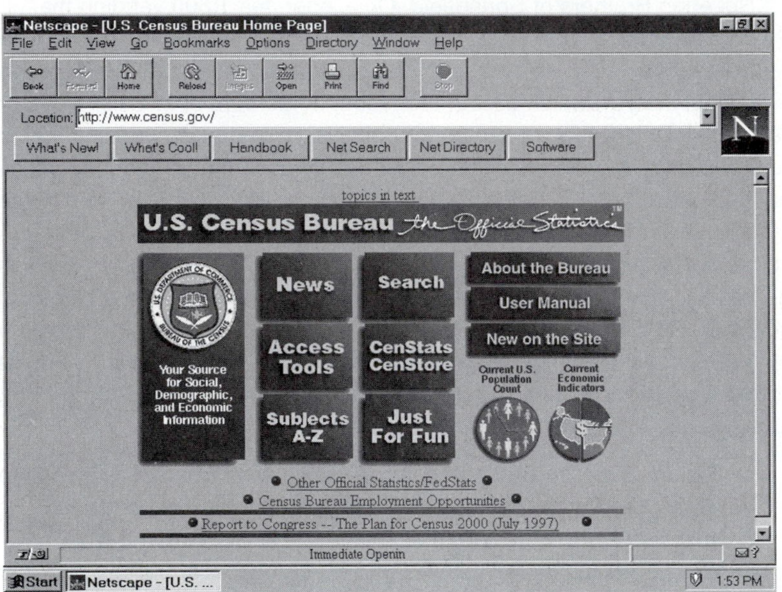

PRACTITIONER VIEWPOINT

Marketing researchers can find a wealth of data that is already gathered, compiled, and perhaps even analyzed, but only if they know where to look. In this "information age," technology is rapidly changing the volume, structure, and availability of these secondary sources. A single outline database can now provide access to thousands of sources, such as newspapers, trade journals, news releases, industry newsletters, and much more. And, with the advent of the global economy, gaining access to information from around the world is crucial; online technology makes this possible.

— Paul Owen, Vice President of Marketing
Predicasts, a Division of Ziff Communications Company

Current Census Data at the Click of a Mouse!

The U.S. government provides a wealth of information in the form of census data. Much of this information is very useful for making marketing decisions, and marketing researchers are very much aware of the value of this information. To the typical user, however, knowing what information is available, knowing where to find it and how to access it has always been a problem. Not to worry! Today, census information is available 24 hours a day at your fingertips. The U.S. Census Bureau maintains an excellent homepage on the Internet. The Internet screen (left) shows this homepage; the homepage address is: http://www.census.gov/. Try accessing this page to find the following information:

- ✔ What is the projected U.S. population right now?
- ✔ How many people live in your state?
- ✔ What is the population of the zip code in which you reside?
- ✔ How many businesses are in your state, and what is the payroll?
- ✔ What were the latest levels of retail sales? How did they change from the previous period?

1. Establish the need for marketing research
2. Define the problem
3. Establish research objectives
4. Determine research design
5. Identify information types and sources
6. Determine methods of accessing data
7. Design data collection forms
8. Determine sample plan and size
9. Collect data
10. Analyze data
11. Prepare and present the final research report

The U.S. Census Bureau homepage example illustrates how today's technology makes current secondary information readily available to decision makers. You should access this homepage and explore the vast amount of information available to you via the Internet. Imagine how this information would help if you were trying to make marketing decisions. You would be able to quickly, and inexpensively, make many marketing decisions by accessing such information even though it was gathered by someone else for some other purpose. In this chapter, we introduce you to the advantages and disadvantages of secondary data, how to evaluate secondary data, and where you can find different types of secondary data. We include a discussion of databases available to you, such as those you can access via the U.S. Census Bureau's homepage. We also provide you with some tips on conducting your own search for secondary information.

SOURCES OF SECONDARY DATA

As presented in chapter 3, data needed for marketing management decisions can be grouped into two types: primary and secondary. **Primary data** refers to information that is developed or gathered by the researcher specifically for the research project at hand. **Secondary data** has previously been gathered by someone other than the researcher and/or for some other purpose than the research project at hand. One example of secondary data is information collected by U.S. customs officials. These officials turn over their documents

Primary data refers to information that is developed or gathered by the researcher specifically for the research project at hand. Secondary data has previously been gathered by someone other than the researcher and/or for some other purpose than the research project at hand.

every month to the U.S. Bureau of the Census, which publishes foreign trade statistics. Information on imports and exports of goods, including data on country of origin/destination, value, quantities, and mode of transportation is available to any marketer needing foreign trade statistics.

There has been an explosion of published data in the past decade.

Since Gutenberg printed the Bible in the middle of the fifteenth century, we have seen a staggering rate of growth in the amount of published information, particularly in this century. In 1986, more than 718,000 books from 20,000 publishers were in print.[1] In 1991, there were over one million books in print from over 40,000 publishers. By 1996, there were 1,265,891 titles in print from over 49,000 publishers.[2] When one considers there were only 85,000 titles in print from 357 publishers in 1948, the growth rate has been phenomenal.[3] The number of journals published has also increased very rapidly, doubling every 15 years for the last 150 years.[4]

With so much secondary information available, every marketing researcher must learn to properly manage this data. In fact, secondary data is more important to the marketing researcher today than ever before because so much of it is available, and it can be extremely useful (see Marketing Research Insight 6.1, pages 143–144). However, the stock of information available can be overwhelming. Marketing researchers must learn to properly handle secondary data. They must know the classifications of secondary data, its advantages and disadvantages, and they must know how to evaluate the information available to them.

Internal data refers to data that has been collected within the firm. Such data includes sales records, purchase requisitions, and invoices.

Secondary data may be broadly classified as either internal or external. **Internal data** refers to data that has been collected within the firm. Such data includes sales records, purchase requisitions, and invoices. Obviously, a good marketing researcher always determines what internal information is already available. You may recall from chapter 1 that we referred to internal data analysis as being part of the internal reports system of a firm's Marketing Information System (MIS). Today, a major source of internal data is databases that contain information on customers, sales, suppliers, and any other facet of business a firm may wish to track. **Database marketing** is the term used to refer to uses of these internal databases to target marketing programs directly to consumers. The use of these databases has grown so dramatically that we have added a section on them in which we discuss both internal and external databases.

External data is obtained from outside the firm. We classify external data into three sources: published, syndicated, and databases.

External data is data obtained from outside the firm. We classify external data into three sources: published, syndicated, and databases. **Published sources** are those that are available from either libraries or other entities such as trade associations. This data is free or obtained for a nominal fee (because the information is available on request). Examples of published data sources include the *Censuses of Wholesale Trade, Retail Trade, Service Industries*, and the *Census of Governments*, which are published by the U.S. government and are provided free to the public. There are also many publications for which there is a cost but that are normally available in libraries. Examples include *Sales & Marketing Management's Survey of Buying Power* and Dun and Bradstreet's *Million Dollar Directory*. **Syndicated sources** are highly specialized and are not available in libraries for the general public. The suppliers syndicate (sell) the information to multiple subscribers, thus making the costs more reasonable to any one subscriber. Examples include National Family Opinion's panel data, Nielsen's television viewing data, and Arbitron's radio listenership studies.

There are so many sources of syndicated data that we have devoted all of chapter 7 to this subject. As previously noted, with this edition, we are adding a third form of external information, **database** sources. Databases are explained more fully in the following section.

Databases

A **database** refers to a collection of interrelated data that may be accessed to meet certain information requirements.[5] Although you can have a noncomputerized database, the majority of databases are computerized because they contain large amounts of information and their use is facilitated by computers' abilities to edit, sort, and analyze the mass of information. Databases have grown so dramatically that it is confusing to understand the different types.

A database refers to a collection of interrelated data that may be accessed to meet certain information requirements.

First, as we previously noted, there are **internal databases.** These are databases consisting of information gathered by a company, typically about its customers. Companies gather information about you when you inquire about a product or service, make a purchase, or have a product serviced. Think about the information you may have provided to marketing firms: your name, address, telephone number, fax number, e-mail address, credit card number, your banking institution and account number, and so on. Coupled with a knowledge of what products you have purchased in the past and with other information provided by government and other commercial sources, many companies know quite a bit about you. Although there are issues here regarding privacy rights of consumers, companies do use their internal databases for purposes of direct marketing and to strengthen relationships with customers.

Internal databases consist of information gathered by a company, typically about its customers.

External databases are simply databases supplied by organizations outside the firm. They may be used as sources for secondary data. Typically, these databases are available from commercial sources who provide subscribers access for a fee. These databases have grown dramatically in recent years as shown in Figure 6.1 on page 142. They are becoming more important facilitators of secondary data searches. We place them in a third category of secondary data because, as a group, they do not fit in either of our categories (published or syndicated) of external data. However, we could consider these published sources of external data because more libraries have them available at a nominal fee or no charge but most are available by subscription.

External databases are simply databases supplied by organizations outside the firm.

As we noted previously, most of these databases are computerized. A **computerized database** is a collection of data records in any electronic medium. Presently, the majority of these databases is accessed either "online"—a direct electronic link to the database supplier or through CD-ROM—a disk containing the data record, which is accessed by the user's CD-ROM reader. A few databases, such as the *1990 Census of Population and Housing*, are available on computer tape as well as CD-ROM. There are four types of databases: bibliographic, numeric, directory, and full-text, which are categorized according to the nature of the data records contained in the database.[6] Databases containing citations to journal articles, newspapers, government documents, and so on are **bibliographic databases.** Examples include the *Business Index*, an index to over 800 business, management, and trade journals, and the *General Academic*

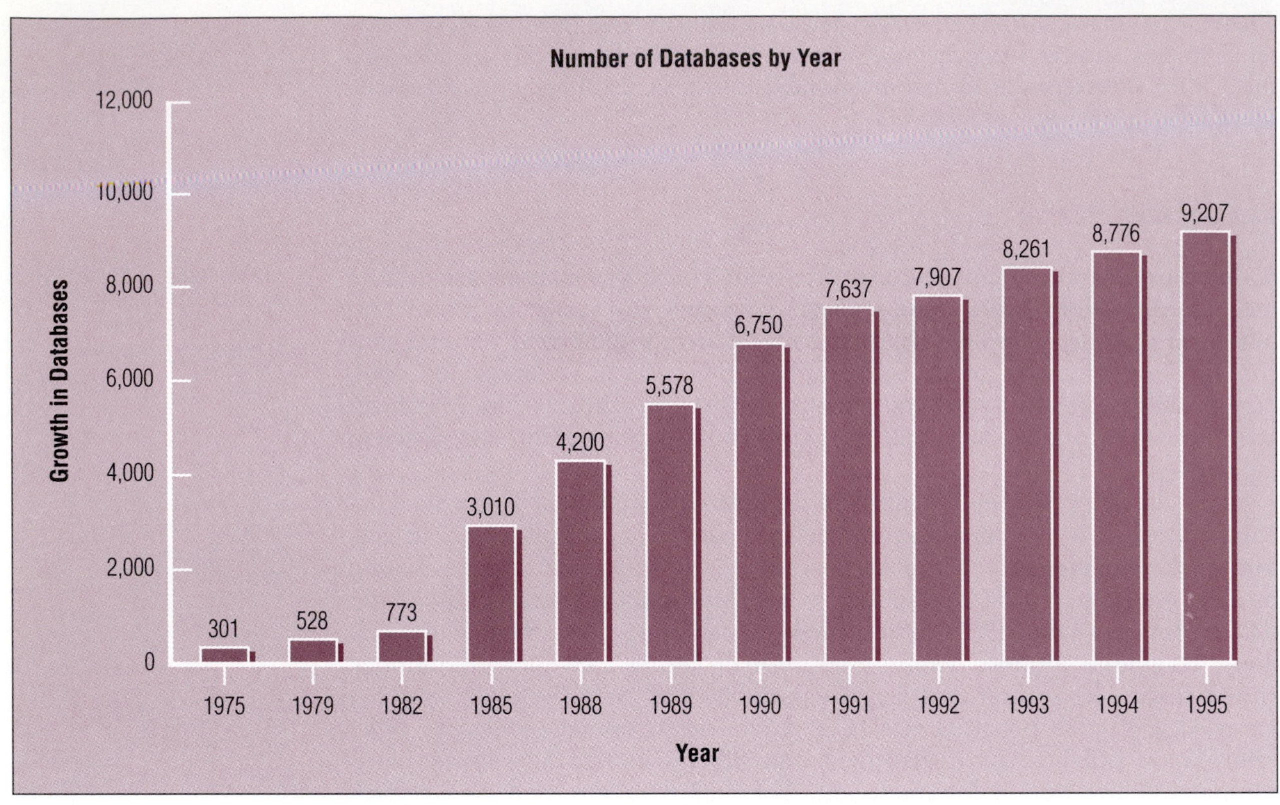

Figure 6.1

The Dramatic Growth of Databases as Sources of External, Secondary Information[7]

Source: Gale Research, *Gale Directory of Databases,* by permission.

Index, an index to over 960 journals. The *Social Science Citation Index,* known as a citation bibliographic database, actually indexes the bibliographies of articles allowing the user to learn which articles "cited" certain sources.

Computerized databases may be bibliographic, numeric, directory, or full-text.

Databases containing numerical data—such as baseball game attendance records or sales for a given industry over some time period—are referred to as **numeric databases.** Examples include the *1990 Census of Population and Housing, National Trade Data Bank,* and *Regional Economic Information System (REIS).* **Directory databases** are those that list information about certain organizations, individuals, government entities, and so on. Examples include *Gale Associations,* which lists more than 80,000 nonprofit membership associations in the United States, and *Phone Disc,* which lists addresses and phone numbers for residences and businesses in the United States. **Full-text databases** offer the complete text of articles appearing in selected publications. The *Disclosure* database, for example, contains detailed reports about major public U.S. corporations. Many of these databases are available through the Internet. Marketing Research Insight 6.1 explains the types of secondary information available on the Internet. Table 6.1 on pages 151–154 contains a listing of some of the more popular databases.

MARKETING RESEARCH INSIGHT 6.1

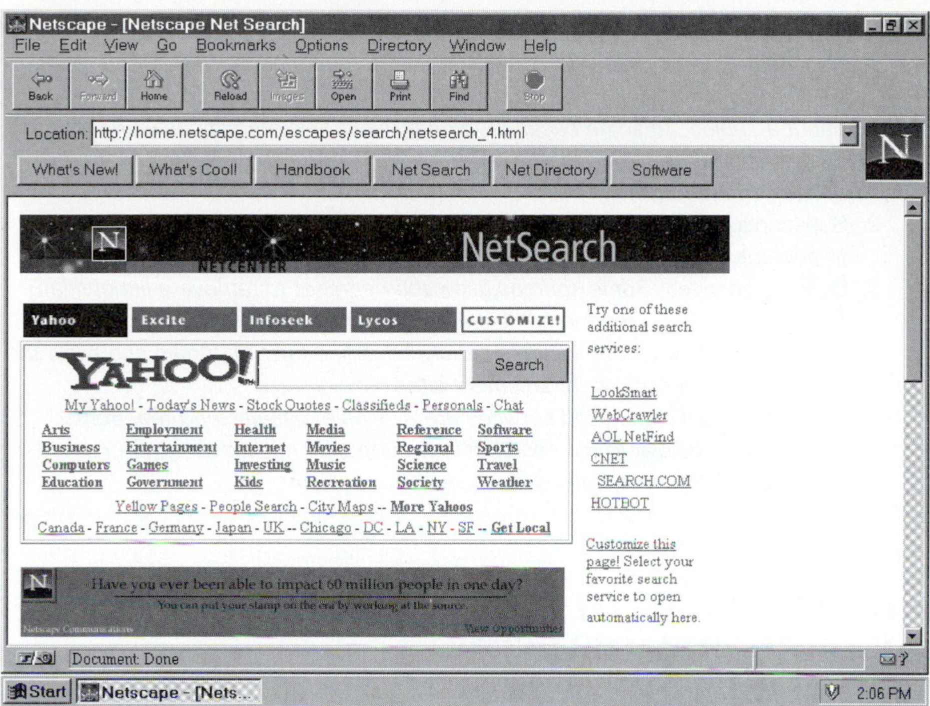

The Internet: A Growing Source of Secondary Data

*The **Internet** is a huge international computer network linking other computer networks from all parts of the world together. The Internet has been around since the 1980s, but until about 1994 it was the well-kept secret of academic, industrial, and government researchers. The Internet is really just the infrastructure (the machinery, computers, lines, and equipment) that supports what has become known as the **World Wide Web** (aka **"The Web"** or the **"WWW"**), which consists of all the linkages of sites containing information and resources. The Web enables anyone who has a personal computer, a modem, an Internet access provider, and the necessary software to access thousands of data sources known as **"Web sites."** (The title page, or first page of a Web site is called a **"homepage."**) It also allows individuals, groups, or companies to create Web sites using a standard programming format. Because there are no restrictions or standards for the content of what is posted on the Internet, the quality of databases varies widely. The software programs that allow access to the WWW are known as **"browsers."** Browsers such as Netscape and Microsoft Explorer are used to move you around the Web. These browsers can call up homepages by their **uniform resource locator addresses** (URL; for example, http://www.dowjones.com) or by linking to **search engines** such as Yahoo (shown in the screen above), Alta Vista, Lycos, and so forth, which allow you to **"surf"** Web sites by subjects or keywords.*

Knowing which databases are reliable requires some amount of expertise, which can be gained by actual experience, reading reviews in business and online journals, or relying on companies that have established reputations such as Reuters, Dow Jones, or Dun and Bradstreet.

Not every source is actually available on the Internet, but most publishers use the Internet to advertise their products. Thus, a searcher may find the following kinds of resources:

1. Free full-text information *such as company annual reports, news, stock quotes, travel information, lists of other Internet sites, and list of articles or books about a subject. In some cases, "E-zines" (electronic magazines/journals) are available in full text, and some printed journals are also published for free access on the Internet.*
2. Subscriptions to Internet services. *Some sources will provide information only to searchers who pay fees.*
3. Delivery services. *Some sources allow the searcher to retrieve a list of titles but will deliver for a fee the full-text article via mail, fax, or modem.*
4. Order information. *Many vendors simply advertise their materials and allow the searcher to order online for shipment later.*
5. Alert services. *Customized services are available, usually for a fee, from vendors who deliver to the searcher's desktop only notices of news or publications that have been defined by the searcher.*

ADVANTAGES/DISADVANTAGES OF SECONDARY DATA

There are four main advantages gained from using secondary data. It may be obtained quickly, it is inexpensive, it is available, and it may be used to enhance primary data collection.

There are four main advantages of using secondary data. First, it can be obtained quickly, in contrast to collecting primary data, which may take several months from beginning to end. Second, it is cheap when compared to collecting primary data. Third, it is usually available. And fourth, it enhances existing primary data. What do we mean by enhancing primary data? Simply because researchers use secondary data does not mean that they will not collect primary data. In fact, in almost every case, the researcher's task of primary data collection is aided by first collecting secondary data. A secondary data search can *familiarize the researcher with the industry*, including its sales and profit trends, major competitors, and the significant issues facing the industry.[8] A secondary data search can *identify concepts, data, and terminology* that may be useful in conducting primary research. A bank's management, for example, hired a marketing research firm and, together, management and the research team decided to conduct a survey measuring the bank's image among its customers. A check of the secondary information available on the measurement of bank image identified the components of bank image for the study. Also, the research team, after reviewing secondary information, determined there were three sets of bank customers: retail customers, commercial accounts, and other correspondent banks. When the researchers mentioned this to bank management, the original objectives of the research were changed in order to measure the bank's image among all three customer groups.

Some of the problems associated with secondary data include mismatch of the units of measurement, differing definitions used to classify the data, the recency of the secondary data, and the lack of information needed to assess the credibility of the data reported.

Although the advantages of secondary data almost always justify a search of this information, there are caveats associated with secondary data. Some of the problems associated with secondary data include mismatch of the units of measurement, differing definitions used to classify the data, the recency of the secondary data, and the lack of information needed to assess the credibility of the data reported. These problems exist because secondary data was not collected specifically to address the researcher's problem at hand; it was collected for some other purpose. Consequently, the researcher must determine the extent of these problems before using the secondary data. This is done by evaluating the secondary data. We discuss the first three disadvantages in the following paragraphs. Evaluation of secondary data is discussed in the next section.

Measurement units in secondary data may not match the researcher's needs.

Sometimes, secondary data are reported in *measurement units that do not match the measurement unit needed by the researcher.* In analyzing markets, for example, marketing researchers are typically interested in income levels. Available studies of income may measure income in several ways: total income, income after taxes, household income, and per capita income. Or, consider a research project that needs to categorize businesses by size in terms of square footage. Secondary data sources, however, classify businesses in terms of size according to sales volume, number of employees, profit level, and so on. Much information in the United States is recorded in American units of measurement (feet, pounds, etc.), yet most of the rest of the world uses metric units (meter, kilograms, etc.) The United States is slowly becoming metric.[9] As illustrated in Marketing Research Insight 6.2 (page 146), the issue of having the proper units of measure is a hotly debated topic as the census for the year 2000 approaches. However, the point is, the researcher must determine which if any of these measurement units is appropriate for his or her specific use.

Visit the Market Statistics homepage, http://www.marketstats.com

The *class definitions of the reported data may not be useable* to a researcher. Secondary data is often reported by breaking a variable into different classes and reporting the frequency of occurrence in each class. For example, the *Survey of Buying Power* reports the variable effective buying income (EBI) in three classes (see Table 6.2). The first class reports the percentage of households having an EBI between $20,000 and $34,999, and the final class reports the percent of households having an EBI of $50,000 and over. For most applications, these classifications are most applicable. However, it is doubtful that Beneteau, Inc., a manufacturer of sailing yachts in South Carolina, could use these income classifications to help them target potential customer markets. Because Beneteau's average customer is thought to have an EBI in excess of $75,000, Beneteau could not use the data reported because of the way the EBI classes were defined. What does the researcher do? Typically, if you keep looking you can find what you need. For example, Beneteau can obtain secondary data that would solve their problem by purchasing *Demographics USA* from *Market Statistics*™, the producers of the *Survey of Buying Power.* They would find that *Demographics USA* provides information on EBI up through categories of $150,000 or more.[10]

Secondary data may be too out of date for a researcher to use.

Sometimes, a marketing researcher will find information reported with the desired unit of measurement and the proper classifications, yet, *the data is "out of date."* Some secondary data is published only once. However, even for secondary data that is published at regular intervals, the time that passed since the last publication can be a problem when applying the data to a current problem. Ultimately, *the researcher must make the decision as to whether or not to use the data.* Consider one of the most important secondary data sources—the *Census of the Population.* The census is taken every 10 years, yet it is so complex that its results typically are not totally available to the public for four years after the census year! Already some of the information is dated. Fortunately, for data that is thought to be very useful for marketers, commercial firms have evolved to help resolve this problem. These firms, such as *Sales & Marketing Management,* col-

MARKETING RESEARCH INSIGHT 6.2

Census 2000: Debates over Units of Measurement

As the census year 2000 rapidly approaches, the government's system of racial and ethnic classifications is under attack. Critics claim the present system is "confusing . . . unscientific . . . and unfair." Public hearings on the matter have been held for several years. Why all the fuss? It is important because federal dollars, for some programs, are allocated based on racial compositions of the population and because ethnic identities are symbols of pride and power. The Office of Management and Budget (OMB) is responsible for defining the racial and ethnic categories used by federal, state, and local governments. OMB officials claim "there are no clear, unambiguous, objective, agreed-upon definitions of the terms 'race' and 'ethnicity.' "

Here are some of the problems related to trying to develop clear units of measurement for race and ethnicity discovered during the 1990 census:

- *When people were asked to write down their own race or ethnic heritage, rather than check a box, they volunteered a bewildering jumble of responses: more than 300 ways to describe race, 600 separate nationalities, and 600 Native American tribes. Hispanics listed 70 different places of origin.*
- *The "white" category included Middle Easterners with skin tones darker than many African Americans listed by the census as "black."*
- *Hispanics overlapped four different groups: whites (from Spain or Portugal); Native Americans (from Mexico); Asian Americans (from the Phillippines), and blacks (from Puerto Rico).*

When it comes to race and ethnicity, we have a complicated country. The government has changed the units of measurement for race and ethnicity in almost every census. Chances are good that they will be different, once again, for Census 2000.

Source: *Adapted from Knight-Ridder, October 13, 1996.*

lect information annually at the local level, and this information, coupled with their own growth rate forecasts, are used to generate secondary data on a more current basis. Therefore, *Sales & Marketing Management's Survey of Buying Power*, containing a large quantity of secondary data, is available each year.

Marketers dealing with international markets are not so fortunate. Think about the difficulties of taking a census in China. The country has limited resources in terms of roads and methods of communication. There are few technological means of taking the census. As a result, China is *thought* to have about 1.2 billion people. The most recent population census was taken in China in 1982. Prior to that, a census had not been taken for 29 years. The first census of industry was taken in 1986.[11]

EVALUATING SECONDARY DATA

By now you should have learned that not everything you read is true. Every time you receive information, you must evaluate that information before you use it as a basis for decision making. To determine the reliability of secondary data, marketing researchers must evaluate it. This is done by answering the following five questions:

Marketers should always evaluate secondary information before using it.

- What was the purpose of the study?
- Who collected the information?
- What information was collected?
- How was the information obtained?
- How consistent is the information with other information?[12]

A discussion of each question follows.

What Was the Purpose of the Study?

Studies are sometimes conducted in order to "prove" some position or advance the special interest of those conducting the study.

Studies are conducted for a purpose. Unfortunately, studies are sometimes conducted in order to "prove" some position or advance the special interest of those conducting the study. Many years ago, chambers of commerce were known for publishing data that exaggerated the size and growth rates of their communities. They did this to "prove" that their communities were a good choice for new business locations. However, after a few years, they learned that few people trusted chamber data and today chambers of commerce publish reliable and valid data. But the lesson is that you must be very careful to determine whether the entity publishing the data acted in a fair and unbiased manner. Consider the example of disposable diapers. The disposable diaper industry was created in the 1960s. But environmental concerns became alarming, and during the late 1980s the number of customers buying old-fashioned cloth diapers doubled. Also, more than a dozen state legislatures were considering various bans, taxes, and even warning labels on disposable diapers. Then research studies were produced on the environmental effects of disposable versus cloth diapers. Soon after several of these studies were made available to legislators, the movement against disposables was dead. Who conducted the studies? Proctor & Gamble, owning the lion's share of the market for disposable diapers, commissioned the consulting firm of Arthur D. Little, Inc. to conduct a study of disposable versus cloth diapers. The study found that disposable diapers were no more harmful to the environment than reusable cotton diapers. A second study conducted by Franklin Associates also produced research showing disposables were not any more harm-

Discovering the sponsor of secondary information may reveal hidden agendas.

ful than cloth diapers. Who sponsored this study? The American Paper Institute, an organization with major interests in disposable diapers. But wait, before you are so critical of the disposable diaper folks, let's consider some other "scientific" studies. In 1988, a study was published that showed disposable diapers as being "garbage" and contributing to massive build-ups of waste that was all but impervious to deterioration. Who sponsored this study? The cloth diaper industry! Another study published in 1991 found cloth diapers to be environmentally superior to disposable diapers. Guess who sponsored this study?[13]

Who Collected the Information?

Evaluating the competence of the organization that gathered secondary data is important in evaluating the validity of the information.

Even when you are convinced that there is no bias in the purpose of the study, you should question the competence of the organization that collected the information. Why? Simply because organizations differ in terms of the resources they command and their quality control. But how do you determine the competency of the organization that collected the data? There are several things that you can do. First, ask others who have more experience in a given industry. Typically, creditable organizations are well known in those industries for which they conduct studies. Second, examine the report itself. Competent firms will almost always provide carefully written and detailed explanations of the procedures and methods used in collecting the information contained in the report. Third, contact previous clients of the firm. Have they been satisfied with the quality of the work performed by the organization?

What Information Was Collected?

Be careful of titles; studies do not always measure what their titles imply. Know exactly what is being measured in a study, and know how it was measured.

There are many studies available on topics such as economic impact, market potential, feasibility, and the like. But what exactly was measured in these studies that constitutes impact, potential, or feasibility? There are many examples of studies that claim to provide information on a specific subject but, in fact, measure something quite different. Consider a study conducted by a transit authority on the number of riders on their bus line. On examination of the methodology used in the study, the number of *riders* was not counted at all. Rather, the number of *fares* was counted. A single rider may pay several fares per day. Is this distinction important? It may be or it may not be; that depends on how the study's user intends to use the information. The important point here is that the user should discover exactly what information was collected!

How Was the Information Obtained?

Understanding the methods used to collect secondary data can be useful in evaluating the information.

You should be aware of the methods used to obtain information reported in secondary sources. What was the sample? How large was the sample? What was the response rate? Was the information validated? As you will learn throughout this book, there are many alternative ways of collecting primary data and each may have an impact on the information collected. Remember that, even though you are evaluating *secondary* data, it was gathered as *primary* data by some organization. Therefore, the alternative ways of gathering the data had an impact on the nature and quality of the data. It is not always easy to find out how the secondary data was gathered. However, as noted earlier, most reputable organizations who provide secondary data also provide information on their data collection methods. If this information is not readily available and your use of the secondary data is very important to your research project, you should make the extra effort to find out how the information was obtained.

How Consistent Is the Information with Other Information?

In some cases, the same secondary data is reported by multiple, independent organizations, which provides an excellent way to evaluate secondary data sources. Ideally, if two or more independent organizations report the same data, you can have greater confidence in the validity and reliability of the data. Demographic data, for example, for MSAs (metropolitan statistical areas), counties, and most municipalities is widely available from more than one source. If you are evaluating a survey that is supposedly representative of a given geographic area, you may want to compare the characteristics of the sample of the survey with the demographic data available on the population. If you know, based on U.S. census data, that there are 45 percent males and 55 percent females in a city and a survey, which is supposed to be representative of that city, reports a sample of 46 percent males and 54 percent females, then you can be more confident in the survey data. It is indeed rare, however, that two organizations will report *exactly* the same results. Here, you must look at the magnitude of the differences and determine what you should do. If all independent sources report very large differences of the same variable, then you may not have much confidence in any of the data. You should look at some of the factors we have already discussed to help you understand why these differences may occur. Marketing Research Insight 6.3 (page 150) serves as a good example of conflicting secondary data and how to evaluate the discrepancies.[14]

Sometimes data from two different secondary sources will conflict. Find out why before you use the information.

LOCATING SECONDARY DATA SOURCES

View: "Coca Cola: Sorting, Searching, and Inserting Variables"

How does one go about the actual task of locating secondary data sources? We suggest you follow the approach outlined here.[15]

Step 1. Identify what you wish to know and what you already know about your topic. This is the most important step in searching for information. Without having a clear understanding of what you are looking for, you will undoubtedly have difficulties. Clearly define your topic; what are relevant facts, names of researchers or organizations associated with the topic, key papers and other publications with which you are already familiar, and any other information you may have. Reference guides such as the *Encyclopedia of Business Information Sources* should be helpful in listing such specialized sources on your topic.

Having a clear understanding of exactly what you wish to know and knowing what you already know about your topic is the most important first step in searching for information.

Step 2. Develop a list of key terms and names. These terms and names will provide access to secondary sources. Unless you already have a very specific topic of interest, keep this initial list long and quite general. Use business dictionaries and handbooks to help develop your list.

Step 3. Begin your search using several of the library sources listed in Table 6.1 on pages 151–154. If you know of a particularly relevant paper or author, you may consult the *Social Science Citation Index* (in print or on CD-ROM) to identify papers by the same author or papers citing the author or work. Use indices such as the *Business Periodicals Index* to compile a list of journal articles for the previous two or three years. Some indices use a specialized list, or thesaurus, of key terms or descriptors. Because many periodical indices are available on CD-ROM or online databases, the use of the thesaurus is important

MARKETING RESEARCH INSIGHT 6.3

When Secondary Information Sources Conflict

Missie Patterson, a marketing researcher, was preparing a sales forecast for a new product. She had developed a model for forecasting that required, as one input, the number of business firms located in the counties for which she was making forecasts. One was Maricopa County, Arizona. The governmental source of information on types and numbers of business firms is the Bureau of the Census's County Business Patterns (CBP). *Data was taken from the latest edition, 1995. Another source is information obtained from the firm, Survey Sampling, Inc. Both of these sources of information fare very well when we evaluate them against some of the criteria we have already discussed. Both are creditable organizations that are known for their objectivity and thoroughness in their work. However, when Missie Patterson received the information from these sources she noted that they were completely different, as illustrated:*

MARICOPA COUNTY, ARIZONA

TOTAL NUMBER OF BUSINESS FIRMS	
County Business Patterns	61,372
Survey Sampling, Inc.	93,265*

**Information provided by permission of Survey Sampling, Inc., 1997.*

How does Patterson reconcile this discrepancy? The answer is found by asking the questions, "What information was actually collected?" and "How was this information obtained?" As it turns out, neither organization actually counts the numbers of businesses in a given area. CBP counts the number of firms submitting payroll information on their employees. Some firms may not report this information and other small firms with "no paid employees" (whose owners are the employees) are excluded from CBP data. Therefore, the CBP surrogate indicator used to count the number of business firms is going to have a downward bias because it does not count all firms. On the other hand, Survey Sampling counts the number of business firms by adding up the number of businesses listed in the Yellow Pages.

This brings up the question, "What is a business firm?" One franchise organization may run the McDonald's in a city, yet the Yellow Pages lists 9 locations. Is this one business or nine? Survey Sampling would list this as nine separate businesses. Therefore, Survey Sampling's estimates of the number of businesses has an upward bias. Which data source should be used? It would depend on the purpose of your study and how the information would be used. Patterson can use either source of information as long as the logic of her forecasting model considers the impact of the data used as an input. The key point is—you must adequately evaluate the various data sources so that you are in a position to select the information that will give you the most valid and reliable results.

to an efficient search. Consider a computerized information search. If you have not already conducted a computerized search, the reference librarian can recommend, in some cases, CD-ROM or online databases that you may search yourself. The reference librarian can assist with such a search but will need your help in the form of a carefully constructed list of key words.

TABLE 6.1

Sources of Secondary Information Sources on Marketing

I. REFERENCE GUIDES

MARKETING INFORMATION: A PROFESSIONAL REFERENCE GUIDE

Atlanta, Ga.: Georgia State University Business Press, 1995. For the marketing researcher, this lists marketing associations, advertising agencies, research centers, agencies, and sources relating to subjects of advertising, consumer behavior, franchising, pricing, promotion, etc.

II. INDEXES

ABI INFORM

Ann Arbor, Mich.: UMI, 1982. Available online and CD-ROM. Indexes and abstracts major journals relating to a broad range of business topics.

BUSINESS INDEX

Menlo Park, Calif.: Information Access Corp, 1982. Available online and CD-ROM. This index covers primarily business and popular journals.

BUSINESS PERIODICALS INDEX

New York: H. W. Wilson, Co, 1958. Available online and CD-ROM. This basic index is useful for indexing the major business journals further back in time than other indexes.

III. DICTIONARIES AND ENCYCLOPEDIAS

DICTIONARY OF MARKETING TERMS

Lincolnwood, Ill.: NTC Business Books, 1995. This dictionary includes brief definitions of popular terms in marketing.

DICTIONARY OF INTERNATIONAL TRADE

New York: Wiley, 1994. By Jerry Rosenberg, this dictionary specializes in definitions of terms that are commonly used in overseas trade.

ENCYCLOPEDIA OF CONSUMER BRANDS

Detroit, Mich.: St. James Press, 1994. For consumable products, personal products, and durable goods, this source provides detailed descriptions of the history and major developments of major brand names.

IV. DIRECTORIES

ADVERTISER AND AGENCY RED BOOK PLUS

New Providence, N.J.: Reed Reference Pub. Annual. Available on CD-ROM. Includes the complete *Standard Directory of Advertisers, Standard Directory of Advertising Agencies*, and the *Standard Directory of International Advertisers and Agencies.*

BRADFORD'S DIRECTORY OF MARKETING RESEARCH AGENCIES AND MANAGEMENT CONSULTANTS IN THE UNITED STATES AND THE WORLD

Middleberg, Va.: Bradford's. Biennial. Indexed by type of service, this source gives scope of activity for each agency and lists names of officers.

(continued)

TABLE 6.1 (continued)

IV. DIRECTORIES (continued)

BROADCASTING AND CABLE YEARBOOK

New Providence, N.J.: R. R. Bowker, Annual. A directory of U.S. and Canadian television and radio stations, advertising agencies, and other useful information.

CONSUMER SOURCEBOOK

Detroit, Mich.: Gale Research, 1996/97. This handbook is a subject guide to over 8,000 government agencies, associations, information centers, clearinghouses, and related resources in all fields.

DIRECTORIES IN PRINT

Detroit, Mich.: Gale Research, 1997. Provides detailed information on business and industrial directories, professional and scientific rosters, online directory of databases, and other lists. This source is particularly useful for identifying directories associated with specific industries or products.

GALE DIRECTORY OF PUBLICATIONS AND BROADCAST MEDIA

Detroit, Mich.: Gale Research. Annual. A geographic listing of U.S. and Canadian newspapers, magazines, and trade publications, as well as broadcasting stations. Includes address, edition, frequency, circulation, and subscription and advertising rates.

POWERFINDER PHONE DISK

1995. Available on CD-ROM. Similar databases are available on the Internet. Includes six regional residential CDs covering every city in the United States. Accessible by product or SIC code, this database can also list companies by product. Each entry includes name, mailing address, telephone number, business heading, SIC code, and number of employees.

V. STATISTICAL SOURCES

DATAPEDIA OF THE UNITED STATES, 1790-2000

Lanham, Md.: Bernan Press, 1994. Based on the *Historical Statistics of the United States from Colonial Times* and other statistical sources, this volume presents hundreds of tables reflecting historical and, in some cases, forecasting data on numerous demographic variables relating to the United States.

DEMOGRAPHICS USA—SURVEY OF BUYING POWER

New York: *Sales and Marketing Management* magazine. Annual. A compilation of data published in *Sales and Marketing Management* magazine (HF 5438 A34), which includes statistics on population, income, retail sales, effective buying income, etc., for counties, cities, and MSAs (this source is discussed at length later in this chapter).

EDITOR AND PUBLISHER MARKET GUIDE

New York: Editor and Publisher. Annual. Provides market data for more than 1,500 U.S. and Canadian newspaper cities covering facts and figures about location, transaction, population, households, banks, autos, etc.

MARKET SHARE REPORTER

Detroit, Mich.: Gale Research, 1994. Provides market share data on products and service industries in the United States.

V. STATISTICAL SOURCES (continued)

SIMMONS STUDY OF MEDIA AND MARKETS

New York: Simmons Market Research Bureau. Annual. Contains detailed analyses of consumer preferences for products. CD-ROM version is entitled *Choices II.*

STANDARD RATE AND DATA SERVICE

Des Plaines, Ill.: SRDS. Monthly. In the SRDS monthly publications (those for consumer magazine and agri-Media, newspapers, spot radio, spot television) marketing statistics are included at the beginning of each state section.

VII. PROFESSIONAL DATABASES

DATASTAR

(http://www.krinfo.com). This online service provides access to several hundred bibliographic, numeric, and full-text databases.

DATATIMES EYEQ

(http://www.enews.com/clusters/datat). Offers more than 5,000 sources from the United States and around the world including newspapers, magazines, newswires, financial data, and newsletters.

DIALOG

(http://www.dialog.com). Featuring many business databases, this service offers several hundred files that can be searched at various prices. A special product of this service is KR BusinessBase.

DOW JONES NEWS/RETRIEVAL

(http://bis.dowjones.com/index.html). Having exclusive full-text access to *The Wall Street Journal,* this source also offers newswires, text libraries of more than 180 publications, company and industry information.

LEXIS-NEXIS

(http://lexis-nexis.com). LEXIS is a comprehensive legal database and NEXIS offers full-text news and business information services. It offers exclusive service to the archival file of the *New York Times.*

NEWSNET

Primarily offers industry-specific business newsletters online.

NTDB—NATIONAL TRADE DATA BANK

Available on CD-ROM. This comprehensive international marketing database includes statistics and full text of publications published by the U.S. government. This disk is useful when searching by country name or product.

VII. CONSUMER DATABASE SERVICES

AMERICA ONLINE

(http://www.blue.aol.com). Provides reference library of business sources and products from Hoover's Business Resources as well as Dow Jones.

(continued)

TABLE 6.1 (continued)

VII. CONSUMER DATABASE SERVICES (continued)

COMPUSERVE

(http://world.compuserve.com). Provides access to *Knowledge Index,* a less expensive product of Dialog as well as many other databases in business, demographic, government publications, etc.

PRODIGY

(http://www.prodigy.com). Contains databases on business, news, consumer reports, etc.

VIII. INTERNET SITES

We are providing you with just a few examples. New sites appear very rapidly; happy "surfing!"

FED WORLD

(http://www.fedworld.gov). Offers links to major sites for government information.

NEW YORK TIMES BUSINESS CONNECTIONS

(http://www.nytimes.com/library/cyber/reference/busconn.html). Links to net resources in business. Free registration.

STAT-USA

(http://www.stat-usa.gov). Provides extensive business statistics to subscribers.

Interlibrary loan networks let you access secondary information not available in your local library.

If the sources are not available in your library, ask for them through interlibrary loan. Interlibrary loan is a procedure whereby one library obtains materials from another. This is accomplished through a network of libraries that have agreed to provide access to their collections in return for the opportunity to obtain materials from other libraries in the network. Most libraries have an interlibrary loan form on which relevant information about requested materials is written.

Step 4. Compile the literature you have found and evaluate your findings. Is it relevant to your needs? Perhaps you are overwhelmed by information. Perhaps you have found little that is relevant. Rework your list of key words and authors. If you have had little success or your topic is highly specialized, consult specialized directories, encyclopedias, and so on, such as the ones listed in this chapter. Again, the librarian may be able to recommend the most appropriate source for your needs. Each reference source performs a certain function; for example, a directory lists companies, people, organizations, sources, telephone numbers, and so on. There is even a directory of directories called *Directories in Print* that lists such sources on specialized topics. You may first need to identify potentially useful primary directories, which will then lead you to other sources.

If your library and Internet searches are unsuccessful, turn to an authority in your field.

Step 5. If you are unhappy with what you have found or are otherwise having trouble, and the reference librarian has not been able to identify sources, use an authority. Identify some individual or organization that might know something about the topic. Such publications as *Who's Who in Finance and Industry, Consultants and Consulting Organizations Directory, Encyclopedia of Associations, Industrial Research Laboratories in the United States,* or *Research*

Centers Directory may help you identify sources. Do not forget university faculty, government officials, or business executives. Such individuals are often delighted to be of help.

There are several keys to a successful search. First, be well informed about the search process. Reading this chapter is a good place to start. Second, you must be devoted to the search. Don't expect information to fall into your lap; be committed to finding the information. Finally, there is no substitute for a good, professional librarian. Do not be afraid to ask for advice.

A reference librarian is an excellent advisor in locating secondary data sources.

KEY SOURCES OF SECONDARY DATA FOR MARKETERS

We hope you understand by now that there are thousands of sources of secondary data that may be relevant to business decisions. However, there are a few sources that are so important that they deserve some attention. In the next few paragraphs we give you additional information about the *Census of the Population*, the North American Industrial Classification System (NAICS), which is replacing the Standard Industrial Classification (SIC) system, and a major private source of information for marketers—the *Survey of Buying Power.*

Census of the Population

First, some may question why we would devote special attention to the census because the 1990 census is dated and information from the Census 2000 is years away. It is because census data serves as a "baseline" for much marketing information that is provided "in between" census years. That is, companies providing market information use census data and then make adjustments each year to report "current" information. However, it is all based on census data. Consequently, census information is the "granddaddy" of market information even between census years. Perhaps the most important government source of secondary data for marketing research applications is the ***Census of the Population.*** Conducted by the U.S. Bureau of the Census, the census, as required by the U.S. Constitution in order to determine appropriate representation, is conducted by mailing a questionnaire to most housing units in the country every 10 years. In some rural areas, the questionnaires are delivered by census takers. Census workers also attempt to count people living in shelters and on the streets. Phone calls or visits are made to households that do not respond or who send in incomplete questionnaires. A local review team reviews returns to determine if any areas in their communities are not represented. Completed questionnaire forms are sent to data processing centers for analysis and report preparation. A number of data products are then made available to the public in the form of reports, computer tapes, microfiche, CD-ROM discs and the Internet.

Census information serves an important function as a baseline data source.

Information from the census is derived either from questions asked of the entire population or from questions asked only of a sample of the population. The questions asked of every person and housing unit are called the 100 percent or short-form questions, whereas the others are called the sample or long-form questions. Therefore, it is important to note that much of the data collected by the census is not census data at all—it is sample data. All 50 states, plus the District of Columbia, Puerto Rico, the U.S. Virgin Islands, Guam,

The Census includes both short-form (census) and long-form (sample) question formats.

the Commonwealth of the Northern Mariana Islands, American Samoa, and Palau are included in the census. In addition to statistical information on states, the census also offers data on several different statistical areas, which you can learn about by accessing http://www.census.gov/td/stf3/append_a.html.

North American Industry Classification System (NAICS)

NAICS is not actually a source of information. It is a classification system that you can use to find information sources.

The **North American Industry Classification System (NAICS)** is not actually a "source" in and of itself, yet all marketing research students should be familiar with it because it will be used by so many secondary data sources. Many readers will not be familiar with NAICS, but they will have heard of the **Standard Industrial Classification (SIC) system,** which NAICS is replacing. (We discuss both here because data based on the SIC will be around for many years.) The SIC was created in the mid-1930s when the government required all agencies gathering economic and industrial data to use the same system for classifying businesses. The SIC was a system that classified establishments by the type of activity in which they were engaged. Codes, describing a type of business activity, were used to collect, tabulate, summarize, and publish data. Each industry was assigned an SIC code number and all firms within that particular industry reported all activities (sales, employment, etc.) by this assigned code. The SIC divides all establishments into 11 divisions: Division A, for agriculture, forestry, and fishing; Division B, for mining; Division C, for construction; Division D, for manufacturing; Division E, for transportation, communications, electric, gas, and sanitary services; Division F, for wholesale trade; Division G, for retail trade; Division H, for finance, insurance, and real estate; Division I, for services; Division J, for public administration; and Division K, for nonclassifiable establishments. Divisions are then subdivided into a second level of classification dividing the industry into "major groups." Major groups are numbered consecutively 01 through 99. Division A, for example, contains major groups 01 through 09. A major group within Division A is Agricultural Production—crops; this is major group 01. Division B contains major groups 10 through 14: 10 is metal mining, 11 is coal mining, and so on. Each major group is further divided into two other categories, each providing greater specificity of classification.[16]

Visit the NAICS home page at http://www.census.gov/epcd/www/naicsusr.html

The SIC is being replaced by NAICS as a result of the North American Free Trade Agreement (NAFTA). The new system will allow reports conducted by the Mexican, Canadian, and U.S. governments to share a common language for easier comparisons of international trade, industrial production, labor costs, and other statistics. NAICS will have improvements over the SIC and yet will allow for comparative analyses with past SIC-based data. NAICS will classify businesses based on similar production processes; special attention is being given to classifying emerging industries such as services and high technology, and more classifications will be assigned to certain industry groups such as eating and drinking places. Under the SIC, all restaurants—beaneries, caterers, hamburger stands, and five-star restaurants—fall under the same category: Eating & Drinking Places. NAICS will break this down into several categories, which will be more useful to researchers.[17]

The NAICS system is composed of 20 broad sectors of the economy.

NAICS groups the economy into 20 broad sectors as opposed to the 11 SIC divisions. Many of these new sectors reflect recognizable parts of the SIC, such as the Utilities and Transportaton section broken out from the SIC Transportation, Communications & Utilities division. Because the service sector of the economy has grown so much in recent years, the SIC division for Services Industries has been broken into several new sectors including Professional, Scientific, and Technical Services; Management, Support, Waste Management & Remediation Services; Education Services; Health & Social Assistance; Arts, Entertainment & Recreation; and Other Services except Public Administration. Other new NAICS sectors are composed of combinations of pieces from more than one SIC division. For example, the new Information sector is composed of components from Transportation, Communications & Utilities (broadcasting and telecommunications); Manufacturing (publishing); and Services Industries (software publishing, data processing, information services, and motion pictures and sound recording).

Each NAICS sector is broken down into a 6-digit classification system for industries.

The NAICS will use a six-digit classification code instead of the old SIC four-digit code. The additional two digits allows for far greater specificity in identifying special types of firms. However, the six-digit code will not be used by all three NAFTA countries. The three countries have agreed on a standard system using the first five digits and the sixth digit will be used by each country in a manner allowing for special user needs in each country. The structure of NAICS is shown in Figure 6.2, which was taken off the Internet. It illustrates how the six-digit code may be used to identify companies in a specific industry. Note that the NAICS code doesn't tell you anything *per se*. However, knowing that 513321 is paging transmissions services will allow you to find all kinds of information about the firms making up this industry.

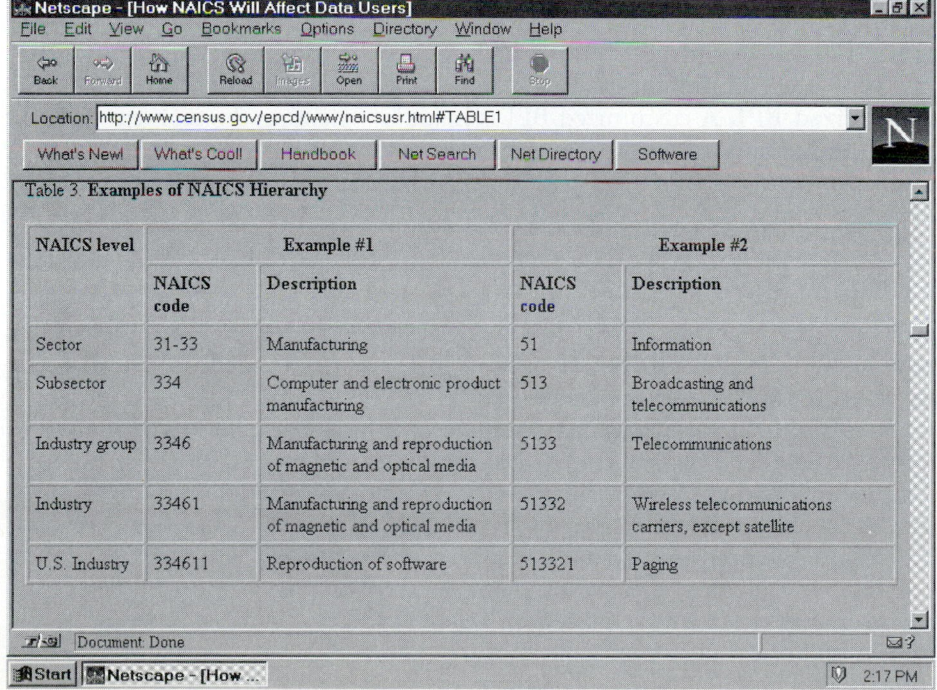

Table 3. **Examples of NAICS Hierarchy**

NAICS level	Example #1		Example #2	
	NAICS code	Description	NAICS code	Description
Sector	31-33	Manufacturing	51	Information
Subsector	334	Computer and electronic product manufacturing	513	Broadcasting and telecommunications
Industry group	3346	Manufacturing and reproduction of magnetic and optical media	5133	Telecommunications
Industry	33461	Manufacturing and reproduction of magnetic and optical media	51332	Wireless telecommunications carriers, except satellite
U.S. Industry	334611	Reproduction of software	513321	Paging

Figure 6.2

The Hierarchy of NAICS

"Survey of Buying Power"

Sales & Marketing Management *magazine publishes the "Survey of Buying Power" every August.*

The **"Survey of Buying Power"** is an annual survey that is published every August in *Sales & Marketing Management* magazine. The survey contains data for the United States on population, income, and retail sales for food, eating and drinking places, appliances, and automotives. These data are broken up into metropolitan, county, and city levels. Because the data for the survey are extrapolated from census data, the data are current with each year's publication. In addition to the general data, the survey also reports the **effective buying income (EBI)** and the **buying power index (BPI).**

EBI is defined as disposable personal income. It is equal to gross income less taxes and therefore reflects the effective amount of income available for expenditure on goods and services. This is important because taxes differ widely depending on geographic location. BPI is an indicator of the relative market potential of a geographic area. It is based on the factors that make up a market: people (population), ability to buy (EBI), and willingness to buy (retail sales is used as a surrogate indicator of what the market actually buys).

The BPI (buying power index) is an indicator of the relative market potential of a geographic area.

It must be remembered that BPI is only an *indicator of market potential* of a place for mass products sold at popular prices. For instance, the BPI of 0.2140 for the metropolitan area of Baton Rouge, Louisiana, indicates Baton Rouge's "ability to buy" expressed as a percentage of the national total. Marketing managers make use of the BPI by looking at the absolute value of a market area's BPI. Thus, the BPI provides a readily available quantification of the "ability to buy" for geographical markets in the United States. Also, managers track BPIs over time for any given market area. This tells them if that market is growing or waning. Being able to assess markets in this way allows management to make many decisions concerning allocation of their resources among the various markets. A problem with the BPI is that it is not necessarily a good indicator of an area's market power for each and every product. This is because it is based on all retail sales, total EBI, and the total population—all age groups. It would not be a good indicator of the market for, say, luxury cars. For such specific products and details, we can adapt the data to create a **customized BPI.** A customized BPI is made by selecting the segment of retail trade, population age groups, and EBI groups that are more meaningful to a given product. We show you how this can be done for luxury cars in the following section.

Creating a Customized BPI

Because the BPI is a general indicator, a marketing researcher may opt to create a customized BPI that better serves his or her purpose.

Consider the example of Mr. Ed Livingston, marketing vice president for a new luxury car about to be introduced in the United States. Mr. Livingston wants to use the "Survey of Buying Power" to determine the market potential for luxury cars in various metropolitan areas. This information will be used to locate dealers for the new car. In the steps that follow, we illustrate how the "Survey of Buying Power" can be used to determine the market potential for luxury cars in one MSA: Pensacola, Florida.

Step 1. We need to determine the levels of the three factors (population, retail sales, and income) that we are going to use. For this, we need to determine the profile of a luxury car customer. It would be reasonable to assume that a typical luxury car customer will be in the 35+ age group, and will be earning more than $50,000 annually. Therefore, the factors we will be using are:

Here is an example of the steps to take in order to create a customized BPI.

Age group: Persons in the age group of 35 and over

Retail sales: Automotive

EBI: Households earning $50,000 and over

Step 2. We need to determine the population, automotive sales, and EBI for the Pensacola MSA. These figures can be found from information shown in Table 6.2 (pages 160–163).

Age group of 35+: $(0.26 + 0.228) \times 397{,}000 = 193{,}736$

Automotive sales: $1,018,505

EBI ($50,000+) households: $.229 \times 143{,}900 = 32{,}953$

Step 3. Next, we calculate the figures from step 2 as a percentage of total U.S. figures. The figures for the total U.S. market can be found in the front end of *Sales & Marketing Management* (see "Market Totals").

$$\text{Age group \%} = \frac{193{,}736 \times 100}{133{,}001{,}200} = 0.14\%$$

$$\text{Automotive sales \%} = \frac{\$1{,}018{,}505{,}000 \times 100}{\$605{,}127{,}843{,}000} = 0.16\%$$

$$\text{EBI households \%} = \frac{32{,}953 \times 100}{29{,}134{,}500} = 0.113\%$$

Step 4. We need to make an assessment of how important each of the three factors (EBI, age group, retail sales) are. For luxury cars, the importance factors could be:

Age group: 30%
EBI: 60%
Automotive sales: 10%

Step 5: Calculate the BPI using figures from steps 3 and 4.

BPI = (% Age group × 0.3) + (% EBI households × 0.6) + (% Automotive Sales × 0.1)

BPI for luxury automobiles in Pensacola = $0.14 \times 0.3 + 0.113 \times 0.6 + 0.16 \times 0.1 = 0.1258$

Ed Livingston can use this information in a variety of ways. First, he can calculate the BPI for several market areas and determine which of these have the greatest buying power for luxury cars. Second, he can use this information to calculate the *sales* potential for any given market area. How can he do this? Let us assume that total firm sales for the new luxury car are estimated to be $xxx billion. The sales potential for Pensacola will be:

$$\frac{\text{Total firm sales} \times \text{Pensacola BPI}}{100}$$

Finally, Mr. Livingston could compare actual sales in Pensacola with the potential just calculated for purposes of evaluating the dealership once it is open and operating.

Table 6.2

Survey of Buying Power

Metro Area / County / City	Population: Total Population (000s)	% of Population by Age Group: 18–24	25–34	35–49	50 +	Households (000s)	Retail Sales by Store Group (0): Total Retail Sales	Food	Eating & Drinking Places	General Mdse.	Furniture/ Furnish. Appliance	Automotive	Effective Buying Income: Total EBI ($000)	Median Hsld. EBI	% of Hslds. by EBI Group: A $20,00–$34,999	B $35,000–$49,999	C $50,000 & Over	Buying Power Index
DAYTONA BEACH	**457.9**	**7.8**	**12.6**	**20.1**	**39.5**	**187.8**	**4,247,725**	**840,071**	**450,725**	**549,169**	**177,336**	**1,092,924**	**6,602,729**	**27,384**	**28.0**	**17.7**	**19.4**	**.1655**
FLAGLER	41.5	5.2	9.9	19.1	46.4	16.7	257,335	84,969	25,262	8,180	7,210	52,007	666,008	31,530	29.9	19.3	24.1	.0143
VOLUSIA	416.4	8.0	12.9	20.3	38.8	171.1	3,990,390	755,102	425,463	540,989	170,126	1,040,917	5,936,721	26,952	28.0	17.5	18.9	.1512
▪Daytona Beach	64.6	14.7	13.6	18.1	37.0	28.3	1,492,286	131,936	140,044	277,836	53,237	542,386	829,401	20,723	25.8	12.8	13.0	.0330
FORT LAUDERDALE	**1,452.7**	**6.9**	**14.9**	**22.7**	**34.9**	**608.7**	**20,467,194**	**2,674,612**	**1,767,772**	**1,876,064**	**1,163,908**	**7,932,368**	**25,662,888**	**32,698**	**24.3**	**17.9**	**28.8**	**.6660**
BROWARD	1,452.7	6.9	14.9	22.7	34.9	608.7	20,467,194	2,674,612	1,767,772	1,876,064	1,163,908	7,932,368	25,662,888	32,698	24.3	17.9	28.8	.6660
Coral Springs	99.6	7.9	12.9	32.1	15.7	33.6	1,031,997	189,939	118,586	205,500	40,338	179,875	1,877,558	46,577	19.3	17.9	46.0	.0426
Davie	63.9	8.7	17.6	27.5	20.9	24.0	1,063,967	165,693	90,364	203,570	43,056	179,668	1,120,509	39,722	22.2	20.2	36.8	.0312
Deerfield Beach	45.0	5.6	13.6	17.5	49.9	22.3	640,132	104,284	73,557	42,446	65,689	112,010	814,628	29,156	25.3	17.9	23.4	.0209
▪Fort Lauderdale	170.4	7.0	16.4	24.3	33.5	75.4	4,178,439	294,885	453,970	149,083	176,046	2,362,042	3,476,251	29,232	24.6	15.1	26.9	.1054
Hollywood	125.4	6.5	13.6	21.6	39.3	54.3	1,798,063	223,544	129,291	109,829	52,665	828,109	2,140,173	29,504	24.9	17.2	24.3	.0570
Lauderhill	51.9	7.5	16.3	21.0	32.7	22.0	1,207,135	55,472	33,936	89,720	91,016	706,169	818,491	28,864	26.8	16.5	23.8	.0284
Margate	50.7	6.5	12.8	20.2	43.4	22.3	805,711	122,300	48,825	27,046	18,979	452,554	806,387	30,580	25.2	18.1	25.8	.0233
Miramar	53.7	7.7	17.9	24.8	23.0	19.1	517,472	103,203	28,257	179,859	11,871	79,855	792,877	38,595	22.0	21.5	33.9	.0198
Pembroke Pines	97.2	6.7	15.4	24.2	34.1	39.3	1,147,064	201,356	106,797	48,718	72,839	403,620	1,715,654	39,159	21.1	21.1	35.2	.0418
Plantation	75.8	7.7	14.4	27.0	30.2	30.1	1,464,448	183,485	105,087	308,379	117,578	376,723	1,693,724	44,863	20.2	19.2	44.3	.0438
Pompano Beach	76.6	6.6	15.3	19.9	40.5	33.7	1,326,929	133,880	89,169	162,550	95,322	573,890	1,396,088	31,635	24.3	17.5	27.4	.0387
Sunrise	78.1	6.6	15.8	22.9	32.0	31.7	989,630	131,393	117,339	130,803	145,256	11,011	1,209,425	34,007	23.3	20.1	28.3	.0324
Tamarac	48.6	4.6	10.2	13.7	62.8	24.7	490,701	128,766	44,566	76,638	29,700	22,339	925,154	28,816	28.6	17.0	22.5	.0207
FORT MYERS-CAPE CORAL	**389.1**	**6.2**	**12.3**	**19.7**	**42.0**	**159.7**	**4,697,312**	**755,032**	**469,952**	**588,433**	**341,035**	**1,228,671**	**6,424,693**	**31,040**	**28.3**	**19.6**	**23.9**	**.1634**
LEE	389.1	6.2	12.3	19.7	42.0	159.7	4,697,312	755,032	469,952	588,433	341,035	1,228,671	6,424,693	31,040	28.3	19.6	23.9	.1634
▪Cape Coral	90.2	6.1	13.1	21.4	36.9	35.1	602,148	178,074	56,029	63,006	31,007	74,550	1,429,886	34,195	28.9	22.6	26.0	.0313
▪Fort Myers	54.3	9.7	15.7	19.6	28.5	21.4	2,027,628	161,039	149,053	299,117	164,706	721,900	716,111	24,514	27.0	15.9	16.4	.0373
FORT PIERCE-PORT ST. LUCIE	**293.7**	**6.1**	**12.8**	**19.9**	**40.0**	**116.7**	**2,834,077**	**541,584**	**232,843**	**344,834**	**130,685**	**837,689**	**4,885,689**	**31,016**	**26.8**	**18.3**	**25.1**	**.1152**
MARTIN	115.7	5.7	11.8	20.1	44.6	48.7	1,437,815	248,493	117,316	207,908	68,191	380,817	2,500,946	35,257	24.3	17.7	32.6	.0562
ST. LUCIE	178.0	6.4	13.4	19.7	37.0	68.0	1,396,262	293,091	115,527	136,926	62,494	456,872	2,384,743	28,587	28.8	18.7	19.7	.0590
▪Fort Pierce	34.9	8.0	12.5	18.5	34.0	13.4	722,293	82,000	48,498	56,996	31,528	368,515	353,575	19,578	24.2	12.0	12.8	.0157
▪Port St. Lucie	79.5	5.9	16.1	21.8	30.6	29.1	495,830	172,805	53,937	39,452	25,477	47,513	1,115,151	33,449	31.4	23.5	23.4	.0254
FORT WALTON BEACH	**166.7**	**9.2**	**17.3**	**22.7**	**24.3**	**61.5**	**1,694,962**	**222,586**	**176,155**	**272,584**	**85,126**	**488,077**	**2,466,882**	**32,140**	**28.6**	**19.6**	**25.6**	**.0629**
OKALOOSA	166.7	9.2	17.3	22.7	24.3	61.5	1,694,962	222,586	176,155	272,584	85,126	488,077	2,466,882	32,140	28.6	19.6	25.6	.0629
▪Fort Walton Beach	25.1	9.1	16.1	21.9	28.9	10.0	634,329	44,954	43,629	81,843	25,541	330,732	387,096	32,449	29.7	19.3	26.2	.0143

GAINESVILLE	**204.0**	**19.0**	**16.1**	**21.9**	**20.3**	**79.8**	**2,041,350**	**346,254**	**252,079**	**367,810**	**104,972**	**452,133**	**2,888,106**	**25,943**	**22.4**	**14.4**	**23.5**	**.0748**
ALACHUA	204.0	19.0	16.1	21.9	20.3	79.8	2,041,350	346,254	252,079	367,810	104,972	452,133	2,888,106	25,943	22.4	14.4	23.5	.0748
■Gainesville	91.3	25.0	15.9	20.4	18.8	34.2	1,228,901	173,919	144,639	164,114	77,541	379,999	1,217,832	24,713	21.9	13.6	22.9	.0364
JACKSONVILLE	**1,025.6**	**8.8**	**16.3**	**23.9**	**24.5**	**385.2**	**10,155,283**	**1,724,123**	**1,085,493**	**1,322,558**	**401,440**	**2,842,087**	**16,566,044**	**34,277**	**24.1**	**19.4**	**29.5**	**.3994**
CLAY	131.2	7.9	14.6	26.9	21.5	44.7	1,151,948	192,290	101,685	193,663	75,608	329,691	1,999,692	39,072	24.3	22.6	34.0	.0479
DUVAL	733.5	9.3	17.0	23.2	23.9	278.8	7,644,507	1,188,370	817,466	1,005,084	271,494	2,222,816	11,524,516	32,914	24.4	19.2	27.7	.2865
■Jacksonville	694.5	9.3	17.1	23.4	23.4	261.8	7,369,565	1,114,161	741,887	947,652	261,671	2,175,208	10,764,842	32,781	24.5	19.3	27.4	.2710
NASSAU	52.1	7.6	14.4	25.2	25.5	19.1	399,511	128,708	43,254	40,451	7,060	68,297	782,662	34,282	22.5	19.6	29.4	.0181
ST. JOHNS	108.8	7.4	13.5	24.3	32.2	42.6	959,317	214,755	123,088	83,360	42,278	221,283	2,259,174	38,007	23.1	17.7	36.4	.0469
LAKELAND-WINTER HAVEN	**457.3**	**7.6**	**12.8**	**21.0**	**34.1**	**175.2**	**4,138,963**	**716,972**	**302,657**	**653,749**	**414,029**	**1,128,914**	**6,008,744**	**27,049**	**28.8**	**17.5**	**18.2**	**.1568**
POLK	457.3	7.6	12.8	21.0	34.1	175.2	4,138,963	716,972	302,657	653,749	414,029	1,128,914	6,008,744	27,049	28.8	17.5	18.2	.1568
■Lakeland	73.4	9.1	12.6	19.6	37.5	30.8	1,712,401	236,838	124,915	401,867	155,417	429,789	1,046,880	26,216	29.0	16.9	16.9	.0389
■Winter Haven	25.4	6.5	11.4	17.5	44.8	11.2	704,356	120,696	58,450	114,471	36,255	201,503	381,257	25,411	27.2	17.7	16.2	.0151
MELBOURNE-TITUSVILLE-PALM BAY	**455.9**	**7.4**	**15.3**	**21.7**	**33.4**	**184.7**	**5,238,840**	**750,563**	**424,964**	**641,732**	**216,134**	**2,057,429**	**7,174,189**	**32,246**	**26.1**	**19.6**	**26.1**	**.1841**
BREVARD	455.9	7.4	15.3	21.7	33.4	184.7	5,238,840	750,563	424,964	641,732	216,134	2,057,429	7,174,189	32,246	26.1	19.6	26.1	.1841
■Melbourne	70.0	9.9	16.1	20.3	33.0	29.6	1,230,253	125,304	89,072	198,543	57,950	537,179	976,624	27,460	27.2	19.0	18.5	.0319
■Palm Bay	78.9	7.3	19.3	22.1	23.0	29.6	411,584	129,964	46,539	40,550	13,723	59,117	1,053,204	31,920	29.2	23.0	21.3	.0236
■Titusville	40.2	7.0	15.4	20.8	33.6	16.6	439,628	96,037	43,219	80,693	12,934	101,799	601,997	30,248	27.0	18.4	23.8	.0156
MIAMI	**2,100.2**	**8.4**	**14.9**	**22.6**	**29.6**	**737.2**	**21,396,408**	**3,213,826**	**2,177,298**	**2,262,050**	**1,736,062**	**5,021,309**	**29,846,745**	**29,176**	**22.7**	**15.9**	**26.2**	**.7760**
DADE	2,100.2	8.4	14.9	22.6	29.6	737.2	21,396,408	3,213,826	2,177,298	2,262,050	1,736,062	5,021,309	29,846,745	29,176	22.7	15.9	26.2	.7760
Coral Gables	42.1	13.8	13.5	23.7	33.3	16.0	760,664	91,911	93,079	38,651	73,436	253,881	1,278,872	50,437	16.5	13.7	50.3	.0278
Hialeah	195.6	8.4	13.6	21.4	32.5	60.6	1,550,512	322,849	129,344	214,605	126,460	151,659	1,867,824	25,748	27.2	16.9	17.3	.0559
■Miami	387.3	7.9	13.9	21.2	33.9	138.2	4,715,982	638,072	532,109	471,613	389,861	1,117,292	4,009,013	18,910	21.9	11.4	14.3	.1345
■Miami Beach	83.7	6.3	13.6	20.0	45.5	43.7	515,654	133,148	151,939	25,212	15,181	10,542	1,426,318	17,085	19.2	9.2	15.3	.0297
North Miami	55.6	8.6	17.1	23.2	27.9	21.9	532,920	110,110	65,369	1,956	46,721	68,458	780,077	26,853	29.1	16.7	18.5	.0200
MIAMI-FORT LAUDERDALE CONSOLIDATED AREA	***3,552.9***	***7.8***	***14.9***	***22.7***	***31.7***	***1,345.9***	***41,863,602***	***5,888,438***	***3,945,070***	***4,138,114***	***2,899,970***	***12,953,677***	***55,509,633***	***30,765***	***23.4***	***16.8***	***27.3***	***1.4420***
NAPLES	**196.0**	**6.5**	**12.8**	**20.3**	**40.1**	**78.5**	**2,854,121**	**535,142**	**320,318**	**351,074**	**286,536**	**535,644**	**4,549,252**	**38,931**	**23.9**	**19.5**	**36.3**	**.1040**
COLLIER	196.0	6.5	12.8	20.3	40.1	78.5	2,854,121	535,142	320,318	351,074	286,536	535,644	4,549,252	38,931	23.9	19.5	36.3	.1040
■Naples	22.9	3.8	5.9	16.5	64.1	11.3	1,163,314	193,874	150,027	170,325	139,909	128,109	985,672	49,342	18.1	14.5	49.4	.0277
OCALA	**236.8**	**6.4**	**11.9**	**20.0**	**39.2**	**94.8**	**2,400,825**	**383,974**	**184,016**	**527,905**	**119,160**	**454,140**	**3,016,164**	**24,716**	**29.3**	**16.2**	**15.5**	**.0831**
MARION	236.8	6.4	11.9	20.0	39.2	94.8	2,400,825	383,974	184,016	527,905	119,160	454,140	3,016,164	24,716	29.3	16.2	15.5	.0831
■Ocala	60.1	7.8	12.5	20.9	34.3	24.9	1,795,848	242,260	142,833	353,536	93,942	409,522	824,723	23,720	25.7	13.2	18.6	.0363
ORLANDO	**1,460.2**	**9.3**	**16.3**	**23.1**	**27.0**	**551.6**	**16,705,324**	**2,666,390**	**2,180,551**	**1,937,681**	**899,253**	**4,582,544**	**23,723,263**	**33,998**	**25.6**	**19.2**	**29.3**	**.5973**
LAKE	189.9	5.6	10.6	18.5	45.2	79.0	1,456,761	311,020	131,263	171,392	51,239	432,371	2,414,922	24,257	30.2	16.0	14.3	.0609
ORANGE	790.8	10.9	18.0	22.8	23.9	297.3	9,559,200	1,416,482	1,414,819	972,037	517,468	2,746,014	12,983,315	34,614	25.6	19.6	29.8	.3315
■Orlando	188.8	15.5	19.8	20.3	23.3	75.2	2,953,525	333,255	515,266	320,534	235,274	795,890	2,982,594	29,982	27.3	18.4	23.7	.0859
OSCEOLA	142.6	8.5	14.9	23.1	27.9	50.7	1,638,102	338,300	289,297	151,601	39,366	420,825	1,794,503	29,015	29.9	20.5	19.1	.0520
SEMINOLE	336.9	8.0	15.9	26.7	23.7	124.6	4,051,261	600,588	345,172	642,651	291,180	983,334	6,530,523	43,172	20.9	19.9	41.5	.1529

(continued)

Table 6.2 (continued)

Survey of Buying Power

Metro Area / County / City	Population: Total Population (000s)	% of Population by Age Group: 18–24	25–34	35–49	50 +	Households (000s)	Retail Sales by Store Group (0): Total Retail Sales	Food	Eating & Drinking Places	General Mdse.	Furniture/ Furnish. Appliance	Automotive	Effective Buying Income: Total EBI ($000)	Median Hsld. EBI	% of Hslds; by EBI Group: A $20,000–$34,999	B $35,000–$49,999	C $50,000 & Over	Buying Power Index
PANAMA CITY	**145.9**	**8.3**	**15.6**	**22.8**	**27.6**	**55.6**	**1,754,244**	**344,156**	**237,513**	**308,397**	**80,635**	**393,314**	**2,039,424**	**28,698**	**26.8**	**17.7**	**21.8**	**.0567**
BAY	145.9	8.3	15.6	22.8	27.6	55.6	1,754,244	344,156	237,513	308,397	80,635	393,314	2,039,424	28,698	26.8	17.7	21.8	.0567
▪Panama City	39.3	8.1	14.2	21.1	31.6	15.8	1,193,786	176,271	123,801	227,648	61,663	360,030	544,312	25,964	24.6	17.2	18.3	.0240
PENSACOLA	**397.0**	**10.1**	**15.2**	**22.8**	**26.0**	**143.9**	**3,692,662**	**587,139**	**393,633**	**563,178**	**221,770**	**1,018,505**	**5,308,247**	**29,077**	**25.7**	**18.1**	**22.9**	**.1384**
ESCAMBIA	288.7	11.0	15.0	22.1	26.5	106.4	3,061,146	455,756	340,623	507,378	199,593	843,523	3,793,700	27,939	25.8	17.5	21.5	.1044
▪Pensacola	61.6	8.9	13.4	22.3	31.9	25.0	1,111,303	97,768	122,764	277,107	94,458	289,673	968,695	27,702	23.3	15.5	24.9	.0298
SANTA ROSA	108.3	7.7	15.9	24.5	24.5	37.5	631,516	131,383	53,010	55,800	22,177	174,982	1,514,547	32,636	25.6	19.5	26.7	.0340
PUNTA GORDA	**131.2**	**4.8**	**9.3**	**16.6**	**53.5**	**56.8**	**1,188,488**	**209,242**	**97,375**	**251,149**	**65,285**	**220,821**	**2,012,296**	**28,000**	**31.7**	**18.4**	**18.6**	**.0483**
CHARLOTTE	131.2	4.8	9.3	15.6	53.5	56.8	1,188,488	209,242	97,375	251,149	65,285	220,821	2,012,296	28,000	31.7	18.4	18.6	.0483
▪Punta Gorda	12.5	3.4	4.9	12.1	69.1	5.9	292,193	54,709	20,486	68,406	5,700	72,941	289,134	36,468	24.8	18.1	34.1	.0080
SARASOTA-BRADENTON	**547.0**	**5.6**	**11.1**	**18.9**	**47.1**	**239.6**	**5,822,928**	**1,038,938**	**593,614**	**612,207**	**439,956**	**1,553,160**	**10,159,499**	**32,347**	**27.2**	**19.0**	**26.7**	**.2338**
MANATEE	238.3	6.1	11.9	18.7	44.0	101.5	2,064,090	353,642	223,169	230,501	150,540	533,316	4,017,527	31,043	27.9	18.6	24.8	.0912
▪Bradenton	49.4	6.7	12.7	18.3	42.9	21.1	618,967	95,458	68,656	65,619	47,686	159,758	802,814	31,093	26.9	20.0	23.1	.0209
SARASOTA	308.7	5.2	10.4	19.1	49.5	138.1	3,758,838	685,296	370,445	381,706	289,416	1,019,844	6,141,972	33,346	26.8	19.3	28.0	.1426
▪Sarasota	57.9	8.1	13.9	20.1	39.5	25.7	1,378,772	183,383	162,159	189,383	135,380	274,279	1,012,086	27,793	28.1	16.6	21.6	.0333
TALLAHASSEE	**271.1**	**16.2**	**15.7**	**23.4**	**20.4**	**101.9**	**2,686,828**	**499,705**	**346,587**	**448,842**	**142,597**	**530,777**	**4,173,529**	**31,239**	**22.4**	**16.5**	**28.4**	**.1030**
GADSDEN	46.4	8.3	13.7	21.6	26.5	15.0	232,712	78,049	13,460	22,891	10,902	50,018	456,772	23,145	23.4	15.5	17.3	.0117
LEON	224.7	17.9	16.1	23.8	19.1	86.9	2,454,116	421,656	333,127	425,951	131,695	480,759	3,716,757	32,826	22.2	16.7	30.4	.0913
▪Tallahassee	140.4	23.7	16.1	21.4	18.7	56.4	2,036,153	342,381	290,257	370,896	119,248	370,311	2,196,337	28,173	22.6	14.9	26.0	.0617
TAMPA-ST. PETERSBURG-CLEARWATER	**2,240.2**	**7.3**	**13.7**	**21.5**	**36.9**	**933.1**	**24,635,275**	**3,739,607**	**2,434,643**	**2,406,275**	**1,355,108**	**6,505,526**	**36,284,306**	**29,922**	**26.4**	**17.8**	**24.4**	**.9033**
HERNANDO	122.3	4.9	9.1	17.8	49.6	50.7	911,725	236,998	80,458	146,201	34,499	212,149	1,608,608	25,816	32.4	16.7	15.4	.0395
HILLSBOROUGH	918.8	9.0	16.3	23.9	26.1	355.4	11,116,928	1,540,384	1,225,797	1,017,688	654,220	2,981,460	15,028,618	33,556	24.0	18.4	29.5	.3846
▪Tampa	291.9	9.5	16.8	21.9	28.4	119.1	5,006,086	516,388	638,516	425,808	329,410	1,683,662	4,469,567	27,031	24.7	16.3	21.9	.1364
PASCO	315.1	5.6	10.3	17.4	48.7	135.3	2,095,013	415,936	186,180	283,254	121,362	559,368	4,278,752	25,272	30.1	16.3	15.6	.1005
PINELLAS	884.0	6.3	12.9	21.1	41.9	391.7	10,511,609	1,546,289	942,208	959,132	545,027	2,752,549	15,368,328	29,716	26.4	17.9	24.0	.3787
▪ Clearwater	101.5	6.7	12.5	21.4	41.4	45.0	1,504,590	147,731	168,723	205,280	99,032	459,588	1,865,035	29,557	25.9	17.5	24.8	.0483
Largo	68.4	6.4	13.3	17.9	48.4	32.9	741,741	214,717	73,707	96,814	89,260	38,090	1,116,093	27,555	30.1	17.9	18.6	.0276
Pinellas Park	46.7	7.4	14.7	20.6	36.6	19.5	661,275	79,414	41,108	174,065	28,538	193,549	673,033	29,374	28.9	20.6	20.1	.0196
▪St. Petersburg	239.7	7.1	14.3	21.6	37.0	105.5	3,527,391	398,507	198,289	233,979	219,686	573,215	3,767,538	26,693	25.7	16.9	20.6	.1061
WEST PALM BEACH-BOCA RATON	**1,001.1**	**6.4**	**13.7**	**20.9**	**39.1**	**420.7**	**12,387,827**	**1,897,778**	**1,310,174**	**1,424,984**	**748,163**	**3,564,424**	**22,154,626**	**37,852**	**22.3**	**17.9**	**35.8**	**.4918**
PALM BEACH	1,001.1	6.4	13.7	20.9	39.1	420.7	12,387,827	1,897,778	1,310,174	1,424,984	748,163	3,564,424	22,154,626	37,852	22.3	17.9	35.8	.4918
▪Boca Raton	69.0	7.7	13.2	24.2	37.6	29.3	1,589,891	301,273	276,286	52,442	194,046	46,722	2,108,617	48,716	18.3	17.0	48.6	.0498
Boynton Beach	53.7	6.1	13.3	18.4	44.0	23.3	666,676	150,014	87,189	136,541	26,370	14,919	1,011,759	33,464	26.0	19.3	28.2	.0243

Delray Beach	52.2	5.9	13.3	18.7	45.9	23.5	1,819,115	77,167	74,563	87,403	60,950	1,322,087	1,230,518	36,144	22.7	16.9	34.6	.0408
▪West Palm Beach	79.7	8.7	17.4	21.6	31.6	33.6	1,898,521	153,406	161,820	213,788	148,314	879,817	1,412,078	30,715	24.5	17.3	26.3	.0460
OTHER COUNTIES																		
BAKER	20.9	8.5	15.8	23.6	20.7	6.5	119,178	44,259	8,149	19,359	4,972	12,181	235,826	29,284	27.3	20.9	19.3	.0059
BRADFORD	24.6	8.0	17.5	24.4	26.2	7.8	138,851	41,631	12,302	14,330	4,388	32,029	307,610	29,453	25.9	19.9	20.2	.0072
CALHOUN	12.3	8.5	13.9	21.6	29.4	4.3	56,717	16,270	5,749	2,125	757	12,531	127,605	21,096	27.7	12.5	12.4	.0032
CITRUS	110.2	4.6	9.1	17.7	50.8	47.6	808,696	173,982	52,799	100,513	29,214	225,026	1,468,598	23,526	28.7	14.7	15.3	.0358
COLUMBIA	53.5	7.7	13.2	22.4	28.5	19.6	531,176	110,841	47,558	81,040	19,188	120,948	604,159	24,022	26.0	17.2	15.7	.0177
DE SOTO	26.7	7.7	12.7	20.3	34.8	9.3	160,737	41,597	10,883	16,974	1,823	60,853	261,821	20,334	29.0	11.9	10.0	.0071
DIXIE	12.6	7.4	12.7	22.6	33.1	4.5	42,634	12,379	4,888	1,467	1,648	11,031	121,691	18,606	23.4	12.2	10.8	.0028
FRANKLIN	10.7	6.2	11.3	21.4	37.1	4.2	60,342	25,188	9,623	1,381	212	5,218	129,313	21,995	27.1	11.9	15.1	.0030
GILCHRIST	12.8	8.0	11.9	22.8	30.7	4.5	19,114	9,299	1,816	732	903	1,204	130,455	20,426	28.5	17.1	5.5	.0029
GLADES	9.8	5.8	10.6	20.3	38.7	3.6	17,497	11,111	1,137		12	1,953	114,518	23,090	29.3	13.1	15.7	.0023
GULF	13.7	7.9	14.0	20.6	33.3	5.0	42,821	17,122	3,976	2,664	3,256	2,113	157,750	25,775	26.4	17.3	18.7	.0034
HAMILTON	13.8	8.9	13.8	21.9	24.8	4.5	58,010	12,777	3,642	1,961	1,634	4,081	126,672	18,805	25.7	12.9	9.1	.0033
HARDEE	23.1	8.2	12.2	20.7	30.2	7.1	151,028	45,522	6,942	17,903	3,718	39,578	185,092	19,994	27.2	13.8	8.9	.0057
HENDRY	30.5	8.7	13.8	20.8	24.7	9.7	201,309	78,474	17,508	18,452	1,924	38,221	289,429	24,396	28.1	16.4	15.0	.0083
HIGHLANDS	78.5	4.8	9.2	15.5	51.5	33.7	818,647	139,948	43,665	55,595	32,249	397,997	948,744	21,512	31.0	12.3	10.5	.0272
HOLMES	18.3	7.8	12.8	22.3	31.9	6.6	55,574	15,643	6,471	2,191	475	7,754	174,696	19,522	24.2	13.6	10.9	.0041
INDIAN RIVER	103.4	5.7	11.2	19.0	44.5	43.1	1,074,936	211,066	97,487	129,187	59,361	246,939	1,909,297	31,002	26.5	18.0	25.9	.0438
JACKSON	49.2	9.3	13.7	22.2	29.8	17.5	348,553	68,546	23,604	42,209	10,061	96,982	587,360	23,759	24.1	15.0	17.6	.0150
JEFFERSON	13.7	7.2	11.7	21.8	31.4	4.5	42,510	15,886	3,373	1,390	327	3,221	141,796	23,809	25.9	15.1	16.8	.0033
LAFAYETTE	7.0	8.9	15.8	21.6	27.3	2.3	8,443	5,283	304	111	342	656	64,972	19,534	28.3	10.6	10.1	.0014
LEVY	31.1	6.5	11.4	21.1	36.5	12.0	218,771	55,686	22,910	36,187	1,768	31,597	323,820	20,835	24.9	14.7	12.0	.0089
LIBERTY	7.6	9.0	16.2	22.8	26.2	2.3	11,893	3,570	910	186	186	549	105,546	26,814	25.1	18.2	19.8	.0020
MADISON	18.9	8.7	13.8	20.7	28.5	6.3	78,767	21,198	7,051	4,542	3,582	3,881	194,134	19,297	23.3	12.6	12.4	.0047
MONROE	84.1	6.7	15.6	26.6	33.7	35.8	1,123,711	223,700	231,156	88,510	39,116	107,096	1,786,380	34,263	25.3	18.3	30.5	.0414
OKEECHOBEE	34.0	7.7	12.9	19.8	31.8	11.4	262,272	73,848	21,282	35,900	7,108	57,998	347,939	23,188	29.2	14.6	13.5	.0099
PUTNAM	70.8	6.6	11.9	20.6	35.2	27.0	439,040	108,797	33,369	73,296	17,756	89,964	884,916	25,200	25.3	14.9	19.8	.0212
SUMTER	42.3	7.2	11.6	18.8	40.0	16.1	194,227	41,646	24,035	15,239	4,301	18,820	478,078	22,749	26.5	15.2	14.0	.0113
SUWANNEE	31.9	6.9	11.4	21.5	33.5	11.9	247,297	58,216	19,015	12,694	4,930	72,165	323,308	20,828	27.7	12.4	11.8	.0093
TAYLOR	19.3	7.3	13.4	21.3	29.5	7.1	117,479	27,214	11,104	11,619	6,945	29,360	219,644	24,323	24.0	16.1	18.2	.0055
UNION	13.2	7.7	19.1	24.6	20.3	3.3	24,043	11,373	1,887	724	1,233	2,681	127,005	23,382	29.6	18.1	9.9	.0027
WAKULLA	18.4	6.8	12.9	25.8	26.1	6.7	59,954	25,926	9,604	1,940	2,465	4,952	230,537	29,078	26.1	20.2	20.4	.0047
WALTON	34.7	6.4	12.4	21.7	36.2	13.7	303,218	70,381	36,980	34,088	27,406	19,395	480,390	27,264	25.8	16.0	21.6	.0121
WASHINGTON	20.0	7.2	11.3	21.7	34.4	7.4	99,776	38,746	10,500	4,593	5,557	3,001	206,282	21,809	26.4	13.6	13.6	.0052
TOTAL METRO COUNTIES	**13,629.6**	**8.0**	**14.4**	**22.0**	**33.2**	**5,373.0**	**151,040,638**	**23,687,694**	**15,438,362**	**17,710,675**	**9,129,190**	**42,440,456**	**221,947,315**	**31,390**	**25.3**	**17.9**	**26.7**	**5.5238**
TOTAL STATE	**14,701.2**	**7.9**	**14.3**	**21.9**	**33.5**	**5,779.9**	**158,977,857**	**25,541,819**	**16,230,041**	**18,539,777**	**9,428,007**	**44,202,431**	**235,742,698**	**30,830**	**25.3**	**17.8**	**26.0**	**5.8661**

Source: *Sales & Marketing Management,* by permission.

WORLDWIDE AVAILABILITY OF SECONDARY DATA

Although secondary data is abundant in the United States and other industrialized countries, this is certainly not the case worldwide. In the global market context of many industries, researchers can be frustrated by the lack of secondary information or the lack of access to secondary information characterizing, for example, most Latin American countries. However, the availability of international information is improving. We provide sources of international information useful in marketing in Table 6.3.

TABLE 6.3

Sources of Information for International Marketing

I. COUNTRY INFORMATION

BACKGROUND INFORMATION

General Encyclopedias

Online library catalog—under name of country (i.e., Sweden—economic conditions, politics and government, social conditions, statistics, population).

COUNTRY DESCRIPTIONS

World Almanac and Book of Facts. New York: Press Pub. Annual.

Countries of the World and Their Leaders Yearbook. Detroit, Mich.: Gale. Annual.

Europa World Yearbook. London: Europa Publications. Annual.

Craighead's *International Business Travel and Guide to Countries.* Detroit, Mich.: Gale, 1995.

Statesman's Yearbook. New York: St. Martin's Press. Annual.

World Factbook. Washington, D.C.: Central Intelligence Agency. Annual.

MARKETING IN SPECIFIC COUNTRIES

Cracking Latin America. Chicago, Ill.: Probus, 1994. Series covers other countires.

China Business: The Portable Encyclopedia for Doing Business With China. Genzberger, Christine. San Rafael, Calif.: World Trade Press, 1994.

Chile, A Country Study. Washington, D.C.: GPO, 1994. Series includes other countries.

STATISTICAL SOURCES

International Financial Statistics Yearbook. Washington, D.C.: International Monetary Fund. Annual.

International Marketing Data and Statistics. London: Euromonitor Pub., 1994.

Statistical Abstract of the United States. Washington, D.C.: GPO. Annual.

U.N. Statistical Yearbook. Annual.

GEOGRAPHICAL SOURCES

Atlases and maps available in libraries in print and CD-ROM.

LEGAL INFORMATION

Martindale–Hubbell International Law Digest. New Providence, N.J.: Martindale–Hubbell. Annual. Gives a summary of each country's laws, including patents, copyrights, trademarks, divorces, marriages, etc.

GOVERNMENT DOCUMENTS (ASK DOCUMENTS LIBRARIAN FOR DETAILS)

Business America. Washington, D.C.: U.S. Dept. of Commerce. Monthly.

Department of State Background Notes. Washington, D.C.: U.S. Dept. of State, irregular series.

CURRENT INDEXES

Newspapers

New York Times Index. New York: New York Times Co.

The Wall Street Journal Index. New York: Dow Jones.

Journals

ABI/INFORM. Ann Arbor, Mich.: UMI.

Business Index. Menlo Park, Calif.: Information Access Corp.

COMPUTERIZED DATABASES

Datastar. A supplier, based in Europe, of international databases.

Dialog. A professional database supplier of hundreds of databases.

Global Trade Outlook. A U.S. government publication about the outlook of international trade.

National Trade Data Bank (NTDB). A CD-ROM library of government documents about U.S. international trade.

II. BUSINESS INFORMATION

INVESTMENT SERVICES

IDD Trade Line. Available on Datastar, etc. Includes international stock information.

Moody's International Manual. Summarizes a country's economic conditions and major companies in each country.

DIRECTORIES OF COMPANIES

Disclosure: A comprehensive database of U.S. company reports. Published by Compact D/SEC [CD-ROM], Bethesda, Md: Disclosure Inc. Annual.

Hoover's Handbook of World Business. Austin, Tex.: Reference Press, 1996.

Principal International Businesses. New York: Dun & Bradstreet. Annual.

EXPORTING/IMPORTING INFORMATION

American Export Register. New York: Thomas International Pub. Co. Annual.

Basic Guide to Exporting. San Rafael, Calif.: World Trade Press, 1994.

Directory of United States Exporters. New York: Journal of Commerce. Annual.

Directory of United States Importers. New York: Journal of Commerce. Annual.

Importers Manual USA. San Rafael, Calif.: World Trade Press. Annual.

SUMMARY

Data needed for marketing management decisions may be grouped into primary and secondary. Primary data is gathered specifically for the research project at hand. Secondary data refers to data that has been previously gathered for some other purpose. Secondary data may be internal, such as data already gathered within the firm for some other purpose (for example, information from sales receipts), or external to the firm (for example, census data provided by the government). Secondary data has the advantages of being quickly gathered and relatively inexpensive. Such data often adds helpful insights should primary data be needed. Disadvantages are that the data is reported in measurement units or class definitions that are incompatible with the researchers' needs, and secondary data may not be recent. Evaluation of secondary data is important; researchers must ask certain questions in order to ensure the integrity of the information they use.

Finding secondary data involves understanding what you need to know and understanding key terms and names associated with the subject. Indices and bibliographies may first be consulted; they list sources of secondary information by subject. Consult the sources and evaluate the information. Make use of computerized data search from databases, if available. Seek the services of a reference librarian.

Much secondary information is now available through the Internet and the World Wide Web. Examples of important secondary data for business decisions are the *Census of the Population* from the U.S. Bureau of the Census and "Survey of Buying Power" published annually in *Sales & Marketing Management* magazine. The North American Industry Classification System (NAICS) is replacing the Standard Industrial Classification (SIC) system as the government's classification system for business.

View: "Your SPSS Data Sets Supplied by Burns and Bush"

KEY TERMS

Primary data (p. 139)
Secondary data (p. 139)
Internal data (p. 140)
Database marketing (p. 140)
External data (p. 140)
Published sources (p. 140)
Syndicated sources (p. 140)
Database (p. 141)
Internal databases (p. 141)
External databases (p. 141)
Computerized database (p. 141)
Bibliographic databases (p. 141)
Numeric databases (p. 142)
Directory databases (p. 142)
Full-text databases (p. 142)
Internet (p. 143)
World Wide Web, The Web, WWW (p. 143)
Web sites (p. 143)
Homepage (p. 143)
Browsers (p. 143)
Uniform resource locator addresses (p. 143)
Search engines (p. 143)
Surf (p. 143)
Census of the Population (p. 155)
North American Industry Classification System (NAICS) (p. 156)
Standard Industrial Classification (SIC) system (p. 156)
Survey of Buying Power (p. 158)
Effective buying income (EBI) (p. 158)
Buying power index (BPI) (p. 158)
Customized BPI (p. 158)

REVIEW QUESTIONS/APPLICATIONS

1. What is secondary data and how does it differ from primary data?
2. Describe how the Internet and World Wide Web may be used to access secondary data?
3. When should the researcher seek out secondary information? Why?
4. Discuss three advantages of secondary data. Discuss three disadvantages of secondary data.
5. How would you go about evaluating secondary data? Why is evaluation important?
6. Discuss how you would go about finding secondary data in your own library.
7. What are the different kinds of computerized databases? Find an example of each in your own library.
8. Briefly identify 10 types of information that are available from the *Census of the Population.*
9. Why is the NAIC system important? How would you use a NAICS code once you have identified the appropriate code? List three industries in which you have a career interest. What are the appropriate NAICS codes for these industries?
10. Taking the NAICS codes you have identified in question 9, find (a) the number of firms in each industry in the United States, (b) the number of firms in each industry in your state, and (c) the number of firms in each industry in your MSA or county.
11. Once again, taking the three industries you have identified in question 9, consult the *Encyclopedia of Associations.* Write down the name(s) and addresses of the trade associations in each industry. (You may want to write to them and find out about their services, membership, and so on if you have an interest in interviewing firms within the industry.)
12. What is the BPI? What is the significance of the BPI?
13. What is the BPI for your MSA or county? What has been the trend in your MSA's (county's) BPI for the last five years? Can you give some rationale for this trend? Do the same for two other nearby MSAs (counties) that you would regard as being similar to yours.

CASE 6.1

The University of West Florida

The dean of the College of Business at the University of West Florida (UWF), Dr. William B. Carper, was interested in knowing the demand for different educational programs during the next couple of years. Specifically, he was interested in knowing the educational plans, including intended fields of study, among residents 18 years and older of the primary service area served by UWF. He asked a marketing research professor if she would consider conducting such a study in her class. Students in the class made over 2,500 telephone calls and completed almost 800 interviews with respondents 18 and over in Escambia and Santa Rosa County, Florida—the Pensacola, Florida, MSA.

The results of the study were very interesting and Dean Carper provided a copy of the survey to the president, Dr. Morris Marx. Sometime later, the president was making plans for the university and he had a number of reports available to him, including the survey conducted by the College of Business. He was interested in using some of the information reported in the survey but he wondered about the reliability of this report. Was the data reported accurate? President Marx did find some information in a section titled "Profile of the Sample." This section provided a demographic profile of the survey's respondents. Among other variables reported, the following information on the age of the respondents was included:

DEMOGRAPHIC PROFILE OF SURVEY RESPONDENTS

AGE (1990 CENSUS CATEGORIES)	*n*	PERCENT
18–20 years	55	7.0
21–24	88	11.3
25–44	309	39.5
45–54	96	12.3
55–59	56	7.2
60–64	55	7.0
65 or greater	119	15.2
Refused to answer	4	0.5
Total	782	100.0

This situation is not all that unusual. A survey, conducted for one entity, ends up in another party's hands and the issue of credibility is raised. President Marx has decided that the credibility of this "secondary data" is very important. He is about to make some major decisions impacting the university based on the study's results.

1. What can President Marx do to evaluate the information in the survey?

CASE 6.2

Cadillac

The marketing vice president of the Cadillac Division of General Motors, Mr. J. Thomas Nesbitt, constantly makes decisions requiring the use of secondary data. In considering sales promotion activities around the United States for the upcoming year, he wants to know which markets have the greatest sales potential. He assigned this task to a new university co-op student working for him, and she has just prepared a report ranking the top 150 markets in the United States based on their BPI as reported in the most recent "Survey of Buying Power."

1. What should Nesbitt say to the co-op student? What suggestions would you have for her?

CHAPTER 7

Syndicated Services

LEARNING OBJECTIVES

- *To learn how to distinguish syndicated services from other types of data in marketing research*
- *To understand the advantages and disadvantages of syndicated services*
- *To distinguish the differences between syndicated data services and standardized services*
- *To know three different applications of syndicated data services*

A salesperson makes a presentation using IRI's expert system, SalesPartner™.

PRACTITIONER VIEWPOINT

The desire of marketers to forge strong one-to-one relationships with existing customers and uncover prospective customers has never been stronger. The challenge is to match the right audience with the right product and the right message. To do that, marketers must accurately answer questions like: "Who are my customers?", "What are they like?", "Where do they live?", and "How can I reach them?"

Syndicated data tools, like lifestyle segmentation systems, provide a reliable framework for profiling consumers and building effective marketing strategies. Additionally, they provide the flexibility needed to link to both in-house client files and secondary data sources. This, in turn, allows companies to target their most profitable customers and prospects and create marketing strategies most likely to reach them.

— Nancy G. Deck
President
Claritas, Inc.

Blue Blood Estates, Gray Power, and Big City Blend

1. Establish the need for marketing research
2. Define the problem
3. Establish research objectives
4. Determine research design
5. **Identify information types and sources**
6. Determine methods of accessing data
7. Design data collection forms
8. Determine sample plan and size
9. Collect data
10. Analyze data
11. Prepare and present the final research report

Ethan Martin works for Mall Development Corporation (MDC). MDC is a large firm involved in shopping center location, development, and management. Ethan's primary responsibility is in the area of finding suitable locations for new shopping centers. Historically, Ethan had used standard demographic data for various locales. Although this information was useful, particularly in providing Ethan with an area's income and population growth trends, Ethan felt he needed more information. The shopping center location decision is complex. It involves a huge capital outlay, and the market appeal of any given shopping center is largely dependent on the types of stores that become the center's tenants. A large discount chain store appeals to a different type of consumer than does an upscale department store.

Ethan felt that the standard secondary data giving him an area's income distribution and population growth rate was not very helpful in understanding the people themselves. By having better information about the people in the market, Ethan felt he could do a much better job of developing the right mix of stores for a shopping center. He wanted information about the types of people in a market area, an understanding of their life-styles, and their likes and dislikes in terms of products and services. This information was not available through secondary data, and Ethan knew that it would be cost prohibitive for MDC to pay for collecting this information in every market area they considered for a shopping center.

Ethan had heard of a company that provided this kind of information—Claritas, Inc. He called Claritas and was visited by Amelia Brown, its account representative. Ms. Brown explained to Ethan that her firm collected the kind of information he was interested in and could provide it at a reasonable cost because the information could be marketed to a number of different firms. This allowed Claritas to spread the expense over many firms that subscribed to the service.

Ms. Brown explained some of the advantages of her firm's information. First, she pointed out that much of the secondary data Ethan had been using was for prespecified geographic areas, such as counties, cities, or MSAs. However, she noted that Ethan was especially interested in information about the geographic area that would become the trading area for the new shopping center. Claritas could provide the needed information for the estimated trading area.

Second, Claritas annually collects and updates information on over 800 demographic variables, and they use this information to classify over 7 million neighborhoods in the United States into 62 categories based on consumer behavior and life-style. Brown explained some of the characteristics of the people in these 62 categories, which have been given descriptive labels such as "Blue Blood Estates," "Gray Power," and "Big City Blend." To illustrate how this information could prove useful, Brown then showed Ethan the table on page 172, which details the differences among three categories of these consumers in terms of their likes and dislikes for several types of goods and services.

Brown summarized by stating, "If you could supply me with a description of the geographic area estimated to make up the trading area for a proposed shopping center, Claritas could help you learn much about the consumers in those areas. This information would be beneficial to you in developing the right mix of shopping center tenants."[1]

	"BLUE BLOOD ESTATES" MORE LIKELY TO . . .	"GRAY POWER" MORE LIKELY TO . . .	"BIG CITY BLEND" MORE LIKELY TO . . .
Life-style	Belong to a country club Go sailing Use maid/ housekeeper Buy classical music	Go to Walt Disney World Go golfing Buy novels Spend $26+ avg. long-dist. bill	Go to baseball games Buy 15+ lottery tickets/month Use a grocery list Eat at a fast food Mexican restaurant
Products & Services	Own mutual funds $100,000+ Have "gold"/premium credit card Eat pita bread Own a BMW Spend $250+ on business suit Drink imported wine	Own annuities Eat Post grape-nuts Use an egg substitute Own a water filter Own a Buick Shop at Wal-Mart	Have first mortgage loan Own a Mitsubishi Drink Pepsi-Free Buy stereo equipment Own a home gym system Buy Adidas shoes
Radio/TV	Listen to news/ talk radio Listen to soft contemporary radio Watch *Seinfeld* Watch The Masters (golf) Watch *MacNeil/ Lehrer News Hour*	Watch morning TV Watch arts and entertainment Listen to news radio Watch *Jeopardy* Watch *Live with Regis & Kathie Lee*	Listen to progressive rock radio Listen to variety radio Watch *Another World* Watch *Entertainment Tonight* Watch MTV
Print	Read *Fortune* Read *Food & Wine* Read *Business Week* Read *Smithsonian*	Read *Southern Living* Read newspaper editorial section Read *Golf Magazine*	Read newspaper general news section Read *Cosmopolitan*

	"BLUE BLOOD ESTATES" MORE LIKELY TO . . .	"GRAY POWER" MORE LIKELY TO . . .	"BIG CITY BLEND" MORE LIKELY TO . . .
Print	Read newspapers often	Read *Modern Maturity* Read *Consumer's Digest*	Read newspaper entertainment section Read *Rolling Stone* Read *Sports Illustrated*

As the Claritas case illustrates, there are some situations in which existing secondary data does not solve the research problem, and yet collecting primary data is not feasible. In many such situations, firms such as Claritas or DMIS (another supplier that collects data on over 1,600 demographic variables classifying all neighborhoods in the United States into 47 life-style categories based on consumer behavior) collect the primary data needed and make this information available at a reasonable cost by selling it to a large number of firms who subscribe to the information service. We refer to these supplier firms as syndicated data service firms. This chapter describes syndicated data services and standardized services. These two types of syndicated services are described, as well as a form of syndicated data service called "single-source" data.

UNDERSTANDING SYNDICATED SERVICES

Syndicated data are a form of external, secondary data that are supplied from a common database to subscribers for a service fee. Recall from our discussion of the types of firms in the marketing research industry in chapter 2 that we call firms providing such data **syndicated data service** firms. Such information is typically detailed information that is valuable to firms in a given industry and is not available in libraries. Firms supplying syndicated data follow standard research formats that enable them to collect the same, standardized data over time. These firms provide specialized, routine information needed by a given industry in the form of ready-to-use, standardized marketing data to subscribing firms. For example, one syndicated data service firm provides syndicated data on the number and types of listeners to the various radio stations in each radio market. This standardized information helps advertising firms reach their target markets; it also helps radio stations define audience characteristics by providing an objective, independent measure of the size and characteristics of their audiences. As another example, Nielsen Media Research supplies syndicated data in the form of TV ratings.

Syndicated data service firms syndicate data.

Standardized service firms syndicate methods of collecting data.

Second, there are **standardized services** that are also syndicated. These services are supplied by firms that provide a standard service and syndicate this service to any firm wishing to subscribe. Audits & Surveys provides a standardized service in the form of prearranged test marketing. The company will provide a subscribing firm with all necessary services to test market a product and will then supply data back to the subscribing firm about the test market. Such data will include information regarding sales, levels of promotion, level of distribution, and so on. Subscribing firms supply the firms offering these services with products and advertisements. SPAR/Burgoyne also offers this service, which they refer to as their mini-market test. Many of the firms in the syndicated services industry supply both syndicated data as well as standardized services. NFO, for example, provides panel data on retail purchases and, at the same time, it offers the Multicard service, described in chapter 2, which is a standardized method of collecting primary information. As we take you through examples in this chapter we, in some cases, note whether the example is referring to a syndicated data service or a standardized service.

ADVANTAGES/DISADVANTAGES OF SYNDICATED SERVICES

The key advantages of syndicated data are shared costs, high quality, and currency of information.

One of the key *advantage of syndicated services* is shared costs. Many organizations may subscribe to the services; thus, the cost of the service is greatly reduced to any one subscriber firm. When costs are spread across several subscribers, other advantages result. Because syndicated data firms specialize in the collection of routine data and because their viability, in the long run, depends on the validity of the data, the quality of the data collected is typically very high. With several companies paying for the service, the syndicating company can go to great lengths to gather a great amount of data as well. Another advantage of syndicated data comes from the routinized systems used to collect and process the data. The data is normally disseminated very quickly to subscribers because these syndicated data firms set up standard procedures and methods for collecting the data over and over again on a periodic basis. The more current the data, the greater its usefulness.

Standardized services not only have the advantage of lowered cost per user but also the service has been through many trials and, consequently, can be regarded as a reliable service.

The disadvantages of syndicated data include no control over what data is collected, its standardized format, availability of same information to everyone, and the cost of commitment.

There are some *disadvantages to syndicated services.* First, for syndicated data services, subscribers have little or no control over the data being collected. Consequently, before becoming a subscriber, you must evaluate commercial data much like secondary data, making sure that the units of measurement are appropriate and that the class definitions are suitable for your needs. This is also true for standardized services. A user cannot, for example, change the population from which a standardized survey sample is drawn. There are certain cities that may not be used as a test market because no standardized service company has facilities in that city.

Second, every prospective subscriber firm must carefully evaluate the information that is provided by syndicated data suppliers because these suppliers often require a long-term contract. Usually, a company must commit to several months, and typically a minimum of a year, of subscription. Last, unlike primary data collection, which enables a firm to collect customized information for its own specific needs, standardized commercial data is available to everyone in the industry. Competing firms make use of the same data. So, whatever you observe in the syndicated data can be observed by your competitors. By the same token, knowing that your competitors subscribe to a particular syndicated source may compel you to subscribe to it as well.

APPLICATION AREAS OF SYNDICATED DATA SERVICES

The four major application areas of syndicated data are measuring consumer attitudes and opinion polls, defining market segments, conducting market tracking, and monitoring media usage and promotion effectiveness.

Measuring Consumer Attitudes and Opinion Polls

Consumer attitude surveys and opinion polls are performed by the Yankelovich monitor, the ABC News/Harris poll, the Gallup poll, and the DDB Needham life-style study.

Several firms offer measurements of consumer attitudes and opinions on various issues. The **Yankelovich monitor** measures changing social values and how these changes affect consumers.[2] The **Harris poll** measures consumer attitudes and opinions on the economy, environment, politics, and so on.[3] The **Gallup poll** surveys public opinion, asking questions on domestic issues, private issues, and world affairs such as, "Did you favor the use of tactical nuclear weapons against Iraq in the Persian Gulf War?" A number of demographic breakdowns are available so that readers may see how opinions differ by sex, age, race, and level of education. The Gallup poll is available each year, and back issues cover each year beginning with 1935.[4] Consumer attitudes have been tracked over an 18-year period by the **DDB Needham life-style study.** Their study shows how attitudes have changed toward family debt, brand names, types of entertainment, and a variety of other subjects.

Defining Market Segments

Defining market segments requires that you place customers sharing certain attributes (age, income, stage in the family life cycle, etc.) into homogenous groups or market segments. Once in these groups, marketers gather information about the members of the market, compiling profiles of the attributes describing the consumers that make up each segment. Marketers can then decide which segments are presently being served or not served by the competition. They can also determine the size, growth trends, and profit potential of each segment. Using this data, a segment, or group of segments, can be targeted for marketing.

Syndicated services firms provide information about members of various market segments in the industrial market as well as the consumer market.

Several syndicated services provide marketers with information about customers in the market. Some of these services provide information on members of the industrial market, and others provide information on members of the consumer market.

Providing Information on Members of the Industrial Market

A great deal about the industrial market can be learned through the use of the **Standard Industrial Classification (SIC) system** and the new **North American Industry Classification System (NAICS),** the government's method of classifying business firms (discussed in chapter 6). Although achieving the basic objectives of allowing you to identify, classify, and monitor standard statistics about certain industries and their member firms, the SIC falls short of allowing you to target customers in a highly specific industry. NAICS will partially remedy this problem by going from the SIC's four-digit code to a six-digit code. However, it is too early to tell what impact NAICS will have on information gathering.

Dun's market identifiers allows researchers to identify certain types of firms in the industrial market.

One syndicated service firm supplies additional information that allows the user to make even better use of the government's classification systems. **Dun's market identifiers (DMI),** published by Dun & Bradsteet, provides information on over four million firms that it updates monthly. The real benefit of DMI is that it provides a service called "2 + 2 enhancement" that provides two additional two-digit codes to the SIC codes. The current four-digit SIC codes allow you to group firms into 1,006 categories. However, with DMI's additional two-digit code, you can examine 2,500 categories and by adding the second two-digit code you can have 15,000 categories. The additional categories allow you to target more specific industries.

For example, one marketing researcher recently worked with a manufacturing firm, BasKet Kases, a manufacturer of wooden gift baskets, to secure a listing of all firms that wholesale gift baskets for the purposes of targeting these firms with a marketing campaign. Using the *SIC Classification Manual*, it was determined that SIC numbers with a 51 prefix were wholesalers of nondurable goods. By examining all of the 51 prefix descriptions, the SIC code of 5199 was found to represent wholesalers of "miscellaneous, nondurable goods," which included baskets. Without additional information, a list of firms with an SIC code of 5199 would have included wholesalers of all types of baskets, including wooden baskets for shipping fruit and freight and so on. However, with the use of the additional codes supplied by DMI, it was found that the eight-digit code 51990603 represented "wholesalers of gift baskets." This was exactly what the researcher was seeking. By finding the firms sharing this eight-digit code, the researcher was able to identify 45 wholesale firms of gift baskets in the United States for BasKet Kases.

Providing Information on Members of the Consumer Market

Information on segmenting consumers by life-style is available through DDB Needham's life-style study[5] and the VALS-2 study, which is the Stanford Research Institute's survey that places consumers in segments based on lifestyles.[6]

Geodemographics combines census data with other survey data for profiling customer defined geographic areas.

Geodemographics is the term used to describe the classification of arbitrary, usually small, geographic areas in terms of the characteristics of their inhabitants. Aided with sophisticated computer programs, geodemographers can access huge databases and construct profiles of consumers residing in geographic areas determined by the geodemographer. Instead of being confined to consumer information recorded by city, county, or state, geodemographers can produce this information for geographic areas thought to be relevant for a given marketing application (such as a proposed shopping center trading area).[7]

Firms specializing in geodemographics combine census data with their own survey data or data that they gather from administrative records, such as motor vehicle registrations or credit transactions, to produce customized products for their clients.[8] Claritas, referred to at the beginning of this chapter, is one such firm. By accessing zip codes and census data regarding census tracks, census block groups, or blocks, which make up a firm's trading area(s), Claritas can compile much information about the characteristics and life-styles of the people within these trading areas. Or, a firm may give Claritas a descriptive profile of its target market and Claritas can supply the firm with geographic areas that most closely match the prespecified characteristics. This service is referred to as Prizm (potential ratings index for Zip+4 markets).

Learn more about Claritas by visiting their website at http://www.claritas.com/index.htm.

Claritas updates census data every year and provides information to subscriber firms. The census provides a snapshot of the demographic state of the nation at 10-year intervals. The problem with these data is that as the decade progresses, the data becomes older and more unreliable for use in business planning. Claritas therefore supplements the base census information with current estimates and projections on an annual basis. The set of variables included in the estimates and projections has been expanded to include a number of labor force characteristics, education, and marital status, as well as extensions to the income estimates to include income by race and ethnic origin.

Claritas also offers the Market Reporter, which is a customized database system that is delivered electronically to users. The Market Reporter offers users a simple way to obtain data on any site in the entire United States. All the user has to do is specify the area of interest. Once the area is specified, Market Reporter provides a variety of reports such as Area, Housing, Population, and Socioeconomic Profiles, as well as Demographic Trends for the years 1980, 1990, 1995, 2000, and 2005 for the chosen area. How can these help the manager? Let's say you are a retailer and are trying to select the best location for your establishment in a certain part of the town. The Shopping Center Data package can give you details on location, gross leasable area, anchor stores, center type, year built, and more. The Traffic Volume Package can provide you with information on how many vehicles actually pass by the business establishment on a daily basis. It can answer questions such as: Are there other areas with similar demographics that have more traffic? (See Marketing Research Insight 7.1 on pages 178–180 for examples of specific reports that can be obtained from the Market Reporter.)

Market Reporter is a geodemographic software product. It is explained in Marketing Research Insight 7.1.

Conducting Market Tracking

Companies conduct **market tracking** to monitor sales and market shares of products/services over time. Although a company may monitor its own sales, sales measured by a firm's own invoices provide an incomplete picture. By monitoring only its own sales, a firm does not know what is going on in the channel of distribution. Products are not distributed instantaneously. Rather, inventories are built up and depleted at various rates among the different distributors. Just because household sales of a product increase does not mean that a producer will experience a sales increase of that product. To really know what is happening in the industry, marketers need to monitor the movement of goods at every level. Recognizing this need, market tracking is conducted at both the retail level and at the household level.

Market Tracking at the Retail Level

There are several services that monitor sales and market shares at the retail level, including those provided by Nielsen Services and SPAR/Burgoyne's national retail tracking index (NRTI). A discussion of these follows.

Market tracking at the retail level provides data on the products.

MARKETING RESEARCH INSIGHT 7.1

Market Reporter

Market Reporter offered by Claritas offers a simple way to get data on any site in the entire United States.

The standard package includes the following data:

1. *Geography:* *U.S. National Coverage by Block Group, Census Tract, County, MSA, State, Place, Zip Code, and U.S.*
2. *Data:* *1970, 1980, 1990 Census Data, Current Year Estimates, Five-Year Projections, Ten-Year Projections.*
3. *Reports:* *Executive Summary, Benchmark Summary, Population Profile, Age 65+, Demographic Updates, Vehicles Available, Demographic Trends, Income Updates, Income Trends, Area Profile, Population Profile (1990), Housing Profile, Socio-Economic Profile, and Travel Time.*

In addition to the standard package, there are other reports available, such as the Merchandise Potential (14 reports), the Traffic Volumes (2 reports), the Shopping Centers (2 reports), and the Business/Daytime Census (3 reports). These reports provide detailed information about any chosen location, comparison of various sites with respect to demographics, and so on.

How does one use this plethora of information to investigate the business potential of a particular site? There are four basic steps to get to the necessary reports for a study. These are:

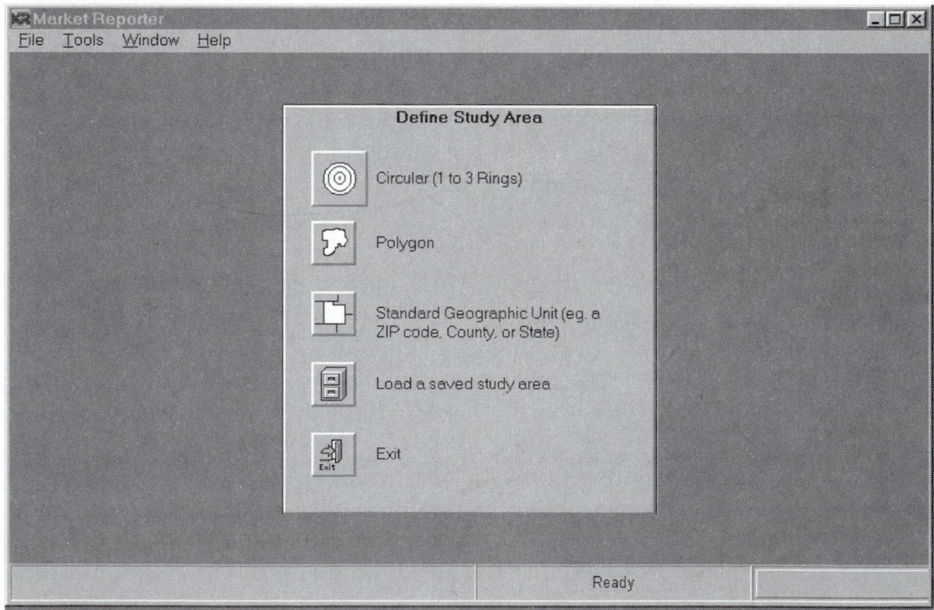

1. Define. *Define the area to be studied. The options available are a circle around the area of interest, a polygon, or a standard geographic unit such as a zip code, county, or state. In this case a circular ring study was chosen.*

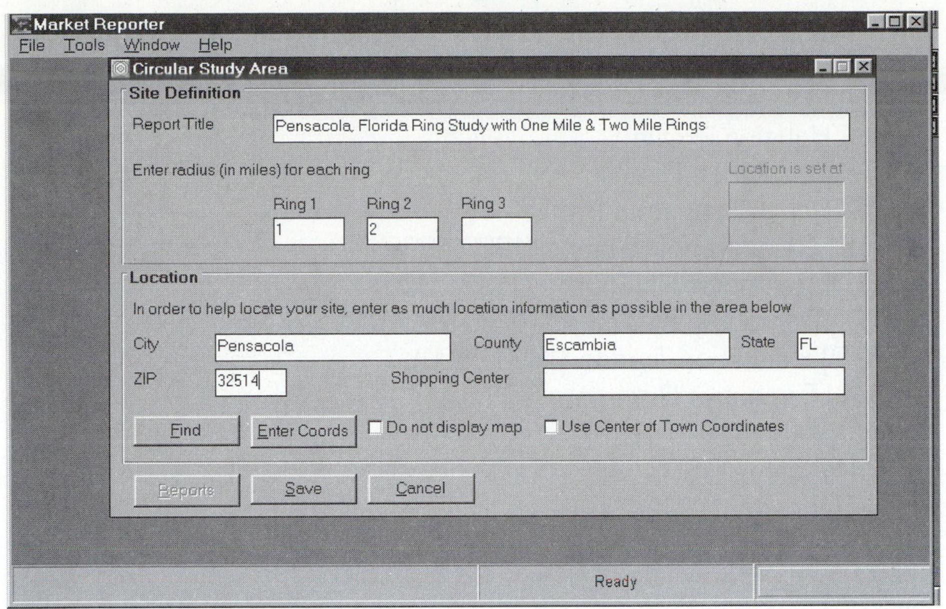

2. Specify. *In the* Study Area *window, provide as much information on your trade area as possible (city, zip code, state, or even a specific shopping mall). In this example the desired city was Pensacola, Florida, with a one-mile and two-mile radius.*

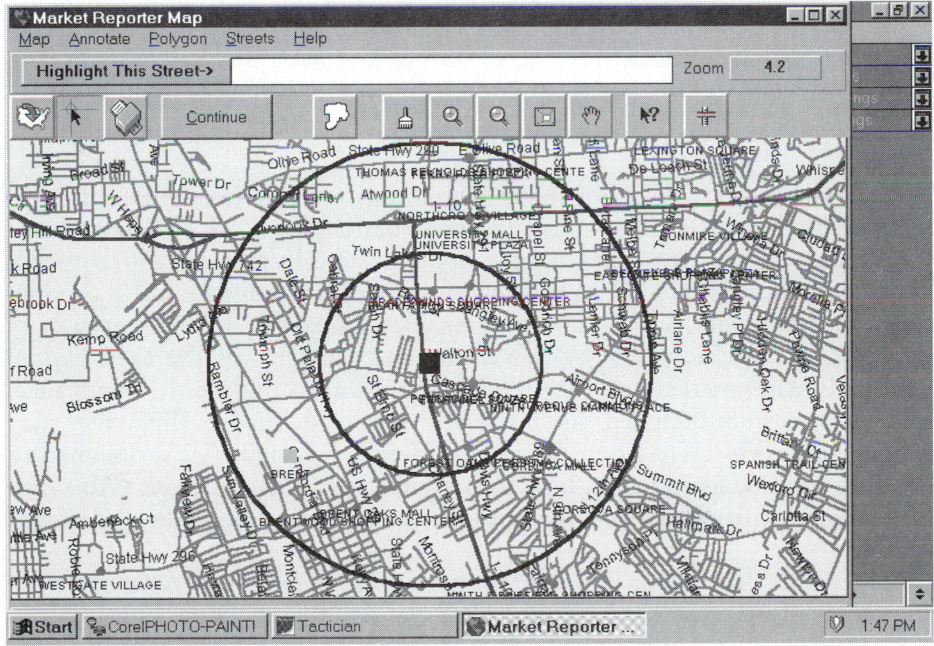

3. Choose. *Once Market Reporter has found your desired location you have to select the center for the circles. The University Mall was chosen as the center for the Pensacola study.*

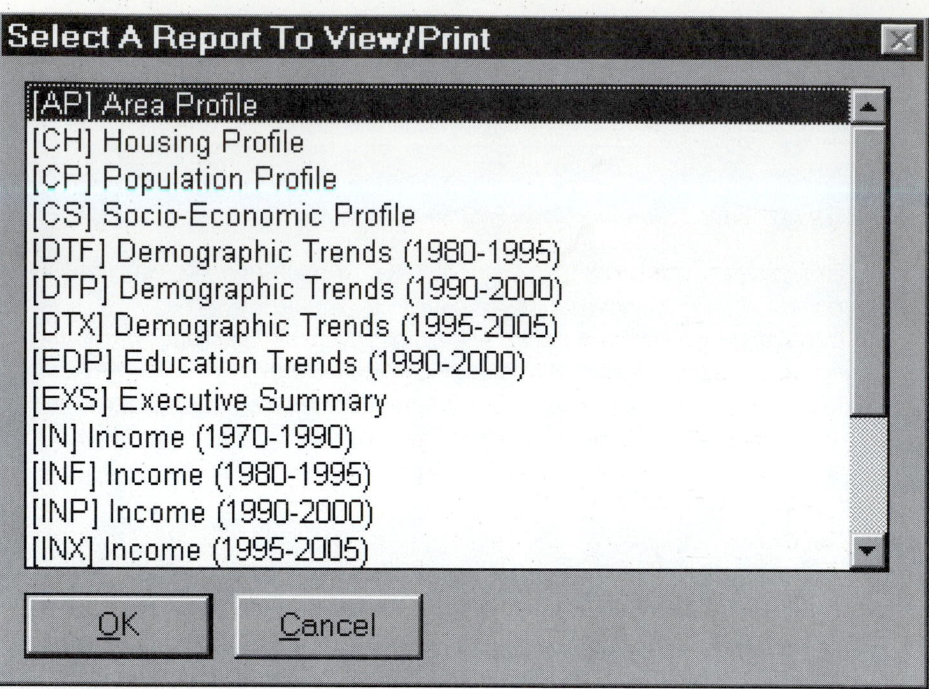

4. Continue/Choose. *Load the corresponding database for the reports. Finally, choose among 18 different standard reports—for example, the 1990 area profile report, which provides demographic information separated by different rings. It shows the household income distribution, age distribution, as well as information on households, sex, school years, vehicles, and rent.*

ACNielsen services include a variety of valuable market tracking monitors.

ACNielsen Services.[9] For many major consumer product firms, the primary research vehicles for evaluating brand performance are **ACNielsen services.** Although internal sales records provide some insight on a given product's sales, they do not measure sales of competitive brands or the product category itself. The ACNielsen report enables a manager to track growth of the category and individual brands within the category for the total United States, 50 major markets, and the remaining sales areas outside the major markets. Also, custom-designed sales areas and retailer-defined trading areas may also be tracked by ACNielsen. Marketing Research Insight 7.2 is designed to give you some suggestions on how to analyze an ACNielsen report. (You may find this particularly useful if you work the ACNielsen case at the end of this chapter.)

Until 1986, the national ACNielsen grocery store report was generated from an audit of 1,050 stores, which comprised the **ACNielsen Food Index (NFI).** The sample consisted of chains as well as all sizes of independents, including convenience stores. Each store was audited bimonthly to produce six reports a year for the total United States, 35 major markets, and the remaining sales areas outside the major markets. Every period, ACNielsen employees would visit sample stores and physically count inventories for all brands and packages of every contracted category. Product "sell-in" (a measure of the quantity of *purchases* of a

MARKETING RESEARCH INSIGHT 7.2

Analyzing an ACNielsen Report

The first step in an ACNielsen analysis is to paint the "big picture" of trends on a national level. Scan the report for the following data:

1. *Total category sales: How much has the category grown in the past year? Is the rate of growth increasing or slowing?*
2. *Total category flavor/package trends: Which flavors and packages are increasing in importance? Which ones are decreasing?*
3. *Your corporate share trends: Is your corporate share increasing or declining? Which of your brands are increasing in share and which ones are declining? Are the increases in your "up" brands sufficient to offset decreases in your "down" brands?*
4. *Competitive corporate share trends: Ask the same questions about your competition as you did about your corporation in number 3.*
5. *Brand-by-brand share trend analysis: For each brand, which flavors and packages are gaining share? Which ones are losing? Are the increases in the "up" flavors and packages sufficient to offset decreases in the "down" flavors and packages?*

Having determined national trends for the category, corporate, and individual brands, the next step is to isolate those local markets that most affect those trends. Rarely will all 51 ACNielsen segments—the 50 Major Markets plus the Remaining United States—reflect the same trend. Therefore, a marketing manager must identify problem markets and formulate an appropriate response for each of those markets. To do so, he or she must determine the following:

1. *Which segments are up in share, and what is the case sales impact of that share increase?*
2. *Similarly, which segments are down and what is their impact?*
3. *What is the case sales impact of all 51 segments in total?*
4. *Which segments are problem markets requiring special attention?*

To calculate the case sales impact of a share change, multiply the share change times the number of cases in the total category. For example, if the category of salad dressing in Detroit was 500,000 cases and Brand A's share decreased from 24.4 a year ago to 23.7 in the current year, the share loss of 0.7 represents −0.7 percent of the total category, or −3,500 cases. Case sales impact can be calculated for an individual brand, as in the example, or for corporate share.

Taking this analysis one step further, compare your performance to that of a competitor, for comparable individual brands or total corporate share, by calculating the share swing. Share swing is defined as your share change minus the share change for your competitor. To illustrate, let us say that in the Detroit salad dressing example, share for your competition, Brand B, increased from 20.2 one year ago to 20.6 in the current year, a gain of 0.4. Share swing is your share change (−0.7) minus their share change (+0.4) equals a share swing of −1.1. The impact of that −1.1 share swing is −1.1 percent of the total category, or −5,500 cases.

Whether you are analyzing the impact of brand or corporate share change, or the impact of brand or corporate share swing, the next step is to rank-order all 51 ACNielsen market segments. Generally, you will list markets with the largest negative impact at the top of the page, because these are the problem markets requiring attention. For each individual market, then, determine the flavors and packages that most affect the trend.

---

given commodity by an outlet) to the outlet for the bimonthly period was determined from delivery tickets collected by the store manager and reports of shipments to the outlet from manufacturers, warehouses, wholesalers, and other sources. Consumer "sell-through" (a measure of the quantity of a given commodity that an outlet has *sold*) for individual sample stores was calculated by adding beginning inventory and bimonthly product sell-in and subtracting ending inventory. Then, the 1,050 individual stores were statistically consolidated. Projections of total U.S. and major market data were generated that included category sales, sales and share of sales for individual brands and packages, item availability, and inventories and share of inventory for individual brands and packages.

Up until 1986, ACNielsen market tracking reports were not prepared quickly because they were based on physical audits.

A major disadvantage of the NFI report was its data collection procedure, which required considerable time and manpower to physically count inventories in sample stores. Each bimonthly period took ACNielsen employees approximately six weeks to audit all the sample outlets. Thus, an "April/May" report actually reflected sales of as early as March 10 through May 10 in some sample outlets and as late as April 21 through June 21 in others. Data tabulation took another two to three weeks, which meant that top-line share and sales from April/May reached a product manager in early July, by which time the data was as much as four months old.

ACNielsen now provides very current market tracking reports based on scanner data.

Since 1986, the ACNielsen reports have been generated from weekly checkout scanner data obtained from 3,000 stores that comprise **ACNielsen SCANTRACK** service. The sample consists of chains and independents with annual all-commodity volume (ACV—a measure of the total sales volume for a given outlet) of at least $2 million. SCANTRACK breaks out 50 major markets—15 more than the NFI. Reports are available on a four-week or weekly basis with custom sales areas developed as needed.

Using scanner data has provided several benefits. First of all, it has eliminated the time-consuming and labor-intensive physical audit. As a result, data are available in a few days rather than in several weeks. Additionally, reporting periods are now exact and precise: All outlets reflect sales for the same designated 28 days of the report period.

However, there are some differences between SCANTRACK and NFI. Most important, because scanning data does not consider inventory information, there is no longer a measure of share of outlet inventory. (Inventory information is available on an *ad hoc* basis through ACNielsen's in-store conditions service.) SCANTRACK provides a qualitative measurement of item availability and can provide quantitative data on the amount of inventory or out-of-stock conditions via the in-store conditions service. Such information is vital for evaluating new item introductions, where it is important to determine whether new items secured incremental space or merely took space from existing items. Such data must now be procured from additional field surveys or other sources. Recall that SCANTRACK's sample of 3,000 stores does not include convenience stores, which need to be audited by field representatives. To account for movement in convenience stores, ACNielsen now offers a service of combining large store scanning with convenience store audits for those clients wishing to track both segments of the grocery store distribution system. This is called C-Store Plus.

ACNielsen's market tracking service for convenience stores is called C-Store Plus.

In 1996, ACNielsen expanded its SCANTRAK Ethnic Services, which evaluate the effectiveness of micro-marketing efforts targeting population segments with specific ethnic characteristics. Because the ethnic population resides in highly concentrated areas (70 percent of U.S. Hispanics reside in just four states, whereas 40 percent of African-Americans live in five states), SCANTRAK Ethnic Services track consumer activity in these key markets by reporting six Hispanic markets and three African-American markets. A report for the total Hispanic or African-American market is also available. Hispanic market reports are available for Los Angeles, Miami, San Antonio, Chicago, New York, and Houston. African-American market reports are available for Chicago, Baltimore/Washington, and Memphis.

By comparing ethnic sales trends with the population at large, management can make informed decisions with respect to distribution, variety of products, pricing, and promotion. This ACNielsen tracking capability, combined with ACNielsen's exclusive Consumer Panel, provides a complete understanding of these unique marketing opportunities.

In July 1994, ACNielsen and Market Decisions entered into a joint venture, creating a powerful custom retail research unit. The services offered by this unit allow manufacturers and retailers to assess high-risk merchandising and product initatives in a live, but tightly controlled, low-risk environment. For example, Controlled Market Testing provides data from nationally recognized retailers across mutiple channels, enabling manufacturers to gauge actual trade and consumer response to changes in marketing strategy.

In 1993, ACNielsen and Promotion Information Bureau (PIB) formed a joint venture, which brought the grocery scanning expertise of SCANTRAK to the liquor store venue. WineScan and LiquorScan provide complete weekly data, ranging from fundamental sales trends to market- and item-level analyses to promotion and pricing evaluations. The results can also be compared across channels including liquor stores, combo stores, and supermarkets. This service is available in 20 key liquor markets across these retail channels. (You can read about WineScan and LiquorScan at http://acnielsen.com/countries/unitedst/explore.htm.)

ACNielsen tracks wine and liquor sales with WineScan and LiquorScan.

Some of the other services provided by ACNielsen include tools that help organizations meet sales and marketing challenges and build retail partnerships at the same time. For instance, **Retail Account Reports (RARs)** offer account specific information as defined by SCANTRAK major market geographic boundaries. These data would be useful for category management across retail chains and geographic markets. **Census Trading Areas** provide information that can be used to review and evaluate marketing tactics on a store-by-store basis. **SCANTRAK Key Account Causal** provides weekly data for over 200 individual accounts. This enables managers to understand how each account supports a product or brand on an ongoing basis. **Efficient Market Services, Inc. (EMS)** provides daily sales and merchandising information on virtually all scanned UPCs in every store. This information allows managers to solve out-of-stock problems, reduce excess inventory, and increase promotion productivity.

Prior to 1991, scanners had not become sufficiently widespread in drug and mass merchandiser accounts to enable Nielsen to initiate scanner-based reports. Thus, the 550-store **Nielsen Drug Index (NDI)** and the 125-store **Nielsen Mass Merchandiser Index (NMMI)** were generated with the traditional physical audit procedure. However, during 1991, enough scanner data was available to enable Nielsen to provide Procision scanner-based reports and analyses for drug and mass merchandiser stores. **Procision** is an integrated information service for the health and beauty aids (HBA) industry. Procision utilizes scanning-based weekly data from all major HBA channels combined with merchandising, television, promotion activity, and consumer purchase information. This design allows clients across various functional areas such as sales, marketing research, media, and top management to fully understand the changes in the marketplace. Within a single database, clients can access the tools and information needed to understand channel differences and the wide range of factors driving sales changes within each channel. For example, marketers can monitor the impact of in-store displays, feature and coupon ads, and temporary price reductions on sales to determine which type of promotion works best.[10]

Services that track retail level sales are offered by ACNielsen, SPAR/Burgoyne, and Information Resources, Inc.

NRTI tracks retail prices, shelf facings, display activity, and more for many types of consumer products.

National Retail Tracking Index. **SPAR/Burgoyne's National Retail Tracking Index (NRTI)** was started in 1969 to provide in-store observation information to manufacturers of consumer products. NRTI data is collected in over 50 markets in a variety of different retail stores (Table 7.1). Data is collected routinely as frequently as every four weeks or quarterly by 800 field auditors. Information is collected on a number of variables, including product availability, retail shelf price, number of shelf facings, shelf location, display activity, presence of point-of-purchase (POP) material, and other information of interest. For each item surveyed, reports are generated that define the percent of distribution, the average retail price, the share of facings, the percent out-of-stock, the average number of shelf facings, the percent of stores displaying the product, and the percent of stores with POP, as well as other items of interest.

TABLE 7.1

SPAR/Burgoyne's NRTI Data Collection

OUTLET TYPE	NUMBER OF MARKETS	NUMBER OF STORES
Supermarkets	64	2,608
Drugstores	64	2,080
Mass merchandisers	64	959
Convenience stores	50	1,774
Home centers	N/A	401
Warehouse clubs	N/A	145
Computer outlets	N/A	316

Source: National Retail Tracking Index: Syndicated In-Store Distribution Surveys *(Mahwah, N.J.: The SPAR/Burgoyne Retail Services, Inc. Group [Undated]). Reprinted by permission.*

Information is tabulated by product category, brand, and types/sizes of brands, and information is reported for the total United States, each individual market, or by retail chains within each market. All of this information is standardized and is available to all firms subscribing to the service in an all-market summary report (Figure 7.1). However, like other firms supplying standardized data for syndication, SPAR/Burgoyne also supplies customized data on request. If a firm wants data reported by their sales territories, for example, SPAR/Burgoyne provides this information.

IRI's InfoScan is a large scanner-based tracking service for grocery and drug products.

InfoScan Daily Census is store-level scanner data that is offered by Information Resources, Inc. (IRI). It provides a daily store-specific record of sales, price, price promotion activity, distribution levels, and sales rates for all prod-

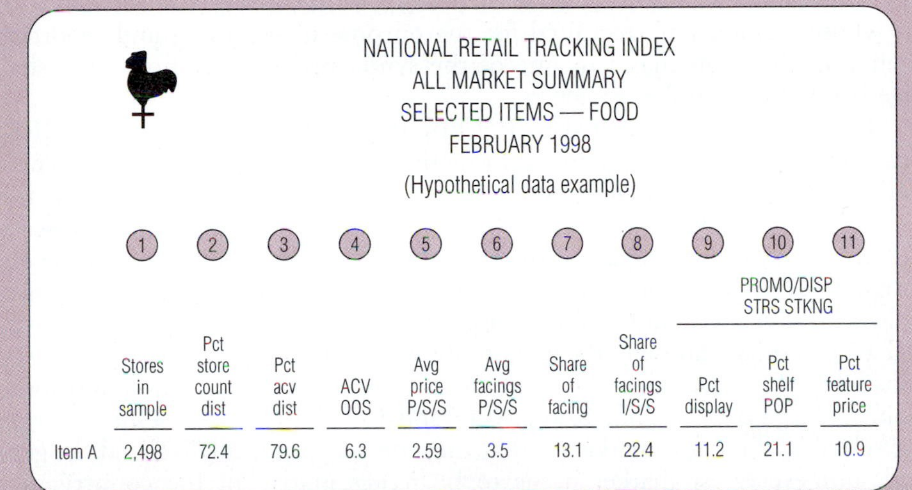

NATIONAL RETAIL TRACKING INDEX
ALL MARKET SUMMARY
SELECTED ITEMS — FOOD
FEBRUARY 1998
(Hypothetical data example)

	(1)	(2)	(3)	(4)	(5)	(6)	(7)	(8)	(9)	(10)	(11)
									PROMO/DISP STRS STKNG		
	Stores in sample	Pct store count dist	Pct acv dist	ACV OOS	Avg price P/S/S	Avg facings P/S/S	Share of facing	Share of facings I/S/S	Pct display	Pct shelf POP	Pct feature price
Item A	2,498	72.4	79.6	6.3	2.59	3.5	13.1	22.4	11.2	21.1	10.9

1. There were **2,498 Supermarkets** surveyed in all markets combined.
2. Of the 2,498 Supermarkets surveyed, **72.4%** of the *stores* had Item A stocked in the selling area.
3. Stores stocking Item A account for **79.6%** of the Supermarket Universe all commodity volume (ACV).
4. Of the stores stocking Item A last period, those accounting for **6.3%** ACV did not have the item available in the selling area this period.
5. The average retail price in stores stocking Item A is **$2.59.**
6. The average number of shelf facings per store stocking Item A is **3.5.**
7. The percent of shelf facings across *all stores* for Item A is **13.1%.**
8. Item A's share of shelf facings within *stores that stock Item A* is **22.4%.**
9. *Of the stores that stock Item A,* **11.2%** had the product on display.
10. *Of the stores that stock Item A,* shelf POP material was found in **21.1%.**
11. *Of the stores stocking Item A,* **10.9%** featured a reduced price.

Figure 7.1
Hypothetical Example of SPAR/Burgoyne's National Retail Tracking Index Report

ucts. Scanner data for over 12,000 grocery stores and 6,000 drug stores are collected. This represents approximately 80 percent of the chain grocery ACV (all commodities volume). At 11 P.M. each night, scanner data is electronically transferred from each store to an IRI facility for processing, cleaning, and database creation. Once the data is checked, client specific databases are made available to users by 5 A.M. the next day on IRI's online software tool, DataServer. Information from this database can help managers identify and quantify lost opportunities by store, evaluate the success of new product introductions, minimize out-of-stocks, and so on.

Market Tracking at the Household Level

Market tracking at the household level provides data on the market; that is, the consumers who buy the various products.

There are two primary ways of tracking the purchase of goods and services by households. One method incorporates the use of scanner data from stores or in-home scanner data. The second method utilizes diaries completed by household members. Both of these methods rely on consumer household panels whose members are recruited for the purpose of recording and reporting their household purchases to one of the syndicated services firms. We shall give you some examples of each.

Syndicated data at the household level is provided by ACNielsen, NFO, and IRI.

BehaviorScan uses a panel of 3,000 households to track and analyze retail purchases in great detail.

BehaviorScan was started in 1979 by Information Resources, Inc. (IRI). Scanner data provides objective information and accurately records purchase data: type of product, quantities purchased, package sizes, date purchased, and so on. This is similar to InfoScan, which was discussed earlier. However, scanner data alone only tells part of the marketing story. It does not record the demographics of who purchased the products—age, gender, education, household size, education, and so on. Hence, in addition to collecting scanner data, IRI also recruits a household panel of 3,000 households in each of six markets: Pittsfield, Mass.; Marion, Ind.; Eau Claire, Wis.; Midland, Tex.; Grand Junction, Colo.; Visalia, Calif.; Rome, Ga.; and Cedar Rapids, Ia. One criterion for selecting these test markets is that they are geographically isolated. In general, not every test market needs to be representative of the country as a whole. However, according to IRI, the combination of test markets comes closer to being representative of the entire country. Also, there is no single large employer in any of these cities.

BehaviorScan panel members present ID cards at scanner-equipped stores. Information from the cards is scanned into computer databases along with products purchased.

Members of each panel household are given an ID card, and they are asked to present this ID card at the checkout in scanner-equipped grocery and drug stores. Goods purchased in stores not scanner-equipped have to be scanned by the panel members themselves with a hand-held scanner. With this system, merchandise purchase can be linked to household demographic information. In each market, key marketing variables can be tested and sales results quantified under tightly controlled, yet close to "real-life" conditions. In addition to the scanned data reporting all goods purchased by the different households, in-store features and displays are observed and recorded by IRI personnel. This makes it possible to analyze correlations between changes in marketing mix variables and sales. A change in POP display, for example, may be easily monitored so as to assess the effectiveness of the new display.

Data are available at the store sales level (e.g., volume, share, pricing, promotion measures, etc.), and at the household level (e.g., trial, repeat purchase, cannibalization, brand cross-purchasing, etc.). These measures are key for developing an early forecast of a brand's national sales potential.

A BehaviorScan panel member presents her card at a supermarket checkout.

BehaviorScan can also test the effects of advertising and POP materials.

BehaviorScan can also be used to assess advertising effects. In many panel homes, a special device is installed on the TV set. This allows IRI to selectively transmit alternative commercials to predesignated subsamples of the panel. This makes it possible to correlate the purchase of a product/brand with test TV commercials. BehaviorScan allows answers to questions like the following:

Here are some questions that BehaviorScan data can answer.

1. How many consumers try my brand and how many buy again?
2. What volume level will my brand achieve in one year? In two years?
3. Will my line extension "steal" share from its parent brand?
4. What flavor mix will maximize trial?
5. Does increased advertising or new copy increase sales?
6. What are the implications of a change in price, package, or shelf placement?
7. Who are my brand's buyers and what else do they buy?

In a BehaviorScan test, two or more test markets are generally used as control groups. We discussed the necessity of control groups in chapter 5. By using control test markets, one has greater confidence that the observed market "reactions" are due solely to the manipulated variable. External effects, or effects due to other extraneous variables can be excluded. In some cases, the experimental test groups and the control panel groups are split within each market. This is the case when the influence of TV commercials is to be tested. IRI can direct different television ads to different panel members. IRI maintains its own TV studio in each market, enabling it to transmit special TV spots to targeted households. The system uses two cable TV channels to override regularly scheduled network, local, and cable TV spots with test TV spots. The system is so precise, it can run a TV spot in one household and skip the next-door neighbor's. When purchases are made, IRI knows if the purchase was made by a panel member of the experimental group or by a member of the control group. For some tests, each city is either a control market or a test market. Care is taken to ensure that the groups of test and control markets are representative of the population of the entire country, according to IRI.

ACNielsen panel members use wands to record information on products they purchase.

The **ACNielsen Household Panel,** begun in 1989, recruits panel members who use hand-held scanners to scan all bar-coded products purchased and brought home from all outlets. Panel members also record the outlet at which the merchandise was purchased and which family member made the purchase, as well as price and causal information such as coupon usage. Nielsen's household panel consists of 40,000 households demographically and geographically balanced and projectable to the total United States. In addition, 16 local markets and approximately 200 retail chains can be tracked. ACNielsen also collects consumer information from 60,000 households in 15 other countries. Supplemental surveys are administered to the panel to develop media consumption profiles based on magazine and newspaper readership, TV viewing and radio listening, as well as to collect consumer attitudes on various topics. All of this information is used to segment consumers and target these segments.

NFO panel members keep records on their purchases and respond to NFO via telephone or mail surveys.

National Family Opinion (NFO) maintains one of the largest household panels with over 500,000 households matched with the U.S. population. Panel members agree to respond to telephone interviews or mail surveys. Panelists do not confuse the NFO inquiries with telemarketing calls or sales literature. This allows NFO to maintain response rates consistently between 70 and 75 percent. Because NFO maintains records on their panel members with demographic and ownership information, marketers using their services can conduct studies of tightly defined market segments classified by demographics, or they can study ownership groups such as families with dogs, VCRs, and cellular car phones.[11]

Share of Intake Panel (SIP) is a tracking service provided by NFO. A nationally matched set of panel members records their beverage consumption both at home and away from home for all household members. SIP reports reveal who is drinking what and the volumes that they are consuming of carbonated soft drinks, coffee, tea, milk, fruit juice, fruit drinks, wine, beer, milk shakes, and so on. SIP data is available from 1980 forward.

NFO's SIP tracks beverage consumption and its SCREEN-TEST tests ad copy and product concepts sent on videotape.

NFO also provides several other data collection services such as SCREEN-TEST and the Chronic Ailment Panel. **SCREEN-TEST** enables marketers to test product concepts, advertising copy, and so on by sending videos to panel members for review. Panel members' evaluations are recorded on mail questionnaires, telephone interviews, or incorporated into the video as the panel member views the video presentation. The **Chronic Ailment Panel** is for pharmaceutical marketers and provides information that allows them to gauge reactions to new product advertising, to measure ad awareness, and to test new products or product reformulations for over-the-counter drugs. In addition, the panel provides information on the number and percentages of population who suffer from illnesses such as asthma, arthritis, diabetes, high blood pressure, migraines, and ulcers.

In response to the rapid changes in technology, NFO Research has introduced the **Technology Monitor.** This service tracks household ownership of more than 30 technology-based products and services, such as cellular phones, fax machines, online services, and home security systems. This tells the marketer which households own what type of consumer technology. This information is particularly useful to marketers of products and services designed to

NFO panel members are matched to U.S. demographics.

access the "information superhighway." Over time, it can also be used to develop forecasts for emerging technology products and services. **Volumetric Concept Screening by Mail** is a joint effort of NFO Research and The Bases Group. This effort enables companies to evaluate early-stage product ideas and carry out rigorous concept testing. The company also offers a database library, the **AMS Concept Testing SmartSystem,** where the manager can view the information, select particular studies for analysis, and compare results to other individual studies. NFO Research in collaboration with ASI Market Research offers **Targeted Print Testing.** This copy testing service includes the test ad in a current issue of a general distribution magazine or one specific to a target population. A copy of this magazine is mailed to select respondents who read and evaluate the magazine at home, the natural environment in which they typically receive information about products and services. The following day, the respondents are contacted by telephone to determine ad recall, purchase intent, and other diagnostic measures.

View: "National Family Opinion Omnibus Panel"

Market Tracking at the Wholesale Level

Market tracking data are no longer available at the wholesale level.

At the beginning of this section we mentioned that marketers needed market tracking information at different levels of the distribution channel, and we discussed tracking studies at the retail level and at the household level. You may have wondered why tracking studies at the wholesale level were not mentioned. For many years, tracking data was collected at the wholesale level. Today, however, it is virtually nonexistent.

There are two reasons tracking data are not collected at the wholesale level. First, prior to scanning data, market tracking studies took several months to collect and process. The time delay between data collection and actual reporting of the data made the data somewhat less reliable. Hence, by collecting the data at several levels of the channel, including the wholesale level, marketing managers could make a better assessment of market trends. With the advent of market tracking studies based on scanning devices, turnaround time on these studies was reduced to a very short time period, giving marketers greater confidence in their knowledge of what was happening "at that point in time." Second, direct store delivery by many large producers meant that the wholesaler was skipped altogether.

Monitoring Media Usage and Promotion Effectiveness

Media firms typically conduct studies to measure their effectiveness, readership, listenership, and so on. This information is useful to firms contemplating advertising expenditures. Because there is a need for some objective measure of promotional effectiveness, several syndicated data service companies have evolved over the years to supply such information to subscribing firms. Some of these services specialize in a particular medium; a few others conduct studies on several forms of media. A discussion of both types of these organizations follows.

Television

Nielsen Media Research is now the sole provider of TV ratings in the United States.

Nielsen Media Research is now the sole provider of TV ratings information in the United States. Nielsen Media Research, whose parent company is Cognizant Corporation, was created when Dun & Bradstreet divested themselves of ACNielsen Marketing Research. The research company now exists as

ACNielsen and is separate from Nielsen Media Research. ACNielsen, however, is still in the TV ratings business in countries other than the United States and Canada. At the time of this writing they are measuring TV ratings in 26 countries. The name Nielsen is synonymous with television audience statistics. It is, in fact, well known for its **Nielsen Television Index (NTI).** Until the last few years, the size and characteristics of TV audiences by program were determined by panels made up of approximately 2,000 families that recorded their TV viewing habits on a diary or through an electronic device, the **audiometer,** that was attached to their TV set. Data was gathered twice a year. (For a discussion of using meters to monitor TV viewership, see Marketing Research Insight 7.3 on page 192).

The data collection period became known as "sweeps" month, and this affected network and cable programming during these periods. Few TV watchers have been unaffected by the Nielsen Television Index; their favorite show has been canceled or, because the index showed a large audience, the show has run for many years. Obviously, firms in the TV industry are constantly trying to achieve higher viewership than their competition. High viewership allows them to charge higher prices to advertise on the "more popular" programs. See Case 7.2 at the end of the chapter for a real example of how TV stations use Nielsen TV ratings.

Nielsen Media Research uses the people meter to compile its television index.

In 1987, in an effort to gain greater objectivity, Nielsen changed the method of measuring the size and characteristics of the audiences to the **people meter,** an electronic instrument that automatically measures when a TV set is on, and who is watching which channel. Family members are asked to enter their names into the people meter each time they watch TV. Data from the people meter is transmitted directly back to Nielsen, allowing the firm to develop estimates of the size of the audience for each program by reporting the percentage of TV households viewing a given show.[12] NTI reports a *rating* and a *share* for each program telecast. A rating is the percentage of households that have at least one set tuned to a given program for a minimum of 6 minutes for each 15 minutes the program is telecast. A share is the percentage of households with at least one set tuned to a specific program at a specific time.

The Nielsen Television Index also provides subscribers with other audience characteristic information that allows potential advertisers to select audiences that most closely match their target markets' characteristics. Ratings are reported as follows: by the number of households, by whether the women are employed outside the home, by age group for women (18+, 12–24, 18–34, 18–49, 25–54, 35–64, 55+), age group for men (18+, 18–34, 18–49, 25–54, 35–65, 55+), and by age group of children (children ages 2 and older, ages 6 to 11, and teenagers).

Nielsen Television Index is used by marketers to compute a "cost per thousand" number.

Marketers using the NTI are not only interested in the programs that reach the largest numbers of a desired target audience, but they are also interested in cost efficiencies in reaching those audiences at the lowest cost. Cost efficiency is measured using the **cost per thousand (CPM)** criterion. It is measured as follows:

$$CPM = \frac{\text{cost of commercial}}{\text{number of target audiences delivered (in thousands)}}$$

Table 7.2 (page 193) illustrates the application of the CPM as it is applied to four TV programs.

Marketing Research Insight 7.3

Television Audience Measurement: An Ethical Issue of the Future?

Two MIT professors, Robert F. Elder and Louis Woodruff, invented a mechanical radiometer to measure the audience size of radio audiences. Named the audiometer, the device was acquired by Arthur C. Nielsen Sr. of the A. C. Nielsen Company. Nielsen launched the first commercial ratings service, the Nielsen Radio Index, in 1942.

Radiometers automatically monitored on/off status and frequency tuned. Every two weeks a Nielsen employee visited consumers' homes to retrieve recorded data. Later, the data was mailed to Nielsen by the consumer. During the 1950s and 1960s, portable radios increasingly meant radio listenership occurred out of the home. Also, TV was becoming increasingly popular with advertisers. In 1964, the radio audiometer was withdrawn. No meter has been used for measuring radio listening since 1964.

During 1949, the first TV audiometer was used by Nielsen. This was an electromechanical device that recorded TV station selection. Families having the audiometer in their homes mailed a cartridge to Nielsen every two weeks. In 1957, Arbitron started a day-after metered service by connecting the meter to phone lines. Nielsen followed this practice in 1959 and the two companies competed for TV viewer ratings throughout the 1980s.

One fault of the original meters was that they did not record who, if anyone, was watching TV. Nielsen and Arbitron both added diaries so that individuals could record their viewing. But as cable TV added so many new channels, consumers did not record their viewing accurately. Hence, paper diaries became suspect. A better system was needed.

In 1983, British AGB Research introduced the "people meter." It provided a beep or verbal message asking the viewer to enter his or her own personal code into a hand-held remote keypad. Information on what TV channel was being watched by which person or persons in the household was automatically downloaded to central computers each day. During the mid-1980s, AGB Research, Nielsen, Percy, and Arbitron offered the people meter service. Today, only Nielsen and MediaFax offer this service in the United States.

The use of people meters has always been controversial. Unlike the old audiometers, which were passive, people meters are considered by some to be invasive because they require active participation by viewers, which could distort viewing behavior. However, another type of controversy may arise in the future if, as some experts believe, we will have sensors implanted under the skin or on permanently worn jewelry. With such sensors some even suggest that marketers will be able to monitor consumers' reactions to commercials and programs in terms of pulse, blood pressure, neurochemistry, and the like. Does the idea of implants create moral and ethical issues?

Source: *Adapted from Laurence N. Gold, "Technology in Television Research: The Meter,"* Marketing Research, *6:1 (Winter 1994), 57–58.*

TABLE 7.2

How Nielsen Media Research Ratings Are Used to Make Media Decisions

Nielsen Media Research ratings may be used to determine the most cost-efficient basis for reaching a targeted audience. CPM, cost per thousand, is the criterion on which many media decisions are made. Assume you have targeted the total audience for your marketing program and you are trying to determine which TV program to use to run two 30-second ads on Mondays during the 8:00 P.M. to 10:00 P.M. time period. A recent Nielsen Media Research rating for four shows indicated the following audience sizes.

CBS	The Nanny	15,700,000
ABC	ABC Monday Night Movie	10,850,000
NBC	Fresh Prince of Bel Air	12,580,000
FOX	Melrose Place	12,340,000

CPM is calculated as: $\frac{\text{cost of ads}}{\text{number of reviewers/1000}}$

CPM for each of the TV shows is calculated as:

The Nanny: $\frac{\$132{,}100}{15.7 \text{ million/1000}} = 8.41$

ABC Monday Night Movie: $\frac{\$62{,}800}{10.85 \text{ million/1000}} = 5.78$

Fresh Prince of Bel Air: $\frac{\$169{,}000}{12.58 \text{ million/1000}} = 5.02$

Melrose Place: $\frac{\$62{,}000}{12.34 \text{ million/1000}} = 5.02$

Here we see the lowest CPM alternative is for Melrose Place. Please note we have used fictitious figures for cost of ads.

Source: *Nielsen Media Research, by permission.*

Radio

Arbitron provides listenership data for the radio industry.

Arbitron provides syndicated data on radio station listening. Since 1964, radio listenership has been measured by Arbitron's national and regional panels whose members complete diaries reporting radio listening for one week. The sample frame for Arbitron radio surveys is designed to include households with telephones. The radio surveys are conducted over a 12-week period, and there are four 12-week surveys in a year. Each selected household is sent a radio diary package. Typically, this package contains a diary for each member of the household who is 12 years or older, a letter thanking the participants for their cooperation, and a cash incentive for each participant. For age groups that have proven difficult to reach in the past, special premiums may be included. The token incentive could be anywhere between $0.25 and $2.00. Hispanic households are sent bilingual diaries and letters. The respondent is required to maintain the diary for seven days.

You count in the radio ratings!

No matter how much or how little you listen, you're important!
You're one of the few people picked in your area to have the chance to tell radio stations what you listen to.
This is *your* ratings diary. Please make sure you fill it out yourself.

Here's what we mean by "listening":
"Listening" is any time you can hear a radio – whether you choose the station or not.
When you hear a radio between Thursday, May 15, and Wednesday, May 21, write it down – whether you're at home, in a car, at work or someplace else.

When you hear a radio, write down:

TIME

Write the time you start listening and the time you stop. If you start at one time of day and stop in another, draw a line from the time you start to the time you stop.

STATION

Write the call letters or station name. If you don't know either, write down the program name or dial setting.

Check AM or FM. AM and FM stations can have the same call letters. Make sure you check the right box.

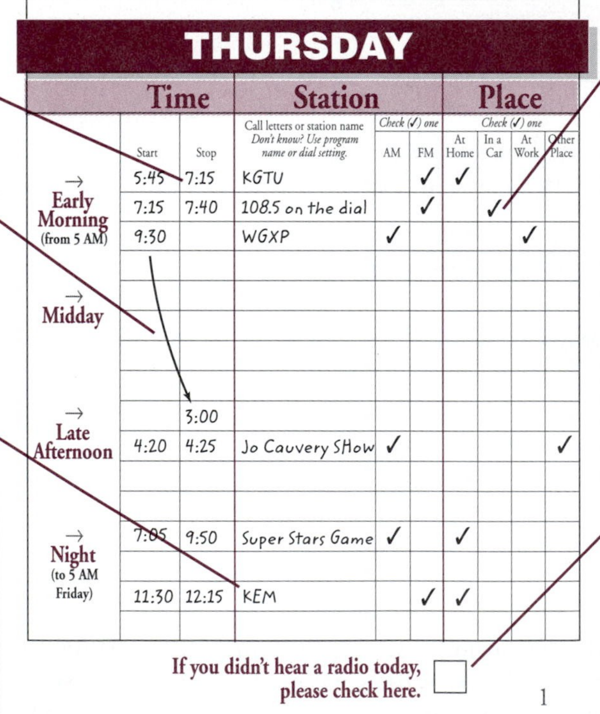

THURSDAY

	Time		Station			Place			
	Start	Stop	Call letters or station name *Don't know? Use program name or dial setting.*	Check (✓) one: AM	FM	Check (✓) one: At Home	In a Car	At Work	Other Place
Early Morning (from 5 AM)	5:45	7:15	KGTU		✓	✓			
	7:15	7:40	108.5 on the dial		✓		✓		
	9:30		WGXP	✓				✓	
Midday									
Late Afternoon		3:00							
	4:20	4:25	Jo Cauvery SHow	✓					✓
Night (to 5 AM Friday)	7:05	9:50	Super Stars Game	✓		✓			
	11:30	12:15	KEM		✓	✓			

If you didn't hear a radio today, please check here. ☐

1

PLACE

Check where you listen:

- at home
- in a car
- at work
- other place

Write down *all* the radio you hear. Carry your diary with you starting **Thursday, May 15.**

No listening?
If you haven't heard a radio all day, check the box at the bottom of the page.

Questions? Call us toll-free at 1-800-638-7091.

Information is recorded in weekly paper-and-pencil diaries to indicate the time of day; how long the station was tuned in; which station was on; where the listening was done (at home, in a car, at work, or other place); and the panel member's age, gender, and home address. Although paper-and-pencil diaries are still being used, Arbitron has invested heavily in an electronic diary, a device similar to a pocket calculator that enables the listener to simply enter where he or she is and the radio station's call letters. Time and date are

Quick questions

1 What is your age?

☐☐ years

2 Are you male or female? *Mark (x) one.*

☐ Male ☐ Female

3 Where do you live?

City ____________

County ____________

State ____________

Zip ☐☐☐☐☐

4 Are you employed, either full time or part time? *Mark (x) one.*

☐ Yes (1) ☐ No (2)

If yes: How many hours per week are you usually employed? *Mark (x) one.*

Less than 35 ☐ (1) 35 or more ☐ (2)

Your opinion counts

Use this space to make any comments you like about specific stations, announcers or programs.

recorded automatically. At the end of the week the panelist transmits the data by dialing a toll-free number and holding the electronic diary to the phone's mouthpiece. Within 10 seconds, all of the data is stored in Arbitron's computers. All diary entries are carefully screened for possible errors.

Data from the diaries is used to measure and report a number of variables indicative of radio listenership. Listenership is measured in 15-minute intervals and data is also reported by age and gender to aid in profiling audience characteristics. Subscribers to Arbitron Radio Market Reports can now view the data on the computer and select the output formats in which they wish to view the data. How can radio stations and businesses use this information to formulate marketing strategy? For instance, knowing where a person is listening may affect the type of message an advertiser wishes to employ. A station with a high concentration of in-car listening may appeal to car dealers, auto-part stores, transmission repair shops, and tire stores. Understanding where the listening occurs is also helpful in determining programming elements such as traffic reports, contests, newscasts, and other information and entertainment segments. Arbitron also conducts other customized marketing research studies to suit individual clients' problems.[13]

Arbitron's Retail Direct measures shopping habits of audiences for different media types.

An extension of the radio listenership service offered by Arbitron is Retail Direct. This service measures the shopping habits of audiences for local radio, television, cable, newspapers, Yellow Pages, and circulars. The audience profile obtained gives users of Retail Direct a detailed profile of the store's customers—where they shop, what competitors they patronize, their media viewing and listening habits, and how they select banks, restaurants, and other local establishments. This enables retailers to spend their advertising dollars more effectively.

Print

The Starch Readership Service reports four different types of magazine advertisement readership based on ads people recall seeing or have read.

The **Starch Readership Service,** a service of Starch INRA Hooper, provides syndicated data and specializes in print media. Trained field interviewers conduct over 100,000 interviews to measure ad effectiveness in magazines and newspapers. The interviewer provides an issue of a given magazine to a respondent and first determines whether or not the respondent read the issue. If so, the interviewer asks if he or she has read selected ads shown in the magazine. Four responses are recorded:

1. *Nonreader.* Respondent does not remember having seen the advertisement before.
2. *Noted.* Respondent remembers having seen the ad in the issue of the magazine in question.
3. *Associated.* Respondent not only noted the ad but also read some part of the ad that cited the brand or the advertiser's identity.
4. *Read most.* Respondent read 50 or more percent of the written material in the ad.[14]

MARKETING RESEARCH INSIGHT 7.4

Using Simmons' Study of Media and Markets

Simmons collects information on hundreds of product and brand categories. It associates usage of a particular category with a number of factors such as demographics, magazine readership, TV viewership, and radio listenership. A key to understanding Simmons' data is its indexing system. An index of 100 refers to the average for a particular attribute; the attribute may be product usage, magazine readership, and so on. For example, for shampoo used at home, the index for all women is 100. The index for female homemakers is 95 and for employed mothers, it is 121. This means that female homemakers use shampoo less than average and employed mothers are above-average users. Simmons data are very helpful in describing "heavy users." Consider the following Simmons indexes for the CDs of various types of music.

The Simmons index compiles information on product usage, demographics, and multimedia usage patterns.

TYPE OF MUSIC

	HEAVY ROCK	GOSPEL
Demographics:		
Age	18–24 = 308	18–24 = 65
	65 or older = 11	45–54 = 130
Education	Attended College = 134	Attended College = 100
	Graduated College = 87	Graduated College = 101
Employment	Employed Part Time = 156	Employed Females = 122
Marital	Single = 228	Single = 81
status	Married = 69	Married = 101
Magazine Readership:		
	Hot Rod = 234	*Ebony* = 283
	Muscle & Fitness = 231	*Essence* = 340
	Architectural Digest = 47	*Barrons* = 21
TV Viewership:		
	Saturday Night Live = 184	Black Entertainment TV = 252
	MTV = 267	*Jane Whitney Show* = 252
	This Week, David Brinkley = 28	*Another World* = 70
	Comedy Central = 230	Comedy Central = 61

Simmons provides much more information than we show here. We have selected this information in order for you to see how useful Simmons data are for discerning differences between the heavy users of different product categories. Can you describe the differences between buyers of heavy rock and gospel music?

There are many other ways that Simmons data may be used. A marketer could gain insights into the readership of a single magazine by users of different products. Smithsonian *is a magazine published by the Smithsonian Institute in Washington, D.C. Note how readership of the* Smithsonian *varies across buyers of different types of music: Rap = 37; Jazz = 221; Classical = 243; Heavy Rock = 63; Gospel = 92; and Country = 92.*

Multimedia

At least one company's service, the **Simmons' Study of Media and Markets,** provides reports on a number of media: magazines, Sunday magazines, newspapers, television, radio, cable, outdoor, Yellow Pages, and syndicated television. They report media audiences, product/brand usage in over 800 product and brand categories, demographic data, and psychographic data. Marketing Research Insight 7.4 explains how Simmons reports may be used by marketers.

SINGLE-SOURCE DATA

Single source data refers to a powerful combination of panel, scanner, and other computerized monitoring methods.

Single-source data are recorded continuously from a panel of respondents to measure their exposure to promotional materials (usually TV as well as in-store promotions) and subsequent buying behavior. Armed with this information, marketers know whether consumers who saw one of their ads actually bought their product. Several technological developments have led to the development of single-source data, including the universal product code (UPC) and scanning equipment that electronically records and stores data gathered at the point of purchase. As we shall explain in the following paragraphs, when coupled with computer and MIS technological developments, powerful "single-source" databases are built that are capable of providing a wealth of information on consumer purchases down to the UPC level.

Although scanner-based databases can provide up-to-the-minute reports on the sale of virtually any consumer product by store, date, time of day, price, and so on, these same powerful databases cannot provide any information at all as to who bought the product. However, as we noted earlier, several marketing research services, such as Information Resource's BehaviorScan, can supply demographic data on the consumers' purchasing of various products.

ACNielsen panelists use scanner wands to record the UPC codes of products they buy.

Several marketing research firms have selected a nationally representative sample (sometimes based on stores, sometimes based on respondents) and supplied consumers in these samples with electronic cards that record their purchases as they check out of participating stores. ACNielsen provides its panel members with electronic scanner wands and asks them to pass this wand over the UPC codes on the products they have purchased from all outlets. Panelists transmit their data each week over the regular telephone lines in their homes. ACNielsen maintains a comprehensive item master file or UPC dictionary containing over one million UPC definitions. As panelists scan and transmit their purchases, ACNielsen decodes each UPC and produces customized reports for each manufacturer, retailer, and agency client. Regardless of which company is collecting the data, we know who bought what.

Single-source data goes beyond knowing who bought what by adding the media-viewing behavior of individual panel members. Media-viewing behavior typically is measured in two ways. First, TV viewing may be monitored via electronic meters on the panel members' TV sets. Information Resource's panel members have their TV sets electronically monitored by IRI every 5 seconds. This television viewing information is automatically sent to IRI's computers. Second, by knowing the store location, date, and time of purchase, the research firm also knows what in-store promotional materials to which the panel member was exposed. IRI has field personnel who monitor stores to make checks on the marketing efforts of various brands. Information on factors such as the level of POP materials, shelf-facings, and prices by sku are then sent to IRI's computers. Consequently, with this database, marketers have not only the ability to determine who is purchasing what, when, and where, but they also know what media[15] and in-store promotions to which the buyers were exposed. Therefore, from this one database (single-source) marketers should have the ability to answer cause-and-effect questions concerning how marketing mix variables actually affect sales.[16]

Single-source data allow managers to determine the effects of price, TV advertising, POP, and other mix variables on sales.

Single-source data may ultimately revolutionize the marketing research industry. Some say it will not reach its full potential until decision support systems (DSSs) actually live up to their potential and become truly user-friendly, staffs learn the new information technology, and supplier firms offer a service that provides a sustainable competitive advantage.[17] Others believe that, even in a world of improved single-source data, there will always be a need for traditional research methods to serve in an *ad hoc* fashion.[18] Critics of single-source data question it on the grounds that it lacks sound sampling procedures (using nonprobability samples), poor response rates (when probability samples have been attempted, only 10 percent of the predesignated sample was willing to cooperate), and that it collects information from a unique sample of volunteers who are willing to subject themselves to a fairly arduous task (that is, passing a wand over all of the products purchased and brought into their home). "They represent nothing besides themselves."[19] The main providers of single-source data, IRI and ACNielsen attempt to overcome some of these problems. The sampling problem of using only data from scanner stores (IRI), for example, ACNielsen claims is overcome by its method of having panel members pass a wand over the bar codes of all purchases made, including those not purchased at a scanner-equipped store. ACNielsen also sends test commercials through the airwaves to its panelists, which means non-cable families can be included. IRI, on the other hand, pioneered the single-source concept and has more experience.

Here are some criticisms of single-source data.

Learn more about these systems by visiting the ACNielsen homepage at http://acnielsen.com/index.cgi and Information Resources, Inc. homepage at http://www.infores.com.

Critcisms notwithstanding, single-source data systems are here to stay. Early uses of the data from these systems resulted in "information overload" for practicing marketing managers. There was simply too much information and it was difficult to make decisions using the reams of information provided. More recently, research companies have been developing expert systems, which use the huge volumes of data generated by single-source systems to provide heuristics useful for decision making. Some examples follow.

Because today's research systems have produced so much information, research firms have developed expert systems that digest all the information and provide managers with heuristics.

ACNielsen Analytical Services has an expert system for category and brand managers. The Marketing Mix Simulator is a Windows-based software application that allows management to estimate profitability arising from proposed variations in marketing mix components. From their desktop PCs, using the Marketing Mix Simulator, managers can make "what-if" decisions and the expert system projects profits for each marketing mix scenario. Other systems, such as the Sales Advisor, allow salespersons to access important factors that have the greatest influence on their client's sales and profits. This gives salespersons important information when making presentations. IRI has a similar product called the Sales Partner (see photo at the beginning of this chapter). IRI has another expert system, called CoverStory, which gleans information from databases and writes managers memos that reflect important "events" taking place among the data.[20]

THE FUTURE OF SYNDICATED SERVICES

The future of syndicated services is indeed bright. The expanding capabilities of computerized and automated information collection, storage, and analysis create the opportunity for new information products such as the expert system products just discussed. Greater depth and broader coverage of markets and customers allow more specific information for decision makers. As opportunities occur and imaginative suppliers develop, new ways of organizing and presenting information on syndicated products will enter the market. Successful research companies are continually looking to develop and acquire the most creative and useful technologies available. We predicted in the first edition of this book that changes in information technology would occur very rapidly. We were correct—and they are still changing rapidly; new products are introduced almost daily.

View: "NFO Panel Data: Making Simple Graphs"

SUMMARY

Syndicated data is a form of external, secondary data that is supplied from a common database to subscribers for a service fee. Information that has value to a company, yet is cost-prohibitive if collected by a single firm, is collected by a syndicated services firm and sold to multiple user firms on a subscription basis. In this way, firms may obtain valuable industry-specific information at a fraction of the costs incurred to collect and process the data. Syndicated services are primarily of two types: (1) syndicated data services, which supply the same data to all subscribers, and (2) standardized services, which provide on-going methods of data collection such as test markets and nationally representative surveys that firms may access for their own data collection needs.

Syndicated data is collected to track consumer attitudes and opinions; to identify various customer groups for purposes of market segmentation or profiling; to track important marketing variables such as brand sales and market share; and for monitoring the number of listeners, viewers, or readers of the various media in order to aid in making decisions relating to promotion. A recent innovation in the industry has been single-source databases, in which information collected by scanning equipment recording sales at the UPC level by brand, store, date, price, and so on, is then coupled with information on the buyer's demographics and media exposure. Having information on who bought what, where, and when after being exposed to promotional materials in one single database may give marketers the ability to answer important cause-and-effect questions on, for example, which marketing mix variable, *X,* caused the sale of product *Y.* single-source databases are now augmented by expert systems, which allow managers to make decisions based on the huge volumes of single-source data.

KEY TERMS

Syndicated data (p. 173)
Syndicated data service (p. 173)
Standardized services (p. 173)
Yankelovich monitor (p. 175)
Harris poll (p. 175)
Gallup poll (p. 175)
DDB Needham life-style study (p. 175)
Standard Industrial Classification (SIC) system (p. 175)
North American Industry Classification System (NAICS) (p. 175)
Dun's market identifiers (DMI) (p. 176)
Geodemographics (p. 176)
Market tracking (p. 177)
ACNielsen services (p. 180)
ACNielsen Food Index (NFI) (p. 180)
ACNielsen SCANTRACK (p. 182)
Retail Account Reports (RARs) (p. 183)
Census Trading Areas (p. 183)
SCANTRAK Key Account Causal (p. 183)
Efficient Market Services, Inc. (EMS) (p. 183)
Nielsen Drug Index (NDI) (p. 184)
Nielsen Mass Merchandiser Index (NMMI) (p. 184)
Procision (p. 184)
SPAR/Burgoyne's National Retail Tracking Index (NRTI) (p. 184)
InfoScan Daily Census (p. 185)
BehaviorScan (p. 186)
ACNielsen Household Panel (p. 188)
National Family Opinion (NFO) (p. 188)
Share of Intake Panel (SIP) (p. 188)
SCREEN-TEST (p. 188)
Chronic Ailment Panel (p. 188)
Technology Monitor (p. 188)
Volumetric Concept Screening by Mail (p. 190)
AMS Concept Testing SmartSystem (p. 190)
Targeted Print Testing (p. 190)
Nielsen Media Research (p. 190)
Nielsen Television Index (NTI) (p. 191)
Audiometer (p. 191)
People meter (p. 191)
Cost per thousand (CPM) (p. 191)
Arbitron (p. 193)
Starch Readership Service (p. 196)
Simmons Study of Media and Markets (p. 196)
Single-source data (p. 198)

REVIEW QUESTIONS/APPLICATIONS

1. What is meant by syndicated services?
2. What are the advantages and disadvantages of syndicated services?
3. Name four broad types of applications of syndicated services and give an example of each.
4. What is geodemography and how can it be used in marketing decisions? Give an example.
5. What is the firm that is best known for conducting studies of radio listenership? Briefly describe the service it provides.
6. What is single-source data? Describe how a marketing manager could make use of single-source data to make (a) pricing decisions and (b) in-store promotions decisions.

7. Contact a radio or TV station or perhaps a newspaper in your town. Ask managers how they measure listenership, viewership, or readership and for what purposes they use this information. In most cases, these firms will be happy to supply you with a standard package of materials answering the above questions.
8. Given what you know about syndicated services, which firm would you call on if you had the following information needs:
   a. You want to know which magazines have the heaviest readership among tennis players.
   b. You have decided to conduct a test market but you have no research department within your firm and no experience in test marketing.
   c. You need to know how a representative sample of U.S. households would answer seven questions about dental hygiene.
   d. You are thinking about a radically new advertising theme but you are very concerned about consumer reaction to the new theme. You want some idea as to how the new theme will impact sales of your frozen dinners.

CASE 7.1

Nielsen Report Analysis[21]

The data in this case is based on ACNielsen data. Prior to analyzing this case you should read Marketing Research Insight 7.3, Analyzing ACNielsen Data. This case analysis requires you to use three tables (A, B, and C) of data:

> Table A: Year 2 category volume and year 2/year 1 annual shares for two competitive brands, Cereal Brand X and Cereal Brand Y, for 16 of the ACNielsen major markets.
>
> Table B: Year 2/year 1 annual shares by package for Cereal Brand X in Houston.
>
> Table C: Four twelve-week periods of year 2 with shares by package for Cereal Brand X in Houston.

Analysis Situation 1. Examine the data in Table A. Calculate the following two items:

1. Share swing (as noted in Marketing Research Insight 7.3, defined as share change for Cereal Brand X minus share change for Cereal Brand Y).
2. Case sales effect of share swing (as noted in Marketing Research Insight 7.3, defined as share swing—expressed as a percentage—times category volume).

Analysis Situation 2. Rank-order the 16 ACNielsen markets by case sales effect of share swing, with the worst market (highest negative case sales effect) as #1 and the best market (highest positive case sales effect) as #16.

Analysis Situation 3. Interpret the data generated in steps 1 and 2.

Analysis Situation 4. Examine Tables B and C. Take a close look at the worst market—Houston. Interpret the data from Tables B and C.

Table A

ACNielsen Major Market Ready-to-Eat Cereal Data

Cities	Year 2 Category Volume	Cereal Brand X		Cereal Brand Y	
		Year 2 Share	Year 1 Share	Year 2 Share	Year 1 Share
Atlanta	73,430	45.6	49.0	10.9	8.9
Baltimore	37,802	21.9	22.4	21.6	21.3
Chicago	100,412	19.0	18.7	23.3	23.8
Cleveland	39,634	17.4	17.8	20.9	20.7
Dallas	78,900	32.3	33.3	8.1	7.8
Denver	54,322	19.1	18.9	12.6	12.4
Detroit	65,324	17.6	16.9	25.5	25.9
Houston	80,022	47.9	54.9	10.0	5.9
Los Angeles	123,131	11.7	11.4	13.4	13.5
Memphis	84,123	39.2	42.3	10.1	9.1
Miami	72,234	31.7	31.6	26.6	24.5
Milwaukee	43,233	19.9	18.5	17.7	20.1
New York	143,244	13.2	13.2	14.3	14.2
St. Louis	45,689	12.4	12.1	29.7	32.3
San Francisco	69,239	17.4	17.0	13.7	14.2
Washington, DC	69,923	25.2	24.6	23.4	24.0

Table B

Cereal Brand X Annual Shares by Package Size, Houston

Package Size	Year 2	Year 1
Single-Serving	7.2	10.6
10-oz. box	11.4	12.4
15-oz. box	9.8	9.9
19-oz. box	8.1	10.2
24-oz. box	7	11.8
3-lb. box	4.4	—
TOTAL	47.9	54.9

TABLE C

CEREAL BRAND X SHARES BY PACKAGE FOR 12-WEEK PERIODS, HOUSTON

	12-WEEK PERIODS ENDING			
PACKAGE SIZE	5/14/YEAR 2	7/9/YEAR 2	10/1/YEAR 2	12/24/YEAR 2
Single-Serving	8.4	7.0	7.2	6.9
10-oz. box	12.2	10.5	11.2	11.5
15-oz. box	9.0	10.8	10.3	9.1
19-oz. box	9.7	9.5	8.7	5.4
24-oz. box	13.0	4.6	4.3	4.1
3-lb. box	—	10.5	4.1	3.0
TOTAL	52.3	52.9	45.8	40.0

Data provided by ACNielsen

CASE 7.2

WBTV Television[22]

Diane Sadler-Diaz is the research director at WBTV, the local ABC-affiliate television station in Atlanta, Georgia. As a research director, Sadler-Diaz's duties include analyzing and presenting research data from a variety of sources. Most of her work involves interpreting and summarizing Nielsen Media Research TV ratings data after each quarterly measurement period, or "sweep," looking for trends and changes from sweep to sweep. Using Nielsen ratings data published after each quarterly sweeps period—November, February, May, and July—Sadler-Diaz will compare programs on WBTV to programs on the other three local television stations in the market and look for areas where WBTV's programs deliver better ratings for various demographic groups. (A rating is a measure of the number of TV households tuned to a particular station; the higher the rating, the more people are viewing a program.) For example, a program that runs on WBTV Monday through Friday from 11:00 A.M. to 12 P.M. may perform well with women 25–54 but may not do as well with men 25–54. On a competing station in the market, however, the same time period may perform extremely well with this male demographic group.

The majority of Sadler-Diaz's job involves highlighting the areas in which WBTV achieves good ratings and interpreting these ratings for presentations that the account executives use to sell advertising spots and packages to their clients. Recently, Sadler-Diaz was approached by one of the station's account executives, Joe Meyers, who had acquired a new client. The new client, Designer Interiors, Ltd.,* is a full-service decorating firm that sells to the general public and provides all levels of decorating needs, from selling draperies and accent pieces to the complete design of a home's decor. Meyers informed Sadler-Diaz that Designer Interiors, Ltd. had never advertised on television before, but that the owner might be interested in beginning a television campaign. Meyers wanted some help from Sadler-Diaz in preparing a presentation that would show the owner of Designer Interiors, Ltd. what advertising on WBTV could do for her business.

1. Taking the role of the research director for WBTV, discuss some of the factors about Designer Interiors, Ltd. that should be considered in preparing this presentation for Meyers.
2. Meyers wants to place an advertising spot for Designer Interiors, Ltd. in a program on WBTV that delivers a 15 rating for a cost of $450. The owner of Designer Interiors, however, is hesitant because she was approached by a competing television station offering a less expensive spot, $300, in a program that delivers a 6 rating. How can Meyers and Sadler-Diaz show the owner of Designer Interiors that advertising on WBTV is the better choice?

*This is an actual case though the TV station and the client, Designer Interiors, Ltd., are both fictitious companies used for illustration purposes only.

CHAPTER 8

Observation, Focus Groups, and Other Qualitative Methods

LEARNING OBJECTIVES

- *To understand basic differences between quantitative and qualitative research techniques*
- *To learn the pros and cons of using observation as a means of gathering data*
- *To discover what focus groups are and how they are conducted and analyzed*
- *To become familiar with other qualitative methods used by marketing researchers*

PRACTITIONER VIEWPOINT

Knowing when to use qualitative research and, importantly, when not to is a crucial skill in a research manager's judgment. Once you have decided to use a qualitative approach, you have to select the right interviewing format and the appropriate questioning tools to come up with the best research design. For example, we do a lot of focus group research that has really opened up our eyes as to why people do or do not buy a particular brand, why they shop for groceries on a particular day, and how a mother acts as the purchasing agent for the rest of the family in many cases. I don't think you could have come to really understand any of these things if you had just run a survey.

— Malcolm Baker, President
The B/R/S Group, Inc.

Getting a Handle on Early Cybercitizens[1]

1. Establish the need for marketing research
2. Define the problem
3. Establish research objectives
4. Determine research design
5. Identify information types and sources
6. **Determine methods of accessing data**
7. Design data collection forms
8. Determine sample plan and size
9. Collect data
10. Analyze data
11. Prepare and present the final research report

Along with other profound changes in communication, the Internet dramatically altered consumer information acquisition and buying patterns. In the mid-1990s, marketers were caught in a dilemma. On one hand, unvalidated reports claimed that tens of thousands of consumers

Market researchers report that consumers are growing more confident in buying on the Internet.

with Internet access were in the process of adapting to its information-saturated services. On the other hand, almost no hard information existed to define these consumers. It was as though legions of phantom consumers had materialized and were poised to pound on every marketer's Internet door. Marketers wrestled with the questions of who were these consumers, where were they searching, and what did they want to find on company Internet homepages?

Traditional marketing research methods were inappropriate for many reasons. For one, the "cybercitizens" constituted less than 1 percent of the U.S. population, so finding them was like looking for a needle in a haystack. For another, they were in the early stages of learning the Internet, and they could not respond to paper-and-pencil questionnaires with any degree of certainty while their behavior was evolving. Finally, Internet marketing was emerging, and Internet marketers did not even know what questions to ask the "cyberpioneer" consumers.

But because of the newness of cybercitizenry, marketers turned to qualitative techniques in order to get a handle on online behavior. Cyberstudies took the forms of in-depth, online interviews as well as moderated chat room conversation exchanges. Insights were remarkable due to the convenience and anonymity factors: Cybercitizens could respond from the familiarity of their own homes and through their own computer systems, and they could hide their identities through computer aliases. Patterns began to emerge: Fully one-half had purchased a product online during the last year, and almost three-quarters planned to use the Internet more often as a shopping vehicle for products and services in the future. The Internet was truly a viable shopping outlet for cybercitizens! As marketers began to appreciate the degree to which consumers were embracing the Internet as a shopping alternative, online surveys were implemented to supplement the qualitative findings with statistical summaries of just how huge and meaningful this phenomenon was to marketers. Armed with hard data from Internet survey users surveys conducted by companies such as Louis Harris, FIND/SV, and Mediamark Research, Inc., Internet marketers orchestrated "cybermarketing's" passage from infancy to maturity in a matter of a few years.

This chapter deals with qualitative methods, referred to by some people as the "soft side" of marketing research. But as the cybercitizen story proves, these methods can be very illuminating. Qualitative methods are techniques that typically do not generate the huge amounts of data associated with surveys. You will find that each qualitative method has its place in the marketing research process, and that each has its unique advantages and disadvantage as well. Because focus groups are a popular qualitative marketing research technique, an in-depth discussion of them is included. We begin with a discussion of qualitative, quantitative, and pluralistic research.

QUALITATIVE, QUANTITATIVE, AND PLURALISTIC RESEARCH

The means of data collection during the research process can be classified into three broad categories: quantitative, qualitative, and pluralistic. There are vast differences between the first two methods, and it is necessary to understand their special characteristics in order to make the right selection. To start, we briefly define these two approaches, and then we describe pluralistic research.

Quantitative research is the traditional mainstay of the research industry, and it is sometimes referred to as "survey research." For our purposes in this chapter, **quantitative research** is defined as research involving the use of structured questions where the response options have been predetermined and a large number of respondents is involved. When you think of quantitative research, you might envision a nationwide survey conducted with telephone interviews. That is, quantitative research often involves a sizable representative sample of the population and a formalized procedure for gathering data. The purpose of quantitative research is very specific, and this research is used when the manager and researcher have agreed that precise information is needed. Data format and sources are clear and well defined, and the compilation and formatting of the data gathered follows an orderly procedure that is largely numerical in nature.

Quantitative research involves a structured questionnaire and a large sample.

Qualitative research, in contrast, involves collecting, analyzing, and interpreting data by observing what people do and say. Observations and statements are in a qualitative or nonstandardized form. Because of this, qualitative data can be quantified but only after a translation process has taken place. For example, if you asked five people to express their opinions on a topic such as gun control or promoting alcoholic beverages to college students, you would probably get five different statements. But after studying each response, you could characterize each one as "positive," "negative," or "neutral." This translation step would not be necessary if you instructed them to predetermined response options such as "yes" or "no." Any study that is conducted using an observational technique or unstructured questioning can be classified as qualitative research.

Qualitative research involves observing and/or asking open-ended questions, usually with a small number of informants.

Why would you want to use such a "soft" approach? Occasionally, marketing researchers find that a large-scale survey is inappropriate. For instance, Procter & Gamble may be interested in improving its Tide laundry detergent, so it invites a group of housewives to sit down with some of Tide's marketing personnel and brainstorm how Tide could perform better, how its packaging could be improved, or discuss other features of the detergent. Listening to the market in this way can generate excellent packaging, product design, or even product positioning ideas. As another example, if the Procter & Gamble marketing group was developing a special end-of-aisle display for Tide, it might want to test one version in an actual supermarket environment. It could place one in a Safeway grocery store located in a San Francisco suburb and videotape shoppers as they encountered the display. The marketing group would then review the videotape and see if the display generated the types of responses they hoped it would. For instance, did shoppers stop there? Did they read the copy on the display? Did they pick up the displayed product and look at it?

Both quantitative and qualitative methods are important to market research but in different situations.

Although there are proponents of both types of research, many marketing researchers have adopted **pluralistic research,** defined as the combination of

Pluralistic research combines the advantages of both qualitative research and quantitative research.

qualitative and quantitative research methods in order to gain the advantages of both. With pluralistic research, it is common to begin with exploratory qualitative techniques as, for example, in-depth interviews of selected dealers or a series of group discussions with customers in order to understand how they perceive your product and service as compared to those of competitors. Even an observational study could be used if it is helpful in understanding the problem and bringing to the surface issues in the research project. These activities often help crystallize the problem or otherwise open the researcher's eyes to factors and considerations that might be overlooked if he or she rushed into a full-scale survey. The qualitative phase serves as a foundation for the quantitative phase of the research project because it provides the researcher with first-hand knowledge of the research problem. Armed with this knowledge, the researcher's design and execution of the quantitative phase is invariably superior to what it might have been without the qualitative phase. With pluralistic research, the qualitative phase serves to frame the subsequent quantitative phase, and in some cases, a qualitative phase is applied after a quantitative study to help the researcher understand the findings in the quantitative phase.

With pluralistic research, the qualitative phase is the foundation for the quantitative phase.

The pluralistic approach is becoming increasingly popular, especially with complex marketing decisions. For example, when the Swedish manufacturer of the Volvo automobile launched its model 850 into the British market in 1992, Great Britain was in the midst of the worst car sales recession ever to hit the industry. Prior research had found that although the Volvo was seen as one of the safest cars on the road, it was also perceived as boring and somewhat snobbish. The 850 model was restyled to reposition Volvo as a more exciting car to drive. Focus groups (to be described later in this chapter), a qualitative research method, found the 850's styling to be sleek, softer, and impressive, evidenced by comments such as, ". . . an air of quality. Solid looking but shapely." Subsequent quantitative research revealed three potential buyer groups: (1) Volvo loyalists who would definitely buy a Volvo 850, (2) "soft" prospects who would consider buying the 850, and (3) "hard" prospects who

The Volvo 850 was designed and perfected using a combination of qualitative and quantitative marketing research methods.

were not attracted to the 850. This research also suggested that the soft prospects would trade up to the 850 from their current smaller Volvo model or from a different automobile make. Aided by an effective advertising campaign emphasizing a rejuvenating theme for Volvo and its new 850 model, Volvo experienced a share gain from 3 percent to about 4.5 percent in Great Britain by the end of the 850's launch year.[2]

OBSERVATION TECHNIQUES

Qualitative techniques include the class of **observation methods**—techniques in which the researcher relies on his or her powers of observation rather than communicating with a respondent in order to obtain information. Observation requires something to observe, and because our memories are faulty, researchers depend on recording devices such as videotapes, audiotapes, handwritten notes, or some other tangible record of what is observed. As we describe each observation technique, you will see that each is unique in how it obtains observations.

Observation methods typically rely on recording devices as the researcher's memory alone can be faulty.

Types of Observation

At first glance, it may seem that observation studies can occur without any structure; however, it is important to adhere to a plan so that the observations are consistent and comparisons or generalizations can be made without worrying about any conditions of the observational method that might confound the findings. There are four general ways of organizing observations: (1) direct versus indirect, (2) disguised versus undisguised, (3) structured versus unstructured, and (4) human versus mechanical.

Direct versus Indirect

Observing behavior as it occurs is called **direct observation.** For example, if we are interested in finding out how much shoppers squeeze tomatoes to assess their freshness, we can observe people actually picking up the tomatoes. Direct observation has been used by Kellogg's to understand breakfast rituals, by a Swiss chocolate maker to study the behavior of "chocoholics," and by the U.S. Post Office's advertising agency to come up with the advertising slogan, "We Deliver."[3]

Observation may be direct or indirect.

In order to observe types of hidden behavior, such as past behavior, we must rely on indirect observation. With **indirect observation,** the researcher observes the effects or results of the behavior rather than the behavior itself. Types of indirect observations include archives and physical traces.

Archives are secondary sources such as historical records that can be applied to the present problem. These sources contain a wealth of information and should not be overlooked or underestimated. Many types of archives exist. For example, records of sales calls may be inspected to determine how often salespersons make cold calls. Warehouse inventory movements can be used to study market shifts. Scanner data may afford insight on the effects of price changes.

Archives and physical traces are forms of indirect observation.

Physical traces are a tangible evidence of some event. For example, we might turn to "garbology" (observing the trash of subjects being studied) as a way of finding out how much recycling of plastic milk bottles occurs. A soft drink company might do a litter audit in order to assess how much impact its aluminum cans have on the countryside. A fast-food company such as Wendy's might measure the amount of graffiti on buildings located adjacent to prospective location sites as a means of estimating the crime potential for each site.[4]

Disguised versus Undisguised

With disguised observation, subjects are unaware they are being studied, whereas with undisguised observation, they are aware they are being studied.

With **disguised observation,** the subject is unaware that he or she is being observed. An example of this method might be a "secret shopper" that is used by a retail store chain to record and report on sales clerks' assistance and courtesy. One-way mirrors and hidden cameras are a few of the other ways that are used to prevent subjects from becoming aware that they are being observed. This disguise is important because if the observees were aware of the observation, it is possible that they would change their behavior, resulting in observations of atypical behavior. If you were a store clerk, how would you act if the department manager told you that he would be watching you for the next hour? You would probably be on your best behavior for the next 60 minutes. Disguised observation has proved illuminating in studies of parents and children shopping together in supermarkets.[5] With direct questions, parents might feel compelled to say that their children are always on their best behavior while shopping.

Sometimes it is impossible for the respondent to be unaware of the observation, and this is a case of **undisguised observation.** Laboratory settings, observing a sales representative's behavior on sales calls, and people meters (a de-

Hidden cameras can record the buying behavior of shoppers who are too busy to remember all of the actions they exhibited in a shopping trip.

The use of observation raises ethical questions. Should people being observed be informed of the observation, and, if so, what changes might they make in their behavior in order to appear "normal" or conform to what they think is expected? The researcher wants to observe behavior as it actually occurs even if it is unusual or out of the ordinary. However, people being observed might feel uncomfortable about their habits or actions and try to act in more conventional ways. For instance, if a family agrees to have its television set wired so a researcher can track what programs the family watches, will the parents make sure that the children watch mainly wholesome shows such as those on The Disney Channel? Sometimes researchers resort to deceit in order to observe people without their knowledge. Nissan Motor Corporation was charged with unethical observation. A couple in California sued Nissan, charging that a Japanese researcher they had invited to stay in their home as part of an exchange program was really spying on them for Nissan to understand their automobile buying behavior.[6]

vice, discussed in chapter 7, that is attached to a television set to record when and to what station a set is tuned), must all be used with the subject's knowledge. Because people might be influenced by knowing they are being observed, it is wise to always minimize the presence of the observer to the maximum extent possible.

Structured versus Unstructured

Observation may be structured or unstructured.

When using **structured observation** techniques, the researcher identifies beforehand which behaviors are to be observed and recorded. All other behaviors are "ignored." Often, a checklist or a standardized observation form is used to isolate the observer's attention to specific factors. These highly structured observations typically require a minimum of effort on the part of the observer.

Unstructured observation places no restriction on what the observer would note: All behavior in the episode under study is monitored. The observer just watches the situation and records what he or she deems interesting or relevant. Of course, the observer is thoroughly briefed on the area of general concern. This type of observation is often used in exploratory research. For example, a company that makes power tools used by carpenters in constructing houses might send one of its representatives to observe carpenters working at various job sites as a means of better understanding how the tools are used and to help generate ideas as to how to design the tools for increased safety.

Human versus Mechanical

Scanners and audiometers are forms of mechanical observation.

With **human observation,** the observer is a person hired by the researcher, or, perhaps, the observer is the researcher. However, it is sometimes possible (or desirable) to replace the human observer with some form of observing device, as in **mechanical observation.** This substitution may be made because of accuracy, cost, or functional reasons. Auto traffic counts may be more accurate and less costly when recorded by machines that are activated by car tires rolling over them. Besides, during rush hour, a human observer could not count the number of cars on most major metropolitan commuter roads. Nor would it be possible to count the number of fans entering a gate at a professional football title game, so turnstile counts are used instead. Scanning devices are used to count the number and types of products sold (see chapter 7). Mechanical devices may also be used when it is be too expensive to use human observers. For example, a people meter is used instead of a human observer to record families' television viewing habits. As these examples illustrate, mechanical observation has moved into the high technology area recently, and the combination of telecommunications, computer hardware, and software programs has created a very useful research tool.

Appropriate Conditions for the Use of Observation

Certain conditions must be met before a researcher can successfully use observation as a marketing research tool. These conditions are: the event must occur in a short time interval, the observed behavior must occur in a public setting, and when the possibility of faulty recall rules out collecting information by asking the person.

Successful observations are of short duration, are public, and when conditions leading to faulty recall are present.

Short time interval means that the event must begin and end within a reasonably short time span. Examples include a shopping trip in a supermarket, waiting in a teller line at a bank, purchasing a clothing item, or observing children as they watch a television program. Some decision-making processes can take a long time (for example, buying a home), and it would be unrealistic in terms of the time and money required to observe the entire process. Because of this factor, observational research is usually limited to scrutinizing activities that can be completed in a relatively short time span or to observing certain phases of those activities with a long time span.

Public behavior refers to behavior that occurs in a setting the researcher can readily observe. Actions such as cooking, playing with one's children, or private worshipping are not public activities and are therefore not suitable for observational studies such as those described here.

Faulty recall occurs when actions or activities are so repetitive or automatic that the respondent cannot recall specifics about the behavior under question. For example, people cannot recall accurately how many times they looked at their wrist watch while waiting in a long line to buy a ticket to a best-selling movie, or which FM radio station they listened to last Thursday at 2:00 P.M. Observation is necessary under circumstances of faulty recall to fully understand the behavior at hand. For instance, an observation technique called "actual radio measurement" using a high-gain antenna, digital frequency scanner, and computer can be used to determine which radio stations were listened to by commuters in their cars.[7]

Advantages of Observational Data

Sometimes observation is the only way to gain an accurate picture of the behavior of interest.

Ideally, the subjects of observational research are unaware they are being studied. Because of this they react in a natural manner, giving the researcher insight into actual, not reported, behaviors. As previously noted, observational research methods also mean that there is no chance for recall error. The subjects are not asked what they remember about a certain action. Instead, they are observed while engaged in the act. In some cases, observation may be the only way to obtain accurate information. For instance, children who cannot yet verbally expresss their opinion of a new toy will do so by simply playing or not playing with the toy. Retail marketers commonly gather marketing intelligence about competitors and about their own employees' behaviors by hiring the services of "mystery shoppers" who pose as customers but who are actually trained observers.[8] In some situations, data can be obtained with better accuracy and less cost by using observational methods as opposed to other means. For example, counts of in-store traffic can often be made by means of observational techniques more accurately and less expensively than by using survey techniques.

Observation can be used to supplement and complement other research techniques.

Such advantages of observational research methods should not be interpreted as meaning that this technique is always in competition with other approaches. A resourceful researcher will use observation techniques to supplement and complement other techniques.[9] When used in combination with other techniques, each approach can serve as a check on the results obtained by the other. Actually, observation of humans in their natural context is the approach that has been used by anthropologists for over 100 years, and has recently become accepted as a method of marketing research.[10]

Limitations of Observational Data

Due to small samples and the need for interpretation, conclusions based on observation are usually considered to be tentative.

The limitations of observation are the limitations inherent in qualitative research in general. With direct observation, typically only small numbers of subjects are studied and usually under special circumstances, so their representativeness is a concern. This factor, plus the subjective interpretation required to explain the observed behavior, usually forces the researcher to consider his or her conclusions to be tentative. Certainly, the greatest drawback of all observational methods is the researcher's inability to pry beneath the behavior observed and to interrogate the person on motives, attitudes, and all of the other unseen aspects of why what was observed took place.

A limitation of observation research is that what people are thinking is hidden from view.

With observation, you cannot tell what is going on beneath the surface behavior.

To recap, a limitation of observation is that motivations, attitudes, and other "internal" conditions cannot be observed. Only when these feelings are relatively unimportant or readily inferred from the behavior is it appropriate to use observational research methods. For example, facial expression might be used as an indicator of a child's attitudes or preferences for various types of fruit drink flavors because children often react with conspicuous physical expressions. But adults and even children usually conceal their reasons and true reactions in public, and this fact necessitates a direct questioning approach because observation alone cannot give a complete picture of why and how people act the way they do.

It is best to consider qualitative and quantitative methods as partners and not as competitors.

Before we describe some of the commonly used qualitative techniques, we need to tell you about two syndromes that should be avoided—Dracula and Frankenstein.[11] The **Dracula syndrome** occurs when you suck all of the substance out of a few and possibly unrepresentative observations; whereas the **Frankenstein syndrome** is when you mindlessly crunch numbers from a survey. Neither extreme approach is correct. What needs to occur is a balance between the two, or better stated, you should use the advantages of one to offset the drawbacks of the other. Using qualitative and quantitative research in partnership rather than as mutually exclusive alternatives is best. When a broad research plan is formulated to use multiple techniques, the best understanding and prediction of consumer behavior results. Zale Corporation, which is the largest retailer of jewelry in the United States, subscribes to this strategy of complementing quantitative research with qualitative research.[12] It combines large-scale surveys with unstructured, in-depth personal interviews.

FOCUS GROUPS

As we indicated, there are several types of qualitative research, but the technique most often associated with this category is the focus group. A **focus group** is a small group of people brought together and guided by a modera-

Focus groups are small group discussions moderated by a trained discussion leader.

tor through an unstructured, spontaneous discussion about some topic. The goal of a focus group is to draw out ideas, feelings, and experiences about a certain issue that would be obscured or stifled by more structured methods of data collection. The use of a small group allows the operation of group dynamics and aids in making the participants feel comfortable in a strange environment. It is called a "focus" group because the moderator serves to focus the discussion on the topic and does not let the group move off onto tangents or irrelevant points. Focus groups have become so popular in marketing research that every large city has a number of companies who specialize in performing focus group research. You can be assured that you will encounter focus group research if you become a practicing marketing manager. "Almost nothing gets done without them"[13] says Bill Hillsman, a successful advertising executive whose campaigns have worked for the Minnesota Twins, the "Dales" shopping centers, and Arctic Cat snowmobiles. Focus groups are an invaluable means of regaining contact with customers when marketers have lost touch, and they are very helpful in learning about new customer groups.

Focus groups are small group discussions led by a trained moderator.

A focus group will help a marketer "get in touch" with target customers.

Some Objectives of Focus Groups

There are four main objectives of focus groups: to generate ideas; to understand consumer vocabulary; to reveal consumer needs, motives, perceptions, and attitudes on products or services; and to understand findings from quantitative studies.

Focus groups have four main objectives.

To generate ideas means to use the focus group as a starting point for new product or service ideas, uses, or improvements. Marketing Research Insight 8.1 on page 218 depicts how this brainstorming can occur in a focus group.

To understand consumer vocabulary means to use the focus group to stay abreast of the words and phrases consumers use when describing one's product so as to improve product or service communication with them. Such information may help in advertising copy design or in the preparation of an instruction pamphlet. This knowledge refines research problem definitions and also helps structure questions for use in later quantitative research.

To reveal consumer needs, motives, perceptions and attitudes on products or services means to use the focus group to refresh the marketing team as to what customers really feel or think about a product or service. This application is useful in generating objectives to be addressed by subsequent research.

To understand findings from quantitative studies means to use focus groups to better comprehend data gathered from other surveys. Sometimes a focus group can reveal why the findings came out a particular way.

Warner-Lambert is a company that has successfully used focus groups to accomplish all four of these objectives. Its consumer health products group, which markets over-the-counter health and beauty products as well as nonprescription drugs, uses focus groups extensively.[14] In fact, Warner-Lambert uses a combination of qualitative research techniques to gain background information, to reveal needs and attitudes related to health and beauty products, to interpret the results of qualitative studies, and to stimulate brainstorming new ideas. Focus groups have been useful in understanding basic shifts in consumer life styles, values, and purchase patterns.

MARKETING RESEARCH INSIGHT 8.1

What a Brainstorming Focus Group "Sounds" Like

Background: Kodak is considering redesigning its cameras and film to make them more "user friendly," and it is using focus group research to understand what problems consumers encounter when using cameras. The 35mm camera is the central topic of this excerpt.

MODERATOR: "What other problems have you encountered with 35mm camera film?"

MARY: "Well, we have a camera that has a lot of automatic features such as focusing and sensing when the flash should be used. It is really convenient to have the camera sense when the film is all used up, and to automatically rewind it.

MODERATOR: "What about the film, itself? Let's just talk about the film itself."

MARY: "Oh, it is a bit of a problem to position a new roll of film into the camera so it will catch on those little cogs and feed through the camera. Sometimes it takes a couple of tries for it to be loaded okay."

SALLY: "Yes, and sometimes they don't feed correctly, but you don't realize it, and when you take that first picture, it won't snap. I have lost one or two good photo opportunities because of misfeeds like this."

GENE: "It's a pain having to pull the end of the film out of the film canister and feed it into the proper place inside the camera."

MARY: "I bet there is some way that they could make the film so it would feed without us having to pull out the film and place it over those little cogs."

GAIL: "Yes, but first I would want them to solve the problem of misfeeds. It would be worse if I put in the film, and it misfed, and then I would have to open up the camera and fix the mess inside."

GENE: "Yes, I agree that it could be a worse mess than the misfeeds I am experiencing, but it seems to me that the camera companies could invent a fail-safe system of just dropping a film cartridge that would automatically set up the feed every time. Everything else on a camera is automated and fail-safe, so why shouldn't the film insertion be the same?"

GAIL: "Yes, that's what we need—a fail-safe and automatic film insertion feature for when we are putting in a new roll of film.

MODERATOR: "Can you think of any other ways that the companies who market 35mm film might be able to change their products so they are more helpful to you?"

SALLY: "I have a problem with the number system they use. What does it mean when it says it is 100, 200, or 400 film? I always get confused, and those clerks at the grocery store are no help at all."

MODERATOR: "What else about the film numbering system? Do you have any ideas on a better system?"

Focus Groups outside the United States

Focus groups are applied differently in Europe.

Focus group research is practiced in Europe as well as in the United States. However, there are some interesting differences in how it is applied and how it is regarded by the respective clients. Qualitative research is becoming known in Europe as the "new qualitative technology." Because most Europeans, and especially British, participants are more reserved, focus groups are applied differently. Also, the great diversity of cultures and peoples in Europe means that

TABLE 8.1

Differences in Qualitative Research between the U.S. and the U.K.

AREA	U.S.	U.K.
Focus group size	10 to 12	6 to 8
Focus group length	2 hours	1.5 to 4 hours
Location	Professional facility	Recruiters' homes
Client viewing	Common	Rare
Topic guides	Long and detailed	Short and flexible
Recruitment	By income/occupation	By social class
Sample size	Of much concern	Of little concern
Credibility	Moderate	High

Source: *Peter Cooper, "Comparison between the UK and US: The Qualitative Dimension,"* Journal of the Market Research Society, *vol. 31, no. 4 (1991), 509–520.*

all qualitative techniques applied must be tailored to the situation. For instance, in France, the moderator is called the "animateur" or animator because he or she enlivens the discussion rather than controls it the way a U.S. moderator does. Table 8.1 lists eight other differences between the United States and British approaches.

In contrast to the culture-specific focus group approaches noted in Table 8.1, recent research has uncovered a strong Western (as opposed to Asian) theme in the use of focus groups worldwide. William McDonald[15] compared focus group research in the United States, Germany, and Japan and found that among moderators the only significant differences were that Japanese moderators had one to two years' less experience, and about 90 percent of Japanese moderators were male, whereas about 60 to 70 percent of American or German moderators were women. McDonald concludes that focus group approaches and objectives do not vary much by country because of (1) the common purpose of all focus group research, which is to explore basic consumer needs and attitudes; (2) the strong effects of Western business practices, especially marketing research techniques, on those in foreign countries; and (3) similarities in business practices of multinational firms, many of which use focus groups.

Operational Questions about Focus Groups

Before a focus group is conducted, certain operational questions should be addressed. It is important to decide how many people should take part in a focus group, who they should be, how they will be selected and recruited, and where they should meet. General guidelines exist for answering these questions. A discussion of each follows.

What Should Be the Size of a Focus Group?

The accepted size of a focus group is 8 to 12 participants.

According to industry wisdom, the optimal size of a focus group is 8 to 12 people. A small group (fewer than eight participants) is not likely to generate the energy and group dynamics necessary for a truly beneficial focus group session. With fewer participants, it is common that one or two of the participants do most of the talking in spite of the moderator's efforts. At the same time, a small group will often result in awkward silences and force the moderator to take too active a role in the discussion just to keep the discussion alive. Similarly, a group with more than 12 will ordinarily prove too large to be conducive to a natural discussion. As a focus group becomes larger in size it tends to become fragmented. Those participating may become frustrated by the inherent digressions and side comments. Conversations may break out among two or three participants while another is talking. This situation places the moderator in the role of disciplinarian in which he or she is constantly calling for quiet or order rather than focusing the discussion on the issues at hand.

With a focus group of less than six participants, group dynamics may not work well, and with more than 12, control of the group is difficult.

Unfortunately, it is often difficult to predict the exact number of people who will attend the focus group interview. Ten may agree to participate and only six may show up. Fourteen may be invited in hopes that 8 will show up, and all 14 will arrive. Of course, if this occurs, the researcher faces a judgment call as to whether or not to send some home. In the worst case, a researcher may run into a situation in which no one attends, despite promises to the contrary. There is no guaranteed method that will ensure a successful participation ratio. Incentives (which will be discussed later) are helpful, but definitely not a certain way of gaining acceptance. So although 8 to 12 is the ideal focus group size range, it is not uncommon to have some groups with fewer than 8 and some with more than 12.

Who Should Be in the Focus Group?

It is generally believed that the best focus groups are ones in which the participants share homogenous characteristics. This requirement is sometimes automatically satisfied by the researcher's need to have particular types of people in the focus group. For instance, the focus group may comprise executives who use laptop computers, it may involve building contractors who specialize in building customer residences over $200,000 in value, or it might involve a group of salespeople who are experiencing some common customer service difficulty.

Focus groups work best with participants who share similar characteristics.

The need for similar demographic or other relevant characteristics in the focus group members is accentuated by the fact that the focus group participants are typically strangers. In most cases, they are not friends or even casual acquaintances, and many people feel intimidated or at least hesitant to voice their opinions and suggestions to a group of strangers. But participants typically feel more comfortable once they realize they have similarities such as their age (they may all be in their early 30s), job situations (they may all be junior executives), family composition (they may all have preschool children), purchase experiences (they may all have bought a new car in the past year), or even leisure pursuits (they may all play tennis). Furthermore, by conducting a group that is as homogenous as possible with respect to demographics and other characteristics, the researcher is assured that differences in these variables will be less likely to confuse the issue being discussed.

How Should Focus Group Participants Be Recruited and Selected?

Focus group participants are often recruited by telephone and provided an incentive for participating.

As you can guess, the selection of focus group participants is determined largely by the purpose of the focus group. For instance, if the purpose is to generate new ideas on product packaging, the participants must be consumers who have used the brand. If the focus group is intended to elicit building contractors' reactions to a new type of central air conditioning unit, it will be necessary to recruit building contractors. It is not unusual for companies to provide customer lists, or for focus group recruiters to work from secured lists of potential participants. For instance, with building contractors, the list might come from the local Yellow Pages or a building contractor trade association membership roster. In any case, it is necessary to initially contact prospective participants by telephone to qualify them, and then to solicit their cooperation in the focus group. Occasionally, a focus group company may recruit by requesting shoppers in a mall to participate, but this approach is rare.

"No shows" are a worry with focus groups.

As we noted earlier, "no shows" are a problem with focus groups, and researchers have at least two strategies to entice prospective participants. First, incentives of various types are used. These range from monetary compensation for the participant's time to free products or gift certificates. Second, many focus group companies use call-backs during the day immediately prior to the focus group to remind prospective participants that they have agreed to take part. If one prospective participant indicates that some conflict has arisen and he or she cannot be there, it is then possible to recruit a replacement. Neither approach works perfectly, as we indicated earlier, and anticipating how many participants will show up is always a concern. Some focus group companies have a policy of over-recruiting, and others have lists of people they can rely on to participate, given that they fit the qualifications.

Over-recruiting is one way to deal with "no shows."

Where Should a Focus Group Meet?

Obviously, if a group discussion is to take place for a period of 90 minutes or more, it is important that the physical arrangement of the group be comfortable and conducive to group discussion. So focus groups ideally are conducted in large rooms set up in a roundtable format. An advertising company confer-

Focus group participants are often recruited by telephone.

ence room, a moderator's home, a respondent's home, the client's office, hotels, and meeting rooms at churches are all locations in which focus groups can be held. Aside from a circular seating arrangement where participants can all see one another, the second critical requirement in selecting a meeting place is to find one quiet enough to permit an intelligible audiotaping of the sessions.

Focus group facilities operated by focus group companies have the best locations for focus groups because of their layouts and equipment.

The ideal setting for a focus group is a **focus group facility,** which is a set of rooms especially designed for focus groups at a marketing research company specializing in conducting focus groups. The focus group room itself contains a large table and comfortable chairs, a relaxing atmosphere, and a one-way mirror so that clients can view the interviewing process. Ample space for video and audio equipment should also be provided. An example of a typical floor plan for a focus group facility is provided in Figure 8.1. Because focus group research is qualitative, it generates many diverse pieces of information. Rather than relying on memory, which can be faulty, or relying on the moderator's taking notes, which can slow down and distract the process, most focus groups are audiotape recorded and many are video recorded. You can see from the floor plan in Figure 8.1 that a focus group company's facilities have recording capabilities designed into them. Microphones are built into the walls or ceiling or otherwise set in the center of the table, and videotape equipment often resides behind a one-way mirror. One-way mirrors also allow clients to observe the focus group as it takes place.

Focus groups are recorded on audiotape and sometimes videotape.

The Focus Group Moderator's Role and Responsibilities

A successful focus group requires an effective moderator.

By now, you realize that the most crucial factor influencing the effectiveness and usefulness of a focus group is the moderator.[16] A **focus group moderator** is a person who conducts the entire session and guides the flow of group dis-

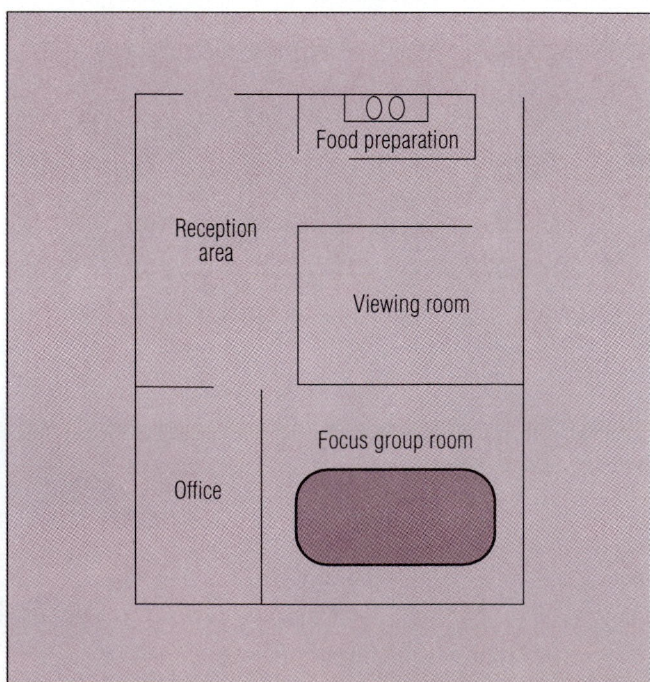

Figure 8.1

The floor plan of a focus group facility reveals how one operates.

In the past, companies have tried to hide or disguise the equipment they used to record respondents' reactions. This was done in an attempt to remove any feelings of self-consciousness or awkwardness that might result in the respondents' interviews by being taped. However, such a practice is unethical, and few participants are tricked anyway. Now, it is common practice to let participants know about the recording aspect when they are recruited. If they have any objections, they can decline at that time.

cussion across specific topics desired by the client. The moderator must strive for a very delicate balance between stimulating, natural discussions among all of the group members while ensuring that the focus of the discussion does not stray too far from the topic. A good moderator must have excellent observation, interpersonal, and communication skills to recognize and overcome threats to a productive group discussion. He or she must be prepared, experienced, and armed with a detailed list of topics to be discussed.[17] It is also helpful if the focus group moderator can eliminate any preconceptions on the topic from his or her mind. Finally, the moderator should be empathetic or sensitive to the participants' situations and comments.[18]

A good moderator is experienced, prepared, unbiased, and empathetic.

The focus group's success depends on the participants' involvement in the discussion and in their understanding of what is being asked of them. Productive involvement is largely a result of the moderator's effectiveness, which in turn is dependent on his or her understanding of the purpose and objectives of the interview. Unless the moderator understands what information the researcher is after and why, he or she will not be able to phrase questions effectively. It is good policy to have the moderator contribute to the development of the project's goals so as to guide the discussion topics. By aiding in the formation of the topics (questions), he or she will be familiar with them and will be better prepared to conduct the group. It is important when formulating questions that they be organized into a logical sequence and that the moderator follow this sequence, to the furthest extent possible. With an incompetent moderator, the focus group can become a disaster. Unfortunately, there are no industry standards or certification systems for focus group moderators, but one writer has identified 10 traits a marketing researcher can use to judge the competency of a moderator (see Table 8.2 on page 225).

The focus group topic guide should be prepared with the moderator's involvement.

The moderator's introductory remarks are influential; they set the tone of the entire session. All subsequent questions should be prefaced with a clear explanation of how the participants should respond, for example, how they really feel personally, not how they think they should feel. This allows the moderator to establish a rapport with participants and to lay the groundwork for the interview's structure.

Reporting and Use of Focus Group Results

As we noted earlier, focus groups report some of the subtle and obscure features of the relationships among consumers and products, advertising, and sales efforts. They furnish qualitative data on such things as consumer language; emotional and behavioral reactions to advertising; life-style; relationships; the product category and specific brand; and unconscious consumer motivations relative to product design, packaging, promotion, or any other

A focus group moderator must be prepared with subject knowledge and a topics outline.

facet of the marketing program under study. But focus group results are qualitative and not perfectly representative of the general population.

Focus group transcripts must be translated before they are reported.

Two important factors must be remembered when analyzing the data. First, some sense must be made by translating the qualitative statements of participants into categories and then reporting the degree of consensus apparent in the focus groups. Second, the demographic and buyer behavior characteristics of focus group participants should be judged against the target market profile to assess to what degree the groups represent the target market.

Focus group information is evaluated by an analyst who carefully observes the recorded tapes several times, transcribing any relevant statements that seem evident. These statements are then subjected to closer evaluation. This evaluation is based on the analyst's knowledge of the history and statement of

TABLE 8.2

Ten Traits of a Good Focus Group Moderator

1. Be experienced in focus group research.
2. Provide sufficient help in conceptualizing the focus group research design, rather than simply executing the groups exactly as the client specifies.
3. Prepare a detailed moderator guide well in advance of the focus group.
4. Engage in advance preparation to improve overall knowledge of the area being discussed.
5. Provide some "added value" to the project beyond simply doing an effective job of conducting the session.
6. Maintain control of the group without leading or influencing the participants.
7. Be open to modern techniques such as visual stimulation, conceptual mapping, attitude scaling, or role-playing, which can be used to delve deeper into the minds of participants.
8. Take personal responsibility for the amount of time allowed for the recruitment, screening, and selecting of participants.
9. Share in the feeling of urgency to complete the focus group while desiring to achieve an excellent total research project.
10. Demonstrate the enthusiasm and exhibit the energy necessary to keep the group interested even when the hour is running late.

Source: *Thomas L. Greenbaum, "Do You Have the Right Moderator for Your Focus Groups? Here Are 10 Questions to Ask Yourself,"* Bank Marketing, *vol. 23, no. 1 (1991), 43.*

the problem plus his or her own interpretation of the responses. A detailed report is prepared for the client's review.

A focus group analysis should identify the major themes as well as salient areas of disagreement among the participants.

The focus group report reflects the qualitative aspect of this research method. It lists all themes that have become apparent, and it notes any diversity of opinions or thoughts expressed by the participants. It will also have numerous verbatim excerpts provided as evidence.[19] In fact, some reports include complete transcripts of the focus group discussion. This information is then used as the basis for further research studies or even for more focus groups. If the information is used for subsequent focus groups, the client uses the first group as a learning experience, making any adjustments to the discussion topics as needed to improve the research objectives. Although focus groups may be the only type of research to tackle a marketing problem or question, they are also used as a beginning point for quantitative research efforts. That is, a focus group phase may be used to gain a feel for a specific survey that will ultimately generate standardized information from a representative sample.

Advantages of Focus Groups

Now that you understand the basics of focus groups, we can turn to a brief description of their advantages, disadvantages, and other issues researchers are confronted with when they rely on focus groups. There are four major advan-

Key advantages of focus groups include the generation of ideas, client interaction, versatility, and the ability to tap special respondents.

tages to using focus groups as a form of qualitative research: They generate fresh ideas, they allow clients to observe the group in action, they are generally versatile, and they work well with special respondents. We describe each in turn.

Generate Fresh Ideas

Creative and honest insights are often the result of focus groups. Because the respondents are not alone with the interviewer, they feel more at ease and free to express honest opinions rather than the ones they think will please the interviewer. The effect of "snowballing," or of one comment triggering another, is also common in a focus group situation. A "group creativity" factor is often observed in brainstorming sessions in which one person's idea stimulates others to generate their own ideas. Focus groups are excellent arenas for this sort of effect.

Allow Clients to Observe the Group

The ability to observe focus groups greatly facilitates client understanding.

A frequent complaint of marketing research clients is that they have difficulty understanding the complex quantitative techniques used and the statistical results produced. This lack of understanding invariably leads to an underutilization of the information provided. However, because managers can be involved throughout the focus group process by helping with the design of objectives and by observing the focus group, the results make more of an impression on them and are more likely to result in action. In fact, managers sometimes formulate and begin executing action plans based on their focus group observations even before the focus group data is analyzed and submitted as a formal report.

Generally Versatile

A virtually unlimited number of topics and issues can be discussed in a focus group interview situation. It is even possible to incorporate the use of other qualitative techniques such as role playing into the session, thus increasing the productivity of the discussion. Prototypes of products can be demonstrated, concepts can be described, and product performance test results can be dis-

A major advantage of a focus group is client observation while it is taking place.

closed. Even advertising copy can be evaluated with a focus group.[20] The moderator is also allowed to probe deeper into the opinions of the participants, something not allowed in highly structured quantitative methods. A different aspect of this advantage is the flexibility of focus groups afforded by technology. Some companies regularly conduct focus groups with participants at diverse geographical locations through the use of videoconferences.[21] Even business supply companies such as Kinko's Copies have videoconference centers available for rent, and focus groups can be conducted with executives for instance with the use of these facilities or the video conferences facilities now in place in many focus group company office areas. Some services are now providing focus groups on the Internet where net users will enter "chat rooms" where certain topics are identified and all chat room members can submit their comments and reactions in a public forum. Some Internet focus groups take place over extended time periods using news group postings.

Focus groups using video-conferencing and Internet "chat rooms" demonstrate the versatility of this technique.

Work Well with Special Respondents

Another major advantage of focus groups is that they permit the researcher to study respondents that might not respond well under more structured situations. In some situations, such as those involving hard-to-interview groups such as lawyers or doctors, the format gives them an opportunity to associate with their peers and to compare notes. Otherwise, they might refuse to take part in a survey. Creative variations of focus groups are successful in studies on children. Both Kid2Kid and Doyle Research Associates have innovative approaches where children interact with children in structured team activities, storytelling, and other interactions that the children treat as games.[22]

Disadvantages of Focus Groups

No research technique is flawless, and focus groups are no exception.[23] Some weaknesses are readily apparent, whereas others are less obvious. There are three major weaknesses: They may not represent the general population, their interpretation is subjective, and their cost per participant is high. A discussion of these weaknesses follows.

May Not Represent the Population

Focus group results should not be viewed as conclusive research because the participants are not likely to be representative of the general population the researcher is studying. Generally, those who agree to participate in focus groups are more outgoing than the average person. They are more accessible and probably more compliant. Coupled with the small sample size and homogenous group design, these unique characteristics render many focus groups unrepresentative of the marketer's target population. Furthermore, because it is not possible to ensure that all of the participants who agree to take part will show up, semi-professional respondents are sometimes "on call" for last-minute emergencies. Consequently, tight controls and a sober evaluation of the representativeness of focus groups' participants are mandatory.

It is important to remember that a focus group may not be representative of the total group under study.

Interpretation Is Subjective

Selective use of the data collected by focus groups is a typical problem. Individuals with preconceived notions can almost always find something to support their views, ignoring anything that does not support their opinions. So focus

Managers may engage in subjective interpretation of a focus group, so it is advisable to use a trained analyst.

The difficulties encountered by focus group companies in recruiting focus group participants have led to some questionable practices. Some people like to participate in focus groups, and a focus group company may keep a list of willing participants. Other participants may want to take part simply for the monetary compensation, and their names may be on the focus group company's list as well. In either case, inclusion of those people who have previously participated in numerous focus groups can lead to serious validity problems. Some researchers will explicitly disallow a focus group company to use these participants because of this concern. As a matter of policy, some focus group companies will always report the last time, if ever, that each focus group member participated in a focus group. Other companies will do so only if the client firm makes an explicit request for this information.

group analysts are constantly on guard against bias entering into qualitative research.[24] The subjectivity problem is compounded by involvement of management personnel during the design and conduct of the focus groups. It is not uncommon for a manager to enter the process with a preconceived notion of what the research will find (or what it should support). Because focus group research typically allows the manager and his or her team to suggest topics and to add specific questions as well as to observe the groups in progress, a danger exists that certain preconceptions will enter into their impressions of the research findings. In fact, as we mentioned earlier, they may even take these impressions and convert them to action before the focus groups are analyzed and the summary report delivered to the client. If a researcher senses that premature actions are a danger, he or she will advise the client to wait until a trained focus group analyst has interpreted the complete set of focus group transcripts, and experienced researchers know that this process takes time.[25]

A danger of focus groups is that clients may take action before objective interpretation takes place.

Cost-per-Participant Is High

Although focus group information is valuable, it bears a high cost-per-participant.

A variety of expensive items contribute to the high cost-per-participant. One is participant recruitment. Numerous telephone calls are usually needed to recruit the desired number of required participants. The average charge for this service is around $25, and more for hard-to-reach or rare respondents. Next is the incentive cost. Some sort of compensation is offered to those who show up (usually around $30 dollars). This should be given to all respondents who arrive, even if they are not required to participate. These costs are minor compared to the moderator and facilities rental fees. A qualified moderator's salary can range from $1,500 to $2,000 per session. This amount includes his or her participation in developing the objectives, conducting the focus groups, transcribing the videotapes, and writing and presenting a full report to management. Last, rental of the focus group facility plus its videotaping equipment are additional costs to be considered. The rental cost varies greatly, depending on where the focus group takes place, but a fully equipped focus group facility usually charges hundreds of dollars per hour of use. A final cost factor involves hidden costs. Such costs include time spent by the marketing manager and his or her team working and traveling that are absorbed by the manager's budget but not necessarily assigned as a cost of the focus groups by the company's accounting system. Sometimes managers may even review all of the videotapes pertaining to a set of focus groups, resulting in many hours of time, which also draws them away from their other responsibilities. Not counting hidden costs that are difficult to estimate, a typical focus group may cost from $150–$200 per participant, whereas a "ballpark" telephone survey cost is between $10 and $15 per respondent.

The Future of Focus Groups

Focus groups are an appealing qualitative research method.

The focus group approach will remain a popular and influential marketing research technique for many years to come. Because they are easy to interpret, of reasonable total cost when compared to large-scale quantitative surveys involving a thousand or more respondents, adaptable to managers' concerns, and capable of yielding immediate results, focus groups are an appealing qualitative research method. They are a unique research method because they permit marketing managers to see and hear the market. Managers become so engrossed in their everyday problems and crises that they find it very refreshing to see their customers in the flesh. It is common for marketing managers to come away from a focus group session observation stimulated and energized to respond to the market's desires.

As was noted earlier, focus group research is becoming more widespread worldwide. In fact, differences among the world's populations necessitate that the research be tailored to the specific culture and people. Marketing Research Insight 8.2 (page 230) notes these differences. The popularity of focus groups has caused a sharp increase in the number of focus group facilities. By one account a five-fold increase in the number of viewing facilities occurred in the mid-1990s in the United Kingdom.[26]

Focus groups have a promising future.

As communications technology advances, focus group research will naturally expand. For instance, some companies have experimented with conference calls where two focus groups interact with one another.[27] Refinements in telecommunications such as videoconferencing[28] are rendering these useful when participants are busy professionals, such as doctors or lawyers, or when they are geographically distant. Computer technology will ultimately reduce the transcript preparation time, and there are computer programs that can perform content analysis of recorded speech. With a few key words, a researcher can gain a tabulation of the topics under discussion in a few minutes. Focus groups were predicted to grow during the 1990s and they did grow.[29] We believe the future of focus groups continues to look bright.

OTHER QUALITATIVE RESEARCH TECHNIQUES

Although focus group interviews and many of the observation methods we have described thus far are clearly the most frequently used qualitative research techniques, they are not the only type of nonstructured research available to marketing researchers. Other popular methods include depth interviews, protocol analysis, various projective techniques, and physiological measurements.

Depth Interviews

Depth interviews with consumers may reveal what they are thinking or why they have acted in a certain way.

A **depth interview** is defined as a set of probing questions posed one-on-one to a subject by a trained interviewer so as to gain an idea of what the subject thinks about something or why he or she behaves in a certain way. It is con-

MARKETING RESEARCH INSIGHT 8.2

Using Focus Groups to Measure Value Systems around the World

Research International (RI), one of the world's largest ad hoc research organizations, recently launched a global qualitative research initiative, called RIO (Research International Observer). Twice a year, participating units from RI's global network select two topics to explore in a qualitative context. They then report their results to their clients, the media, and other interested parties.

The first RIO research was completed in early 1992. Twenty-six countries participated: The United States, Canada, Argentina, Brazil, Japan, the Philippines, Malaysia, New Zealand, Australia, Kenya, Nigeria, South Africa, France, Portugal, Spain, Italy, Greece, Belgium, The Netherlands, Germany, United Kingdom, Austria, Sweden, Norway, Denmark, and Hungary. In each country, two focus groups were conducted with between 8 and 10 women in each group. The two topics selected for the first wave were the role of women and nutritional trends.

Researchers found that the role of women in all societies is moving along two major dimensions: from self-denial toward self-fulfillment, and from submission toward assertion. California, Germany, Canada, Sweden, and Norway are furthest along in these two dimensions. In virtually all societies, the major impact has been the influx of women into the workforce. Where this change is fairly recent, for example in Africa, Latin America, or the Far East, women greet it with a high level of enthusiasm, explaining it represents a newly achieved independence. At the other extreme, there is even a feeling that women may have become too successful, emasculating men and their roles.

The traditional woman's role still survives in countries such as South Africa and the Philippines. In these countries, the ideal woman is feminine, motherly, self-denying, and submissive. The more advanced nations of Africa and South America can be termed "Action Movers," with a forceful and aggressive attitude toward change. The "Superwoman" is the ideal in these countries.

The "Emancipated" woman is found throughout much of Southern Europe and the Antipodes. The predominant feeling in these areas is that women have finally arrived on the scene, although much has still to be done in terms of true equality. For example, women still have to face enormous pressures balancing their professional and domestic lives—all too often with little help from men. For some women, there is a dawning of a realization that working so hard at being Superwoman is foolish—"(woman) is the victim of a condition she has created for herself."

"Self-achievers" are at least moving toward a better balance of roles. In fact, women's ability in the workforce now valorizes their family commitment. This self-confidence on the part of women creates strong pressures for part-time work and government-supported services such as child care and maternity leave. The true self-achiever, exemplified by many women in Canada, California, and Northern Europe, is most concerned to be "at ease with herself." She readily acknowledges that it is now men who have the hardest time adjusting to the new realities—still focused on their superseded role of aggressive breadwinner and struggling with their role of supportive, equal partner.

It would be dangerous to draw firm conclusions from a study of only 500 people. However, RIO does provide a stimulating look at issues often only examined on a national basis and, importantly, it also gives us a framework to explore and manage data globally.

Source: *This description was provided by Malcolm Baker, President, The B/R/S Group, Inc.*

ducted in the respondent's home or possibly at a central interviewing location such as a mall-intercept facility where several respondents can be interviewed in depth in a relatively short time period. The objective is to obtain unrestricted comments or opinions and to ask questions that will help the marketing researcher better understand the various dimensions of these opinions as well as the reasons for them. Of primary importance is the compilation of the data into a summary report so as to identify common themes. New concepts, designs, advertising, and promotional messages can arise from this method. If used properly, depth interviews can offer great insight into consumer behavior.[30,31] Depth interviews are especially useful when the researcher wants to understand decision making on the individual level, how products are used, or the emotional and sometimes private aspects of consumers' lives.[32]

The depth interview is typically conducted by a trained field worker who is equipped with a list of topics or, perhaps, open-ended questions. In other words, the respondent is not provided a list of set responses and then instructed to select one from the list. Rather, the respondent is encouraged to respond in his or her own words, and the interviewer is trained in asking probing questions such as, "Why is that so?," "Can you elaborate on your point?," or "Would you give me some specific reasons?" These questions are not intended to tap subconscious motivations; rather, they simply ask about conscious reasons to help the researcher form a better picture of what is going on in the respondent's head. The interviewer may tape record responses or may take detailed notes. Depth interviews are versatile, but they require careful planning, training, and preparation.[33]

A depth interview uncovers conscious reasons that interviewees may not disclose without probing questions.

The summary report will look very similar to one written for a focus group study. That is, the analyst looks for common themes across several depth interview transcripts, and these are noted in the report. Verbatim responses are included in the report to support the analyst's conclusions, and any significant differences of opinion that are found in the respondents' comments are noted as well. Again, it is vital to use an analyst who is trained and experienced in interpreting the qualitative data gathered with depth interviews.

Protocol Analysis

Protocol analysis involves placing a person in a decision-making situation and asking him or her to verbalize everything he or she considers when making a decision. It is a special-purpose qualitative research technique that has been developed to peek into the consumer's decision-making processes. Often, a tape recorder is used to maintain a permanent record of the person's thinking. After several people have provided protocols, the researcher reviews them and looks for commonalities such as evaluative criteria used, number of brands considered, types and sources of information utilized, and so forth.

Protocol studies require subjects to "think aloud."

Protocol studies are useful in two different purchase situations. First, they are helpful for purchases involving a long time frame in which several decision factors must be considered such as buying a house. By having people verbalize the steps they went through, a researcher can piece together the whole process. Second, where the decision process is very short, recall may be faulty and protocol analysis can be used to slow down the process. For example, most people

Protocol studies require subjects to tell what they are thinking as they go about shopping or considering a purchase.

do not give much thought to buying chewing gum, but if Dentine wanted to find out why people buy Spearmint gum, protocol analysis might provide some important insights regarding this purchasing behavior.

Projective Techniques

With a projective technique, people often divulge something about themselves they would not divulge in a direct questioning situation.

Projective techniques involve situations in which participants are placed in (projected into) simulated activities in the hopes that they will divulge things about themselves that they might not reveal under direct questioning. Projective techniques are appropriate in situations in which the researcher is convinced that respondents will be hesitant to relate their true opinions. Such situations may include behaviors such as tipping waitresses, socially undesirable behaviors such as smoking or alcohol consumption, questionable actions such as littering, or even illegal practices such as betting on football games.

There are five common projective techniques used by marketers: the word association test, the sentence completion test, the picture test, the cartoon or balloon test, and role-playing activity. A discussion of each follows.

Word Association Test

A **word association test** involves reading words to a respondent who then answers with the first word that comes to his or her mind. These tests may contain over 100 words and usually combine neutral words with words being tested in ads or words involving product names or services. The researcher then looks for hidden meanings or associations between responses and the words being tested on the original list. This approach is used to uncover people's real feelings about these products or services, brand names, or ad copy. The time taken to respond, called "response latency," and/or the respondents' physical reactions may be measured and used to make inferences. For exam-

TABLE 8.3

Results of a Word Association Test with Alternative Brand Names for a New Fruit-Flavored Sparkling Water Drink

POSSIBLE BRAND NAME	ASSOCIATED WORDS
Ormango	Green, tart, jungle
Tropical Fruit	Juice, sweet, island
Orange Sparkle	Light, bubbly, cool
Paradise Passion	Fruity, thick, heavy

ple, if the response latency to the word "duo" is long, it may mean that people do not have an immediate association with the word.

Word association tests can help marketers to analyze potential brand names.

One company used a word association test to help determine a new product's name. It had narrowed the brand name down to four alternatives: Ormango, Tropical Fruit, Orange Sparkle, or Paradise Passion. They then invited university students to take a word association test of the proposed product names. The words they tended to associate with each possible brand name are provided in Table 8.3.

Which brand name is associated with the notion of a refreshing drink? It appears that Paradise Passion is not and Tropical Fruit seems more like a breakfast juice. Ormango might qualify, but Orange Sparkle definitely made students think of a sparkling drink more than the other names did.

Sentence Completion Test

With a **sentence completion test,** respondents are given incomplete sentences and asked to complete them in their own words. The researcher then inspects these sentences to identify themes or concepts that exist. The notion here is that respondents will reveal something about themselves in their responses. For example, suppose that Lipton Tea was interested in expanding its market to teenagers. A researcher might recruit high school students and instruct them to complete the following sentences:

Someone who drinks hot tea is ______________________.

Tea is good to drink when ______________________.

Making hot tea is ______________________.

My friends think tea is ______________________.

Write in words to complete these sentences. What does it tell you about your attitude toward drinking hot tea?

The researcher would look at the written responses and attempt to identify central themes. For instance, the theme identified for the first sentence might be "healthy," which would signify that tea is perceived as a drink for those who are health conscious. The theme for the second sentence might be "hot," indicating that tea is perceived as a cold weather drink, whereas the theme for the third sentence may turn out to be "messy," denoting the students' reaction to using a tea bag. Finally, the last sentence theme might be found as "okay," suggesting there are no peer pressures working to cause high school students to avoid drinking tea. Given this information, Lipton might deduce that there is room to capitalize on the hot tea market with teens.

Picture Test

Picture tests are useful ways to test potential advertisements for impact and reactions.

With a **picture test,** a picture is provided to participants who are instructed to describe their reactions by writing a short story about the picture. The researcher analyzes the content of these stories to ascertain feelings, reactions, or concerns generated by the picture. Such tests are useful when testing pictures being considered for use in brochures, advertisements, and on product packaging. For example, a test advertisement might depict a man holding a baby, and the ad headline might say, "Ford includes driver and passenger airbags as standard equipment because you love your family." A picture test may well divulge something about the picture that is especially negative or distasteful. Perhaps unmarried male respondents cannot relate to the ad because they do not have children and have not experienced strong feelings for children. On the other hand, it may turn out that the picture has a much more neutral tone than Ford's advertising agency intended. It may be that the picture does not generate feelings of concern and safety for the family in married respondents with young children. In any case, without the use of a picture test, it would be very difficult to determine the audience's reactions.

Cartoon or Balloon Test

Take the balloon test on the next page. What does it reveal about your concern for UV rays?

With a **balloon test,** a line drawing with an empty "balloon" above the head of one of the actors is provided to subjects who are instructed to write in the balloon what the actor is saying or thinking. The researcher then inspects these thoughts to find out how subjects feel about the situation described in the cartoon. For example, when shown a line drawing of a situation in which one of the characters is making the statement, "Here is a pair of patent leather dress shoes on sale for $39.99," the participant is asked how the other character in the drawing would respond. Feelings and reactions of the subject are judged based on their answers. An example of a cartoon test is provided in Figure 8.2. Feel free to fill in the balloon. It may interest you to know that some undergraduate students have written quotes indicating that this sunbather is not worried about skin damage from the sun, whereas others have written quotes about how this woman would not dare recline like this in the sun unless she had a very powerful sun block on.

Role-Playing Activity

Role play this: What would your best friend say if you bought a pair of $200 "Astronaut" Ray-Bans?

With **role playing,** participants are asked to pretend they are a "third person," such as a friend or neighbor, and to describe how they would act in a certain situation or to a specific statement. By reviewing their comments, the researcher can spot latent reactions, positive or negative, conjured up by the situation. It is believed that some of the respondents' true feelings and beliefs will be revealed by this method because they can pretend to be another individual. For example, if Ray-Ban is thinking about introducing a new "Astronaut" sunglasses model with superior ultraviolet light filtration, space-age

Figure 8.2

A balloon test: What is she saying about her protection from the sun's ultraviolet rays?

styling, and a cost of about $200, role playing might be used to fathom consumers' initial reactions. In this use of role playing, subjects could be asked to assume the role of a friend or close workmate and to indicate what they would say to a third person when they learned that their friend had purchased a pair of Astronaut sunglasses. If consumers felt the Astronaut model was overpriced, this feeling would quickly surface. On the other hand, if the space-age construction and styling was consistent with these consumers' lifestyles and product desires, this fact would be divulged in the role-playing comments.

As with depth interviews, all of these projective techniques require highly qualified professionals to interpret the results. This increases the cost per respondent compared to other survey methods. Because of this aspect, projective techniques are not used extensively in commercial marketing research, but each one has value in its special realm of application.[34]

Physiological Measurement

Physiological measures are sometimes used in marketing research, but they are unnatural and difficult to interpret.

Physiological measurement involves monitoring a respondent's involuntary responses to marketing stimuli via the use of electrodes and other equipment. Most people who are monitored find the situation strange and may experience uneasiness during the monitoring. Because of this factor, and the necessary hardware, this technique is rarely used in marketing research.

We briefly describe two physiological measures to round out this chapter on qualitative research: the pupilometer and the galvanometer. The **pupilometer** is a device that attaches to a person's head and determines interest and attention by measuring the amount of dilation in the pupil of the eye. It actually photographs the movement of a person's iris when he or she views different pictures. Theoretically, a person's iris enlarges more with an interesting image than when an uninteresting one is viewed. The **galvanometer** is a device that determines excitement levels by measuring the electrical activity in the respondent's skin. It requires electrodes or sensing pads to be taped to a person's body in order to monitor this activity. When a person encounters an interesting stimulus, the electrical impulses in the body become excited. Physiological measures are useful under special circumstances, such as testing sexually oriented stimuli where many people are embarrassed or may not tell the truth, and they require special skills to be administered correctly. There are two disadvantages to using physiological measurement techniques. First, the techniques are unnatural in nature, and subjects may become nervous and emit false readings. Second, even though we know that the respondent reacted to the stimulus, we do not know if the response was positive or negative.[35]

SUMMARY

This chapter described the various qualitative research techniques employed by marketing researchers. Qualitative research is much less structured than are quantitative approaches. We described the various types of observation alternatives possible such as disguised versus undisguised, structured versus unstructured, and human versus mechanical. We noted the circumstances most suitable to observational studies are instances of (1) short time interval, (2) public behavior, and (3) lack of recall.

The chapter next described the use of focus groups, or moderated small group discussions, which is a very popular form of research. We noted that a focus group should include from 8 to 12 participants sharing similar characteristics. Recruiting and selection may be problems due to "no shows." Focus group facilities exist in most major cities, but any large room with a central table can be used. The moderator's role is key to a successful focus group. There are, however, a few drawbacks to focus groups, and assessing the representativeness of the group is one of them. Also, interpretation is subjective and the cost-per-participant is high. Nevertheless, the future of focus group research is bright.

We wrapped up the chapter with descriptions of some of the other qualitative techniques used in marketing research. Depth interviews, for instance, have been adapted to probe into consumer motivations and hidden concerns. Protocol analysis induces participants to "think aloud" so the researcher can map the decision-making process being used while a consumer goes about making a purchase decision. Projective techniques, such as word association, sentence completion, or role playing, are also useful in unearthing motivations, beliefs, and attitudes that subjects may not be able to express well verbally. Finally, there are some physiological measurements such as pupil movement or electrical activity in the skin that can be used in special circumstances to better understand consumer reactions.

KEY TERMS

Quantitative research (p. 209)
Qualitative research (p. 209)
Pluralistic research (p. 209)
Observation methods (p. 211)
Direct observation (p. 211)
Indirect observation (p. 211)
Archives (p. 211)
Physical traces (p. 211)
Disguised observation (p. 212)
Undisguised observation (p. 212)
Structured observation (p. 213)
Unstructured observation (p. 213)
Human observation (p. 213)
Mechanical observation (p. 213)
Dracula syndrome (p. 216)
Frankenstein syndrome (p. 216)
Focus group (p. 216)
Focus group facility (p. 222)
Focus group moderator (p. 222)
Depth interview (p. 229)
Protocol analysis (p. 231)
Projective techniques (p. 232)
Word association test (p. 232)
Sentence completion test (p. 233)
Picture test (p. 234)
Balloon test (p. 234)
Role playing (p. 234)
Physiological measurement (p. 235)
Pupilometer (p. 235)
Galvanometer (p. 236)

REVIEW QUESTIONS/APPLICATIONS

1. Define quantitative research. Define qualitative research. List the differences between these two research methods. What is pluralistic research?
2. What is meant by an "observation technique?" What is observed, and why is it recorded?
3. Indicate why disguised observation would be appropriate for a study on how parents discipline their children when dining out.
4. Describe at least three different uses of focus groups.
5. How are focus group participants recruited, and what is a common problem associated with this recruitment?
6. Should the members of a focus group be similar or dissimilar? Why?
7. Describe what a focus group company facility looks like and how a focus group would take place in one.
8. Should the marketing manager client be a focus group moderator? Why or why not?
9. What should be included in a report that summarizes the findings of a focus group?
10. Indicate the advantages and disadvantages of client interaction in the design and execution of a focus group study.
11. What is meant by the term "projective" as in projective techniques?
12. Describe (a) sentence completion, (b) word association, and (c) balloon test.
13. Johnny Walker Red Label Scotch is concerned about the shifting attitudes of the public regarding the consumption of alcohol. However, managers think that scotch

whiskey may be seen differently because it is normally consumed in small quantities as opposed to beer, wine, or even other hard liquors such as vodka. Select two projective techniques. First, defend your use of a projective technique. Second, describe in detail how your two chosen techniques would be applied to this research problem.

14. Your university is considering letting an apartment management company build an apartment complex on campus. To save money, the company proposes to build a common cooking area for every four apartments. This area would be equipped with an oven, burners, microwave oven, sink, food preparation area, garbage disposal, and individual mini-refrigerators with locks on them for each apartment. Two students would live in each apartment. You volunteer to conduct focus groups with students to determine their reactions to this concept and to brainstorm suggestions for improvements. Prepare the topics list you would have as a guide in your role as moderator.
15. Indicate how a focus group moderator should handle each of the following cases: (a) A participant is loud and dominates the conversation; (b) a participant is obviously suffering from a cold and goes into coughing fits every few minutes; (c) two participants who, it turns out, are acquaintances, persist in a private conversation about their children; and (d) the only minority representative participant in the focus group looks very uncomfortable with the group and fails to make any comments.

CASE 8.1

Getaway Travel Agencies, Inc.

Getaway Travel Agencies, Inc. is a franchise system of travel agencies that operates in major cities throughout the United States. It specializes in the "cruise trade," or trips that are conducted on cruise ships operating in the Caribbean, Gulf of Mexico, Pacific Coast from Mexico to Alaska, and, recently, the Mediterranean. Getaway package trips include air fare to and from the port of departure/return, all transfers, and all cruise costs. Getaway prides itself on negotiating with the cruise ship operators and buying in volume to bring the costs down to be among the lowest in the market. Over the past two years, Getaway system sales have not been as strong as Getaway top management would like to see. In fact, the whole Getaway franchise system experienced a 5 percent decrease in total bookings last year. Getaway has commissioned a company to conduct focus groups as a way to gain a feel for the problem. Here is an excerpt from the transcript of the first focus group. This group comprised single males between the ages of 22 and 30.

John: "I don't like package cruises. I prefer to go out on my own and find what each location has to offer. Sometimes, I just rent a moped or car and drive around."

Jim: "Well, I don't really care to go that way. I much prefer to have someone else worry about where I need to be and when, and to just tell me where to catch the next bus or van out or back."

Jerry: "Yes, I do want that for the most part. But I do want some personal exploration time like the time they give us in native shopping areas or to explore the town or sights. I like a little adventure on my cruises, but in a controlled way, so I know that I don't waste all of my time searching for something special that doesn't exist."

Moderator: "Does anyone else have a reaction to the cruises?"

John: "Yes, I really prefer to make up my own cruise. Getaway has only about three to pick from in each of its cruise areas. I have done Jamaica, and the Bahamas, and . . . where was that other place? Anyway, there are no more places to go in the Caribbean with Getaway. Plus, I think they are a little pricey for what you get."

Jim: "No, they aren't. You pay more for those Delta Vacations or the American Airlines Fly-Aways than you do for a typical Getaway trip."

Jerry: "Getaway is cheaper by the package. But it is because Getaway crams so much into a trip. You don't have a spare moment to yourself, so you feel that you are getting a lot for the price you pay. That's still quite a bargain by the way I figure it."

John: "Getaway is a limited cruise travel agency—the Caribbean and Alaska are the only places they go. I want a lot more variety when I plan my vacation, and so I go to other travel agencies. In fact, last week I experimented with a build-it-yourself trip that a travel agency has on the Internet. It let me pick and choose where I wanted to go, and then it gave me a total cost."

Jim: "Those systems are way too complicated. There are just too many things to pick from. Besides, I think it is just a trick to make you think you are planning your trip, but in the end you just plug into trips that the agency has already set up. All I need to pick from is trip A, B, or C."

Jerry: "Yes, that's a lot more appealing as long as there is some free time for exploration every day or so. I don't want to punch minute-by-minute choices on a computer menu screen."

Using these excerpts as representative of the entire focus group transcript, answer the following questions.

1. How is Getaway perceived? That is, what is different about Getaway's trips compared to other travel services?
2. What are some areas of possible service improvement for Getaway?
3. What misperceptions about Getaway should management worry about? What do you recommend to correct these misperceptions?
4. Should Getaway consider establishing its cruise selection and purchasing service on the Internet? What are the pros and cons?

CASE 8.2

Home Depot

Home Depot is a large, self-service home, garden, and building supply store operation. It buys products in great volume and stores them in large warehouse-like stores. On any given day, hundreds of customers can be seen wandering through the warehouse, pulling merchandise ranging from houseplants, PVC piping, plywood, paint cans, kitchen sinks, lawn mowers, electrical supplies, and practically any other do-it-yourself building or fix-up product and placing them in oversized shopping carts or even on heavy-duty hand trucks.

To better understand its customers, Home Depot commissioned Observations, Inc. to perform an observational study and to describe the typical customer's trip through the store. Observations, Inc. performed direct observations using human observers who followed customers through the store. The observers carried clipboards and masqueraded as Home Depot employees who were checking merchandise, but in reality they followed each customer under observation and made notations on a structured observation form. A summary of their findings is as follows:

OBSERVATION ITEM	FINDING
Shopper/Store Use Profile	
Average time in store:	32.4 (minutes)
Customer party size:	1.2 (persons)
Average expenditures:	57.34 (dollars)
Payment method:	73.0% (cash)
Number of aisles traveled:	5.7
Requests for assistance:	0.5
Stops and looks at items:	5.4
Items handled per stop:	2.1

OBSERVATION ITEM	FINDING
Shopper/Store Use Profile (cont.)	
Total items handled:	11.3
Items purchased:	2.5
Product Categories of Purchases	
Appliances	10%
Hand tools	22%
Electrical	31%
Plumbing	14%
Roofing	3%
Garden	35%
Other	26%

(Totals greater than 100% are due to multiple purchases.)

1. What are the implications of these findings for (a) aisle design, (b) in-store promotion, and (c) merchandise mix?
2. List five questions these observation findings suggest that can be answered only through quantitative research methods.

CHAPTER 9

Survey Data Collection Methods

LEARNING OBJECTIVES

- *To learn about advantages and disadvantages of surveys*
- *To become knowledgeable of the details of different types of survey data collection methods such as personal interviews, telephone interviews, and computer-assisted interviews*
- *To comprehend factors researchers consider when choosing a particular survey method*

PRACTITIONER VIEWPOINT

A researcher has several options available for gathering data. They range from face-to-face interviews to very sophisticated computer-driven questioning systems. I'm excited about the high-technology options that are becoming more available and reasonable from a cost standpoint. I would not be surprised to see data collection methods revolutionized in the next decade. Even now, major companies are building extensive databases on their customers by capturing the electronic trails people leave as they make credit card purchases, have their purchases scanned in retail stores, and subscribe to cable television systems. These systems may be the ways the research industry overcomes the growing reluctance on the part of consumers to take part in surveys.

— Bill Jameson
Polaris Marketing Research

A Revolution in Survey Data Collection

Laptops and other computer technology have changed the way interviewers record a respondent's answers.

The continual adoption of the Internet by tens of thousands of businesses and households has led to what some describe as a "paradigm shift," or a completely different way to think about and to execute data collection, in the marketing research industry. Companies such as Decisive Technology Corporation have developed products such as its Decisive Survey that are radically changing the face of data collection.[1] Decisive Survey is a Windows-based computer program that allows the researcher to create a questionnaire, send it to any number of e-mail addresses, receive the responses, perform simple tabulations, and make graphs of findings. The company claims that e-mail eliminates the tedium associated with filling out printed forms by hand, and it eliminates the interruptions of phone interviewers. Further, surveys by e-mail dramatically reduce the costs of conventional survey data collection as duplication, postage, phone, and manual data entry costs are eliminated. It also greatly reduces the time it takes to get survey results. Further, Decisive Technology Corporation claims that respondents view electronic surveys as more important, more interesting, more enjoyable, and more relaxing than the paper-and-pencil versions. You can examine and experience Decisive Survey by visiting Decisive Technology's homepage at http://www.decisive.com.

There are three general ways of obtaining primary data in marketing research—survey, observation, and experiment. Although exact figures are not available, it is well known that surveys are the most widely used method of data collection in commercial marketing research. The bulk of marketing research surveys are sometimes called "cross-sectional" studies or surveys of large cross-sections of populations. Consequently, we devote much attention to collecting data via surveys in this chapter. First, we note the advantages of surveys. Next, we describe the pros and cons of the three basic survey modes: (1) person-administered surveys, (2) computer-assisted surveys, and (3) self-administered surveys. After these, we give descriptions of several commonly used data collection methods such as mall intercepts, telephone interviews, and mail surveys. Finally, we discuss factors a market researcher should consider when deciding which data collection method to use.

ADVANTAGES OF SURVEYS

Key advantages of surveys include standardization, ease of administration, ability to tap the "unseen," suitability to tabulation and statistical analysis, and sensitivity to subgroup differences.

Compared to observation or other qualitative methods, survey methods allow the collection of significant amounts of data in an economical and efficient manner; and they typically allow for much larger sample sizes. There are five advantages of using survey methods: (1) standardization, (2) ease of administration, (3) ability to tap the "unseen," (4) suitability to tabulation and statistical analysis, and (5) sensitivity to subgroup differences (see Table 9.1).

Standardization

Because questions are preset and organized in a particular arrangement on a questionnaire, survey methods ensure that all respondents are asked the same questions and are exposed to the same response options for each question. Moreover, the researcher is assured that every respondent will be confronted with questions that address the complete range of information objectives driving the research project.

TABLE 9.1

Five Advantages of Survey Research

ADVANTAGES	DESCRIPTIONS
Standardization	All respondents react to questions worded identically and presented in the same order. Response options (scales) are the same, too.
Administration ease	Interviewers read questions to respondents and record their answers quickly and easily. In some cases, the respondents fill out the questionnaires themselves.
Tap the "unseen"	It is possible to ask questions about motives, circumstances, sequences of events, or mental deliberations.
Tabulation/analysis	Large sample sizes and computer processing allows quick tallies, cross-tabulations, and other statistical analyses.
Subgroup differences	Respondents can be divided into segments or subgroups for comparisons in the search for meaningful differences.

Ease of Administration

Sometimes an interviewer is used, and survey modes are easily geared to such administration. On the other hand, the respondent may fill out the questionnaire unattended. In either case, the administration aspects are much simpler than, for instance, conducting a focus group or utilizing depth interviews. Perhaps the simplest case is a mail survey in which questionnaires are sent to prospective respondents. There is no need for tape recording, taking notes, or analyzing projective or physiological data; there is not even a need to read the questions to the respondent. All the researcher needs to do is mail the questions to prospective respondents.

Mail surveys are self-administered, the simplest form of administration for researchers.

Ability to Tap the "Unseen"

The four questions of what, why, how, and who help uncover "unseen" data. For instance, we can ask a working parent to tell us how important the location of a preschool was in his or her selection of the child's preschool. We can inquire as to how many different preschools he or she seriously considered before deciding on one, and we can easily gain an understanding of the person's financial or work circumstances with a few questions on income, occupation, and family size. Much information is unobservable and requires direct questions.

Suitability to Tabulation and Statistical Analysis

The marketing researcher ultimately must interpret the patterns or common themes sometimes hidden in the raw data he or she collects. Statistical analysis, both simple and complex, is the preferred means of achieving this goal, and large cross-sectional surveys perfectly complement these procedures. Qualitative methods, in contrast, prove much more frustrating in this respect because of their necessarily small samples, need for interpretation, and general approach to answering marketing managers' questions. Increasingly, questionnaire design software includes the ability to perform simple statistical analyses, such as tabulations of the answers to each question, as well as the ability to create color graphs summarizing these tabulations. The Decisive Survey program described in the introduction of this chapter is one such program.

Questionnaire design programs include statistical analysis packages as a natural extension of survey research.

Sensitivity to Subgroup Differences

Because surveys involve large numbers of respondents, it is relatively easy to "slice" up the sample into demographic groups or other subgroups and then to compare them for market segmentation implications. In fact, the survey sample design may be drawn up to specifically include important subgroups as a means of looking at market segment differences. In any case, the large sample sizes that characterize surveys facilitate subgroup analyses and comparisons of various groups existing in the sample.

THREE ALTERNATIVE DATA COLLECTION MODES

There are three major ways to collect information from respondents: (1) Have a person ask the questions, (2) have a computer assist or direct the questioning, or (3) allow respondents to fill out the questionnaire themselves. We will

Three data collection modes are person-administered, computer-administered, and self-administered.

refer to these three alternatives as person-administered, computer-administered, and self-administered surveys, respectively. Each one has special advantages and disadvantages that we describe in general before discussing the various types of surveys found within each category. Specific advantages and disadvantages on these various types are discussed later.

Person-Administered Surveys

A **person-administered survey** is one in which an interviewer reads questions to the respondent and records his or her answers. It was the primary administration method for many years. However, its popularity has fallen off as communications systems have developed and technology has advanced. Nevertheless, person-administered surveys are still used, and we describe the advantages and disadvantages associated with these surveys next.

Advantages of Person-Administered Surveys

Person-administered surveys have the four unique advantages of feedback, rapport, quality control, and adaptability.

Person-administered surveys have four unique advantages: They offer feedback, rapport, quality control, and adaptability.

1. *Feedback.* Interviewers often must respond to direct questions from respondents during an interview. Sometimes respondents do not understand the instructions, or they may not hear the question clearly, or they might become distracted by some outside factor during the interview. A human interviewer may be allowed to adjust his or her questions according to verbal or nonverbal cues. When a respondent begins to fidget or look bored, the interviewer can say, "I have only a few more questions." Or if a respondent makes a comment, the interviewer may jot it down as a side note to the researcher.

Market researchers sometimes use face-to-face personal interviews.

2. *Rapport.* Some people distrust surveys in general, or they may have some suspicions about the survey at hand. It is often helpful to have another human being present to develop some rapport with the respondent early on in the questioning process. Once a bridge of trust and understanding has been established, most respondents will become visibly more relaxed with the interview and will open up more to the various questions being posed.

Personal interviewers can build rapport with respondents who are initially distrustful or suspicious.

3. *Quality control.* An interviewer sometimes must select certain types of respondents based on sex, age, or some other distinguishing characteristic. Personal interviewers may be used to ensure respondents are selected correctly. Alternatively, some researchers feel that respondents are more likely to be truthful when they respond face-to-face.
4. *Adaptability.* Personal interviewers can adapt to respondent differences. It is not unusual, for instance, to find an elderly person who must be initially helped step-by-step through the answering process in order to understand how to respond to question asking if the respondent "strongly agrees," "somewhat agrees," "somewhat disagrees," or strongly disagrees." By the same token, an engineer quickly grasps very complicated numerical rating scales. An interviewer may be allowed to adjust the directions accordingly or have the respondent do tasks such as sorting cards with brand names into piles or examining a mock-up of an ad.

Personal interviews can easily adapt to the needs and styles of different respondents.

Disadvantages of Person-Administered Surveys

The drawbacks to using human interviewers are precisely those we list as advantages for computer-administered systems (see the following section). That is, personal interviewers are slower; they are prone to errors; and although pictures, videos, and graphics can be handled by personal interviewers, they cannot accommodate them as easily as a computer. Often, personal interviewers simply record respondents' answers using pencil and paper, which necessitates a separate data-input step to build a computer data file. Naturally, the use of a face-to-face interviewer is more expensive than interviewing on the telephone or mailing the questionnaire to respondents. Ideally, personal interviewers are highly trained and skilled and their use overcomes the expense factor. Of course, poorly trained or low-skilled personal interviewers are not desirable.

Person-administered surveys are relatively slow and/or expensive.

Computer-Administered Surveys

As our introductory example illustrates, computer technology represents a viable option with respect to survey mode, and new developments occur almost every day. Although person-administered surveys are still the industry mainstay, it is important to discuss computer-administered survey methods as we are certain that this approach will grow and become common in the foreseeable future. Computer-assisted surveys are in an evolutionary state, and they are spreading to other survey types. For instance, a computer may house questions asked by a telephone interviewer, or a questionnaire disk may be mailed to respondents for self-administration. Basically, a **computer-administered survey** is one in which computer technology plays an essential role in the interview work. Here, either the computer assists an interview, or it interacts directly with the respondent. In the case of Internet questionnaires, the com-

Computer technology increasingly changes the character of data collection.

puter acts as the medium by which potential respondents are approached, and it is the means by which respondents return their completed questionnaire. As with person-administered surveys, computer-administered surveys have their advantages and disadvantages.

Advantages of Computer-Administered Surveys

Computer-administered surveys are fast, error-free, capable of using pictures or graphics, able to capture data in real time, and less threatening for some respondents.

At least five advantages of computer-administered surveys are evident: speed; error-free interviews; use of pictures, videos, and graphics; real-time capture of data; and reduction of "interview evaluation" concern in respondents.

1. *Speed.* The computer-administered approach is much faster than the human interview approach. Computers can quickly jump to questions based on specific responses, they can rapidly dial random telephone numbers, and they can easily check on answers to previous questions to modify or otherwise custom tailor the interview to each respondent's circumstances. The speed factor translates into cost savings, and there is a claim that Internet surveys are about one-half the cost of mail or phone surveys.[2]
2. *Error-free interviews.* Properly programmed, the computer-administered approach guarantees zero interviewer errors such as inadvertently skipping questions, asking inappropriate questions based on previous responses, misunderstanding how to pose questions, recording the wrong answer, and so forth. Also, the computer neither becomes fatigued nor cheats.
3. *Use of pictures, videos, and graphics.* Computer graphics can be integrated into questions as they are viewed on a computer screen. So rather than having an interviewer pull out a picture of a new type of window unit air conditioner, for instance, computer graphics can show it from various perspectives. CD-ROM disk capabilities allow high-

quality video windows to appear so the respondent can see the product in use or can be shown a wide range of visual displays.

4. *Real-time capture of data.* Because respondents are interacting with the computer and not a human who is recording their answers on a questionnaire, the information is directly entered into a computer's data storage system and can be accessed for tabulation or other analyses at any time. Once the interviews are completed, final tabulations can be completed in a matter of minutes. This feature is so beneficial that some interview companies have telephone interviewers directly linked to computer input when they conduct their interviews.

The real-time capture of data by computer-administered surveys is an important advantage of this data collection method.

5. *Reduction of "interview evaluation" concern in respondents.* Some people, when they are involved in responding to questions in a survey, become anxious about the possible reaction of the interviewer to their answers. Questions about personal hygiene, political opinions, financial matters, and even age are considered to be "personal" by many people, and the presence of a human interviewer may deter them from answering, or they may give false answers that they believe the interviewer will accept. On the other hand, some respondents try to please the interviewer by saying what they think the interviewer wants to hear. In any case, some researchers believe that respondents will provide more truthful answers to potentially sensitive topics when interacting with a machine.

Disadvantages of Computer-Administered Surveys

Obviously, computer-assisted surveys must have some disadvantages; otherwise, more surveys would make use of computer technology. Although computers are relatively inexpensive at present, there are significant costs involved in computer design, programming, debugging, and set up, which must be incurred with each survey. These costs, including the time factor associated with them, often render computer-administered delivery systems for surveys unattractive relative to other data collection options. However, set-up costs are falling rapidly with user-friendly programs such as Decisive Survey.

Computer-administered surveys incur relatively high set-up costs, but these costs are falling rapidly.

Self-Administered Surveys

A **self-administered survey** is one in which the respondent completes the survey on his or her own. It is different from other survey methods in that there is no agent—human or computer—administering the interview. So, we are referring to the prototypical "pencil and paper" survey here. Instead, the respondent reads the questions and responds directly on the questionnaire. Normally, the respondent goes at his or her own pace, and in most instances he or she selects the place and time to complete the interview. He or she also may decide when the questionnaire will be returned. As with other survey methods, those that are self-administered have their advantages and disadvantages.

Advantages of Self-Administered Surveys

Self-administered surveys have three important advantages: reduced cost, respondent control, and no interviewer-evaluation apprehension.

Self-administered surveys are attractive because they are low in cost, they give respondents control, and they avoid interviewer-evaluation apprehension.

1. *Reduced cost.* By eliminating the need for an interviewer or an interviewing device such as a computer program, there can be significant savings in cost.

2. *Respondent control.* Respondents can control the pace at which they respond, so they may not feel rushed. Ideally, a respondent should be relaxed while responding, and a self-administered survey may effect this state.
3. *No interviewer-evaluation apprehension.* As we just noted, some respondents feel apprehensive when answering questions. The self-administered approach takes the administrator, whether human or computer, out of the picture, and respondents may feel more at ease.

Disadvantages of Self-Administered Surveys

As you can see, self-administration places control of the survey in the hands of the prospective respondent. Hence, this type of survey is subject to the possibilities that respondents will not complete the survey, will answer questions erroneously, will not respond in a timely manner, or will refuse to return the survey at all.

There is potential for respondent error with self-administered surveys.

The major reason for these drawbacks is that no opportunity exists to monitor or interact with the respondent during the course of the interview. For example, in conducting a survey for a mass transit system, one question might be, "Have you used this city's subway system to commute to and from work in the past three months?" The questionnaire may then instruct respondents who indicate "no" to skip the next set of questions, whereas those responding "yes" would continue on and answer questions about the subway's cleanliness, the degree of crowding, its adherence to published schedules, and so on. If a respondent who indicated "no" somehow failed to realize that he or she should skip these questions, there is the possibility that he or she would become frustrated at the questions about the subway's features and throw the questionnaire away. Alternatively, in conducting a survey of aspirin use, one question might ask the respondent to rank five different brands of aspirin from "most preferred" to "least preferred" by writing the rank number beside each brand. However, the respondent might misunderstand and just check off his or her most-preferred brand. In either case, if an interviewer were present, the error would be quickly spotted and resolved; but, because the interviewer is not present, the respondent may well commit numerous similar errors while fully believing that he or she has responded properly.

If respondents misunderstand or do not follow directions, they may become frustrated and quit.

Due to the absence of the interviewer, the burden of respondent understanding falls on the questionnaire itself. It must have very clear instructions, examples, and reminders throughout. Although questionnaire design is a complete topic that we take up in chapter 11, the point to remember here is that the respondent, not the interviewer, has control with self-administered surveys. Thus, the potential for error is very high, and market researchers must take great care to reduce this error factor.

DESCRIPTIONS OF REPRESENTATIVE DATA COLLECTION MODES

Now that you have an understanding of the pros and cons of person-, computer-, and self-administered surveys, we can describe the various interviewing techniques used in each method. There are 10 different data collection methods used by marketing researchers:

1. In-home interview
2. Mall-intercept interview
3. In-office interview
4. "Traditional" telephone interview
5. Central location telephone interview
6. Computer-assisted telephone interview (CATI)
7. Fully computerized interview
8. Group self-administered survey
9. Drop-off survey
10. Mail survey (Table 9.2)

A discussion of each follows.

TABLE 9.2

Ways to Gather Data

In-home interview	The interviewer conducts the interview in the respondent's home. Appointments may be made ahead by telephone.
Mall-intercept interview	Shoppers in a mall are approached and asked to take part in the survey. Questions may be asked in the mall or in the mall-intercept company's facilities located in the mall.
In-office interview	The interviewer makes an appointment with business executives or managers to conduct the interview at the respondent's place of work.
"Traditional" telephone interview	Interviewers work out of their homes to conduct telephone interviews with households or business representatives.
Central location telephone interview	Interviewers work in a data collection company's office using cubicles or work areas for each interviewer. Often the supervisor has the ability to "listen in" to interviews and to check that they are being conducted correctly.
Computer-assisted telephone interview (CATI)	With a central location telephone interview, the questions are programmed for a computer screen and the interviewer then reads them off. Responses are entered directly into the computer program by the interviewer.
Fully computerized interview	A computer is programmed to administer the questions. Respondents interact with the computer and enter in their own answers by using a keyboard, by touching the screen, or by using some other means.
Group self-administered survey	Respondents take the survey in a group context. Each respondent works individually, but they meet as a group and this allows the researcher to economize.
Drop-off survey	Questionnaires are left with the respondent to fill out. The administrator may return at a later time to pick up the completed questionnaire, or it may be mailed in.
Mail survey	Questionnaires are mailed to prospective respondents who are asked to fill them out and return them by mail.

Person-Administered Interviews

There are at least four variations of person-administered interviews, and their differences are largely based on the location of the interview. These variations include the in-home interview, the mall-intercept interview, the in-office interview, and the telephone interview (which includes the "traditional" and central location telephone interviews).

In-Home Interviews

In-home interviews are conducted in the security and comfort of respondents' homes.

Just as the name implies, an **in-home interview** is conducted in the home of the respondent. Two important factors justify the use of in-home interviews. First, the marketing researcher must believe that personal contact is essential to the success of the interview. Second, he or she must be convinced that the in-home environment is conducive to the questioning process.

In-home interviews facilitate interviewer–interviewee rapport.

Let us analyze these factors more completely. With respect to the first factor, the survey may incorporate a set of advertisements the researcher wants viewed, it might require the respondent to see and touch a product, the respondent may have to perform a complicated task such as sorting cards with brand names on them into piles, or it might be vital that the interviewer make visual confirmation of the respondent's qualifying characteristics or nonverbal cues. On the second factor, it is often believed that conducting an interview in the home greatly improves the quality of responses and facilitates the rapport between interviewer and interviewee. When a respondent is in a secure, comfortable environment, the likelihood of distraction is reduced, and it is believed that respondents take more care in responding to various questions.

In-home interviews require the interviewer to enter the interviewee's home to ask questions or demonstrate product concepts.

Also, most in-home interviews take considerable time, and by allowing the interview to take place in his or her home, the respondent is implicitly expecting it to take some time, certainly longer than would be expected for a telephone survey, for instance. It is interesting to note that the in-home, personal interview is the most common type used in Great Britain, but as Marketing Research Insight 9.1 notes, the situation is changing.

Mall-Intercept Interviews

Mall-intercept interviews are conducted in large shopping malls, and they are less expensive per interview than are in-home interviews.

Although the in-home interview has important advantages, it has the significant disadvantage of cost. The expense of in-home interviewer travel is high, even for local surveys. Patterned after "man-on-the-street" interviews pioneered by opinion-polling companies and other "high-traffic" surveys conducted in settings where crowds of pedestrians pass by, the **mall-intercept interview** is one in which the respondent is encountered and questioned while he or she is visiting a shopping mall. This approach has given birth to a new breed of survey interview companies. A mall-intercept company generally has

MARKETING RESEARCH INSIGHT 9.1

Why There Is a Shift away from Personal Interviewing in Great Britain

The traditional form of data collection in Great Britain is face-to-face, in-home interviews, which account for slightly more than one-half of all data collection methods. However, some observers believe that this pattern will shift, and greater percentages of data collection will be accounted for by telephone and mail survey in the future. One British marketing research executive sees four problems that could accelerate the shift away from face-to-face, in-home interviews:

1. *More women moving into employment. With the increased number of British women taking on full-time or part-time paid employment, fewer are interested in earning "pin" money through irregular marketing research fieldworker jobs.*
2. *Evidence of decreased cooperation by prospective respondents. National statistics document a long-term trend of decline in survey response rates. In the late 1980s, the Great Britain National Readership Survey response rate declined to 67 percent. Moreover, the London rate declined to below 55 percent. This trend continues.*
3. *Uninteresting and complicated surveys. British market researchers should endeavor to make their interviews interesting, and they should use visuals and prompt cards as memory aids. Also, researchers should keep their surveys to reasonable lengths.*
4. *Right to privacy. Although data privacy legislation is less restrictive in Great Britain than in some other European countries, it is possible that pressures will be brought on the industry with new legislation. Also, British subjects are exhibiting a greater desire for privacy, which is impacting cooperative rates.*

Source: *Tim Bowles, "Data Collection in the United Kingdom,"* Journal of the Market Research Society, *vol. 31, no. 4 (1991), 467–476.*

its offices located within a large shopping mall, usually one that draws from a regional rather than a local market area. Typically, the interview company negotiates exclusive rights to do interviews in the mall and thus forces all marketing research companies who wish to do mall intercepts in that area to use that interview company's services. In any case, the travel costs are eliminated because the respondents incur the costs themselves by traveling to the mall.

Mall-intercept interview companies make this method easy and popular.

Mall-intercept interviewing has acquired a major role as a survey method due to its ease of implementation.[3] Shoppers are intercepted in the pedestrian traffic areas of shopping malls and either interviewed on the spot or asked to move to a permanent interviewing facility located in the mall office. Although some malls do not allow marketing research interviewing because they view it as a nuisance to shoppers, many do permit mall-intercept interviews and may rely on these data themselves to fine-tune their own marketing programs.

The representativeness of mall interview samples is always an issue.

In addition to low cost, mall interviews have most of the advantages associated with in-home interviewing. Perhaps the most important advantage is the presence of an interviewer who can interact with the respondent.[4] However, a few disadvantages are specifically associated with mall interviewing, and it is necessary to point them out here. First, sample representativeness is an issue, for most malls draw from a relatively small area in close proximity to their location. Some people shop at malls more frequently than others and therefore have a greater chance of being interviewed.[5] Recent growth on non-mall retailing concepts such as catalogs and stand-alone discounters such as Wal-

Mall-intercept interviews often take place in the corridors of large, regional shopping malls.

Mart have shifted mall shoppers to be less convenience oriented and more recreational shoppers, resulting in the need to scrutinize mall-intercept samples as to what consumer groups they actually represent.[6] Also, many shoppers refuse to take part in mall interviews for various reasons. Nevertheless, special selection procedures called quotas, which are described in chapter 12, may be used to counter the problem of nonrepresentativeness.

A second shortcoming of mall intercept interviewing is that a shopping mall does not have a comfortable home environment that is conducive to rapport and close attention to details. The respondents may feel uncomfortable because passersby stare at them; they may be pressed for time or otherwise preoccupied by various distractions outside the researcher's control. These factors may adversely affect the quality of the interview. As we indicated earlier, some interview companies attempt to counter this problem by taking respondents to special interview rooms located in the interview company's mall offices. This procedure minimizes distractions and encourages respondents to be more relaxed.

Mall interview companies use rooms in their small headquarters areas to conduct private interviews in a relaxed setting.

In-Office Interviews

In-office interviews are conducted at executives' or managers' places of work because they are the most suitable locations.

Although the in-home and mall-intercept interview methods are appropriate for a wide variety of consumer goods, marketing research conducted in the business-to-business or organizational market typically requires interviews with business executives, purchasing agents, engineers, or other managers. Normally, **in-office interviews** take place in person while the respondent is in his or her office, or perhaps in a company lounge area. Interviewing businesspersons face-to-face has essentially the same advantages and drawbacks as in-home consumer interviewing. For example, if Texas Instruments wanted information regarding user preferences for different features that might be offered in a new ultra-high-speed laser printer designed for business accounting firms, it would make sense to interview prospective users or purchasers of these printers. It would also be logical that these people would be interviewed at their places of business.

In-office personal interviews incur costs due to difficulties in accessing qualified respondents.

As you might imagine, in-office personal interviews incur relatively high costs. Those executives qualified to give opinions on a specific topic or individuals who would be involved in product purchase decisions must first be located. Sometimes names can be obtained from sources such as industry directories or trade association membership lists. More frequently, screening must be conducted over the telephone by calling a particular company that is believed to have executives of the type needed. However, locating those people within a large organization may be time consuming. Once a qualified person is located, the next step is to persuade that person to agree to an interview and then set up a time for the interview. Finally, an interviewer must go to the particular place at the appointed time. Even with appointments, long waits are sometimes encountered and cancellations are not uncommon because businesspeople's schedules sometimes shift unexpectedly. Added to these cost factors is the fact that interviewers who specialize in businessperson interviews are more costly in general because of their specialized knowledge and abilities. They have to navigate around gatekeepers such as secretaries, learn technical jargon, and be conversant on product features when the respondent asks pointed questions or even criticizes questions as they are posed to him or her.

Telephone Interview

As we have mentioned previously, the need for a face-to-face interview is often predicated on the necessity of the respondent's actually seeing a product, advertisement, or packaging sample. On the other hand, it may be vital that the interviewer watch the respondent to ensure correct procedures are followed or otherwise to verify something about the respondent or his or her reactions. If, however, physical contact is not necessary, telephone interviewing is an attractive option. There are a number of advantages as well as disadvantages associated with telephone interviewing.

Advantages of telephone interviews are cost, quality, and speed.

The advantages of telephone interviewing are many, and they explain the popularity of phone surveys. First, the telephone is a relatively inexpensive way to collect survey data. Long-distance telephone charges are not high to begin with, and WATS lines lower them significantly. A second advantage of the telephone interview is that it has the potential to yield a very high-quality sample. If the researcher employs random dialing procedures and proper callback measures, the telephone approach may produce a better sample than any other survey procedure. A third and very important advantage is that telephone surveys have very quick turnaround times. Most telephone interviews are of short duration anyway, but a good interviewer may complete several interviews per hour. Conceivably, a study could have the data collection phase executed in a few days with telephone interviews. In fact, in the political polling industry where real-time information on voter opinions is essential, it is not unusual to have national telephone polls completed in a single night.

Disadvantages of telephone interviews are inability of respondents to see questions, inability to observe respondents, and limitations on information quality and quantity.

Unfortunately, the telephone survey approach has several inherent shortcomings. First, the respondent cannot be shown anything. This shortcoming ordinarily eliminates the telephone survey as an alternative in situations requiring that the respondent view product prototypes, advertisements, packages, or anything else. A second disadvantage is that the telephone interview does not permit the interviewer to make the various judgments and evaluations that can be made by the face-to-face interviewer. For example, judgments regarding respondent income based on the home they live in and other outward signs of economic status cannot be made. Similarly, the telephone does not allow for the observation of body language and facial expressions, nor does it permit eye contact. On the other hand, some may argue that the lack of face-to-face contact is helpful. Self-disclosure studies have indicated that respondents provide more information in personal interviews, except when the topics are threatening or potentially embarrassing. Questions on alcohol consumption, contraceptive methods, racial issues, or income tax reporting will probably generate more valid responses when asked in the relative anonymity of the telephone than when administered face-to-face.[7]

A third disadvantage of the telephone interview is that the marketing researcher is more limited in the quantity and types of information he or she can obtain. Very long interviews are inappropriate for the telephone, as are questions with lengthy lists of response options that respondents will have difficulty remembering when they are read over the telephone. Respondents short on patience may hang up during interviews, or they may utter short and convenient responses just to speed up the interview. Obviously, the telephone is a poor choice for conducting an interview with many open-ended questions.

The telephone is a poor choice of conducting a survey with many open-ended questions.

A last problem with telephone interviews is the growing use of answering machines and caller recognition devices being adopted by consumers. The research industry is concerned about these gatekeeping methods, and it is just beginning to study ways around them.[8] Another difficulty is that legitimate telephone interviewers must contend with the negative impression people have of telemarketers.[9]

Telephone interviewers must contend with the negative impression people have of telemarketers.

There are two types of telephone interviews: traditional and central location. As you can guess, telephone interviewing has been and continues to be greatly impacted by advances in telephone systems and communications technology. As you will see, the traditional telephone approach has largely faded away, whereas the central location approach has embraced technological advances in telephone systems.

Traditional Telephone Interviewing. Technology has radically changed telephone surveys; however, it is worthwhile to describe this form of telephone interviewing as a starting point. Prior to central location and computer-assisted telephone interviewing, these **traditional telephone interviews** were those that were conducted either from the homes of the telephone interviewing staff or, perhaps, from telephone stalls located in the data collection company's offices. Everything was done mechanically. That is, interviewers dialed the telephone number manually, they read questions off a printed questionnaire, they were responsible for following special instructions on how to administer the questions, and they checked off the respondent's answers on each questionnaire. Quality control was limited to training sessions, sometimes in the form of a dress rehearsal by administering the questionnaire to the supervisor or another interviewer, and to callback checks by the supervisor to verify that the respondent had taken part in the interview.

Obviously, the traditional telephone interview method offers great potential for errors. In addition to the possibilities of misdialing and making mistakes in administering the questions, there are potential problems of insufficient callbacks for not-at-homes, and a host of other problems. Also, because the actual hours worked performing telephone interviews are difficult to track, most interview companies opt for a "per completion" compensation system. That is, the interviewer is compensated for each questionnaire delivered to the office completely filled out. As you can imagine, there have been instances of dishonest interviewers turning in falsified results.

Traditional telephone interviewing has great potential for errors.

Central Location Telephone Interviewing. This form of telephone interviewing is in many ways the research industry's standard. With **central location telephone interviewing,** a field data collection company installs several telephone lines at one location, and the interviewers make calls from the central location. Usually, interviewers have separate enclosed work spaces and lightweight headsets that free both hands so they can record responses. Everything is done from this central location, which is usually equipped with WATS long-distance lines. Obviously, there are many advantages to operating from a central location. For example, resources are pooled, and interviewers can handle multiple surveys, such as calling plant managers in the afternoon and households during the evening shift.

Central location interviewing is the current telephone survey standard.

The reasons for the growing prominence of the central location phone interview are savings and control. Apart from cost savings, perhaps the most

A concern with traditional telephone interviewing is interviewer cheating. Although most traditional telephone interviewers are honest, only minimal control and supervision can be used with this method. Consequently, there are temptations for cheating such as turning in bogus completed questionnaires or conducting interviews with respondents who do not qualify for the survey at hand. When traditional telephone interviewing is used, checks should be more extensive and may include the following:

1. *Have an independent party call back a sample of each interviewer's respondents to verify that they took part in the survey.*
2. *Have interviewers submit copies of their telephone logs to validate that the work was performed on the dates and in the time periods required.*
3. *If long-distance calls were made, have interviewers submit copies of their telephone bill with long-distance charges itemized to check that the calls were made properly.*
4. *If there is a concern about a particular interviewer's diligence, request that the interviewer be taken off the project.*

A researcher should always check the accuracy and validity of interviews, regardless of the data collection method used.

Central location telephone interviewing affords good control of interviewers.

important reason is quality control. To begin, recruitment and training is performed uniformly at this location. Interviewers can be oriented to the equipment, they can study the questionnaire and its instructions, and they can simulate the interview among themselves over their phone lines. Also, the actual interviewing process can be monitored. Most telephone interviewing facilities have monitoring equipment that permits a supervisor to listen in on interviewing as it is being conducted. Interviewers who are not doing the interview properly can be spotted and the necessary corrective action taken. Ordinarily, each interviewer will be monitored at least once per shift, but the supervisor may focus attention on newly hired interviewers to ensure they are doing their work correctly. The fact that each interviewer never knows when the supervisor will listen in guarantees more overall diligence than would be seen otherwise. Also, completed questionnaires are checked on the spot as a further quality control check. Interviewers can be immediately informed of any deficiencies in filling out the questionnaire. Finally, there is control over interviewers' schedules. That is, interviewers report in and out and work regular hours, even if they are evening hours, and make calls during the time periods stipulated by the researcher as appropriate interviewing times.

Computer-Administered Interviews

Computer technology has impacted the telephone data collection industry significantly. There are two variations of computer-administered telephone interview systems. In one, a human interviewer is used, but in the other, a computer, sometimes with a synthesized or tape-recorded voice, is used. At the same time, there are important computer-assisted interview methods that have recently emerged, which we describe in this section as well.

Computer-Assisted Telephone Interview (CATI)

The most advanced companies have computerized the central location telephone interviewing process; such systems are called **computer-assisted telephone interviews (CATI).** Although each system is unique, and new developments occur almost daily, we can describe a typical situation. Here, each interviewer is equipped with a "hands-free" headset and is seated in front of a computer screen that is driven by the company's computer system. Often, the computer dials the prospective respondent's telephone automatically, and the computer screen provides the interviewer with the introductory comments. As the interview progresses, the interviewer moves through the questions by pressing a key or a series of keys on the keyboard. Some systems use light pens or pressure-sensitive screens. The questions and possible responses appear on the screen one at a time. The interviewer reads the question to the respondent, enters the response code, and the computer moves on to the next appropriate question. For example, an interviewer might ask if the respondent owns a dog. If the answer is "yes," there could appear a series of questions regarding what type of dog food they buy. If the answer is "no," these questions would be inappropriate. Instead, the computer program skips to the next appropriate question, which might be "Do you own a cat?" In other words, the computer eliminates the human error potential that would exist if this survey were done in the traditional paper-and-pencil telephone interview mode. The human interviewer is just the "voice" of the computer.

With CATI, the interviewer reads the questions off a computer screen and enters respondents' answers directly into the computer program.

With CATI, the interviewer is the "voice" of the computer.

The computer can even be used to customize questions. For example, in the early part of a long interview you might ask a respondent the years, makes, and models of all cars he or she owns. Later in the interview you might ask questions about each specific car owned. The question might come up on the interviewer's screen as follows: "You said you own a 1997 BMW. Who in your family drives this car most often?" Other questions about this car and others owned would appear in similar fashion. Questions like this can, of course, be dealt with in a traditional or central location manual interview, but they are handled much more efficiently in the computerized version because the interviewer does not need to physically flip questionnaire pages back and forth or remember previous responses.

The CATI approach also eliminates the need for editing completed questionnaires and creating computer data files by later manually entering every response with a keyboard. There is no checking for errors in completed questionnaires because there is no physical questionnaire. More to the point, in most computerized interview systems it is not permitted to enter an "impossible" answer. For example, if a question has three possible answers with codes "A," "B," or "C," and the interviewer enters a "D" by mistake, the computer will ask for the answer to be reentered until an acceptable code is entered. If a combination or pattern of answers is impossible, the computer will not accept an answer, or it may alert the interviewer to the inconsistency and move to a series of questions that will resolve the discrepancy. Data entry for completed questionnaires is eliminated because data is entered directly into a computer file as the interviewing is completed.

Most CATI systems are programmed to make wrong answers impossible.

This second operation brings to light another advantage of computer-assisted interviewing. Tabulations may be run at any point in the study. Such real-time reporting is impossible with the pencil-and-paper questionnaire in

CATI systems integrate telephones and computers to perform very efficient interviewing systems with many advantages.

which there can be a wait of several days following interviewing completion before detailed tabulations of the results are available. Instantaneous results available with computerized telephone interviewing provide some real advantages. Based on preliminary tabulations, certain questions may be dropped, saving time and money in subsequent interviewing. If, for example, over 90 percent of those interviewed answered a particular question in the same manner, there may be no need to continue asking the question.

CATI systems permit tabulation in mid-survey.

Tabulations may also suggest the addition of questions to the survey. If an unexpected pattern of product use is uncovered in the early interviewing stages, questions can be added to further delve into this behavior. So the computer-administered telephone survey affords an element of flexibility unavailable in the traditional paper-and-pencil survey methods. Finally, managers may find the early reporting of survey results useful in preliminary planning and strategy development. Sometimes survey project deadlines run very close to managers' presentation deadlines, and advance indications of the survey's findings permit managers to organize their presentations in advance rather than all in a rush the night before. The many advantages and quick turnaround of CATI and CAPI (computer-assisted personal interviewing) make them mainstay data collection methods for many syndicated omnibus survey services.[10]

In sum, computer-administered telephone interviewing options are very attractive to marketing researchers because of the advantages of cost savings, quality control, and time savings over the paper-and-pencil method.[11] With computer prices falling and questionnaire design software becoming available, more companies are adopting this high-technology approach. Some researchers expect the integration of voice recognition technology to be an exciting new feature that will assist market researchers.[12] The prospect for CATI is very good, and marketing researchers can be assured that when they consider telephone interviews in the future, the computer-assisted option will be an attractive option available to them.[13]

CATI is the wave of the future due to cost savings, quality control, and time savings.

Fully Computerized Interview

Some companies have developed **fully computerized interviews,** in which the survey is administered completely by a computer. With one such system, a computer dials a phone number and a recording is used to introduce the survey. The respondent then uses the push buttons on his or her telephone to make responses, thereby interacting directly with the computer. In the research industry, this approach is known as **CATS, completely automated telephone survey.** CATS has been successfully employed for customer satisfaction studies, service quality monitoring, election day polls, product/warranty registration, and even in-home product tests with consumers who have been given a prototype of a new product.[14]

CATS eliminates the need for a human interviewer.

In another system, the respondent sits or stands in front of the computer unit and reads the instructions off the screen. Each question and its various response options appear on the screen, and the respondent answers by pressing a key or touching the screen. For example, the question may ask the respondent to rate how satisfied, on a scale of 1 to 10 (where 1 is very unsatisfied and 10 is very satisfied), he or she was the last time he or she used a travel agency to plan a family vacation. The instructions would instruct the respondent to press the key with the number appropriate to his or her degree of satisfaction. So, the respondent might press a "2" or a "7," depending on his or her experience and expectations. If, however, a "0" or some other ineligible key were pressed, the computer could be programmed to beep, indicating that the response was inappropriate, and instruct the respondent to make another entry. Advanced Data Research uses a pad and wand system, and claims that 90 percent of the people involved in their research preferred it to paper questionnaires.[15] Another example is Mediamark Research, Inc., which has developed a completely computerized system with audio features for its print readership measurement studies.[16]

With fully computerized interviewing, respondents interact directly with the computer and enter their responses manually.

Several varieties of computer-assisted interview formats are emerging.

All of the advantages of computer-driven interviewing are found in this approach, plus the interviewer expense or extra cost of human voice communication capability for the computer is eliminated. Because respondents' answers are saved in a file during the interview itself, tabulation can take place on a daily basis. Even if the interviews are conducted in remote locations across the United States, it is a simple matter to download the files via telephone lines and high-speed modems to the central facility for daily tabulations. Some researchers believe that the research industry should move to replace pen-and-paper questionnaires with computer-based ones.[17]

Other Computer-Assisted Interview Formats

It was noted earlier that computer-assisted interviewing is in a development phase. As examples of this evolution, Scott Dacko[18] identified several methods of computerized interviewing that are available to marketing researchers. These are: (1) computer-assisted personal interviewing in which the interviewer reads questions off a laptop computer screen and keys the respondent's answers in, (2) computerized self-interviewing in which the respondent reads the questions and keys them into the computer, (3) computer-assisted telephone interviewing (CATI), (4) completely automated telephone surveys (CATS), (5) computer disks sent by mail for respondents to respond to on their own computers and mail back, (6) e-mail surveys such as the one described in our introduction of this chapter, and (7) computer-based fax of a questionnaire to the respondent, who completes it and faxes or mails it back. In general, all of these computer-assisted interview formats are superior to manual methods in the ways that are identified in Table 9.3. Significant advantages of computer-assisted interview formats include the ability to accommodate branching types of questions, use respondent-generated words in the questionnaire, measure response times, display graphics, minimize recording errors, and speed up data collection. The idea of e-mail surveys is very appealing, although questions of response rate and representativeness of respondents are troublesome right now.[19] The Internet is an exciting new interview medium, and some believe it will replace mail and telephone surveys and become the most common survey mode in the future.[20]

Self-Administered Surveys

Probably the most popular type of self-administered survey is the mail survey; however, there are other variations—the group self-administered surveys and drop-off surveys—that are discussed first.

Group Self-Administered Survey

Group self-administered surveys economize in time and money because a group of respondents participates at the same time.

Basically, a **group self-administered survey** entails administering a questionnaire to respondents in groups, rather than individually, for convenience or to gain certain economies. One way to be more economical is to have respondents self-administer the questions. For example, 20 or 30 people might be recruited to view a TV program sprinkled with test commercials. All respondents would be seated in a viewing room facility, and a videotape would run on a large television projection screen. Then they would be given a questionnaire to fill out regarding their recall of test ads, their reactions to the ads, and so on. As you would suspect, it is handled in a group context primarily to re-

TABLE 9.3

Features of Various Computer-Assisted Data Collection Methods

	PERSONAL	ON-SITE	TELEPHONE		MAIL	E-MAIL	FAX
BENEFITS	COMPUTER-ASSISTED PERSONAL INTERVIEWING	COMPUTERIZED SELF-INTERVIEWING	COMPUTER-ASSISTED TELEPHONE INTERVIEWING	COMPLETELY AUTOMATED TELEPHONE SURVEY	COMPUTER DISKS BY MAIL	E-MAIL SURVEY	COMPUTER-GENERATED FAX SURVEY
Respondent needs no computer skills.	✔		✔	✔			✔
Respondent can choose own schedule for responding.		✔			✔	✔	✔
Allows for complex branching questions in survey.	✔	✔	✔	✔	✔	✔	
Can use respondent-generated words in questions throughout the survey.	✔	✔	✔		✔	✔	
Can measure response times to key questions.	✔	✔	✔	✔	✔	✔	
Can display graphics and relate them to questions.	✔	✔			✔	✔	
No need to encode data from paper surveys—reduces these errors.	✔	✔	✔	✔	✔	✔	

Modified from: Scott G. Dacko, *"Data Collection Should Not Be Manual Labor,"* Marketing News, *vol. 29, no. 18 (August 28, 1995), 31.*

duce costs and to provide the ability to interview a large number of people in a short time.

Variations for group self-administered surveys are limitless. Students can be administered surveys in their classes; church groups can be administered surveys during meetings; social clubs and organizations, company employees, movie theater patrons, and any other group can be administered surveys during meetings, work, or leisure time. Often, the researcher will compensate the group with a monetary payment as a means of recruiting the support of the group's leaders. In all of these cases, each respondent works through the questionnaire at his or her own pace. Granted, a survey administrator may be present, so there is some opportunity for interaction concerning instructions or how to respond, but the group context often discourages the respondents from asking all but the most pressing questions.

With a self-administered survey, each respondent works at his or her own pace.

Drop-Off Survey

Another variation of the self-administered survey is the **drop-off survey,** in which the survey representative approaches a prospective respondent, introduces the general purpose of the survey to the prospect, and leaves it with the respondent to fill out on his or her own. Essentially, the objective is to gain the prospective respondent's cooperation. The respondent is told the questionnaire is self-explanatory, and it will be left with him or her to fill out at leisure. Perhaps the representative will return to pick up the questionnaire at a certain time, or the respondent may be instructed to complete and return it by prepaid mail. Normally, the representative will return on the same day or the next day to pick up the completed questionnaire. In this way, a representative can cover a number of residential areas or business locations in a single day with an initial drop-off pass and a later pick-up pass. Drop-off surveys are especially appropriate for local market research undertakings in which travel is necessary but limited. They have been reported to have quick turnaround, high response rates, minimal interviewer influence on answers, and good control over how respondents are selected; plus, they are inexpensive.[21]

Drop-off surveys must be self-explanatory.

Variations of the drop-off method include handing out the surveys to people at their places of work, asking them to fill them out at home, and then to return them the next day. Some hotel chains have questionnaires in their rooms with an invitation to fill them out and turn them in at the desk on checkout. Stores sometimes have short surveys on customer demographics, media habits, purchase intentions, or other information that customers are asked to fill out at home and return on their next shopping trip. A gift certificate drawing may even be used as an incentive to participate. As you can see, the term "drop-off" can be stretched to cover any situation in which the prospective respondent encounters the survey as though it were "dropped off" by a research representative.

Several variations of drop-off surveys exist.

Mail Survey

A **mail survey** is one in which the questions are mailed to prospective respondents who are asked to fill them out and return them to the researcher by mail. Part of its attractiveness stems from its self-administered aspect: There are no interviewers to recruit, train, monitor, and compensate. Similarly, mailing lists are readily available from companies that specialize in this business, and it is possible to access very specific groups of target respondents. For example, it is possible to obtain a list of physicians specializing in family practice who operate clinics in cities larger than 500,000 people. Also, one may opt to purchase computer files, printed labels, or even labeled envelopes from these companies. In fact, some list companies will even provide insertion and mailing services. On a per-mailed respondent basis, mail surveys are very inexpensive. In fact, they are almost always the least expensive survey method in this regard. But mail surveys incur all of the problems associated with not having an interviewer present, which we discussed earlier in this chapter.

For an example of a mailing list firm visit: http:/www./soft.com/lists/listref.html

The mail survey is plagued by two major problems. The first is **nonresponse,** which refers to questionnaires that are not returned.[22] The second is **self-selection bias,** which means that those who do respond are probably dif-

Mail surveys suffer from low response rates and self-selection bias.

Mail surveys are sent directly to prospective respondents' homes, often with incentives to entice recipients to take part in the survey.

ferent from those who do not fill out the questionnaire and return it, and therefore the sample gained through this method is nonrepresentative of the general population. To be sure, the mail survey is not the only survey method that suffers from nonresponse and self-selection. Failures to respond are found in all types of surveys, and marketing researchers must be constantly alert to the possibilities that their final samples are somehow different from the original list of potential respondents because of some systematic tendency or latent pattern of response. Whatever the survey mode used, those who respond may be more involved with the product, they may have more education, they might be more or less dissatisfied, or they may even be more opinionated in general than the target population of concern.[23]

Measuring the nonresponse rate is discussed in chapter 14.

Self-selection means respondents to a mail survey may differ from the original sample.

When informing clients of data collection alternatives, market researchers should inform them of the nonresponse problems and biases inherent in each one being considered. For example, mail surveys are notorious for low response, and those respondents who do fill out and return a mail questionnaire are likely to be different from those who do not. At the same time, there are people who refuse to answer questions over the telephone, and consumers who like to shop are more likely to be encountered in mall-intercept interviews than are those who do not like to shop. Each data collection method has its own nonresponse and bias considerations, and a conscientious researcher will help his or her client understand the dangers represented in the methods under consideration.

TABLE 9.4

Various Methods Are Used to Increase Mail Survey Response

INDUCEMENT	EXAMPLES
Preliminary notification	Advanced letter or postcard, telephone prenotification
Foot-in-the-door	Use of small initial request and then a larger subsequent request to those who comply with the small request
Personalization	Hand-addressed envelope, personal signature, individually typed/addressed cover letter
Anonymity	Assurance of anonymity, use/nonuse of ID number
Response deadline	Different due dates following receipt of questionnaire
Appeals	Social utility, help the sponsor, egoistic
Sponsorship	Company, trade association, university researcher
Incentives	Nonmonetary (for example, ballpoint pens, summary of findings), monetary (for example, given to sample member, donated to charity)
Questionnaire length	Printing of both sides of sheet, white space related to perceived length
Questionnaire size, reproduction, and color	8½ × 11, 8½ × 14, printed, mimeographed, various colors
Type of postage (outgoing)	Commemorative stamp, metered postage, first class, third class
Type of postage (return envelopes)	Business reply permit, regular stamps, metered postage
Follow-ups	Different intervals, postcard, letter, replacement questionnaire

Source: *Jeffrey Connant, Denise Smart, and Bruce Walker, "Mail Survey Facilitation Techniques: An Assessment and Proposal Regarding Reporting Practices,"* Journal of the Market Research Society, *vol. 32, no. 4 (1990), 569–580.*

The nonresponse rate and subsequent danger of self-selection bias is greatest with mail surveys. Typically, mail surveys of households achieve response rates of less than 20 percent. Even though there are strategies, such as those listed in Table 9.4, used by mail survey researchers to increase response rates and reduce self-selection bias, nonresponse remains a major concern to survey researchers. Unfortunately, despite a great deal of academic research,[24,25] we still do not have a clear understanding of the effectiveness and efficiency of these various techniques.[26] Despite this situation, mail surveys are viable in countries with high literacy rates and dependable postal systems.[27] Marketing Research Insight 9.2 identifies four factors that marketing researchers should emphasize in their mail survey research tactics. Remember, however, that consumers and business respondents are constantly changing, and the inducement that works today may not necessarily work the same way in the future. One way research companies have sought to cope with the low response for mail surveys is to create a mail panel in which respondents agree to respond to several questionnaires mailed to them over time, and some see this approach as a preferred option.[28] Of course, the panel members are carefully prescreened to ensure that the mail panel represents the company's target market or consumers of interest.

To cope with low response to mail surveys, some companies have turned to mail panels.

MARKETING RESEARCH INSIGHT 9.2

How to Increase Mail Survey Response Rates

M. Chris Paxton, a professor of hotel and restaurant administration at Washington State University, examined a number of studies on mail survey response rates, and he has identified four factors that are critical. He offers the following recommendations for specific tactics that will maximize the response rates of mail surveys.

FOUR FACTORS AND ASSOCIATED WAYS TO INCREASE MAIL SURVEY RESPONSE RATES

FACTOR	DEFINITION	TO MAXIMIZE IMPACT . . .
Saliency	The importance of the survey topic to the potential respondent	■ Put a sharp focus on the research topic. ■ Design a good questionnaire, cover letter, and survey process.
Sponsorship	The organization that develops or implements the survey	■ Have a legitimate, prestigious organization or agency sponsor the survey, and make clear that this agency's motive is not to sell a product or service. ■ Use the sponsor's normal business stationery.
Follow-up	A series of planned additional contacts with potential respondents by mail or telephone	■ Make courteous contacts to thank respondents and remind nonrespondents to participate in the survey. ■ Include a postcard, another mailing, or a telephone follow-up contact as part of the survey.
Incentives	Tangible rewards for participating in the survey, even if they are token	■ Send cash or a small gift, preferably before the questionnaire is completed. ■ Offer to send a copy of the results back to respondents.

Source: *Adapted from M. Chris Paxton, "Increasing Survey Response Rates,"* Hotel and Restaurant Administration Quarterly, *vol. 36, no. 4 (August 1995), 66–73.*

FACTORS DETERMINING THE CHOICE OF A PARTICULAR SURVEY METHOD

At the outset of the discussion of the various types of interviewing used in marketing research, we made the comment that the marketing researcher is faced with the problem of selecting the one survey mode that is optimal in a given situation. As you can see in Table 9.5, each data collection method has unique advantages, disadvantages, and special features. How do you decide which is the best survey mode? There are several considerations that answer this question. For purposes of convenience, we have identified three categories of considerations, along with some factors within each category, to help answer this question. This breakdown, which is outlined in Table 9.6 (page 270), reveals that the primary considerations are the researcher's resources and objectives, the characteristics of the respondents who are to be interviewed, and the characteristics of the specific questions that the marketing researcher wishes to ask of these respondents. We first discuss each of the various considerations.

Researcher's Resources and Objectives

In selecting a data collecting mode, the researcher balances quality against cost and time.

As you now realize from having read the section on defining the purpose of the research project, every marketing research project has specific objectives. In the case of data collection, the driving objective is translated into a single concern: the quality of information desired. Balanced against this objective are two critical constraints—namely, the time deadline and the budget available for the data collection phase.

The Survey Data Collection Time Horizon

A short deadline may dictate what data collection method is to be used.

Regardless of its nature, every marketing management decision has a deadline when it must be resolved, and this deadline directly impacts the amount of time allowed, or the time horizon, for a particular marketing research survey. In some instances, the deadline is distant, and the marketing researcher is allowed the luxury of choosing his or her data collection methods. Frequently, however, the time period is compressed, and the researcher is forced into choosing a data collection method that may not be his or her first choice but is one that does a reasonable job within the permissible time horizon.

By their very natures, some survey data collection methods take longer than others.

As we described the various interviewing methods, you probably realized intuitively that some approaches, such as mail surveys, door-to-door, and personal interviews, require long time periods; whereas others, principally telephone studies and mall intercept surveys, typically take much less time. An example will help you understand the impact of time deadlines on the choice of survey method.

The marketing director of a large bank was informed on Tuesday by the bank president that a number of complaints had been telephoned in by anonymous callers. The complaints focused on a new advertising campaign that used an old Beatles melody called, "Getting Better All the Time." The advertising schedule allowed for a two-week radio ad before the television spots appeared, meaning that the television spots would begin in 10 days. The marketing director, under pressure from the president, thought of inviting people to view the prospective television ads along with other ads and to ask their opinions, but there was insufficient time to recruit respondents and run them through the viewings. The local mall-intercept firms were booked

TABLE 9.5

Key Advantages and Disadvantages of Alternative Data Collection Methods

METHOD	KEY ADVANTAGES	KEY DISADVANTAGES	COMMENT
In-home interview	Conducted in privacy of the home, which facilitates interviewer–respondent rapport	Cost per interview can be high; interviewers must travel to respondent's home	Often much information per interview is gathered
Mall-intercept interview	Fast and convenient data collection method	Only mall patrons are interviewed; respondents may feel uncomfortable answering questions in the mall	Mall intercept company often has exclusive interview rights for that mall
In-office interview	Useful for interviewing busy executives	Relatively high cost per interview; gaining access is sometimes difficult	Useful when respondents must examine prototypes or samples of products
Central Location Telephone Interview	Fast turnaround; good quality control; reasonable cost	Restricted to telephone communication	Long distance calling is not a problem
CATI	Computer eliminates human interviewer error; simultaneous data input to computer file; good quality control	Set-up costs can be high	Will advance with new computer and telecommunications technology
Computer-assisted interview types	Respondent responds at his/her own pace; computer data file results	Respondent must have access to a computer or be computer literate	Many variations and an emerging data collection method with exciting prospects
Group self-administered survey	Cost of interviewer eliminated; economical for assembled groups of respondents	Must find groups and secure permission to conduct the survey	Prone to errors of self-administered surveys; good for pretests or pilot tests
Drop-off survey	Cost of interviewer eliminated; appropriate for local market surveys	Generally not appropriate for large-scale national surveys	Many variations exist with respect to logistics and applications
Mail survey	Economical method; good listing companies exist	Low response rates; self-selection bias; slow	Many response rate increase strategies exist

up for the next week, so this method was eliminated. About the only method left was telephone, which disallowed visual exposures. Because the complaints had all been leveled at the radio spots, it was decided to use the telephone and to have respondents listen to the ad over the telephone. Then their reactions could be solicited even if they had not heard the ad on the ra-

TABLE 9.6

When Deciding on a Survey Data Collection Method, a Researcher Should Take Most of These Factors into Consideration

1. Researcher's Resources and Objectives
   a. Survey data collection time horizon
   b. Survey data collection budget
   c. Desired quality of data
      i. Generalizability
      ii. Completeness
2. Respondent Characteristics
   a. Incidence rate
   b. Willingness to participate
   c. Ability to participate
   d. Diversity of respondents
3. Characteristics of Questions Asked by Researcher
   a. Complexity
   b. Amount of information required per respondent
   c. Topic sensitivity

A telephone survey helped this bank test its radio ads in a few days.

dio. They quickly generated a list of respondents from bank customer files, and the interviewing was completed in two evenings. It turned out that no one objected strongly to the theme, and the marketing director concluded that the complaints were competitors trying to unsettle the president. The television ads were shown on schedule without incident. In this example, the short survey time horizon disqualified certain survey data collection modes. In other instances, the time horizon may be longer, which permits consideration of these modes that require more time to implement and complete.

The Survey Data Collection Budget

Budget constraints may disallow consideration of the more expensive data collection methods.

The commercial marketing researcher frequently encounters situations in which the budget available for a study greatly influences the survey method used. In truth, the budget alone does not dictate the choice of a survey interviewing method; rather, the budget constraint in combination with other considerations influence the survey mode choice. For example, if a researcher wanted to have a final sample of 500 respondents, and the data collection portion of the budget was $5,000, it would be infeasible to hire personal interviewers if the going rate was in excess of $20 per completed interview because the interviewing bill alone would be $10,000. On the other hand, mall-intercept, telephone, and self-administered methods are more within the expense limit for this example. Budgets are sometimes set more arbitrarily than we would prefer, and a budget constraint such as the one described here must be dealt with by selecting a workable data collection mode if the survey is to be done.

Desired Quality of Data Collected

Data quality has many facets, which we discuss in the chapters on questionnaire design, sample design, data editing, and statistical analysis. Still, we have made several comments in our previous descriptions alluding to the quality of the data. Some market researchers claim that quality, not quantity, of data is the main issue in deciding on which data collection method to use.[29] For instance, you are aware that mail surveys suffer from low response and self-selection problems. Obviously, if the researcher desires a comprehensive sample and an extremely accurate sample, a mail survey is unlikely to achieve this objective because of nonresponse. Similarly, for sensitive topics, the face-to-face alternatives may create embarrassment for the respondent, who will then give socially desirable answers rather than the truth, thus compromising the results. In fact, one study on patient satisfaction found that a mail survey generated less acquiescense bias than did a telephone survey for recently discharged hospital patients.[30]

For the purpose of discussion here, we identify two aspects of data quality. The first is **"generalizability,"** which is the confidence that the researcher has that the data collected from a particular method garners respondents who accurately describe the population under study. The second aspect of data quality is **"completeness,"** which is defined as the depth and breadth of information obtained from each person. Mall-intercept interviewing, for example, has the potential to generate highly complete information, but telephone interviews perform lower on the completeness criterion due to the necessary brevity of the questions and the short duration of the interview. On the other hand, mall-intercept interviews have generalizability shortcomings because they are conducted only with mall shoppers, whereas telephone interviews cover the population better and are therefore more generalizable if the survey is aimed at all types of shoppers. Mail surveys can garner completeness, but they suffer on the generalizability criterion because of nonresponse and self-selection problems, which eliminate certain types of potential respondents.

Data collection methods represent varying degrees of generalizability and completeness.

Respondent Characteristics

Every survey targets the types of people who will be questioned. Each targeted group has certain characteristics that have some bearing on the most appropriate method of data collection. At least four characteristics of the targeted group must be considered in the choice of a data collection mode: (1) incidence rate, (2) willingness to participate, (3) ability to participate, and (4) the diversity of respondents.

Respondent characteristics that determine the survey data collection mode are the incidence rate, willingness to take part, ability to take part, and their diversity.

Incidence Rate

The **incidence rate** is the percentage of people in the general population that fits the qualifications of those people the marketing researcher desires to have interviewed. For example, if we were doing a concept test of a new low-calorie microwave dinner line, we might target only those households who own microwave ovens and who have purchased low-calorie meals in the last six months. Some quick calculations using sales and census figures on the number of households might determine that only 5 percent of all households fall in this "qualified" category. This incidence rate means that only 1 out of every 20 households contacted at random would qualify for questioning. To elaborate, if a researcher wanted to have 500 completed telephone surveys of households in a circumstance in which the incidence rate was 5 percent, it would take approximately 20 times 500 or 10,000 telephone calls to reach the target of 500 households that qualify to take the survey, and this amount assumes that every household called answers on the first call attempt.

As you can imagine, the data collection process in this example would incur substantial search costs, and the time spent trying to locate qualified respondents may actually exceed the time spent actually interviewing. In other words, performing a low incidence rate study on a face-to-face basis could result in a very high cost-per-interview search, and would only be elected if some other overriding consideration such as the need for a long, in-depth interview compelled this approach. Perhaps the lowest cost alternative for a low geographic density population is the mail survey. Here, self-selection may actually work in a positive manner because we do not want responses from nonqualifiers. With a creative incentive, careful wording, and appropriate checks, a mail survey may well result in the desired sample of prospective low-calorie microwave dinner buyers. To summarize our point, for situations in which the researcher expects incidence rates to be low and search costs to be high, it is important that the interviewing method employed does not end up with highly paid interviewers searching rather than interviewing.

A low incidence rate means the researcher must find an inexpensive way to identify potential respondents.

Telephone interviewing offers an efficient device to screen the population and identify low-incidence prospective respondents. In fact, it is common to use telephone screening as a qualifying phase. Then individuals who satisfy the criteria for participating in the survey are subsequently interviewed at home, or invited to take part in a focus group, or interviewed by whatever other method is most suitable.

Willingness to Participate

Respondent willingness is a serious consideration in any survey. High refusal rates always alert the marketing researcher to question the representativeness of the results. Two types of unwillingness will be encountered in any survey. The first concerns a generalized suspicion or desire for privacy in many people: They simply do not like to participate in surveys. The second pertains to topic-specific tendencies. That is, some people will participate in surveys when the topic is one they want to discuss. (Likewise, some people will not participate because the topic is something they do not want to discuss.) In any case, self-selection takes place. Willingness can be affected by the survey method. For example, people find it more difficult to refuse a face-to-face request to participate than to decline a telephone request or a mailed questionnaire.

Researchers should do everything in their power to increase the willingness of prospective respondents to participate in a survey.

Generally, the marketing researcher attempts to do everything in his or her power to increase the willingness of prospective respondents to participate. The various tactics listed earlier illustrate how survey researchers have endeavored to increase response rates by attempting to effect willingness. So, it is not unusual for mail survey respondents to be offered incentives such as monetary payment, putting their names in for a grand prize drawing, or to be given small gifts such as pens or coupons as means of soliciting cooperation. Other examples include the drop-off method, which combines a personally delivered appeal with the informality of responding to a mail survey. Group self-administered approaches try to apply social dynamics to enhance willingness to participate when a researcher believes that unwillingness is a concern.

Ability to Participate

Nothing is more frustrating to an interviewer than to have a prospective respondent qualified and willing to participate in the survey but unable to do so at that time. Numerous instances of this situation can be cited. The mall-intercept interviewer finds out that the respondent has a dental appointment in 15 minutes or that she must pick up her child at school. The businessperson interviewer realizes on arriving for a scheduled interview that the manager was called to an emergency meeting. A prospective mail respondent puts the questionnaire in a drawer and then forgets about it, or a telephone interviewer encounters a respondent whose favorite television show is about to begin.

As a general rule, personal contact should increase the ability of prospective respondents to participate because respondents will make time available more readily when approached in person. A mail survey, on the other hand, has no such social facilitator. With telephone surveys, lack of participation can be lessened through a rescheduling of the interview or a call-back policy for nonrespondents. However, the mall-intercept and other self-administered approaches do not have call-back or rescheduling provisions because respondents are encountered away from their homes.

Willing survey respondents may be unable to participate due to schedule conflicts, time demands, or their routines.

Diversity of Respondents

Diversity refers to the degree to which some key trait is possessed by prospective respondents. For example, if everyone in the target population goes on shopping trips to shopping malls, then the mall-intercept alternative surely will be considered. On the other hand, if only a small percentage of the target population patronizes shopping malls, the mall-intercept approach would be less suitable because it would generate an unrepresentative sample. That is, the respondents would be suspiciously different from the others in the population by virtue of their mall-shopping behavior. To use telephones as another example, you can see in Marketing Research Insight 9.3 on page 274 that the incidence of unlisted numbers ranges dramatically from a low of 7.0 percent in Sarasota–Bradenton, Florida, to a high of 69.8 percent in Oakland, California. Obviously, there are profound differences between areas in the United States with regard to the desire for telephone privacy, and a telephone survey, even one in which the numbers are dialed randomly, would encounter different reactions in Knoxville, Tennessee, than in San Diego, California.

Telephone listings and cooperation differ markedly across U.S. cities.

In general, the more diverse the target group, the greater the necessity for the marketing researcher to use a person-administered approach to solicit the cooperation of the prospective respondent. This conclusion should explain why telephone surveying is common in public opinion polling as most people have views on politics, road repairs, public education, and national issues. At the same time, it should help you to realize why mail surveys perform poorly in diverse populations in which there exists the strong possibility of overrepresentation by a particular minority.

Characteristics of Questions Asked by Researchers

Because all interviews concern questions, it is necessary to look at the complexity of the tasks asked of respondents, the amount of information sought from a particular respondent, and the sensitivity of the topics surveyed.

Characteristics affecting the choice of the survey data collection mode include how complex they are, how many there are, and how sensitive the topics are for respondents.

MARKETING RESEARCH INSIGHT 9.3

Unlisted Numbers and Cooperation Rates for Telephone Surveys Vary across the United States

Survey Sampling, Inc., located in Fairfield, Connecticut, provides the following statistics on telephone surveys.

10 MSAS WITH LOWEST UNLISTED NUMBERS		10 MSAS WITH HIGHEST UNLISTED NUMBERS	
Sarasota–Bradenton, Fla.	7.0%	Oakland, Calif.	69.8%
Daytona Beach, Fla.	10.9	Sacramento, Calif.	69.8
West Palm Beach–Boca Raton, Fla.	11.0	Fresno, Calif.	69.3
Melbourne–Titusville–Palm Bay, Fla.	15.4	Los Angeles–Long Beach, Calif.	69.2
Nassau–Suffolk, N.Y.	15.6	San Jose, Calif.	68.6
Knoxville, Tenn.	16.4	San Diego, Calif.	67.3
Minneapolis–St. Paul, Minn.	16.6	Orange County, Calif.	64.9
Mobile, Ala.	16.8	Riverside–San Bernardino, Calif.	64.2
Bridgeport–Stamford–Norwalk–Danbury, Conn.	16.8	Bakersfield, Calif.	63.7
Monmouth–Ocean, N.J.	17.2	Ventura, Calif.	63.3

10 MSAS DEEMED MOST COOPERATIVE FOR PHONE SURVEYS

1. *Knoxville, Tenn.*
2. *Greenville–Spartanburg, S.C.*
3. *York, Pa.*
4. *Charlotte–Gastonia–Rock Hill, N.C.*
5. *Fort Wayne, Ind.*
6. *Birmingham, Ala.*
7. *Norfolk–Virginia Beach–Newport News, Va.*
8. *Syracuse, N.Y.*
9. *Dayton–Springfield, Ohio*
10. *Harrisburg–Lebanon–Carlisle, Pa.*

10 MSAS DEEMED LEAST COOPERATIVE FOR PHONE SURVEYS

1. *Miami–Hialeah, Fla.*
2. *Fort Lauderdale–Hollywood–Pompano Beach, Fla.*
3. *Los Angeles-Long Beach, Calif.*
4. *Houston, Tex.*
5. *Anaheim–Santa Ana, Calif.*
6. *New York, N.Y.*
7. *Bergen–Passaic, N.J.*
8. *Nassau–Suffolk, N.Y.*
9. *Newark, N.J.*
10. *Bridgeport–Stamford–Norwalk–Danbury, Conn.*

Source: *Survey Sampling, Inc. Reprinted by permission.*

Complexity of Tasks

The more complex the tasks asked of respondents, the more the need for a personal interviewer.

Some marketing research studies have fairly complicated preparation and administration procedures. Taste tests or TV ad tests fall into this category. Taste tests, for example, typically require food presentation done under controlled conditions so that the researcher can be certain that each person interviewed responded to the same stimulus. Thus, the most commonly used survey method for these types of tests is the mall intercept. Variations include recruiting people to come to a properly equipped central location, such as a church or community center, to sample the product and to be interviewed. Similarly, TV ad testing can be done in the mall-intercept context, but it requires a central viewing room. Because much TV ad testing depends on the use of videotaped versions of commercials, the lack of portability of video equipment practically compels a mall location study or a group-administered, central location study. In general, the more complex the tasks and preparation activities in the interview, the greater the need for personal administration.

Amount of Information Required per Respondent

The amount of information sought from each respondent varies greatly from study to study. One study may include extensive product- and brand-purchasing information and have a battery of life-style questions along with detailed demographic questions, whereas another may simply seek to find out what respondents remembered about an end-of-aisle display in their supermarket (if they saw it). Marketing researchers have wrestled with the appropriate amount of information problem for years, and some creative strategies have emerged from time to time.

Phone interviews are typically short, whereas in-home personal interviews are long.

Traditionally, phone surveys are short, whereas in-home personal interviews are long, and other data collection modes fall in between. Strategies range from scheduling a series of interviews to combining different data collection methods, such as merging a telephone interview and a follow-up mail survey. Monetary or other incentives have also been used to entice respondents to "stay with" the interview. If the researcher does not have the opportunity to re-interview, and must collect a great deal of information from each respondent in one interview, then two options exist. The first option is to use a personal interviewer whose physical presence compels the respondent to complete the interview. The other option is to allow the respondent to complete the survey at his or her own pace and without interviewer presence. Here, the mail survey or drop-off method would fit, probably augmented with a sizable incentive to reduce nonresponse bias.

Topic Sensitivity

The sensitivity of the topic is rarely a consideration for the vast majority of marketing research studies. With the exception of a question on income level, which most studies include, the remaining questions on brands purchased, stores patronized, satisfaction with present products, or buying intentions, for example, are typically very low in sensitivity. Occasionally, however, a researcher finds himself or herself working with topics that are inherently sensitive. Such topics include prescription medication abuse, blood donation, racial issues, personal hygiene, and charity contributions. Industry wisdom suggests that for sensitive issues, face-to-face interviews are less appropriate than alternatives such as telephone interviews or computer-administered interviews in which the respondent will not feel ill at ease when divulging some personal habit or sensitive answer to a machine.

SELECTING A SURVEY MODE

The selection of a particular survey mode is accomplished by simultaneously considering all of the previously mentioned factors. Of course, certain considerations will take priority over others. Sometimes the deadline for completing the research is close, and this disallows consideration of personal interviews or a mail survey, for instance, which take more time than a telephone interview. On the other hand, there may be a great number of complicated questions and tasks that are involved in a survey, and telephone administration is eliminated from consideration for this reason. At the same time, a researcher may have a favored survey mode with which he or she feels especially comfortable, and this factor may largely determine the selection. It is important that the manager allow the marketing researcher to decide on the survey mode because he or she has a unique understanding of how question characteristics, respondent characteristics, and survey resources and objectives come into play. We have described these factors in very general terms, but the researcher can envision how they specifically help or hinder the entire marketing research process. Choice of survey method can be made by answering the question, "What data collection method will generate the most complete and generalizable information within the time horizon and without exceeding the allowable expenditure for data collection?"

Quality, time, and budget are usually combined in the objective, "What data collection method will generate the most complete and generalizable information within the time horizon and without exceeding the allowable expenditure for data collection?"

SUMMARY

This chapter described the various methods available to marketing researchers to survey respondents. Surveys provide the important advantages of standardization, easy administration, getting at motives for behaviors, simple tabulation, and ability to investigate subgroupings of respondents. We noted that personal interviews are advantageous because they allow for feedback, permit rapport building, facilitate certain quality controls, and capitalize on the adaptability of a human interviewer. However, they are slow and prone to human errors. Computer-administered interviews, on the other hand, are faster, error free, may have pictures or graphics capabilities, allow for real-time capture of data, and may make respondents feel more at ease because another person is not listening to their answers.

We described 10 different survey data collection methods: (1) in-home interviews, which are conducted in respondents' homes; (2) mall-intercept interviews, conducted by approaching shoppers in a mall; (3) in-office interviews, conducted with executives or managers in their places of work;

(4) "traditional" telephone interviews, conducted by an interviewer working in his or her home; (5) central location telephone interviews, conducted by workers in a telephone interview company's facilities; (6) computer-assisted telephone interviews, in which the interviewer reads questions off a computer screen and enters responses directly into the program; (7) fully computerized interviews, in which the respondent interacts directly with a computer; (8) group self-administered surveys, in which the questionnaire is handed out to a group for individual responses; (9) drop-off surveys, in which the questionnaire is left with the respondent to be completed and picked up or returned at a later time; and (10) mail surveys, in which questionnaires are mailed to prospective respondents who are requested to fill them out and mail them back. The specific advantages and disadvantages of each data collection mode were discussed.

Researchers must take into account several considerations when deciding on a survey data collection mode. The major concerns are (1) the researcher's resources and objectives of the survey, (2) special characteristics of the respondents, and (3) unique aspects of the questions being asked. With the first concern, the research project deadline, money available for data collection, and desired quality of data are taken into consideration. With the second concern, the incidence or prevalence of qualified respondents is a consideration, as are the willingness and ability of respondents to take part in the survey. Finally, for question concerns, the researcher must think about the complexity of the questions or tasks to be performed by respondents, the sheer amount of information sought for each respondent, and the degree to which the topics in the survey touch on sensitive issues that might deter respondents in some way. Ultimately, the researcher will select a data collection mode with which he or she feels comfortable and one that will result in the desired quality and quantity of information without exceeding time or budget constraints.

KEY TERMS

Person-administered survey (p. 246)
Computer-administered survey (p. 247)
Self-administered survey (p. 249)
In-home interview (p. 252)
Mall-intercept interview (p. 253)
In-office interviews (p. 255)
Traditional telephone interviews (p. 257)
Central location telephone interviewing (p. 257)
Computer-assisted telephone interviews (CATI) (p. 259)
Fully computerized interviews (p. 261)
CATS (completely automated telephone survey) (p. 261)
Group self-administered survey (p. 262)
Drop-off survey (p. 264)
Mail survey (p. 264)
Nonresponse (p. 264)
Self-selection bias (p. 264)
Generalizability (p. 271)
Completeness (p. 271)
Incidence rate (p. 271)
Diversity (p. 273)

REVIEW QUESTIONS/APPLICATIONS

1. List the major advantages of survey research methods over qualitative methods. Identify the major drawbacks.
2. What aspects of computer-administered surveys make them attractive to marketing researchers?
3. What are the advantages of person-administered surveys over computer-administered ones?
4. Indicate the differences between: (a) in-home interviews, (b) mall-intercept interviews, and (c) in-office interviews. What do they share in common?
5. Why are telephone surveys so popular?
6. Indicate the pros and cons of self-administered surveys.
7. How does a drop-off survey differ from a mail survey?
8. What are three aspects of the researcher's resources and objectives that have much influence in the determination of which survey mode will be used? How does each one affect the decision?
9. Differentiate "incidence rate" from "diversity of respondents."
10. Is a telephone interview inappropriate for a survey that has as one of its objectives a complete listing of all possible advertising media a person was exposed to in the last week? Why or why not?
11. NAPA Car Parts is a retail chain specializing in stocking and selling both domestic and foreign automobile parts. It is interested in learning about its customers, so the marketing director sends instructions to all 2,000 store managers telling them that whenever a customer makes a purchase of $150 or more, they are to write down a description of the customer who made that purchase. They are to do this just for the second week in October, writing each description on a separate sheet of paper. At the end of the week, they are to send all sheets to the marketing director. Comment on this data collection method.
12. Discuss the feasibility of each of the 10 types of survey mode for each of the following cases:
    a. Fabergé, Inc. wants to test a new fragrance called "Lime Brut."
    b. Kelly Services needs to determine how many businesses expect to hire temporary secretaries for those who go on vacation during the summer months.
    c. The Encyclopedia Britannica requires information on the degree to which mothers of elementary school-aged children see encyclopedias as worthwhile purchases for their children.
    d. AT&T is considering a television screen phone system and wants to know people's reaction to it.
13. With a telephone survey, when a potential respondent refuses to take part or is found to have changed his or her telephone number or moved away, it is customary to simply try another prospect until a completion is secured. It is not standard practice to report the number of refusals or noncontacts. What are the implications of this policy for the reporting of nonresponse?
14. Compu-Ask Corporation has developed a stand-alone computerized interview system that can be adapted to almost any type of survey. It can fit on a notebook-sized computer, and the respondent directly answers questions using the keyboard once the interviewer has turned on the computer and booted up the

program. Indicate the appropriateness of this interviewing system in each of the following cases:

a. A survey of plant managers concerning a new type of hazardous waste disposal system.

b. A survey of high school teachers to see if they are interested in a company's videotapes of educational public broadcast television programs.

c. A survey of consumers to determine their reactions to a nonrefrigerated variety of yogurt.

15. A researcher is pondering what survey mode to use for a client who markets a home security system for apartment dwellers. The system comprises sensors that are pressed onto all of the windows and magnetic strips that are glued to each door. Once plugged into an electric socket and activated with a switch box, the system emits a loud alarm and simulates a barking guard dog when an intruder trips one of the sensors. The client wants to know how many apartment dwellers in the United States are aware of the system, what they think of it, and how likely they are to buy it in the coming year. Which consideration factors are positive and which ones are negative for each of the following survey modes: (a) in-home interviews, (b) mall intercepts, (c) drop-off survey, and (d) telephone survey?

CASE 9.1

Skinner's Knife Shop

Skinner's Knife Shop is a family-owned business located in Butte, Montana. The shop was opened in 1975 by Bill "Skinner" Roberts whose personal knife collection became too large to keep in his mobile home, so he decided to go into the knife trading business. For five years, Skinner traveled from swap meet to swap meet in his Ford pickup truck selling his knives around Montana and in neighboring states. Eventually, Skinner tired of traveling and decided to open up a knife store in Centerville, a suburb of Butte.

In the last 15 years, Skinner's Knife Shop has grown steadily, and now its line includes quality knife manufacturers such as Al Mar, Beretta, Ka-Bar, Kershaw, and Spyderco. Customers range from retail "walk-in" trade, which includes hunters, fishermen, tradespersons, collectors, and homemakers, to wholesale "UPS Delivery" trade where Skinner's Knife Shop supplies bulk shipments to approximately 50 different hardware or sporting goods stores located in the western United States, and Skinner supplies special-order knives to about 200 other retailers who order in small quantities from time to time. Sales are divided 40 percent–60 percent, retail–wholesale.

Knife sales are seasonal or nonseasonal, depending on the type of knife. Hunting and fishing knives are in greater demand at the beginning of hunting and fishing seasons, whereas kitchen knives are fairly constant across the year. Specialty knives, such as those sold to collectors, are not seasonal.

Skinner is contemplating using the Internet as a selling channel. He has heard that a great deal of business can be gained by opening up an Internet homepage shop. One of Skinner's employees is Jason Pyle, and Jason is a marketing major at nearby Montana Tech. Jason convinces Skinner that he can do marketing research as part of a marketing internship to determine the feasibility of a Skinner's Knife Shop homepage. Skinner agrees to let Jason do this as long as Jason maintains one-half of his time selling knives and doing his regular duties around the store.

1. To understand the attitudes and intentions of the retail trade, Jason is considering a mail survey of all customers who have purchased a knife at Skinner's Knife Shop in the past three years. This list has about 750 names on it. What is your reaction to this data collection alternative? What are the pros and cons in this case? Is there another data collection method that would be more appropriate, and if so, what and why?
2. There are two categories of wholesale trade: (1) the hardware stores who are regular reorder customers, and (2) the special-order retailers. Jason proposes personal interviews with 20 of the owners of reorder stores and 30 personal interviews with the special order retailers. What is your reaction to this data collection alternative? What are the pros and cons in this case? Is there another data collection method that would be more appropriate, and if so, what and why?
3. A third alternative being considered by Jason is to place a questionnaire on the Internet itself. Jason took a course in Internet programming, and he can perform a survey on the Internet. What is your reaction to this data collection alternative?

CASE 9.2

Boy Scouts of America

The Knox Council of the Boy Scouts of America is responsible for scout activities in six counties in central Tennessee. The council has decided to conduct two surveys, one with its scouts and the other with volunteers who serve as scoutmasters and in other support roles. The purposes of the research are to find (1) scout activities that the boys enjoy and (2) volunteers' opinions of the quality and quantity of information being supplied to them by the council. The council has budgeted $3,000 to accomplish both surveys.

There are approximately 500 scout units ranging from Webelos groups with 2 or 3 boys in the 6- to 8-year-old age range to Boy Scout troops with up to 25 boys in the 12- to 16-year-old range. Also included are Cub Scout units that have 10 to 12 boys who are between the Webelos and the Boy Scouts in age. All units meet at least once per month, and some meet as often as every week.

Approximately 7,500 volunteers have been involved in the Knox Council Boy Scout units over the past 10 years. There is a list with all 7,500 names in the council's headquarters. The council estimates that about one-third of the volunteers are currently actively working with scouts. The remaining two-thirds either have permanently stopped volunteering because their boys no longer belong to the scouts, or they are temporarily involved with other work and may become active volunteers in the future.

Answer the following questions by reviewing the selection factors discussed in the textbook, and be sure to note important strengths or weaknesses of the method you have chosen in each case.

1. What data collection method do you think is appropriate for the volunteers, assuming that only active volunteers' opinions are desired?
2. What data collection method do you think is appropriate for the scouts?

CHAPTER 10

Measurement in Marketing Research

LEARNING OBJECTIVES

- *To appreciate the considerations used by the researcher to determine which question format will be used for a particular question*
- *To understand the basics of measurement regarding people, places, and things*
- *To recognize the four types of scales used by marketing researchers*
- *To examine question formats commonly used in marketing research*
- *To comprehend why reliability and validity are a concern when designing and administering questions intended to measure concepts*

PRACTITIONER VIEWPOINT

In most cases, we must actually measure concepts that we are studying as we conduct marketing research. How we measure "sales potential," "demand," "attitudes," "intentions," and so on is very important when it comes time to interpret our study. The way the researcher decides how to measure a concept greatly impacts what he or she can or cannot say about these concepts. For instance, brand loyalty can be defined as the last brand acquired, or it can be defined as the person's most-preferred brand. If a competitor is giving away free samples, the first definition will give a false reading on brand loyalty, while the second one will yield a truer measurement. A good understanding of measurement is basic knowledge among marketing researchers.

— William H. Neal, Senior Executive Officer
Sophisticated Data Research, Inc.

Measuring Soft Drink Users to Determine Target Markets

1. Establish the need for marketing research
2. Define the problem
3. Establish research objectives
4. Determine research design
5. Identify information types and sources
6. Determine methods of accessing data
7. **Design data collection forms**
8. Determine sample plan and size
9. Collect data
10. Analyze data
11. Prepare and present the final research report

Mediamark has devised a way to measure the differences between diet and regular cola and non-cola drinkers.

Competition is fierce in the soft drink industry, and marketers must identify specific soft drink users or target markets in order to pinpoint their efforts to retain present users or convert new ones. Mediamark Research specializes in target market profile research. In a recent study, Mediamark used an index of 100 to evaluate the likelihood of purchase of various types of colas and non-colas. It applied this index to develop demographic profiles of the most likely consumers of various soft drinks. Here are the results of Mediamark's study.[1]

Demographic Factor	Regular Cola Drinker	Regular Non-cola Drinker	Diet Cola Drinker	Diet Non-cola Drinker
Age	18 to 44	18 to 44	35 to 64	35 to 64
Gender	Male	Male	Female	Female
Race	Black or Hispanic	Black	White	White
Education	No high school degree	Attended college	College degree or post-secondary education	Some post-secondary education or college degree

DEMOGRAPHIC FACTOR	REGULAR COLA DRINKER	REGULAR NON-COLA DRINKER	DIET COLA DRINKER	DIET NON-COLA DRINKER
Marital status	Single or parents	Single or parents	Married	Married
Household	3 or more persons with children of all ages	3 or more persons with children of all ages	2 or more persons with children 6 and up	2 or more persons with children age 2 to 11
Employment	Full or part-time	Full or part-time	Full or part-time	Full or part-time
Annual income	$10,000–$49,000	$20,000–$74,500	$40,000 or less	$40,000 or less
Lives in (U.S.):	South	Northeast, North Central, or West	North Central or Northeast	North Central

How did Mediamark design a questionnaire to measure all of the constructs reported in their study? This chapter is the first of two devoted to the questionnaire design phase of the marketing research process. Its primary goal is to develop the foundation for understanding measurement in marketing research. This is done by first describing the six question–response formats available, then defining basic concepts in measurement, and, finally, explaining the various scale formats commonly used in marketing research.

BASIC QUESTION-RESPONSE FORMATS

Question response formats can be open-ended, close-ended, or scaled.

Designing a questionnaire from the ground up is akin to Eric Clapton's composing a song, Stephen King's writing a short story, or an artist's painting a landscape. That is, it requires creativity. Still, there are some basic aspects to questionnaire design that can be described. This chapter is concerned with the response side of the question, and it will introduce you to measurement issues. To begin, you should be aware of the three basic question–response formats from which a researcher has to choose: open-ended, closed-ended, and scaled-response questions. Figure 10.1 illustrates the three types and indicates two variations for each one. Pros and cons of each format are provided in Table 10.1 on page 286. A description of each format follows.

Open-ended Response Format Questions

An **open-ended question** presents no response options to the respondent. Rather, the respondent is instructed to respond in his or her own words. The response depends, of course, on the topic. An **unprobed format** seeks no additional information from the respondent. Sometimes the researcher wants a

There are many question types available to a researcher composing a survey questionnaire.

comment or statement from the respondent, or perhaps the researcher simply wants the respondent to indicate the name of a brand or a store. In this case, the researcher uses a **probed format,** which includes a **"response probe"** instructing the interviewer to ask for additional information, saying, for instance, "Can you think of anything more?" The intent here is to encourage the respondent to provide information beyond the initial and possibly superficial first comments.

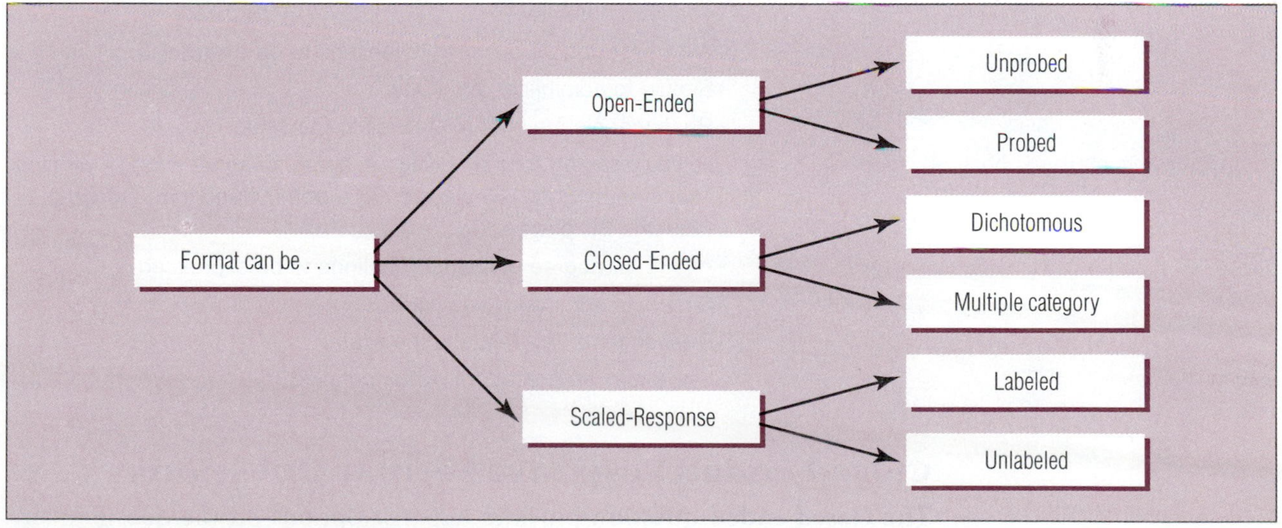

Figure 10.1

A Diagram of Six Alternative Question Response Formats

TABLE 10.1

Pros and Cons of Alternative Response Formats

RESPONSE FORMAT	EXAMPLES: PROS (+) AND CONS (−)
Unprobed open-ended question	"What was your reaction to the Sony CD player advertisement you saw on television last?" +Allows respondent to use his or her own words. −Difficult to code and interpret. −Respondents may not give complete answers.
Probed open-ended question	"Did you have any other thoughts or reactions to the advertisement?" +Elicits complete answers. −Difficult to code and interpret.
Dichotomous closed-ended question	"Do you agree or disagree with the statement, 'Sony CD players are better than Panasonic CD players'?" +Simple to administer and code. −May oversimplify response options.
Multiple category closed-ended question	"If you were to buy a CD player tomorrow, which brand would you be most likely to purchase? Would it be: a. Panasonic b. General Electric c. Sony d. JVC, or e. Some other brand?" +Allows for broad range of possible responses. +Simple to administer and code. −May alert respondents to response options of which they were unaware. −Must distinguish "pick one" from "pick all that apply."
Unlabeled scaled-response question	"On a scale of 1 to 7, how would you rate the Sony CD player on ease of operation?" +Allows for degree of intensity/feelings to be expressed. +Simple to administer and code. −Respondents may not relate well to the scale.
Labeled scaled-response question	"Do you disagree strongly, disagree, agree, or agree strongly with the statement, 'Sony CD players are a better value than General Electric CD players'?" +Allows for degree of intensity/feelings to be expressed. +Simple to administer and code. +Respondents can relate to the scale. −Scale may be "forced" or overly detailed.

Closed-Ended Response Format Questions

The **closed-ended question** provides response options on the questionnaire. A **dichotomous closed-ended question** has only two response options, such as "yes" or "no." If there are more than two options for the response, then the researcher is using a **multiple category closed-ended question.** Both the dichotomous and multiple category closed-ended question formats are very common on questionnaires because they facilitate the questioning process as well as data entry. They also standardize these questions on the questionnaire.

Scaled-Response Questions

The **scaled-response question** utilizes a scale developed by the researcher to measure the attributes of some construct under study. The response options are identified on the questionnaire. With an **unlabeled scaled-response format,** the scale may be purely numerical or only the end points of the scale are identified. The **labeled scaled-response format** uses a scale in which all of the scale positions are identified with some descriptor. We describe both of these formats in detail later in this chapter.

CONSIDERATIONS IN CHOOSING A QUESTION-RESPONSE FORMAT

Six basic response format options are available to the researcher.

All of the six different question formats we have just described are eligible formats for any question on a questionnaire. So how does the researcher decide on which option to use? At least five considerations serve to narrow the choice down: (1) the nature of the property being measured, (2) previous research studies, (3) the data collection mode, (4) the ability of the respondent, and (5) the scale level desired.

Nature of the Property Being Measured

The properties of the construct being measured often determine the appropriate response format.

As will become clear later in the chapter when we describe basic concepts in measurement, the inherent nature of the property of a construct often determines the question-response format. For example, if Alka Seltzer wants to know if respondents have bought its brand of flu relief medicine in the last month, the only answers are "yes," "no," or perhaps "do not recall." If we ask marital status, a woman is married, separated, divorced, widowed, single, or she may be cohabitating. But when we ask how much a person likes Hershey's chocolate, we can use a scaled-response approach, because "liking" is a subjective property with varying degrees. A special challenge encountered when conducting cross-cultural research is to make sure that the translation of the concept is what the researcher wants. We have included Marketing Research Insight 10.1 (page 288) to illustrate some of the translation problems that can be encountered.

Previous Research Studies

Researchers try to use question formats that are tried and true.

On some occasions, a survey follows an earlier one, and there may be a desire to explicitly compare the new findings with the previous survey. In this case, it is customary to simply adopt the question format used in the initial study. On the other hand, a particular scale or question format may have been developed by others who have measured the construct. Some scales are published or available for use by marketing researchers at no cost, whereas others may reside within the researcher's own company as a result of its work with several clients over time. For instance, some research companies specialize in customer satisfaction studies, and they have refined their own scales tapping this construct.[2] In any case, if a researcher believes a question format to be reliable and valid, and it suits the purpose of the study at hand, it is good practice to adopt or adapt it rather than inventing a new one.

MARKETING RESEARCH INSIGHT 10.1

Are You Saying What You Meant to Say?

According to Professor David A. Ricks, professor at the Thunderbird American Graduate School of International Management, translation errors cause the greatest number and variety of blunders in international business. There are three types of translation errors: carelessness, multiple-meaning words, and idioms.

CARELESSNESS

The most prevalent type of translation blunder is careless rendering of a company's communication message into another language. The results may range from embarrassment to a significant injury to sales. Consider the following examples. When KFC promoted its "finger lickin' good" message in China, the message was read by the Chinese as "eat your fingers off." It certainly did not help the bankrupt-headed Eastern Airlines when their message, "We earn our wings daily," translated into Spanish in such a way as to imply that passengers often ended up dead. In Quebec one company attempted to describe its pens as terrific, but their translation was "terrifiantes," which means terrifying.

MULTIPLE MEANINGS

Parker Pen Company prepared ads for its Latin American markets using the word "bola" to describe its ball-point pens. Fortunately, the company learned before the ads were released that in some countries bola does mean ball but in other countries bola means revolution. Still, in other countries bola means lie or fabrication. An American toothpaste manufacturer wanted to promote the idea that its toothpaste would make customers more interesting. However, in some Latin American countries the word "interesting" is a euphemism for pregnant. When a Swedish company bought the highly successful vacuum cleaner company, Electrolux, they prepared ads for the American market that proclaim "Electrolux sucks better."

IDIOMS

Idioms characterize every language and present especially difficult problems in translation. An American hosiery firm proclaimed to Spanish markets that ". . . anyone who didn't wear its hosiery simply wouldn't have a leg to stand on." Unfortunately, the translation in Spanish meant that the wearer of its hosiery ". . . would only have one leg." The idiom "Out of sight, out of mind" was translated by a naïve translator in Thailand as "Invisible things are insane." The lesson is to not translate idioms literally. "You can't teach an old dog new tricks" literally translates into French-Canadian as "One does not teach an old monkey to make faces."

These examples of promotional messages illustrate the difficulties in selecting words that have identical meanings between cultures. As one final example, consider a marketing research study that concluded that more spaghetti was consumed by West Germans and French than by Italians—a finding that certainly lacks face validity but one supported by the data. However, the error of the research was tracked back to the meaning attached to the specific wording in the questionnaire. The questionnaire asked respondents to report the amount of branded and packaged spaghetti they purchased. It was no wonder that the Italians scored low in these purchases; they eat so much spaghetti they usually buy it in bulk! Marketing researchers must be certain they are truly measuring the concept they want to measure.

Source: *David A. Ricks,* Blunders in International Business *(Cambridge, Mass.: Blackwell Publishers, Inc., 1997), 71–87, 142–143. By permission.*

Data Collection Mode

The method of data collection determines the appropriate response format.

As you know, certain data collection modes are better suited for certain question formats. For instance, a telephone interview is hampered by the respondent's inability to see the response categories, so the interviewer must read them off. It is very difficult to administer certain types of response formats over the telephone as some require detailed explanation before the respondent can envision the response-scale items.[3] On the other hand, a mail or other self-administered questionnaire accommodates scaled-response questions well because the respondent can see the response categories on the questionnaire itself.

Ability of the Respondent

Some respondents may relate better to one type of response format than another.

It is advantageous to match the question format with the abilities of the respondents. For instance, if a researcher feels that the respondents in a particular study are not articulate or that they will be reluctant to verbalize their opinions, the open-ended option is not a good choice. Similarly, if the respondent is unaccustomed to rating objects on numerical scales, it is appropriate to use a label format, or perhaps to move back to a dichotomous closed-ended question format in which the respondent simply indicates "agree" or "disagree."[4]

Scale Level Desired

As you will learn in subsequent chapters, certain statistical analyses incorporate assumptions about the nature of the measures being analyzed, so the researcher must bear these requirements in mind when selecting a question format. For example, if the response options are simply "yes" or "no," the researcher can report the percentage of respondents who answered in each way, but if the question asks how many times respondents used an ATM machine in the past month, the researcher could calculate an average number of times. An average is different from a percent; one reason being that a dichotomous yes–no response option is less informative than a scaled-response option such as "0," "1," "2," and so on. If a researcher desires to use higher-level statistical analyses, the question's response format must embody the correct scale assumptions. This point brings us to the concepts involved with measurement.

BASIC CONCEPTS IN MEASUREMENT

Measurement is determining how much of a property is possessed by an object.

Questionnaires are designed to collect information. How is this information collected? It is gathered via **measurement,** which is defined as determining the amount or intensity of some characteristic of interest to the researcher. For instance, a marketing manager may wish to know how a person feels about a certain product, or how much of the product he or she uses in a certain time period. This information, once compiled, can help solve specific questions such as brand usage.

But what are we really measuring? We are measuring properties—sometimes called attributes or qualities—of objects. *Objects* include consumers, brands, stores, advertisements, or whatever construct is of interest to the researcher working with a particular manager. *Properties* are the specific features or characteristics of an object that can be used to distinguish it from another object. For example, assume the object we want to research is a consumer. As depicted in Table 10.2, the properties of interest to a manager who is trying to define who buys a specific product are a combination of demographics such as age; income level; gender; and buyer behavior, which includes such things as the buyer's impressions or perceptions of various brands. Note that each property has the potential to further differentiate consumers. For example, Table 10.2 also compares three consumers' ages, income levels, perceptions, and sexes. Once the object's designation on a property has been determined, we say that the object has been measured on that property. If you recall in our introductory case, Mediamark Research measured cola and noncola preferences and revealed the target market profile for each type of soft drink user.

Objective properties are observable and tangible. Subjective properties are unobservable and intangible, and they must be translated onto a rating scale through the process of scale development.

On the surface, measurement may appear to be a very simple process. It is simple as long as we are measuring **objective properties,** which are physically verifiable characteristics such as age, income, number of bottles purchased, store last visited, and so on. However, marketing researchers often desire to measure **subjective properties,** which cannot be directly observed because they are mental constructs such as a person's attitude or intentions. In this case, the marketing researcher must ask a respondent to translate his or her mental constructs onto a continuum of intensity—no easy task. To do this, the marketing researcher must develop question formats that are very clear and that are used identically by the respondents. This process is known as scale development.

TABLE 10.2

Measuring the Properties of an Object and Differentiating among Three Consumers' Properties

THE OBJECT	PROPERTIES	MEASUREMENT DESIGNATIONS
A consumer (Mr. Able)	Age	35 years
	Income level	$35,000
	Gender	Male
	Brand last bought	Gillette
	Evaluation of "our" brand	"Fair"

PROPERTIES	MEASUREMENT DESIGNATIONS		
	Mr. Able	*Ms. Black*	*Mr. Colby*
Age	35	42	21
Income	$35,000	$45,000	$25,000
Gender	Male	Female	Male
Brand last bought	Gillette	Schick	Gillette
Evaluation of "our" brand	"Fair"	"Good"	"Excellent"

SCALE CHARACTERISTICS

Scale development is designing questions to measure the subjective properties of an object. There are various types of scales, each of which possesses different characteristics. The characteristics of a scale determine the scale's level of measurement. The level of measurement, as you shall see, is very important. There are four characteristics of scales: description, order, distance, and origin.

Scale characteristics are description, order, distance, and origin.

Description

Description refers to the use of a unique descriptor, or label, to stand for each designation in the scale. For instance, "yes" and "no," "agree," and "disagree," and the number of years of a respondent's age are descriptors of a simple scale. All scales include description in the form of characteristic labels that identify what is being measured.

Order

Order refers to the relative sizes of the descriptors. Here, the key word is "relative" and includes such descriptors as "greater than," "less than" or "equal to." A respondent's least-preferred brand is "less than" his or her most-preferred brand, and respondents who check the same income category are the same ("equal to"). Not all scales possess order characteristics. For instance, is a "buyer" greater than or less than a "nonbuyer?" We have no way of making a relative size distinction.

An ordered scale has descriptors that are "greater than," "less than," and "equal to" one another.

Distance

A scale has the characteristic of **distance** when absolute differences between the descriptors are known and may be expressed in units. The respondent who purchases three bottles of diet cola buys two more than the one who purchases

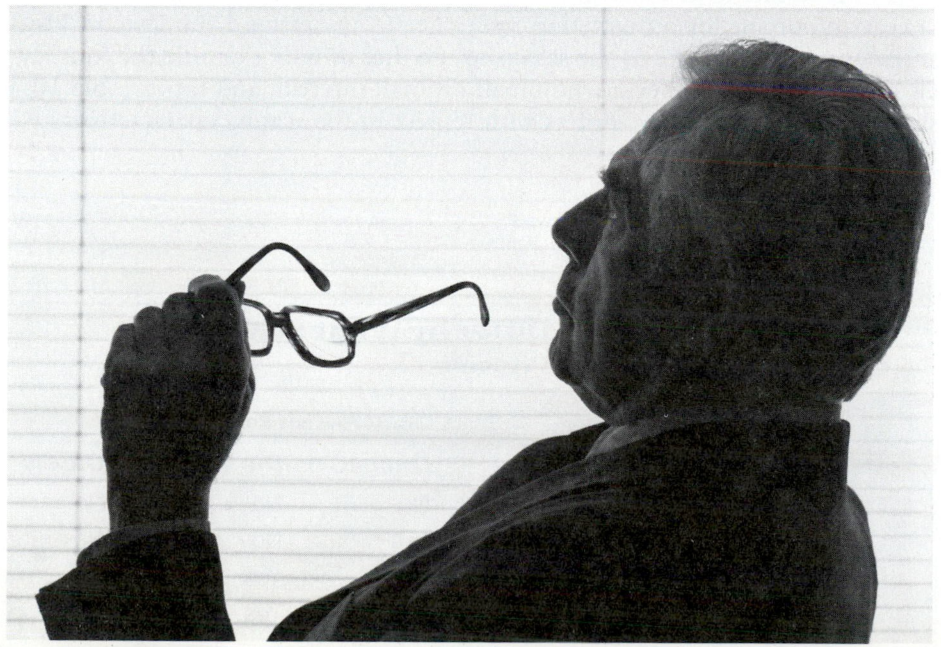

To understand markets, researchers must measure both objective and subjective aspects of buyers.

only one bottle; a three-car family owns one more automobile than a two-car family. Note that when the characteristic of distance exists, we are also given order. We know not only that the three-car family has "more than" the number of cars of the two-car family, but we also know the distance between the two (1 car).

Origin

A neutral category is not a true zero value for a scale.

A scale is said to have the characteristic of **origin** if there is a unique beginning or true zero point for the scale. Thus, 0 is the origin for an age scale just as it is for the number of miles traveled to the store or for the number of bottles of soda consumed. Not all scales have a true zero point for the property they are measuring. In fact, many scales used by marketing researchers have arbitrary neutral points, but they do not possess origins. For instance, when a respondent says "No opinion" to the question, "Do you agree or disagree with the statement, 'The Lexus is the best car on the road today?'," we cannot say that the person has a true zero level of agreement.

Perhaps you noticed that each scaling characteristic builds on the previous one. That is, description is the most basic and is present in every scale. If a scale has order, it also possesses description. If a scale has distance, it also possesses order and description, and if a scale has origin, it also has distance, order, and description. In other words, if a scale has a higher-level property, it also has all lower-level properties. But the opposite is not true, as is explained in the next section.

LEVELS OF MEASUREMENT OF SCALES

There is a hierarchy of scales; ratio scales are the "highest" and nominal scales are the "lowest."

You may ask, "Why is it important to know the characteristics of scales?" The answer is that the characteristics possessed by a scale determine that scale's level of measurement. Throughout this chapter, we try to convince you that it is very important for a marketing researcher to understand the level of measurement of the scale he or she selects to use. Let us now examine the four levels of measurement. They are nominal, ordinal, interval, and ratio. Table 10.3 shows how each scale type differs with respect to the scaling characteristics we have just discussed.

TABLE 10.3

Measurement Scales Differ by What Scale Characteristics They Possess

LEVEL OF	SCALE CHARACTERISTICS POSSESSED			
MEASUREMENT	DESCRIPTION	ORDER	DISTANCE	ORIGIN
Nominal scale	Yes	No	No	No
Ordinal scale	Yes	Yes	No	No
Interval scale	Yes	Yes	Yes	No
Ratio scale	Yes	Yes	Yes	Yes

Nominal Scales

Nominal scales simply label objects.

Nominal scales are defined as those that use only labels; that is, they possess only the characteristic of description. Examples include designations as to race, religion, type of dwelling, gender, brand last purchased, buyer/nonbuyer; answers that involve yes–no, agree–disagree; or any other instance in which the descriptors cannot be differentiated except qualitatively. If you describe respondents in a survey according to their occupation—banker, doctor, computer programmer—you have used a nominal scale. Note that these examples of a nominal scale only label the consumers. They do not provide other information such as "greater than," "twice as large," and so forth. Examples of nominal scale questions are found in Table 10.4A on page 294.

Ordinal Scales

Ordinal scales indicate only relative size differences between objects.

Ordinal scales permit the researcher to rank-order the respondents or their responses. For instance, if the respondent was asked to indicate his or her first, second, third, and fourth choices of brands, the results would be ordinally scaled. Similarly, if one respondent checked the category "Buy every week or more often" on a purchase-frequency scale and another checked the category "Buy once per month or less," the result would be an ordinal measurement. Ordinal scales indicate only relative size differences among objects. They possess description and order, but we do not know how far apart the descriptors are on the scale because ordinal scales do not possess distance or origin. Examples of ordinal scale questions are found in Table 10.4B.

Interval Scales

Interval scales use descriptors that are equal distances apart.

Interval scales are those in which the distance between each descriptor is known. The distance is normally defined as one scale unit. For example, a coffee brand rated "3" in taste is one unit away from one rated "4." Sometimes the researcher must impose a belief that equal intervals exist between the descriptors. That is, if you were asked to evaluate a store's salespeople by selecting a single designation from a list of "extremely friendly," "very friendly," "somewhat friendly," "somewhat unfriendly," "very unfriendly," or "extremely unfriendly," the researcher would probably assume that each designation was one unit away from the preceding one. In these cases, we say that the scale is "assumed interval." As shown in Table 10.4C, these descriptors are evenly spaced on a questionnaire; as such, the labels connote a continuum and the check lines are equal distances apart.[5] By wording or spacing the response options on a scale so they appear to have equal intervals between them, the researcher achieves a higher level of measurement than ordinal or nominal. With higher-order scales, the researcher is permitted to apply more powerful statistical techniques such as correlation analysis.

Ratio Scales

Ratio scales have a true zero point.

Ratio scales are ones in which a true zero origin exists—such as an actual number of purchases in a certain time period, dollars spent, miles traveled, number of children, or years of college education. This characteristic allows us to construct ratios when comparing results of the measurement. One person may spend twice as much as another, or travel one-third as far. Such ratios are

TABLE 10.4

Examples of the Use of Different Scaling Assumptions in Questions

A. NOMINAL-SCALED QUESTIONS

1. Please indicate your gender. Male Female

2. Check all the brands you would consider purchasing.
_____ Sony
_____ Zenith
_____ RCA
_____ Curtis Mathes

3. Do you agree or disagree that "Delta is ready when you are"? Agree Disagree

B. ORDINAL-SCALED QUESTIONS

1. Please rank each brand in terms of your preference. Place a "1" by your first choice, a "2" by your second choice, and so on.
_____ Arrid
_____ Right Guard
_____ Mennen

2. For each pair of grocery stores, circle the one you would be more likely to patronize.
Kroger versus First National
First National versus A&P
A&P versus Kroger

3. In your opinion, would you say the prices at Wal-Mart are
_____ Higher than Sears
_____ About the same as Sears
_____ Lower than Sears

C. INTERVAL-SCALED QUESTIONS

1. Please rate each brand in terms of its overall performance.

BRAND	RATING (CIRCLE ONE)									
	Very Poor									Very Good
Mont Blanc	1	2	3	4	5	6	7	8	9	10
Parker	1	2	3	4	5	6	7	8	9	10
Cross	1	2	3	4	5	6	7	8	9	10

2. Indicate your degree of agreement with the following statements by circling the appropriate number.

STATEMENT	STRONGLY DISAGREE				STRONGLY AGREE
a. I always look for bargains.	1	2	3	4	5
b. I enjoy being outdoors.	1	2	3	4	5
c. I love to cook.	1	2	3	4	5

TABLE 10.4 (continued)

3. Please rate PONTIAC FIREBIRD by checking the line that best corresponds to your evaluation of each item listed.

Slow pickup	_____	_____	_____	_____	Fast pickup
Good design	_____	_____	_____	_____	Bad design
Low price	_____	_____	_____	_____	High price

D. RATIO-SCALED QUESTIONS

1. Please indicate your age.
_____Years

2. Approximately how many times in the last month have you purchased anything over $5 in value at a 7-11 store?
0 1 2 3 4 5 More (specify:_____)

3. How much do you think a typical purchaser of a $100,000 term life insurance policy pays per year for that policy?
$_________

4. What is the probability that you will use a lawyer's services when you are ready to make a will?
_____ percent

inappropriate for interval scales, so we are not allowed to say that one store was one-half as friendly as another. Examples of ratio scale questions are presented in Table 10.4D.

WHY THE MEASUREMENT LEVEL OF A SCALE IS IMPORTANT

Why all the fuss over scale characteristics and the level of measurement? There are two important reasons. First, the level of measurement determines what information you will have about the object of study; it determines what you can say and what you cannot say about the object. For example, nominal scales measure the lowest information level, and therefore they are sometimes considered the crudest scales. Nominal scales allow us to do nothing more than identify our object of study on some property. Ratio scales, however, contain the greatest amount of information; they allow us to say many things about our object. Yet, it is not always possible to have a true zero point. A second important reason for understanding the level of measurement your scale possesses is that the level of measurement dictates what type of statistical analyses you may or may not perform. Low-level scales necessitate low-level analyses whereas high-level scales permit much more sophisticated analyses. In other words, the amount of information contained in the scale dictates the limits of statistical analysis. You will read more about this in chapters 15 through 18.

Measurement level is important because it determines (a) what you can or cannot say about your object and (b) which statistical analyses you may use.

As a general recommendation it is desirable to construct a scale at the highest appropriate level of measurement possible. Of course, appropriateness is determined by the properties of the object being scaled and to some extent by the mental abilities of your respondents. You can, for example, always "collapse" a scale down to a lower level, but it is practically impossible to climb to a higher level once the data is collected. For instance, the intensity of disagreement or negativism represented by responses such as "strongly disagree" or "somewhat disagree" on an interval scale can be collapsed into the "disagree" category found on a nominal scale, but the reverse is not true.

SCALED-RESPONSE QUESTION FORMS

Scaled-response questions are used to measure unobservable constructs.

We noted in our opening comments that marketing researchers often wish to measure subjective properties of consumers. There are many variations of these properties, but usually they are concerned with the psychological aspects of consumers. There are many different terms and labels given to these constructs, including attitudes, opinions, evaluations, beliefs, impressions, perceptions, feelings, and intentions. All of these constructs share the measurement difficulty we discussed earlier. That is, because these constructs are unobservable, the marketing researcher must develop some means of allowing respondents to express the direction and the intensity of their impressions in both a convenient and understandable manner. To do this, the marketing researcher uses scaled-response questions, which are designed to measure unobservable constructs.

View: "Piccadilly Cafeterias: Using Templates"

Because most of these psychological properties exist on a continuum ranging from one extreme to another in the mind of the respondent, it is common practice to design scaled-response questions in an assumed interval-scale format. Sometimes numbers are used to indicate a single unit of distance between each position on the scale. Usually, but not always, the scale ranges from an extreme negative, through a neutral, and to an extreme positive designation (Table 10.5). The neutral point is not considered zero, or an origin; instead, it is considered a point along a continuum.

TABLE 10.5

The Intensity Continuum Underlying Scaled-Response Question Forms

EXTREMELY NEGATIVE			NEUTRAL			EXTREMELY POSITIVE
Strongly Disagree	Somewhat Disagree		Neither Agree nor Disagree	Somewhat Agree		Strongly Agree
1	2		3	4		5
Extremely Dissatisfied	Very Dissatisfied	Somewhat Dissatisfied	No Opinion	Somewhat Satisfied	Very Satisfied	Extremely Satisfied
1	2	3	4	5	6	7
Extremely Unfavorable	Very Unfavorable	Somewhat Unfavorable	Neutral	Somewhat Favorable	Very Favorable	Extremely Favorable
____	____	____	____	____	____	____

As we noted earlier, it is not good practice to invent a novel scale format with every questionnaire. Instead, marketing researchers often fall back on standard types used by the industry. Such standards include the modified Likert scale, the life-style inventory, and the semantic differential, all three of which we describe next. Of course, sometimes no previous scale exists; or if one exists, it may have been developed in a context different from the one the researcher has in mind. Marketing Research Insight 10.2 describes the difficulties encountered when researchers attempt to develop scales that will be used across more than one country.

Marketing researchers use standard scales rather than inventing new ones for each research project.

The Modified Likert Scale

A scaled-response form commonly used by marketing researchers is the **modified Likert scale,** in which respondents are asked to indicate their degree of agreement or disagreement on a symmetric agree–disagree scale for each of a series of statements. The value of the modified Likert scale should be apparent because respondents are asked *how much* they agree or disagree with the statement. That is, the scale captures the intensity of their feelings.

The Likert scale format measures intensity of agreement or disagreement.

MARKETING RESEARCH INSIGHT 10.2

Problems in Developing a Scale for International Research

Language differences are only one of the many difficulties encountered when a market researcher develops a scale to be used across countries. Here are some guidelines for developing a scale to be used in different cultures.

1. *First, undertake extensive qualitative research to understand the similarities and differences among the cultures. Focus groups conducted by native-speaking moderators and held in the countries under study are recommended.*
2. *Ensure that the basic concepts being researched are equivalent. For example, in the United States gardening is often a leisure hobby, but in certain countries, such as China, maintaining a garden is essential to life. Sometimes consultants who are very knowledgeable of the particular cultures are used to evaluate the equivalence of concepts.*
3. *Look for differences in ways cultures react to the scale points. Some cultures, such as Japan, disapprove of extremism, and the endpointss of a scale will rarely be used; whereas other cultures value strong opinions, so the neutral point will be avoided.*
4. *Watch for translation errors. The accepted procedure is to write the question in English and have a native-speaking person translate it into the foreign language. Then, a second native speaker should back-translate it into English, and the back-translated version should be compared with the original for discrepancies.*
5. *Control administration factors that may influence the responses. Researchers doing a survey in Thailand, where women are traditionally passive and nonpolitical, found that respondents gave excessively positive answers in a survey administered by a Thai woman professor who had a progressive reputation.*

TABLE 10.6

The Likert Question Format Can Be Used in Telephone Surveys, But Respondents Must Be Briefed on Its Format or Otherwise Prompted

(INTERVIEWER: READ) I have a list of statements that I will read to you. As I read each one, please indicate whether you agree or disagree with it.

Are the instructions clear? (IF NOT, REPEAT)

(INTERVIEWER: READ EACH STATEMENT. WITH EACH RESPONSE, ASK) "Would you say that you (dis)agree STRONGLY or (dis)agree SOMEWHAT?

	RESPONSE (CIRCLE)				
STATEMENT	STRONGLY AGREE	SOMEWHAT AGREE	NEUTRAL	SOMEWHAT DISAGREE	STRONGLY DISAGREE
(a) Levi's 501 jeans are good looking.	1	2	3	4	5
(b) Levi's 501 jeans are reasonably priced.	1	2	3	4	5
(c) Your next pair of jeans will be Levi's 501s.	1	2	3	4	5
(d) Levi's 501s are easy to identify on someone.	1	2	3	4	5
(e) Levi's 501s make you feel good.	1	2	3	4	5

Table 10.6 presents an example of its use in a telephone interview. You should notice the directions given by the interviewer to properly administer this scale.

The Likert-type of response format, borrowed from a formal scale development approach developed by Rensis Likert, has been extensively modified and adapted by marketing researchers, so much, in fact, that its definition varies from researcher to researcher. Some assume that any intensity scale using descriptors such as "strongly," "somewhat," "slightly," or the like is a Likert variation. Others use the term only for questions with agree–disagree response options. We tend to agree with the second opinion, and prefer to refer to any scaled measurement other than an agree–disagree dimension as a "sensitivity" or "intensity" scale. But this convention is only our preference, and you should be aware that different researchers embrace other designations.

The Life-Style Inventory

Life-style measures a person's activities, interests, and opinions with a Likert scale.

There is a special application of the modified Likert question form called the **life-style inventory** (or psychographics inventory), which takes into account the values and personality traits of people as reflected in their unique activities, interests, and opinions (AIOs) toward their work, leisure time, and purchases. The technique was originated by advertising strategists who wanted to obtain descriptions of groups of consumers as a means of establishing more effective advertising. The underlying belief is that knowledge of consumers' life-styles, as opposed to just demographics, offers direction for marketing decisions.

Life-style questions measure consumers' unique ways of living.

Life-style questions measure consumers' unique ways of living. These questions can be used to distinguish among types of purchasers such as heavy versus light users of a product, store patrons versus nonpatrons, or media vehicle users versus nonusers. They can assess the degree to which a person is price-conscious, fashion-conscious, an opinion giver, a sports enthusiast, child oriented, home centered, or financially optimistic. These attributes are mea-

A consumer's life-style may be measured in terms of their activities, interests, and opinions.

sured by a series of AIO statements, usually in the form presented in Table 10.7.[6] Each respondent indicates his or her degree of agreement or disagreement by responding to the Likert-like categories. In some applications, the questionnaire may contain a large number of different life-style statements ranging from very general descriptions of the person's AIOs to very specific statements concerning particular products, brands, services, or other items of interest to the marketing researcher. Ideally, more than one statement for each life-style dimension should be used. Each respondent's indications on the related items are then usually added or averaged together. Then, a single score is given for each person on each life-style dimension. A valuable feature of life-style questions is that they are adaptable to practically every developed culture in the world. Marketing Research Insight 10.3 details psychographic segmentation as it has been researched by Market Decisions, Inc.

TABLE 10.7

Examples of Life-Style Statements on a Questionnaire

Please respond by circling the number that best corresponds to how much you agree or disagree with each statement.

STATEMENT	STRONGLY AGREE	AGREE	NEITHER AGREE NOR DISAGREE	DISAGREE	STRONGLY DISAGREE
1. I shop a lot for "specials."	1	2	3	4	5
2. I usually have one or more outfits that are of the very latest style.	1	2	3	4	5
3. My children are the most important thing in my life.	1	2	3	4	5
4. I usually keep my house very neat and clean.	1	2	3	4	5
5. I would rather spend a quiet evening at home than go out to a party.	1	2	3	4	5
6. It is good to have a charge account.	1	2	3	4	5
7. I like to watch or listen to baseball or football games.	1	2	3	4	5
8. I think I have more self-confidence than most people.	1	2	3	4	5
9. I sometimes influence what my friends buy.	1	2	3	4	5
10. I will probably have more money to spend next year than I have now.	1	2	3	4	5

MARKETING RESEARCH INSIGHT 10.3

Psychographic Segmentation in South America

Market Decisions, Inc. of San Diego has developed its "MDI COMPASS" psychographic segmentation system for application in South American countries. By asking questions about attitudes, life-styles, and product interests to consumers living in Santiago, Chile; Buenos Aires, Argentina; São Paulo, Brazil; and Mexico City, Mexico, Market Decisions has identified five distinct South American life-style segments. A summary of each follows.

SEGMENT NAME	SIZE	DESCRIPTION
Careful copers	29%	Cautious and pessimistic
		Not adventurous in decisions or buying
		Prefer products they know and trust
		Dominate Chile; least prevalent in Mexico
Cosmopolitan climbers	24%	Young and upscale
		Enthusiastic about new and imported products
		Willing to spend for quality
		Most common in Brazil and Mexico; less common in Chile and Argentina
Hopeful homebodies	23%	Value appearance, propriety, and civility
		Most likely to say things have changed for the worse
		Least likely to buy imported products
Relaxed realists	17%	More relaxed and less driven
		Not given to planning
		Considered the emerging middle class
Hurried handlers	7%	Mainly modern Latin women with busy lives
		Goal oriented and highly educated
		Demand value
		Common in Chile and Argentina

Source: *American Demographics (September 1996), [http://www.demographics.com/Publications/NN/96_NN/9609_FC/9609F09.htm]*

The Semantic Differential Scale

The semantic differential is a good way to measure a brand, company, or store image.

A specialized scaled-response question format that has sprung directly from the problem of translating a person's qualitative judgments into quantitative estimates is the semantic differential. Like the modified Likert scale, this one has been borrowed from another area of research, namely semantics. The **semantic differential scale** contains a series of bipolar adjectives for the various properties of the object under study, and respondents indicate their impressions of each property by indicating locations along its continuum. The focus

A semantic differential scale will identify image differences between two competing establishments or brands.

of the semantic differential is on the measurement of the meaning of an object, concept, or person. Because many marketing stimuli have meaning, mental associations, or connotations, this type of scale works very well when the marketing researcher is attempting to determine brand, store, or other images.

The construction of a semantic differential scale begins with the determination of a concept or object to be rated. The researcher then selects bipolar pairs of words or phrases that could be used to describe the object's salient properties. Depending on the object, some examples might be "friendly–unfriendly," "hot–cold," "convenient–inconvenient," "high quality–low quality," or "dependable–undependable." The opposites are positioned at the endpointss of a continuum of intensity, and it is customary, although not mandatory, to use seven separators between each point. The respondent then indicates his or her evaluation of the performance of the object, say a brand, by checking the appropriate line. The closer the respondent checks to an endpoint on a line, the more intense is his or her evaluation of the object being measured.

When using the semantic differential, you should control for the "halo effect."

Table 10.8 shows how this was done for a survey for Red Lobster. The respondents also rated Jake's Seafood Restaurant on the same survey. You can see that each respondent has been instructed to indicate his or her impression of various restaurants, such as Red Lobster by checking the appropriate line between the several bipolar adjective phrases. As you look at the phrases, you should note that they have been randomly flipped to avoid having all of the "good" ones on one side. This flipping procedure is used to avoid the **halo effect,**[7] which is a general feeling about a store or brand that can bias a respondent's impressions on its specific properties (see Marketing Research Insight 10.4 on page 304). For instance, suppose you have a very positive image of Red Lobster. If all of the positive items were on the right-hand side and all the negative ones were on the left-hand side, you might be tempted to just check all of the answers on the right-hand side. But it is entirely possible that some specific aspect of the Red Lobster might not be as good as the others. Perhaps the

TABLE 10.8

The Semantic Differential Scale Is Useful When Measuring Store, Company, or Brand Images

Indicate your impression of RED LOBSTER restaurant by checking the line corresponding to your opinion for each pair of descriptors.

High prices	___	___	___	___	___	___	___	Low prices
Inconvenient location	___	___	___	___	___	___	___	Convenient location
For me	___	___	___	___	___	___	___	Not for me
Warm atmosphere	___	___	___	___	___	___	___	Cold atmosphere
Limited menu	___	___	___	___	___	___	___	Wide menu
Fast service	___	___	___	___	___	___	___	Slow service
Low-quality food	___	___	___	___	___	___	___	High-quality food
A special place	___	___	___	___	___	___	___	An everyday place

PRESENTATION OF THE RESULTS

High prices	___	___	___	___	___	___	___	Low prices
Inconvenient location	___	___	___	___	___	___	___	Convenient location
For me	___	___	___	___	___	___	___	Not for me
Warm atmosphere	___	___	___	___	___	___	___	Cold atmosphere
Limited menu	___	___	___	___	___	___	___	Wide menu
Fast service	___	___	___	___	___	___	___	Slow service
Low-quality food	___	___	___	___	___	___	___	High-quality food
A special place	___	___	___	___	___	___	___	An everyday place

——— Red Lobster

_ _ _ _ Jake's Seafood Restaurant

restaurant is not located in a very convenient place, or the menu is not as broad as you would like. Randomly flipping favorable and negative ends of the descriptors in a semantic differential scale minimizes the halo effect. There is some evidence that when respondents are ambivalent in the survey topic, it is best to use a balanced set of negatively and positively worded questions.[8]

View: "Red Lobster: Recording and Computing Variables"

With a semantic differential, a researcher can plot the average evaluation on each set of bipolar descriptors.

One of the most appealing aspects of the semantic differential is the ability of the researcher to compute averages and then to plot a "profile" of the brand or company image. Each check line is assigned a number for coding. Usually, the numbers 1, 2, 3, and so on, beginning from the left side, are customary. Then, an average is computed for each bipolar pair. The averages are plotted as you see them, and the marketing researcher has a very nice graphical communication vehicle with which to report the findings to his or her client. The semantic differential scale format can be applied in various ways. We have included Marketing Research Insight 10.5 (page 305) to show how it has been adapted to help an advertiser assess the perceived credibility of a celebrity being considered to endorse a brand or product line.

MARKETING RESEARCH INSIGHT 10.4

If You Do Not Mix the Favorable and Unfavorable Endpoints of a Semantic Differential, a Bias Will Result

What happens when a researcher places all of the positive or favorable ends of a rating scale on the right-hand side? What if they are all on the left-hand side of the scale? Researchers are told that, unless they mix the positive and negative ends of a scale, a generalized halo effect will occur.

To test this theory, researchers had college students rate different aspects of their university. One group was administered a seven-point rating scale with all of the favorable items on the left, and another group responded to the same scale but with all of the favorable items on the right-hand end. A third group was given a mixed arrangement.

A definite halo effect was observed with the left-hand side group. They exhibited a strong tendency to respond more on the left end of the scale. Placing all of the favorable descriptors on the right side of the page produced a less pronounced shift to the right. Researchers concluded that, by randomly mixing right-to-left and left-to-right scales, they will minimize any halo effects that might creep in to contaminate the findings.

Source: *Hershey H. Friedman, Linda Weiser Friedman, and Beth Gluck, "The Effects of Scale-Checking Styles on Responses to a Semantic Differential Scale,"* Journal of the Market Research Society, *vol. 30, no. 4 (October 1988), 477–481.*

Composite Scales

Composite scales may be either formative or reflective.

On many occasions marketing researchers find themselves studying constructs that require the use of **composite scales,** defined as instances in which multiple items are required to completely measure the construct. For instance, in many attitude scales, perceptual scales, or opinion scales, a number of items are used and then combined to obtain a complete measure of the construct. There are two types of composite scales: a formative scale and a reflective scale. With a **formative composite scale,** each item measures some part of the whole; for example, in a store image scale in which each item pertains to a different aspect of the store such as: competitive prices, location convenience, friendliness of sales clerks, variety of merchandise, quality for the price, or speedy checkouts. The sum of all these parts forms the complete, or formative composite, scale that measures the store's image. With a **reflective composite scale,** multiple items are used to measure a single dimension of a construct. For example, in a study of the service quality provided by a travel agency, the friendliness of its agents can be measured on a Likert agree–disagree scale with items such as, "The travel agent knows me by name," "The agents are always cheerful," and "These travel agents have a friendly manner." Here, each item reflects friendliness, and an averaging of the reflective composite scale items will measure the degree of service–quality friendliness in the travel agency being researched. If other dimensions of the construct are under study, multiple items should be used to reflect each of them as well.[9] Of course, with both formative and reflective composite scales, any negatively worded items must be reverse scored by the researcher so that all fall consistently along the negative-to-positive intensity continuum.

Formative composites are summed, whereas reflective composite scales are averaged.

MARKETING RESEARCH INSIGHT 10.5

What Do Madonna, John McEnroe, and Tom Selleck Have in Common with a Semantic Differential Scale?

A researcher has developed a source credibility scale using celebrities such as Madonna, John McEnroe, Tom Selleck, and Linda Evans, and he has created a source credibility scale that is reliable and valid. Using college students plus "real" consumers, he tested the following celebrity product endorsement pairings:

Madonna promoting a new line of jeans
Tom Selleck promoting a new men's cologne
John McEnroe promoting a line of tennis rackets
Linda Evans promoting a new perfume

The preliminary semantic differential scale measured the spokesperson's credibility on the three dimensions of (1) attractiveness, (2) trustworthiness, and (3) expertise. Five bipolar adjective items were used to define each dimension. The endorser's source credibility scale is as follows:

ATTRACTIVENESS								
Attractive	___	___	___	___	___	___	___	*Unattractive*
Classy	___	___	___	___	___	___	___	*Not classy*
Beautiful	___	___	___	___	___	___	___	*Ugly*
Elegant	___	___	___	___	___	___	___	*Plain*
Sexy	___	___	___	___	___	___	___	*Not sexy*

TRUSTWORTHINESS								
Dependable	___	___	___	___	___	___	___	*Undependable*
Honest	___	___	___	___	___	___	___	*Dishonest*
Reliable	___	___	___	___	___	___	___	*Unreliable*
Sincere	___	___	___	___	___	___	___	*Insincere*
Trustworthy	___	___	___	___	___	___	___	*Untrustworthy*

EXPERTISE								
Expert	___	___	___	___	___	___	___	*Not an expert*
Experienced	___	___	___	___	___	___	___	*Inexperienced*
Knowledgeable	___	___	___	___	___	___	___	*Unknowledgeable*
Qualified	___	___	___	___	___	___	___	*Unqualified*
Skilled	___	___	___	___	___	___	___	*Unskilled*

Advertisers now have an instrument that can be used to assess the credibility of people they are considering to use as spokespersons for brands or products.

Source: *Roobina Ohanian, "Construction and Validation of a Scale to Measure Celebrity Endorsers' Perceived Expertise, Trustworthiness, and Attractiveness,"* Journal of Advertising, *vol. 19, no. 3 (1990), 39–52.*

Issues in the Use of Sensitivity Scales

Use a neutral response option when you think respondents have a valid "no opinion" response.

Using scaled-response formats requires the researcher to confront two issues. First is the question of whether or not to include the middle, neutral response option. Our modified Likert scale, life-style, and semantic differential examples all have a neutral point, but some researchers prefer to leave out the neutral option on their scales. Valid arguments exist for both options.[10] Those arguing for the inclusion of a neutral option believe that some respondents do not have opinions formed on that item, and they must be given the opportunity to indicate their ambivalence. Proponents of not including a neutral position, however, believe that respondents may use the neutral option as a dodge or a method of hiding their opinions.[11] Eliminating the neutral position forces these respondents to indicate their opinions or feelings.

Use common sense in deciding whether to have a completely symmetric scale.

The second issue concerns the need to have a completely symmetric scale. Sometimes, common sense causes the researcher to conclude that only the positive side is appropriate. For example, when you think of how important something is to you, you do not usually think in terms of degrees of "unimportance." Consequently, some scales contain only the positive side, because very

TABLE 10.9

Scaled-Response Question Formats Can Have Various Forms

SCALE NAME	DESCRIPTION AND EXAMPLES
Graphic rating scale	*Use of a line or pictorial representation to indicate intensity of response:* Unimportant ______________________ Extremely Important ☺ ☺ ☺ ☺
Itemized rating scale	*Use of a numbered or labeled continuous scale to indicate intensity of response:* ☐ 1 Poor ___ ☐ 2 Fair ___ ☐ 3 Good ___ ☐ 4 Very Good ___ ☐ 5 Excellent ___
Stapel scale	*Use of numbers, usually –5 to +5 to indicate the intensity of response:* Fast checkout service –5 –4 –3 –2 –1 +1 +2 +3 +4 +5
Percentage scale	*Use of percentages to indicate the intensity of response:* Unlikely to purchase ... Likely to purchase 0% 10% 20% 30% 40% 50% 60% 70% 80% 90% 100% Very dissatisfied ______________________ Very satisfied 0% 25% 50% 75% 100%

few respondents would make use of the degrees of intensity on the negative side. When in doubt, a researcher can pretest both the complete and the one-sided versions to see whether the negative side will be used by respondents.

Other Scaled-Response Question Formats

There are a great many variations of scaled-response question formats used in marketing research. If you choose a career in the marketing research business, you will realize that each marketing research company or marketing research department tends to rely on "tried-and-true" formats that they apply from study to study. Several examples are provided in Table 10.9.

Researchers tend to rely on "tried and true" scale formats.

There are some very good reasons for this practice of adopting a preferred question format. First, it expedites the questionnaire design process. That is, by selecting a standardized scaled-response form that has been used in several studies, there is no need to be creative and to invent a new form. This saves both time and costs.[12] Second, by testing a scaled-response format across several studies, there is the opportunity to assess its reliability as well as its validity. Both of these topics are discussed in detail in the next sections of this chapter, which introduce the basic concepts involved with reliability and validity of measurements and illustrate the methods used to assess reliability and validity.

RELIABILITY OF MEASUREMENTS

In a nutshell, **reliability** is the tendency in a respondent to respond in the same or in a very similar manner to an identical or near-identical question. To state the concept of reliability somewhat differently, a measure is reliable when it elicits an identical or very similar response from the same person with suc-

Reliability is the consistency of responses to a question.

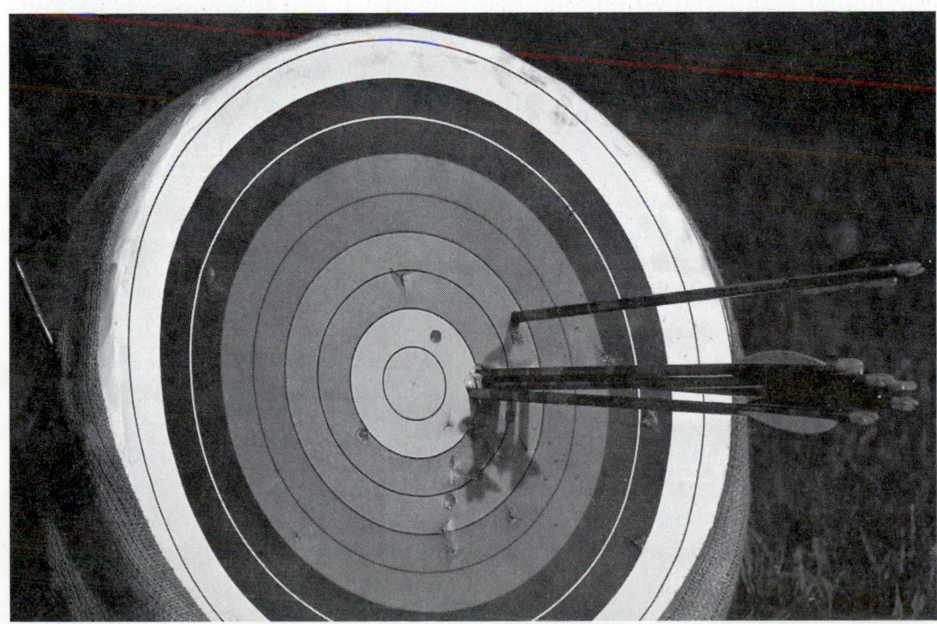

Reliability of measurements means that they are highly consistent or very similar.

cessive administrations. Marketing researchers use their own jargon and say that the instrument is free from "random response error," or, stated more simply, each person is consistent and does not respond randomly.

Reliable measures obtain identical or very similar responses from the same respondent.

Reliability is a matter of degree. Some measures will exhibit perfectly consistent responses, some will show wild swings, and some will generate responses that are somewhat the same. The great danger of unreliable measurements should be obvious to you. The marketing researcher cannot place any faith in them; they are just meaningless numbers. An unreliable measure will obtain different responses from respondents who have identical feelings or opinions. Precisely why the measurement is unreliable is never quite certain. Perhaps the instructions on the questionnaire are unclear. Possibly, the respondents are not motivated to pay attention. An interviewer may not have stated the question the same way each time, or the respondents may have been confused by the wording of a question. Notice that researchers initially assume that the measure determines reliability. In other words, if responses are unreliable, we first look at the question, instruction, response options, and so forth, to be at fault before looking at the respondent. At the same time, researchers realize that respondent groups differ in their abilities to "handle" each measure. So a question that is reliable for a sample of consulting engineers with graduate degrees may not be reliable for a sample of automobile mechanics with vocational school diplomas. This fact necessitates reliability assessment for every survey performed.

Assessment methods for reliable measures include test–retest, equivalent forms, and split-half.

There are a number of options available to the marketing researcher to assess reliability. A favorite approach is called the test–retest method. Other methods include equivalent forms and split-half. Each of the various reliability assessment methods is briefly described following.

Test–Retest Reliability

For test–retest reliability, administer the same question at a later, but not too much later, time.

Test–retest reliability requires that respondents be administered the identical question(s) at some later time, and that the original and retest answers be compared. Some researchers, for example, will instruct the interviewer to finish the interview with a retest section. The interviewer may say something like, "That concludes our survey, but let me just glance back over the questions to make sure I did not skip any or forget to check your answers. Oh, yes, here's one." He or she then repeats the question asked earlier and notes the second response. Obviously, not all questions can be repeated, so a few critical questions are selected and retested in this manner. A verification call-back is a variation of this approach. You should realize that the test–retest approach rides on the horns of a time dilemma. If the time interval between test and retest is too short, respondents may simply remember their responses, but if the time period is too long, some real changes may have occurred in the respondents' opinions. Most researchers opt for a short time interval over a long one and assume that respondents' memory is not involved.

Computer technology coupled with database management systems have opened up a new type of test–retest reliability assessment. In it, respondents are tracked over successive surveys and examined for response reliability. With this approach, a respondent's answers to identical or similar questions can be compared across studies for consistency, and inconsistent respondents can be pulled out of the database.[13]

Equivalent Forms Reliability

Equivalent forms reliability relies on the "similar" aspect of the definition of reliability and uses equivalent forms of questions typically embedded in the same questionnaire. Here, the attempt is to make respondents think that each question is different, when in truth they are tapping the same opinion or attitude dimension. One favorite device is to flip a question or statement. For instance, if a modified Likert form were used, one statement could be, "Progressive Savings and Loan makes you feel like a friend." Later on, the statement could be, "Progressive Savings and Loan makes you feel like a stranger." Reflective composite scales have equivalent forms reliability automatically built in as the reflective items are constructed to be highly similar to one another. The danger of this method lies in the degree of equivalence between two questions; during measure development, if respondents fail to treat them as equivalents, the usual assumption is that the measure is unreliable, not the respondents.

With equivalent forms reliability, be certain the two questions are identical in meaning.

Split-Half Reliability

Split-half reliability requires that the marketing researcher separate the total sample into two groups and compare one group's responses to the other's responses. Here, the assumption is that the two groups are identical in composition, or homogenous, and that their averages for the various scaled-response questions will be very similar. Statistical tests can be used to determine the degree of similarity. The basic complaint against this approach is its inability to reveal subgroup problems because all comparisons are done on a group-to-group basis. The following example illustrates this problem.

With a split-half reliability test, the pattern of responses should be compared as well as the two group averages.

In a survey of college students about to graduate, we asked them to respond to the following modified five-point agree–disagree Likert statement: "I believe I will have an exciting career." The responses were then converted to numbers with a 1 for "strongly disagree," a 2 for "disagree," and so forth. We divided the sample into two groups and computed the averages: both groups' means were exactly 3.0. So we concluded they were equivalent, and that the measure was reliable. But just to check, we looked at the two groups' responses more closely and found that in one group, all of our students responded "neither agree nor disagree," but in the other one, 50 percent responded "strongly agree" and the other half responded "strongly disagree." These responses are not equivalent even though the comparison of means says they are. For this reason, split-half reliability is the least-popular reliability assessment method.

How to Develop Reliable Measures

Regardless of the method used, the marketing researcher has four avenues to develop and report reliable measures. First, in the instance of greatly unreliable measurements, the marketing researcher should throw out the questions completely, and they should be revamped and reevaluated before the actual survey. You will note that reliability assessment here should occur during the development of the questionnaire, probably in the form of a series of pilot tests aimed at improving the measures. Although perhaps laborious, the development and testing of questions for acceptable reliability is a necessary step in the marketing research process.

Development of reliable questions is a necessary step in the marketing research process.

Measurement reliability can be improved by revising question(s), collapsing scales, and throwing out respondent(s).

Second, the researcher can "collapse" scales that have too many gradations. For instance, the modified Likert responses can be collapsed into the three categories of "agree," "disagree," and "no opinion," or the semantic differential responses can be collapsed into a five-point scale by combining the 1s and 2s and the 6s and 7s into single categories. Such collapsing usually increases reliability. You will note that this step takes place after the survey has been administered but while measure reliability is still a concern.

Third, as an alternative to the second step or to be performed after the second step, reliability assessment may be done on an individual basis, such as a direct comparison of each respondent's test answer with the retest or equivalent answer. It may be possible to identify those unreliable respondents and pull them out from the final analysis. But you should throw out respondents only if you are certain the measure is reliable in the first place for most respondents.

Fourth, after the first three steps have been applied, the researcher can report the reliability levels. Normally, the measurement of reliability is a coefficient analogous to a proportion in which 1.00 indicates perfect reliability. Some disagreement exists for an "acceptable" minimum, but levels of 0.65 or 0.70 are often considered acceptable for measures that are being used for the first time, whereas higher reliability levels are expected for measures that have been used before and have undergone fine-tuning over successive administrations and improvements.

VALIDITY OF MEASUREMENTS

Validity is the accuracy of responses to a measure.

Validity operates on a completely different plane than reliability; it is possible to have measurements perfectly reliable but that are invalid. **Validity** is defined as the accuracy of the measurement: It is an assessment of the exactness of the measurement relative to what actually exists. To illustrate this concept and its difference from reliability, think of a respondent who is embarrassed by a question about his income. This person makes under $25,000 per year, but he does not want to tell it to the interviewer. Consequently, he responds with the highest category, "Over $100,000." In a retest of the questions, the respondent persists in his lie by stipulating the highest income level again. Here, the respondent has been perfectly consistent, but he has also been completely untruthful. Of course, lying is not the only reason for invalidity. The respondent may have a faulty memory, may have a misconception, or may even be a bad guesser, which causes his responses to be inexact from reality.[14]

How do you remember the difference between reliability and validity? Think of your wristwatch. If you set your watch incorrectly, it will say 1:00 every 12 hours (reliable), but it will be inaccurate (not valid). But how would you determine whether a person was accurate in his or her response? Naturally, you would need some means of verification. For income, an income tax form or verification from the employer would serve to determine the validity. Of course, either of these items would be very difficult to obtain, but what about an estimate of the person's income from another family member? Regardless of the source used, this example demonstrates the basic concept in validation: The identical answer must be obtained from a different source of data collection. This approach is known as convergent validation, or assessing

Validity of measurements means that they are "right on target."

the validity of information of using two different methods to obtain the information. Convergent validation is described more fully later in this section.

Actually, there are a number of different types of validity involved in measurement. The ones most commonly considered by marketing researchers are face, predictive, convergent, and discriminant.

Types of validity are face, predictive, convergent, and discriminant.

Face Validity

Face validity is concerned with the degree to which a measurement "looks like" it measures that which it is designed to measure. It is a judgment call by the researcher and is made as the questions are designed. Thus, as each question is developed, there is an implicit assessment of its face validity. Revisions enhance the face validity of the question until it passes the researcher's subjective evaluation. Unfortunately, this method of assessing validity is the weakest. It can be strengthened somewhat by having other researchers critique the questions.

Face validity: Does the question "look like" it measures what it is supposed to measure?

Predictive Validity

Predictive validity pertains to the extent to which a particular measure predicts or relates to other measures. For instance, we might ask respondents to indicate their purchase intentions for onion dip on a probability scale. Those

Predictive validity: Does the measure predict another measure as we expect?

who indicate high likelihoods of purchasing the product or brand should have high incidence of actual purchasing, whereas those with low likelihoods should have a low incidence of actual onion dip purchasing. So we ask them to tell us how many onion dips they have purchased in the last month to validate their responses. You would predict that a respondent who says she dislikes purchasing onion dip would not have purchased as much onion dip as one who likes purchasing onion dip. Those with strong positive attitudes toward a brand should have good things to say about that brand, and so forth. If your logical predictions are supported by the findings, predictive validity has been demonstrated for those measures.

Convergent Validity

Convergent validity: Do two methods of collecting the same information agree?

When the researcher uses two different methods or sources of data collection for the same piece of information, **convergent validity** is being assessed. For example, field research companies often use a telephone validation technique to verify respondents who were interviewed by their interviewers in a mall-intercept study. If the two different methods produce similar results, convergent validity is demonstrated.

In another example of convergent validity, a drop-off survey was delivered by college students to every tenth house in a medium-sized city. The students explained the survey and left the questionnaire with a head of the household. They returned later that day to pick up the completed questionnaires. The convergent validity was assessed by follow-up telephone calls. In the drop-off phase, 386 homeowners responded, and the average age of the home was 14.2 years. Thirty questionnaires were selected at random, and follow-up telephone calls were made to these homes. This time, the other head of the household was questioned, and the average home age was determined as 14.6 years. The closeness of the two averages (14.2 and 14.6) indicates convergent validity. (A statistical test revealed no significant difference.)

Discriminant Validity

Discriminant validity: Do measures of different constructs differ as you expect them to?

Discriminant validity means that dissimilar constructs should differ. In other words, questions that measure different objects should yield different results. When the researcher knows that real differences do exist, he or she should find that the responses differ. Otherwise, there is some doubt as to the validity of the measurements.

Discriminant validity was also assessed in the homeowners' survey just described. One question on the survey asked how concerned homeowners were about home security. They were to indicate concern using a scale from 1, meaning "not concerned at all," to 7, meaning "very concerned." Another question asked about their concern about home fire safety using the same seven-point scale. The averages were found to be 4.3 and 5.6, respectively. Thus, they were more worried about fire safety than about break-ins, and this difference seems reasonable because fires can happen any time, but break-ins are more rare. These are two different constructs, and their discriminant validity was demonstrated by the difference between the averages.

How to Develop Valid Measures

What does the marketing researcher do about validity? Face validity becomes second nature to the researcher, and it should be constantly evaluated throughout the design of the questionnaire. Unfortunately, in most cases, face validity is the only assessment used to determine the validity of research measures.

As you can see, developing valid measures with face, predictive, convergent, and discriminant validity can be a time-consuming task. Consequently, typically only research companies who have developed proprietary scales and instruments that are used over and over engage in rigorous scale-development activities. Academic marketing studies appearing in top-rated marketing journals, however, must satisfy strict criteria for measure reliability and validity, and these studies are excellent sources for marketing researchers who are vitally concerned about the reliability and validity of their measurements.

There is very good reason to be vitally concerned about reliability and validity of measurements in marketing research: If a measure is unreliable or invalid, the entire study falls apart. Consequently, we have provided a quick reference summary of the various tests discussed in this section and you will find these summaries in Table 10.10 on page 314.

Researchers face an ethical dilemma in scale development. The proper way to develop a scale is very lengthy and expensive. For instance, the book Handbook of Marketing Scales *(Newbury Park, Calif.: Sage Publications, 1993), by William Bearden, Richard Netemeyer, and Mary Ann Mobley stipulates 12 different criteria that should be used to assess the quality of a scale. To meet these criteria, it is expected that a scale will be developed over a series of administrations. Statistical tests are used after each one to refine the scale, and each subsequent administration tests the new version, which leads to further refinement. It is not unusual for scales that are published in academic journals to go through three or four administrations involving hundreds of respondents.*

Marketing research practitioners do not have the time and their clients are unwilling to supply the monetary resources necessary to thoroughly develop scales. A few research firms have pursued scale development, and they have developed proprietary instruments that are protected by copyright. The ethical dilemma is especially evident when a marketing researcher is attempting to maximize his or her profit. Reliability and validity assessment can be omitted or treated superficially because clients do not understand the involved procedures that should be applied in these evaluations. In fact, they may not even believe these procedures are warranted and will refuse to pay for them, meaning that if such tests are performed, they will reduce the marketing researcher's profits. However, these are rare cases. The vast majority of marketing researchers are forced to design their measures by relying on face validity alone. The unfortunate truth is that some researchers do not concern themselves at all with reliability or validity measurements. On the other hand, it is unethical for a researcher to find reliability and/or validity problems and not strive to resolve them. Some researchers hold that not assessing reliability and validity is an unethical practice in itself. However, a conscientious market researcher will devote as much time and energy as possible to ensure the reliability and validity of the research throughout the entire process.

TABLE 10.10

Criteria for Reliability and Validity Tests Used in Marketing Research

TEST	CRITERION
Test–retest reliability	Most respondents give an identical response to the same question administered with some time interval between.
Equivalent forms reliability	Most respondents give an equivalent response to near-identical questions administered at different times.
Split-half reliability	The responses of one-half of the sample are highly similar to the responses of the other half when key questions are compared.
Face validity	The researcher judges that a question "looks like" it is measuring what it is supposed to measure.
Predictive validity	One measure that logically should predict another measure is found to do so statistically (usually correlation).
Convergent validity	Two completely different methods of measuring the same variable are found to yield similar statistical findings (usually means or correlation).
Discriminant validity	One measure that logically should not be related to another measure is found not to do so statistically (usually correlation).

SUMMARY

This chapter discussed the concepts involved in measurement of the subjective properties of marketing phenomena. We began by reviewing the three basic question–response option formats of open-ended, closed-ended, and scaled-response and then we introduced you to the four types of scales used in marketing research: (1) nominal or simple classifications; (2) ordinal or rank order; (3) interval scales, which include number scales and other equal-appearing spaced scales; and (4) ratio scales, which have a true zero point. As you move from the lowest (nominal) to the highest (ratio) type of scale, you gain more information in measurement.

Marketing researchers have a set of commonly used scale types, and the chapter included descriptions of three of these. First, there is the modified Likert scale, which appears as an agree–disagree continuum with five to seven positions. Next, we described life-style questions, which use a modified Likert approach to measure people's attitudes, interests, and opinions. Third, we illustrated how the semantic differential scale uses bipolar adjectives to measure the image of a brand or a store.

Reliability and validity of measurement were discussed. Reliability is the degree to which a respondent is consistent in his or her answers. It can be assessed any of three ways: (1) test–retest, in which identical questions are administered at two different points in time and then compared; (2) equivalent forms, in which answers to similar questions are compared; and (3) split-half, in which one portion of the sample is compared to another for consistency. Validity, on the other hand, is the accuracy of responses. It is possible to have reliable measures that are inaccurate. There are four forms of validity: (1) face validity, in which the researcher judges the validity of a measure by its face value; (2) predictive validity, in which the accuracy of one measure predicting another is assessed; (3) convergent validity, in which two different approaches are used to measure the same object; and (4) discriminant validity, in which measures of different objects are compared for their expected differences.

KEY TERMS

Open-ended question (p. 284)
Unprobed format (p. 284)
Probed format (p. 285)
Response probe (p. 285)
Closed-ended question (p. 286)
Dichotomous closed-ended question (p. 286)
Multiple category closed-ended question (p. 286)
Scaled-response question (p. 287)
Unlabeled scaled-response format (p. 287)
Labeled scaled-response format (p. 287)
Measurement (p. 289)
Objective properties (p. 290)
Subjective properties (p. 290)
Scale development (p. 291)
Description (p. 291)
Order (p. 291)
Distance (p. 291)
Origin (p. 292)
Nominal scales (p. 293)
Ordinal scales (p. 293)
Interval scales (p. 293)
Ratio scales (p. 293)
Modified Likert scale (p. 297)
Life-style inventory (p. 298)
Semantic differential scale (p. 301)
Halo effect (p. 302)
Composite scales (p. 304)
Formative composite scale (p. 304)
Reflective composite scale (p. 304)
Reliability (p. 307)
Test–retest reliability (p. 308)
Equivalent forms reliability (p. 309)
Split-half reliability (p. 309)
Validity (p. 310)
Face validity (p. 311)
Predictive validity (p. 311)
Convergent validity (p. 312)
Discriminant validity (p. 312)

REVIEW QUESTIONS/APPLICATIONS

1. List each of the three basic question–response formats. Indicate the two variations for each one, and provide an example for each.
2. Identify at least four considerations that determine a question's format and indicate how each one would determine the format.
3. What is measurement? In your answer, differentiate an object from its properties, both objective and subjective.
4. Distinguish the four scale characteristics that determine the level of measurement with a scale.
5. Define the four types of scales and indicate the types of information contained in each.
6. Explain what is meant by a continuum along which a subjective property of an object can be measured.
7. What are the arguments for and against the inclusion of a neutral response position in a symmetric scale?
8. Distinguish among a modified Likert scale, a life-style scale, and a semantic differential scale.
9. What is the halo effect, and how does a researcher control for it?

10. How does reliability differ from validity? In your answer, define each term.

11. What are three methods of assessing reliability? What are three methods of assessing validity?

12. When should a researcher assess reliability and validity of a scale?

13. Mike, the owner of Mike's Market, which is a convenience store, is concerned about low sales. He reads in a marketing textbook that the image of a store often has an impact on its ability to attract its target market. He contacts the All-Right Research Company and commissions it to conduct a study that will shape his store's image. You are charged with the responsibility of developing the store image part of the questionnaire.

Design a semantic differential scale that will measure the relevant aspects of Mike's Market's image. In your work on this scale, you must do the following: (a) brainstorm the properties to be measured, (b) determine the appropriate bipolar adjectives, (c) decide on the number of scale points, and (d) indicate how the scale controls for the halo effect.

14. Each of the examples listed below involves a market researcher's need to measure some construct. Devise an appropriate scale for each one. Defend the scale in terms of its scaling assumptions, number of response categories, use or nonuse of a "no opinion" or neutral response category, and face validity.

- **a.** Mattel wants to know how preschool children react to a sing-along video game in which the child must sing along with an animated character and guess the next word in the song at various points in the video.
- **b.** TCBY is testing five new flavors of yogurt and wants to know how its customers rate each one on sweetness, flavor strength, and richness of taste.
- **c.** A pharmaceutical company wants to find out how much a new federal law eliminating dispensing of free sample prescription drugs by doctors will affect their intentions to prescribe generic versus brand-name drugs for their patients.

15. Harley-Davidson is the largest American motorcycle manufacturer, and it has been in business for several decades. Harley-Davidson has a clothing line, and it is expanding into other "signature" products such as shirts that prominently display the Harley-Davidson logo. Some people have a negative image of Harley Davidson because it was the motorcycle favored by the Hell's Angels and other motorcycle gangs. There are two research questions here. First, do consumers have a negative feeling toward Harley-Davidson, and, second, are they inclined toward the purchase of Harley-Davidson signature products such as shirts, belts, boots, jackets, sweatshirts, lighters, and key chains? Design a Likert measurement scale that can be used in a nationwide telephone study to address these two issues.

16. In conducting a survey for the Equitable Insurance Company, Burke Marketing Research assesses reliability by selecting a small group of respondents, calling them back, and readministering five questions to them. One question asks, "If you were going to buy life insurance sometime this year, how likely would you be to consider the Equitable Company?" Respondents indicate the likelihood on a probability scale (0% to 100% likely). Typically, this test–retest approach finds that respondents are within 10 percent of their initial response. That is, if a respondent indicated that he or she was 50 percent likely in the initial survey, he or she responded in the 45 percent to 55 percent range on the retest.

The survey has been going on for four weeks, and it has two more weeks before the data collection will be completed. Respondents who are retested are called back exactly one week after the initial survey. In the last week, reliability results have been very different. Now Burke is finding that the retest averages are 20 percent higher than the initial test. Has the scale become unreliable? If so, why has its previous good reliability changed? If not, what has happened, and how can Burke still claim that it has a reliable measure?

17. General Foods Corporation includes Post, which is the maker of Fruit and Fibre Cereal. The brand manager is interested in determining how much Fruit and Fibre consumers think it is helping them toward a healthier diet. But the manager is very concerned that respondents in a survey may not be entirely truthful about health matters. They may exaggerate what they really believe so they "sound" more health conscious than they really are, and they may say they have healthy diets when they really do not.

The General Foods Corporation marketing research director suggests a unique way to overcome the problem. He suggests that they conduct a survey of Fruit and Fibre customers in Pittsburgh, Atlanta, Dallas, and Denver. Fifty respondents who say that Fruit and Fibre is helping them toward a healthier diet and who also say they are more health conscious than the average American will be selected, and General Foods will offer to "buy" their groceries for the next month. To participate, the chosen respondents must submit their itemized weekly grocery trip receipts. By reviewing the items bought each week, General Foods can determine what they are eating and make judgments on how healthy their diets really are. What is your reaction to this approach? Will General Foods be able to assess the validity of its survey this way? Why or why not?

CASE 10.1

Fleetwood Manufactured Homes

Fleetwood is one of the largest manufacturers and marketers of manufactured homes in the United States. It enjoys about 20 percent market share, and it has benefited from steady growth of manufactured, or "mobile," homes for the past 20 years. Located in Riverside, California, the company was orginally a recreational vehicle manufacturer that saw an opportunity to move into the manufactured homes market during the 1970s, and the decision to branch into that business has served Fleetwood very well.

John Pulse, the vice president of Marketing, is concerned at this time, however, because competition is increasing and gaining inroads, and customers are becoming more sophisticated in their mobile home buying processes. John believes that a critical element of Fleetwood's success lies in the numerous independent retailers who represent Fleetwood to all potential buyers, and Pulse wants a marketing research study to determine the "ideal" manufactured homes retail business profile.

Prior research has identified three types of mobile home buyers: One type is young working-class families, typically tradespersons, who are buying their first home, and who have severe financial constraints. This segment is characterized primarily by high school or less education, two working parents, and both employed in blue-collar or low-level service occupations. The second segment comprises retirees or about-to-be-retirees who are moving into retirement communities. These communities are typically found in Sunbelt states such as

Florida and Arizona. The retirees are identified by their varied educational background (from less than high school to graduate degrees); accumulated "nest egg," such as a large annuity to live on and cash from sale of their last home with which to buy a mobile home; and a strong desire to live with others who are retired. The third segment is made up of recreationists who want to buy a mobile home as a "camp" or as a second home. These buyers are locating their mobile homes on lakes, rivers, close to the ocean or gulf, or somewhere close where they can pursue a strong avocation such as hunting, fishing, golfing, or snow skiing. This segment is characterized by the fact that most are in their prime earning years, young or middle-aged, and confident in their job or career circumstances.

Pulse and Fleetwood believe that the location of a manufactured home dealer determines to a great extent the market segment to which it caters, and the research needs to be tailored to that market segment clientele.

1. From a marketing research standpoint, translate the three manufactured home segments into their implications for measurement scales. For instance, what level of measurement is appropriate for each segment and why?
2. What would be the implications of the findings if the researchers opted to use (1) the modified Likert scale on how the retailer should have acted versus (2) a semantic differential scale on how the retailer did act?

CASE 10.2

Amos Brown Chevrolet of Reno

The Amos Brown Chevrolet dealership, located in Reno, Nevada, wanted to know how people who intended to buy a new American-made automobile in the next 12 months view their purchase. The owner, Amos Brown, called the marketing department at the University of Nevada–Reno and arranged for a class project to be taken on by Professor Thomas Clary's undergraduate marketing research students. Professor Clary had a large class that semester, so he decided to divide the project into two groups and to have each group compete against the other to see which one designed and executed the better survey.

Both groups worked diligently on the survey over the semester. They met with Mr. Brown, discussed the dealership with his managers, conducted focus groups, and consulted the literature on brand, store, and company image research. Both teams conducted telephone surveys, whose findings are presented in their final reports.

Professor Clary offered to grant extra credit to each team if it gave a formal presentation of its research design, findings, and recommendations.

1. Contrast the different ways these findings can be presented in graphical form to the Amos Brown Dealership management group. Which student team has the ability to present its findings more effectively? How and why?
2. What are the managerial implications apparent in each team's findings? Identify the implications and recommendations for Amos Brown Chevrolet as they are evident in each team's findings.

FINDINGS OF PROFESSOR CLARY'S MARKETING RESEARCH TEAMS

TEAM ONE'S FINDINGS FOR AMOS BROWN CHEVROLET

IMPORTANCE OF FEATURES OF DEALERSHIP IN DECIDING TO BUY THERE

FEATURE	PERCENT
Competitve prices	86%
No high pressure	75%
Good service facilities	73%
Low-cost financing	68%
Many models in stock	43%
Convenient location	35%
Friendly salespersons	32%

IMAGE OF AMOS BROWN CHEVROLET DEALERSHIP: PERCENT RESPONDING "YES"

Competitve prices	45%
No high pressure	32%
Good service facilities	80%
Low-cost financing	78%
Many models in stock	50%
Convenient location	81%
Friendly salespersons	20%

TEAM TWO'S FINDINGS FOR AMOS BROWN CHEVROLET

IMPORTANCE AND IMAGE OF AMOS BROWN CHEVROLET DEALERSHIP

FEATURE	IMPORTANCE[a]	RATING[b]
Competitive prices	6.5	1.3
No high pressure	6.2	3.6
Good service facilities	5.0	4.3
Low-cost financing	4.7	3.9
Many models in stock	3.1	3.0
Convenient location	2.2	4.1
Friendly salespersons	2.0	1.2

[a]Based on a seven-point scale where 1 = unimportant and 7 = extremely important.

[b]Based on a five-point scale where 1 = poor and 5 = excellent performance.

CHAPTER 11

Designing Data Collection Forms

LEARNING OBJECTIVES

- To appreciate the basic functions of a questionnaire
- To learn the basics of questionnaire organization
- To know the "shoulds" and "should nots" of phrasing questions
- To find out what should go into a cover letter or survey opener
- To understand the advantages of computer-assisted questionnaire design software
- To learn the basics of observation form design

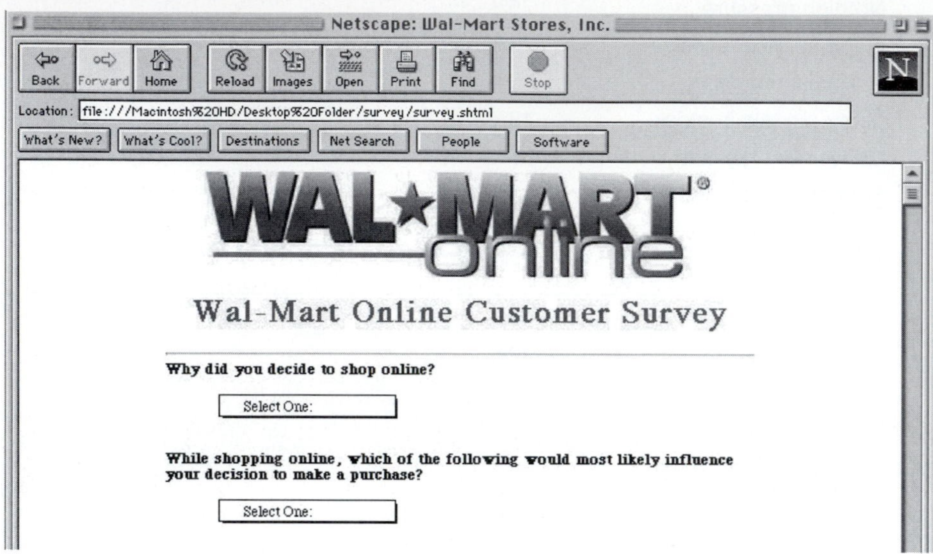

Some firms, such as Wal-Mart, are designing innovative questionnaires that can be answered by customers on the Internet.

PRACTITIONER VIEWPOINT

In many situations, the questionnaire is the key information-gathering tool. Unfortunately, even when a researcher has carefully designed a questionnaire to obtain the information sought by the client in a clear and unbiased manner, a lack of similar expertise on the part of the client often results in changes that may seriously jeopardize the results. This chapter provides an overview of not only the goal and strategy behind questionnaire design, but also the examples of specific questions and designs that aid in both the flow of the questionnaire and in the solicitation of respondent cooperation. Even if you do not believe that you will be designing questionnaires, this chapter should still be studied so you can evaluate the objectivity and value of test results depending upon the quality of the questionnaire used in the study.

— Lee Weinblatt
The PreTesting Company

Striving for Consistent Meaning

Although we hear that the world is getting smaller due to telecommunications, researchers must remember that the world is still made up of thousands of different subcultures. Designing a questionnaire to elicit responses from any group of people must take these subcultural differences into consideration. Even within subcultures, there are affinity groups, and these differences create headaches for market researchers. For instance, there are over 16 million Hispanic consumers in the continental United States representing over $100 billion in purchasing power. However, Hispanics comprise subgroups such as people of Cuban, Tex-Mex, Cal-Mex, and Puerto Rican descent. Although members of these groups speak Spanish, differences exist across the subgroups' language forms and idioms. Researchers must prepare questionnaires so that proper translation is made by all the Hispanic subgroups.[1]

Care in preparing questionnaires is especially important when dealing with international markets. Winston Churchill once noted of the United

1. Establish the need for marketing research
2. Define the problem
3. Establish research objectives
4. Determine research design
5. Identify information types and sources
6. Determine methods of accessing data
7. **Design data collection forms**
8. Determine sample plan and size
9. Collect data
10. Analyze data
11. Prepare and present the final research report

Isabel Valdés is President of Hispanic Market Connections in Los Altos, California. Her company specializes in providing client firms with information on the growing Hispanic market.

States and England that "We are two nations divided by a common language." Joel Axelrod of BRX/Global, Inc., a marketing research firm, sent a fax to his colleagues in France who were conducting a survey for a cosmetic manufacturer. Dr. Axelrod asked his French counterparts to interview 150 Caucasian women. The next day BRX/Global received a panicky phone call: How could they conceivably be expected to locate 150 women in Paris who were born and raised in the Caucusus?! Caucasians to the French are people from the Caucasus mountain system. This term for white is so commonly accepted that even when Dr. Axelrod described the situation to an American researcher, there was a blank look on the part of the listener as though to say that it was impossible for anybody to misunderstand his request. Conducting another study in Germany for this same manufacturer, it took BRX/Global three days to identify the precise translation in German for "pancake makeup." In an industrial study done in Italy, BRX/Global designed a questionnaire asking, in the English version, for comments about a certain brand of industrial seals. When they received the Italian translation and translated it back to English, seals had been converted to bee's wax.[2]

Striving for consistency of meaning among all respondents is a desirable goal in designing a questionnaire. The many cultures and languages of the world, however, make this a difficult task for marketing researchers.

In this chapter, we are concerned with designing the forms on which data will be recorded. This includes both questionnaires, which are used to ask respondents questions, as well as observation forms, which are designed to record the respondents' actions. You should be aware of the pitfalls in designing data collection instruments. The choice of questions, words, and even their order can be very influential in affecting how respondents react to a survey. You should have an appreciation of all of the preparation and thought that goes into the creation of the final version. For this reason, we describe the six functions of a questionnaire, and we introduce you to the questionnaire development process. We relate the "shoulds" and "should nots" of question development and indicate options for questionnaire organization. Last, we describe how a researcher goes about developing a form to be used in an observational study.

THE FUNCTIONS OF A QUESTIONNAIRE

The questionnaire serves six key functions.

A questionnaire serves six key functions. (1) It translates the research objective into specific questions that are asked of the respondents. (2) It standardizes those questions and the response categories so every participant responds to identical stimuli. (3) By its wording, question flow, and appearance, it fosters cooperation and keeps respondents motivated throughout the interview. (4) Questionnaires serve as permanent records of the research. (5) They speed up the process of data analysis. For instance, some companies use questionnaires that can be scanned by machines and quickly converted into raw data files. (6) They contain the information upon which reliability assessments such as test–retest or equivalent-form questions may be made, and they are used in follow-up validation of respondents' participation in the survey.

Scantron is an example of a company that provides questionnaire scanning services. See: http:/www.scantron.com/

Given that it serves all of these functions, the questionnaire is a very important element in the research process. In fact, research has shown that questionnaire design directly affects the quality of the data collected. Even experienced interviewers cannot compensate for questionnaire defects.[3] The time and effort invested in developing a good questionnaire are well spent. As you will soon learn, questionnaire development is a systematic process in which the researcher contemplates various question formats, considers a number of factors characterizing the survey at hand, and ultimately words the various questions very carefully. Questionnaire design is really a process that requires the researcher to go through a series of interrelated steps.

Good questionnaire design is essential to the high quality of a survey.

THE QUESTIONNAIRE DEVELOPMENT PROCESS

We now turn to a discussion of the steps a researcher goes through and how the questionnaire fits into this process. Figure 11.1 on page 324 offers a flow chart of the various phases in a typical marketing research survey. The first two steps have already been covered in this book. During the problem definition phase, the researcher and manager will have determined the survey objectives for the study, and the researcher knows the resources to be applied to the project plus any special circumstances or constraints involved (see chapter 4). The primary data collection method will be agreed on in the early stages of this process (see chapter 9). Questionnaire design begins, as shown by the interior outlined box in Figure 11.1, after these issues are resolved. Also, we considered basic question response formats in chapter 10.

A questionnaire will ordinarily go through a series of drafts before it is in acceptable final form. In fact, even before the first question is constructed, the researcher mentally reviews alternative question formats to decide which ones are best suited to the survey's respondents and circumstances. As the questionnaire begins to take shape, the researcher continually evaluates each question and its response options for face validity. Changes are made, and the question's wording is reevaluated to make sure that it is asking what the researcher intends. Also, the researcher strives to minimize **question bias,** defined as the ability of a question's wording or format to influence respondents' answers.[4]

Questionnaire development is an iterative process.

Questions must be designed with minimum bias so they will not influence respondents' answers.

We will describe aspects of this iterative process in more detail in succeeding sections of this chapter. For now, it is important only that you realize that with a custom-designed research study, the questions on the questionnaire, along with its instructions, introduction, and general layout, are systematically evaluated for potential error and revised accordingly. Generally, this evaluation takes place at the researcher's end, and the client will not be involved until after the questionnaire has undergone considerable development and evaluation by the researcher.

The client is given the opportunity to comment on the questionnaire during the client approval step, in which the client reviews the questionnaire and agrees that it covers all of the appropriate issues. This step is essential, and some research companies require the client to sign or initial a copy of the

Client review ensures that the questionnaire covers all of the appropriate issues.

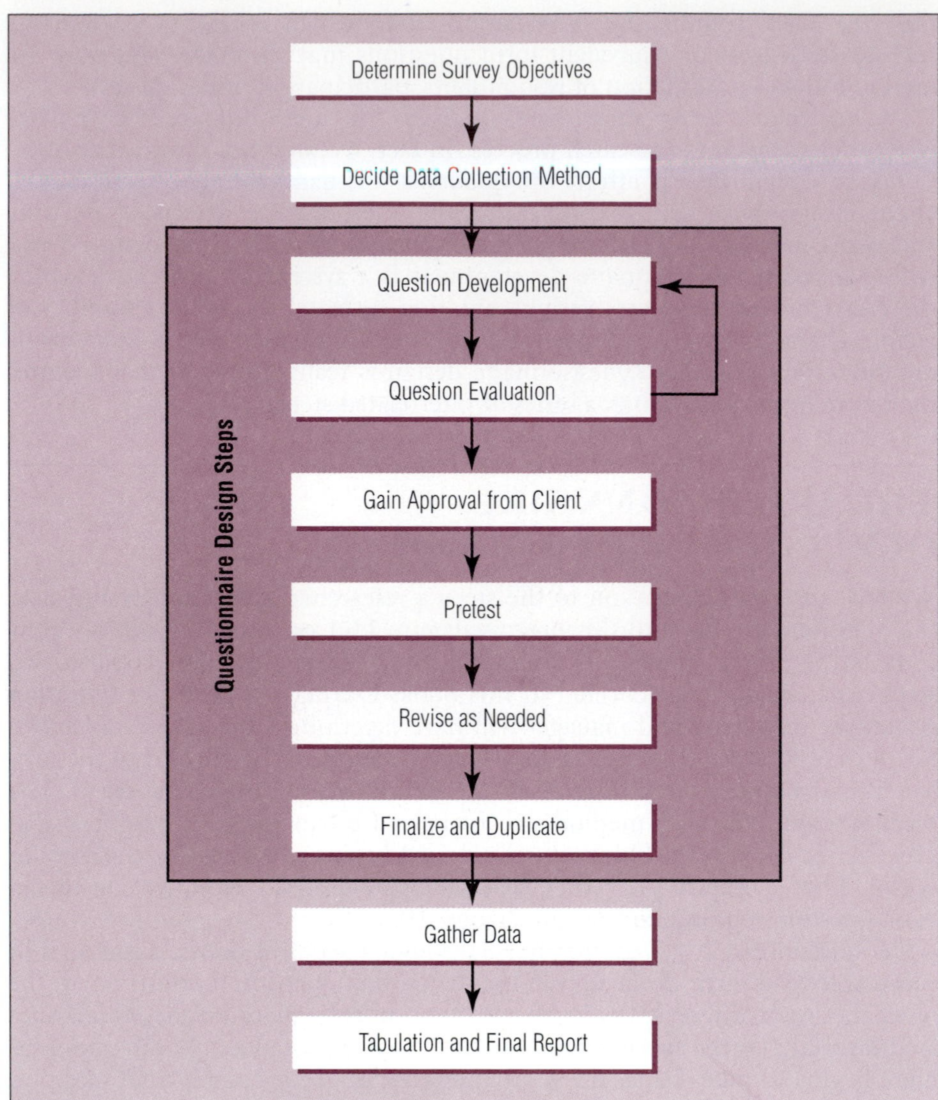

Figure 11.1

Steps in the Questionnaire Development Process

questionnaire as verification of approval. There are several good reasons for client approval of a proposed questionnaire. First, it serves as a check that the researcher is still in tune with the survey's objectives. The client may not appreciate all of the technical aspects of questionnaire design, but he or she is vitally concerned with the survey's objectives, and he or she can comment on the degree to which the questions on the questionnaire appear to address these objectives. Second, client approval ensures that the client will be apprised of the survey's progress. Third, approval and the initialed questionnaire ensure that the researcher is protected against the remote possibility that the manager will claim that the questions were incomplete or done incorrectly after the findings are revealed.

Following client approval, the questionnaire normally undergoes a pretest, which is an actual field test using a very limited sample to reveal any difficulties that might still lurk in wording, instructions, administration, and so on. We describe pretesting more fully later in this chapter.[5] Revisions are made based on the pretest results, and the questionnaire is finalized.

DEVELOPING QUESTIONS

Developing a question's precise wording is not easy. We have claimed that developing questions for a questionnaire is an art. But just as there is good art and bad art, there are good questions and bad questions. In developing any question, the ultimate goal is to devise a way to tap the person's true response without influencing him or her either overtly or subtly. Compounding this problem is the fact that the researcher will have only one chance to accomplish this goal, so the wording of each question is critical.

Unfortunately, there is far greater potential to generate unreliable or inaccurate responses than we care to admit.[6] Table 11.1, on pages 326–329, illustrates how certain words cause problems in questionnaires.

As we noted earlier, question bias occurs when the phrasing of a question influences a respondent to answer unreliably or with other than perfect accuracy. Ideally, every question should be examined and tested according to a number of crucial factors known to be related to question bias. For convenience, we discuss these factors as "shoulds" and "should nots."[7] A summary can be found in Table 11.2 on page 330.

Question wording should be scrutinized for bias or undue influence on respondents' answers.

The Five "Shoulds" of Question Wording

There are five "shoulds" of question wording: (1) The question should be focused on a single issue or topic; (2) the question should be brief; (3) the question should be interpreted the same way by all respondents; (4) the question should use the respondent's core vocabulary; and (5) the question should be a grammatically simple sentence if possible. A discussion of these "shoulds" follows.

The Question Should Be Focused on a Single Issue or Topic

The researcher must stay focused on the specific issue or topic. For example, take the question, "What type of hotel do you usually stay in when on a trip?" The focus of this question is hazy because it does not narrow down the *type* of trip or *when* the hotel is being used. For example, is it a business or a pleasure trip? Is the hotel at a place en route or at the final destination? A more focused version is, "When you are on a family vacation and stay in a hotel at your destination, what type of hotel do you typically use?" As a second example, consider how "unfocused" the following question is: "When do you typically go to work?" Does this mean when do you leave home for work or when do you actually begin work once at your workplace? A better question would be, "At what time do you ordinarily leave home for work?"

Sharply focused questions are desirable.

The Question Should Be Brief

Unnecessary and redundant words should always be eliminated, regardless of the data collection mode. This requirement is especially important when designing questions that will be administered verbally, such as over the telephone. Brevity will help the respondent to comprehend the central question and reduce the dis-

Brief questions are desirable.

TABLE 11.1

Problem Words in Questionnaire Design

PROBLEM WORD	REASON FOR DIFFICULTY
All	A "dead giveaway" word. Some people have a negative reaction to opinion questions that hinge on all-inclusive or all-exclusive words. They may be generally in agreement with a proposition, but nevertheless hesitate to accept the extreme idea of *all, always, each, every, never, nobody, only, none,* or *sure.* *Would you say that all cats have four legs?* *Is the mayor doing all he can for the city?* It is correct, of course, to use an all-inclusive word if it correctly states the alternative. But you will usually find that such a word produces an overstatement.
Always	Another dead giveaway word. *Do you always observe traffic signs?* *Is your boss always friendly?*
America, American	Be careful of two things with words like these. First, they may be heavily loaded emotional concepts. Answers may be given in terms of patriotism instead of the issue at hand. Second, these are very indefinite words referring to whole continents or parts of continents, to Native Americans, or even to that sometimes misused phrase—100% Americans.
Any	The trouble with "any" is that it may mean "every," "some," or "one only" in the same sentence or question, depending on the way you look at it. Another difficulty with "any" is that when used in either the "every" or the "not any" context it becomes as much a dead giveaway word as are "every" and "none."
Anybody	Words with the "any" root are subject to the same trouble as "any" itself. "Anybody" can mean everybody or some one person. *Do you think that anybody could do this job?* "Sure, it's so simple that anyone could do it." "Yes, probably Superman could."
Bad	Experience indicates that people are generally less willing to criticize than they are to praise. Because it is difficult to get them to state their negative views, sometimes the critical side needs to be softened. For example, after asking, *What things are good about your job?,* we may be wise not to apply the "bad" stigma but to ask, *What things are not so good about it?*
Best	This is a dead giveaway word. Few people do the *best* they can, for example.
Could	It should not be confused with "should" or "might." "Could" means that something *can* be done.
Country	What is meant by this word—the nation as a whole, or rural areas?
Daily	Which is intended—five days a week, or all seven?
Dinner	Dinner, the main meal of the day, comes at noon for some families whereas in some areas, it is the evening meal. The question should not assume that it is either the one or the other.
Ever	Tends to be a dead giveaway. "Ever" is such a long time and so inclusive that it makes it seem likely that something may have happened during the time period of "ever." *Have you ever seen Seinfeld?* "Yes—I suppose I must have at some time or other."

PROBLEM WORD	REASON FOR DIFFICULTY
Every	Another dead giveaway. Putting forth *every* effort is pretty extreme, for example.
Everybody	Another dead giveaway. "Everybody" includes billions of people.
Everything	Another dead giveaway.
Fair	When used in the sense of "just" or "reasonable" it can be taken to mean "average."
Few	We cannot assume that this word has definite limits. One person's few is another's several.
Government	It is sometimes used as a definite word meaning the U.S. federal government; sometimes as an inclusive term for federal, state, and local government, sometimes as an abstract idea; and sometimes as the party in power as distinct from the opposition party. The trouble is that the respondent does not always know which "government" is meant.
It, Its	These words necessarily refer to some antecedent, and it is best to repeat the full antecedent except where it is unmistakably clear.
Just	A word with conflicting meanings. "Just as much," for example, may mean "only" as much or "fully" as much.
Know	Knowing varies greatly in degree, from mere recognition to full information. Some respondents may hesitate to say they know something when they don't know it for sure or completely. A person may know a song without knowing the words.
Less	This word is usually used as an alternative to "more," where it may cause a minor problem. The phrase "more or less" has a special meaning all its own in which some respondents do not see an alternative. Thus, they may simply answer "yes, more or less" to a question such as *Compared with a year ago, are you more or less happy in your job?* The solution to this problem is to break up the "more or less" expression by introducing an extra word or so or to reverse the two: *Compared with a year ago, are you more happy or less happy in your job?* *Compared with a year ago, are you less or more happy in your job?*
Like	This word is a problem only because it is sometimes used to introduce an example. The problem with bringing an example into a question is that the respondent's attention may be directed toward the particular example and away from the general issue it is meant to illustrate. The choice of an example can affect the answers to the question—in fact, it may materially change the question, as in these two examples: *Do you think that leafy vegetables like spinach should be in the daily diet?* *Do you think that leafy vegetables like lettuce should be in the daily diet?* Because many people do not like spinach, they would answer "no" to the first question.
Might	Do not think of this as synonymous with "could" or "should." Whereas "could" refers to whether something *can* be done, "might" refers to a *probability* that something *will* be done.
More	This word has more or less been discussed under the word "less." It is a problem for another reason also: When "more" is used in the comparative sense, it is usually advisable to indicate the basis for comparison—more than what? *Are you finding question wording more complicated?*
Most	This word can introduce tricky double thoughts as shown by this question: *Where would you be doing the most useful work?* Which is meant—the most work that is useful or work that is the most useful?

(continued)

TABLE 11.1 (continued)

Problem Words in Questionnaire Design

PROBLEM WORD	REASON FOR DIFFICULTY
Much	"Much" is an indefinite word. The "how much" type of question leads to unnecessarily wide variations in response—questions should be worded such that it is clear that the responses are expressed in specific terms of dollars, doughnuts, percents, fractions, and other measures.
Never	A dead giveaway word.
Nobody	This is yet another dead giveaway word. Nobody can use "nobody" with impunity.
None	This also can be a dead giveaway word.
Now	For a word that appears reasonably clear, "now" can be almost too definite in the sense of "right this minute," leading to situations like this: *What kind of work are you doing now?* "I'm answering foolish questions."
Own	This definite-sounding word is not always so definite. Some homeowners think that they will not own their homes until they pay off the mortgage. Some stockholders have no feeling of owning part of their company.
Possible	An alternative that uses "possible" in the ultimate sense ("as much as possible") is a dead giveaway.
Quite	This word is quite frequently misused. "Quite a little," for example, has no sensible meaning. If in a question the word "entirely" can be substituted for "quite" without changing the meaning, then "quite" is being properly used. However, in such proper use, "quite" may become a dead giveaway word.
Saw, See, Seen	These words are sometimes used in the sense of visiting someone, but they may be interpreted literally. *When did you see your dentist last?* "Yesterday, on the golf course."
Service	Here is another indefinite word. Try, for example, to put down exactly what you mean when you speak of the "service" of the electric utility company.
Should	This is one of the three words that should not, could not, might not be used as though synonymous.
Such	Beware of this word because it is often used to introduce examples. When we discussed "like" we pointed out that the particular example may supplant the general issue in the minds of respondents. "Would you use such a product to clean your carpet?" may deflect the respondent's attention from *this* product to another one.
That, These, This, Those	These are antecedent words. Do not use them except when you are reasonably sure that their antecedents are clear.
Today	This may be interpreted too literally, just as "now" may be. *Are farmers getting a fair price for milk today?* "Do you mean right today? You know the price dropped this morning."
Trip	This word needs to be qualified—"one-way trip" or "round-trip," for example.

PROBLEM WORD	REASON FOR DIFFICULTY
Where	The frames of reference in answers to a "where" question may vary greatly. *Where did you read that?* "In the *New York Times*." "At home in front of the fire." "In an advertisement."
You	In most questions, "you" gives no trouble whatever. However, the word may sometimes have a collective meaning as in a question asked of computer repairpersons: *How many computers did you repair last month?* This question seemed to work all right until one repairperson in a large shop countered with, "Who do you mean, me or the whole shop?" Sometimes "you" needs the emphasis of "you yourself," and sometimes it just isn't the right word to use, as in the aforementioned situation.

Source: Adapted from Stanley L. Payne, *The Art of Asking Questions,* First printing, 1951, Princeton University Press. These examples were taken from the 1980 edition, chapter 10. By permission of Princeton University Press.

traction of wordiness. Here is a question that suffers from a lack of brevity: "What are the considerations that would come to your mind while you are confronted with the decision to have some type of repair done on the automatic icemaker in your refrigerator assuming that you noticed it was not making ice cubes as well as it did when you first bought it?" A better, brief form would be, "If your icemaker were not working right, how would you correct the problem?"

The Question Should Be Interpreted the Same Way by All Respondents

Questions should be clear.

All respondents should "see" the question identically. For example, the question, "How many children do you have?," might be interpreted in various ways. One respondent might think of only those children living at home, whereas another might include children from a previous marriage. A better question is, "How many children under the age of 18 live with you in your home?"

The Question Should Use the Respondent's Core Vocabulary

The question should be worded in respondents' everyday vocabulary.

The core vocabulary is the everyday language respondents use to converse with others like themselves, but it does not include slang or jargon. Obviously, if a question includes words with which some but not all respondents are familiar, these words are a potential source of error for those who do not interpret them properly. Sometimes, the technical aspects of a product or marketing activity will slip into a question and violate the rule of using core vocabulary. For instance, "Did the premiums offered by the store attract you to it?," assumes that respondents know what premiums are and can relate them to being attracted to the store. So a better question would be, "Was the offer of a free gift a reason for your last visit to The Village clothing store?"

The Question Should Be a Grammatically Simple Sentence if Possible

Grammatically simple questions are desirable.

A simple sentence is preferred because it has only a single subject and predicate, whereas compound and complex sentences are busy with multiple subjects, predicates, objects, and complements. The more complex the sentence, the greater the potential for respondent error. There are more conditions to remember, and more information to consider simultaneously, so the respondent's attention may wane or he or she may concentrate on only one part of the question. To avoid these problems, the researcher should strive to use only simple sentence structure—even if two separate sentences are necessary to communicate the essence of the question. Take the question, "If you were looking for an automobile that would be used by the head of your household who is primarily responsible for driving your children to and from school, music lessons, and friends' houses, how much would you and your spouse discuss the safety features of one of the cars you took for a test drive?" A simple approach is, "Would you and your spouse discuss the safety features of a family car?" followed by (if yes), "Would you discuss safety 'very little,' 'some,' 'a good deal,' or 'to a great extent'?"

The Eleven "Should Nots" of Question Wording

There are more "should nots" than "shoulds" in question construction. In fact, there are 11. They are listed under "Errors to Avoid When Developing Questions" in Table 11.2. A discussion of these "should nots" follows.

TABLE 11.2

Shoulds and Should Nots Regarding Question Development

FIVE DESIRABLE QUALITIES OF QUESTION WORDING

1. The question should be focused on a single issue or topic.
2. The question should be brief.
3. The question should be interpreted the same way by all respondents.
4. The question should use the respondent's core vocabulary.
5. The question should be a grammatically simple sentence if possible.

ERRORS TO AVOID WHEN DEVELOPING QUESTIONS

1. The question should not assume criteria that are not obvious.
2. The question should not be beyond the respondent's ability or experience.
3. The question should not use a specific example to represent a general case.
4. The question should not ask the respondent to recall specifics when only generalities will be remembered.
5. The question should not require the respondent to guess a generalization.
6. The question should not ask for details that cannot be related.
7. The question should not use words that overstate the condition.
8. The question should not have ambiguous wording.
9. The question should not be "double-barreled."
10. The question should not lead the respondent to a particular answer.
11. The question should not have "loaded" wording or phrasing.

The Question Should Not Assume Criteria That Are Not Obvious

A question that implies that the respondent should always answer for people in general is undesirable.

Questions frequently require respondents to make judgments, and judgment assumes that certain criteria are being applied. But sometimes the criteria on which the judgments are to be made are not obvious, and a danger exists in respondents' using criteria different from those assumed by the question designer. A frequently omitted criterion is the respondent's frame of reference. The question, "How important do you think it is for a Circle K convenience store to have a well-lighted parking lot?" has the potential for respondents to think in terms of the needs of others rather than their own. Perhaps a respondent never goes to a Circle K after dark, but he or she thinks that those who do should have good lighting. The better approach is to phrase the question as, "How important is it for you that a Circle K store has a lighted parking lot?"

The Question Should Not Be Beyond the Respondent's Ability or Experience

A question transcending the respondent's experience is undesirable.

Questions should not transcend the respondent's experience. For example, it makes little sense to ask teenagers what type of family automobile they will purchase when they are married, just as it makes little sense to ask their parents about whether their teenagers would drink nonalcoholic beer at a party. Teenagers cannot predict this purchase decision accurately because they are not (usually) married and are unlikely to have bought a new automobile, and the conditions for a family automobile purchase are unknown. Similarly, most parents do not know what goes on at teenagers' parties, so their answers would be guesses at best.

The Question Should Not Use a Specific Example to Represent a General Case

Questions using a specific example to represent a general case or class are undesirable.

The danger in using a specific example to measure a broader situation lies in the possibility that the respondent will concentrate only on that example. The question, "Do you recall any advertising for Sears in the last week such as the inserts that are sometimes placed in your newspaper?" will cause some respondents to concentrate only on the newspaper inserts, but the intent of the question is to ask about all advertising. A better version is, "Did you notice any newspaper, television, radio, or mailed advertising for Sears in the last week?" See the word "like" in Table 11.1 on page 327.

The Question Should Not Ask the Respondent to Recall Specifics When Only Generalities Will Be Remembered

Questions that ask the respondent to recall specifics when only generalities will be remembered are undesirable.

Sometimes a question designer forgets that people do not have perfect memory, and the detail requested in the question is beyond the respondent's abilities to reconstruct what actually happened. For instance, "How much was the price per gallon of gasoline when you last bought some at a convenience store?" certainly will require some respondents to think back several months, and it is very unlikely that they will recall the exact price per gallon. A more appropriate way to ask this question is to tap the generalities that the respondent will remember. For example, "The last time you bought gasoline at a convenience store, do you recall it costing more, less, or about the same per gallon as at a gasoline station?"[8]

The Question Should Not Require the Respondent to Guess a Generalization

Questions that make respondents guess are undesirable.

When asked to respond to a question involving a generality, respondents may be inclined to respond with what they think "must" have happened or what "should" happen. This encourages guessing. Although guesses may be accurate, they are more likely to be inaccurate. Consider these two examples: "When you buy fresh fish at the supermarket, do you worry about its freshness?" and "If you bought a new 35-millimeter automatic focus camera at a catalog showroom store, would you ask the store clerk about its warranty?" Both of these encourage the respondent to answer in the affirmative by tapping into generalizations. One generalization is that freshness is virtually always assessed when buying seafood, and the other is that a common concern of buyers of expensive cameras should be the warranty. A strategy for avoiding the generalization factor is to require specificity from the respondent. For instance, with the fresh fish example, the question might be posed as, "In the last five times you bought fresh fish at the supermarket, how many times did you worry about its freshness?" For the camera question, it would be advantageous to use a likelihood scale: "Would you be 'unlikely,' 'somewhat likely,' 'likely,' or 'extremely likely' to ask the clerk about the camera's warranty?"

The Question Should Not Ask for Details That Cannot Be Related

Questions asking respondents to recall minor details are undesirable.

Marketers sometimes ask for information that is impossible to remember, forgetting that consumers have more important things to worry about than consumption. If Sunbeam Bread were interested in knowing whether Sunbeam customers compare prices with other brands, a question might be developed as follows, "How many and what brands of bread did you compare to Sunbeam before deciding to buy Sunbeam?" Few respondents will be able to supply this detailed information accurately. Probably the only accurate information Sunbeam could obtain is whether respondents recall comparing prices, so the question should be phrased, "Do you recall comparing the price of Sunbeam with another brand of bread before deciding to buy Sunbeam?"

The Question Should Not Use Words That Overstate the Condition

Questions with overstatement in them are undesirable.

Avoid using words that overstate conditions. It is better to present the question in a neutral tone rather than in a positive or a negative tone. Here is an example that might be found in a survey conducted for Ray-Ban sunglasses. An overstated question might ask, "How much do you think you would pay for a pair of sunglasses that will protect your eyes from the sun's harmful ultraviolet rays, which are known to cause blindness?" As you can see, the overstatement concerns the effects of ultraviolet rays, and because of this overstatement, respondents will be compelled to think about how much they would pay for something that can prevent their blindness and not about how much they would pay for the sunglasses. A more toned-down and acceptable question wording would be, "How much would you pay for sunglasses that will protect your eyes from the sun's rays?"

The Question Should Not Have Ambiguous Wording

Ambiguous questions are undesirable.

Ambiguity in wording allows respondents to apply their own situations, experiences, or interpretations to them. Two forms of ambiguous wording can occur: First, the question designer might use a word that has several legitimate connotations for any one respondent. For example, a Society for the Prevention of

Cruelty to Animals survey may ask, "When your puppy has an accident, do you discipline it?" There are two ambiguous words in this question. An "accident" could mean urinating on the floor, or spilling water out of the feeding dish, or any number of different mishaps. The definition of "discipline" is vague, and as you can imagine, the nature and severity of canine discipline can vary greatly. A series of questions would be needed to reduce the ambiguity by specifying the types of accidents and nature of the discipline applied. Second, the question designer might inadvertently select a word that has different interpretations for different subgroups of respondents. For example, ambiguous questions are evident in regional differences in the use of words. Let's say Oscar Mayer wants to perform a survey on the use of meats in sandwiches. A type of sandwich that is called a "grinder" in New England is referred to as a "submarine," a "hero," "hoagie," or a "poor boy" in other parts of the United States. New Englanders cannot relate to a "poor boy" any more than someone living in New Orleans can relate to a "grinder." Obviously, Oscar Mayer would need to be concerned about the regional ambiguity of these words.

The Question Should Not Be "Double-Barreled"

A **"double-barreled" question** is really two different questions posed in one question. With two questions posed together, it is difficult for a respondent to answer either one directly. Here is an example for a Toys-Я-Us survey. "Did you know that Toys-Я-Us sells mainly educational toys, and it is the only American toy retailer selling toys in Japan?" The first question concerns the educational aspects of these toys, whereas the second concerns the international nature of the company. Double-barreled questions are improved by either breaking them into two separate questions, or by specifying one question as a condition of the other. For instance, "Did you know that Toys-Я-Us is the only American toy retailer in Japan?" and "Did you know these toys are primarily educational?" could be used.

Double-barreled questions, which ask two questions at once, are undesirable.

The Question Should Not Lead the Respondent to a Particular Answer

A **leading question** is worded in such a way as to give the respondent a clue as to how to answer. Therefore, they bias responses. Consider the question used by Alreck and Settle to illustrate a leading question: "Don't you see some danger in the new policy?"[9] Obviously, the respondent is led to expect that there are dangers in the new policy and, therefore, will likely respond with some of these dangers. Rephrasing the question as "Do you see any danger in the new policy?" is a much more objective request of the respondent. Here the respondent is free—that is, not led—to respond "yes" or "no."

Questions that lead respondents to answer a certain way are undesirable.

The Question Should Not Have "Loaded" Wording or Phrasing

Leading questions direct the respondent to answer in a predetermined way. By contrast, a **loaded question** is more subtle. Identifying this type of bias in a question requires more judgment, because a loaded question has buried in its wording elements that allude to universal beliefs or rules of behavior. It may even apply emotionalism or touch on a person's inner fears. For example, a company marketing mace for personal use may use the question, "Should people be allowed to protect themselves from harm by using mace as self-defense?" Obviously, most respondents will agree with the need to protect oneself from harm, and self-defense is an acceptable and well-known legal defense. Eliminating the loaded aspect of this question would result in the

Loaded questions, which use subtle emotional appeals or prey on respondents' inner fears, are undesirable.

Marketing Research Insight 11.1

The Science of Wording Questions to Create Intentional Bias!

A young monk was once rebuffed by his superior when he asked if he could smoke while he prayed. Ask a different question, a friend advised. Ask if you can pray while you smoke.

The Wall Street Journal *reporter and editor, Cynthia Crossen, believes that many surveys are conducted simply to further the interests of their sponsors. By carefully wording questions, enough bias is introduced so that survey results may be predetermined . . . always supporting the sponsor's interest. Consider the following examples Ms. Crossen provides:*

If you are conducting a survey, consider the impact of the following word choices on how you might respond to a survey question:

. . . The legislation would generate more revenue . . .	*vs.*	*. . . The legislation would generate more taxes . . .*
Are you in favor of the MX missle?	*vs.*	*Are you in favor of the Peacekeeper?*
Are you in favor of abortion?	*vs.*	*Are you in favor of Pro-Choice?*
Are you in favor of welfare?	*vs.*	*Are you in favor of public assistance?*
Are you in favor of a Department of War?	*vs.*	*Are you in favor of a Department of Defense?*
Should the president have the line item veto to prevent waste?	*vs.*	*Should the president have the line item veto, or not?*

Consider this question in a mail survey sponsored by Greenpeace, the environmental guerrilla group:

"Depletion of the earth's protective ozone layer leads to skin cancers and numerous other health and environmental problems. Do you support Greenpeace's demand that DuPont, the world's largest producer of ozone-destroying chemicals, stop making unneeded ozone-destroying chemicals immediately?"

A representative from Connecticut presented a survey on his constituent's views of universal versus private health care. His survey results were based upon the following question: "Would you support universal health care if it would mean the loss of thousands of jobs, particularly in Connecticut?"

How we select the wording for our questions has a great deal to do with how people will respond to our questions. Good research should be based on questions that are clear and unbiased.

Source: *Cynthia Crossen,* Tainted Truth: The Manipulation of Fact in America *(New York: Simon & Schuster, 1994). By permission.*

question, "Do you think carrying a mace product is acceptable for people who are worried about being attacked?" Marketing Research Insight 11.1 illustrates how questions may be worded to intentionally bias results.

As you can see, the phrasing of each question should be examined almost microscopically to guard against the various sources of question bias error. Seasoned researchers develop a sixth sense about the pitfalls we have just described; however, because the researcher can become caught up in the research process, slips do occur. This danger explains why many researchers use "experts" to review drafts of their questionnaires. For example, it is common for the questionnaire to be designed by one employee of the research company and then given to another employee who understands questionnaire design for a thorough inspection for question bias as well as face validity.

QUESTIONNAIRE ORGANIZATION

The Introduction

The introduction is very important in questionnaire design. The **introduction** serves five functions:

The introduction serves five functions.

1. Identification of the surveyor/sponsor
2. Purpose of the survey
3. Explanation of respondent selection
4. Request for participation/provide incentive
5. Screening of respondent

If the introduction is written to accompany a mail survey, it is normally referred to as a **cover letter.** If the introduction is to be verbally presented to a potential respondent, as in the case of a personal interview, it may be referred to as the **opening comments.** Of course, each survey and its target respondent group is unique, so a researcher cannot use a standardized introduction. In this section, we discuss the five functions to be provided by the introduction.

Sometimes the sponsor of a survey is disguised.

First, it is not only common courtesy, but it is also expected that you will introduce yourself at the beginning of a conversation. Some research companies opt for the direct approach with a statement such as, "Hello, my name is ______, and I am a telephone interviewer working with Nationwide Opinion Research Company here in Milwaukee. I am not selling anything." Here, the researcher has identified himself or herself and the prospective respondent has been made aware that this is a bona fide survey and not a sales pitch. Additionally, the "sponsor" of the survey should be identified. There are two options with respect to sponsor identity. The sponsor may be "undisguised" or "disguised." With an **undisguised survey,** the sponsoring company is identified, but with a **disguised survey,** the sponsor's name is not divulged to respondents. The choice of which approach to take rests with the survey's objectives or with the researcher and client who agree whether disclosure of the sponsor's name or true intent can in some way influence respondents' answers. Another reason for disguise is to prevent alerting competitors to the survey.

The purpose of the survey should be described clearly and simply.

Second, the purpose of the survey should be described clearly and simply. In a cover letter, the purpose may be expressed in one or two sentences: "We are conducting a survey on personal computer presentation graphics packages used by successful executives such as yourself." Note that respondents aren't interested in the specific purposes of the survey. Rather, they are interested in knowing the subject you will address as you ask them questions. Consider a bank having a survey conducted by a marketing research firm. The actual purpose of the survey is to determine the bank's image relative to that of its competitors. However, the research firm need only say "We are conducting a survey on customers' perceptions of financial institutions in this area." This satisfies the respondent and does not divulge the name of the bank. Also, it doesn't bore the prospective respondent with details of the actual purpose of the survey.

Respondents should be told how they were selected.

Third, prospective respondents must be made aware of how and why they were selected. Just a short sentence to answer the repondent's question of "Why me?" will suffice. Telling them that they were "selected at random" usually is sufficient. Of course, you should be ethical and tell them the actual method that was used. If their selection wasn't random, you should inform them as to which method was used.

Ask for participation.

Fourth, you must ask for their participation. "Will you please take five minutes to complete the attached questionnaire and mail it back to us in the postage-paid, preaddressed envelope provided?" If you are conducting a personal interview or a telephone interview, you might say something like "I would now like to ask you a few questions about your experiences with automotive repair shops. OK?" You should be as brief as possible yet let the respondent know that you are getting ready for him or her to participate by answering questions. This is also the appropriate time to say something that will reduce the probability that the respondent will refuse to participate in the survey. There are various incentives that may be used by the researcher to encourage participation. Offering a monetary incentive, a sample of a product, or a copy of study results are examples. A more complete list is found in chapter 14, which deals with nonresponse error and how it can be minimized. Other incentives encourage respondent participation by letting them know the importance of their participation: "You are one of a select few, randomly chosen, to express your views on how the proposed tax increase should be spent." Or the topic itself can be highlighted for importance: "It is important that the people let our elected representatives know their wishes."

Incentives may be used to encourage participation.

Other forms of incentives address respondent anxieties concerning privacy. Here again, there are methods that tend to reduce these anxieties and, therefore, increase participation. The first is **anonymity,** in which the respondent is assured that neither the respondent's name nor any identifying designation will be associated with his or her responses. The second method is **confidentiality,** which means that the respondent's name is known by the researcher, but it is not divulged to a third party, namely the client. Anonymous surveys are most appropriate in data collection modes where the respondent responds directly on the questionnaire. Any self-administered survey qualifies for anonymity as long as the respondent does not indicate his or her identity and provided the questionnaire does not have any covert identification tracing mechanism. However, when an interviewer is present, appointments and/or call-backs are usually necessary, so there typically is an explicit designation of the respondent's name, address, telephone number, and so forth on the questionnaire. In this case, confidentiality may be required. Often, questionnaires have a call-back notation area for the interviewer to make notes indicating, for instance, whether the phone is busy, the respondent is not at home, or a time at which to call back when the respondent will be available. Here, the respondent will ordinarily be assured of confidentiality, and it is vital that the researcher guard against the loss of that confidentiality.

Respondents are screened for their appropriateness to take part in the survey.

Fifth, respondents are screened for their appropriateness to take part in the survey. Whether you screen respondents depends on the research objectives. If the survey's objective is to determine the factors used by consumers to select an automobile dealer for the purpose of purchasing a new car, you may want to screen out those who have never purchased a new car or those who have not purchased a new car within the last, say, two years. "Have you purchased a new car within the last two years?" For all those who answer "no," the survey is terminated with a polite "Thank you for your time." Some would argue that you should put the screening question early on so as to not waste the time of the researcher or the respondent. This should be considered with each survey. We place it here as last because we have found it awkward to begin a conversation with a prospective respondent without first taking care of the first four items we just discussed.

The creation of the introduction of a questionnaire requires great care in its design.

As you can see, the creation of the introduction should entail just as much care and effort as the development of the questions on the questionnaire. The first words heard or read by the prospective respondent will largely determine whether he or she will take part in the survey. It makes sense, therefore, for the researcher to labor over a cover letter or opening until it has a maximum chance of eliciting the respondent's cooperation to take part in the survey. If the researcher is unsuccessful in persuading prospective respondents to take part in the survey, all of his or her work on the questionnaire itself will have been in vain. Marketing Research Insight 11.2 on page 338 shows a cover letter used by Burke Marketing Research. In this study, telephone calls were first made to solicit participation to a mail survey. This technique has been shown to increase the response rate. Also, notice the strong incentives used by Burke, their explicit instructions, and the provision of an 800 number should the respondents have any questions.

Typical Question Sequence

A questionnaire starts out with screening and warm-up questions.

Each research objective gives rise to a question or a set of questions. As a result, questions are usually developed on an objective-by-objective basis. However, to facilitate the questioning process, the organization of these sets of questions should follow some understandable logic. A commonly seen sequence of questions found in questionnaires is presented in Table 11.3 (page 339). As we discussed in the previous section, the first few questions are normally **screening questions,** which will determine whether the potential respondent qualifies to participate in the survey based on certain selection criteria that the researcher has deemed essential.[10] For instance, if a mall-intercept approach is used in a survey being conducted for Arm & Hammer baking soda, screening questions might be used to qualify respondents who buy the

MARKETING RESEARCH INSIGHT 11.2

Cover Letters Provide Several Functions

In the cover letter shown here, Burke Marketing Research provides additional information and an incentive to encourage response. If a research project is very important, research firms will go to great lengths to increase the response rate. In this example, Burke has used a method referred to as "prenotification." Potential respondents were called and told about a forthcoming survey and were provided with a description of the incentive to participate in the survey. What you see here is the cover letter that arrived at the respondent's home a few days later. Notice that the respondent is reminded that he or she had a phone conversation with Burke. Also, notice that the $10 incentive check has been provided to "demonstrate appreciation." An additional incentive is provided if the respondent completes the interview. Explicit instructions are provided, and even an 800 number is made available should the respondent have any questions. No doubt, the survey resulted in a very high response rate, which significantly reduced nonresponse error.

Burke Marketing Research 805 Central Avenue, Cincinnati, Ohio 45202
Telephone: (513) 241-5663, Fax: (513) 684-7500

Dear Information Superhighway Customer,

Thank you very much for participating in this important survey. As you may recall when we first talked on the phone, we promised you $10 when you completed the survey and mailed it back. For efficiency and in order to demonstrate our appreciation to you for your help, we have included the $10 at this time. Your completed interview will also be entered into a drawing for a chance to win a $1500 home entertainment system, a $1500 personal computer, or the cash equivalent.

The first thing to do is watch the videotape. Then complete the blue questionnaire booklet. The red dictionary is included in case you need more information when answering question #6.

When you have completed the booklet be sure to mail it back in the postage-paid envelope. Please do not return the videotape.

If you have any questions about how to complete any of the questionnaire you may call me at 1-800-688-2674, extension 7594.

Sincerely,

Jeanne Vennemeyer

Jeanne Vennemeyer
Senior Project Manager
Burke Marketing Research

Source: *Burke Inc., by permission.*

TABLE 11.3

The Location of Questions on a Questionnaire Is Logical

QUESTIONNAIRE ORGANIZATION			
QUESTION TYPE	**QUESTION LOCATION**	**EXAMPLES**	**RATIONALE**
Screens	First questions asked	"Have you shopped at the Gap in the past month?" "Is this your first visit to this store?"	Used to select the respondent types desired by the researcher to be in the survey
Warm-ups	Immediately after any screens	"How often do you go shopping?" "On what days of the week do you usually shop?"	Easy to answer; shows respondent that survey is easy to complete; generates interest
Transitions (statements)	Prior to major sections of questions or changes in question format	"Now, for the next few questions, I want to ask about your family's TV viewing habits." "Next, I am going to read several statements and, after each, I want you to tell me if you agree or disagree with this statement."	Notifies respondents that the subject or format of the following questions will change.
Complicated and difficult-to-answer questions	Middle of the questionnaire; close to the end	"Rate each of the following 10 stores on the friendliness of their salespeople on a scale of 1 to 7." "How likely are you to purchase each of the following items in the next three months?"	Respondent has committed himself or herself to completing the questionnaire; can see (or is told) that there are not many questions left
Classification and demographic questions	Last section	"What is the highest level of education you have attained?"	Questions that are "personal" and possibly offensive are placed at the end of the questionnaire

cooking ingredients for their family, do most of the cooking, and make a baked food item at least once a month. Of course, not all surveys have screening questions. A survey of all charge account customers for a department store, for example, may not require screening questions. This is true because, in a sense, all potential respondents have already been qualified by virtue of having charge accounts with the store.

Once the individual is qualified by the screening questions, the next questions may serve a "warm-up" function. **Warm-ups** are simple and easy-to-answer questions that may or may not pertain to the research objectives. These questions really perform the task of heightening the respondent's interest while making the person feel that the questions can be answered easily and quickly. Here, a warm-up may be, "Have you baked anything in the past month?"

Questionnaire flow must move the respondent smoothly through the questions.

Transitions are typically statements made to let the respondent know that changes in question topic or format are forthcoming. A statement such as "Now, I would like to ask you a few questions about your family's TV viewing habits" is an example of a transition statement. Such statements aid in making certain that the respondent understands the line of questioning. Transitions include **"skip" questions** to determine which question or set of questions will be asked next. Using our Arm & Hammer baking soda example, a transition question may be, "When you bake a cake, do you usually do it from scratch or do you use a box mix?" If the person responds that he or she uses a box mix, questions asking more details about baking from scratch are not appropriate, and the questionnaire will instruct the respondent (or the interviewer, if one is being used) to skip over or to bypass those questions. "Skip" questions are tricky. It's a wise idea to check them over several times before finalizing a questionnaire.

Complicated and/or difficult-to-answer questions are best placed deep in the questionnaire.

Deeper in the questionnaire you will find the most complicated and difficult-to-answer questions. Scaled-response questions such as semantic differential scales, Likert-type response scales, or other questions that require some degree of mental activity such as evaluation, voicing opinions, recalling past experiences, indicating intentions, or responding to "what if" questions are found here. There are at least two reasons for this placement. First, by the time the respondent has arrived at these questions, he or she has answered several relatively easy questions and is now caught up in a responding mode in which he or she feels some sort of commitment. Even though the questions in this section require more mental effort, the person will feel more compelled to complete the questionnaire than to break it off. Second, if the questionnaire is self-administered, the respondent will see that only a few sections of questions remain to be answered. That is, once he or she is through the present difficult section, the respondent will be finished. If the survey is being administered by an interviewer, the questionnaire will typically have prompts included for the interviewer to notify the respondent that the interview is in its last stages. Also, experienced interviewers can sense when respondents' interest levels sag, and they may voice their own prompts, if permitted, to keep the respondent on task.

Demographic and other classification questions are traditionally placed at the end of the questionnaire.

The last section of a questionnaire is reserved for **classification questions.** The word "classification" is used because these questions are normally used to classify respondents into various groups for purposes of analysis. For instance, the researcher may want to classify respondents into categories based on age, gender, income level, and so on. Therefore, demographic items are normally placed here. This placement is industry tradition, and it embodies the strategy of placing questions that may cause respondents to break off the survey at the end of the interview. Some respondents will consider certain demographic questions "personal," and they may refuse to give answers to questions about the highest level of education they attained or about their income level. In these cases, if the respondent refuses to answer, the refusal comes at the very end of the questioning process. If it occurred at the very beginning, the interview would begin with a negative vein, perhaps causing the person to think that the survey will be asking any number of personal questions. As a result, the respondent may very well refuse to take part in the survey at that point.

Approaches to Question Flow

The flow of questions we have just described is generally used by questionnaire designers, but there are at least three specific approaches to questionnaire organization that we can describe: the funnel approach, the work approach, and the sections approach. The **funnel approach** uses a wide-to-narrow or general-to-specific flow of questions that places inquiries at the beginning of a topic on the questionnaire that are general in nature, and those requiring more specific and detailed responses later on.[11] The **work approach** is employed when the researcher realizes that respondents will need to apply mental effort to a group of questions. When questions tap responses that are deeper than simple recall, respondents must apply a certain degree of concentration in answering them. Difficult questions are customarily placed deep in the questionnaire. Scaled-response questions are often placed here because their forms are complicated and require respondents to work harder than when answering simple format questions. As we just noted, when the respondent encounters the work questions, he or she should be caught up in the responding mode or otherwise committed to completing the questionnaire. If this is the case, the respondent will be more inclined to expend the extra effort necessary to answer them. Perhaps the simplest format is to arrange the questions in logical sets on the questionnaire, referred to as the **sections approach.** Sometimes the objectives define the sections, but in other instances, question formats are used for this demarcation. For example, with our Arm & Hammer survey, we could have separate sections of questions for baking cakes, baking pies, baking cookies, baking from scratch, baking with box mixes, and so forth. Elsewhere on the questionnaire, the researcher may want to know respondents' opinions of baking by conventional oven, baking by microwave, and how well Arm & Hammer brand baking soda performs—all of these items can be placed in a single section in which the respondent is instructed to indicate his or her agreement with each statement along a seven-point, agree–disagree scale.

The funnel approach uses a general-to-specific question flow.

The work approach requires that difficult-to-answer questions be placed deep in the questionnaire.

The sections approach arranges the questionnaire into sections or topic category divisions.

Which approach is best? There is no single questionnaire format that fits all cases. In fact, the three approaches we have just described are not mutually exclusive, and there is no reason a researcher cannot use a combination of approaches in a single questionnaire. In fact, a researcher may find that the survey topics influence the placement or approach used in question flow.[12] To illustrate this, we have included Marketing Research Insight 11.3 (page 342), which describes how "sensitive" questions can be handled.

As we indicated earlier, designing a questionnaire is a blend of creativity and adherence to simple, commonsense guidelines. The most important principle to keep in mind, though, is to design the questionnaire's flow of questions so as to make it respondent-friendly[13] by minimizing the amount of effort necessary to respond to it while maximizing the probability that each respondent will fill it out reliably, accurately, and completely.[14] To achieve these results, the researcher selects logical response formats, provides clear directions, makes the questionnaire appearance visually appealing, and numbers all sections plus all items in each section.[15]

MARKETING RESEARCH INSIGHT 11.3

How to Ask Sensitive Questions

Occasionally a market researcher finds that a client wants sensitive information from consumers. To gather this information, sensitive questions must be asked of respondents. Here are a few examples.

Goodyear wants to know how much over the speed limit drivers typically drive.

Colgate toothpaste wants to know who brushes daily.

Lady Stetson wants to know if its fragrance is sexy to men.

Jockey wants to know about respondents' use of pantyhose.

H&R Block wants to know who cheats on their income tax.

Swatch wants to know how much peer pressure is involved with wearing its watches.

Sandals All Inclusive Resorts of Jamaica wants to know if singles are looking for a romantic adventure.

Bufferin wants to know if people abuse the use of aspirin.

How does a researcher ask these sensitive questions?
Here are four options:

- Hide *the sensitive question among a group of more innocent questions.*
- *State the behavior or attitude is* not unusual *before asking the question.*
- *Phrase the question to ask* how others *might feel or act.*
- *Present the responses in categories that the respondent simply checks* without verbalizing *the behavior.*

Source: *Jamshid C. Hosseini, and Robert L. Armacost, "Randomized Responses: A Better Way to Obtain Sensitive Information,"* Business Horizons *(May–June, 1990), 82–86.*

PRECODING THE QUESTIONNAIRE

Precodes are code numbers placed on the questionnaire to facilitate data entry after the survey has been conducted.

A final task in questionnaire design is **precoding** questions, which is the placement of numbers on the questionnaire to facilitate data entry after the survey has been conducted. Precodes are included as long as they are not confusing to respondents or interviewers.

The logic of precoding is simple once you know the ground rules. The primary objective of precoding is to associate each possible response with a unique number or letter. Ordinarily, a number is preferred for two reasons. First, numbers are easier and faster to keystroke into a computer file. Second, computer tabulation programs are more efficient when they process numbers. Table 11.4 illustrates code designations for selected questions. When words such as "yes" or "no" are used as literal response categories, precodes are normally placed alongside each response and in parentheses. With scaled-response questions in which numbers are used as the response categories, the numbers are already on the questionnaire, so there is no need to use precodes for these questions.

There is one instance in which precoding becomes slightly complicated; but, again, once you learn the basic rules, the precoding is fairly easy to understand. Occasionally, a researcher uses a question that asks the respondent to

TABLE 11.4

Examples of Precodes on the Final Questionnaire

1. Have you purchased a Godfather's pizza in the last month?
_____ Yes (1) _____ No (2) _____ Unsure (3)

2. The last time you bought a Godfather's pizza, did you (check only one):

_____	Have it delivered to your house?	(1)
_____	Have it delivered to your place of work?	(2)
_____	Pick it up yourself?	(3)
_____	Eat it at the pizza parlor?	(4)
_____	Purchase it some other way?	(5)

3. In your opinion, the taste of a Godfather's pizza is (check only one):

_____	Poor	(1)
_____	Fair	(2)
_____	Good	(3)
_____	Excellent	(4)

4. Which of the following toppings do you typically have on your pizza? (Check all that apply.)

_____	Green pepper	(0;1)
_____	Onion	(0;1)
_____	Mushroom	(0;1)
_____	Sausage	(0;1)
_____	Pepperoni	(0;1)
_____	Hot peppers	(0;1)
_____	Black olives	(0;1)
_____	Anchovies	(0;1)

(Note: the 0;1 indicates the coding system that will be used. Typically, no precode such as this is placed on the questionnaire. Each response category must be defined as a separate question.)

5. How do you rate the speediness of Godfather's in-restaurant service once you have ordered? (Circle the appropriate number if a 1 means very slow and a 7 means very fast.)

Very Slow	1	2	3	4	5	6	7	Very Fast

6. Please indicate your age: __________ Years *(Note: No precode is used as the respondent will write in a two-digit number.)*

indicate "all that apply" from a list of possible responses. For example, if Fruit of the Loom were interested in the type and color of underpants men own, there might be a question in a mail survey such as, "What type or types of underpants do you own? (Please check all that apply.)" The response categories could be: (1) plain white boxer style, (2) colored boxer style, (3) colored brief style, (4) plain white brief style, and (5) colored bikini style. You should note that if the respondent was instructed to select only one style, the precodes would be 1, 2, 3, 4, and 5; but because more than one response category can be checked, there are numerous different possible combinations (1 and 2; 1 and 3; 1, 2, and 3; and so on). Rather than list all possible combinations with a unique code number for each, the standard approach is to have each response category option coded with a 0 or a 1. The designation "0" will be used if the category is not checked, whereas a "1" is used if it is checked by a respondent. In other words, there would be five separate precodes of 0 or 1, each associated with one of the response options. Question number 4 in Table 11.4 is an example of multiple-answer precoding. Note that each response category must be defined as a separate question for data analysis purposes.

It is becoming less common, however, for precodes to appear on the final questionnaire as the marketing research industry moves further into the high-technology side of questionnaire design and administration. There is no need for precodes to appear on the questionnaire, for instance, with a CATI system or a questionnaire that will be scanned because the coding has been taken care of by the computer programs themselves.

COMPUTER-ASSISTED QUESTIONNAIRE DESIGN

Technology is impacting questionnaire design. **Computer-assisted questionnaire design** is an area of exciting growth in recent years. A handful of companies has developed computer software that bridges the gap between composing questions on a word processor and generating the final, polished version complete with boxes, circles, and coded questions. In fact, most of these special-purpose personal computer programs have the ability to interface with statistical analysis packages such as SPSS for Windows.

Features of Computer-Assisted Questionnaire Design Systems

Key advantages of computer-assisted questionnaire design programs include a conversation feature, the creation of data files, and other special features.

There are several significant advantages of computer-assisted questionnaire design: They are easier, faster, and "friendlier" than using a word processor. In fact, research companies that do a great deal of survey research have found the cost of buying these programs well worth their expense when spread across several marketing research projects. In addition to simplifying the process of questionnaire layout, these programs also have the ability to link to other software systems. This facilitates coding of responses and data analysis. Just to give you a feel for the power of computer-assisted questionnaire design, we describe three major advantages of these programs: conversation feature, creation of data files, and other special features.

Conversation Feature

The typical questionnaire design program will query the designer on, for example, type of question, number of response categories, whether multiple responses are permitted, if skips are to be used, and how responses are to be coded. The conversation feature sometimes takes the form of a menu of choices, or it might appear as a sequence of format inquiries for each section of the questionnaire. For example, SNAP, a questionnaire design program offered by Mercator Corporation, allows you to enter the question and select the desired response format. Sample response formats that are offered include multiple choice, open-ended, and grid table. Once you have keyed in your question, the program formats the layout, and automatically adds boxes wherever necessary. Using the library of layouts available, you can match your data collection requirements with the type of survey you plan to carry out. The same program can be used for paper questionnaires, personal interviews, or computer-based telephone interviews. Figure 11.2 shows the format of a mutiple-choice question created using SNAP.

Computer-assisted questionnaire design programs have menus for selecting the desired question response format.

Creation of Data Files

Computer-assisted questionnaire design may provide for a direct path from responses to a computer file for all respondents' answers. With CATI systems that we described in chapter 9, the questionnaire is administered by the telephone interviewer who is prompted for each question by the computer screen, and as the respondent's answers are keystroked by the interviewer, they are immediately written to a data file. Even with mail surveys, computer-assisted questionnaire design can create a final version that can be scanned and converted to a data file in a matter of seconds. In some cases where responses have to be keyed in, the software program provides all the required data fields. This facilitates the process of data entry. The program can also check for errors. Figure 11.3 on page 346 shows the SNAP data entry form for the question on items ordered.

Most computer-assisted questionnaire design programs allow for the creation of data files as data is collected.

Data Analysis and Reports

Many of the software programs for questionnaire design also have provisions for data analysis, graphic presentation, and report formats of results. Using the previous question on fast-food eating habits, we show in Figure 11.4 (page 346) the

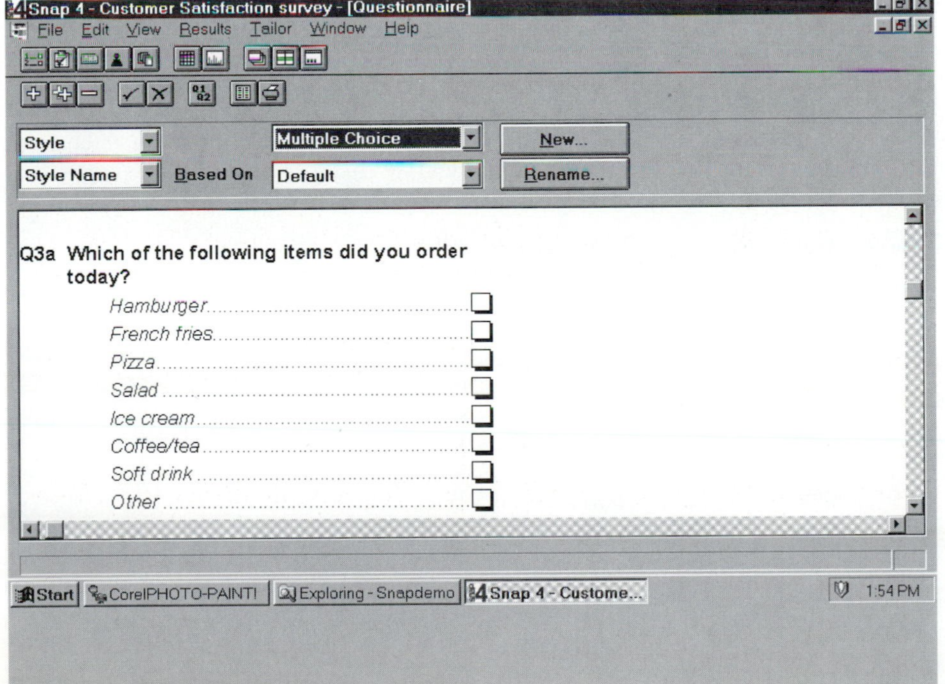

Figure 11.2

Computer-assisted questionnaire design software allows users to select the question format.

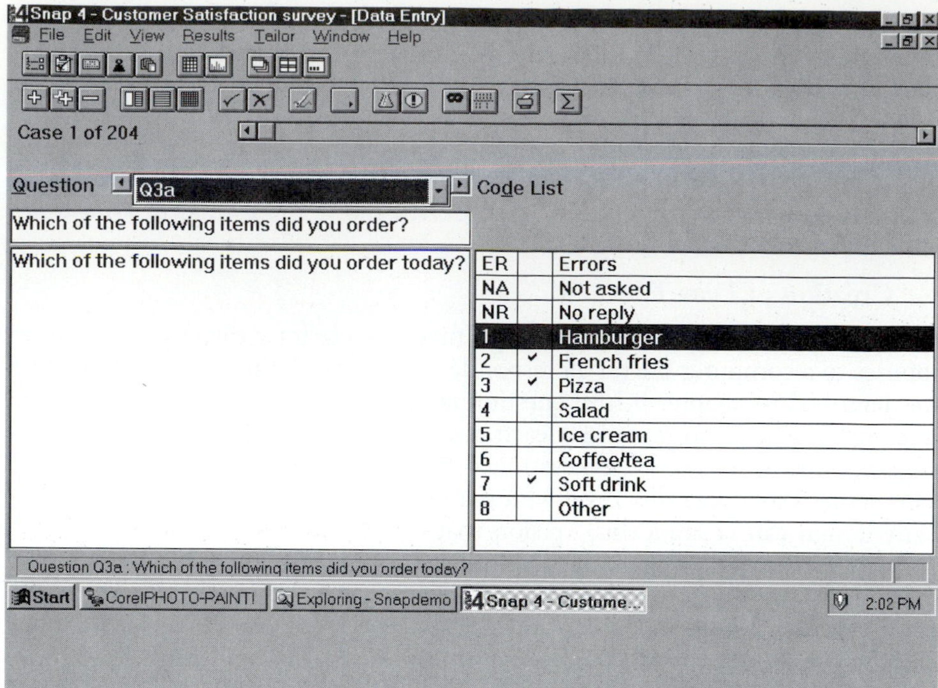

Figure 11.3

Some computer-assisted questionnaire design programs allow users to enter responses during an interview, directly to a data file.

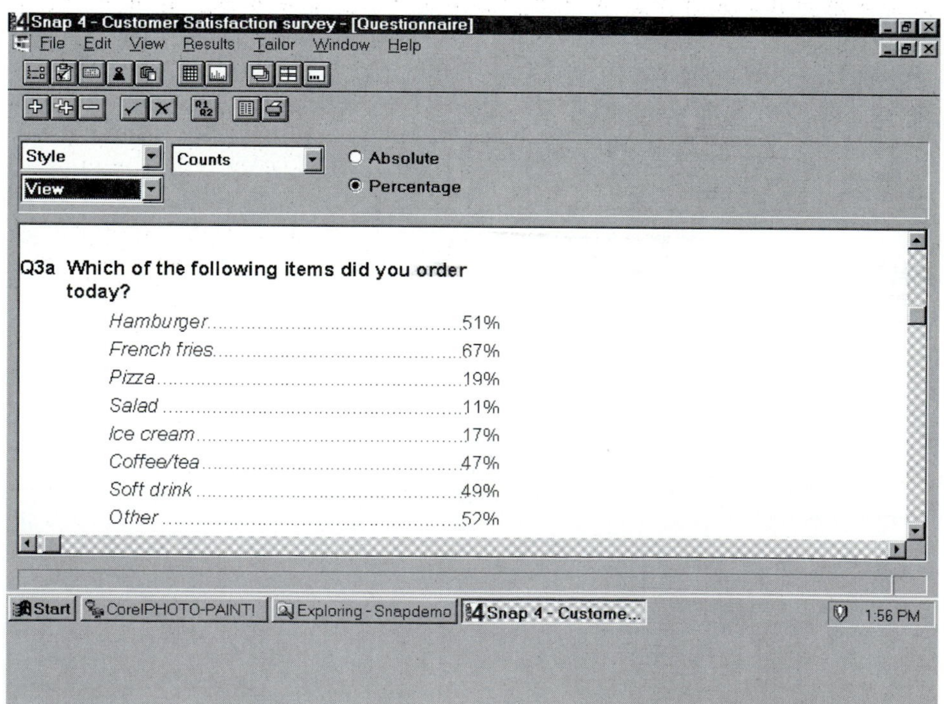

Figure 11.4

Some computer-assisted questionnaire design programs allow users to analyze data and to write reports.

percentage value for each option in the question. Basically, what we have done with SNAP is to display the results of the survey in the form of a questionnaire. The tabulated results can also be exported to other data analysis packages, such as SPSS for Windows, for further processing.

Other Special Features

A variety of special aspects of questionnaires designed with computer assistance are helpful in various ways. For instance, if color monitors are used, there may be the option of using color coding to emphasize certain words or instructions. Some provide for a clock function to track how long interviews are taking or how long it takes to administer groups of questions. Notepad features allow for the interviewer to make comments in a window on the screen that can be activated or deactivated by a single keystroke. Randomization of the presentation of response categories or even questions across respondents may be available to counter presentation sequence bias. Some even include a tabulation feature that provides for real-time summaries of specific questions, quota status (to be discussed in chapter 12), or other breakdowns of interest while the survey is conducted.

PERFORMING THE PRETEST OF THE QUESTIONNAIRE

A pretest can reveal questionnaire errors before the survey is launched.

Pretests should only be administered on actual members of a study's targeted population.

Before finalizing the questionnaire, one final evaluation should be conducted on the entire questionnaire. Such an evaluation uses a pretest to ensure that the questions will accomplish what is expected of them. A **pretest** involves conducting a dry run of the survey on a small, representative set of respondents in order to reveal questionnaire errors before the survey is launched. As our Figure 11.5 illustrates, it is very important that pretest *participants* are in

Figure 11.5

"Excuse me, co-workers. Could I have your help in pretesting this questionnaire that the Acme Toy Company wants us to administer to 7- to 12-year-old kids? First, can you rank order the six most important attributes of your four most preferred toys? Second, can you recall whether your most recent toy purchase included an explicit or implied product warranty? Third, . . . "

fact representative, that is, selected from the target population under study. Before the questions are administered, participants are informed of the pretest, and their cooperation is requested in spotting words, phrases, instructions, question flow, or other aspects of the questionnaire that appear confusing, difficult to understand, or otherwise a problem.

A pretest of 5 to 10 representative respondents is usually sufficient to identify problems with a questionnaire.

Normally, from 5 to 10 respondents are involved in a pretest, and the researcher looks for common problem themes across this group.[16] For example, if only one pretest respondent indicates some concern about a question, the researcher probably would not attempt modification of its wording, but if three mention the same concern, the researcher would be alerted to the need to undertake a revision. Ideally, when making revisions, researchers should place themselves in the respondent's shoes and ask the following questions: "Is the meaning of the question clear?," "Are the instructions understandable?," "Are the terms precise?," and "Are there any loaded or charged words?" However, because researchers can never completely replicate the respondent's perspective, a pretest is extremely valuable.[17]

DESIGNING OBSERVATION FORMS

You should recall that a survey is only one of the ways primary information can be gathered. Another means is through observation. As we indicated in our discussion on qualitative research techniques in chapter 8, there is one class of qualitative research in which a human observer watches some episode of behavior and takes notes on what he or she sees. The remainder of this chapter describes some considerations and guidelines pertaining to recording observations. First, we discuss why it is important to develop a useful structure or categorization scheme for the observations, and then we contrast the build-up and break-down approaches to developing observation categorization systems.

Structuring Observational Studies

Let us do some role playing to help you understand the importance of structuring observational studies. Let us assume that you are working part-time for a marketing research company that is being used by Minute Maid orange juice to do an observational study on how consumers buy juice in the grocery store. When you come to work, your supervisor tells you to go to the nearby Kroger grocery store. She has arranged with the Kroger store manager for you to dress as a clerk so you will not be conspicuous to shoppers.

You begin your observations by selecting a shopper as she enters the store. This shopper happens to be a woman about in her early thirties, and she has two children with her, both of whom are girls, aged about seven and three. The seven-year-old girl walks alongside her mother, and the three-year-old girl sits in the child seat of the grocery cart being pushed by the mother. Your shopper starts shopping with the normal flow of shoppers, and stops at the vegetable bins. She picks up an orange. Now, you are thinking that the observation might be relevant, so you make a note. As you do, she puts it back down and picks up another, apparently squeezing it to determine its freshness. She does this several more times before selecting a total of six oranges that she places in her cart.

She moves on, selecting various other items, and finally arrives at the aisle with juices. She immediately picks out a large Welch's grape juice bottle and puts it in her cart. She picks up a can of V-8 Light and seems to read the label with interest. Meanwhile, the seven-year-old girl picks up a can of Donald Duck orange juice and asks the mother to buy it. The mother says no, puts the V-8 Light and Donald Duck cans back, and moves on. You make a note of this episode.

Now, you notice that she has arrived at the diary products. After selecting low-fat milk, she reaches for a carton of Tropicana orange juice. When she does, the three-year-old girl begins crying because the seven-year-old girl has grabbed her doll. The mother turns, and sternly tells the seven-year-old girl to stop. The older child gives the doll back to the little one who stops crying. Your shopper then continues on, apparently forgetting about the Tropicana she was about to pick up. You make a note of this incident.

Last, when she passes the frozen foods, your shopper stops and buys a container of Sealtest brand rocky road flavor ice cream. As she puts it in her cart, you notice her spot the frozen fruit juices. She looks back at the dairy counter and seems to think for a minute. Then, she picks up the largest frozen Minute Maid orange juice container in that section of the frozen foods and puts it in her cart. You make a note of this event. By the end of your day observing shoppers in that Kroger grocery store, you have followed 20 shoppers on their trips, and you have about a dozen pages of scribbled notes from your observations.

How would you structure these observations of an orange juice buyer's travels through a grocery store?

How do you structure your observational study so you can summarize your observations into a coherent report? Certainly, the first task would be to group them into logical categories. One scheme you might begin with is to group them by the type of juice bought: (1) fresh oranges, (2) bottled, (3) canned, (4) refrigerated fresh, and (5) frozen. Then, for each one of these, you might identify alternative approaches to selection of a brand such as: (1) picked brand immediately, (2) picked brand after inspecting others, (3) inspected but did not buy, or (4) did not stop at this area. A separate categorical scheme would be the shopping party. Was it one shopper, two adults, one adult and child(ren), or some other grouping, and what were the sexes and apparent ages of the shoppers? Did they use a shopping cart, a carry basket, or neither?

Build-Up and Break-Down Approaches

An observation form indicates what behavior is to be watched and how it should be recorded.

Your work in creating this categorization system might be referred to as the **"build-up" approach** in which you must perform the observations first, and then the categories for reporting them are built on these observations. An opposite method might be called the **"break-down" approach** in which the categories are created before the observer goes into the field, and they are provided on an observation record form. This approach requires the researcher to think through and map out all of the relevant behaviors before the actual observation phase is undertaken. Figure 11.6 on page 350 is a break-down form for observing orange juice purchasing in a grocery store. As you inspect it, you should notice the various details that are constant across all observations. For example, the observer always records the (1) time of day the observation begins, (2) size and composition of shopping party, (3) use/nonuse of shopping

Observer: ______________ Location: ______________

Date: ______________ Time of Day: ______________

Shopping Party Composition

Number in Party: ______ Adults ______ Children

Note by Sex: Adults: ______ Male(s) ______ Female(s)

Children: ______ Male(s) ______ Female(s)

Use of: ______ Shopping Cart ______ Shopping Basket ______ None

Shopping Behaviors (record of each)

Behavior	Fresh oranges	Bottled juice	Canned juice	Frozen juice
Pass by/ enter aisle?				
Comparisons (note type, if any)				
Brand(s)/ item(s) selected				
Brand(s)/ item(s) examined				
Interactions with shopping party members				
Other specific to purchase/ nonpurchase				

Use of: ________ List ________ Calculator ________ Coupons

Time completed shopping: ________ Total purchases: ________

Figure 11.6

A Sample Observation Recording Form for Minute Maid Orange Juice

cart or handheld basket, and (4) types of other groceries purchased. In addition, it has sections with recording areas for (1) fresh oranges, (2) bottled juice, (3) canned juice, (4) refrigerated fresh juice, and (5) frozen juice.

Well-designed observation forms achieve consistency, structure, and completeness.

In general, a break-down approach is better than a build-up method for at least three reasons. First, it offers consistency. That is, because the form has specific observation categories, some comment should be on each category for every shopper observed. Without the form, observations are vulnerable to observer distraction or fatigue. Second, it offers structure. In other words, the observer does not make random or arbitrary comments. Instead, the observations are structured, and even though the researcher is working with qualitative data, there is some inherent logic to the categories that will help make sense out of the multitude of observations when they are analyzed. Third, it offers completeness. If the observation form designer has done all of the necessary planning, the form will have a thorough inventory of all of the relevant behaviors. In this way, the researcher will not be concerned about the differences among observers when they are left on their own to decide what to itemize in their notes or what to leave out of their records. Differences among observers will be minimized.

SUMMARY

This chapter described questionnaire design and the creation of observation forms. We began by describing the questionnaire development process. Next, developing questions became the focus, and we listed five different "shoulds" and eleven separate "should nots" regarding question wording. The introduction of the questionnaire serves several functions including identification, purpose, request for participation, and it screens potential respondents to ensure that they are qualified to take part in the survey. There are alternative question flow approaches, so we described the typical sequence along with the funnel approach, the work approach, and the sections approach. We also showed you that a pretest is helpful in fine-tuning the questionnaire into final form.

The chapter also introduced you to the notion of precoding, or placing the codes to be put in the computer data file on the questionnaire itself. In addition, some companies have developed computer software that performs questionnaire design, and the chapter briefly described the features of these programs. We discussed observational studies and illustrated how important it is to design a structured observation form that is easy for observers to record the various behaviors that are of interest to the researcher.

KEY TERMS

Question bias (p. 323)
Double-barreled question (p. 333)
Leading question (p. 333)
Loaded question (p. 333)
Introduction (p. 335)
Cover letter (p. 335)
Opening comments (p. 335)
Undisguised survey (p. 335)
Disguised survey (p. 335)
Anonymity (p. 336)
Confidentiality (p. 336)
Screening questions (p. 337)
Warm-ups (p. 339)
Transitions (p. 340)
Skip questions (p. 340)
Classification questions (p. 340)
Funnel approach (p. 341)
Work approach (p. 341)
Sections approach (p. 341)
Precoding (p. 342)
Computer-assisted questionnaire design (p. 344)
Pretest (p. 347)
Build-up approach (p. 349)
Break-down approach (p. 349)

REVIEW QUESTIONS/APPLICATIONS

1. What is meant by the statement that questionnaire design is an "iterative" process?
2. What is meant by question bias? Write two biased questions.
3. Explain the client's role during questionnaire development.
4. Indicate the functions of (a) screening questions, (b) warm-ups, (c) transitions, (d) "skip" questions, and (e) classification questions.
5. Differentiate the funnel approach from the work approach to questionnaire design.
6. Using a campus escort service as the topic of a survey, define and give examples of questions that (a) are loaded, (b) are leading, (c) are double-barreled, and (d) use assumed criteria.
7. What is meant when questions (a) overstate the condition, (b) require the respondent to guess a generalization, (c) lack focus, (d) use a specific example to represent a general class, and (e) use a complex sentence?
8. Describe precoding and give examples of the precoding for a (a) closed-ended question, (b) scaled-response question, and (c) "check-all-that-apply" question.
9. Why should the researcher expend so much effort on the cover letter or opening comments of a questionnaire?
10. Distinguish anonymity from confidentiality.
11. Differentiate the "build-up" from the "break-down" approach to observational studies.
12. Take five of the problem words identified in this chapter and write a question for each word selected. Describe why the word is a problem word for your question.
13. Listed here are five different aspects of a questionnaire to be designed for the crafts guild of Maui, Hawaii. It is to be administered by personal interviewers who will intercept tourists as they are waiting at the Maui Airport in the seating areas of their departing flight gates. Indicate how the arrangement of these items could differ on a questionnaire if the researcher used the funnel approach, the work approach, the sections approach, or some combination of these approaches.
    - **a.** Determine how they selected Maui as a destination.
    - **b.** Discover what places they visited in Maui and how much they liked each one.
    - **c.** Describe what crafts they purchased, where they purchased them, when they bought them, how much they paid, who made the selection, and why they bought those particular items.
    - **d.** Specify how long they stayed and where they stayed while on Maui.
    - **e.** Provide a demographic profile of each tourist interviewed.
14. The Marketing Club at your university is thinking about undertaking a money-making project. Coeds will be invited to compete and 12 will be selected to be in the "Girls of (insert your school) University" calendar. All photographs will be taken by a professional photographer and tastefully done. Some club members are concerned about the reactions of other students who might think that the calendar will degrade women. Taking each "should not," phrase questions that violate the "should not" such that the response would tend to support the view that such a calendar would be degrading. Indicate how the question is in error, and provide a version that is in better form.
15. Go to a local movie theater and observe the food-buying behavior exhibited by the patrons. Be sure to note the following:
    - **a.** When the food was bought.

b. What food was bought.
c. Who bought what food.
d. How buying differed for adults versus children.
e. How it differed for mixed sex versus same sex groups of teenagers.
f. How movie goers reacted to the theater's popcorn and soft drink prices.

Write up your observations and present your summary in class. (*Note:* It is a good idea to ask the manager's permission to observe the movie goers for a class exercise ahead of time.)

CASE 11.1

Park Place Psychiatric Hospital

Park Place Hospital opened last year in Tucson, Arizona. It specializes in psychiatric care and mental health services. Both inpatient and outpatient services are provided, although the hospital is quite small and can only accommodate up to 20 inpatients at any one time. Because the hospital is new and its location is in the desert on the outskirts of Tucson, it has invested in an extensive advertising campaign using billboards, newspaper, and radio spots. By the end of its first year of operation, Park Place has experienced only 45 percent occupancy, but it is optimistic about the future.

The management of Park Place has decided that in order to grow, it must reach out to its patient population in Tucson by being more aggressive in its program offerings. Among the services being considered is a series of seminars on selected mental health care problems and a set of companion programs that will cover the various topics more extensively. The marketing manager contacts a local research company and works with some of its personnel to formulate a list of research objectives. These objectives address his concerns about the effectiveness of the marketing program, the hospital's location situation, the decision-making process for a family member who detects another family member having a problem, and an interest in various programs and seminars. These objectives include the following:

- To determine the level of interest in each of the following two-hour evening seminars that cost $25 each: stop smoking, weight control, stress management, substance abuse, Alzheimer's disease, understanding anxiety, and coping with teenagers.
- To assess the degree of interest in enrolling in any of the two-month-long programs listed above that cost $250 each.
- To evaluate where a person or family would seek help if a mental health problem requiring professional counseling were evident.
- To determine if prospective clients recall Park Place Hospital advertising, and if so, in which advertising medium.
- To evaluate the importance of location in the selection of a mental health care facility for a family member, either as an inpatient or an outpatient.
- To obtain target market information.

Random digit dialing will be used to select prospective respondent households.

1. Design a questionnaire suited for a telephone survey of 500 Tucson households to be conducted with the "adult head of the household who is responsible for the family's health care."
2. Justify your choice of the type of question response format for each question. If you have used the same format for a group of related questions, you should indicate your rationale for the group rather than for each question in the group.
3. Identify the organization aspects of your questionnaire. Identify the question flow approach you have used and indicate why. Also, identify all screening questions, warm-ups, transition questions, and skip questions that you have used.

CASE 11.2
Kendalures

About 10 years ago, Larry Kendall, a retired postal worker living in Maine, began experimenting with the design of a new fishing lure in the hopes that he would invent one that would become as successful as the Johnson Silver Spoon or the Jitterbug. Because of his familiarity with coldwater fish such as trout, Larry's lure took the shape of a wavy spoon with a treble hook on the end. Its action in the water when retrieved or trolled at slow speed simulates a wounded minnow. He paid a machine shop to make a die and stamp out 500, and a paint shop to paint them either gold, silver, metallic red, or metallic green.

Although Larry has used the lure with success, and he has given many away to his friends who report that they have caught fish with it, he has had great difficulty convincing retailers to stock the lure. Despite much effort on Larry's part, only about 10 small bait shops in New Hampshire and Maine stock the item, and most of these have only bought one display card that holds 24 lures for sale. The lure sells for $2.50 retail for the 1/4-ounce size and $3.00 for the 1/2-ounce size. Larry has made inquiries with Kmart, Wal-Mart, Sears, and L.L. Bean, but all have declined to buy his lures.

One of Larry's nephews is a marketing manager with New England Bell, and the nephew suggests that if Larry had some convincing marketing research results about the desirability of the lure, he might have a stronger case to present to the large retail chains. The nephew recommends a "product placement" approach where fishermen would be given the lure with the promise that they would try it. Reactions Larry would like to know about his lure include its action; its colors; how well it casts; its appearance; what and how many fish, if any, the fishermen caught with it; how much they used the lure; and the weather conditions. There is also a number of other factors that might be helpful in marketing the Kendalure. These items include its appropriate price, what causes fishermen to try a new lure, where they buy lures, sizes of lures purchased, and how much fishing they do.

The plan is to intercept fishermen at boat launches, secure their cooperation to use the lure sometime during their fishing trip that day, meet them when they return, and verbally administer questions to them. As an incentive, each respondent will receive three lures to try that day, and five more will be given to each fisherman who answers the questions at the end of the fishing trip.

1. Design the questionnaire for fishermen who will use the lures.
2. What opening comments should be verbalized when approaching fishermen who are launching their boats? Draft a script to be used when asking these fishermen to take part in the survey.

CHAPTER 12

Determining the Sample Plan

LEARNING OBJECTIVES

- *To become familiar with sample design terminology*
- *To learn about practical and "sufficiency of information" reasons for selecting a sample*
- *To understand the differences between "probability" and "nonprobability" sampling methods*
- *To acquire the skills to administer different types of samples*
- *To be able to develop a sample plan*

PRACTITIONER VIEWPOINT

When you think about it, in conducting a research study, you are just not getting correct answers when you are not interviewing the right population or when you are not sampling that population correctly. A situation could result in which the finest of questionnaires, very carefully administered, and combined with state-of-the-art analysis and reporting, provides very misleading, sometimes damaging, results. There is a real danger that, because of the pressures of time or budget, an overemphasis on technology, or a lack of senior management understanding, the sampling plan does not get sufficient attention. You have got to be talking to the right people.

This chapter will teach you how to do that. You'll learn how one of the least expensive aspects of the study's design is the keystone that holds the study together. Careful attention to this chapter will help you distinguish a good sample from a bad sample.

— Terrence F. Coen
Survey Sampling[1]

WebBank Learns How to Sample Internet Users[2]

1. Establish the need for marketing research
2. Define the problem
3. Establish research objectives
4. Determine research design
5. Identify information types and sources
6. Determine methods of accessing data
7. Design data collection forms
8. Determine sample plan and size
9. Collect data
10. Analyze data
11. Prepare and present the final research report

Doing surveys on Internet users requires special sampling procedures.

The Internet has become a viable marketing medium. Thousands of consumers use it each hour, and marketers have turned to it as a convenient advertising medium. Some marketers have created their own homepages where consumers can purchase merchandise. In the financial industry, banks have moved to the Internet as it is a very convenient, 24-hour "virtual teller," which is always available for a bank customer.

WebBank is an innovator in cyberbanking, and early in its experience with the Internet, it put up a survey page asking important questions about how consumers were using the Internet and how they perceived WebBank services. The WebBank survey page afforded significant advantages over traditional survey methods. For one, it garnered a huge sample size in a short time. In one week, over 3,000 people filled in the WebBank survey page and submitted it. Because they were electronic in nature, the survey responses were converted into raw data almost instantaneously, and real-time tabulations were made on a daily basis. Perhaps the greatest plus of the WebBank survey page was its low cost as it avoided use of interviewers, copies of the questionnaire, and all of the costs associated with drawing a sample.

After a short time, however, a significant problem became apparent with this method of market research. That is, there was no control on the respondents as anyone with an Internet connection could come to the

WebBank survey page and fill it out. In fact, the same person could fill it out and submit it multiple times. Children could fill it out. Competitors could answer it, and even foreign country residents could fill it out. As these problems became more apparent, the usefulness of the WebBank survey page information plummeted.

Necessary measures were then taken to improve the representativeness of the WebBank survey. A significant one involved the creation of a questionnaire file that was e-mailed periodically to a sample of WebBank customers. These customers filled out the questionnaire on their computers and e-mailed it back to the WebBank marketing research department.

Realizing an opportunity, WebBank changed the purpose of its ongoing survey page. The questions were altered to gather demographics, life-style, financial services usage, and other consumer characteristics, and each respondent was added to the WebBank Internet users' database. This database quickly amounted to over 100,000 names, and it grows daily. When special research needs arise, the database is used as a handy listing of potential WebBank customers, and a sample is drawn from it. Because much information is known about each person in the database, highly specialized samples can be drawn from it. For example, only those people who have children in college or people who are retired can be selected from the database. The selected individuals are sent an e-mail questionnaire that has been designed to address the research questions at hand.

International markets are measured in hundreds of millions of people, national markets comprise millions of individuals, and even local markets may constitute hundreds of thousands of households. To obtain information from every single person in a market is usually impossible and obviously impractical. For these reasons, marketing researchers make use of a sample. This chapter describes how researchers go about taking samples. We begin with definitions of basic concepts such as population, sample, and census. Then we discuss the reasons for taking samples. From here, we distinguish the four types of probability sampling methods from the four types of nonprobability sampling methods. Last, we present a step-by-step procedure for taking a sample, regardless of the sampling method used.

BASIC CONCEPTS IN SAMPLES AND SAMPLING

To begin, we acquaint you with some basic terminology used in sampling. The terms we discuss here are population, sample and sample unit, census, sampling error, sample frame, and sample frame error.

Population

The population is the entire group under study as defined by research objectives.

A **population** is defined as the entire group under study as specified by the objectives of the research project. Managers tend to have a vaguer definition of the population than do researchers. This is because the researcher must use the description of the population very precisely, whereas the manager uses it in a more general way.

For instance, let us examine this difference for a research project performed for Terminix Pest Control. If Terminix were interested in determining how prospective customers were combating roaches, ants, spiders, and other insects in their homes, the Terminix manager would probably define the population as "everybody who might use our services." However, the researcher in charge of sample design would use a definition such as "heads of households in those metropolitan areas served by Terminix who are responsible for insect pest control." Notice that the researcher has converted "everybody" to "households" and has indicated more precisely who the respondent will be in the form of "heads of households." The definition is also made more specific by the requirement that the household be in a metropolitan Terminix service area. Population definition error can be devastating to a survey, as you will see by reading Marketing Research Insight 12.1.

Sample and Sample Unit

The sample is a subset of the population, and the sample unit pertains to the basic level of investigation.

A **sample** is a subset of the population that should represent that entire group. Once again, there is a difference in how the manager uses this term versus how it is used by the researcher. The manager will often overlook the "should" aspect of this definition and assume that any sample is a representative sample. However, the researcher is trained in detecting sample errors and is very careful in assessing the degree of representativeness of the subgroup selected to be the sample.

As you would expect, a **sample unit** is the basic level of investigation. That is, in the Terminix example, the unit is a household. For a Weight Watchers survey, the unit would be one person, but for a survey of hospital purchases of laser surgery equipment, the sample unit would be the hospital because hospital purchases are being researched.

MARKETING RESEARCH INSIGHT 12.1

What's Wrong with Defining Foreign Populations in American Terms?

Differences exist between cultures, even for the simplest product. Such differences can be disastrous, as described by Joel Axelrod, President of BRX/GLOBAL, INC., in the following excerpt.

> *It is all too easy to assume that those products that are used in the United States are also used in Western Europe, which is obviously similar to us. In one study, the client shipped a large volume of brownie mix to Germany so that we could ask local housewives to compare the brownies produced via this American mix with the housewives' homemade brownies. Unfortunately, we ran into one small problem. The German consumers did not know what a brownie was, much less how to prepare brownie mixes. No one had walked the supermarket aisles checking to determine if brownies were a known product in Germany.*

Source: *Joel Axelrod, by permission*

Census

A census requires information from everyone in the population.

Although a sample is a subset of a group, a **census** is defined as an accounting of the complete population. Perhaps the best example of a census is the United States Census taken every 10 years by the U.S. Census Bureau. The target population in the case of the U.S. Census is all households in the United States. In truth, this definition of the population constitutes an "ideal" census, for it is virtually impossible to obtain information from every single household in the United States. At best, the Census Bureau can reach only a certain percentage of households, obtaining a census that provides information within the time period of the census-taking activity. Even with a public-awareness promotional campaign budget of several hundred thousand dollars that covered all of the major advertising media forms such as television, newspaper, and radio, and an elaborate follow-up procedure method, the Census Bureau admits that its numbers are inaccurate.[3]

The difficulties encountered by U.S. census takers are identical to those encountered in marketing research. For example, there are instances of individuals who are in transition between residences, without places of residence, illiterate, incapacitated, illegally residing in the United States, or unwilling to participate. Marketing researchers undertaking survey research face all of these problems and a host of others. In fact, researchers long ago realized the impracticality and outright impossibility of taking a census of a population. Consequently, they turned to the use of subsets, or samples, which were chosen to represent the target population.

Sampling Error

Whenever a sample is taken, the survey will reflect sampling error.

Sampling error is any error in a survey that occurs because a sample is used. Sampling error is caused by two factors: (1) the method of sample selection and (2) the size of the sample. You will learn in this chapter that some sampling methods minimize this error, whereas others do not control it well at all. Also, in the next chapter, we show you the relationship between sample size and sampling error.

Sample Frame and Sample Frame Error

A sample frame is a master list of the entire population.

To select a sample, you will need a **sample frame,** which is some master list of all the sample units in the population. For instance, if a researcher had defined a population to be all shoe repair stores in the state of Montana, he or she would need a master listing of these stores as a frame from which to sample. Similarly, if the population being researched were certified public accountants, a sample frame for this group would be needed. In the case of shoe repair stores, a list service such as American Business Lists of Omaha, Nebraska, which has compiled its list of shoe repair stores from Yellow Pages listings, might be used. For CPAs, the researcher could use the list of members of the American Institute of Certified Public Accountants, located in New York City, which contains a listing of all accountants who have passed the CPA exam. Sometimes the researcher is hampered by the lack of a physical list, and the sample frame becomes a matter of whatever access to the population the researcher can conceive of, such as "all shoppers who purchase at least $25 worth of merchandise at a Radio Shack store during the second week of

Organization and association directories are handy sample frames.

March." Here, because some shoppers pay by credit card, some by check, and some with cash, there is no physical master list of qualified shoppers, but there is a stream of shoppers that can be sampled.

A listing of the population may be inaccurate and thus contain sample frame error.

A sample frame invariably contains **sample frame error,** which is the degree to which it fails to account for all of the population. A way to envision sample frame error is by matching the list with the population and seeing to what degree the list adequately matches the targeted population. What do you think is the sample frame in our shoe repair store sample frame? The primary error involved lies in using only Yellow Pages listings. Not all shops are listed in the Yellow Pages, as some have gone out of business, some have come into being since the Yellow Pages were published, and some may not be listed at all. The same type of error exists for CPAs, and the researcher would have to determine how current the list is that he or she is using.

Whenever a sample is drawn, the amount of potential sample frame error should be judged by the researcher.[4] Sometimes the only available sample frame contains much potential frame error, but it is used due to the lack of any other sample frame. It is a researcher's responsibility to seek out a sample frame with the least amount of error at a reasonable cost. The researcher should also apprise the client of the degree of sample frame error involved.

REASONS FOR TAKING A SAMPLE

Taking a sample is less expensive than taking a census.

There are two general reasons a sample is almost always more desirable than a census. First, there are practical considerations such as cost and population size that make a sample more desirable than a census. Taking a census is expensive as consumer populations may number in the millions. If the population is restricted to a medium-sized metropolitan area, hundreds of thousands of individuals can be involved. Even when using a mail survey, accessing the members of a large population is cost prohibitive.

Second, typical research firms or the typical researcher cannot analyze the huge amounts of data generated by a census. Although computer statistical programs can handle thousands of observations with ease, they slow down appreciably with tens of thousands, and most are unable to accommodate hundreds of thousands of observations. In fact, even before a researcher considers the size of the computer or tabulation equipment to be used, he or she must consider the various data preparation procedures involved in just handling the questionnaires or responses and transferring these responses into computer files. The sheer physical volume places limitations on the researcher's staff and equipment.

National opinion polls rarely have sample sizes of more than 1,200 respondents.

How large a group is considered "sufficient" to represent a specific population? The numbers are surprisingly small. Statisticians refer to "large samples" as anything greater than 30 observations! Most national political polls use samples of between 1,100 and 1,300 respondents to represent the population of over 265 million U.S. citizens. Apparently, the opinion polling industry believes that "sufficient" information can be obtained with a sample that represents a tiny fraction of the population. (Chapter 13 describes sample size determination in detail.)

Approaching sufficiency of information from a different tack, we can turn to an informal cost–benefit analysis to defend the use of samples. If a project director had chosen a sample of 500 respondents at a cost of $10,000 and had determined the average family size to be 3.2 individuals, what would be the result if he or she chose a completely different sample of the same size in identical fashion to determine the same characteristic? For example, suppose the second sample resulted in an estimate of 3.3 members per family. He or she has spent $10,000 more, but what has been gained with the second sample? Common sense suggests that very little in the form of additional information has been gained, for if he or she combined the two samples he or she would come up with an estimate of 3.25 family members. In effect, $10,000 more has been spent to gain .05 family members' worth of information. It is extremely doubtful that this additional precision offsets the additional cost.

TWO BASIC SAMPLING METHODS: PROBABILITY VERSUS NONPROBABILITY

With probability sampling, the chances of selection are "known," but with nonprobability sampling, they are not known.

In the final analysis, all sample designs fall into one of two categories: probability or nonprobability. **Probability samples** are ones in which members of the population have a known chance (probability) of being selected into the sample. **Nonprobability samples,** on the other hand, are instances in which the chances (probability) of selecting members from the population into the sample are unknown. Unfortunately, the terms "known" and "unknown" are misleading for, in order to calculate a precise probability, one would need to know the exact size of the population, and it is impossible to know the exact size of the population in most marketing research studies. If we were targeting, for example, readers of the magazine *People,* the exact size of the population changes from week to week as a result of new subscriptions, old ones running out, and fluctuations in counter sales as a function of whose picture is on the cover. You would be hard pressed, in fact, to think of cases in which the population size is known and stable enough to be associated with an exact number.

The essence of a "known" probability rests in the sampling method rather than in knowing the exact size of the population. Probability sampling methods are those that ensure that, if the exact size of the population were known for the moment in time that sampling took place, the exact probability of any member of the population being selected into the sample *could* be calculated. In other words, this probability value is really never calculated in actuality, but we are assured by the sample method that the chances of any one population member being selected into the sample could be computed.

With nonprobability methods there is no way to determine the probability even if the population size is known because the selection technique is subjective. So it is the sampling method rather than the knowledge of the size of the sample or the size of the population that determines probability or nonprobability sampling.

With probability sampling, the method determines the chances of a sample unit being selected into the sample.

Probability Sampling Methods

There are four probability sampling methods: simple random sampling, systematic sampling, cluster sampling, and stratified sampling (Table 12.1). A discussion of each method follows.

TABLE 12.1

Four Different Probability Sampling Methods

SIMPLE RANDOM SAMPLING

The researcher uses a table of random numbers, random digit dialing, or some other random selection procedure that guarantees that each member of the population has an identical chance of being selected into the sample.

SYSTEMATIC SAMPLING

Using a list of the members of the population, the researcher selects a random starting point for the first sample member. A constant "skip interval" is then used to select every other sample member. A skip interval must be used such that the entire list is covered, regardless of the starting point. This procedure accomplishes the same end as simple random sampling, and it is more efficient.

CLUSTER SAMPLING

The population is divided into geographic areas, each of which must be considered to be very similar to the others. The researcher can then randomly select a few areas and perform a census of each one. Alternatively, the researcher can randomly select more areas and take samples from each one. This method is desirable when highly similar areas can be easily identified.

STRATIFIED SAMPLING

If the population is believed to have a skewed distribution for one or more of its distinguishing factors (for instance, income or product ownership), the researcher identifies subpopulations called strata. A simple random sample is then taken of each stratum. Weighting procedures may be applied to estimate population values such as the mean. This approach is better suited than other probability sampling methods for populations that are not distributed in a bell-shaped pattern.

Simple Random Sampling

With **simple random sampling,** the probability of being selected into the sample is "known" and equal for all members of the population. This sampling technique is expressed by the following formula:

$$\text{Probability of selection} = \frac{\text{sample size}}{\text{population size}}$$

With simple random sampling, the probability of selection into the sample is "known" and equal for all members of the population.

There are a number of examples of simple random sampling, including the "blind draw" method and the table of random numbers method.

The "blind draw" is a form of simple random sampling.

The "Blind Draw" Method. The **"blind draw" method** involves blindly choosing participants by their names or some other unique designation. For example, suppose that you wanted to determine the attitudes of students in your marketing research class toward a career in marketing research. Assume that the particular class that you have chosen as your population has 30 students enrolled. To do a blind draw, you first write the name of every student on a 3-by-5 index card, then take all of these cards and put them inside a container of some sort. Next, you place a top on the container and shake it very vigorously. This procedure ensures that the names are thoroughly mixed. You then ask some person to draw the sample. This individual is blindfolded so that he or she cannot see inside the container. You would instruct him or her to take out ten 3-by-5 cards as the sample. (For now, let us just concentrate on sample selection methods. We cover sample size determination in the next

Lotteries use selection methods that embody simple random sampling assumptions.

chapter.) In this sample, every student in the class has a known and equal probability of being selected with a probability of 10/30 or 0.33. In other words, each student has a 1 out of 3 chance of being selected into that sample. Of course, you could use ID numbers or some other designation for each population member as long as there were no duplicates.

A random number table embodies simple random sampling assumptions.

The Table of Random Numbers Method. A more sophisticated application of simple random sampling is to use a **table of random numbers** which is a listing of numbers whose random order is assured. If you look at a table of random numbers, you will not be able to see any systematic sequence of the numbers regardless of where on the table you begin and whether you go up, down, left, right, or diagonally across the entries.

To use a table of random numbers to draw the sample in your careers in marketing research study, assign each student in the class a number, say 1 through 30. Granted, we will select only 10 students, but every member of our population must be uniquely identified before we begin the selection process. Or you might use Social Security numbers because these are unique to each person. If each student is given a number from 1 to 30, it is a simple matter to use a table of random numbers to draw the sample.

Marketing Research Insight 12.2 on page 366 shows the steps involved in using a table of random numbers to select students from this 30-member population. Beginning with any starting point, you would progress through the table of random numbers seeking numbers from 1 to 30. As each of the qualifying numbers is encountered, it would constitute a student drawn into the sample. All numbers greater than 30 are automatically skipped. If you encounter the same number twice within the same sample draw, the number is skipped over, because it is improper to collect information twice from the same person. Such an occurrence would constitute overrepresentation of that person in the sample and violate our "and equal" requirement.

Advantages and Disadvantages of Simple Random Sampling. Simple random sampling is an appealing sampling method simply because it embodies the requirements necessary to obtain a probability sample and therefore to derive unbiased estimates of the population's characteristics. This sampling method guarantees that every member of the population has a known and equal chance of being selected into the sample; therefore, the resulting sample, no matter what the size, will be a valid representation of the population.

Using a table of random numbers to draw a simple random sample requires a complete accounting of the population.

However, there are some disadvantages associated with simple random sampling. To use either the blind draw or the table of random numbers approach, it is necessary to predesignate each population member. In the blind draw example, each student's name was written on a 3-by-5 card, whereas in the random numbers example, each student was assigned a specific number. In essence, simple random sampling necessarily begins with a complete listing of the population, and current and complete listings are often difficult to obtain. It is also very cumbersome to provide unique designations for each population member. Numbering from 1 through an unknown total population size (N) is tedious and invites administrative errors. Using names is unsatisfactory due to duplicates, and nine-digit Social Security numbers are not amenable to random number tables.

Simple Random Sampling Used in Practice. Still, it would be improper for you to leave this section with the notion that simple random sampling is impossible to use in marketing research as there are cases in which simple ran-

MARKETING RESEARCH INSIGHT 12.2

How to Use a Table of Random Numbers to Select a Simple Random Sample

STEP 1: Assign all members of the population a unique number.

NAME	NUMBER
Adams, Bob	1
Baker, Carol	2
Brown, Fred	3
Chester, Harold	4
Downs, Jane	5
Zimwitz, Roland	30

STEP 2: Select any starting point in the table of random numbers and find the first number that corresponds to a number on the list of the population. In the following example, number 32 has been chosen as the starting point.

23	15	75	48	59	01	
65	54	55	50	43	10	
03	87	16	30	28	32	← *Starting point: move left to*
38	97	29	49	51	94	*the end of the row, then*
96	31	26	17	18	99	*down to the next row;*
11	74	27	93	81	44	*move right to the end, then*
43	36	58	05	59	09	*down to the next row, and so on.*

STEP 3: Select the person corresponding to that number into the sample.

#28—White, Ann

STEP 4: Continue to the next number that qualifies and select that person into the sample.

#30—Zimwitz, Roland

STEP 5: Continue on in the same manner until the full sample is selected. If you encounter a number selected earlier, simply skip over it.

dom sample designs are employed quite successfully. There are three practical applications of simple random sampling: small populations, random digit dialing, and computerized lists.

Three practical applications of simple random sampling are small populations, random digit dialing, and computerized lists.

Obviously, one of the most troublesome aspects of simple random sampling is a listing of the population. Consequently, in those marketing research studies where "small" and stable populations are involved, it is wise to use simple random sampling. For instance, the owner/operator of a hair styling shop once wanted to know how his customers would react to a proposed location change. He hoped to move from the present location on a secondary commercial street to a minimall being developed on a main thoroughfare. Over time, the owner had carefully maintained a computer file on each customer with specifics on services used, dates, and basic personal information. The population of 471 customers was quite amenable for simple random sampling with the aid of a table of random numbers. Each customer was numbered from 1 to 471 based on location in the computer file, and 50 random numbers between 1 and 471 were drawn from the table to create the sample.

Other situations in which simple random sampling is commonly used rely on a computer to generate the numbers and select the sample. One instance in which simple random sampling is employed quite successfully is through the use of random digit dialing. **Random digit dialing** is used in telephone surveys to overcome the problems of unlisted and new telephone numbers. Unlisted numbers are a growing concern not only for researchers in the United States, but in all industrialized countries such as those in Europe as well.[5] In random digit dialing, telephone numbers are generated randomly with the aid of a computer. Telephone interviewers call these numbers and administer the survey to the respondent once the person has been qualified. However, random digit dialing may result in a large number of calls to nonexisting tele-

Random digit dialing overcomes problems of unlisted and new telephone numbers.

CATI systems typically have random digit dialing systems built into them.

Plus-one dialing is a convenient variation of random digit dialing.

phone numbers. A popular variation of random digit dialing that reduces this problem is the **plus-one dialing procedure** in which numbers are selected from a telephone directory and a digit, such as a "1," is added to each number to determine what telephone number is then dialed.[6]

SPSS allows you to randomly select subsets of cases in a file.

Finally, there is the possibility of selecting respondents from computer tapes, company files, or commercial listing services, which are then converted into computer input. All computers can be programmed to provide a random number generator. This random number generator may be applied against the population list in order to draw a sample. This procedure is occurring more frequently because population lists are becoming more available in the form of tapes or computer files. The computer routine can work with random numbers of as many digits as are necessary, so even Social Security numbers with nine digits are no problem. Companies with credit files, subscription lists, or MISs have the greatest opportunity to use this approach, or a research company may turn to specialized sampling companies such as Survey Sampling to have it draw a random sample of households or businesses in a certain geographic area.

These three cases—small populations, random digit dialing, and sampling from computerized lists—constitute the bulk of the use of simple random sampling in marketing research. In other instances, the practical problems of embodying simple random sampling assumptions overwhelm its advantages. The most prevalent frustration is the need to obtain a complete listing of the population. It is difficult, particularly in the case of marketing research projects involving consumer goods, to be able to secure such a listing. In the instance of industrial marketing research, listings are more prevalent, particularly if trade organization member listings, industrial directories, or commercially available mailing lists exist.

Without computer assistance, simple random sampling has practical implementation problems to overcome.

Even with a complete listing of the population in hand, it may not be in computer file form, so there is the practical problem of employing a device that embodies simple random sampling assumptions. Using someone to select names from a box full of 3-by-5 cards, for example, would not be appropriate, for that individual would be subject to fatigue and other subtle biases (for instance, always drawing from the right-hand side of the box), which would violate the requirements of known and equal probability of selection. Beyond using a person, there is the opportunity to use mechanical or electronic devices to draw the sample. Such devices include large drums, which are used to draw lottery winners as well as the computer random number generators we just described.

Both of these examples, however, require time and effort to set up for implementation. Plus, once the random numbers are selected, someone must match them up with the associated members of the population. Often, the additional time and expense required to use simple random sampling eliminates it from consideration. Typically, a more economical probability sampling method is used such as systematic sampling.

Systematic Sampling

Systematic sampling is more efficient than simple random sampling.

Systematic sampling is one of the most prevalent types of sampling techniques used in place of simple random sampling. Its popularity over simple random sampling is based primarily on the "economic efficiency" that it represents; systematic sampling can be applied with less difficulty and accomplished in a shorter time period than can simple random sampling. Furthermore, in many instances, systematic sampling has the potential to create a sample that is almost identical in quality to samples created from simple random sampling.

To use systematic sampling, it is necessary to obtain a listing of the population, just as in the case of simple random sampling. However, it is not necessary to transcribe names, numbers, or any other designations onto slips of paper or computer files. Instead, the researcher decides on a **"skip interval,"** which is calculated by dividing the number of names on the list by the sample size. Names are selected based on this skip interval. The skip interval is computed very simply through the use of the following formula:

One must calculate a "skip interval" to use systematic sampling.

$$\text{Skip interval} = \frac{\text{population list size}}{\text{sample size}}$$

For example, if one were using the local telephone directory and calculated a skip interval of 250, every 250th name would be selected into the sample. The use of this skip interval formula ensures that the entire list will be covered. Marketing Research Insight 12.3 shows how to take a systematic sample.

Researchers would not actually count every listing in a telephone directory. Rather, they estimate the population list size by randomly selecting several pages and determining the average listings per page.

Why Systematic Sampling Is Efficient. Systematic sampling is probability sampling because it employs a random starting point, which ensures there is sufficient randomness in the systematic sampling to approximate a known and equal probability of any person or item in the population being selected into the sample. In essence, systematic sampling envisions the list as a set comprising mutually exclusive samples, each one of which is equally representative of the listed population.

MARKETING RESEARCH INSIGHT 12.3

How to Take a Systematic Sample

STEP 1: Identify a listing of the population that contains an acceptable level of sample frame error.
Example: The telephone book for your city.

STEP 2: Compute the skip interval by dividing the number of names on the list by the sample size.
Example: 25,000 names in the phone book, sample size of 500, so skip interval = every 50th name

STEP 3: Using random number(s), determine a starting position for sampling the list.
Example: Select: Random number for page number.
Select: Random number of column on that page.
Select: Random number for name position in that column (say, Jones, William P.).

STEP 4: Apply the skip interval to determine which names on the list will be in the sample.
Example: Jones, William P. (Skip 50 names.)
Lathum, Ferdinand B.

STEP 5: Treat the list as "circular"; that is, the first name on the list is now the initial name you selected, and the last name is now the name just prior to the initially selected one.
Example: When you come to the end of the phone book names (Zs), just continue on through the beginning (As).

How does systematic sampling work? If you were using a telephone directory, it would be necessary to use a random number to determine the page on which you will start. Suppose page 53 is drawn. Another random number would be drawn to decide the column on that page. Assume the 3rd column is drawn. A final random number would be used to determine the actual starting position in that column. Let us say the 17th name is selected. From that beginning point, the skip interval would be employed. The skip interval would ensure that the entire list would be covered, and the final name selected would be approximately one skip interval before the starting point. It is convenient to think of the listing as a circular file, like a Rolodex file, such that A actually follows Z if the list were alphabetized, and the random starting point determines where the list "begins."

Systematic sampling is more efficient than simple random sampling because only one or a very few random numbers need to be drawn at the beginning.

The essential difference between systematic sampling and simple random sampling is apparent in the use of the words "systematic" and "random." The system used in systematic sampling is the skip interval, whereas the randomness in simple random sampling is determined through the use of successive random draws. Systematic sampling works its way through the entire population from beginning to end, whereas random sampling guarantees that the complete population will be covered but without a systematic pattern. The efficiency in systematic sampling is gained by two features: (1) the skip interval aspect and (2) the need to use random number(s) only at the beginning.

Systematic sampling is used widely in certain types of marketing research. The key to the use of systematic sampling lies in the availability of lists, directories, or other listlike specifications of the population. The most prevalent example is the one previously indicated in which names are drawn from a telephone directory. Other commonly used lists are city directories, company customer files, and association membership lists. One variation is systematically sampling from a stream of visitors or customers with interviewers stationed at entrances or exits.[7]

With systematic sampling the small loss in sampling precision is counterbalanced by its economic savings.

Disadvantages of Systematic Sampling. Although systematic sampling is simpler, less time consuming, and less expensive to employ than simple random sampling, it is less representative in the final analysis than simple random sampling because it arbitrarily places population members into groups before the sample is selected. Nonetheless, the small loss in sample precision is more than counterbalanced by the economic savings, so systematic sampling is often chosen when simple random sampling is impractical or too expensive. The greatest danger in the use of systematic sampling lies in the listing of the population. Sample frame error can be bothersome, plus a list may contain hidden patterns or "periodicities." For example, the skip pattern used to draw a sample from a city directory could result in drawing a disproportionate number of homes on corner lots. If the survey was on lawn care products, the results could be biased because corner lots are normally larger.

Cluster Sampling

A cluster sampling method divides the population into groups, any one of which can be considered a representative sample.

Another form of probability sampling is known as **cluster sampling,** in which the population is divided into subgroups, each of which represents the entire population. Note that the basic concept behind cluster sampling is very similar to the one described for systematic sampling, but the implementation differs. The procedure identifies identical clusters. Any one cluster, therefore, will be a satisfactory representation of the population. If you were to take a series of independent simple random samples from any population, the various samples would be clusters. However, cluster sampling goes a step further in striving to gain economic efficiency over simple random sampling by simplifying the sampling procedure used. We illustrate cluster sampling by describing a type of cluster sample known as area sampling.

Area sampling employs either a one-step or two-step approach.

In area sampling, geographic areas (clusters) are selected by a random method.

Area Sampling as a Form of Cluster Sampling. In **area sampling,** the researcher subdivides the population to be surveyed into areas, such as census tracts, cities, neighborhoods, or any other convenient and identifiable geographic designation. The researcher has two options at this point: a one-step approach or a two-step approach. In the **one-step** approach, the researcher may believe the various geographic areas to be sufficiently identical to permit him or her to concentrate his or her attention on just one area and then generalize the results to the full population. But the researcher would need to select that one area randomly and perform a census of its members. Alternatively, he or she may employ a **two-step** approach to the sampling process. That is, for the first step, the researcher could select a random sample of areas, and then for the second step, he or she could decide on a probability method to sample individuals within the chosen areas. The two-step approach is preferable to the one-step approach because there is always the possibility that a single cluster may be less representative than the researcher believes. But the two-step method is more costly because more areas and time are involved. Marketing Research Insight 12.4 on page 372 illustrates how to take an area sample using subdivisions as the clusters.[8]

Area grid sampling is a variation of the area sampling method. To use it, the researcher imposes a grid over a map of the area to be surveyed. Each cell within the grid then becomes a cluster. The difference between area grid sampling and area sampling lies primarily in the use of a grid framework, which cuts across natural or artificial boundaries such as streets, rivers, city limits, or

Area sampling can be used effectively when groups in the population are highly similar.

MARKETING RESEARCH INSIGHT 12.4

How to Take an Area Sampling Using Subdivisions

STEP 1: Determine the geographic area to be surveyed, and identify its subdivisions. Each subdivision cluster should be highly similar to all others.

Example: Ten subdivisions within five miles of the proposed site for our new restaurant; assign each a number.

STEP 2: Decide on the use of one-step or two-step cluster sampling.

Example: We decide to use two-step cluster sampling.

STEP 3: (Assuming two-step) Using random numbers, select the subdivisions to be sampled.

Example: Select four subdivisions randomly, say numbers 3, 5, 2, and 9.

STEP 4: Using some probability method of sample selection, select the members of each chosen subdivision to be included in the sample.

Example: Identify a random starting point; instruct field workers to drop off the survey at every fifth house (systematic sampling).

other separations normally used in area sampling. Geodemography has been used to describe the demographic profiles of the various clusters.[9] Regardless of how the population is sliced up, the researcher has the option of a one-step or a two-step approach.

Stratified Sampling

With stratified sampling, the population is separated into different strata and a sample is taken from each stratum.

All of the sampling methods we have described thus far implicitly assume that the population has a normal or bell-shaped distribution for its key properties. That is, there is the assumption that every potential sample unit is a fairly good representation of the population, and any who are extreme in one way are perfectly counterbalanced by opposite extreme potential sample units. Unfortunately, it is common to work with populations in marketing research that contain unique subgroupings; you might encounter a population that is not distributed symmetrically across a normal curve. With this situation, unless you make adjustments in your sample design, you will end up with a sample described as "statistically inefficient" or, in other words, inaccurate. One solution is **stratified sampling,** which separates the population into different subgroups and then samples all of these subgroups.

Stratified sampling is appropriate when we expect that responses will vary across strata.

Working with "Skewed" Populations. A **"skewed" population** deviates quite a bit from what is assumed to be the "normal" distribution case in the use of simple random, systematic, or cluster sampling. Because of this abnormal distribution, there exists the potential for an inaccurate sample. For example, let's take the case of a college that is attempting to assess the quality of its educational programs. A researcher has formulated the question, "To what extent do you value a college degree?" The response options are along a 5-point scale where 1 equals "not valued at all" and 5 equals "very highly valued." The population of students is defined by year: freshman, sophomore, junior, and senior. It is believed that the means will differ by the respondent's year status because seniors probably value a degree more than do juniors who value a degree more than do sophomores, and so on. At the same time, it is expected that seniors would be more in agreement (have less variability) than would underclasspersons. This belief is due to the fact that freshmen are students who are trying

Stratified sampling should be used because college students' attitudes toward their education change as they approach graduation.

out college, some of whom are not serious about completing it and do not value it highly, but some of whom are intending to become doctors, lawyers, or professionals whose training will include graduate degree work as well as their present college work. The serious freshmen students would value a college degree highly, whereas the less serious ones would not. So, we would expect much variability in the freshmen students, less in sophomores, still less in juniors, and the least with college seniors. The situation might be something similar to the distributions illustrated in Figure 12.1 on page 374.

What would happen if we used a simple random sample of equal size for each of our college groups? Because sample accuracy is determined by the variability in the population, we would be least accurate with freshmen and most accurate with seniors. To state this situation differently, we would be statistically overefficient with seniors and statistically underefficient with freshmen because we would be oversampling the seniors and undersampling the freshmen. To gain overall statistical efficiency, we should draw a larger sample of freshmen and a smaller one of seniors. We might do this by allocating the sample proportionately based on the total number of the freshmen, sophomores, juniors, and seniors, each taken as a percentage of the whole college population. (Normally, there are fewer seniors than juniors than sophomores than freshmen in a college.) Thus, we would be drawing the smallest sample from the seniors group, who have the least variability in their assessments of the value of their college education, and the largest sample from the freshmen, who have the most variability in their assessments. We discuss this more fully in the next chapter.

With stratified random sampling, one takes a skewed population and identifies the subgroups or **strata** contained within it. Simple random sampling, systematic sampling, or some other type of probability sampling procedure is then applied to draw a sample from each stratum. The stratum sample sizes can differ based on knowledge of the variability in each population stratum and with the aim of achieving the greatest statistical efficiency.

Stratified sampling is used when the researcher is working with a "skewed" population divided into strata and wishes to achieve high statistical efficiency.

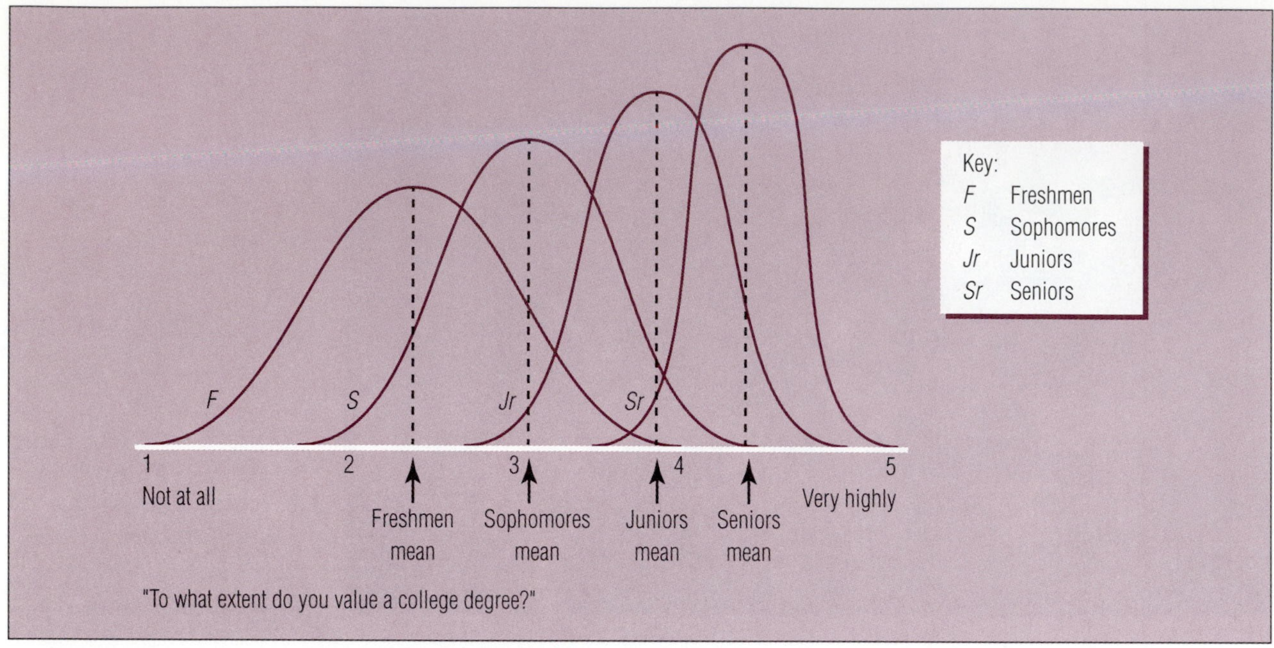

Figure 12.1

Stratified Simple Random Sampling: Using College Year Status as a Stratification Factor

Accuracy of Stratified Sampling. How does stratified sampling result in a more accurate overall sample? Actually, there are two ways this accuracy is achieved. First, stratified sampling allows for explicit analysis of each stratum. The college degree example illustrates why a researcher would want to know about the distinguishing differences between the strata in order to assess the true picture. Each stratum represents a different response profile, and by allocating sample size based on the variability in the strata profiles, a more efficient sample design is achieved.

A stratified sample may require the calculation of a weighted mean to achieve accuracy.

Second, there is a procedure that allows the estimation of the overall sample mean by use of a **weighted mean,** whose formula takes into consideration the sizes of the strata relative to the total population size and applies those proportions to the strata's means. The population mean is calculated by multiplying each stratum by its proportion and summing the weighted stratum means. This formula results in an estimate that is consistent with the true distribution of the population when the sample sizes used in the strata are not proportionate to their shares of the population. Here is the formula that is used for two strata:

$$Mean_{Population} = (mean_A)(proportion_A) + (mean_B)(proportion_B)$$

where A signifies stratum A, and B signifies stratum B.

To apply stratified sampling, researchers often use an easily identified surrogate as the stratification mechanism.

How to Apply Stratified Sampling. There are a number of instances in which stratified sampling is used in marketing research because skewed populations are often encountered. Prior knowledge of populations under study, augmented by research objectives sensitive to subgroupings, sometimes reveals that the population is not normally distributed. Under these circumstances, it is advantageous to apply stratified sampling to preserve the diversity of the various subgroups. Usually, a **surrogate measure,** which is some observable or easily determined characteristic of each population member, is used to help partition or separate the population members into their various subgroupings. For example, in the instance of the college, the year classification of each student is a handy surrogate. With its internal records, the college could easily identify students in each stratum, and this determination would be the stratification method. Of course, there is the opportunity for the researcher to divide the population into as many relevant strata as necessary to capture different subpopulations. For instance, the college might want to further stratify on college of study, gender, or grade point average (GPA) ranges. Perhaps professional school students value their degrees more than do liberal arts students, female more than male students, and high GPA students more than average GPA or failing students. The key issue is that the researcher should use some basis for dividing the population into strata which results in different responses across strata. There is no need to stratify if all strata respond alike.

Researchers should select a basis for stratification that reveals different responses across the strata.

If the strata sample sizes are faithful to their relative sizes in the population, you have what is called a **proportionate stratified sample** design. Here you do not use the weighted formula because each stratum's weight is automatically accounted for by its sample size. But with **disproportionate stratified sampling,** the weighted formula needs to be used because the strata sizes do not reflect their relative proportions of the population. We have provided a step-by-step description of stratified sampling in Marketing Research Insight 12.5.

The weighted mean formula is not needed with a proportionate sample.

MARKETING RESEARCH INSIGHT 12.5

How to Take a Stratified Sample

STEP 1: Be assured that the population's distribution for some key factor is not bell-shaped and that separate subpopulations exist.

Example: Cellular automobile telephone owners differ from nonowners in their use of long-distance calls.

STEP 2: Use this factor or some surrogate variable to divide the population into strata consistent with the separate subpopulations identified.

Example: Use a screening question on ownership/nonownership of a cellular automobile telephone. This may require a screening survey using random digit dialing to identify respondent pools for each stratum.

STEP 3: Select a probability sample from each stratum.

Example: Use a computer to select simple random samples for each stratum.

STEP 4: Examine each stratum for managerially relevant differences.

Example: Do owners differ from nonowners in their long-distance calls? Answer: Owners average 35 minutes per month; nonowners average 20 minutes per month.

STEP 5: If stratum sample sizes are not proportionate to the stratum sizes in the population, use the weighted mean formula to estimate the population value(s).

Example: If owners are 20% and nonowners are 80% of the population, the estimate is $(35)(.20) + (20)(.80) = 23$ minutes per month.

Nonprobability Sampling Methods

With nonprobability sampling methods, every member of the population does not have a chance of being included in the sample.

All of the sampling methods we have described thus far embody probability sampling assumptions. In each case, the probability of any item being selected from the population into the sample is known, even though it cannot be calculated precisely. The critical difference between probability and nonprobability sampling methods is the mechanics used in the sample design. With a nonprobability sampling method, selection is not based on probability. That is, you cannot calculate the probability of any one person in the population being selected into the sample. Still, each nonprobability sampling method strives to draw a representative sample. There are four nonprobability sampling methods: convenience samples, judgment samples, referral samples, and quota samples (Table 12.2). A discussion of each method follows.

Convenience Samples

Convenience samples may misrepresent the population.

Convenience samples are samples drawn at the convenience of the interviewer. Accordingly, the most convenient areas to a researcher in terms of time and effort turns out to be "high-traffic" areas such as shopping malls or busy pedestrian intersections. The selection of the place and, consequently, prospective respondents is subjective rather than objective. Certain members of the population are automatically eliminated from the sampling process. For instance, there are those people who may be infrequent or even nonvisitors of the particular high-traffic area being used. On the other hand, in the absence

TABLE 12.2

Four Different Types of Nonprobability Sampling Methods

CONVENIENCE SAMPLING

The researcher or interviewer uses a "high-traffic" location such as a busy pedestrian area or a shopping mall to intercept potential respondents. Error occurs in the form of members of the population who are infrequent or nonusers of that location.

JUDGMENT SAMPLING

The researcher uses his or her judgment or that of some other knowledgeable person to identify who will be in the sample. Subjectivity enters in here, and certain members of the population will have a smaller chance of selection than will others.

REFERRAL SAMPLING

Respondents are asked for the names or identities of others like themselves who might qualify to take part in the survey. Members of the population who are less well known, disliked, or whose opinions conflict with the respondent have a low probability of being selected.

QUOTA SAMPLING

The researcher identifies quota characteristics such as demographic or product use factors and uses these to set up quotas for each class of respondent. The sizes of the quotas are determined by the researcher's belief for the relative size of each class of respondent in the population. Often, quota sampling is used as a means of ensuring convenience samples will have the desired proportion of different respondent classes.

Convenience sampling is used when large numbers of potential respondents are found at a convenient location.

of strict selection procedures, there are members of the population who may be omitted because of their physical appearance, general demeanor, or by the fact that they are in a group rather than alone.

Mall intercepts are convenience samples.

Mall-intercept companies often use a convenience sampling method to recruit respondents. For example, shoppers are encountered at large shopping malls and quickly qualified with screening questions. For those satisfying the desired population characteristics, a questionnaire may be administered or a taste-test performed. Alternatively, the respondent may be given a test product and asked if he or she would use it at home. A follow-up telephone call some days later solicits his or her reaction to the product's performance. In this case, the convenience extends beyond easy access of respondents into considerations of set-up for taste tests, storage of products to be distributed, and control of the interviewer workforce. Additionally, large numbers of respondents can be recruited in a matter of days. The screening questions and geographic dispersion of malls may appear to reduce the subjectivity inherent in the sample design, but in fact the vast majority of the population was not there and could not be approached to take part. Yet, there are ways of controlling convenience sample selection error using a quota system, which we discuss shortly.

Judgment Samples

With a judgment sample, one "judges" the sample to be representative.

Judgment samples are somewhat different from convenience samples in concept because they require the judgment or an "educated guess" as to who should represent the population. Often, the researcher or some individual helping the researcher who has considerable knowledge about the population will choose those individuals that he or she feels constitute the sample.

Focus group studies often use judgment sampling rather than probability sampling. In a recent focus group concerning the need for a low-calorie, low-fat microwave oven cookbook, 12 women were selected as representative of the present and prospective market. Six of these women had owned a microwave oven for three or more years; three of the women had owned the oven for less than three years; and three of the women were in the market for a microwave oven. In the judgment of the researcher, these 12 women represented the population adequately for the purposes of the focus group. It must be quickly pointed out, however, that the intent of this focus group was far different from the intent of a survey. Consequently, the use of a judgment sample was considered satisfactory for this particular phase in the research process for the cookbook. The focus group findings served as the foundation for a large-scale regional survey conducted two months later that relied on a probability sampling method.

Referral Samples

A referral sample asks respondents to provide the names of additional respondents.

Referral samples, sometimes called "snowball samples," require respondents to provide the names of additional respondents. Such lists begin when the researcher compiles a short list of sample units that is smaller than the total sample he or she desires for the study. After each respondent is interviewed, he or she is queried about the names of other possible respondents. In this manner, additional respondents are referred by previous respondents. Or, as the other name implies, the sample grows just as a snowball grows when it is rolled downhill.

Referral samples are most appropriate when there is a limited and disappointingly short sample frame and when respondents can provide the names of others who would qualify for the survey. The nonprobability aspects of referral sampling comes from the selectivity used throughout. The initial list

Judgment samples can be unethically applied to marketing research, as in the case of readership research. Readership research is high stakes in that the publication that claims the most readership can make the pitch to potential advertisers that their publications will get them the biggest bang for their bucks. As stated by David Forsyth, chairman of the Business Advertising Committee of the Advertising Research Foundation, "Abuse of the research process, whether intentionally or unknowingly, has become so commonplace that all studies are now suspect and disregarded." The article goes on to describe unethical audience researchers as foxes who are counting chickens.

The foxes commit a number of sins, and one of them is sample selection. Here are ways foxes pick samples so as to ensure that the findings will be positive for the publications paying for the research.

- *Ask the sponsoring publication's staff to handpick a group of "representative" subscribers.*
- *Select the sample from a list of those readers who have returned a reader reply card.*
- *Choose the sample only from among those who have been subscribing for a long time.*
- *Draw the sample from lists advertisers supply that were compiled based on prior responses to their ads in the publication.*

An ethical sample selection procedure would select subscribers at random from the publication's entire, recently verified circulation list.[10]

may also be special in some way, and the primary means of adding people to the sample is by tapping the memories of those on the original list. Referral samples are often useful in industrial marketing research situations.[11]

Quota Samples

The **quota sample** establishes a specific quota for various types of individuals to be interviewed. It is a form of nonprobability sampling used prevalently by marketing researchers. The quotas are determined through application of the research objectives and are defined by key characteristics used to identify the population. In the application of quota sampling, a field worker is provided with screening criteria that will classify the potential respondent into a particular quota cell. For example, if the interviewer is assigned to obtain a sample quota of 50 each for black females, black males, white females, and white males, the qualifying characteristics would be race and gender. Assuming our field workers were working mall intercepts, each would determine through visual inspection where the prospective respondent falls and work toward filling the quota in each of the four cells. So a quota system overcomes much of the nonrepresentativeness danger inherent in convenience samples.

Quota samples rely on key characteristics to define the composition of the sample.

Quota samples are often used by companies that have a firm grasp on the features characterizing the individuals they wish to study in a particular marketing research project. A large bank, for instance, might stipulate that the final sample be one-half adult males and one-half adult females because in their understanding of their market, the customer profile is about 50–50, male and female.

Quota samples are appropriate when you have a detailed demographic profile of the population on which to base the sample.

Sample quotas are sometimes used to facilitate field worker control. Often, there is considerable opportunity for field workers to apply their own judgment in the selection of respondents. However, if the field worker is given guidelines establishing quotas for various types of individuals to be included in the sample, the researcher has an assurance that the final sample composition will be faithful to his or her prior specifications. In no way does this approach eliminate the subjectivity or the nonprobability aspects of the sampling method; however, it does gain the necessary control to ensure that the final sample will include people within the marketing researcher's definition of the population. Or it may guarantee that he or she has sufficient subsample sizes for meaningful subgroup analysis.

DEVELOPING A SAMPLE PLAN

Up to this point, we have discussed various aspects of sampling as though they were discrete and seemingly unrelated decisions. However, they are logically joined together, and there is a definite sequence of steps, called the **sample plan,** that the researcher goes through in order to draw and ultimately arrive at the final sample. These steps are illustrated in Figure 12.2 on page 380. Now that you are acquainted with basic terms, definitions, and concepts involved with sampling, we can describe these steps in detail.

Step 1: Define the Relevant Population

As you know, the very first step to be considered in the sampling process requires a definition of the target population under study. We indicated earlier in the chapter that the target population is identified by the marketing re-

A sample plan begins with the population definition.

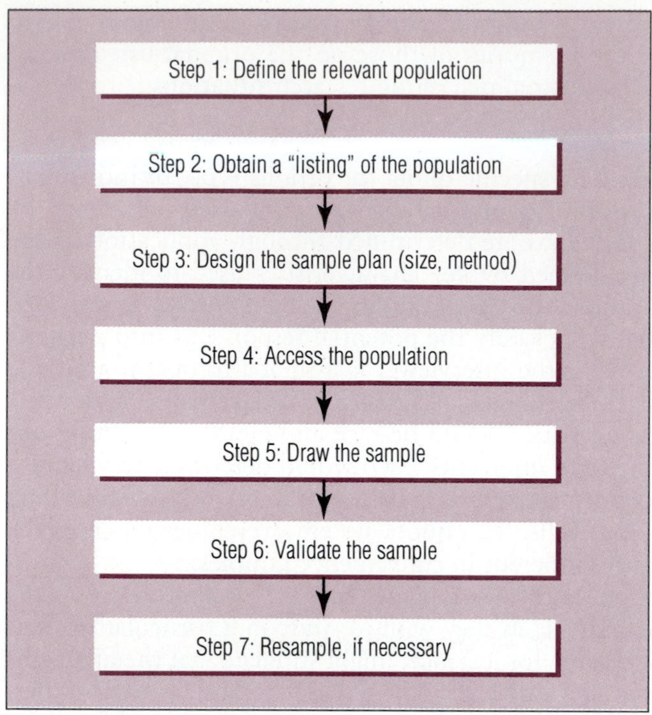

Figure 12.2

Steps in the Sampling Process

search study objectives; however, typically at the beginning of the sampling phase of a research project, the focus on the relevant population is necessarily sharpened. This sharpening involves the translation of nebulous descriptions of the target population into fairly specific demographic or other characteristics that separate the target population from other populations. The task here is for the researcher to specify the sample unit in the form of a precise description of the type of person to be surveyed.

Demographic descriptions, such as age range, income range, educational level, and so forth, are typically used in population definitions. They are also used in target market definitions that, by the way, are excellent starting points for population definitions. Life-style descriptions may also be included. Finally, other types of descriptions are available. Most of these are product-specific or company-specific. That is, they are particular to the purchasing or buying phenomenon under study. For example, with a fast-food restaurant survey done for Taco Bell, it might be assumed that an important descriptor helping to define the relevant population is that its members have very limited time for lunch—many of them have only 30 minutes (actually less, if one were to consider driving or walking time). A population description can result from previous studies, or it may be the collective wisdom of marketing decision makers who have catered to this particular population for a number of years and have had the opportunity to observe members' behaviors and to listen to their comments.

Step 2: Obtain a "Listing" of the Population

Once the relevant population has been defined, the researcher begins searching for a suitable list to serve as the sample frame. In some studies, candidate lists are readily available in the forms of directories of various sorts—company files or records, either public or private, that are made available to the researcher. In other instances, the listing is available at a price from a third party. Unfortunately, it is rare that a listing is perfectly faithful to the target population. Most lists suffer from sample frame error; or, as we noted earlier, the listing does not contain a complete enumeration of members of the population. Alternatively, the listing may be a distorted accounting of the population in that some of those listed may not belong to the population.

Lists to be considered as sample frames should be assessed in terms of sample frame error.

A good example of working with sample frame error is a survey that might be conducted for the independent gasoline distributors in your state. As a means of winning new customers, the independent gasoline dealers might consider marketing an "automobile travelers' maintenance and emergency kit." This kit comes in a tough plastic case about 10 inches long, 6 inches wide, and 4 inches deep. Inside are found various car maintenance devices such as a tire pressure gauge, a quart of oil, a bottle of windshield wiper solvent, a road flare, and a waterless cleaner for your hands. A marketing research company is contacted and asked to come up with a proposal for a consumer acceptance survey. This company claims that the most appropriate list of the population would be voter registration records. What sample frame error is evident here, and how severe is it?

Two forms of sample frame error include the names of people on the list who are not part of the population and members of the population who are not on the list.

The answer should be apparent once you realize a list of registered voters is incomplete in that it omits new state residents. Also, it would not be a complete listing of all drivers in your state because, prior to President Clinton's motor voter registration act, not everyone who drove bothered to register to vote. Motor vehicle registration records, on the other hand, would be a more accurate listing of this population. Furthermore, most states mandate that a new resident must acquire state license plates within 60 days of acquiring an address in that state. Obviously, the motor vehicle registration list would be more complete and more current, not to mention more relevant. So why did the research company not recommend motor vehicle registrations as its sample frame? Unfortunately, vehicle registration records typically are not available for outside inspection or sampling procedures. Voter registration records, on the other hand, are available. Consequently, the use of a less accurate list is necessary because of the impracticality involved in securing a more complete listing.

The key to assessing sample frame error lies in two factors: (1) judging how different the people listed in the sample frame are from the population, and (2) estimating what kinds of people in the population are not listed in the sample frame. With the first factor, screening questions at the beginning of an interview will usually suffice as a means of disqualifying those contacted who are not consistent with the population definition. As we noted in an earlier chapter, the percentage of people on a list who qualify as members of the population is referred to as the **"incidence rate."** With the second consideration, if the researcher cannot find any reason that those population members that were left off the list would adversely affect the final sample, the degree of frame error is judged tolerable. In the emergency highway kit example using voter registration records, the incidence rate should be high, and unregistered state residents constitute only a tiny portion of drivers in most states, plus they probably do not differ from registered residents in their gasoline purchasing. So voter registration records would serve as an acceptable sample frame for this survey.

Lists with high "incidence rates" are good candidates for use as sample frames.

Step 3: Design the Sample Plan (Size, Method)

Armed with a precise definition of the population and an understanding of the availability and condition of lists of the target population, the researcher progresses directly into the design of the sample itself. At this point, the cost of various data collection method factors come into play. That is, the researcher begins to simultaneously balance sample design, data collection costs, and sample size. We discuss sample size determination in the next chapter, and you will learn that it is a trade-off between the desire for statistical precision and the requirements of efficiency and economy.

Sample size and sample method are separate steps in the sample plan.

Regardless of the size of the sample, the specific sampling method or combination of sampling methods to be employed must be stipulated in detail by the researcher. There is no one "best" sampling method. The sample plan varies according to the objectives of the survey and its constraints.[12]

The sampling method description includes all of the necessary steps to draw the sample. For instance, if we decided to use systematic sampling, the sampling method would detail the sample frame, the sample size, the skip interval, how the random starting point would be determined, qualifying questions, recontracts, and replacement procedures. That is, all eventualities and contingencies should be foreseen and provisions should be made for each of them. These contingency plans are most apparent in the directions given to interviewers or provided to the data collection company. Obviously, it is vital to the success of the survey that the sampling method be adhered to throughout the entire sampling process.

Step 4: Access the Population

Because many marketing research studies involve subcontracting data collection services, it is sometimes left up to the policies of the data collection firm to determine how the population will be accessed. For example, telephone interviewing companies have their own policies concerning the number of callback attempts made to telephone numbers that do not answer or are busy. They also may have specific policies regarding the number of telephone rings that the interviewer will allow before giving up. Personal interviewers may be trained to make "cold calls" on potential respondents, and to leave a small postcard or memo on the door for those people who are not home. These prospective respondents are instructed to mail in the postcard or to call a certain number to set up an interview time and date. Field data collection companies are tolerant of reasonable respondent access instructions requested by research clients, but they prefer to maintain their own policies whenever possible. If incidence rates are unusually low or cooperation is less than expected and either necessitates a departure from its standard policies, the data collection company may renegotiate the price or basis of payment. For example, it may wish to move from a "per completion" basis to an hourly rate.

Data collection companies have policies on how much effort will be applied to access potential respondents.

Step 5: Draw the Sample

Drawing the sample is a two-phase process. First, the sample unit must be selected. Second, information must be gained from that unit. Simply put, you need to choose a person and ask him or her some questions. However, as you realize, not everyone will agree to answer. So there comes the question of substitutions.[13] Substitutions occur whenever an individual who was qualified to

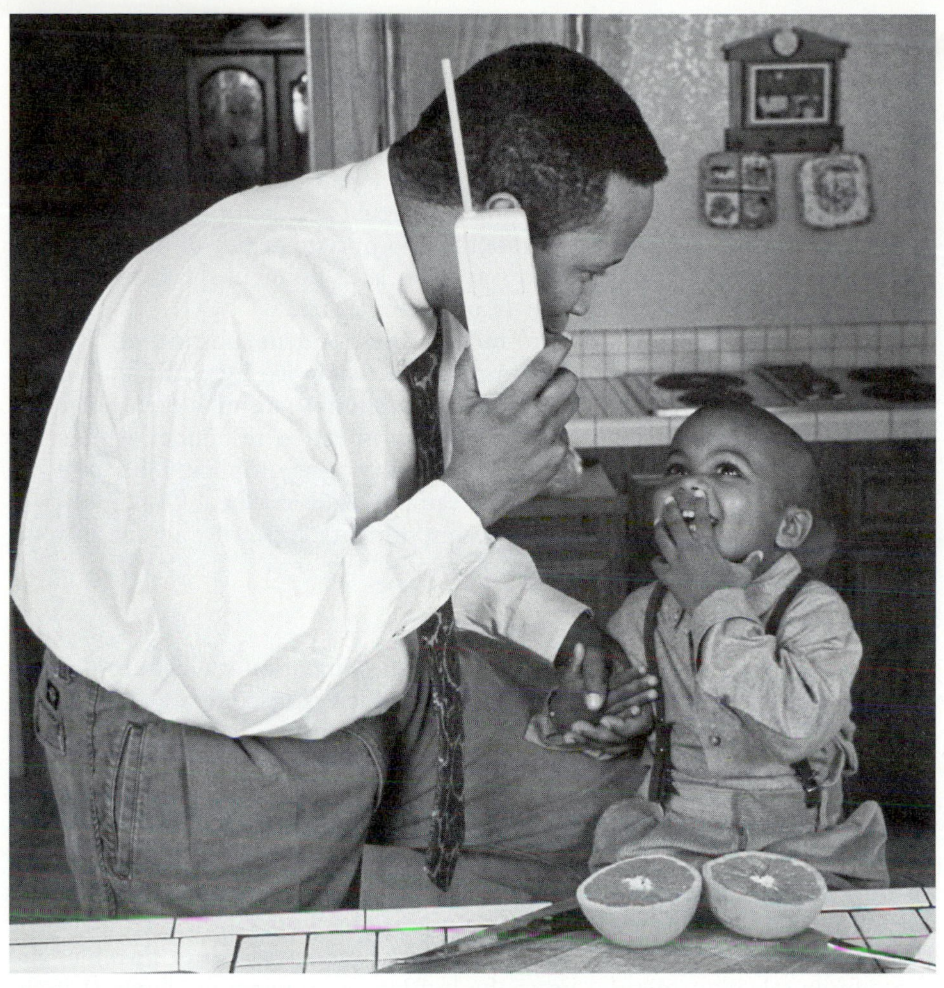

Because some respondents refuse or don't have the time to answer questions, it is necessary to have a substitution provision in a sample plan.

be in the sample proves to be unavailable, unwilling to respond, or unsuitable. The question here is, "How is the substitution respondent determined?" If the marketing research project director wishes to ensure that a particular sampling method is used faithfully, the question of substitutions must be addressed. There are three substitution methods in practice: "drop-downs," oversampling, and resampling.

Substitutions in the sample may be effected with "drop-downs," oversampling, or resampling.

The **drop-down substitution** is often used with systematic sampling. Let us say that we are using a telephone directory as our sample frame, and you are the interviewer who is instructed to call every 100th name. On your first call, the person qualifies but refuses to take part in the survey. If the drop-down method of substitution is in effect, your responsibility is to call the name immediately following the one you just called. You will not skip 100 names, but just drop down to the next one below the refusal. If that person refuses to take part, you will drop down another name and so on until you find a cooperative respondent. Then you will resume the 100 skip interval, using the original name as your beginning point. Obviously, interviewers must be provided the complete sample frame to use drop-down substitution.

Oversampling is an alternative substitution method, and it takes place as a result of the researcher's knowledge of incidence rates, nonresponse rates, and unusable responses. For example, if the typical response rate for a mail survey questionnaire hovers around 20 percent, in order to obtain a final sample of 200 respondents, 1,000 potential respondents must be drawn into the mailout sample. Each data collection method constitutes separate oversampling implications, and it is up to the marketing research project director to apply his or her wisdom to determine the appropriate degree of oversampling. Otherwise, resampling will be necessary at a later point in the marketing research study in order to obtain the desired sample size.

Incidence rates and response rates determine the need for sample substitutions.

Resampling constitutes a third means of respondent substitution. Resampling is a procedure in which the sample frame is tapped for additional names after the initial sample is drawn. Here, the response rate may turn out to be much lower than anticipated, and more prospective respondents must be drawn. CATI random digit dialing uses resampling implicitly because the numbers are generated until the desired sample size is reached. Of course, provision must be made that prospective respondents appearing in the original sample are not included in the resample.

Step 6: Validate the Sample

Sample validation assures the client that the sample is representative, but sample validation is not always possible.

The final activity in the sampling process is the validation stage. **Sample validation** can take a number of forms, one of which is to compare the sample's demographic profile with a known profile such as the census. With quota sample validation, of course, the researcher must use a demographic characteristic other than those used to set up the quota system. The essence of sample validation is to assure the client that the sample is, in fact, a representative sample of the population about which the decision maker wishes to make decisions. Although not all researchers perform sample validation, it is recommended when prior knowledge exists about the population's demographic profile. When no such prior information exits, validation is not possible, and the sample selection method bears the burden of convincing clients that the sample is representative of the population. (For an example of sample validation, see case 6.1 on page 167.)

Step 7: Resample, If Necessary

When a sample fails the validation, it means that it does not adequately represent the population. This problem may arise even when sample substitutions are incorporated.[14] Sometimes when this condition is found, the researcher can use a weighting scheme in the tabulations and analyses to compensate for the misrepresentation. On the other hand, it is sometimes possible to perform resampling by selecting more respondents and adding them to the sample until a satisfactory level of validation is reached.

SUMMARY

This chapter described various sampling methods. It began by acquainting you with various terms such as population, census, and sample frame. A sample is taken because it is too costly to perform a census, and there is sufficient information in a sample to allow it to represent the population. We described four probability sampling methods where there is a known chance of a member of the population being selected into the sample: (1) simple random sampling, (2) systematic sampling, (3) cluster sampling using area sampling as an example, and (4) stratified sampling. We also described four nonprobability sampling methods: (1) convenience sampling, (2) judgment sampling, (3) referral sampling, and (4) quota sampling. Finally, we described seven steps needed to develop a sample plan: (1) define the relevant population; (2) obtain a "listing" of the population; (3) design the sample plan (size, methods); (4) access the population; (5) draw the sample; (6) validate the sample; and (7) resample, if necessary.

KEY TERMS

Population (p. 358)
Sample (p. 359)
Sample unit (p. 359)
Census (p. 360)
Sampling error (p. 360)
Sample frame (p. 360)
Sample frame error (p. 361)
Probability samples (p. 362)
Nonprobability samples (p. 362)
Simple random sampling (p. 364)
Blind draw method (p. 364)
Table of random numbers (p. 365)
Random digit dialing (p. 367)
Plus-one dialing procedure (p. 368)
Systematic sampling (p. 368)
Skip interval (p. 369)
Cluster sampling (p. 370)
Area sampling (p. 371)
One-step area sample (p. 371)
Two-step area sample (p. 371)
Stratified sampling (p. 372)
Skewed population (p. 372)
Strata (p. 373)
Weighted mean (p. 374)
Surrogate measure (p. 375)
Proportionate stratified sample (p. 375)
Disproportionate stratified sampling (p. 375)
Convenience samples (p. 376)
Judgment samples (p. 377)
Referral samples (p. 378)
Quota sample (p. 379)
Sample plan (p. 379)
Incidence rate (p. 381)
Drop-down substitution (p. 383)
Oversampling (p. 384)
Resampling (p. 384)
Sample validation (p. 384)

REVIEW QUESTIONS/APPLICATIONS

1. Distinguish a nonprobability from a probability sampling method. Which one is the preferable method and why? Indicate the pros and cons associated with probability and nonprobability sampling methods.
2. List and describe briefly each of the probability sampling methods described in the chapter.
3. What is meant by the term "random"? How does each of the following embody randomness: (a) table of random numbers, (b) "blind draw," (c) use of random digit dialing, and (d) use of a computer?
4. In what ways is a systematic sample more efficient than a simple random sample? In what way is systematic sampling less representative of the population than simple random sampling?

5. Distinguish cluster sampling from simple random sampling. How are systematic sampling and cluster sampling related?
6. Differentiate one-step from two-step area sampling, and indicate when each one is preferred.
7. What is meant by a "skewed" population? Illustrate what you think is a skewed population distribution variable and what it looks like.
8. Briefly describe each of the four nonprobability sampling methods.
9. Why is quota sampling often used with a convenience sampling method such as mall intercepts?
10. Describe each of the three methods of substitution for individuals who are selected into the sample but refuse to participate in the survey or who did not qualify.
11. Provide the marketing researcher's definitions for each of the following populations:
    - **a.** Columbia House, a mail order house specializing in tapes and compact discs, wants to determine interest in a 10-for-1 offer on hard rock CDs.
    - **b.** The manager of your student union is interested in determining if students desire a "universal" checking account ID card that will be accepted anywhere on campus and in many stores off campus.
    - **c.** Joy Manufacturing Company decides to conduct a survey to determine the sales potential of a new type of air compressor used by construction companies.
12. Here are four populations and a potential sample frame for each one. With each pair, identify: (1) members of the population who are not in the sample frame, and (2) sample frame items that are not part of the population. Also, for each one, would you judge the amount of sample frame error to be acceptable or unacceptable?

POPULATION	SAMPLE FRAME
a. Buyers of Scope mouthwash	Mailing list of *Consumer Reports* subscribers
b. Listeners of a particular FM radio classical music station in your city	Telephone directory
c. Prospective buyers of a new day planner and prospective clients tracking kit	Members of the Sales and Marketing Executives International (a national organization of sales managers)
d. Users of weatherproof decking materials (to build outdoor decks)	Individuals' names registered at a recent home and garden show

13. Taco Bell approaches an official at your university and proposes to locate one of its restaurants on the campus. Because it would be the first commercial interest of this sort on your campus, the administration requires Taco Bell to conduct a survey of full-time students to assess the desirability of this operation. Analyze the practical difficulties encountered with doing a census in this situation, and provide specific examples of each one. For instance, how long might such a census take, how much might it cost, what types of students are more accessible than others, and what capacity constraints might be operating here?
14. A state lottery (weekly lottery in which players pick numbers from 1 to 20) player is curious about the randomness of winning lottery numbers. He has kept track of the winning numbers in the past 5 weeks and finds that most numbers were

selected 25 percent of the time, but the number 6 was one of the winning numbers 50 percent of the time. Will he be more or less likely to win if he picks a 6 in this week's lottery, or will it not make any difference in his chances? Relate your answer to simple random sampling.

15. Pet Insurers Company markets health and death benefits insurance to pet owners. They specialize in coverage for pedigreed dogs, cats, or expensive and exotic pets such as miniature Vietnamese pot-bellied pigs. The veterinary care costs of these pets can be high, and their deaths represent substantial financial loss to their owners. A researcher working for Pet Insurers finds that a listing company can provide a list of 15,000 names, which includes all current subscribers to *Cat Lovers, Pedigreed Dog,* and *Exotic Pets Monthly.* If the final sample size is to be 1,000, what should be the skip interval in a systematic sample for each of the following: (a) a telephone survey using "drop-down" substitution, (b) a mail survey with an anticipated 30 percent response rate, and (c) resampling to select 250 more prospective respondents. Also, assess the incidence rate for this sample frame.

16. A market researcher is proposing a survey for the Big Tree Country Club, a private country club that is contemplating several changes in its layout to make the course more championship caliber. The researcher is considering three different sample designs as a way to draw a representative sample of the club's golfers. The three alternative designs are:

   a. Station an interviewer at the first hole tee on one day chosen at random, with instructions to ask every 10th golfer to fill out a self-administered questionnaire.

   b. Put a stack of questionnaires on the counter where golfers check in and pay for their golf carts. There would be a sign above the questionnaires, and there would be an incentive for a "free round of golf" for three players who fill out the questionnaires and whose names are selected by a lottery.

   c. Using the city telephone directory, a "plus-one" dialing procedure would be used. With this procedure a random page in the directory would be selected, and a name on that page would be selected, both using a table of random numbers. The plus-one system would be applied to that name and every name listed after it until 1,000 golfers are identified and interviewed by telephone.

   Assess the representativeness and other issues associated with this sample problem. Be sure to identify the sample method being contemplated in each case. Which sample method do you recommend to use and why?

17. A financial services company wants a survey of Internet users to see if they are interested in using the company's financial-planning and asset-tracking Internet services. Previous studies have shown that Internet usage differs greatly by age, education, and gender. The total sample size will be 1,000. Using actual information about Internet usage, or supplying reasonable assumptions, indicate how stratified simple random sampling should be applied for each of the following stratification situations: (1) age ranges of 18–25, 26–50, and 51–65; (2) education levels of high school diploma, some college, college degree, and graduate degree; and (3) gender: males versus females.

CASE 12.1

OLOL Caregivers

Our Lady of the Lake (OLOL) is a regional hospital located in a medium-sized southern city. OLOL has many divisions, with almost all managed as though they were separate entities sharing a multipurpose medical building. One division is called Elderly Services, and part of the mission of this division is to assist OLOL's 5,000 employees. There are several programs under Elderly Services, including a center for the aging, which includes resources that provide literature, counseling, and activities for the elderly; a mail order pharmacy service; a senior companions support group; a geriatric service; Lake Line, which is a daily telephone contact service with elderly patients; and St. Francis House, which is a short-term inpatient ambulatory care facility located on OLOL's grounds. From experience, the division knows that "caregivers" are a vital aspect of the elderly's use of its services. A caregiver is a family member, typically a son or daughter but sometimes a sister or brother, who assumes the health care decision-making role for an elderly person. As the elderly become older, the caregiver takes on more and more of this role, and it is estimated that over 90 percent of all elderly defer health care decisions to their caregivers.

Craig Wishman, the Elderly Services Division manager, is considering a package service in which all of the division's services would be made available to OLOL employees at a nominal cost and as an employee benefit. Mr. Wishman has two concerns that require research: (1) what should be the "core" services that are desired by the majority of OLOL caregivers, and (2) how many potential elderly patients would be represented by OLOL full-time employees over the next 10 years? Below is a comparison of OLOL's employee profile and the profile of the typical caregiver based on a national survey published in *Elder Med America Magazine.*

CHARACTERISTIC	OLOL EMPLOYEES	CAREGIVER SURVEY
Age range	20–68 years	40–55 years
Marital status	80% married	90% married
Sex	70% female	60% male
Race	70% white	90% white
Income range	\$25,000–\$100,000	\$45,000–\$100,000
Own/rent home	50% own	75% own

1. Specify a population definition for an OLOL employee caregivers' survey.
2. Recommend a probability sampling method to select a representative sample of OLOL employees who qualify as caregivers.
3. If Mr. Wishman sent his assistant with questionnaires to the hospital cafeteria with instructions to hand them out to every tenth OLOL employee who buys lunch, what type of sampling method would be incorporated here? If the assistant were instructed to begin handing out the questionnaires at a random time between 11:30 A.M. and 12.30 P.M. to every tenth person, what sampling method would be applied?
4. How would you use simple random sampling in this case? Indicate the specific steps that would be necessary for its application.

CASE 12.2

University of Nebraska at Omaha Food Service Survey

The University of Nebraska at Omaha is located in Omaha, Nebraska, and it has an enrollment of about 15,000 students. About one-half are part-time students, and about one-half of these take only evening classes. Almost no on-campus housing exists at UNO, so virtually all students are commuters. Many UNO students prefer to take their classes in the mornings, because they work in the afternoons, but many students commute from home, and their classes are typically scheduled in the late morning and early afternoon sessions.

The UNO Student Union is the congregating place for these students for lunch, which is served cafeteria style the way it has been served to them for the past 40 years. Jim "Jazzbo" Gantry is the new food service manager, and Jazzbo wants the UNO food service to be in tune with his student consumers. For example, by reading an article in *Frozen Food Digest,*[15] Jazzbo has just found out that almost 15 percent of U.S. college students choose vegetarian offerings at campus dining halls. This figure is about three times what is found in the general U.S. population, so Jazzbo is thinking about adding several vegetarian items on the menu. Reading the article in more detail, Jazzbo learns that in a survey of members of the National Association of College and University Food Services, almost all have added meatless portions to their daily menus, and about 90 percent offer vegetarian dishes at every meal.

Jazzbo looks at today's UNO Food Services menu and notes that the only vegetarian option on it is the french fries. "After all," he muses to himself, "Nebraska is known for its beef, so why should we put hay and grass on the menu?" But Jazzbo's concern for students' preferences is stronger than his loyalty to the Nebraska beef industry, and he formulates some research questions. Jazzbo contacts the chairman of the UNO Marketing Department, who agrees to have a student team perform a survey. The team meets with Jazzbo, brainstorms, conducts a focus group, and comes up with the following objectives.

- To determine the typical student's perception of the UNO Food Services operation
- To ascertain the students' preferences for vegetarian dishes and menu items
- To identify what vegetarian items should be added to the UNO Food Services menu and how often they should be offered

The student team has decided to design a self-administered questionnaire to collect its data in this survey, and it is now debating the sample plan. Somehow the plan must allow for the research team members to access all UNO students who might use UNO Food Services for lunch, hand the questionnaire to each potential respondent, and retrieve the questionnaire once it is completed.

1. Specify a sample plan for each of the following types of probability sampling methods: simple random sampling, systematic sampling, cluster sampling, and stratified sampling.
2. Specify a sample plan for each of the following types of nonprobability sampling methods: convenience sampling, judgment sampling, and quota sampling.

Don't forget to include all of the necessary mechanics of each plan.

CHAPTER 13

Determining the Size of a Sample

LEARNING OBJECTIVES

- *To understand why a marketing manager should comprehend the basic concepts involved with determining the size of a sample*
- *To be able to describe five different methods commonly used to decide sample size*
- *To know how to compute sample size using the confidence interval approach*
- *To become aware of practical considerations in sample size determination*

PRACTITIONER VIEWPOINT

Marketing research clients frequently do not understand sample size. Almost every time we have a new client, we invariably spend a great deal of time wrestling with sample size and sample misconceptions. A typical client question is, "With 170,000 customers, what percentage will we need for an accurate sample?" Then we begin an education process that demonstrates why sample size decisions are more directly related to client budget, study objectives, applications of the data, and report deadlines than to size of the universe.

— Verne R. Kennedy, Ph.D.
Marketing Research Institute

Omni Group

1. Establish the need for marketing research
2. Define the problem
3. Establish research objectives
4. Determine research design
5. Identify information types and sources
6. Determine methods of accessing data
7. Design data collection forms
8. **Determine sample plan and size**
9. Collect data
10. Analyze data
11. Prepare and present the final research report

Omni Group is an insurance broker company specializing in business insurance. Jim Kirby, president, sensed a marketing opportunity when he noticed growth in companies specializing in health care services such as skilled nursing care, homemaker aides, and even adult day care provided in patients' homes. These companies have substantial professional liability, workers' compensation, and employee medical risks because they employ many nurses and other specialists responsible for patient health, plus the heath care workers must travel extensively from home to home.

Marketing research was used to determine the insurance needs of home health care companies.

Jim approached the state home health care association and proposed that it endorse Omni as the insurance provider for its 1,500 member companies. With this endorsement, Omni could put the home health companies in a special insurance pool and save them considerable amounts in reduced premiums. Also, Omni could develop specialized seminars, a newsletter, and other services geared to this industry. Jim suggested that the association conduct a survey to assess members' risk profiles, insurance needs, desires for specialized services, and reactions to the endorsement concept. The home care association agreed, but bids for a telephone survey with a sample of 500 members far exceeded the association's budget allowance. Jim consulted with his marketing research specialist and proposed to pay for the survey himself, but with a sample of 30 of the largest member companies. The association agreed to the pilot study, and

after six weeks, Jim presented the results to the association board of directors. The findings indicated almost unanimous support for the reduced premiums and increased service that could be gained by endorsement and pooled risk.

The selection method determines a sample's representativeness and not the size of the sample.

The Omni Group example illustrates how factors such as cost and practical considerations may affect sample size, which deals with the number of respondents in a survey or experiment rather than the way these respondents are selected. In other words, the size of the sample has nothing to do with how representative that sample is of the population. Unfortunately, many managers falsely believe that sample size and sample representativeness are related, but they are not. Here is a way to convince yourself that there is no relationship between the size of a sample and its representativeness of the population from which it is drawn. Suppose we want to find out what percentage of the U.S. workforce uses a personal computer at their place of employment. So we take a convenience sample by standing on a corner of Wall Street in New York City. We ask everyone who will talk to us about whether or not they have easy access to a personal computer at work. At the end of one week, we have questioned over 5,000 respondents in our survey. Are these people representative of the U.S. population? No, they are not. In fact, conceivably they are not even representative of New York City workers because an uncontrolled nonprobability sampling method was used. What if we had asked 10,000 New Yorkers? The sample would still be unrepresentative for the same reason.

The accuracy of a sample is a measure of how closely it reports the true values of the population it represents.

Instead of determining representativeness, the size of the sample affects the accuracy of results. **Sample accuracy** refers to how close the sample's statistic (for example, mean of the responses to a particular question) is to the true population's value it represents. Sample size will have a direct bearing on how accurate the sample's findings are relative to the true values in the population. If a random sample of U.S. Social Security card holders had 5 respondents, it would be more accurate than if it had only 1; 10 respondents would be more accurate than 5, and so forth. Common sense tells us that larger random samples are more accurate than smaller random samples. But 5 is not 5 times more accurate than 1, and 10 is not twice as accurate as 5. The important points to remember at this time are that (1) sample size is not related to representativeness, but (2) sample size is related to accuracy. Precisely how accuracy is affected constitutes a major section of this chapter.

This chapter is concerned with sample size determination. To begin, we describe five different methods used to decide on a sample's size. The confidence interval approach is the best one to use, so we describe its four underlying notions of variability, confidence intervals, sampling distribution, and standard error. These are combined into a simple formula to calculate sample size, and we give some examples of how the formula works. Last, there are practical considerations and special situations that affect the final sample size, and we briefly mention some of these.

METHODS OF DETERMINING SAMPLE SIZE

How the number of respondents or number of subjects observed in a particular sample is determined is actually one of the simplest decisions within the marketing research process; however, because formulas are used, it often appears to be very bewildering. In reality, a sample size decision is usually a compromise between what is theoretically perfect and what is practically feasible. Although it is not the intent of this chapter to make you a sampling expert, it is important that you understand the fundamental concepts that underlie sample size decisions.

There are two good reasons a marketing practitioner should have a basic understanding of sample size determination. First, as we just described, many practitioners have a false belief that sample size determines a sample's representativeness. Such practitioners ask questions such as, "How large a sample should we have to be representative?" However, as you just learned, there is no relationship between sample size and representativeness. So, you already know one of the basics of sample size determination. Second, a marketing manager should have a basic understanding of sample size determination because the size of the sample is often a major cost factor, particularly for personal interviews but even with telephone surveys. Consequently, understanding how sample size is determined will help the manager manage his or her resources better.

The size of a sample has nothing to do with its representativeness. Representativeness is dependent on the sample plan. Sample size affects the sample accuracy.

In practice, a number of different methods are used to determine sample size. Each method is described briefly in this section. In the first three methods we describe, each has a critical flaw that makes it undesirable, even though you may find instances in which it is used and proponents who argue for its use. But although we have not explained the exact relationship between sample size and the accuracy of that sample in estimating the population's characteristics, this concept should underlie sample size determination, and we refer to it frequently in pointing out the problems associated with each method.

Arbitrary Approach

The **arbitrary approach** may take on the guise of a "rule of thumb" statement regarding sample size: "A sample should be at least 5 percent of the population in order to be accurate." In fact, it is not unusual for a marketing manager to respond to a marketing researcher's sample size recommendation by saying, "But that is less than 1 percent of the entire population!"

The arbitrary percentage rule of thumb approach certainly has some intuitive appeal in that it is very easy to remember, and it is simple to apply. But consider the following example. Suppose Nike marketed a training shoe called the "Triathlon Trainer," which was especially designed for triathletes to wear during the running part of their training program, and they estimated that 10,000 triathletes lived in the United States. If the 5 percent rule were applied, the sample size would be 500. However, if Nike's survey was on the "Air Jordan," and they thought there were 2,000,000 potential basketball shoe buyers in the United States, the sample size would be 100,000, or 200 times larger that the Triathlon Trainer sample size. Do you really believe that the Air Jordan survey must have 200 times more respondents than the Triathlon Trainer survey in order to achieve the same accuracy level? To phrase the ques-

Arbitrary sample size approaches rely on erroneous rules of thumb.

tion differently, are basketball players 200 times different from triathletes? Also, what if basketball suddenly had a surge in popularity, and the population doubled by next year? This increase would result in a sample size of 200,000 in next year's survey to achieve the same accuracy as this year's survey with 100,000 respondents. Surely there must be some fundamental flaw in the percentage rule of thumb approach to sample size determination.

Arbitrary sample sizes are simple and easy to apply, but they are neither efficient nor economical.

To be sure, arbitrary sample sizes are simple and easy to apply, but they are neither efficient nor economical. With sampling, we wish to draw a subset of the population in an economical manner and to estimate the population values with some predetermined degree of accuracy. Arbitrary methods lose sight of the accuracy aspect of sampling, and, as you just saw, they certainly are not economical when the population under study is large.

Conventional Approach

The **conventional approach** follows some "convention" or number believed somehow to be the right sample size. A manager may be knowledgeable of national opinion polls and notice that they are often taken with sample sizes of between 1,000 and 1,200 respondents. This may appear to the manager as a "conventional" number, and he or she may question a market researcher whose sample size recommendation varies from this convention. On the other hand, the survey may be one in a series of studies a company has undertaken on a particular market, and the same sample size may be applied each succeeding year simply because it was used last year. The convention might be an average of the sample sizes of similar studies, it might be the largest sample size of previous surveys, or it might be equal to the sample size of a competitor's survey that the company somehow discovered.

Using conventional sample size can result in a sample that may be too small or too large.

The basic difference between an arbitrary and a conventional sample size determination is that the arbitrary approach has no defensible logic, whereas the conventional approach appears logical; however, the logic is faulty. We just illustrated how an arbitrary approach such as a 5 percent rule of thumb explodes into huge sample sizes very quickly; however, the national opinion poll precedent of 1,200 respondents would be constant regardless of the population size. Still, this characteristic is one of the conventional sample size determination method's weaknesses, for if a company were in the industrial market, the population might well be less than 1,000 prospective buyers. For example, if Alcoa wished to survey soft drink producers in the eastern United States, it would find fewer than 200 companies total. Also, if you read the fine print associated with national opinion polls that polled 1,100 respondents, you will find they claim they are "accurate to plus or minus 3 percent." So if a marketing researcher adopts this convention, assuming he or she has a large population being researched, this accuracy level should be the desired level. But it may be that this much precision is unnecessary. Why pay for a more accurate sample than is required? On the other hand, more than plus or minus 3 percent precision may be desired, and the conventional sample will be too small.

Adopting past sample sizes or taking those used by other companies can be criticized as well, for both approaches assume that whoever determined sample size in the previous studies did so correctly. (That is, not with a flawed method.) If a flawed method was used, you simply perpetuate the error by copying it, and if the sample size method used was not flawed, the circumstances and assumptions surrounding the predecessor's survey may be very different from those encompassing the present one. So, the conventional sample size approach ignores the circumstances surrounding the study at hand and may well prove to be much more costly than would be the case if the sample size were determined correctly.

Conventional sample sizes ignore the special circumstances of the survey at hand.

Cost Basis Approach

The **cost basis approach** uses cost as a basis for sample size. Most managers and marketing research professionals are constantly hindered by survey costs. If there were no sampling costs of marketing research, everything could be accomplished with a census, and there would be no concern about sample accuracy. Unfortunately, costs are very relevant, and the costs of data collection, particularly for personal interviews, telephone surveys, and even for mail surveys in which incentives are included in the envelopes mailed out, can mount quickly. So it is not surprising that cost sometimes becomes the basis for sample size.

Exactly how the cost basis approach is applied varies a great deal. In some instances, the marketing research project budget is determined in advance, and set amounts are specified for each phase. Here, the budget may have, for instance, $10,000 for "interviewing," or it might specify $5,000 for "data collection." A variation is for the entire year's marketing research budget amount to be set, and to have each project carve out a slice of that total. With this approach, the marketing research project director is forced to stay within the total project budget, but he or she can allocate the money across the various cost elements, and the sample size ends up being whatever is affordable within the budget.

Using cost as the sole determinant of sample size seems wise, but it is not.

A cost-based sample size is a case of the tail wagging the dog. That is, instead of the value of the information to be gained from the survey being a pri-

Letting the available budget dictate the sample size is backward thinking.

mary consideration in the sample size, the sample size is determined by budget factors that usually ignore the value of the survey's results to management. Alternatively, because many managers harbor a strong sample size bias, it is possible that their marketing research project budgets are overstated for data collection when smaller sample sizes could have sufficed quite well. Still, we cannot ignore cost altogether.

The appropriateness of using cost as a basis for sample size depends on when cost factors are considered.

How can we decide on sample size without taking cost into consideration? The answer to this question lies in *when* we consider cost. In the cost basis examples we just described, cost drives the sample size completely. When we have $5,000 for interviewing and a data collection company tells us that they charge $25 per completed interview, our sample is set at 200 respondents. Another, better approach is to consider cost relative to the value of the research to the manager. If the manager requires extremely precise information, the researcher will surely suggest a large sample, and then estimate the cost of obtaining the sample. The manager, in turn, should then consider this cost in relation to how much the information is actually worth. The researcher and manager can then discuss alternative sample sizes, different data collection modes, costs, and other considerations. This is a healthier situation, for now the manager is assuming some ownership of the survey and a partnership arrangement is being forged between the manager and the researcher. The net result will be a better understanding on the part of the manager as to how and why the final sample size was determined. This way cost will not be the only means of determining sample size, but it will be given the consideration it deserves.

A healthy dialog takes place when the researcher and the manager discuss sample size costs.

Statistical Analysis Approach

On occasion, a sample's size will be determined using a **statistical analysis approach** because there is some overriding statistical analysis consideration. We have not discussed statistical procedures as yet in this text, but we can assure

Marketing managers and other clients of marketing researchers do not have a thorough understanding of sample size. In fact, they tend to have a belief in a false "law of large sample size." That is, they often confuse the size of the sample with the representativeness of the sample. As you know from learning about sample selection procedures, the way the sample is selected determines its representativeness, not its size. Also, as you have just learned, the benefits of excessively large samples are typically not justified by their increased costs.

It is an ethical marketing researcher's responsibility to try to educate a client on the wastefulness of excessively large samples. Occasionally, there are good reasons for having a very large sample, but whenever the sample size exceeds that of a typical national opinion poll (1,200 respondents), justification is required. Otherwise, the manager's cost will be unnecessarily inflated. Unethical researchers may recommend very large samples as a way to increase their profits, which may be set at a percentage of the total cost of the survey. They may even have ownership in the data collection company slated to gather the data at a set cost per respondent. It is important, therefore, that marketing managers know the motivations underlying the sample size recommendations of the researchers they hire.

you that some advanced techniques require certain minimum sample sizes in order to be reliable, or to safeguard the validity of their statistical results.

Sometimes the researcher's desire to use particular statistical techniques influences sample size.

Statistical analysis is used to analyze subgroups within a sample. Many marketing research projects are undertaken to gain a sensitivity for segments of people within a population. This case is clearly evident in the example of the U.S. Army, which recently researched a proposed military-owned and -run hotel in the Orlando, Florida, area. After extensive focus groups on about a dozen bases, the Army conducted a large survey using a sample of over 2,000 respondents to determine reactions to the concept, amenities desired, prices perceived as reasonable, times of year the facility would be used, reactions to a military-only hotel, and much more. The final report had a great many different breakdowns by rank, age, family situation, distance stationed away from Orlando, and more. A driving consideration in the sample size decision was the need for these subgroups to be of certain minimum sample sizes to perform valid statistical comparisons.

The widespread availability and ease of access to large computers enhances extensive "subgroup analysis," which is nothing more than a reasonably thorough investigation of subsegments within the population such as the U.S. Army example. As you would expect, the desire to gain knowledge about subgroups has direct implications for sample size. It should be possible to look at each subgroup as a separate population and to determine sample size for each subgroup, along with the appropriate methodology and other specifics to gain knowledge about that subgroup. Once this is accomplished, all of the subgroups can be combined into a large group in order to obtain a complete population picture.[1]

Confidence Interval Approach

The confidence interval approach to sample size includes the concepts of variability, confidence interval, sampling distribution, and standard error of a mean or percentage.

The final method of determining sample size is the **confidence interval approach,** which applies the concepts of variability, confidence interval, sampling distribution, and standard error of a mean or percentage to create a valid sample. Because it is the theoretically most correct method, it is the one used by national opinion polling companies and most marketing researchers. To describe the confidence interval approach to sample size determination, we first describe the four underlying concepts.

The Notion of Variability

When we find a wide dispersion of responses—that is, when we do not find one response item accounting for a large number of respondents relative to the other items—we say that the results have much variability. **Variability** is defined as the amount of dissimilarity (or similarity) in respondents' answers to a particular question. If most respondents indicated the same position on the response scale, the distribution would be indicative of little variability. On the other hand, if respondents were found to be evenly spread across the question's response options, there would be much variability.

Variability refers to how similar or dissimilar responses are to a given question.

Conceptualizing variability changes depending on the data used. With nominal data, or data in which the response items are categorical, the responses may be lopsided. The greater this lopsidedness, the less the variability in the responses. For example, we may find that the question, "The next time you order a pizza, will you use Domino's?" yields a 90 to 10 percent distribution split on yes versus no. In other words, most of the respondents gave the

A sample must be larger for a population containing many different types of members than for one with mostly similar members.

A 50/50 split in response signifies maximum variability (dissimilarity) in the population, whereas a 90/10 split signifies little variability.

same answer, meaning that there is much similarity in the responses, and the variability would be low. In contrast, if the question had resulted in a 50 to 50 percent split, the overall response pattern would be (maximally) dissimilar, and there would be much variability.

Interval data, and especially ratio data, have many response options, so envisioning variability is slightly different. With the Domino's yes–no question example just described, you can picture the responses as a bar graph. With the 90 to 10 percent split, the graph would have one high side (90%) and one low side (10%), or it would have both sides at even levels (50%–50%). Suppose, however, we were conducting a survey for Goodyear to determine the number of miles that automobile owners estimate they drive their automobiles in a typical year. This would be an open-ended ratio scale because respondents would write in the number of miles. Each response would be unique, but we could still look for the underlying variability pattern. On inspection, we find that most respondents drive their automobiles 12,000 miles per year, and that large numbers but successively lower percentages, drive 13,000 and 14,000, and 11,000 and 10,000 miles per year.

A normal distribution is shaped like a bell.

Such answers given by respondents can be graphed. We could use a bar graph, but it is customary to rely on a line graph. Figure 13.1 illustrates what the graph might look like. When 50 percent of respondents answer on either side of a middle point, we call this a **bell-shaped distribution** or a **normal distribution.** Bell-shaped distributions can occur with interval or continuous data because such data allows for many possible responses that are exact distances away from the middle value. The resultant distribution is therefore much smoother (bell-shaped).

Just as with nominal data, variability in continuous data such as miles driven per year, years of age, number of gallons of gasoline used per month, and so forth is indicated by the shape of the distribution. If most of the responses

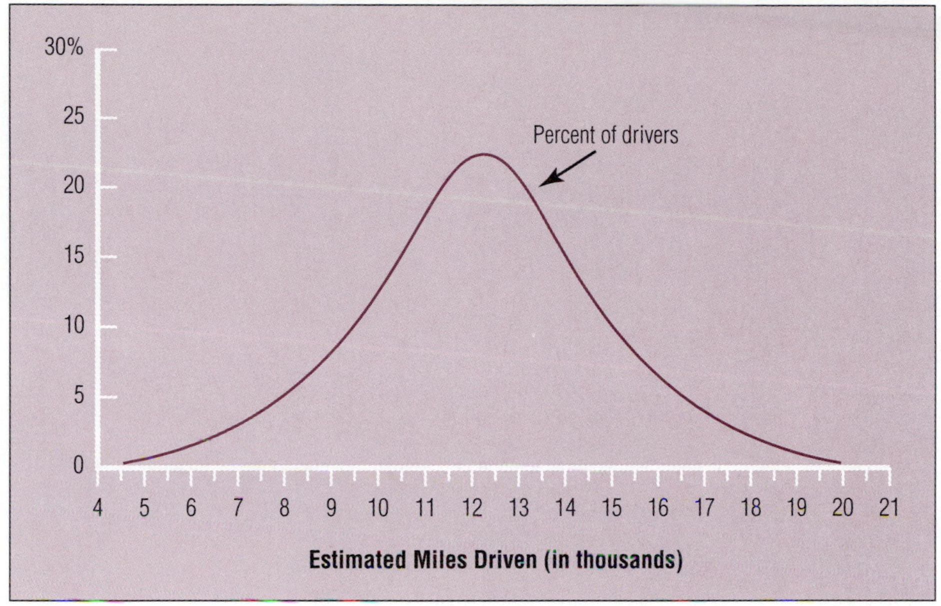

Figure 13.1

A distribution of number of miles driven in a year illustrates variability.

fall close to the same number and a large majority of respondents is found within a small range, there is little variability; if the opposite is true, there is much variability. Figure 13.2 on page 400 illustrates two possible distributions for our number of miles question, one with little variability and one with great variability. Again, the basic concept of variability pertains to how similar the responses are. Little variability means they are quite similar, whereas much variability denotes much dissimilarity. Regardless of whether you are working with question responses relying on nominal, ordinal, interval, or ratio scaling assumptions, if a graph of the responses reveals a large concentration or a "spike," variability is low. If the graph reveals respondents who are spread somewhat evenly across the range of possible responses, variability is high.

The normal distribution has important properties that are related to sample size determination.

Both Figure 13.1 and Figure 13.2 illustrate two important properties associated with the normal distribution that relate to variability. The first property is that the mean or average response falls exactly in the middle of the distribution, at its highest point under the bell curve. This means that 50 percent of the responses are above the mean, while the other 50 percent are below the mean. To state this property differently, the highest number of miles driven shown in Figure 13.1 (20,000) is exactly 8,000 miles away from the mean (12,000), and the lowest number of miles driven (4,000) is also exactly 8,000 miles away from the mean. Because a bell-shaped distribution is symmetric, equal distances above and below the mean account for the identical percentages of the distribution to the right and left of the mean, respectively.

A computed standard deviation indicates the amount of variability in a sample.

Statisticians make extensive use of the normal curve assumption of the distribution of data, and they have devised a simple way of assessing variability without the necessity of graphing the data as we have done. They compute a measure, known as the **standard deviation,** which approximates the average distance away from the mean for all respondents to a particular question. The computation of the standard deviation may look complicated, but it is actually easy to understand. Here is the formula:

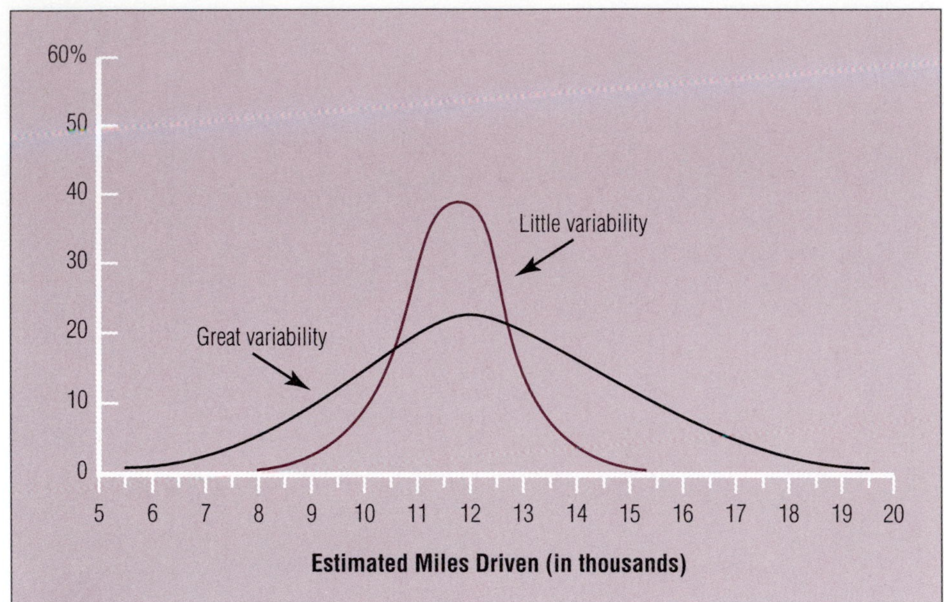

Figure 13.2

The amount of variability is reflected in the spread of the distribution.

$$\text{Standard deviation} = \sqrt{\frac{\sum_{i-1}^{n}(x_i - \bar{x})^2}{n-1}}$$

where n is the sample size, x_i is the value of the ith respondent in the sample, and $\bar{x}$ is the mean.

To illustrate how the standard deviation formula works, we use our Goodyear miles-driven-per-year survey example. Here is how the calculations are performed. First, you calculate the average number of miles driven per year, which is 12,000. Next, take each respondent's answer and subtract this average from it. However, if one-half of the respondents are above the mean and one-half are below it, and if the distribution is perfectly symmetric, what would be the sum of all of the differences of all of our respondents' answers from the mean? Those far above the mean would be counterbalanced by those far below it, and those just above the mean would be counterbalanced by those just below it. The average would be zero! But we know that there is some variability in our distribution because we can see it in our graph.

The standard deviation formula uses a squaring operation to avoid cancellation of +'s and –'s.

To adjust for the cancellation effect that you have just realized will occur, it is necessary to square each respondent's difference from the mean score. This procedure translates all of the negative differences into positive ones and avoids our cancellation problem. Then we add up all of the squared differences and divide them by the number of respondents (minus one to adjust for bias). Finally, because we still have the squared differences in our computations, we take the square root of the result to revert it to the original, unsquared units of measure. The result is a single, positive value known as the standard deviation, and it is indicative of the amount of variability in the distribution under examination. For our example, let us assume the standard deviation is found to be 3,000 miles.

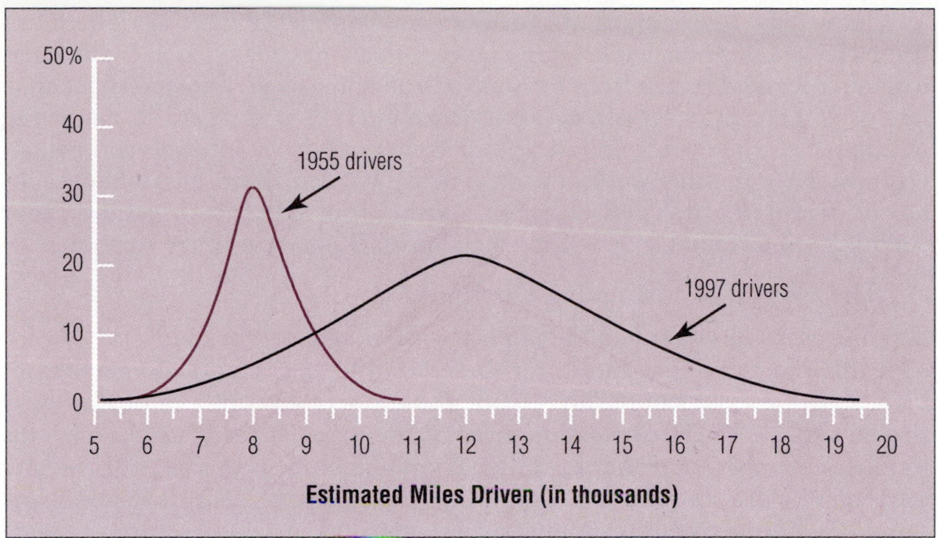

Figure 13.3

A Comparison of 1955 Drivers to 1997 Drivers

How do we use the standard deviation as a measure of variability? There are two ways. First, we could make a comparison of the standard deviations of two samples to judge relative variability. In Figure 13.3, we compare our present study on driving to one done in 1955. Note that in the 1955 study, the average was lower (8,000), and the standard deviation was smaller. The 1955 curve is found to the left of our present study, and it is more compressed. It must be taller, too, because it represents 100 percent of the responses, just as does our present study. In other words, 1955 car owners drove fewer miles (on average) and there was not much variability (the standard deviation), but today's drivers average more miles per year and there is greater variability among them.

Standard deviations of distributions can be used to compare their variabilities.

The Notion of a Confidence Interval

The second property associated with normal distribution relates to confidence intervals. A **confidence interval** is a range whose endpoints define a certain percentage of the responses to a question. The properties of the normal curve are such that 1.96 times the standard deviation theoretically defines the endpoints for 95 percent of the distribution, whereas 2.58 times the standard deviation defines the endpoints for 99 percent of the distribution. We take the 95 percent case to illustrate. In our present-day example, the mean is 12,000 miles, and the standard deviation is 3,000 miles. To find the range that describes 95 percent of the sample, we multiply 1.96 times the standard deviation value, to yield 5,880. Then we add that number to the mean to find the high value, and subtract it to find the low value. So the range is 6,120 miles to 17,880 miles, and it theoretically describes 95 percent of the responses to our miles driven per year question. This range is sometimes referred to as the **95 percent confidence interval,** defined as the range described by the mean ±1.96 times the standard deviation. In other words, because we are using the normal curve interpretation and accepting all of the statistical assumptions underlying it, we can say that we are confident that 95 percent of the respondents' answers fall between 6,120 and 17,880 miles per year.

A confidence interval defines endpoints based on knowledge of the area under a bell-shaped curve.

The term z is used to represent the chosen level of confidence.

Let us take a closer look at variability and confidence intervals. The number associated with the level of confidence, usually designated as *z*, is a mandatory number determined from the statistician's knowledge of the normal curve. Use of 95 percent or 99 percent confidence intervals is standard in marketing research. So, when you compute a 95 percent confidence interval, you will always use 1.96. In other words, the only factor that can affect the confidence interval's size is the standard deviation. With larger standard deviations, your confidence interval must be wider to encompass 95 percent of the responses.

The Notion of a Sampling Distribution

Suppose that Goodyear had the opportunity to take a great many, say 50, independent samples. The means for these 50 different samples are graphed in Figure 13.4. As you can readily see, they align themselves in a normal or bell-shaped curve with the population mean as the mean of the distribution. This profile, remember, is neither the original population distribution, nor is it any one sample's distribution. It is a **sampling distribution,** because it is a distribution of sample means if we took many independent samples from the same population. It is a *theoretical* concept that underlies sample size determination as well as many other statistical procedures. When you look at the sampling distribution in Figure 13.4, you see that a great many of the sample means fall very close to the true population mean, whereas a small percentage of them fall some distance away from the mean. Stated in a different manner, the sampling distribution presented here shows that there is a small probability that any given sample's mean will be a great distance away from the true population mean. Stated differently, there is a high probability that any given sample result will be close to the population mean.

The sampling distribution refers to what would be found if the researcher could take many, many independent samples.

Because the sampling distribution is theoretical, we provide an example that may make it more understandable. Suppose Blockbuster Video wanted to

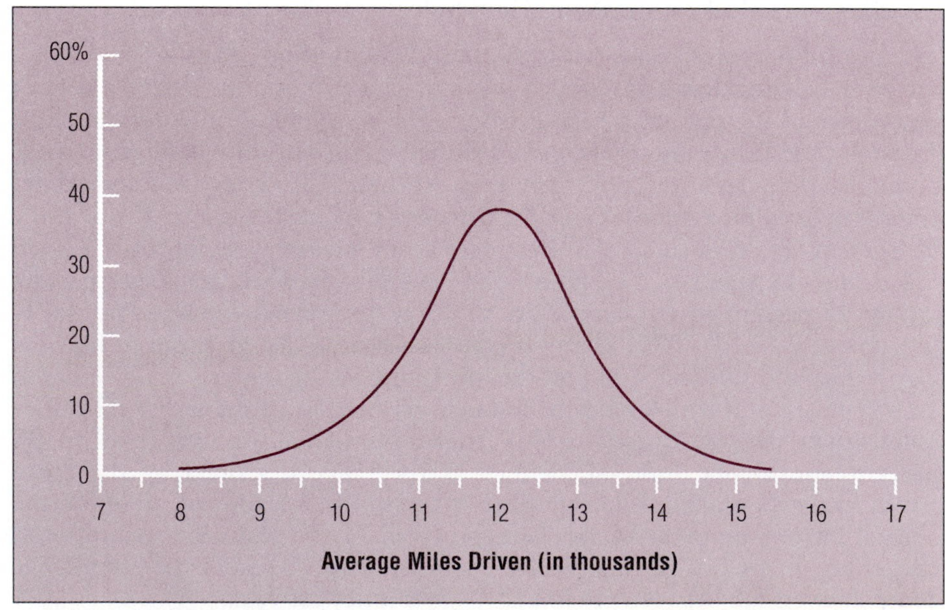

Figure 13.4

The sampling distribution is based on theoretically taking many samples and plotting the distribution of their means.

know how many videos, on average, its customers rented per month, so it instructed every one of its store managers to ask this question of every customer and to put the answer into the store's database. Each of Blockbuster Video's 1,000+ stores would be the same as a sample, and the average number of videos rented by customers at each store could be computed. Many of these stores would have similar averages, and these similar averages would be very close to the overall average number of videos rented for all customers in all stores. If the stores' average number of videos were rounded to whole numbers (you cannot rent a part of a video), the number of stores determined for each average number, and a bar chart created to show the distribution, it would approximate a bell-shaped curve.

The Notion of Standard Error of a Mean or Percentage

The standard error indicates how far away from the true population value a typical sample result is expected to fall.

Obviously, no company would underwrite the cost to undertake a multitude of samples as we have described. In reality, we would do only one survey. Fortunately, it is possible to obtain some indication of the sampling distribution simply through knowledge of the variability of just one sample drawn from the population. The **standard error** is an indication of how far away from the true population value a typical sample result is expected to fall.

There are two ways to compute a standard error, and the formula to use depends on whether you are working with a mean or a percentage. The **standard error of the mean** is computed using the following formula:

$$S_{\bar{x}} = \frac{s}{\sqrt{n}}$$

where

$S_{\bar{x}}$ = standard error of the mean

s = standard deviation of the sample

n = sample size

As you can see, the standard error of the mean is computed by dividing the sample standard deviation by the square root of the sample size. So, if in our Goodyear driving survey, we found a standard deviation of 3,000 miles with a sample of 100 drivers, the standard error of the mean would be calculated as

$$S_{\bar{x}} = \frac{s}{\sqrt{n}}$$

$$S_{\bar{x}} = \frac{3000}{\sqrt{100}}$$

$$S_{\bar{x}} = \frac{3000}{10}$$

$$S_{\bar{x}} = 300$$

Standard error can be measured using either a mean or a percentage.

The standard error concept also pertains to surveys in which we are researching percentages. It is referred to as the **standard error of a percentage.** For example, we might want to estimate the percentage of Goodyear radial tire owners. To determine a percentage, the formula is as follows:

$$S_p = \sqrt{\frac{p \times q}{n}}$$

where

S_p = standard error of the percentage

p = percentage found in the sample

q = (100 – p)

n = sample size

As an example, let us assume that 40 percent of our 100 drivers indicated that they had radial tires on their cars. The standard error of the percentage would be calculated as

$$S_p = \sqrt{\frac{p \times q}{n}}$$

$$S_p = \sqrt{\frac{40 \times 60}{100}}$$

$$S_p = \sqrt{\frac{2400}{100}}$$

$$S_p = \sqrt{24}$$

$$S_p = 4.899$$

Sample size has a direct bearing on the standard error because the size of the sample constitutes the denominator of the formula. As sample size increases, the standard error decreases.

Variability has a direct bearing on the standard error. As variability increases, standard error increases.

We want to point out that for both cases, the size of the sample constitutes the denominator of the formula. Because of this, sample size has a direct bearing on the standard error. Large sample sizes will make the standard error smaller, whereas small sample sizes will make it larger. At the same time, our knowledge of the sample's variability provides us with some idea of the population's variability. The variability in the cases of these two formulas may be expressed in terms of s, the standard deviation, or p, the expected percentage, respectively. For any given sample size, the sample variability will have a predictable effect. If the variability is high, it will cause the standard error to be high; whereas if the variability is low, it will cause the standard error to be low.

Because the most current information available on the population is the sample, the sample statistic (mean or percentage) becomes our best estimate of the population value. This is why we took the sample in the first place. Using the sample information, we compute confidence intervals as the range in which a given population value is expected to fall. The sample statistic ±1.96 times the standard error defines the range in which the population value is estimated to be found in 95 percent of the repeated samplings. Or, in more practical terms, the marketing researcher envisions a probability of 0.95 that the true population mean is included in that range. This relationship underlies statistical inference, which we discuss in chapter 16.

COMPUTING SAMPLE SIZE USING THE CONFIDENCE INTERVAL APPROACH

To compute sample size, only three factors need to be considered: accuracy, variability, and confidence level.

You are now acquainted with the basic concepts essential to understanding sample size determination using the confidence interval approach. To calculate the proper sample size for a survey, only three factors need be considered: (1) the amount of variability believed to be in the population, (2) the desired accuracy, and (3) the level of confidence required in your estimates of the population values.

A researcher can calculate sample size using either a percentage or a mean. We describe the percentage approach first, and then we show you how to determine sample size using a mean. Although the formulas are different, the basic concepts involved are identical.

Determining Sample Size Using a Percentage

As you would expect, there is a formula that includes our three considerations. When determining a percentage, the formula is as follows:

$$n = \frac{z^2(pq)}{e^2}$$

where

n = the sample size

z = standard error associated with the chosen level of confidence

p = estimated variability in the population

q = (100 – p)

e = acceptable error

The sample size using a percentage is applicable if you are concerned with the nominally scaled questions in the survey such as "yes or no" questions.

This formula is used if we are focusing on some nominally scaled question in the survey. For instance, when conducting the Goodyear tire survey, our major concern might be the percentage of radial tire owners. There are two possible answers: those who own radials and those who do not own radials. If we suspect that our population has very *little variability,* that is, if almost everyone owns radial tires, this belief will be reflected in the sample size. With little variation in the population, we know that we can take smaller samples. So how is this accommodated by the formula? The estimated variability in the population, p, is the mechanism that performs this translation. If you look at the formula, you will see that p and q are multiplied together. Their product expresses the variability you believe characterizes the population.

Let us take two cases. First, let us assume that we believe 90 percent of the population use radial tires. This means that the product will be (90%) times (100% – 90% = 10%), or 900. Now, let us assume that we believe that there is more variation in our population, or that only 70 percent own radial tires. This translates into (70%) times (100% – 70% = 30%), or 2,100. Notice that 2,100 is larger than 900, and because these values are in the numerator of the equation, the ultimate result will be a larger sample for 70 percent than for 90 percent.

The case of greatest variability with percentages is 50–50.

The case of greatest variation using a percentage is when a 50 to 50 percent split occurs. You can verify this claim. Experiment with any combination of p and q, and you will find that 50 percent times (100% – 50% = 50%), which equals 2,500, is in fact the largest possible value you can come up with.

Accuracy with percentages is expressed as a ± acceptable error value.

Next, let us address the second factor—*desired accuracy.* **Accuracy** pertains to how precise our sample estimate (%) is of the population value (%). That is, if we performed our survey and found that, say, 44 percent of the respondents own radial tires, the researcher needs to indicate the precision level by saying, "The percentage of automobile owners who have radial tires is 44 percent, plus or minus e percent." Accuracy is the e in this statement as well as in our equation, and the manager determines how accurate he or she want the results to be. So, with nominal measures, accuracy is simply a plus or minus percentage. *High* accuracy translates into a *small* percent such as ±2 percent, whereas *low* accuracy translates into a *large* percent such as ±15 percent.

In marketing research, a 95 percent or 99 percent level of confidence is standard practice.

Last, we need to decide on a *level of confidence,* and as we indicated earlier, researchers typically only worry about the 95 percent or 99 percent level of confidence. A 99 percent level of confidence allows the researcher to state that he or she is 99 percent confident that the true population percentage falls in the range $\pm e$ percent around the percentage he or she finds in the sample (the sample estimate). Remember that the z value associated with 99 percent level of confidence is 2.58, whereas the z value associated with 95 percent level of confidence is 1.96. (For now, do not be overly concerned about how you would estimate variability, about what degree of accuracy is correct, or even what level of confidence is proper. We discuss these topics later in the chapter.)

We are now ready to calculate sample size. Let us assume there is great expected variability (50%) and we want ±10 percent accuracy at the 95 percent level of confidence. To determine the sample size needed, we calculate as follows:

$$
\begin{aligned}
n &= \frac{1.96^2(50 \times 50)}{10^2} \\
&= \frac{3.84(2500)}{100} \\
&= \frac{9600}{100} \\
&= 96
\end{aligned}
$$

Just to convince you of the use of the confidence interval approach, recall our previous comment that most national opinion polls use sample sizes of about 1,100 and they claim ±3 percent of accuracy. Using the 95 percent level of confidence, the computations would be:

$$
\begin{aligned}
n &= \frac{1.96^2(50 \times 50)}{3^2} \\
&= \frac{3.84(2500)}{9} \\
&= \frac{9600}{9} \\
&= 1067
\end{aligned}
$$

In other words, if these national polls were to be ±3 percent accurate at the 95 percent confidence level, they would need to have sample sizes of 1,067 (or about 1,100 respondents).

What if the researcher wanted a 99 percent level of confidence in his or her estimates? The computations would be as follows:

$$n = \frac{2.58^2(50 \times 50)}{3^2}$$

$$= \frac{6.66(2500)}{9}$$

$$= \frac{16650}{9}$$

$$= 1850$$

Thus, if a survey were to be ±3 percent accurate at the 99 percent level of confidence, it would need to have a sample size of 1,850, assuming the maximum variability (50%).

Determining Sample Size Using a Mean

Now let us discuss how to determine sample size using a mean. The formula used is as follows:

$$n = \frac{s^2 z^2}{e^2}$$

where

n = the sample size

z = the level of confidence (indicated by the number of standard errors associated with it)

s = variability indicated by an estimated standard deviation

e = the amount of precision or allowable error in the sample estimate of the population

As you can see, the formula determines sample size by multiplying the squares of the variability (s) and level of confidence values (z) and dividing that product by the square of the desired precision value (e). Although this formula looks different from the one for a percentage, it applies the same logic and key concepts in an identical manner.

The sample size formula for a mean applies the same logic as the sample size formula for a percentage.

First, let us look at how *variability* of the population is a part of the formula. It appears in the form of s, or the estimated standard deviation of the population. This means that, because we are going to estimate the population mean, we need to have some knowledge of or at least a good guess at how much variability there is in the population. We must use the standard deviation because it expresses this variation. Unfortunately, unlike our percentage sample size case, there is no "50 percent equals the most variation" counterpart, so we have to rely on some prior knowledge about the population for our estimate of the standard deviation. Next, we must express e, which is the *accuracy range* we desire around the sample mean when we ultimately estimate the

With the sample size for a mean formula, variability is expressed as the assumed standard deviation, and accuracy is expressed as a range around the mean that is acceptable.

population mean from our survey. This value, as we indicated before, is the responsibility of the manager, who eventually will have to use the survey results and wrestle with their accuracy when making decisions. Finally, the sample size formula requires a *level of confidence*, and we can use either 95 percent or 99 percent, using the same interpretation we used in the percentage sample size formula.

To apply this formula, let us assume our decision maker wants a 95 percent level of confidence (1.96), and we estimate from previous studies the standard deviation to be 100. Finally, our desired precision is ±10. Here are the computations to determine the sample size.

$$n = \frac{100^2 \times 1.96^2}{10^2}$$

$$= \frac{10000 \times 3.84}{100}$$

$$= \frac{38400}{100}$$

$$= 384$$

PRACTICAL CONSIDERATIONS IN SAMPLE SIZE DETERMINATION

Although we have discussed how variability, precision, and confidence level are used to calculate sample size, we have not discussed the criteria used by the marketing manager and researcher to determine these factors. General guidelines follow.

How to Estimate Variability in the Population

To estimate variability, you can use prior research, experience, and/or intuition.

Surprisingly, information about the target population often exists in many forms. There are census tract descriptions available in the form of secondary data, and there are compilations and bits of information that may be gained from groups such as Chambers of Commerce, local newspapers, state agencies, groups promoting commercial development, and a host of other similar organizations. Moreover, many populations under study by firms are known to them either formally through prior research studies or informally through prior business experiences. But what if you had to include several countries in your sample plan? Sometimes a country will have a number of cultural groups within its borders, and the sample size must be inflated to cover all of them.[2] This was the situation encountered by Citibank when conducting research for its worldwide operations (Marketing Research Insight 13.1).

All of this information combines to help the research project director to grasp the variability in the population. That is, some populations are highly consistent in the sense that all potential respondents are very similar in their demographics, attitudes, purchasing intentions, or whatever the salient characteristics under study happen to be. A good example of a population that has relatively little variability is the "tweens." Tweens are consumers between the ages of 10 and 13 who are undergoing the transition from child to young

MARKETING RESEARCH INSIGHT 13.1

Global Marketing Research Complicates the Sample Size Issue for Citibank

Patricia Botwinick of MPG International, Ltd., which specializes in global financial services consultations, provides the following description of worldwide marketing research.

The Citibank Private Bank has operations around the world. In order to assess the size of the global wealth market, the Private Bank Strategic Marketing Department commissioned an international research firm to establish an estimate of their target market, namely individuals with substantial private wealth, using consistent criteria country by country.

Fifty-four countries were evaluated in this study. They were selected based on presence of significant individual wealth. They comprise 82 percent of the world Gross Domestic Product and 49 percent of the world population.

As might be expected, the amount of hard information and its quality (relevance to the assignment) varied greatly by country. The research challenge was to harmonize a vast collection of national country data, spanning political, cultural, economic, and marketing intelligence, and devise a model that could provide a quantitative forecast of private wealth, while taking into account country-by-country market dynamics.

Countries for which there was enough hard data to develop reasonably reliable estimates of individual wealth were used as baseline models for countries with inadequate data. Reliable hard data included, but was not limited to, government reports of taxes paid by individuals, published rankings of individuals with the largest amount of private wealth, personal investment data, and the like. When a country's data was inadequate, a model country most similar to it in socioeconomic, cultural, and political stability was used as a baseline against which an additional series of factors were applied as needed to fill in the missing data.

Once preliminary estimates for all countries were prepared, the crucial next step was to have Citibank country experts review the assumptions for their market/region. Reformulations of initial estimates were made on the basis of first-hand market experience drawn from working in the local business environment.

The results of the Global Wealth Market Model in total, by region and country, helped to identify where corporate resources should be positioned to garner the greatest lift in potential new business.

Source: *Patricia Botwinick, MPG International, Ltd., by permission.*

adult; they are literally "between" stages in their physical and mental development. In recent years, companies such as McDonald's have undertaken aggressive and creative marketing campaigns aimed at the tween market. Besides exhibiting little variability in age (10–13 years old), the tween population also shows little variability in education (junior high school) or in physical development. Moreover, research has revealed that a great majority of them require constant social support from their peers. Consequently, it is extremely important that they adhere to the norms of their tween group. Additionally, the tween, in his or her desire for recognition, often turns to physical achievement or athletic feats that gain peer recognition. In fast food, snacks, clothing, and even magazine reading, most members show fairly consistent buying behavior.

However, if one were to take into consideration all buyers of, say, McDonald's products, there would be a great deal more variability; this population

"Tweens" are consumers between the ages of 10 and 13 who are undergoing the transition from child to young adult.

would include not only tweens but also working men and women who eat breakfast there in the morning, mothers who take their children there for Saturday outings, and travelers who are taking day trips. Intuition should lead you to expect to draw a larger sample from this population than from the tween population because there are so many varieties of people contained within the full market.

The range divided by 6 can be used to estimate variability when computing sample size using a mean.

Still, estimating the variability of a population in which a mean is being researched is often problematic. Consequently, a researcher should take into account all available information about variability and even consider the use of a pilot study to better understand the nature of a population's variability before committing to a final sample size.[3] If information on the population variability is truly unknown and a pilot study is out of the question, a researcher can use a range estimate and knowledge that the range is approximated by the mean ± 3 standard deviations. Suppose, for example, that a critical question on the survey involved a scale in which respondents rated their satisfaction with the client company's products on a scale of 1 to 10. If respondents use this scale, the theoretical range would be 10, and 10 divided by 6 equals a standard deviation of 1.7, which would be the variability estimate. Note that this would be a conservative estimate as respondents might not use the entire 1–10 scale, or the mean might not equal 5, the midpoint, meaning that 1.7 is the largest variability estimate possible in this case.

With a percentage, the decision is much simpler because we know that the maximum possible variability is the 50 percent case. From a practical standpoint, most researchers will opt for the 50 percent level of p because it is the worst possible case, but it does not dramatically impact the sample size. In fact, as we indicated earlier, the manager may protest the small sample size even when 50 percent is used in the formula, and the researcher can use the example of national opinion polls using this approach as a defense.

How to Determine the Amount of Precision Desired

You know that sample findings are nothing more than estimates of population values. The act of estimating incurs a certain degree of error because an estimate will not be precisely the population value; however, it will be close to the population value. From our description of the formulas, you should know that the size of the sample has a direct bearing on the accuracy of the sample statistic value. Small samples are less accurate, on the average, than are large samples, particularly for populations with high variability. Translated in terms of precision, the more precise the marketing decision maker desires the estimate to be, the larger must be the sample size. So, it is the task of the marketing project director to extract from the marketing decision maker the acceptable range of allowable error sufficient for him or her to make a decision.

Marketing researchers often must help decision makers understand the sample size implications of their requests for high precision, expressed as allowable error.

Usually the precision desired is specified as a plus or minus percent. That is, the decision maker might say, "I can live with an estimate that is within ±10 percent of the actual figure." This is translated by the researcher determining the sample size into the relative precision, or relative accuracy, of the final estimate of the population parameter.

For sample size determination situations in which the percentage is the focal statistic, a "±*e* percent" is easy for a manager to understand. For example, if Citibank were testing consumer response to a new type of credit card loss insurance, and the manager indicated that he or she wanted the results to be accurate to ±5 percent, the marketing researcher would translate this in his or her mind into a range around the sample percentage. So if he or she found 30 percent of the sample to indicate a favorable opinion for the credit card loss insurance option, the sample size would, through computation of the standard error of the percentage, effect from 25 percent to 35 percent as a range in which the population percentage most likely falls. Of course, if the precision were less, say ±15 percent, the sample size would be smaller, and if the same 30 percent result occurred, the range would then be 15 percent to 45 percent.

The notion of precision when estimating a percentage is easier to relate to than when estimating a mean.

When using a mean, the precision factor is a bit more complicated, for here we are dealing with different units of measurement with each case. That is, we might be concerned with miles driven per year as in the Goodyear example, number of Big Macs consumed each week by the tweens, or expected annual fee level for the credit card loss insurance example. Obviously, the absolute values of the population means will vary greatly from 12,000 miles per year to perhaps 2.5 Big Macs per week. A way of overcoming this problem is to use a ratio of the mean, sometimes called the **relative error,** which is defined as a percentage of the mean. For instance, if the relative error were 10 percent and we were deciding sample size for the Goodyear survey, it would mean that the precision required would be ±120 miles. For the tweens, it would translate into ±0.25 Big Macs. So we can work with either an exact number or a ratio to indicate desired precision, or allowable error (e), when working with a mean.

Relative error can be used to estimate precision in sample size determination for a mean.

How to Calculate the Level of Confidence Desired

All marketing decisions are made under a certain amount of risk, and it is mandatory to incorporate the estimate of risk, or at least some sort of a notion of uncertainty, into sample size determination. Because sample statistics are estimates of population values, the proper approach is to use the sample information to generate a range in which the population value is anticipated to fall. Because the sampling process is imperfect, it is appropriate to use an estimate of sampling error in the calculation of this range. Using proper terminology, the range is what we have called the confidence interval. The researcher reports the range and the confidence he or she has that the range includes the population figure.

Use of 95 percent or 99 percent level of confidence is standard in sample size determination.

As we have indicated, the typical approach is to use standard confidence intervals of either 99 percent or 95 percent. As we have also indicated, these levels translate to *z*s of 2.58 and 1.96, respectively. If we had calculated the confidence interval for the average number of Big Macs consumed in a month per tween to fall between five and seven hamburgers, at the 99 percent level of confidence, we are saying in effect to the manager that if we had the opportunity to repeat the sampling process 100 independent times, 99 out of 100 of those sample means would fall between five and seven Big Macs. If we had used the 95 percent level of probability, we would be saying that 95 out of 100 of those sample results would fall between five and seven Big Macs.

SPECIAL SAMPLE SIZE DETERMINATION SITUATIONS

The final section of this chapter takes up two special cases: sample size when sampling from small populations and sample size when using a nonprobability sampling method.

Sampling from Small Populations

Implicit to all sample size discussions thus far in this chapter is the assumption that the population is very large. This assumption is reasonable because there are multitudes of households in the United States, millions of registered drivers, hundreds of thousands of persons over the age of 65, and so forth. So it is common, especially with consumer goods marketers, to draw samples from very large populations. Occasionally, however, the population is much smaller, and this is not unusual in the case of industrial marketers.

With small populations, you should use the finite multiplier to determine sample size.

As a general rule, a small population situation is one in which the sample exceeds 5 percent of the total population size. Notice that a small sample is defined by the size of the population under consideration. If the sample is less than 5 percent of the total population, you can consider the population to be of large size, and you can use the procedures described earlier in this chapter. On the other hand, if it is a small population, the sample size formula needs some adjustment with what is called a **"finite multiplier,"** which is an adjustment factor that is approximately equal to the square root of that proportion of the population not included in the sample. For instance, suppose our population size was considered to be 1,000 companies, and we decided to take a sample of 400. That would result in a finite multiplier of about 0.77, or the square root of 0.6, which is ((1,000 – 400)/1,000). That is, we could use a sample of only 308 (or .77 times 400) companies, and it would be just as accurate as one of size 400 if we had a large population.

The formula for computation of a sample size using the finite multiplier is as follows:

$$\text{Sample size} = \text{Sample size formula} \times \sqrt{\frac{N-n}{N-1}}$$

Here is an example using the 1,000 company population. Let us suppose we want to know the percentage of companies that are interested in a substance abuse counseling program for their employees offered by a local hospital. We are uncertain about the variability, so we use our 50–50 "worst case" approach. We decide to use a 95 percent level of confidence, and the director of Counseling Services at Claremont Hospital would like the results to be accurate ±5 percent. The computations are as follows:

$$n = \frac{z^2(pq)}{e^2}$$

$$= \frac{1.96^2(50 \times 50)}{5^2}$$

$$= \frac{3.84 \times 2500}{25}$$

$$= 384$$

Now, applying the finite multiplier

$$n = 384 \times \sqrt{\frac{N-n}{N-1}}$$

$$= 384 \times \sqrt{\frac{1000-384}{1000-1}}$$

$$= 384 \times \sqrt{\frac{616}{999}}$$

$$= 384 \times 0.79$$

$$= 303$$

In other words, we need a sample size of 303, not 384, because we are working with a small population. By applying the finite multiplier, we can reduce the sample size by 81 respondents and achieve the same accuracy level. If this survey required personal interviews, we would gain a considerable cost savings.

Appropriate use of the finite multiplier formula will reduce a calculated sample size and save money when performing research on small populations.

Sample Size Using Nonprobability Sampling

All sample size formulas and other statistical considerations treated in this chapter assume that some form of probability sampling method has been used. In other words, the sample must be unbiased with regard to selection, and the only sampling error present is due to sample size. Remember, sample size determines the accuracy, not the representativeness, of the sample. The sampling method determines the representativeness. All sample size formulas assume that representativeness is guaranteed with use of a probability sampling procedure.

When using nonprobability sampling, sample size is unrelated to accuracy, so cost–benefit considerations must be used.

The only reasonable way of determining sample size with nonprobability sampling is to weigh the benefit or value of the information obtained with that sample against the cost of gathering that information. Ultimately, this is a very subjective exercise, as the manager may place significant value on the information for a number or reasons. For instance, the information may crystallize the problem, it may open the manager's eyes to vital additional considerations, or it might even make him or her aware of previously unknown market segments. But because of the unknown bias introduced by a subjective sample selecting process, it is inappropriate to apply sample size formulas. For nonprobability sampling, sample size is a judgment based almost exclusively on the value of the biased information to the manager, rather than desired precision, relative to cost.

View: "Noxema Skin Cream: Selecting Cases"

SUMMARY

We began this chapter by notifying you of the "large sample size" bias that many managers hold. There are at least five different methods of determining sample size: (1) designating size arbitrarily, (2) using a "conventional" size, (3) letting cost determine the size, (4) basing size on the requirements of statistical procedures to be used, and (5) calculating size with the confidence interval formula. The last method is more complicated than the others, and it requires an understanding of four underlying concepts: (1) variability, (2) standard error, (3) confidence interval, and (4) the sampling distribution. There are formulas for calculating the sample size given a level of confidence, the precision desired, and the anticipated amount of variablity in the population. We provided the formulas for when you are estimating a percentage and when you are estimating an average.

When using the confidence interval approach to sample size determination, the researcher must estimate variability, precision, and confidence level. We indicated that for confidence level, typically 95 percent or 99 percent levels are applied. These equate to z values of 1.96 and 2.58, respectively. For variability with percentage estimates, the researcher can fall back on a 50–50 split, which is the greatest variability case possible. If an average is being estimated, the researcher may rely on prior experience or he or she may use a pilot study to gain a feel for variability. Precision is the allowable amount of error based on sample size, and normally the researcher and manager will discuss the alternative levels to come to agreement on an acceptable level. Finally, the chapter discussed two special sampling situations. With a small population, the finite multiplier should be used to adjust the sample size determination formula. Last, with nonprobability sampling, a cost–benefits analysis should take place.

KEY TERMS

Sample accuracy (p. 392)
Arbitrary approach (p. 393)
Conventional approach (p. 394)
Cost basis approach (p. 395)
Statistical analysis approach (p. 396)
Confidence interval approach (p. 397)

Variability (p. 397)
Bell-shaped distribution (p. 398)
Normal distribution (p. 398)
Standard deviation (p. 399)
Confidence interval (p. 401)
95 percent confidence interval (p. 401)
Sampling distribution (p. 402)
Standard error (p. 403)
Standard error of the mean (p. 403)
Standard error of a percentage (p. 403)
Accuracy (p. 406)
Relative error (p. 411)
Finite multiplier (p. 412)

REVIEW QUESTIONS/APPLICATIONS

1. Describe each of the following methods of sample size determination and indicate a critical flaw in the use of each one.
   a. Using a "rule of thumb" percentage of the population size.
   b. Using a "conventional" sample size such as the typical size pollsters use.
   c. Using the amount in the budget allocated for data collection to determine sample size.
2. Describe and provide illustrations of each of the following notions: (a) variability, (b) bell-shaped distribution, (c) standard deviation, (d) confidence interval, (e) sampling distribution, and (f) standard error.
3. What are the three fundamental considerations involved with the confidence interval approach to sample size determination?
4. When calculating sample size, how can a researcher decide on the level of accuracy to use? What about level of confidence? What about variability with a percentage?
5. Using the formulas provided in your text, determine the approximate sample sizes for each of the following cases, all with precision (allowable error) of ±5 percent:
   a. Variability of 30 percent, confidence level of 95 percent.
   b. Variability of 60 percent, confidence level of 99 percent.
   c. Unknown variability, confidence level of 95 percent.
6. Indicate how a pilot study can help a researcher understand variability in the population.
7. Why is it important for the researcher and the marketing manager to discuss the accuracy level associated with the research project at hand?
8. What are the benefits to be gained by knowing that a proposed sample is more than 5 percent of the total population's size? In what marketing situation might this be a common occurrence?
9. A researcher knows from experience the average costs of various data collection alternatives:

DATA COLLECTION METHOD	COST/RESPONDENT
Personal interview	$15.00
Telephone interview	$33.50
Mail survey	$ 0.50 (per mailout)

   If $2,500 is allocated in the research budget for data collection, what are the levels of accuracy for the sample sizes allowable for each data collection method? Based on your findings, comment on the inappropriateness of using cost as the only means of determining sample size.

10. Last year, Lipton Tea Company conducted a mall-intercept study at six regional malls around the country and found that 20 percent of the public preferred tea over coffee as a midafternoon hot drink. This year, Lipton wants to have a nationwide telephone survey performed with random digit dialing. What sample size should be used in this year's study in order to achieve an accuracy level of ±2.5 percent at the 99% level of confidence? What about at the 95% level of confidence?
11. Spring break is celebrated by many college students in the eastern United States by a pilgrimage to Florida. In recent years, Daytona Beach has been the preferred destination. Miller Lite Beer has conducted a survey of beer consumption of college students on spring break each year for the past four years. In each survey, 1,000 randomly selected college students have been asked to estimate their total beer consumption. The results are as follows:

	Years Ago			
Bottles of Beer Consumed	**1**	**2**	**3**	**4**
Average	45	60	70	80
Standard deviation	30	25	20	15

What are the sample size implications of these data?
12. American Ceramics, Inc. (ACI) has been developing a new form of ceramic that can stand high temperatures and sustained use. Because of its improved properties, the project development engineer in charge of this project thinks that the new ceramic will compete as a substitute for the ceramics currently used in spark plugs. She talks to ACI's market research director about conducting a survey of prospective buyers of the new ceramic material. During their phone conversation, the research director suggests a study using about 100 companies as a means of determining market demand. Later that day, the research director does some background using the *Thomas Register* as a source of names of companies manufacturing spark plugs. A total of 312 companies located in the continental United States are found in the *Register.* How should this finding impact the final sample size of the survey?
13. Here are some numbers that you can use to sharpen your computational skills for sample size determination. Crest toothpaste is reviewing plans for its annual survey of toothpaste purchasers. With each case below, calculate the sample size pertaining to the key variable under consideration. Where information is missing, provide reasonable assumptions.

Case	Key Variable	Variability	Acceptable Error	Confidence Level
1	Market share of Crest toothpaste	23% share last year	4%	95%
2	How often people brush their teeth per week	Unknown	1 time	99%
3	How likely Crest buyers are to switch brands	30% switched last year	5%	95%
4	Number of minutes of prime time television viewing per night	120 minutes	10 minutes	99%

CASE	KEY VARIABLE	ACCEPTABLE VARIABILITY	CONFIDENCE ERROR	LEVEL
5	Percent of people who want tartar-control features in their toothpaste	20% two years ago; 40% one year ago	3.5%	95%
6	Willingness of people to adopt the toothpaste brand recommended by their family dentist	Unknown	6%	99%
7	Annual amount people pay for dental work	Recent report says some people spend up to $3,000 in a year on dental work	$50	95%

14. Do managers really have a "large sample size bias"? Because you cannot survey managers easily, this exercise will use surrogates. Ask any five seniors majoring in business administration who have not taken a marketing research class the following questions. Indicate whether each of the following statements is true or false.

a. A random sample of 500 is large enough to represent all of the full-time college students in the United States.

b. A random sample of 1,000 is large enough to represent all of the full-time college students in the United States.

c. A random sample of 2,000 is large enough to represent all of the full-time college students in the United States.

d. A random sample of 5,000 is large enough to represent all of the full-time college students in the United States.

What have you found out about sample size bias?

15. The Andrew Jergens Company markets a "spa tablet" called ActiBath, which is a carbonated moisturizing treatment for use in a bath. From previous research, Jergens management knows that 60 percent of all women use some form of skin moisturizer and 30 percent believe their skin is their most beautiful asset. There is some concern among management that women will associate the drying aspects of taking a bath with ActiBath and not believe that it can provide a skin moisturizing benefit. Can these facts about use of moisturizers and concern for skin beauty be used in determining the size of the sample in the ActiBath survey? If so, indicate how. If not, indicate why and how sample size can be determined.

16. Donald Heel is the Microwave Oven Division Manager of Sharp Products. Don proposes a $40 cash rebate program as a means of promoting Sharp's new crisp-broil-and-grill microwave oven. However, the Sharp president wants evidence that the program would increase sales by at least 25 percent, so Don applies some of his research budget to a survey. He uses National Phone Systems Company to conduct a nationwide survey using random digit dialing. National Phone Systems is a fully integrated telephone polling company, and it has the capability of providing daily tabulations. Don decides to use this option, and instead of specifying a final sample size, he chooses to have National Phone Systems perform 50 completions each day. At the end of five days of field work, the daily results are as follows:

	Day				
	1	2	3	4	5
Total sample size	50	100	150	200	250
Percentage of respondents who would consider buying a Sharp microwave with a $40 rebate	50	40	35	30	33

For how much longer should Don continue the survey? Indicate your rationale.

CASE 13.1

Peaceful Lake Subdivision

Located on the outskirts of a large city, the subdivision of Peaceful Lake comprises approximately 600 upscale homes. The subdivision came about 10 years ago when a developer built an earthen dam on Peaceful Brook and created Peaceful Lake, a meandering five-acre body of water. The lake became the centerpiece of the subdivision, and the first 100 one-half acre lots were sold as lakefront property. Now Peaceful Lake Subdivision is fully developed, and its residents are primarily young, professional, dual-income families with one or two school-age children.

Controversy has come to Peaceful Lake. The Subdivision Steering Committee has recommended that a subdivision swimming pool, tennis court, and meeting room facility be constructed on four adjoining vacant lots in the back of the subdivision. Cost estimates range from $250,000 to $500,000, depending on how large the facility will be. Currently, every Peaceful Lake Subdivision homeowner pays a voluntary $150 annual fee for maintenance, security, and upkeep of the subdivision. To construct the proposed recreational facility, each homeowner would be expected to pay a one-time fee of $500, and annual fees would increase by $100.

Objections to the recreational facility come from various quarters. For some, the one-time fee is unacceptable; for others, the notion of a recreational facility is not appealing. Some have their own swimming pools, belong to local tennis clubs, or otherwise have little use for a meeting room facility. Other Peaceful Lake Subdivision homeowners see the recreational facility as a wonderful addition where they could have their children learn to swim, play tennis, or just hang out under supervision.

The president of the Subdivision Association has decided to conduct a survey to poll the opinions and preferences of Peaceful Lake Subdivision homeowners regarding the swimming pool, tennis court, and meeting room facility concept.

1. If the Steering Committee agrees to a survey that is accurate to ±5 percent and at a 95 percent level of confidence, what sample size should be used?
2. Should the survey be a sample or a census of Peaceful Lake Subdivision homeowners? Defend your choice. Be certain to discuss any practical considerations that enter into your choice.

Case 13.2
Plant City

Plant City is a regional chain positioned as a discount "nursery–garden–landscape center." It specializes in bulk purchases of live plants, trees, flowers, and shrubs from large commercial growers and then sells them at anywhere from 25 to 50 percent lower than its smaller, local competitors. It also carries garden equipment, fertilizers, pesticides, and just about anything else you might need to landscape, garden, or improve your yard. Plant City outlets are found throughout the southeastern states, and it is the recognized market share leader in Louisiana, Mississippi, Alabama, Florida, Georgia, and Tennessee. On any given day, you can find landscape hobbyists, amateur gardeners, professional landscapers, and homeowners hoping to save money on their lawn and shrubbery, or even company purchasing agents browsing and buying Plant City merchandise.

The owner of Plant City knows that every spring is a bonanza for his business, for customers will flock to the nurseries in the spring to buy plants to replace those that died in the cold months. The questions concerning the owner each spring include the following:

- How many plants should be stocked?
- How many customers should be anticipated?
- What will they buy?

Each question has important consequences for Plant City purchasing, inventory, and pricing. The owner decides to do a survey to find out the answers to these questions. But he is especially concerned because an error in the survey could cause Plant City either to grossly underestimate sales and lose business or to greatly overestimate sales and end up with large amounts of inventory that will die on the lot as the planting season ends.

1. Using the confidence interval method, how can his concerns about error be reflected in (a) the level of confidence, and (b) the allowable error?
2. Recommend a sample plan that will derive a representative sample of the states where Plant City is the market leader. In this plan, you must determine and justify sample size. You must also describe the survey method and sample plan with all of its parts, along with rationale that convinces the owner of its validity.

CHAPTER 14

Data Collection in the Field, Nonresponse Error, and Questionnaire Screening

LEARNING OBJECTIVES

- *To learn about total error and how nonsampling error is related to it*
- *To understand the sources of nonsampling errors and how to minimize them*
- *To learn about the various types of nonresponse error and how to calculate response rate in order to measure nonresponse error*
- *To read about questionnaire inspection procedures used during and after data collection*

PRACTITIONER VIEWPOINT

We are facing difficult times. There is a growing reluctance on the part of the public to participate in surveys. Our company has tried many different incentives, gimmicks, and inducements, but the number of "uncooperatives" just seems to keep rising. I don't think it is the research industry's fault; rather, it is a need in people to maintain their privacy. Long ago, people learned that if they didn't want to talk to a stranger, all they needed to do was not open their door. The same phenomenon has arrived for telephone calls with answering machines acting as guardians of privacy. Gathering survey data is challenging, and it will continue to be challenging for the long term.

— Diane Sadler-Diaz
ABC TV Affiliate Station

Who Slams the Door on Research?

Who refuses to participate in surveys? How do we find out who these "refusniks" are? The answer is found in geodemography, which is the combination of demographic and geographic characteristics of consumers. Geodemographic groups comprise individuals who live in the same region and share distinguishing demographic traits. Geodemography has identified that the most cooperative folks are all found to be blue-collar farm workers living in small towns or rural areas in the south. Their geodemographic group names and cooperation rates are as follows: Tobacco Roads (92%), Share Croppers (88%), Norma Rae-Ville (83%), and Back Country Folks (82%). The next cooperative group is Agri-Business (81%), comprising mainly ranching, farming, lumbering, and mining communities in the Great Plains and mountain states.

The least responsive groups included: Urban Gold Coast (62%), Money & Brains (60%), Blue-Blood Estates (59%), Gray Power (58%), and Bohemian Mix (56%). The Urban Gold Coast has the highest concentration of one-person households living in high-rise apartment buildings. Money & Brains people tend to live in swank townhouses. Blue-Blood Estates are CEOs and heirs to "old money." Gray Power includes nearly 2 million affluent retirees. Bohemian Mix is a hodgepodge of white-collar workers, students, divorced people, and artists.

When the researchers looked for a universal theme, only one significant correlation was found: responsiveness increases as median home value decreases. A higher proportion of retired and relatively well-off householders will lower a neighborhood's response rate.[1]

We previously learned that we can *expect* to have sampling errors and that we can control for the level of sampling error. However, other errors exist. We refer to these other errors as nonsampling errors. You must understand the sources of these nonsampling errors and learn how they may be minimized. This chapter teaches you the sources of nonsampling errors. Along with a discussion of each source of error, we make suggestions on how you can minimize the negative effect of each type of error. We also teach you how to calculate the response rate in order to measure the amount of nonresponse error. We relate what a researcher looks for in preliminary questionnaire screening after the survey has been completed in order to spot respondents whose answers may exhibit bias, such as always responding positively or negatively to questions.

NONSAMPLING ERROR IN MARKETING RESEARCH

Nonsampling error is defined as all errors in a survey except those due to the sample plan and the sample size.

Data collection has the potential to greatly increase the amount of nonsampling error in a survey.

In the two previous chapters, we discussed sampling. We learned that the sample plan and sample size are important in *predetermining* the amount of sampling error that you will experience. The significance of understanding sampling is that we may control sampling error. However, sampling error is only one of the two components of total error in a survey. The counterpart to sampling error is **nonsampling error,** which is defined as all errors in a survey except those due to the sample plan and the sample size. Nonsampling error includes the following: (1) all types of nonresponse error, (2) data gathering errors, (3) data handling errors, (4) data analysis errors, and (5) interpretation errors. It also includes errors in problem definition, question wording, and, in fact, anything other than sampling error. Generally, the greatest potential for large nonsampling error occurs during the data collection stage, so we discuss errors that can occur during this stage at some length. Also, because nonsampling error cannot be measured by a formula as easily as sampling error can, we describe the various controls that can be imposed on the data collection process to minimize the effects of nonsampling error.[2]

POSSIBLE ERRORS IN FIELD DATA COLLECTION

Nonsampling errors are committed by fieldworkers and respondents.

As we stated before, many nonsampling errors occur during data collection. We divide these errors into two general types and further specify errors within each general type. The first general type is **fieldworker error,** defined as errors committed by the persons who administer the questionnaires. It is important to keep in mind that fieldworker error can occur with the professional data

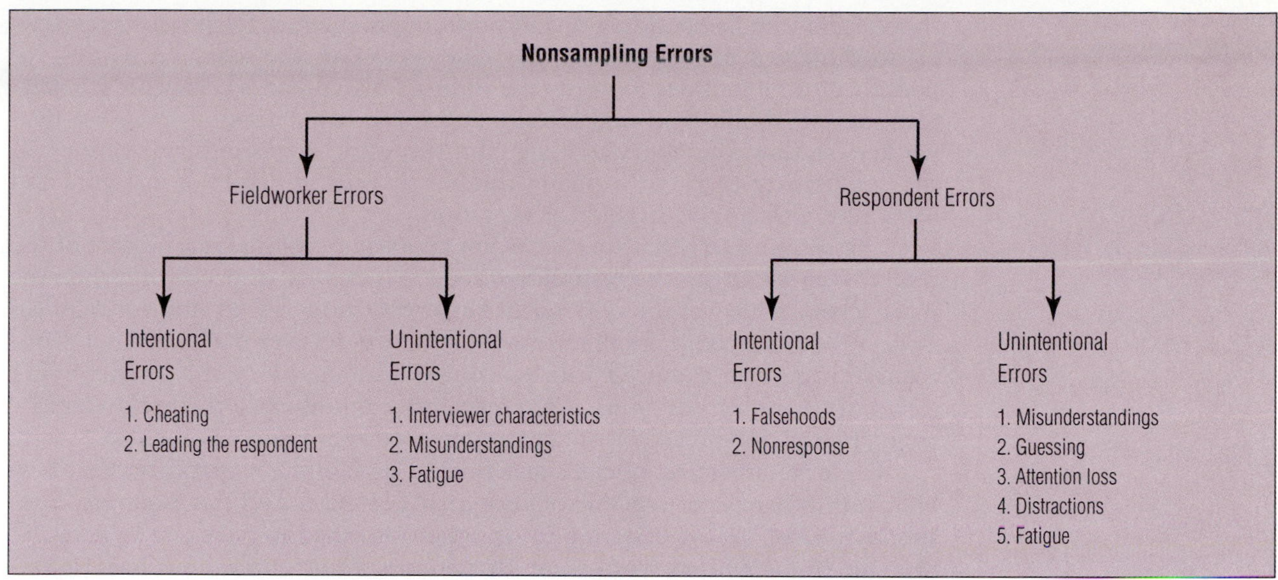

Figure 14.1

Nonsampling Errors

collection worker as well as with the do-it-yourselfer. The other general type is **respondent error,** which refers to errors on the part of the respondent. These, of course, can occur regardless of the method of data collection. Within each general type, we identify two classes of error: **intentional errors,** or errors that are committed deliberately, and **unintentional errors,** or errors that occur without willful intent.[3] Figure 14.1 lists the various errors/types of errors described in this section under each of the four headings.

Intentional Fieldworker Errors

Intentional fieldworker errors occur whenever a data collection person willfully violates the data collection requirements set forth by the researcher. There are two variations of intentional fieldworker errors that we describe: interviewer cheating and leading the respondent. Both are constant concerns of all researchers.

Interviewer cheating is a concern, especially when compensation is based on a per-completion basis.

Interviewer cheating occurs when the interviewer intentionally misrepresents respondents. You might think to yourself, "What would prompt an interviewer to intentionally falsify responses?" The cause is often found in the compensation system.[4] Interviewers may work by the hour, but a common compensation system is to reward them by completed interviews. That is, a telephone interviewer or a mall-intercept interviewer may be paid at a rate of $3.50 per completed interview, so at the end of an interview day, he or she simply turns in the completed questionnaires, and the number is credited to the interviewer.

There is some defensible logic for a paid-by-completion compensation system. Interviewers do not always work like production-line workers. With mall intercepts, for instance, there are periods of inactivity, depending on mall shopper flow and respondent qualification requirements. Telephone interviewers working out of their homes may take breaks, or they may be waiting for periods of time in order to satisfy the number of call-backs policy for a particular survey. Also, as you may already know, the compensation levels for field workers are low, the hours are long, and the work is frustrating at times.[5] So the temptation to turn in bogus completed questionnaires is present, and some interviewers give in to this temptation.

Interviewers should not influence respondents' answers.

The second error that we are categorizing as intentional on the part of the interviewer is **leading the respondent,** and it is defined as occurring when the interviewer influences the respondent's answers through wording, voice inflection, or body language. In the worst case, the interviewer may actually reword a question so it is leading. For instance, consider the question, "Is conserving electricity a concern for you?" An interviewer can influence the respondent by changing the question to "Isn't conserving electricity a concern for you?"

There are other, less obvious instances of leading the respondent. One way is to subtly signal the type of response that is expected. If, for example, a respondent says "yes" in response to our question, the interviewer might say, "I thought you would say 'yes' as over 90 percent of my respondents have agreed on this issue." A comment such as this plants a seed in the respondent's head that he or she should continue to agree with the majority.

Another area of subtle leading occurs in the interviewer's cues. In a personal interview, for instance, the interviewer might ever so slightly shake his or her head "no" to questions he or she disagrees with and "yes" to those he or she agrees with while posing the question. The respondent may perceive these cues and begin responding in the expected manner signaled by the interviewer's head movements while he or she reads the questions. Over the telephone, an interviewer might give verbal cues such as "unhuh" to responses he or she disagrees with or "okay" to responses he or she agrees with, and this continued reaction pattern may subtly influence the respondent's answers. Again, we have categorized this example as an intentional error because professional interviewers are trained to avoid them, and if they commit them, they should be aware of their violations.

Unintentional Fieldworker Errors

Interviewer errors can occur without the interviewer's being aware of them.

An unintentional interviewer error occurs whenever an interviewer commits an error while believing that he or she is performing correctly. There are three general sources of unintentional interviewer errors. These sources are: interviewer personal characteristics, interviewer misunderstandings, and interviewer fatigue. Unintentional interviewer error is found in the interviewer's **personal characteristics** such as accent, sex, and demeanor. We have included Marketing Research Insight 14.1 to illustrate this topic. Under some circumstances, even the interviewer's gender can be a source of bias.[6]

Unintentional interviewer errors include misunderstanding and fatigue.

Interviewer misunderstanding occurs when an interviewer believes he or she knows how to administer a survey, but instead does it incorrectly. As we have described, a questionnaire may include various types of instructions for the interviewer, varying response scale types, directions on how to record responses, and other complicated guidelines that must be adhered to by the interviewer. As you can guess, there is a considerable education gap between marketing researchers who design questionnaires and interviewers who administer them. This gap may translate into a communication problem in which

MARKETING RESEARCH INSIGHT 14.1

How an Interviewer's Accent Can Create "Communication Static"

Almost every American's vocabulary features some slang, jargon, or region-specific terminology and expressions. Observers claim that interviewers with accents tend to experience higher refusal and termination rates than do others working on the same study. In addition to not participating in the survey, respondents who identify an interviewer's accent may apply preconceived biases to the interviewer and the survey.

William G. Eggington, a linguistics professor at Brigham Young University, says, "In a telephone situation like telephone research interviewing, the speaker's voice is the only information the listener gets. Very often, if the speaker has an accent, listeners will stereotype the speaker. To many listeners, a Bostonian accent sounds upper-class. To some people, a Texan accent brings to mind images of cattle ranches and oil wells." In other words, an accent may cause respondents to form negative impressions of the interviewer, which they then project onto the survey through the answers they give to the questions.

Eggington has cataloged nine major regional accents. Americans in these areas generally have similar pronunciation and speech patterns, with some regions closer to "standard American" than others. Standard American is defined as neutral and universally acceptable—like that used by TV newscasters. The map displays numbers indicating the closeness of the region to American standard. A score of zero means the accent is very similar to, whereas a score of 10 means it is very different from, standard American.

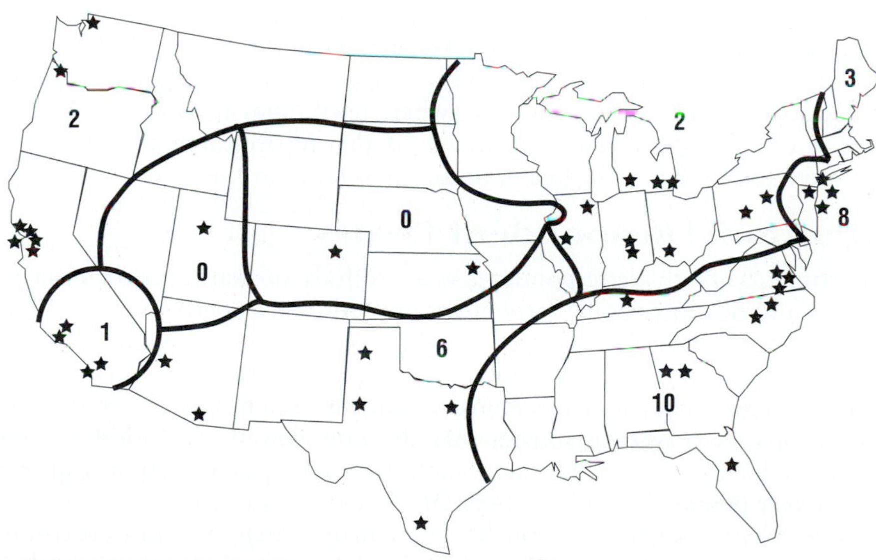

★ = Telephone data collection companies with 50 or more long distance interviewing stations

Accent rankings
0 = Close to standard American
10 = Distant from standard American

Field services hire interviewers from the local workforce where the regional accent is strongest. On the map, the stars identify cities where at least one interview company with 50 or more telephone lines is located. You should notice that many fall in regions where the accent is especially far from American standard. That is, interviewers with strong regional accents conduct the majority of telephone interviewing in the United States.

One practitioner has termed a noticeable interviewer accent as "communication static." This interference diminishes the quality of the interview as it is a source of nonresponse and other biases. It also increases interviewing costs due to refusals and terminations. The implication is that a researcher should either use standard American interviewers or otherwise match regional accents of interviewers to the accents of the respondents, if possible.

Source: *Eric DeRosia, "Accents Boost Nonresponse to Telephone Interviews,"* Marketing News, *25:18 (1992), 38, 41.*

the instructions on the questionnaire are confusing to the interviewer. In this circumstance, the interviewer will usually struggle to comply with the researcher's wishes, but may fail to do so to some degree or another.

The third type of unintentional interviewer error pertains to **fatigue-related mistakes,** which can occur when an interviewer becomes tired. Fatigue sets in because interviewing can become tedious and monotonous. It is repetitious at best. Toward the end of a long interviewing day, the interviewer may be less mentally alert than earlier in the day, and this condition can cause slip-ups and mistakes to occur. The interviewer may fail to obey a skip pattern, might forget to check the respondent's reply to a question, might hurry through a section of the questionnaire, or might appear or sound weary to a potential respondent who refuses to take part in the survey as a result.

The whole issue of interviewer error takes on new meaning when marketing research is conducted in countries where telephones are primitive and illiteracy rates are high. We have included Marketing Research Insight 14.2 to give you a feel for what it is like to be an interviewer in India.

Intentional Respondent Errors

Sometimes respondents do not tell the truth.

Unfortunately, there are respondents who willfully misrepresent themselves in surveys, and this intentional respondent error must be guarded against. There are at least two major intentional respondent errors that require discussion: falsehoods and refusals. **Falsehoods** occur when respondents fail to tell the truth in surveys. They may feel embarrassed, they might want to protect their privacy, or they may even suspect that the interviewer has a hidden agenda such as suddenly turning the interview into a sales pitch. Certain topics denote greater potential for misrepresentation. For instance, the income level of the respondent is a sensitive topic for many people, marital status disclosure is a concern for women living alone, age is a delicate topic for some, and personal hygiene questions may offend some respondents. Energy conservation is a normative topic, and because respondents know what they should be doing to conserve, some of them may resort to lying so they will not be perceived as wasteful or unpatriotic.

Nonresponse is defined as failure on the part of a prospective respondent to take part in a survey or to answer a question.

The second type of intentional respondent error is **nonresponse.** Nonresponse is defined as a failure on the part of a prospective respondent to take

MARKETING RESEARCH INSIGHT 14.2

The Problems Encountered while Doing Research in India

The following description of India's marketing research environment was provided by Surendra Singh, professor of marketing, Oklahoma State University, and by Ms. Pushkala Raman, doctoral candidate at Texas A&M University.

To most Americans, India is still a country with immense poverty and little industrial development of any consequence. However, India, with a population of over 800 million and a sizeable middle class, is a giant market for consumer products, and many foresighted American companies have maintained a significant presence in India for quite some time. Among these are Johnson & Johnson, General Electric, Cummins, Cyanamid, and Procter & Gamble.

Since India's independence from Britain some 45 years ago, the Indian government has centrally planned and managed large sections of the Indian economy with disastrous economic results. Plagued by chronic shortages of consumer products, India has until recently remained a sellers' market for most products. Historically, therefore, marketing research has played a very limited role in the Indian economy, and its customers have been unaccessible to the foreign corporations and advertising agencies doing business in India. However, lately things have begun to change dramatically. The Indian government has loosened its grip on private business, private enterprise has expanded, and competition among firms is fierce. Understandably, in order to gain a competitive advantage and to know their customers better, many Indian companies are turning to marketing research.

Even though the Indian marketing research industry is very small in comparison to that in the United States—one estimate places the size of marketing research activity in India at about $7 million—it has had a very impressive growth rate. Also, according to Mr. Ramesh Thadani, general manager of the Indian Market Research Bureau, marketing research in India today is not limited to ad hoc-sponsored research only but includes a wide range of syndicated research: store audits, consumer panels, readership surveys, and TV audience studies.

An entire issue (April 1992) of the Journal of the Market Research Society *was devoted to the Indian contributions to marketing research. An examination of this issue showed the scope of research undertaken by the Indian marketing researchers. The research areas included opinion polling, impact of clutter on television advertising, pricing research, research among children, semiotics, psychographics, and conjoint analysis applied to personal selection.*

Conducting marketing research in India is unlike conducting research in any other western country. Consider the logistical nightmare in opinion polling described by Sopariwala and Roy (1992). India's large and ethically, culturally, and linguistically diverse electorate is spread over 3,245 towns and 600,000 villages. Given this diversity, the sample size has to be larger than the typical U.S. national poll samples.

With 15 major languages and more than 1,600 dialects, questionnaires have to be translated into several major languages. Telephone and mail interviews are out of the question due to lower telephone penetration rate (less than 2% of the population) and the high illiteracy rate (64%), respectively. Thus, the only polling option is face-to-face interviews. Reaching the survey respondents is not easy either. Consider this.

> *The sample village may be in the back of beyond (meaning "very remote") or have poor transportation links. To reach it, the intrepid interviewer may have to ford a river, wade through slush, commandeer a bullock cart, or hang on for dear life on the footboard of an overcrowded bus or train. (Sopariwala and Roy, 1992, pp. 175–6.)*

In addition to infrastructural problems, simple factors like the sex and cultural characteristics of the interviewer can make a difference to respondent cooperation in completing the survey. In a multicultural city like Bombay (the commercial capital of India), there are people from different states speaking different languages and coming from a variety of cultural backgrounds. In order to get a representative sample, market researchers need to include people from all these diverse backgrounds. Obtaining information from them is not so easy. First, you need to get interviewers who can speak all those languages (typically, there can be as many as five or six major language groups). Also, you have to deal with conservative traditions where a housewife may not speak to a male interviewer unless her husband is present.

Despite these problems, marketing researchers have made impressive gains in the Indian market and have displayed great sophistication and creativity in applying marketing research tools to the Indian conditions.

Sources: Journal of the Market Research Society, *vol. 32, no. 2 (April 1992); Meenahhi Behara and C. P. Chandrasekhar, eds.,* India: In an Era of Liberalization, *London, Euromoney Publications, 1988; Dorab R. Sopariwala and P. L. Roy, "Opinion Polling in India,"* Journal of the Market Research Society, *vol. 32, no. 2 (1992), 173–86.*

---

part in the survey or to answer specific questions on the questionnaire. In fact, nonresponse of various types is probably the most common intentional respondent error that researchers encounter. Some observers believe that survey research is in for tough times ahead because of a growing distaste for survey participation, increasingly busy schedules, and a desire for privacy.[7] Marketing Research Insight 14.3 illustrates the severity of this noncooperation problem. Telephone surveyors are most concerned.[8] In fact, declining cooperation rates are changing the face of the industry,[9] so much so that by the year 2000 traditional surveying may be obsolete.[10] Nonresponse in general, and refusals in particular, are encountered in virtually every survey conducted. We devote an entire section to this important source of error in a following section of this chapter.

Unintentional Respondent Errors

Unintentional respondent errors include misunderstanding, attention loss, distractions, guessing, and fatigue.

An unintentional respondent error occurs whenever a respondent gives a response that is not valid, but he or she believes is the truth. There are five instances of unintentional respondent errors: respondent misunderstanding, guessing, attention loss, distractions, and respondent fatigue. First, **respondent misunderstanding** is defined as situations in which a respondent gives an answer without comprehending the question and/or the accompanying instructions. Potential respondent misunderstandings exist in all surveys. Such misunderstandings range from simple errors, such as checking two responses to a question when only one is called for, to complex errors, such as misunderstanding terminology. For example, a respondent may think in terms of net income for the past year rather than income before taxes as desired by the researcher. Any number of misunderstandings such as these can plague a survey.

Sometimes a respondent will answer without understanding the question.

Whenever a respondent guesses, error is likely.

A second form of unintentional respondent error is **guessing,** in which a respondent gives an answer when he or she is uncertain of its accuracy. Occasionally, respondents are asked about topics they have little knowledge of or low recall about, but they feel compelled to provide an answer to the questions being posed. Here, the respondent might guess the answer. All guesses are likely to contain errors. Here is an example of guessing. If you were a respondent and were asked to estimate the amount of electricity in kilowatt hours you used last month, how many would you say you used?

Marketing Research Insight 14.3

Societal Shifts and the Desire for Privacy Threaten Survey Research

The future may hearken the death of the traditional marketing research survey. Observers have documented an increasing reluctance in Americans to participate in surveys. In fact, more than one-third of Americans now refuse to be surveyed.

A number of social, demographic, and practical considerations have accelerated this noncooperation trend. These factors include: (1) fear of strangers on the part of low-income people; (2) security systems, unlisted numbers, and answering phones used by affluent consumers; and (3) growth of two-income, single-person, and single-parent households too busy to respond to a survey.

At the same time, researchers may be creating the problem themselves as they increasingly rely on telephone surveys in which answering machines are naturally encountered and consumers are suspicious of sales pitches disguised as surveys. Observers also note bad timing and inconvenience.

The research industry is changing in response to the crisis. First, it is moving toward "passive" data collection with the use of scanning wands, people meters, and other methods in which the respondent does not need to verbally respond to questions. However, these methods bring up issues of privacy. Other, more direct approaches include cajoling respondents by telling them how beneficial their cooperation will be. Some research companies are even trying to make surveys more fun by including puzzles, cartoons, sketches, and graphics on their questionnaires to improve response rates. As you read in chapter 2, marketing researchers are very interested in regulating telemarketers who are not in the research business, but who give the research industry a black eye because of their aggressiveness and abuses.

But the real problem may rest with respondents. By refusing to cooperate, Americans may be saying that the industry has not responded to their changing life-styles, their increasing fears of privacy abuse, and their desire for control over their time.

Source: *Adapted from Martha Farnsworth Riche, "Surveys Confront the Sounds of Silence,"* American Demographics, *vol. 12, no. 12 (1990), 19–21.*

A third unintentional respondent error occurs when a respondent's interest in the survey wanes, known as **attention loss.** The typical respondent is not as excited about the survey as is the researcher, and some respondents will find themselves less and less motivated to take part in the survey as they work their way through the questionnaire.

Fourth, **distractions,** such as interruptions, may occur while the questionnaire administration takes place. For example, during a mall-intercept interview, a respondent may be distracted when an acquaintance walks by and says hello. A parent answering questions on the telephone might have to attend to a toddler, or a mail survey respondent might be diverted from the questionnaire by a telephone call. A distraction may cause the respondent to get "off track" or otherwise not take the survey as seriously as is desired by the researcher.

Fifth, unintentional respondent error can take the form of **respondent fatigue,** in which the respondent becomes tired of participating in the survey.

Whenever a respondent tires of a survey, deliberation and reflection will abate. The respondent might even opt for the "no opinion" response category just as a means of quickly finishing the survey because he or she has grown tired of answering questions.

FIELD DATA COLLECTION QUALITY CONTROLS

Fortunately, there are precautions that can be implemented to minimize the effects of the various types of errors just described. Please note that we said "minimize" and not "eliminate," as the potential for error always exists. However, by instituting or otherwise insisting on the following controls, a researcher can be assured that the nonsampling error factor involved with data collection will be diminished. The field data collection quality controls we describe are listed in Table 14.1.

Control of Intentional Fieldworker Error

Intentional fieldworker error can be controlled with supervision and validation procedures.

There are two general strategies to guard against cases in which the interviewer might intentionally commit an error. These strategies are supervision and validation.[11] **Supervision** uses administrators to oversee the work of field data collection workers. Most centralized telephone interviewing companies have a "listening in" capability that the supervisor can use to tap into and monitor any interviewer's line during an interview. The respondent and the interviewer may be unaware of the monitoring, so the "listening in" samples a representa-

TABLE 14.1

How to Control Data Collection Errors

	TYPES OF ERRORS	CONTROL MECHANISMS
Intentional fieldworker errors	Cheating Leading respondent	Supervision Validation
Unintentional fieldworker errors	Interviewer characteristics	Selection and training of interviewers
	Misunderstandings	Orientation sessions and role playing
	Fatigue	Require breaks and alternate surveys
Intentional respondent errors	Falsehoods	Assuring anonymity and confidentiality Incentives Validation checks "Third-person" technique
	Nonresponse	Assuring anonymity and confidentiality Incentives Third-person technique
Unintentional respondent errors	Misunderstandings	Well-drafted questionnaire Direct questions
	Guessing	Well-drafted questionnaire Response options, e.g., "unsure"
	Attention loss Distractions Fatigue	Reversal of scale endpoints Prompters

tive interview performed by that interviewer. If the interviewer is leading or unduly influencing respondents, this procedure will spot the violation, and the supervisor can take corrective action such as a reprimand of that interviewer. With personal interviews, the supervisor might accompany an interviewer to observe that interviewer while administering a questionnaire in the field. Because "listening in" without the consent of the respondent could be considered a breach of privacy, many companies now inform respondents that all or part of the call may be monitored and/or recorded.

Validation verifies that the interviewer did the work. This strategy is aimed at the falsification/cheating problem. There are various ways to validate the work. One type of validation is for the supervisor to recontact the respondent to find out whether he or she took part in the survey. An industry standard is to randomly select 10 percent of the completed surveys for purposes of making a call-back to validate that the interview was actually conducted. A few sample questions might even be readministered for comparison purposes. In the absence of call-back validation, some supervisors will inspect completed questionnaires, and, with a trained eye, they may spot patterns in an interviewer's completions that raise suspicions of falsification. Interviewers who turn in bogus completed questionnaires are not always careful about simulating actual respondents. The supervisor might find inconsistencies, such as very young respondents with large numbers of children, that raise doubts as to a questionnaire's authenticity.

Control of Unintentional Fieldworker Error

Unintentional fieldworker errors can be reduced with supervised orientation sessions and role playing.

The supervisor is instrumental in minimizing unintentional interviewer error as well. We describe three mechanisms commonly used by professional field data collection companies in this regard: selection and training, orientation sessions, and role playing. Interviewer personal characteristics that can cause unintentional errors are best taken care of by *careful selection of interviewers.* Following selection, it is important to *train them well* so as to avoid any biases resulting from manner, appearance, and so forth. **Orientation sessions** are meetings in which the supervisor introduces the survey and questionnaire administration requirements to the fieldworkers. The supervisor might highlight qualification or quota requirements, note skip patterns, or go over instructions to the interviewer that are embedded throughout the questionnaire. Finally, often as a means of becoming familiar with a questionnaire's administration requirements, interviewers will conduct **role-playing sessions,** which are dry runs or dress rehearsals of the questionnaire with the supervisor or some other interviewer playing the respondent's role. Successive role-playing sessions serve to familiarize interviewers with the questionnaire's special administration aspects. To control for interviewer fatigue, some researchers require interviewers to take *frequent breaks* and/or *alternate surveys,* if possible.

Control of Intentional Respondent Error

Tactics useful in minimizing intentional respondent error include anonymity, confidentiality, validation checks, and third-person technique.

To control intentional respondent error, it is important to minimize falsehoods and nonresponse on the parts of respondents. Tactics useful in minimizing intentional respondent error include anonymity, confidentiality, incentives, validation checks, and third-person technique.[12] **Anonymity** occurs when the respondent is assured that his or her name will not be associated with his or her answers. **Confidentiality** occurs when the respondent is given assurances that his or her answers will remain private. Both assurances are believed to be helpful in forestalling falsehoods. The belief here is that when respondents are guaranteed they will remain nameless, they will be more comfortable in self-disclosure and will refrain from lying or misrepresenting themselves.

Incentives sometimes compel respondents to be more truthful, and they also discourage nonresponse.

Another tactic for reducing falsehoods is the use of **incentives,** which are cash payments, gifts, or something of value promised to respondents in return for their participation. For participating in a survey, the respondent may be paid cash or provided with a redemption coupon. He or she might be given a gift such as a ballpoint pen or a tee shirt. Here, in a sense, the respondent is being induced to tell the truth by direct payment. The respondent may now feel morally obligated to tell the truth because he or she will receive compensation. Or, he or she may feel guilty at receiving an incentive and then not answering truthfully. Unfortunately, practitioners and academic researchers are only beginning to understand how to entice prospective respondents to take part in a survey.[13] Incentives also encourage respondents to take part in surveys which reduces nonresponse.

A different approach for reducing falsehoods is the use of **validation checks,** in which information provided by a respondent is confirmed. For instance, in an in-home survey on baldness medication, the interviewer might ask to see the respondent's medication as a verification or validation check. A more unobtrusive validation is to have the interviewer, who is trained to be alert to untrue answers, check for old-appearing respondents who say they are young, shabbily dressed respondents who say they are wealthy, and so on. A well-trained interviewer will note suspicious answers in the margin of the questionnaire.[14]

With an embarrassing question, the third-person technique may make the situation less personal.

Finally, there is a questionnaire design feature that a researcher can use to reduce intentional respondent errors. Sometimes the opportunity arises where a **third-person technique** can be used in a question, in which instead of directly quizzing the respondent, the question is couched in terms of a third person who is similar to the respondent. For instance, a question posed to a middle-aged man might be, "Do you think a person such as yourself uses Minoxidil as a baldness medication?" Here, the respondent will most probably think in terms of his own circumstances, but because the subject of the question is some unnamed third party, the question is not seen as personal. In other words, he will not be divulging some personal and private information by talking about this fictitious other person. The third-person technique may be used to reduce both falsehoods and nonresponse.

Control of Unintentional Respondent Error

Ways to combat unintentional respondent error include well-drafted questionnaire instructions and examples, reversals of scale endpoints, and use of "prompters."

The control of unintentional respondent error takes various forms as well, including *well-drafted questionnaire instructions and examples,* reversals of scale endpoints, and use of prompters. With regard to misunderstanding, well-drafted questionnaire instructions and examples are commonly used as a way of avoiding respondent confusion. We described these in chapter 11 on questionnaire design. Also, researchers sometimes resort to *direct questions* to assess respondent understanding. For example, after describing a five-point agree–disagree response scale in which 1 = strongly agree, 2 = agree, 3 = neither agree nor disagree, 4 = disagree, and 5 = strongly disagree, the interviewer might be instructed to ask, "Are these instructions clear?" If the respondent answers in the negative, the instructions are repeated until the respondent understands them. Guessing may be reduced by alerting respondents to *response options such as "no opinion," "do not recall," or "unsure."*

A tactic we described when we discussed the semantic differential is **reversals of scale endpoints** in which instead of putting all of the negative adjectives on one side and all the positive ones on the other side, a researcher will switch the positions of a few items. Such reversals are intended to warn respondents that they must respond to each bipolar pair individually. With agree–disagree statements, this tactic is accomplished by negatively wording a statement every now and then to induce respondents to attend to each statement individually. Both of these tactics are intended to heighten the respondent's attention.

Finally, long questionnaires often use **"prompters,"** such as "We are almost finished," or "That was the most difficult section of questions to answer," or other statements strategically located to encourage the respondent to remain on track. Sometimes interviewers will sense an attention lag or fatigue on the part of the respondent and provide their own prompters or comments intended to maintain the respondent's full participation in the survey.

"Prompters" are used to keep respondents on task and alert.

Final Comment on the Control of Data Collection Errors

As you can see, a wide variety of nonsampling errors can occur on the parts of both interviewers and respondents during the data collection stage of the marketing research process. Similarly, a variety of precautions and controls are used to minimize nonsampling error. Each survey is unique, of course, so we cannot provide universally applicable guidelines. We will, however, stress the importance of good questionnaire design in reducing these errors. Also, professional field data collection companies whose existence depends on how well they can control interviewer and respondent error are commonly relied on by researchers who understand the true value of their services. Finally, technology is dramatically changing data collection and helping in the control of its errors.[15]

NONRESPONSE ERROR

Although nonresponse was briefly described earlier in our discussion of mail surveys, we will now describe the nonresponse issue more fully, including various types of nonresponse, how to assess the degree of nonresponse error, and some ways of adjusting or compensating for nonresponse in surveys. The identification, control, and adjustments necessary for nonresponse are critical to the success of a survey. Nonresponse has been labeled the marketing research industry's biggest problem,[16,17] and it is multinational in scope.[18] Compounding the problem has been the increase in the numbers of surveys, which means the likelihood of being asked to participate in a survey has increased. With several researchers chasing the same population, there is always a constant battle to keep response rates from dropping. Some industry observers believe that the major problems leading to nonresponse are caused by fears of invasion of privacy, skepticism of consumers regarding the benefits of participating in research, and the use of research as a guise for telemarketing. (At this point, you may want to recall our discussion of sugging and frugging in chapter 2).

Nonresponse is defined as a failure on the part of a prospective respondent to take part in the survey or to answer specific questions on the questionnaire. There are at least three different types of potential nonresponse error lurking in any survey: **refusals** to participate in the survey, **break-offs** during the interview, and refusals to answer specific questions, or **item omission.** Table 14.2 (on page 434) briefly describes each type of nonresponse.

There are three types of nonresponse error: refusals to participate in the survey, break-offs during the interview, and refusals to answer specific questions (item omissions).

TABLE 14.2

The Three "Faces" of Nonresponse

- A prospective respondent may refuse to participate in the survey.
- A respondent may break off or stop answering in the middle of the survey.
- A respondent may refuse to answer a particular question but continue to answer following questions.

Refusals to Participate in the Survey

Refusals to participate in surveys are increasing worldwide.

Our introductory case alerted you to the fact that refusal rates differ by area of the country as well as by demographic differences. The reasons for refusals are many and varied. The person may be busy, he or she may have no interest in the survey, something about the interviewer's voice or approach may have turned the person off, or the refusal may simply reflect how that person always responds to surveys. Part of the problem for a refusal to participate is because the respondents do not want to take the time or because they regard it as an intrusion of their privacy.

As we previously mentioned, one way to overcome refusals is to use incentives as a token of appreciation. In a review of 15 different mail surveys, researchers found that inclusion of a small gift, such as a $1.50 rollerball pen, increased response rates by nearly 14 percent. A second feature that contributes to refusals is the length of the questionnaire.[19] The study previously cited found that for every additional minute it takes to fill out the questionnaire, the response rate drops by 0.85 percent. Response rates to mail surveys are also influenced by the type of appeal that is made in the cover letter. Results from one study indicated that a social utility appeal was more effective in increasing response rates when an educational institution was the sponsor. On the other hand, an egoistic appeal was more effective when the sponsor was a commercial organization. An egoistic appeal is a suggestion that the respondent's individual responses are highly important in completing the research task.[20]

Break-Offs during the Interview

If tired, confused, or uninterested, respondents may "break off" in the middle of an interview.

Break-off occurs when a respondent reaches a certain point, and then decides not to answer any more questions for the survey. Reasons for break-offs, as you would expect, are varied. The interview may take longer than the respondent initially believed, the topic and specific questions may prove to be distasteful or too personal, the instructions may be too confusing, a sudden interruption may occur, or the respondent may choose to take an incoming call on call-waiting and stop the interview. Sometimes with self-administered surveys, a researcher will find a questionnaire in which the respondent has simply stopped filling it out.

It is critical that well-trained interviewers be employed to carry out the surveys. In a discussion on how to improve respondent cooperation, Howard Gershowitz, senior vice president of MKTG, said, "I think the interviewers have to be taken out of the vacuum and be included in the process. Companies that are succeeding right now realize that the interviewers are the key to their success."[21] Increasingly, research providers are focusing on improved training techniques and field audits.

Refusals to Answer Specific Questions (Item Omission)

Occasionally, a respondent will refuse to answer a particular question that he or she considers too personal or a private matter.

Even if a failure to participate or break-off situation does not occur, a researcher will sometimes find that specific questions have lower response rates than others. If fact, if a marketing researcher suspects ahead of time that a particular question, such as the respondent's annual income for last year, will have some degree of refusals, it is appropriate to include the designation "refusal" on the questionnaire. Of course, it is not wise to put these designations on self-administered questionnaires, because respondents may use this option simply as a cop-out, when they might have provided accurate answers if the designation were not there. "Item omission" is the phrase sometimes used to identify the percentage of the sample that refused to answer a particular question.

Measuring Nonresponse Error in Surveys

Most marketing research studies report their **response rate.** The response rate essentially enumerates the percentage of the total sample with which interviews were completed. It is, therefore, the opposite of the nonresponse rate (a measure of nonresponse error). If you have a 75 percent response rate, then you have a nonresponse error in the amount of 25 percent.

The research industry has an accepted way to calculate a survey's response rate.

For many years there was much confusion about the calculation of response rates. There was no one universally accepted definition, and different firms used different methods to calculate response rates. In fact, there were many terms in common usage including completion rate, cooperation rate, interview rate, at-home rate, and refusal rate, among others. In 1982, however, CASRO (Council of American Survey Research Organizations) published a special report in an attempt to provide a uniform definition and method for calculating the response rate.[22]

According to the CASRO report, response rate is defined as the ratio of the number of completed interviews to the number of eligible units in the sample. Or,

$$\text{Response rate} = \frac{\text{Number of completed interviews}}{\text{Number of eligible units in sample}}$$

Example 1. All Units Are Eligible, There Are No Substitutions

Population: Charge account customers for a department store
Sample frame: List of current charge account customers
Sample plan: A systematic sample
Sample size: 1,000
Method of interview: Personal *or* mail *or* telephone

Results:

CALL #	ATTEMPTS	NUMBER OF INTERVIEWS COMPLETED	CUMULATIVE	RESPONSE RATE
1	1,000	600	600	60.0%
2	400	200	800	80.0%
3	200	50	850	85.0%

In this example, all of the 1,000 sampled customers were eligible. Three rounds of calls were made in an attempt to get the not-at-homes and busy signals to respond. The problem with this approach is that the desired sample size was 1,000 yet only 850 completions were obtained. The consequence of this is that the desired level of allowable error (*e*) will not be obtained. There will be more sampling error than desired when the researcher determines that the sample size should be 1,000 and completes a sample of only 850. The following examples include substitutions to the original sample size in order to obtain the predetermined sample size, which allows for the desired level of allowable error.

Example 2. All Units Are Eligible, There Are Substitutions

Sometimes it is desirable to obtain a predetermined sample size. Imagine that in the department store survey shown in example 1, we must have a sample size of 1,000 in order to meet our desired level of allowable error. Because the sample frame contains many more names than our sample size, we have the opportunity to draw additional names for sampling purposes. There are two primary methods we can use to obtain our desired sample of 1,000 interviews:

The calculation of response rate differs for oversampling versus substitution.

a. Oversample: select a larger sample to begin with. This is often done in order to allow for a certain percentage of nonresponse and yet end up with the desired number of completions. Experience with surveys gives you an idea as to how much to oversample. For instance, had we conducted the survey previously reported, we would know that we needed 1,000/0.85 = 1,176 calls in order to complete a sample of 1,000.

If this method is used, the response rate is:

Response rate = 1000/1176 = 85%

b. A second method of obtaining a desired sample size is achieved through substitution. For each nonresponse, after *n* attempts, select the next name from the sample frame, make a single attempt, and, if not successful, take the next one and continue until a completed interview is obtained. For instance, assume that to obtain the additional 150 interviews to bring the sample size up to 1,000, 300 additional names were substituted for original nonrespondents.

If this method is used, the:

Response rate is *NOT* = 1,000/1,300 = 76.9%

but

Response rate is = 850/1,000 = 85.0%

Note that the recommended response rate is based on how you performed on the *original* sample of 1,000 (850 completions out of 1,000). Although it ignores the fact that you substituted an additional 300 sample units, it also does not recognize the increase in sample size generated by the substitutions.

Example 3. Some Units Are Not Eligible

Ineligible people, those who refuse the survey, and those who cannot be reached are included in the formula for response rate.

In many studies respondents may or may not be eligible as respondents. If we were conducting a survey of department store customer satisfaction with shopping in a particular department, we would determine their eligibility for the survey by asking them the screening question, "Have you shopped in department *X* at any time during the last three months?" We have our sample of 1,000 shoppers, and the results of the survey are:

Completions = 400

Ineligible = 300

Refusals = 100

No answer, busy, not at home = 200

This information allows you to calculate the number of sample units that are (a) eligible, (b) noneligible, and (c) not ascertained. When calculating the response rate we have the number of completions in the numerator (as usual). However, in the denominator we have the number of completions plus the percentage of those who refused and who were busy, and not-at-homes who were *eligible.* Since we do not talk to those who refuse, don't answer, have busy signals, or who are not at home, how do we determine the percentage of these people that would have been eligible? We multiply their number by the percentage of those that we did talk with that *are* eligible. By doing this, we are assuming that the same percentage of eligibles exist in the population of those that we did talk with (of the 700 we talked with, 0.57 were eligible) as exist in the population of those that we did not get to talk with (due to refusals, no answers, busy, or not-at-homes). The formula for calculating the response rate for this situation is:

$$\text{Response rate} = \frac{\text{completions}}{\text{completions} + (\text{completions}/(\text{completions} + \text{ineligible})) \times (\text{refusals} + \text{not reached})}$$

$$\text{Response rate} = \frac{400}{400 + \{400/(400 + 300)\}\ \{100 + 200\}}$$

$$= \frac{400}{400 + (0.57)\ (300)}$$

$$= 70.0\%$$

Whereas the CASRO formulas seems simple and straightforward, questions arise as to exactly how to interpret them when dealing with individual research projects. We provide you with a complete example of calculation of response rate for a telephone survey in Marketing Research Insight 14.4 on pages 438–439.

Completed Interview

You must define a "completed" interview.

As we learned earlier, you will experience both break-offs and item omissions. At which point does a break-off still constitute a completed interview? At which level of item omission do we deem a survey to be incomplete? You must determine your definition for a completed interview. Almost all interviews will have some questions for which the subject does not wish to (or cannot) answer. However, simply because a few questions remain unanswered does not mean you do not have a completed interview. But, how many questions must be answered before you have a completed interview? This will vary with each marketing research project. In some cases, it may be necessary that the respondent has answered all of the questions. In others, you may adopt some decision rule to allow you to define completed versus not completed interviews. For example, in most research studies there are questions directed at the primary purpose of the study. Also, there are usually questions asked for purposes of adding additional insights into how respondents answered the primary

MARKETING RESEARCH INSIGHT 14.4

How to Calculate a Response Rate

We are providing you with this example because it seems that all research projects are unique when we are trying to calculate a response rate. For example, although the situation we present here is fairly common, we incorporate two of the response rate formulas discussed in this chapter. Our attempt here is to provide you with a generic telephone survey and to give you as much detail as possible so that you will understand how to calculate a response rate.

Population: *Survey of car-buying attitudes and behavior in households with telephones in Anytown, USA*

Sampling frame: *Anytown, USA, telephone directory*

Desired sample size: *400 completions*

Sample plan: *Systematic sample, which uses oversampling in order to achieve the 400 desired completion. (See example 2.a on page 436.)*

Eligibility of respondents: *The survey seeks information about car dealers and recent car-purchasing behavior. Your client wants only information collected from individuals who have purchased an automobile within the last year. Consequently, a screening question was asked at the beginning of the survey to determine if the respondent, or anyone in the household, had purchased a car within the last year. (See example 3 on pages 436–437.)*

Assume you are doing this survey as a class project and you have been assigned the task of completing five interviews. You have been instructed to draw 25 telephone listings from the directory for Anytown, USA. Your instructor asks you to draw 25 numbers because she has learned that it takes approximately 5 calls to make a completed interview. You draw your 25 numbers from the directory using a systematic sample.

As you call each number, record one of the following codes by the number:

- ***D*** = *Disconnected; message from phone company stating number no longer in service.*
- ***WT*** = *Wrong target (ineligible); i.e., number is a business phone and you are interested only in residences.*
- ***IR*** = *Ineligible respondent; no one in household has purchased an automobile within last year.*
- ***R*** = *Refusal; subject refuses to participate.*
- ***T*** = *Terminate; subject begins survey but stops before completing all questions.*
- ***C*** = *Completed; questionnaire is completed.*

For each of the following codes you will need to make at least two call-back attempts.

- ***BSY*** = *Busy signal; record the time and attempt call-back at later time.*
- ***NA*** = *No answer; record time and attempt call-back at a later time. This includes TADs (telephone answering devices). You may leave a message and state that you will call back later.*

CB *= Subject has instructed you to call back at more convenient time; record call-back time and date and return call.*

When you have reached your quota of completions you are ready to calculate your response rate. Let's assume that your list of numbers and codes looks like the following:

	1st Attempt	2nd Attempt	3rd Attempt
474-2892	NA	NA	C
474-2668	BSY	IR	
488-3211	D		
488-2289	C		
672-8912	WT		
263-6855	BSY	BSY	BSY
265-9799	T		
234-7160	R		
619-6019	CB	BSY	BSY
619-8200	IR		
474-2716	IR		
774-7764	NA	NA	R
474-2654	D		
488-4799	WT		
619-0015	BSY		C
265-4356	NA	NA	C
265-4480	WT		
263-8898	NA	NA	NA
774-2213	C		
474-2651			
474-3351			
488-1322			
474-2323			
234-8347			
234-7125			

Now you should draw a line under the last listing used, 774-2213. You will discard the remaining numbers (6 listings). Look at the ***last*** *code you recorded for each number and count the number of each code. Insert these numbers into the following response rate formula:*

$$\text{Response rate} = \frac{C}{C + \left(\dfrac{C}{C + IR + WT}\right)(BSY + D + T + R + NA)}$$

$$= \frac{C(5)}{C(5) + \left(\dfrac{C(5)}{C(5) + IR(3) + WT(3)}\right)(BSY(2) + D(2) + T(1) + R(2) + NA(1))}$$

$$= \frac{5}{5 + (.455)\ (8)}$$

$$= 57.9\%$$

Note how ineligibles were handled in the formula. Both IR and WT were counted as ineligibles. The logic is that the percentage of eligibles among those who were talked with is the same as among those not talked with (BSY, D, T, R, and NA).

questions. Such secondary questions often include a list of demographic questions. Demographics, because they are more personal in nature, are typically placed at the end of the questionnaire. Because they are not the primary focus of the study, a **completed interview** may be defined as one in which all the primary questions have been answered. In this way, you will have data for your primary questions and most of the data for your secondary questions. Interviewers can then be given a specific statement as to what constitutes a completed survey such as, "If the respondent answers through question 18, you may count it as a completion." (The demographics begin with question 19.) Likewise, the researcher must adopt a decision rule for determining the extent of item omissions necessary to invalidate a survey.

REDUCING NONRESPONSE ERROR

Tactics such as advance notification, monetary incentives, and follow-up mailings are used to increase response rates.

We have now learned the sources of nonresponse error and how to calculate the extent of nonresponse error by calculating the response rate. Now, what can we do to ensure that we minimize nonresponse (maximize the response rate)? Each survey data collection mode represents a unique potential for nonresponse. Mail surveys historically represent the worst case, but even with these, there are many strategies employed by marketing researchers to increase response rates. Such strategies include **advance notification** via postcard or telephone, **monetary incentives,** and **follow-up mailings.** Identification of respondents prior to mailing the survey can increase response rates for a 10-minute survey from 27.5 percent to 33.7 percent. In addition to respondent identification, if respondent cooperation can be secured in advance, the response rate can be improved to 40 percent. Researchers are now experimenting with other data collection methods such as faxes, e-mail, etc., as means of increasing response rates. However, one has to contend with other problems such as a restricted population, loss of anonymity, and inability to have longer questionnaires.[23]

To reduce the not-at-homes, busy signals, and no answers, several **call-back** attempts should be made. Interviewers should be trained to write the time and date when the respondent is not at home, the phone is busy, or there is no answer. Call-back attempts, usually three or four, should be made at a later time and/or date. Marketing research firms have designed special forms that can keep track of the several call-back attempts that may be made to obtain a completed survey from a particular respondent. An example of one such sheet from Survey Sampling, Inc., is shown in Figure 14.2.

Call-back forms are essential tools tracking attempts to reduce nonresponses.

This sheet allows for a total of four call-back attempts. There are provisions to mark the time and date of the call as well as the result. The results are coded so that the data analyst can find out whether the nonresponse was due to a disconnected number, language problems, refusal to answer, and so on.

We discussed using replacement samples during our discussion of calculating response rates and also in chapter 12. There are many methods that may be followed to replace samples. Essentially, they all strive to replace a nonrespondent (noncontact or refusal) with an equivalent respondent during the survey. For instance, if a telephone interviewer is given a telephone book and instructed to interview every 25th name, he or she may find that one of these people refuses to participate in the survey. To replace the nonrespondent, the interviewer can be directed to use the "drop-down" replacement procedure we described in

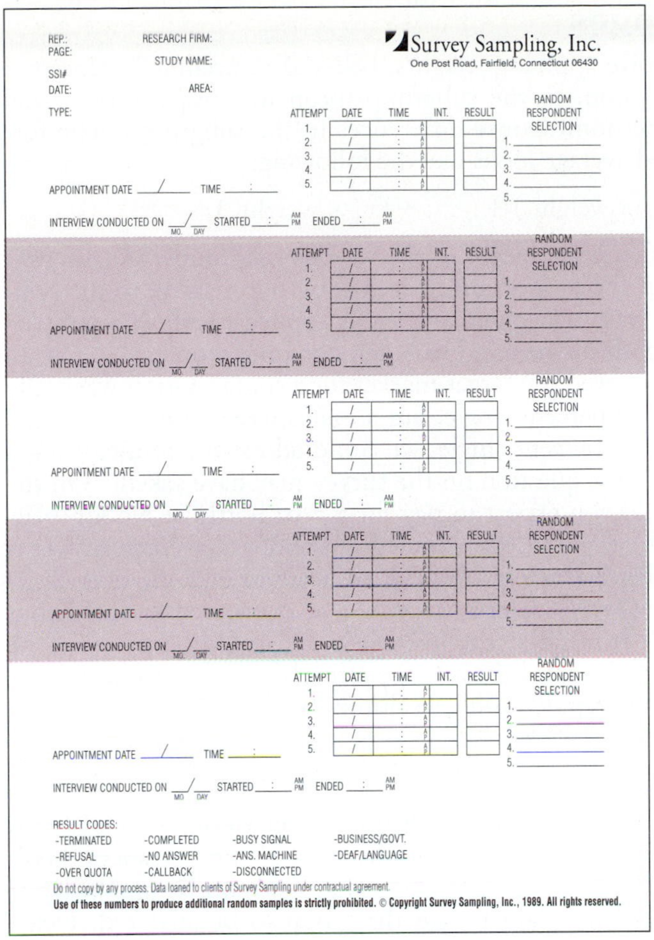

REP.: RESEARCH FIRM: **Survey Sampling, Inc.**
PAGE: STUDY NAME: One Post Road, Fairfield, Connecticut 06430
SSI#
DATE: AREA:
TYPE:

ATTEMPT DATE TIME INT. RESULT — RANDOM RESPONDENT SELECTION
1. 2. 3. 4. 5. — 1. 2. 3. 4. 5.
APPOINTMENT DATE / TIME :
INTERVIEW CONDUCTED ON MO. / DAY STARTED : AM PM ENDED : AM PM

ATTEMPT DATE TIME INT. RESULT — RANDOM RESPONDENT SELECTION
1. 2. 3. 4. 5. — 1. 2. 3. 4. 5.
APPOINTMENT DATE / TIME :
INTERVIEW CONDUCTED ON MO. / DAY STARTED : AM PM ENDED : AM PM

ATTEMPT DATE TIME INT. RESULT — RANDOM RESPONDENT SELECTION
1. 2. 3. 4. 5. — 1. 2. 3. 4. 5.
APPOINTMENT DATE / TIME :
INTERVIEW CONDUCTED ON MO. / DAY STARTED : AM PM ENDED : AM PM

ATTEMPT DATE TIME INT. RESULT — RANDOM RESPONDENT SELECTION
1. 2. 3. 4. 5. — 1. 2. 3. 4. 5.
APPOINTMENT DATE / TIME :
INTERVIEW CONDUCTED ON MO. / DAY STARTED : AM PM ENDED : AM PM

ATTEMPT DATE TIME INT. RESULT — RANDOM RESPONDENT SELECTION
1. 2. 3. 4. 5. — 1. 2. 3. 4. 5.
APPOINTMENT DATE / TIME :
INTERVIEW CONDUCTED ON MO. / DAY STARTED : AM PM ENDED : AM PM

RESULT CODES:
-TERMINATED -COMPLETED -BUSY SIGNAL -BUSINESS/GOVT.
-REFUSAL -NO ANSWER -ANS. MACHINE -DEAF/LANGUAGE
-OVER QUOTA -CALLBACK -DISCONNECTED

Figure 14.2

Forms provided by professional sampling firms make provisions for call-back attempts.

chapter 12. That is, the interviewer will call the next name below that one rather than skipping to the next 25th name. He or she can continue calling names in this manner until a replacement is secured for the refusal. On finding a replacement, the original 25-name skip interval would be resumed. The basic strategy for treating nonresponse error during the conduct of the survey involves a combination of judicious use of incentives and persuasion to cooperate; repeated attempts to reach the original prospective respondent; and systematic replacement of those respondents who, for whatever reason, do not take part in the survey.

ADJUSTING RESULTS TO REDUCE NONRESPONSE ERROR[24]

Nonresponse error should always be measured, and if we assess the degree of nonresponse to be a problem, we are obliged to make adjustments. Of course, if we do not find significant nonresponse error, there is no reason to make adjustments. But, if some exists, there are at least two methods of compensating for its presence: weighted averages and oversampling.

Weighted Averages

Weighting responses by subgroup sizes is a way to compensate for nonresponse error.

Weighted averages involve applying weights, believed to accurately represent subgroups in the population, to the subgroup mean to compute an overall score that adjusts for the nonresponse differences in the subgroups. The formula for such a weighted average looks like the following:

$$x = (x_a \times \text{weight}_a) + (x_b\text{weight}_b) + \ldots + (x_m \times \text{weight}_m)$$

where x_a, x_b, and so forth are the means of the various subgroups, and $weight_a$, $weight_b$, and so on reflect the proportion of each subgroup relative to the population's total size. This way, a weighted average is applied to adjust a sample's results to be consistent with the believed true demographic profile.

For example, if we believed the target market for a suntan lotion was really 50 percent married and 50 percent single, but a mail survey sample contained 25 percent married and 75 percent single, we could adjust the results using a 50:50 weighted average. One question on the survey may have asked, "On the average, how much would you expect to pay for a 5-oz bottle of NoSun Natural Tanning Lotion?" We find that the married respondents' average answer is $2.00, whereas the singles' average is $3.00. If we were to take the overall average of the mail survey (25:75) sample, it would be computed as $2.75, but if we applied the 50:50 true ratio, the average price would turn out to be $2.50. Nonresponse error distorted the average price, but we have adjusted using the believed true demographic profile to eliminate that source of error.

Oversampling

If a researcher believes that nonresponse will be a problem, he or she may opt to oversample in order to compensate.

The second general strategy for dealing with nonresponse error in a survey is typically more expensive, but it is applied under certain circumstances. With the second strategy, the marketing researcher uses **oversampling,** which involves drawing a sample that is larger than the group to be analyzed. Please note that we are referring to an instance in which the final sample will be a good deal larger than the target sample size and not a case of drawing a large number of potential respondents in order to achieve the target sample size. The researcher then draws a *subsample* of respondents to match the believed profile of the target group. Alternatively, with high refusal rates for specific questions, oversampling may generate sufficient numbers of respondents who do answer these questions.

For example, using the suntan lotion example, we might send out 10,000 questionnaires and receive 2,000 back, still with the incorrect 75 percent singles and 25 percent married distribution. Now, we would use our computer capabilities to select a 50:50 sample of marrieds to singles (that is, 500 of each type) out of our respondent group data set. We would not need to perform the weighted averaging because the sample being analyzed is in the proper proportions. In essence, however, we would be throwing away 1,000 questionnaires returned by marrieds to bring our sample into conformity with the married:single population ratio. In fact, if we greatly oversampled, we would have the opportunity to draw a subsample from the respondents that matched our believed population along several demographic factors such as sex, age, education, income, and so forth. But with more factors, the final sample size could decrease, and more returned questionnaires would be left out of our analyses. Obviously, it is the best policy to strive to reduce nonresponse error of all types to as low a level as possible by appropriate survey method choice, use of incentives, and whatever other inducements are available to the researcher so that adjustments are not necessary.

PRELIMINARY QUESTIONNAIRE SCREENING

As we have indicated, nonresponses appear in practically every survey. At the same time, there are respondents whose answers have a suspicious pattern to them. Both of these necessitate a separate phase of the data collection stage in the marketing research process that involves the inspection of questionnaires as they are being prepared for entry into a computer file for tabulation and analysis. Researchers develop a sixth sense about the quality of responses, and they can often spot errors just by inspecting raw questionnaires. Granted, some data collection companies provide for direct entry of responses to a computer file, and this option is becoming commonplace. It is also likely that a stack of completed questionnaires is the result, and this stack is sent to the researcher whose office might be in Omaha, Little Rock, or Boston. In either case, it is good practice to perform a screen step to catch respondent errors before tabulation of the data takes place.

Unsystematic and Systematic Checks of Completed Questionnaires

Completed questionnaires should be screened for errors.

Despite the ongoing checks of questionnaires by supervisors during the data collection phase, it is worthwhile to perform a more complete inspection at this time. There are two options available: unsystematic and systematic checks. With an **unsystematic check,** the researcher flips though the stack in an arbitrary fashion. With a **systematic check,** the researcher selects questionnaires with a random or systematic sampling procedure. Alternatively, he or she may draw a sample for each interviewer or even opt for a full inspection of every completed questionnaire depending on time, resources, and judged necessity.

What to Look for in Questionnaire Inspection

What is the purpose of questionnaire checks? Despite all of the precautions described thus far, the danger still exists that problem questionnaires are included in the completed stack. So the purpose of completed questionnaire inspection is to determine the degree of "bad" questionnaires and, if deemed advisable, to pull the ones with severe problems. Problem questionnaires are ones that fall into the following categories: They have questionable validity; they have unacceptable patterns of incompleteness; they have unacceptable amounts of apparent respondent misunderstanding; or they have other complications such as illegible writing, damage in transit, or some other obvious problem. Five different problems that can be identified with screened completed questionnaires can be described: incomplete questionnaires, nonresponses to specific questions, yea- or nay-saying patterns, middle-of-the-road

TABLE 14.3

Types of Response Problems Found during Questionnaire Inspection

PROBLEM TYPE	DESCRIPTION
Incomplete questionnaire	Questionnaire is incompletely filled out. The respondent apparently stopped answering questions at some point.
Nonresponse to specific questions	The respondent refused to answer particular question(s), but answered others before and after it.
Yea- or nay-saying patterns	Respondent exhibits a persistent tendency to respond favorably or unfavorably, respectively, regardless of the questions.
Middle-of-the-road patterns	Respondent indicates "no opinion" to most questions.
Unreliable responses	Respondent is not consistent on test–retest, equivalent forms, or some other reliability check.

patterns, and unreliable responses. We describe each problem, and Table 14.3 summarizes each one. In industry jargon, these are "exceptions," and they signal possible field data collection errors to a researcher.

Incomplete Questionnaires

Some questionnaires may be only partially completed.

Incomplete questionnaires are those in which the later questions or pages of a questionnaire are left blank. We just described this type of nonresponse error as a "break-off," which is its common label with personal or telephone interviews. That is, the researcher might find that a respondent answered the first three pages of questions, and then, for some reason, the respondent stopped. Perhaps the respondent became bored, or the questions might have been too complicated, or perhaps he or she thought the topic was too personal. The reason that the questionnaire was not completed may never be known.

Nonresponses to Specific Questions—(Item Omissions)

When a respondent does not answer a particular question, it is referred to as an "item omission."

Also, as we just noted in our descriptions of the various types of nonresponse, for whatever reasons, respondents will sometimes leave a question blank. In a telephone interview, they may decline answering a question, and the interviewer might note this occurrence with the designation "ref" or some other code.

Yea- or Nay-Saying Patterns

Yea-saying and nay-saying are seen as persistent tendencies on the parts of some respondents to agree or disagree, respectively, with most of the questions asked.

Even when questions are answered, there can be signs of problems. A **yea-saying** pattern may be evident on one questionnaire in the form of all "yes" or "strongly agree" answers.[25] The yea-sayer has a persistent tendency to respond in the affirmative regardless of the question, and yea-saying implies that the responses are not valid. The negative counterpart to the yea-saying is **nay-saying,** identifiable as persistent responses in the negative.

Middle-of-the-Road Patterns

The **middle-of-the-road** pattern is seen as a preponderance of "no opinion" responses. No opinion is in essence no response, and prevalent no opinions on a questionnaire may signal low interest, lack of attention, or even objections to being involved in the survey. True, a respondent may not have an opinion on a topic, but if one gives a great many no opinion answers, questions arise as to how useful that respondent is to the survey.

Some respondents will hide their opinions by indicating "no opinion" throughout the survey.

Unreliable Responses

We defined reliability in a previous chapter as the consistency in a respondent's answers. Sometimes a researcher will deliberately include an internal consistency check. For instance, if a respondent encountered the question, "Is the amount of electricity used by your kitchen appliances a concern to you?," the person might respond with a "yes." Later in the survey, this question appears: "When you use your electric coffee maker, toaster, or electric can opener, do you think about how much electricity is being used?" Now, suppose that respondent answers with a "no" to this question. This signals an inconsistent or unreliable respondent.

Problems found when screening completed questionnaires include incomplete questionnaires, nonresponses to specific questions, yea- or nay-saying patterns, middle-of-the-road patterns, and unreliable responses.

There are other bothersome problems that can pop up during questionnaire screening. For example, you might find that a respondent has checked more than one response option when only one was supposed to be checked. Another respondent may have failed to look at the back of a questionnaire page and thus missed all of the questions there. A third respondent may have ignored the agree–disagree scale and written in comments about energy conservation. Usually, detecting these errors requires physically examining the questionnaires.

View: "Getting SPSS Help"

SUMMARY

Total error in survey research is a combination of sampling error and nonsampling error. Sampling error may be controlled by the sample plan and the sample size. Researchers must know both the sources of nonsampling error and how to minimize the effect on total errors. The data collection phase of marketing research holds great potential for nonsampling errors. There are intentional as well as unintentional errors on the parts of both interviewers and respondents that must be regulated. Dishonesty, misunderstanding, and fatigue affect fieldworkers; whereas falsehoods, refusals, misunderstanding, and fatigue affect respondents. We described the several controls and procedures used to overcome these sources of error.

At the same time, nonresponse errors of various types are encountered in the data collection phase. Nonresponse error is measured by the calculation of the response rate. There are several methods for improving the response rate and thereby lowering nonresponse error. A weighted average method or oversampling may be applied to bring the sample back into alignment with the population. Once the interviews are completed, the researcher must screen them for errors. Invariably, incomplete questionnaires and refusals are present, and tendencies such as yea-saying may be seen as well.

KEY TERMS

Nonsampling error (p. 422)
Fieldworker error (p. 422)
Respondent error (p. 423)
Intentional errors (p. 423)
Unintentional errors (p. 423)
Intentional fieldworker errors (p. 423)
Interviewer cheating (p. 423)
Leading the respondent (p. 424)
Personal characteristics (p. 424)
Interviewer misunderstanding (p. 424)
Fatigue-related mistakes (p. 426)
Falsehoods (p. 426)
Nonresponse (p. 426)
Respondent misunderstanding (p. 428)
Guessing (p. 428)
Attention loss (p. 429)
Distractions (p. 429)
Respondent fatigue (p. 429)
Supervision (p. 430)
Validation (p. 431)
Orientation sessions (p. 431)
Role-playing sessions (p. 431)
Anonymity (p. 431)
Confidentiality (p. 431)
Incentives (p. 432)
Validation checks (p. 432)
Third-person technique (p. 432)
Reversals of scale endpoints (p. 433)
Prompters (p. 433)
Nonresponse (p. 433)
Refusals (p. 433)
Break-offs (p. 433)
Item omission (p. 433)
Response rate (p. 435)
Completed interview (p. 440)
Advance notification (p. 440)
Monetary incentives (p. 440)
Follow-up mailings (p. 440)
Call-backs (p. 440)
Weighted averages (p. 442)
Oversampling (p. 442)
Unsystematic check (p. 443)
Systematic check (p. 443)
Yea-saying (p. 444)
Nay-saying (p. 444)
Middle-of-the-road (p. 445)

REVIEW QUESTIONS/APPLICATIONS

1. Distinguish sampling error from nonsampling error.
2. Since we cannot easily calculate nonsampling errors, how must the prudent researcher handle nonsampling error?
3. Identify different types of intentional fieldworker error and the controls used to minimize them. Identify different types of unintentional fieldworker error and the controls used to minimize them.
4. Identify different types of intentional respondent error and the controls used to minimize them. Identify different types of unintentional respondent error and the controls used to minimize them.
5. Define "nonresponse." List three types of nonresponse found in surveys.
6. If a survey is found to have resulted in significant nonresponse error, what should the researcher do?
7. Why is it necessary to perform preliminary screening of completed questionnaires?
8. Identify five different problems that a researcher might find while screening completed questionnaires.
9. What is an "exception," and what is typically done with each type of exception encountered?

10. Your church is experiencing low attendance with its Wednesday evening Bible classes. You volunteer to design a telephone questionnaire aimed at finding out why church members are not attending these classes. Because the church has limited funds, members will be used as telephone interviewers. List the steps necessary to ensure good data quality in using this "do-it-yourself" option of field data collection.

11. A new mall-intercept company opens its offices in a nearby discount mall, and its president calls on the insurance company where you work to solicit business. It happens that your company is about to do a study on the market reaction to a new whole life insurance policy it is considering to add to its line. Make an outline of the information you would want from the mall-intercept company president in order to assess the quality of its services.

12. Acme Refrigerant Reclamation Company performs large-scale reclamation of contaminated refrigerants as mandated by the U.S. Environmental Protection Agency. It wishes to determine what types of companies will have use of this service, so the marketing director designs a questionnaire intended for telephone administration. Respondents will be plant engineers, safety engineers, or directors of major companies throughout the United States. Should Acme use a professional field data collection company to gather the data? Why or why not?

13. You work part time in a telemarketing company. Your compensation is based on the number of credit card applicants you sign up with the telemarketing approach. The company owner has noticed that the credit card solicitation business is slowing down, and so she decides to take on some marketing research telephone interview business. When you start work on Monday, she says that you are to do telephone interviews and gives you a large stack of questionnaires to have completed. What intentional fieldworker errors are possible under the circumstances described here?

14. Indicate what specific intentional and unintentional respondent errors are likely with each of the following surveys.

   a. The Centers for Disease Control sends out a mail questionnaire on attitudes and practices concerning prevention of AIDS.

   b. Eyemasters has a mall-intercept survey performed to determine opinions and uses of contact lenses.

   c. Boy Scouts of America sponsors a telephone survey on Americans' views on humanitarian service agencies.

15. How do you define a "completion," and how does this definition help a researcher deal with "incomplete questionnaires?"

16. What is nay-saying and how does it differ from yea-saying? What should a researcher do if he or she suspects a respondent of being a nay-sayer?

17. On your first day as a student marketing intern at the O-Tay Research Company, the supervisor hands you a list of yesterday's telephone interviewer records. She tells you to analyze them and to give her a report by 5 P.M. Well, get to it!

	Ronnie	**Mary**	**Pam**	**Isabelle**
Completed	20	30	15	19
Refused	10	2	8	9
Ineligible	10	3	10	9
Wrong target	5	1	4	6
Busy	20	10	21	23
Disconnected	0	1	3	2
Terminate	5	2	7	9
No answer	3	2	4	3

CASE 14.1

Associated Grocers, Inc.

Associated Grocers, Inc. (AG) is a food store wholesaler cooperative located in Whitewater, Wisconsin. AG operates a large warehouse distribution center and serves approximately 100 independent grocery stores in the state of Wisconsin. Most of these grocery stores are family-owned, medium-sized supermarkets such as Jacob's, Cravitt's, or Wimberly's, but about one-quarter are banned together in local chainlike associations such as Hi Neighbor, Blue Bonnet, or Associated Food Stores. All compete against the national food store chains such as Winn-Dixie, SuperFresh, or Kroger.

A recent statewide survey done by the University of Wisconsin–Madison has revealed that the major chains dominate the market, accounting for over 90 percent of the market. AG stores have very low awareness and represent less than 5 percent of grocery purchases. This finding prompted AG executives to begin a corporate identity program. They talked to a professor of marketing from the University of Wisconsin–Whitewater, who suggested that the first step is to ascertain the positions of the major grocery chains and the desires of grocery shoppers as a way of identifying positioning alternatives for AG. The professor advised AG to do a statewide survey on the grocery market as a first step. He also informed AG that he advises a student marketing group called Pi Sigma Epsilon that does various types of marketing projects. He suggested that AG use the Pi Sigma Epsilon members for data collection in a telephone survey as a means of holding costs down.

AG officials were skeptical of the ability of students to execute this survey, but they had very little money to devote to this project. The professor proposed a meeting with AG officials, the marketing research projects director of Pi Sigma Epsilon, and himself to discuss the matter. When he returned to campus, he informed the Pi Sigma Epsilon president of the opportunity, and told her to have the marketing research projects director draft a list of the quality control safeguards that would be used in a statewide telephone survey in which 20 student interviewers would be calling from their apartments or dorm rooms.

1. Take the role of the marketing research projects director, and draft all of the interviewer controls you believe are necessary to effect data collection comparable in quality to that gathered by a professional telephone interviewing company.
2. The Pi Sigma Epsilon chapter president calls the marketing research projects director, and says, "I'm concerned about the questionnaire's length. It will take over 20 minutes for the typical respondent to complete over the phone. Isn't the length going to cause problems?" Again, take the role of the marketing research projects director. Indicate what nonresponse problems might result from the questionnaire's length, and recommend ways to counter each of these problems.

Case 14.2

Pacific States Research, Inc.

Pacific States Research, Inc. is a full-service interview company located in 10 regional malls throughout the northwest and extending as far south as San Diego. Each location is equipped with a complete focus group facility that accounts for approximately 25 percent of Pacific States' revenues. Another 25 percent is derived from Pacific States' mall-intercept interviewing, and the remaining 50 percent of the business is obtained from centralized telephone interview services. Work has been reasonably steady in all three areas over the past five years. The company has continually wrestled with quality problems in its telephone interview area. The major difficulty is retention of interviewers. An internal study has revealed that the average location needs six telephone interviewers to work full time and another six part timers who are hired as the volume of work requires. When work is slack, the full-time interviewers are laid off, and when the workload increases beyond the ability of the full-time interviewers, the part timers are used for the time when they are needed. The study also found that the average length of time full-time telephone interviewers work for Pacific States is just under six months.

Quality control problems have affected business. One major account recently informed Pacific States that it would no longer use its services when a major error was found in how Pacific States' interviewers administered a critical question on its survey. The account has also threatened not to pay for the work. Other accounts have complained that Pacific States is slow in turning telephone interview work around, and they have also noted errors in the work that has been done.

Ned Allen, the manager responsible for telephone interviewing, has met with various computer services companies about the problem. Ned is thinking of recommending that Pacific move away from centralized telephone interviewing to computer-assisted telephone interviewing (CATI). Ned has done some preliminary analysis, and he figures that CATI would greatly eliminate errors because the interviewer must go through the questionnaire in the proper order and punch in acceptable responses. Otherwise, the program will not allow the interviewer to move to the next question until the error is corrected. He thinks that the ease of a CATI system will probably entice interviewers to stay with Pacific longer. Also, because CATI can be integrated across all 10 locations, it would serve to spread the work evenly across the full-time interviewers. Right now, each location operates like a stand-alone data collection company, but work is allocated to each through Pacific States' main office located in San Francisco.

On the downside, a fully integrated CATI system would require over $200,000 in installation costs. Also Pacific States would need to levy clients a setup charge of $250 per page to convert the questionnaire to a CATI format. Ned hopes to make a preliminary recommendation to the president in 10 days.

1. Using your knowledge of the data collection concepts and issues described in this chapter, make a pro and con list for Ned.
2. What other considerations should Ned bear in mind while mulling over his recommendation?

CHAPTER 15

Basic Data Analysis: Descriptive Statistics

Learning Objectives

- *To learn about the concept of data reduction and the four functions it provides*
- *To appreciate the five basic types of statistical analysis used in marketing research*
- *To use measures of central tendency and dispersion customarily used in describing data*
- *To learn how to obtain descriptive statistics with SPSS for Windows*

PRACTITIONER VIEWPOINT

Most market researchers will tell you that they are always gathering data. But, the successful researcher knows how to use that data to answer difficult marketing questions. Knowing what to analyze, how to analyze, and how to interpret the results are what makes your research worthwhile. Understanding the basics of statistical analysis is a must for a successful career in the marketing research field.

In this chapter, you will learn the basics of statistical data analysis in marketing research. You will learn what data to use, how to prepare that data for analysis, how to determine what type of analysis to perform, and how to conduct descriptive analyses of your data using your statistical analysis package—SPSS® for Windows™.

— Jack Noonan
President, SPSS®, Inc.

Who Reads Newspapers Anymore?

With the onslaught of cable and satellite television channels, inroads by the Internet as a means of learning about the world, and declining literacy rates, are newspapers moving onto the endangered species list? In a survey conducted for *USA Weekend,* the Yankelovich organization found the following:[1]

- ✔ 60 percent of Americans read newspapers "a lot";
- ✔ 72 percent of those reading newspapers the most are college graduates;
- ✔ 40 percent of "Generation Xers" read newspapers, and 69 percent of those aged 50–59 read them;
- ✔ 83 percent find newspaper advertising helpful when deciding what to buy; and
- ✔ 61 percent pay attention to newspaper ads when actively in the market for a purchase.

Analysis determined five subgroups of newspaper reader types. Their descriptions follow.

Networkers	Professional, affluent, well-educated, in control of their lives
Interfacers	Affluent, educated, sophisticated, fun-loving, ethnically diverse
Retroactives	Oldest group, many are retired, least affluent, mostly white females
Neo-bytes	Youngest group, easygoing, creative, impulsive, open to new things
Disconnecteds	Least educated, retired or blue-collar workers, old-fashioned

1. Establish the need for marketing research
2. Define the problem
3. Establish research objectives
4. Determine research design
5. Identify information types and sources
6. Determine methods of accessing data
7. Design data collection forms
8. Determine sample plan and size
9. Collect data
10. Analyze data
11. Prepare and present the final research report

Are people reading newspapers now that we are in the "electronic age"? Research has been applied to this question.

Here are some newspaper usage descriptions for each newspaper reader group.

USAGE ITEM	NET-WORKERS	INTER-FACERS	RETRO-ACTIVES	NEO-BYTES	DIS-CONNECTEDS
Percentage of all newspaper readers	23%	15%	17%	23%	22%
Read the newspaper "a lot"	72%	59%	59%	57%	50%
Read every day or almost every day	68%	50%	56%	56%	48%
Strongly agree advertising is helpful when deciding what to buy	30%	48%	38%	32%	34%
Induced to buy a new product by newspaper advertising	17%	16%	17%	15%	9%
Mailed in a newspaper or magazine coupon in the past year	41%	39%	43%	38%	17%

This chapter begins our discussion of the various statistical techniques available to the marketing researcher. As you will soon learn, these really are devices to convert formless data into meaningful information just as was done for the newspaper industry in the previous example. These techniques summarize and communicate patterns found in the data sets marketing researchers analyze. We begin the chapter by describing data reduction and the four functions it accomplishes. Then, we preview five different types of statistical analyses commonly used by marketing researchers. Next, we define descriptive analysis and discuss measures of central tendency such as the mode, median, and mean. We also discuss measures of variability, including the frequency distribution, range, and standard deviation. It is important to understand when each measure is appropriate, so this topic is addressed. Last, we show you how to obtain the various descriptive statistics available in SPSS for Windows.

CODING DATA AND THE DATA CODE BOOK

After questionnaires are screened and exceptions are dealt with, the researcher moves to data entry stage of the data analysis process. **Data entry** refers to the creation of a computer file that holds the raw data taken from all of the questionnaires deemed suitable for analysis. A number of data entry options exist, ranging from keyboard entry of each and every piece of data to computer scanning systems that scan entire sets of questionnaires and convert them to a data file in a matter of minutes. There are, in fact, integrated questionnaire design and analysis software programs that include computer scanning operations in their systems. For example, Apian Software of Berkeley, California, offers "Survey Pro," which can be used with Principia Products of optimal mark recognition programs. Survey Pro includes tabulation capabilites. The "Snap" program marketed by Mercator Corporation of Newburyport, Massachusetts, is a software program that develops PC-based questionnaires and includes tabulation and graphical capabilities.[2]

Data entry requires an operation called **data coding,** defined as the identification of codes that pertain to the possible responses for each question on the questionnaire. Typically, these codes are numerical because numbers are quick and easy to input, and computers work with numbers more efficiently than they do with alphanumeric codes. Recall that we discussed *precoding* the questionnaire in chapter 11. You have also encountered data codes in your work with SPSS for Windows thus far using your SPSS Student Assistant. In large-scale projects, and especially in cases in which the data entry is performed by a subcontractor, researchers utilize a **data code book,** which identifies all of the variable names and code numbers associated with each possible response to each question that makes up the data set. With a code book that describes the data file, any researcher can work on the data set, regardless of whether or not that researcher was involved in the research project during its earlier stages. The remainder of this chapter will instruct you on how basic data analysis takes place.

Researchers utilize data coding when preparing and working with a computer data file.

DATA REDUCTION

As you have learned through using SPSS, experimenting with the data sets we have provided, and answering the SPSS for Windows tests in previous chapters, marketing researchers work with data matrices. A **data matrix** is the coded raw data from a survey. This data is arranged in columns, representing answers to the various questions on the survey questionnaire, and rows, repre-

Data that exists in huge computer files is simplified through the process of "data reduction."

senting each respondent or case. The problem confronting the marketing researcher when faced with a data matrix is **data reduction,** which is defined as the process of describing a data matrix by computing a small number of measures that characterize the data set. Data reduction condenses the data matrix while retaining enough information so the client can mentally envision its salient characteristics. Descriptive data analysis is a common means of data reduction. Basically, a researcher analyzes a data matrix with the objective of finding patterns and relationships within it and, at the same time, with the goal of summarizing the information in a highly concise manner.

Four Functions of Data Reduction

The four functions of data reduction are summarization, conceptualization, communication, and interpolation.

There are at least four essential functions of data reduction: summarization, conceptualization, communication, and interpolation. A brief description of each follows.

Summarization

Summarizing means condensing raw data into meaningful computations or conclusions.

Because of our inability to cope with large masses of information found within a typical data matrix, it is necessary to somehow summarize the information. **Summarization** is the condensing of raw data into a few meaningful computations. When you are told that the average rating of the Mazda Miata's style was 8.2 on a 10-point scale, you have been provided a summary of these ratings. Similarly, if you are told that Visine was the most popular brand of eyedrops found in a survey of allergy sufferers, the survey's findings have been summarized for you. A number of other descriptive statistics and analytical tools available for summarizing data are discussed in this chapter and subsequent chapters. Each has a unique way of summarizing the data.

Conceptualization

Conceptualization means envisioning what a statistical measure represents.

Most statistical measures are based on certain assumptions. These assumptions, once you learn them, become the foundations of ways to envision the information. **Conceptualization** is the visualization of what these measures represent. When you are told that the range of grades on the last marketing research examination was from a 72 to an 86, you can envision something about your classmates' performances on this exam; and for a range of 25 to 98, you would picture something quite different. Alternatively, a health care company looking for growth opportunities might ask for research on retirement centers, and a researcher might make a scatter diagram comparing the number of people over 60 years of age with the number of retirement centers in the United States. If you looked at this scatter diagram, you might notice that the points lie along what closely resembles a straight line. The use of a simple statistical measure called the correlation coefficient (which we describe in a later chapter) would apply this straight line conceptualization and determine the degree to which the points actually form a straight line. However, it is entirely unnecessary to make a scatter diagram if one understands the basic conceptualization or logic underlying the correlation coefficient.

Most statistical measures have reasonably intuitive conceptualizations underlying them, and it is the intent of this chapter as well as subsequent chapters to help you to understand the conceptual aspects of the various statistical measures used by marketing researchers. Data analysis not only summarizes, but it also gives form to the numbers and indicates relationships among the variables in data matrices.

Communication

Communication means understanding statistical analysis.

The marketing researcher is really a hybrid of sorts. He or she must understand fully the nuances of statistical analysis while being highly sensitive to the level of analytical sophistication of the manager/client. As we discussed in chapter 4, the statistician and the manager do not have much common ground, and it is up to the marketing researcher to serve as an intermediary. **Communication** is the translation of the statistical analysis results into a form that is understandable and, more important, useful to the marketing manager.

Certain types of statistical analysis serve vital communication purposes. There are basic types of analysis that are understandable to most managers and that are beneficial in comprehending the basic patterns and relationships within a data matrix. Take, for instance, our eyedrops survey in which Visine was found to be the most popular brand. In the statistician's jargon, this is the "modal category." If the marketing researcher believes that the marketing manager understands the concept of mode, he or she may use the term "mode" in his or her presentation or description of the data matrix. On the other hand, if the marketing researcher believes that the use of this term would be more confusing than helpful, he or she could rely on simple English and say, "A majority of allergy sufferers in the survey bought Visine." As long as the manager understands the terminology selected by the researcher, communication is effected through the use of statistical analysis measures and concepts.

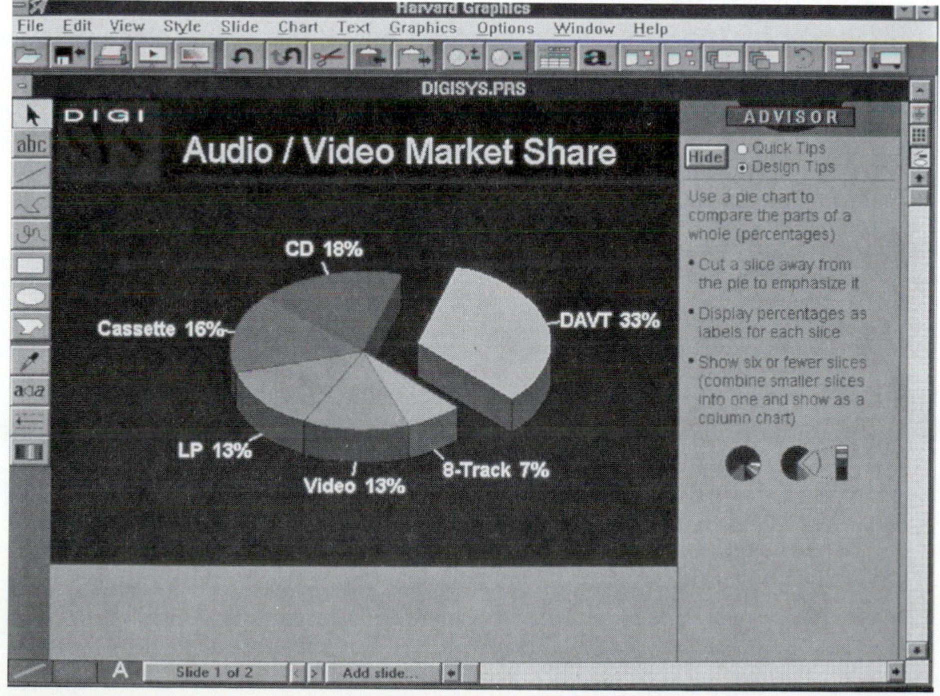

Data reduction transforms raw data into an understandable shape.

Interpolation

Interpolation means applying a sample's statistical analysis to its population.

The information contained in a data matrix is useful in many ways, but one of the most important uses is when it is applied to a target population. The concept is a fairly broad one, but, for our purposes here, **interpolation** pertains to an assessment of the degree to which patterns in, or characteristics of, a sample's data matrix are generalizable to the population. When a researcher discovers that 70 percent of a sample of 1,000 homeowners considers "junk" mail to be a waste of paper, there is evidence that a majority of all homeowners share this opinion. Hence, we interpolate the findings from the sample data to the population. In this way, we "learn" about the characteristics, preferences, and so forth, of the population. Or, to state it differently, the sample's findings can be interpolated, or projected, to make estimates of the population's true values.

Consequently, a number of statistical analysis techniques discussed in the following chapters are ones used to interpolate information from a data matrix and apply it to the parent population from which the sample was drawn. Many statistical techniques pertain to the application of knowledge gained about a sample to other, similar populations or other, similar situations. Interpolation, you will soon find out, is certainly one of the most useful facets of data analysis available to the marketing researcher because the researcher almost always works with samples but must translate the results to pertain to the target population, which is the manager's ultimate concern.

TYPES OF STATISTICAL ANALYSES USED IN MARKETING RESEARCH

There are five basic types of statistical analyses used at one point or another and to some degree or other by marketing researchers: descriptive analysis, inferential analysis, differences analysis, associative analysis, and predictive analysis (Table 15.1). Each one has a unique role in the data analysis process; moreover, they are usually combined into a complete analysis of the information in order to satisfy the research objectives. These introductory comments will provide a preview of the subject matter that will be covered in this and other chapters. Because this is an introduction, we use the names of statistical procedures, but we do not define or describe them here. The specific techniques are all developed later in this textbook. It is important, however, that you understand each of the various categories of analysis available to the marketing researcher and comprehend generally what each is about.

Descriptive Analysis

Descriptive analysis is used to describe the variables (question responses) in a data matrix (all respondents' answers).

Certain measures such as the mean, mode, standard deviation, or range are forms of **descriptive analysis** used by marketing researchers to describe the sample data matrix in such a way as to portray the "typical" respondent and to reveal the general pattern of responses. Descriptive measures are typically used early in the analysis process and become foundations for subsequent analysis.

Inferential Analysis

Inferential analysis is used to generate conclusions about the population's characteristics based on the sample data.

When statistical procedures are used by marketing researchers to generalize the results of the sample to the target population that it represents, the process is referred to as **inferential analysis.** In other words, such statistical procedures

TABLE 15.1

Five Types of Statistical Analysis Used by Marketing Researchers

TYPE	DESCRIPTION	EXAMPLE	STATISTICAL CONCEPTS
Descriptive	Data reduction	Describe the typical respondent, describe how similar respondents are to the typical respondent	Mean, median, mode frequency distribution, range, standard deviation
Inferential	Determine population parameters, test hypotheses	Estimate population values	Standard error Null hypothesis
Differences	Determine if differences exist between groups	Evaluate statistical significance of difference in the means of two groups in a sample	*t* test of differences, analysis of variance
Associative	Determine associations	Determine if two variables are related in a systematic way	Correlation, cross-tabulation
Predictive	Forecast, based on a statistical model	Estimate the level of *Y*, given the amount of *X*	Time series analysis, regression

Statistical analysis is used to find out what people have in common, how they differ, and to predict how they will act in the future.

allow a researcher to draw conclusions about the population based on information contained in the data matrix provided by the sample. Inferential statistics include hypothesis testing and estimating true population values based on sample information. We describe basic statistical inference in chapter 16.

Differences Analysis

Differences analysis is used to compare the mean of the responses of one group to that of another group, such as satisfaction ratings for "heavy" users versus "light" users of a product or service.

Occasionally, a marketing researcher needs to determine whether two groups are different. For example, the researcher may be investigating credit card usage and want to see if high-income earners differ from low-income earners in how often they use American Express. The researcher may statistically compare the average annual dollar expenditures charged on American Express by high- versus low-income buyers. Important market segmentation information may come from this analysis. Or he or she may run an experiment to see which of several alternative advertising themes garners the most favorable impression from a sample of target audience members. The researcher uses **differences analysis** to determine the degree to which real and generalizable differences exist in the population in order to help the manager make an enlightened decision on which advertising theme to use. Statistical differences analyses include the *t* test for significant differences between groups and analysis of variance. We define and describe them in chapter 16.

Associative Analysis

Associative analysis determines the strength and direction of relationships between two or more variables (questions in the survey).

Other statistical techniques are used by researchers to determine systematic relationships among variables. **Associative analysis** investigates if and how two variables are related. For instance, are advertising recall scores positively associated with intentions to buy the advertised brand? Are expenditures on salesforce training positively associated with salesforce performance? Depending on the statistic used, the analysis may indicate the strength of the association and/or the direction of the association between two questions on a questionnaire in a given study. Techniques are also available if the researcher is interested in determining complex patterns of associations; these procedures are beyond the scope of this textbook. We devote chapter 17 to descriptions of cross-tabulations and correlations that are basic associative analysis methods used in marketing research.

Predictive Analysis

Predictive analysis allows one to make forecasts of future events.

Statistical procedures and models are available to the marketing researcher to help him or her make forecasts about future events, and these fall under the category of **predictive analysis.** Regression analysis or time series analysis are commonly used by the marketing researcher to enhance prediction capabilities. Because marketing managers are typically worried about what will happen in the future given certain conditions such as a price increase, prediction is very desirable. Predictive analysis is described in depth in chapter 18.

It is not our intention to make you an expert in statistical analysis. Rather, the primary objective of our chapters on statistical analysis is to acquaint you with the basic concepts involved in each of the selected measures. You will certainly do basic statistical analysis throughout your marketing career, and it is very likely that you will encounter information summarized in statistical terms. So it is important for you to have a conceptual understanding of the commonly used statistical procedures. Our descriptions are intended to show you when and where each measure is appropriately used, and to help you interpret the meaning of the statistical result once it is reported. We also rely heavily on computer statistical program output because you will surely encounter statistical program output in your company's marketing information system and/or summarized in a marketing research study report.

UNDERSTANDING DATA VIA DESCRIPTIVE ANALYSIS

Commonly used descriptive analyses reveal central tendency (typical response) and variability (similarity of responses).

We now turn to the several tools in descriptive analysis available to the researcher to describe the data obtained from a sample of respondents. Suppose that you were the marketing researcher confronted with a data matrix such as the one illustrated in Table 15.2 (page 460). It is from a study on automobile usage and tune-up costs that compares the use of synthetic versus regular oil. Synthetic automobile engine oil does not have the detrimental environmental impacts associated with regular oil. As you know from your work with SPSS for Windows, these numbers could be input via the Data Editor, and assigned variable names such as "user," "gastype," "tuneamt," and so forth. If you performed this operation, you would be creating your own informal data code book. A preliminary step in data reduction is to find measures that capture the general patterns of the numbers under each variable. We need to find some convenient means of summarizing the numbers in each column while communicating as much about the nature of this set of numbers as possible.

Two sets of measures are used extensively to describe the information obtained in a sample. The first set involves measures of "central tendency" or measures that describe the "typical" respondent or response. The second set involves measures of "variability" or measures that describe how similar (dissimilar) respondents or responses are to (from) "typical" respondents or responses. Other types of descriptive measures such as measures of skewness or measures of peakedness are available, but they do not enjoy the popularity of central tendency and variability. In fact, they are rarely reported to clients.

Measures of Central Tendency

Three measures of central tendency are mode, median, and mean.

The basic data reduction goal involved in all **measures of central tendency** is to report a single piece of information that describes the most typical response to a question. The term central tendency applies to any statistical measure used that somehow reflects a typical or frequent response. Three such measures of central tendency are commonly used as data reduction devices. They are the mode, the median, and the mean. We describe each one in turn.

Mode

With a string of numbers, the mode is that number appearing most often.

The **mode** is a descriptive analysis measure defined as that value in a string of numbers that occurs most often. In other words, if you scanned a list of numbers constituting a field in a data matrix, the mode would be that number that appeared more than any other. For example, in Table 15.2 there are seventeen 0s and thirteen 1s under the user versus nonuser column labeled B. This means the mode is a 0, which pertains to "nonuser" of synthetic oil.

TABLE 15.2

The Data Matrix for the Synthetic Oil Use Survey

THE DATA MATRIX

A	B	C	D	E	F	G	H	I	J	K	L
01	0	1	20	1050	5	0	28	89	49	709	2
02	0	0	50	1175	14	0	28	30	62	711	1
03	1	1	105	1230	7	0	39	53	47	724	2
04	1	1	150	1680	9	0	35	48	42	728	2
05	0	1	40	1310	14	1	29	59	66	713	1
06	0	0	125	1500	8	1	32	78	49	723	1
07	0	1	110	1600	12	0	35	87	47	722	2
08	1	1	45	1720	10	0	35	59	76	703	2
09	0	0	250	1750	8	1	32	87	56	714	1
10	0	1	60	1770	11	1	32	41	100	710	1
11	1	1	20	2275	5	1	33	90	63	713	1
12	1	1	120	2500	10	1	38	43	64	705	1
13	0	1	70	1030	3	1	29	100	41	729	1
14	1	0	35	1100	7	0	32	31	26	736	1
15	0	0	70	1185	8	1	30	54	40	715	1
16	1	0	80	1225	12	1	28	41	48	723	2
17	0	0	100	1262	11	1	28	44	73	718	2
18	0	1	85	1295	7	0	32	60	77	724	1
19	1	0	220	1300	4	1	32	100	80	714	1
20	0	0	130	1550	6	1	31	54	54	725	1
21	1	0	155	1820	10	0	32	86	24	734	2
22	0	0	175	1890	8	1	31	51	36	725	1
23	0	1	50	1940	4	0	33	86	39	727	2
24	1	0	100	2200	10	0	36	100	120	734	1
25	0	0	80	2270	8	0	38	98	52	717	2
26	0	1	150	2440	8	1	35	35	44	720	2
27	1	1	20	2560	6	1	36	95	46	716	1
28	0	0	75	2730	7	1	37	46	52	714	1
29	1	1	55	1130	8	1	30	92	46	726	2
30	1	1	90	1575	12	1	31	52	37	731	2

EXPLANATIONS OF VARIABLES

A = Respondent ID number
B = User (=1) vs. nonuser (=0)
C = Premium (=1) vs. regular gasoline (=0)
D = $ paid for last tune-up
E = Miles driven last month
F = Gallons of gas in last fill-up
G = Pays with credit card (=1) or cash (=0)
H = Age of respondent
I = Recreational miles driven last week
J = Work miles driven last week
K = Last three digits of zip code
L = Gender of respondent: male (=1) or female (=2)

Note: It is not necessary to separate the variable columns with blanks. We have done so here simply to make the variables in the matrix easier for you to identify. Also, we are using single letters rather than SPSS variable names such as ID, USER, GAS, etc. to conserve space.

You should note that the mode is a relative measure of central tendency, for it does not require that a majority of responses occurred for this value. Instead, it simply specifies the value that occurs most frequently. For example, in Table 15.2, under column F for the number of gallons last bought, there are seven 8s, which is the largest frequency of any number. So the mode is 8, but

8s are not a majority; there are 30 entries in the column. By the way, if a tie for the mode occurs, the distribution is considered to be "bimodal." Or it might even be "trimodal" if there is a three-way tie. A simple method is available to find the mode. First, the frequency or percentage distribution for each number in the string is tabulated, and then the researcher scans for the largest incidence, or he or she may use a bar chart or histogram as a visual aid.

Median

An alternative measure of central tendency is the **median,** which expresses that value whose occurrence lies in the middle of an ordered set of values. That is, it is the value such that one-half of all of the other values is greater than the median and one-half of the remaining values is less than the median. So, the median tells us the approximate halfway point in a set or string of numbers that are arranged in ascending or descending order while taking into account the frequency of each value. With an odd number of values, the median will always fall on one of the values, but with an even number of values, the median may fall between two adjacent values.

The median expresses the value whose occurrence lies in the middle of a set of ordered values.

To determine the median, the researcher creates a frequency or percentage distribution with the numbers in the string in either ascending or descending order. In addition to the raw percentages, he or she computes cumulative percentages and by inspecting these, finds where the 50–50 break occurs. Let us just take the first five respondents listed in Table 15.2. Arranging column D, the amount each paid for his or her last tune-up, in descending order, the values are $150, $105, $50, $40, and $20. The median is $50 because there are two values above it ($150 and $105) and two values below it ($40 and $20). You should notice that the median supplies more information than does the mode, for a mode may occur anywhere in the string, but the median must be at the halfway point.

Mean

A third measure of central tendency is the mean. The **mean** is the arithmetic average value characterizing a set of numbers. It differs from the mode and the median in that a computation is made to determine the arithmetic average. The mean is computed through the use of the following formula:

The mean is the arithmetic average of a set of numbers.

$$\textit{Arithmetic mean } (\bar{x}) = \frac{\sum_{i-1}^{n} x_i}{n}$$

where

n = is the number of cases

x_i = each individual value, and

Σ signifies that all the x_i values are summed.

As you can see, all of the members in the set of n numbers, each designated by x_i, are summed and that total is divided by the number of members in that set. The resulting number is the mean, a measure that indicates the central tendency of those values. It approximates the typical value in the set. As an illustration, let us compute the mean of miles driven last month in column E of Table 15.2 for all 30 respondents in our synthetic oil data set. The sum of all 30 numbers is 50,062, and when this sum is divided by 30, the mean is found to be 1,668.7 miles. Because the mean is determined by taking every member of the set of numbers into account through this formula, it is more informative than the median.

Measures of Variability

Measures of variability reveal the typical difference between the values in a set of values.

Although they are extremely useful, measures of central tendency are incomplete descriptors of the variety of values in a particular set of numbers. That is, they do not indicate the variability of responses to a particular question or, alternatively, the diversity of respondents on some characteristic measured in our survey. To gain sensitivity for the diversity or variability of values, the marketing researcher must turn to measures of variability. All **measures of variability** are concerned with depicting the "typical" *difference* between the values in a set of values.

Measures of variability include frequency distribution, range, and standard deviation.

It is one matter to know the mean or some other measure of central tendency, but it is quite another matter to be aware of how close to that mean or measure of central tendency the rest of the values fall. For example, in a survey of Internet homepage users, a catalog sales company might find that the average user makes 5 purchases from Internet homepages per year. However, this measure of central tendency paints only part of the picture as some users may make more than 20 purchases yearly, so knowledge of the variety of users can help the company target "heavy users" with its marketing strategies. Thus, knowing the variability of the data could greatly impact a marketing decision based on the data because it expresses how similar the respondents are to one another on the topic under examination. There are three measures of variability: frequency distribution, range, and standard deviation. Each measure provides its own unique version of information that helps to describe the diversity of responses.

Frequency Distribution

A frequency (percentage) distribution reveals the number (percent) of occurrences of each number in a set of numbers.

A **frequency distribution** is a tabulation of the number of times that each different value appears in a particular set of values. Frequencies themselves are raw counts, and normally these frequencies are converted into percentages for ease of comparison. The conversion is arrived at very simply through a quick division of the frequency for each value by the total number of observations for all of the values, resulting in a percent, called a **percentage distribution.** For instance, we stated in the example of a mode that there are 17 respondents who indicated they were not users of synthetic oil, and 13 respondents indicated that they were users. These numbers are the frequency counts for each type of user. By dividing the frequencies by the total number of cases analyzed (30 in our example), the percentages become 56.7 percent and 43.3 percent, respectively.

In sum, a frequency distribution affords an accounting of the responses to values in a set. It quickly communicates all of the different values in the set, and it expresses how similar the values are. The percentage distribution is often used here. Figure 15.1 illustrates how quickly percentage distributions communicate variability when they are converted to bar charts. For instance, if our percentage distribution happened to have only a few, very similar values in it, it would appear as a very steep, spike-shaped histogram to such as the one for our "little variability" bar graph; however, if the set of values happened to be made up of many dissimilar numbers, the histogram would be much

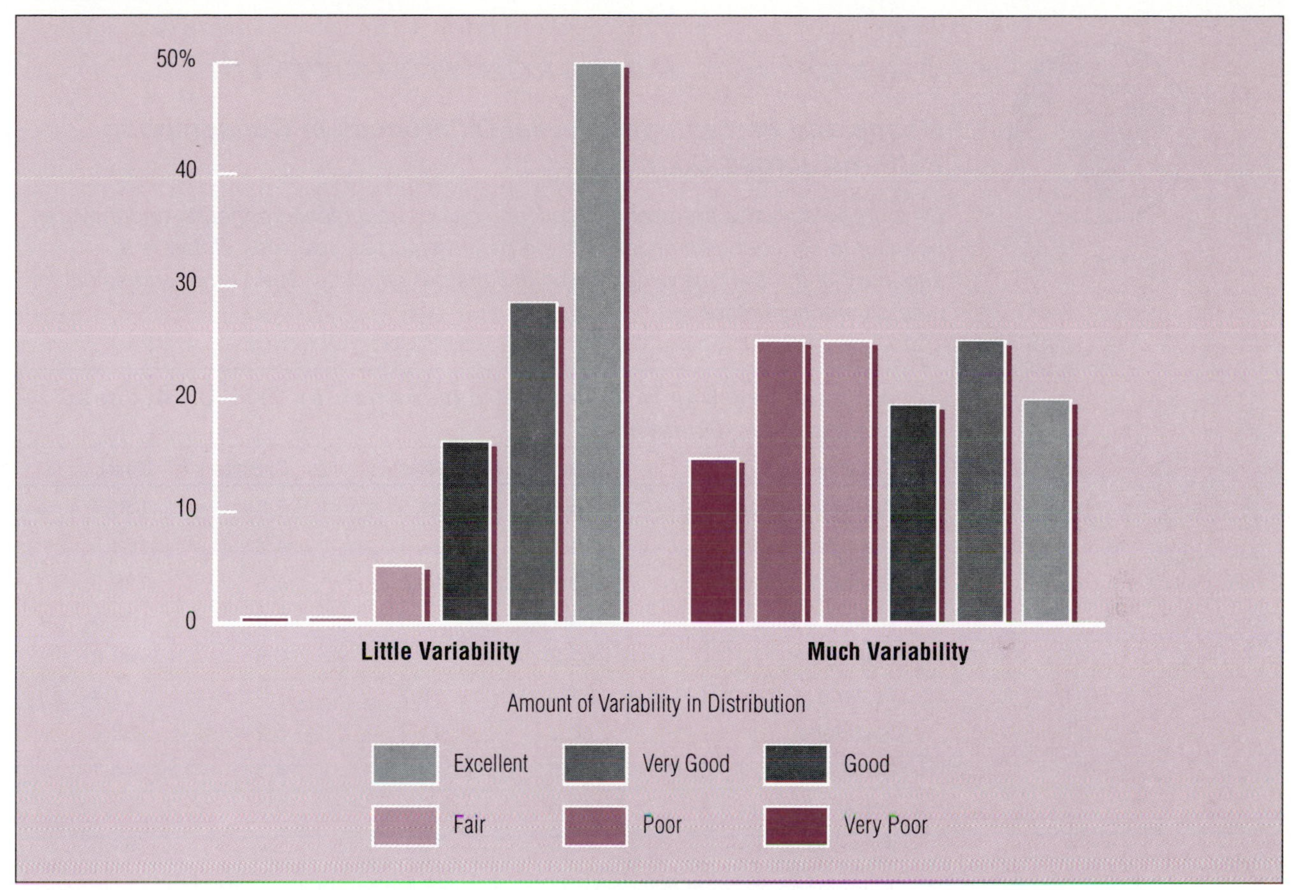

Figure 15.1

Bar charts based on percentage distributions quickly communicate the amount of variability in responses to a question in a survey.

more spread out, with small peaks and valleys. This is the case with the "much variability" bar graph. This pattern indicates a great deal of dispersion in the numbers, whereas the spiked distribution indicates little variability in the set of numbers.

Means and percentage distributions can be used together to communicate consumption patterns that characterize nations. These patterns can be compared for marketing strategy implications. We have included Marketing Research Insight 15.1 (pages 464–465), which deals with comparisons of beer, wine, and spirits consumption in Europe, North America, and Japan.

Range

The range identifies the maximum and minimum values in a set of numbers.

The **range** identifies the distance between lowest value (minimum) and the highest value (maximum) in an ordered set of values. Stated somewhat differently, the range specifies the difference between the endpoints in a distribution of values arranged in order. The range does not provide the same amount of information supplied by a frequency distribution; however, it identifies the in-

MARKETING RESEARCH INSIGHT 15.1

Means and Percentages Reveal Differences in Consumption Patterns across Countries

Descriptive statistics are useful to describe basic consumption patterns, and they can be used to contrast differences in these patterns across countries. Below is a summary of the average consumption in liters per capita for beer, wine, and spirits for nine different countries.

TABLE A

AVERAGE PER CAPITA ALCOHOL CONSUMPTION BY TYPE OF ALCOHOL ACROSS NINE COUNTRIES

COUNTRY	BEER	WINE	SPIRITS	TOTAL
Australia	114.6	21.3	2.8	138.7
New Zealand	114.8	14.4	4.3	133.5
United Kingdom	108.6	16.0	4.3	128.9
United States	89.7	9.0	6.8	105.5
Canada	82.2	10.2	6.6	99.0
Finland	61.7	8.7	7.0	77.4
Sweden	46.8	11.7	5.2	63.7
Norway	47.5	5.1	3.5	56.1
Japan	40.6	0.8	6.0	47.4
Average	78.5	10.8	5.2	94.5

Comparing the total alcohol consumption column for each country to the average of all nine countries reveals the high-consumption countries to be New Zealand, Australia, and the United Kingdom; whereas the low alcohol–consumption countries are Japan, Norway, Sweden, and Finland. The United States falls in the average-to-high range, whereas Canada is close to the average for total alcohol consumption per capita.

These rankings hold true for beer consumption, but interesting differences are apparent when wine or spirits are taken alone. With wine, Americans fall below the average, whereas Swedes fall above it—both reversing their total and beer consumption relative positions. Japanese average consumption of wine per capita is extremely low, but it is above the average for spirits. Australia, the highest average per capita alcohol-consumption country for beer, wine, and total, has the lowest average spirits consumption at about one-half of the nine-country average.

These comparative descriptive statistics have marketing implications for breweries, wine makers, distillers, and alcohol importers and exporters as they reveal

terval in which the distribution occurs. The range also does not tell you how often the maximum and minimum occurred, but it does provide some information on the dispersion by indicating how far apart the extremes are found. For example, if you scan column F in Table 15.2 pertaining to the number of gallons of gas last bought, you will find the lowest number to be 3, whereas the largest is 14. So the range is 3 to 14 gallons, or 11 gallons wide.

relative quantity of alcohol consumption differences. However, another descriptive analysis provides even more interesting information. Percentages can be computed based on the average liters consumed per capita and the average price of each liter of beer, wine, or spirits in each country. Below is a description of expenditures on beer, wine, and spirits in each country as a percentage of average total expenditures on alcohol by that country's citizens.

TABLE B

PERCENT OF ALCOHOL EXPENDITURES BY TYPE OF ALCOHOL ACROSS NINE COUNTRIES

COUNTRY	BEER	WINE	SPIRITS	TOTAL
Australia	62.6	21.7	15.7	100.0
New Zealand	57.2	19.3	23.5	100.0
United Kingdom	53.4	19.2	27.4	100.0
United States	51.5	11.9	36.6	100.0
Canada	39.2	16.2	44.6	100.0
Finland	37.5	13.7	48.8	100.0
Sweden	26.8	18.8	54.4	100.0
Norway	42.8	14.4	42.8	100.0
Japan	38.0	31.2	30.8	100.0
Average	45.4	18.5	36.1	100.0

Now, expenditure differences caused by consumption amounts, inflation, scarcity, or market controls in consumer expenditure patterns can be compared across countries. In the United States, New Zealand, Australia, and the United Kingdom, one-half or more of average expenditures on alcohol products are on beer. However, beer accounts for lower percentages in other countries such as Canada, Finland, Sweden, and Norway where spirits account for close to one-half of average expenditures on alcohol products. Swedes spend proportionately more on spirits and less on beer than do members of any of the other eight countries, and Japanese spend proportionately much more on wine than do consumers in the other eight countries.

These two tables reveal how simple descriptive measures such as averages and percentages can summarize and communicate a picture of the typical consumer—of alcohol in this case—and facilitate cross-national comparisons to help marketers understand the differences across global markets.

Source: *These tables were adapted from data found in E. A. Selvanatha, "Cross-Country Alcohol Consumption Comparison: An Application of the Rotterdam Demand System,"* Applied Economics, *vol. 23, no. 10 (1991), 1613–1622.*

Standard Deviation

A standard deviation indicates the degree of variation in a way that can be translated into a bell-shaped curve distribution.

The **standard deviation** indicates the degree of variation or diversity in the values in such a way as to be translatable into a normal or bell-shaped curve distribution. Although marketing researchers do not always rely on the normal curve interpretation of the standard deviation, they often encounter the standard deviation on computer printouts, and they usually report it in their tables. So it is worthwhile to digress for a moment to discuss this statistical concept.

The standard deviation embodies the properties of a bell-shaped distribution of values.

Table 15.3 shows the properties of a bell-shaped or normal distribution of values. As we have indicated in our chapter on sample size determination, the usefulness of this model is apparent when you realize that it is a symmetric distribution: exactly 50 percent of the distribution lies on either side of the midpoint (the apex of the curve). With a normal curve, the midpoint is also the mean. Standard deviations are standardized units of measurement that are located on the horizontal axis. They relate directly to assumptions about the normal curve. For example, the range of one standard deviation above and one standard deviation below the midpoint includes about 68 percent of the total area underneath that curve. Because the bell-shaped distribution is a theoretical or ideal concept, this property never changes. Moreover, the proportion of area under the curve and within plus or minus any number of standard deviations from the mean is perfectly known. For the purposes of this presentation, normally only two or three of these values are of interest to marketing researchers. Specifically, ±2.58 standard deviations describes the range in which 99 percent of the area underneath the curve is found, ±1.96 standard deviations is associated with 95 percent of the area underneath the curve, and ±1.64 standard deviations corresponds to 90 percent of the bell-shaped curve's area. Remember, we must assume that the shape of the frequency distribution of the numbers approximates a normal curve, so keep this in mind during our following examples.

It is now time to review the calculation of the standard deviation. The equation typically used for the standard deviation is as follows:

$$\textit{Standard deviation } (s) = \sqrt{\frac{\sum_{i-1}^{n}(x_i - \bar{x})^2}{n-1}}$$

In this equation, x_i stands for each individual observation and $\bar{x}$ stands for the mean, as indicated earlier. We use the synthetic oil survey data to illustrate

TABLE 15.3

Normal Curve Interpretation of Standard Deviation

NUMBER OF STANDARD DEVIATIONS FROM THE MEAN	PERCENT OF AREA UNDER CURVE*	PERCENT OF AREA TO RIGHT (OR LEFT)†
±1.00	68	16.0
±1.64	90	5.0
±1.96	95	2.5
±2.58	99	0.5
±3.00	99.7	0.1

*This is the area under the curve with the number of standard deviations as the lower (left-hand) and upper (right-hand) limits and the mean equidistant from the limits.

†This is the area left outside of the limits described by ± the number of standard deviations. Because of the normal curve's symmetric properties, the area remaining below the lower limit (left-hand tail) is exactly equal to the area remaining above the upper limit (right-hand tail).

the calculations for a standard deviation. We already know that the mean number of miles driven last month is 1,668.7. Applying the standard deviation formula, the computations are as follows:

$$s = \sqrt{\frac{\sum_{i-1}^{n} (x_i - \bar{x})^2}{n-1}}$$

$$= \sqrt{\frac{(1050 - 1668.7)^2 + (1175 - 1168.7)^2 + \ldots + (1575 - 1668.7)^2}{30 - 1}}$$

$$= 501.0 \text{ miles}$$

The squaring operation in the standard deviation formula is used to avoid the cancellation effect.

It may seem strange to square differences, add them up, divide them by $n - 1$, and then take the square root. If we did not square the differences, we would have positive and negative values; and if we summed them, there would be a cancellation effect. That is, large negative differences would cancel out large positive differences, and the numerator would end up being close to zero. But this result is contrary to what we know is the case with large differences: There is variation, which is expressed by the standard deviation. The formula remedies this problem by squaring the subtracted differences before they are summed. Squaring converts all negative numbers to positives and, of course, leaves the positives positive. Next, all of the squared differences are summed and divided by 1 less than the number of total observations in the string of values; 1 is subtracted from the number of observations to achieve what is typically called an "unbiased" estimate of the standard deviation. But we now have an inflation factor to worry about because every comparison has been squared. To adjust for this, the equation specifies that the square root be taken after all other operations are performed. This final step adjusts the value back down to the original measure (miles rather than squared miles). By the way, if you did not take the square root at the end, the value would be referred to as the **variance.** In other words, the variance is the standard deviation squared.

Now, whenever a standard deviation is reported along with a mean, a specific picture should appear in your mind. Assuming that the distribution is bell-shaped, the size of the standard deviation number helps you envision how similar or dissimilar the typical responses are to the mean. If the standard deviation is small, the distribution is greatly compressed. On the other hand, with a large standard deviation value, the distribution is consequently stretched out at both ends. With our synthetic oil sample the standard deviation was found to be 501 miles. Assuming that the responses approximate a bell-shaped distribution, the range for 95 percent of the responses would be calculated to be 1668.7 ± (1.96 × 501), which turns out to be 1668.7 ± 982, or 686.7 to 2650.7. Incidentally, there is only one mileage value in Table 15.2 that falls out of this range, and 1 in 30 translates to about 3 percent of the respondents, so our standard deviation interpretation is accurate even though we are working with a fairly small sample. We have prepared Marketing Research Insight 15.2 (see pages 468–470) as a means of helping you remember the various descriptive statistics concepts that are commonly used by marketing researchers.

With a bell-shaped distribution, 95 percent of the values lie within ±1.96 times the standard deviation away from the mean.

MARKETING RESEARCH INSIGHT 15.2

Descriptive Statistics: What They Mean and How to Compute Them

Invariably, a researcher has to make "sense" out of a set of numbers that represents the ways respondents answered the questions in the survey. The answers are normally coded; that is, they are converted to numbers such as 1 for "yes," 2 for "no," and 3 for "maybe." Sometimes the numbers pertain to responses on a scale such as when a respondent indicates that his or her personal computer rates a "4" on a 5-point scale where 1 means "very slow" and a 5 means "very fast," or the number might be the actual number of years he or she has owned that computer.

Descriptive statistics are basic to marketing research and essential to the researcher's understanding of how the respondents answered each question. Here is a data set comprising the answers 10 different respondents gave when asked to rate the speed of their personal computers.

RESPONDENT	RATING
1	4
2	5
3	4
4	2
5	3
6	4
7	3
8	4
9	5
10	4

To illustrate the nine descriptive statistics concepts, the ratings of our 10 respondents are analyzed in the following table.

STATISTICAL CONCEPT	WHAT IS IT?	HOW DO YOU COMPUTE IT?	USING THE RATINGS EXAMPLE
Frequency	The number of times a number appears in the data set	Count the number of times the number appears in the set of numbers	The number 4's frequency is 5
Frequency distribution	The number of times each different number in the set appears	Count the number of times each different number appears in the set, and make a table that shows each number, its count, and the total count (all counts totaled)	Rating / Count 2 1 3 2 4 5 5 2 Total 10

STATISTICAL CONCEPT	WHAT IS IT?	HOW DO YOU COMPUTE IT?	USING THE RATINGS EXAMPLE
Percentage distribution	The presence of each different number expressed as a percent	Divide each frequency count for each rating number by the total count, and report the result as a percent	Rating Percent 2 10% 3 20% 4 50% 5 20% Total 100%
Cumulative distribution (frequency or percentage)	A running total of the counts or percentages	Arrange all the different numbers in descending order and indicate the sum of the counts (percentages) of all preceding numbers plus the present one	Rating Percent Cum. Percent 2 10% 10% 3 20% 30% 4 50% 80% 5 20% 100% Total 100%
Median	The number in the set of numbers such that 50% of the other numbers are larger, and 50% of the other numbers are smaller	Use the cumulative percentage distribution to locate where the cumulative percent equals 50% or where it includes 50%	Rating Cum. Percent 2 10% 3 30% 4 80% ← Median 5 100%
Mode	In a frequency or a percentage distribution, the number that has the largest count or percentage (ties are acceptable)	By inspection, determine which number has the largest frequency or percentage in the distribution	The number 4 accounts for 50%, the largest of any other rating
Mean	The arithmetic average of the set of numbers	Add up all the numbers and divide this sum by the total number of numbers in the set	(4 + 5 + 4 + 2 + 3 + 4 + 3 + 4 + 5 + 4)/10 = 3.8
Range	An indication of the "spread" or span covered by the numbers	Find the lowest and highest numbers in the set and identify them as the minimum and maximum, respectively	The minimum is 2, and the maximum is 5; so the range is 5-2, or 3.

(continued)

MARKETING RESEARCH INSIGHT 15.2 (continued)

Descriptive Statistics: What They Mean and How to Compute Them

STATISTICAL CONCEPT	WHAT IS IT?	HOW DO YOU COMPUTE IT?	USING THE RATINGS EXAMPLE
Standard deviation	An indication of how similar or dissimilar the numbers are in the set, interpretable under the assumptions of a normal curve	Sum the square of each number subtracted from the mean, divide that sum by the total number of numbers less one, and then take the square root of that result	$\{((4-3.8)^2+(5-3.8)^2+\ldots+(4-3.8)^2)/(10-1)\}^{1/2} = .84$

Ethical Issues in Descriptive Data Analysis

It is sometimes said, "Statistics do not lie, but liars can use statistics." This caution is especially pertinent to communication of basic data analysis findings in which the audience is unfamiliar with statistical concepts and misperceptions can distort meanings. Here are some statements that might be made by a researcher, what each statement means in terms of descriptive analysis, and possible misperceptions that might occur in a manager who is not accustomed to working with survey findings.

WHAT IS SAID	WHAT IT MEANS	POSSIBLE MISPERCEPTIONS
"The modal answer was . . ."	The answer given by more respondents than any other answer	Most or all of the respondents gave the answer
"A majority responded . . ."	More than 50% of the respondents answered this way	Most or all of the respondents gave the answer
"A plurality responded . . ."	The answer was given by more respondents than any other answer, but less than 50% gave that answer	A majority of respondents gave the answer
"The median response was . . ."	The answer such that 50% answered above it and 50% answered below it	Most respondents gave this answer
"The mean response was . . ."	The arithmetic average of all respondents' answers	Most respondents gave this answer or responded very close to this answer

WHAT IS SAID	WHAT IT MEANS	POSSIBLE MISPERCEPTIONS
"There was some variability in the responses . . ."	Respondents gave a variety of responses with some agreement	There was no agreement among the respondents
"Missing values were omitted from the analysis."	Respondents who did not answer were not included, and thus the sample size for that question was reduced	An adjustment was made to allow for respondents who did not answer, but the sample size was not affected
"The standard deviation was . . ."	The value was computed by applying the standard deviation formula	No comprehension

Remember, these are very basic statistical concepts, and there are a great many more sophisticated statistics that a researcher may use to completely analyze a data set. Obviously, clients will differ in their familiarity and comprehension of statistical concepts. Here are some approaches that can be used to make certain that the audience will not misunderstand the researcher's words.

1. *Some companies have prepared handbooks or glossaries that define marketing research terms, including statistical concepts. They are given to clients at the onset of work.*
2. *Some researchers include an appendix in the final report that defines and illustrates the statistical concepts mentioned in the report.*
3. *Definitions of statistical concepts are included in the text of the final report where the concept is first mentioned.*
4. *Footnotes and annotations are included in the tables and figures that explain the statistical concepts used.*

No ethical researcher would intentionally mislead a client in reporting findings, and because statistical concepts have high potential for misperceptions such as those illustrated above, ethical researchers go to considerable lengths to prevent misunderstandings.

Other Descriptive Measures

It would be misleading to leave this section without admitting to the existence of other measures of central tendency. The rationale for omitting them is that they are used for special purposes; consequently, marketing researchers use them infrequently. However, there are at least two additional descriptive measures that are sometimes used by marketing researchers: measure of skewness and kurtosis.

Measure of skewness reveals the degree and direction of asymmetry in a distribution.

Measure of skewness reveals the degree and direction of asymmetry in a distribution. Remember, the symmetric bell-shaped distribution assumption underlies the standard deviation, and it is sometimes necessary to assess the degree to which the frequency distribution is really bell-shaped. If it is not, it will be skewed to one side or the other. The measure of skewness appears in the form of a single number. The closer that number is to zero, the closer the distribution is to being symmetric. A positive skewness number means the distribution has a tail to the right, whereas a negative skewness value means that it has a tail to the left.

Kurtosis indicates how pointed or peaked a distribution appears.

Kurtosis indicates how pointed or peaked a distribution appears. A kurtosis value of zero or close to zero signifies that the distribution is bell-shaped, whereas values falling to the negative or positive indicate that the distribution is flatter than or more peaked than a bell-shape, respectively. Both types of measures, along with central tendency and dispersion measures, can communicate a complete portrayal of a distribution to a researcher who knows how to interpret them.

WHEN TO USE A PARTICULAR DESCRIPTIVE MEASURE

The scaling assumptions underlying a question determine which statistic is appropriate.

You should be aware from your current knowledge of scaling assumptions underlying various types of question forms used in marketing research that the amount of information contained within a particular question form is directly related to its scaling assumptions. Remember, for instance, that nominal question forms contain much less information than do those questions with interval scaling assumptions. Similarly, the amount of information provided by each of the various measures of central tendency and dispersion differs. As a general rule, statistical measures that communicate the most amount of information should be used with scales that contain the most amount of information, and measures that communicate the least amount of information should be used with scales that contain the least amount of information. The scaling assumptions determine the appropriate measure; otherwise, the measure will be uninterpretable.

At first reading, this rule may seem confusing, but on reflection it should become clear that the scaling assumptions of each question dictate the measure that should be used. It is precisely at this point that you must remember the arbitrary nature of coding schemes. For instance, if on a demographic question concerning religious preference, "Catholic" is assigned a "1," "Protestant" is assigned a "2," "Jewish" is assigned a "3," and so forth, a mean could be computed. But what would be the interpretation of an average religion of 2.36? It would have no practical interpretation because the mean assumes interval or ratio scaling, whereas the religion categories are nominal. The mode would be the appropriate central tendency measure for these responses.

Table 15.4 indicates the appropriate scaling situations to use with each of the three measures of central tendency and measures of variation. The table

TABLE 15.4

Appropriate Scaling Situations for Various Descriptive Statistics

	TYPE OF SCALE		
TYPE OF MEASUREMENT	NOMINAL	ORDINAL	INTERVAL OR RATIO
Central tendency (Characterizes the most typical response)	Mode	Median	Mean
Dispersion (variability) (Indicates how similar the responses are)	Frequency or percentage distribution	Cumulative percentage distribution	Standard deviation Range

Knowing the scaling assumptions underlying questions clarifies what measures of central tendency and variability are appropriate.

should remind you that a clear understanding of the scaling assumptions for each question on the questionnaire is essential because the researcher must select the statistical procedure and direct the computer to perform the procedure. The computer cannot distinguish scaling assumptions because we typically convert all of our data to numbers for ease of entry.

CELLULAR ONE: OBTAINING DESCRIPTIVE STATISTICS WITH SPSS FOR WINDOWS

Beginning with this chapter and all subsequent chapters dealing with statistical analyses, we provide illustrations with the use of SPSS for Windows in two ways. First, in your textbook descriptions, we indicate step-by-step the procedures used with SPSS for Windows to obtain the statistical analyses being described. Plus, we have included examples of SPSS output in these sections. The second way is with the use of your SPSS Student Assistant. By now, you are well acquainted with the Student Assistant and the movies we prompt you to look at with these statistical analysis sections also illustrate how to operate SPSS for Windows, as well as how to find specific statistical results in SPSS output.

To help you understand these procedures and their output, we are going to use a survey conducted recently for a Cellular One company. Cellular One is a nationwide association of companies that markets cellular telephone equipment. Their primary business concerns the sale of mobile telephone equipment and the cellular telephone network it utilizes. The cellular telephone industry is a successful growth industry, with national sales expanding at a rapid rate over the past five years. Traditionally, cellular telephone sales have relied on salesperson presentations to prospective buyers. However, the Cellular One company involved in this survey was considering an innovation in the marketing mix by opening retail sales centers where customers could browse, ask questions, and inspect Cellular One's line of mobile telephones. The marketing strategy being considered by Cellular One was to operate a specialty store, but there were many unanswered questions in the minds of Cellular One principals. Among them were issues such as: (1) do consumers see a specialty store as having good value, (2) are customers likely to buy from a specialty store, (3) do customers know how much a car phone costs on a monthly use basis, or (4) what types of features do consumers expect to find at this retail center?

Cellular One commissioned a custom research study. The research company concluded that Cellular One's market potential area was approximately the same size as the metropolitan telephone directory, and it used the directory as the sample frame for a telephone survey. A systematic sample of 500 households was drawn and potential respondents were qualified as to (1) those not owing a car telephone, (2) total household income of at least $25,000, and (3) one adult member working full time. A total of 503 usable questionnaires were available for analysis.

Descriptive statistics are needed to see the Cellular One study's basic findings.

In the following sections we describe how to generate descriptive statistics with SPSS for Windows. Specifically, we show you how to obtain a frequency distribution, mode, median, mean, range, and standard deviation using data from the Cellular One survey.

Obtaining a Frequency Distribution and the Mode with SPSS for Windows

There were many questions on the Cellular One survey that had categorical response options, and thus embodied nominal scaling assumptions. With a nominal scale, the mode is the appropriate measure of central tendency, and dispersion must be assessed by looking at the distribution of responses across the various response categories.

A frequency distribution and mode are appropriate for nominal scales.

In the survey, respondents were informed of three options available for retail cellular telephone purchase: (1) a specialty store selling only car phones, (2) an electronics store, and (3) an electronics department in a large store. They were asked, "Of these three types, which store would you expect to find the best value for the price of a car phone?" They were also asked, "If each type of store had the same car phone prices, at which type of store would you most likely purchase your car phone?" For each question, respondents were allowed to select only one alternative. In the SPSS for Windows Data Editor, these questions were assigned the variable names bestvalu and mlpurch, respectively.

To obtain either one or both, first select STATISTICS on the SPSS Main Menu, then click on SUMMARIZE, and select FREQUENCIES. Once you have selected this option, you must then select the two variables bestvalu and mlpurch. Then, from the selection options, click on "Statistics," and a panel will appear with all of the central tendency, dispersion, and distribution options. Click the box beside "Mode" and continue. Then click OK to instruct SPSS to compute the frequency distributions and to find the mode.

Use the STATISTICS-SUMMARIZE-FREQUENCIES procedure to produce descriptive statistics for variables with nominal or ordinal scaling.

View: "Cellular One: Obtaining Descriptive Statistics"

Table 15.5 on page 476 presents the output created in response to this command. As you look at the output, you should notice that the variable labels and value labels were defined, and they appear on the output. The SUMMARIZE-FREQUENCIES procedure creates a frequency distribution and associated percentage distribution of the responses for each question. Its output includes a statistics table and a table for each variable that includes the variable label, value labels, frequencies, percent, valid percent, and cumulative percent. The valid percentages are determined after any missing values are removed. Note in Table 15.5 that there were five respondents who failed to answer the first question, and they are noted in the statistics table as well as the frequency table for "Best Value for the Price of a Phone" table. With the second question, 15 respondents failed to answer, so there were 488 valid cases. "Missing cases" are those instances in which a respondent did not answer a particular question because: (1) the question did not apply, (2) it was overlooked, or (3) the respondent refused to answer that question. Normally, missing cases are input as blanks or special codes in the data set that the statistical analysis software is programmed to identify as missing data and to exclude in any analysis. With SPSS frequency distributions, this exclusion is noted under the column called "Valid Percent."

"Valid cases" pertain to those who answered the question, whereas "missing cases" are those who did not.

Inspection of the valid percentages reveals the central tendency for each question. About 50 percent and 67 percent, respectively, selected the specialty store in both cases. Thus, the store selling only car phones was the modal response. Actually, you do not need to look at the percentages, because we specified that the mode be identified, and the code value for the mode is identified as "1" in the statistics table.

Finding the Median with SPSS

It is also a simple matter to determine the median using the SUMMARIZE-FREQUENCIES procedure. As we indicated, in order for the median to be a sensible measure of central tendency, the values must have some logical order to them. One of the demographic questions at the end of the Cellular One survey asked for the respondent's age; however, instead of indicating his or her exact age, age ranges were used. These were coded from 1 for "under 20 years old" to a 6 for "over 60 years old." To determine the median, all you need to do is to select the "Median" option from the FREQUENCIES-STATISTICS panel with age chosen as the variable to be analyzed.

The output generated by SPSS in response to this option is provided for you in Table 15.6 (page 477). As you can see in the statistics table, the median is indicated as the value code of 3.00, which corresponds to the 31-to-40-year-old category. You can confirm the median by looking at the Cumulative Percent

TABLE 15.5

Frequency Distribution and Mode Printout for SPSS

STATISTICS

	N		Mode
	Valid	Missing	
BEST VALUE FOR THE PRICE OF A PHONE	498	5	1
MOST LIKELY PURCHASE WITH SAME PRICES	488	15	1

BEST VALUE FOR THE PRICE OF A PHONE

		Frequency	Percent	Valid Percent	Cumulative Percent
Valid	STORE SELLING ONLY CAR PHONES	251	49.9	50.4	50.4
	ELECTRONICS STORE	148	29.4	29.7	80.1
	ELECTRONICS DEPARTMENT	99	19.7	19.9	100.0
	Total	498	99.0	100.0	
Missing	System Missing	5	1.0		
	Total	5	1.0		
Total		503	100.0		

MOST LIKELY PURCHASE WITH SAME PRICES

		Frequency	Percent	Valid Percent	Cumulative Percent
Valid	STORE SELLING ONLY CAR PHONES	327	65.0	67.0	67.0
	ELECTRONICS STORE	87	17.3	17.8	84.8
	ELECTRONICS DEPARTMENT	74	14.7	15.2	100.0
	Total	488	97.0	100.0	
Missing	System Missing	15	3.0		
	Total	15	3.0		
Total		503	100.0		

TABLE 15.6

Using SPSS to Find the Median of a Frequency Distribution

STATISTICS

	N		
	Valid	Missing	Median
AGE OF RESPONDENT	502	1	3.00

AGE OF RESPONDENT

		Frequency	Percent	Valid Percent	Cumulative Percent
Valid	UNDER 20	5	1.0	1.0	1.0
	21-30	93	18.5	18.5	19.5
	31-40	177	35.2	35.3	54.8
	41-50	126	25.0	25.1	79.9
	51-60	65	12.9	12.9	92.8
	OVER 60	36	7.2	7.2	100.0
	Total	502	99.8	100.0	
Missing	System Missing	1	.2		
	Total	1	.2		
Total		503	100.0		

column and determining where 50 percent is approximated. You will see that 54.8 cumulative percent is associated with the third age category, or 31 to 40 years old.

Finding the Mean, Range, and Standard Deviation with SPSS for Windows

When using SPSS DESCRIPTIVES, always bear in mind the variables being analyzed should be interval or ratio scaled.

As we have mentioned, computer statistical programs cannot distinguish the scaling assumptions of various questions. Consequently, it is incumbent on the analyst to discern the scaling assumptions and to select the correct procedure(s). One question in the survey asked, "What would you expect the base monthly charge including the access fee and airtime to be?" Respondents answered with a specific dollar amount, so we have a ratio scale. Let us assume that the SPSS variable designation for this question is "month," which stands for "monthly base price." Here, we do not want a frequency table for two reasons. First, month is ratio scaled, and second, a frequency table will have to be quite large to accommodate all of the different monthly fees. So we will use the STATISTICS-SUMMARIZE-DESCRIPTIVES commands, and click on the Options button after we have selected month as the variable for analysis. In the Options panel, you can select the mean, standard deviation, range, and so forth.

TABLE 15.7

The DESCRIPTIVES Command of SPSS for Windows Allows You to Select the Descriptive Statistics You Desire Except for a Frequency or Percentage Distribution

Descriptive Statistics

	N	Range	Minimum	Maximum	Mean	Std. Deviation
BASE MONTHLY CHARGE	290	95	5	100	48.63	23.52
Valid N (listwise)	290					

Table 15.7 presents the output generated from this option. In our Cellular One survey, the output reveals that the average base price estimate was \$48.63, and the standard deviation was \$23.52. You can also see that the lowest estimate (minimum) was \$5, and the highest (maximum) was \$100, making the range equal to 95. A total of 290 respondents provided an estimate. The remaining respondents either were not asked the question because they had indicated earlier that they had little interest in owning a cellular telephone, or they were uncertain and failed to indicate a dollar amount in response to the question. If we multiply the standard deviation by 1.96($1.96 \times 23.52 = 46.10$) and use this value to estimate the 95 percent endpoints, we find them to be \$2.52 and \$94.72, which are quite consistent with our range information. Actually, the standard deviation is fairly large, and it signifies that there was much variability among the respondents. Or to say this differently, there was not much agreement on what the respondents expected the base monthly cost to be.

SUMMARY

This chapter introduced you to the descriptive statistics researchers use to inspect basic patterns in data sets. These measures help researchers summarize, conceptualize, interpolate, and communicate their findings. We also previewed the five types of statistical analysis: descriptive, inferential, differences, associative, and predictive. Descriptive analysis is performed with measures of central tendency such as the mean, mode, or median, each of which portrays the typical respondent or the typical answer to the question being analyzed. Measures of variability, including the frequency distribution, range, and standard deviation, provide bases for envisioning the degree of similarity of all respondents to the typical respondent. Basically, descriptive analysis yields a profile of how respondents in the sample answered the various questions in the survey. The chapter also provides instruction on how to access descriptive statistics with SPSS for Windows under the STATISTICS-SUMMARIZE Main Menu option.

KEY TERMS

Data entry (p. 452)
Data coding (p. 453)
Data code book (p. 453)
Data matrix (p. 453)
Data reduction (p. 454)
Summarization (p. 454)
Conceptualization (p. 454)
Communication (p. 455)
Interpolation (p. 456)
Descriptive analysis (p. 456)
Inferential analysis (p. 456)
Differences analysis (p. 458)
Associative analysis (p. 458)
Predictive analysis (p. 458)
Measures of central tendency (p. 459)
Mode (p. 459)
Median (p. 461)
Mean (p. 461)
Measures of variability (p. 462)
Frequency distribution (p. 462)
Percentage distribution (p. 462)
Range (p. 463)
Standard deviation (p. 465)
Variance (p. 467)
Measure of skewness (p. 471)
Kurtosis (p. 472)

REVIEW QUESTIONS/APPLICATIONS

1. Indicate what data reduction is and why it is useful.
2. Define and differentiate each of the following: (a) descriptive analysis, (b) inferential analysis, (c) associative analysis, (d) predictive analysis, and (e) differences analysis.
3. Indicate why a researcher might refrain from reporting the use of highly sophisticated statistical analyses and opt for simpler forms of analysis.
4. What is a data matrix and how does it appear?
5. What is a measure of central tendency and what does it describe?
6. Indicate the concept of variability and relate how it helps in the description of responses to a particular question on a questionnaire.
7. Using examples, illustrate how a frequency distribution (or a percentage distribution) reveals the variability in responses to a Likert-type question in a lifestyle study. Use two extreme examples of much variability and little variability.
8. Indicate what a range is and where it should be used as an indicator of the amount of dispersion in a sample.
9. With explicit reference to the formula for a standard deviation, show how it measures how different respondents are from one another.
10. Why is the mean an inappropriate measure of central tendency in each of the following cases: (a) gender of respondent (male or female); (b) marital status (single, married, divorced, separated, widowed, other); (c) a taste test in which subjects indicate their first, second, and third choices of Miller Lite, Bud Light, and Coors Silver Bullet.
11. For each of the cases in question 10, what is the appropriate central tendency measure?
12. In a survey on magazine subscriptions, respondents write in the number of magazines they subscribe to regularly. What measures of central tendency can be used? Which is the most appropriate and why?

13. If you use the standard deviation as a measure of the variability in a sample, what statistical assumptions have you implicitly adopted?

14. A manager has commissioned research on a special marketing problem. He is scheduled to brief the board of directors on the problem's resolution in a meeting in New York tomorrow morning. Unfortunately, the research has fallen behind schedule, but the research director works late that night in the downtown San Francisco headquarters and completes the basic data analysis, which will be sufficient for the presentation. However, he now has stacks of computer output and less than an hour before the manager calls him for an early-morning briefing on the survey's basic findings. The researcher looks around at the equipment in his office and an idea flashes in his head. He immediately grabs a blank questionnaire. What is he about to do to facilitate the quick communication of the study's basic findings to the manager?

CASE 15.1

American National Bank

Mary Smith graduated from college in December 1994. On graduation, she took a job as a marketing research assistant with American National Bank. It was not the position she wanted, but she did want to work in a large bank, and she figured she would be promoted into a marketing management position in a year or two if she did well.

When Mary began working, the Marketing Research Department was in the middle of a huge telephone survey of all bank customers across the state. The objectives of the survey included: (1) to determine why people select a particular bank, (2) to identify how many and why people use more than one bank, (3) to investigate satisfaction or dissatisfaction with their present bank's services, (4) to generate suggestions for improved bank services, and (5) to compare profiles of various banks' customers' bases.

Mary was assigned the responsibility of data analysis because she was fresh out of college. She was informed that American National Bank uses a statistical analysis program called WINCOMP for its data analysis. All of the 5,000 respondents' answers have been put on the computer, and all that is left is for someone to instruct WINCOMP as to what analyses to perform. Of course, someone has to interpret the results, too. It is Mary's responsibility to do the analysis and to interpret it.

The questionnaire designers created a master sheet of the scales used in the survey. This code list is duplicated in the following table:

VARIABLE	RESPONSE SCALE USED
Age	Actual age in years
Income	Ranges in $10,000 increments
Sex	Male, female
Marital status	Single, married, other

VARIABLE	RESPONSE SCALE USED
Satisfaction with service	10-point scale from "poor" to "excellent"
10 Possible improvements in service	A 5-point, disagree–agree scale for each improvement
Current bank used	Name of bank written in by interviewer
Usage of various services	Yes or no for each of 15 different services
Bank loyalty	Total number of different services used at that bank (0 to 15)
Exposure to mail advertising	Yes or no to recall receiving it last month from American National Bank

1. What type of descriptive data analysis should Mary instruct WINCOMP to perform to determine basic patterns in the factors listed on the master sheet? For each variable, identify the type of descriptive analysis, describe its aspects, and indicate why it is appropriate.
2. Give an example of what each result might "look like" and how it should be interpreted.

CASE 15.2
Interstate Fair Survey

The following case requires the use of SPSS for Windows, and it is intended to help you learn how to generate the various descriptive statistics available in SPSS. We have conducted the survey, and created an SPSS for Windows data file. It is called "FAIR.SAV." This file contains the variable names, variable labels, and some value labels.

Inspect the questionnaire provided here to understand the issues and types of questions involved in this survey. There are specific questions following the questionnaire that you should answer by using SPSS for Windows to perform descriptive analysis on the data matrix.

INTERSTATE FAIR SURVEY

IID#____

QID#____

Note: Information in bold print is for interviewer only. This is not to be read to respondents.

Hello, my name is___________. I'm a student at the university. My class is conducting a research project for the fair. May I ask you a few questions? It'll only take about three minutes. **(If *YES*, then continue; If *NO*, then terminate and record on a separate sheet of paper.)**

Qualifying question: Ask only if respondent appears to be young.

Are you 16 years old or older? **(If *YES,* then continue; If *NO,* then terminate and record on a separate sheet of paper.)**

1. Not counting yourself, how many people came to the fair with you?
____

2. Counting today, how many days have you been, or will you be coming, to the fair this year? _________ DK _________ (99)

3. Counting this year, how many years out of the past five have you been to this fair? **Circle One:** 1 year 2 years 3 years 4 years 5 years
If only *1 year,* skip to Question 5.

4. In a typical year, how many days do you come to the fair when it is in town?
______ DK ______
(1–11) (99)

5. Do you plan on coming back to the fair next year?
Yes ______ No ______ DK ______
(1) (2) (99)

6. I'm interested in knowing where you got any information about the fair such as the dates and times the fair would be open or the types of entertainment. Can you tell me if you heard or saw any information? **(*Read each* and circle *all* that apply.)**

On Television	***On Radio***	***In the Newspaper***	***On Billboards***	***On a Flyer***	***By Word of Mouth***

Any Other Place? __________________ DK ______
(99)

7. Which radio station do you listen to the most? **Check *One* below:**

WBLX ___ (1)	WMEZ ___ (2)	WKSJ ___ (3)	"Rocket" ___ (4)	WABB ___ (5)
WWSF ___ (6)	WMXC ___ (7)	WXRG ___ (8)	"Arrow" ___ (9)	WTKX ___ (10)
WXBM ___ (11)	WDWG ___ (12)	WAVH ___ (13)	WOWW ___ (14)	CNN ___ (15)
WCOA ___ (16)	WGCX ___ (17)	WJKY ___ (18)	OTHER ___ (20)	

Don't listen to Radio _________ DK ______
(19) (99)

8. Which television station do you watch the most? **Check *One* below:**

WEAR 3 ___ (1)	WKRG ___ (2)	FOXTV ___ (3)	WALA ___ (4)
BLAB ___ (5)	WJTC ___ (6)	OTHER: _______ (8–20)	

Don't watch television _______
(7)

9. How many days (or weeks) ago did you decide to attend the fair this year?______ ________________ DK
(99)

10. a. What *main* attraction drew you to the fair this year? **Read each, then assign a *1*.**
b. What would you say is second? **Read remaining, assign a *2*.**

Livestock ______	Exhibits ______	Music ______	Rides ______
(1)	(2)	(3)	(4)
Games ______	Food ______	Other ______	
(5)	(6)	(7)	
DK ______			
(99)			

11. Approximately how much money, including admission, did you or will you spend on yourself at the fair this year? $______

12. Do you live in Escambia or Santa Rosa County? Yes ______ (1) No _____ (2)

If *YES,* then skip to question 16; If *NO,* then continue.

13. Will you spend the night at a hotel/motel in this city?
Yes ______ (1) No ______ (2) DK ______ (99)

14. Which of the following businesses will you shop at while you are visiting this area? ***Read* and Circle *all* that apply:**

Gas station ______	Convenience store ______
Restaurant ______	Supermarket ______
Any Others? _________	DK ______

15. How much *total* money will you spend on your trip, *not* including money spent at the fair? $_____

Now, I have just a few more questions. . . .

16. How many miles did you travel, *one way,* to get to the fair? _________

17. On a scale from 1 to 10, with 1 being POOR and 10 being EXCELLENT, how would you rate:
EMPLOYEES that operate the RIDES & GAMES. . . .
1.......2......3.......4.......5.......6.......7.......8.......9.......10
POOR EXCELLENT

18. On a scale from 1 to 10, with 1 being POOR and 10 being EXCELLENT, how would you rate:
OTHER FAIR EMPLOYEES. . . .
1.......2......3.......4.......5.......6.......7.......8.......9.......10
POOR EXCELLENT

19. On the same scale from 1 to 10, how would you rate:
THE SECURITY AT THE FAIR. . . .
1.......2......3.......4.......5.......6.......7.......8.......9.......10
POOR EXCELLENT

20. On the same scale from 1 to 10, how would you rate:
THE FAIR OVERALL. . . .
1.......2......3.......4.......5.......6.......7.......8.......9.......10
POOR EXCELLENT

21. What do you think could be done to improve the Interstate Fair?
____
____
____
____

22. What is the zip code where you live?__________

23. Which of the following categories best describes your age?
16–17 __________ (1)
18–24 __________ (2)
25–34 __________ (3)
35–49 __________ (4)
50+ __________ (5)
Refused to Answer __________ (6)

Thank you for your time. Please enjoy the rest of your day/night at the fair!

Note the following:

24. Gender: Male ______ Female ______
(1) (2)

25. Time Completed _________ (To nearest hour)

26. Date Completed _________ (Date)

Thanks for your help in the survey.

Here are some questions you can answer by using SPSS for Windows.

1. What is the attendance profile of the typical fair attendee? By this, we mean how long has he/she been coming to the fair; how many days has or will he/she be attending; what is the group size; and does he/she plan to come next year?
2. How did respondents gain information about the fair, and what are their radio station listening and television station viewing habits?
3. What attracts people to the fair, and how much money do they anticipate spending while at it? Also, how far in advance do people plan on coming to the fair?

4. How much and what kinds of benefits do businesses located in the fair's city location gain from the fair?
5. How do fairgoers rate the quality of the fair's various aspects addressed in the survey?
6. What is the demographic profile of fair attendees who participated in the survey?

CHAPTER 16

Inferring Sample Findings to the Population and Testing for Differences

LEARNING OBJECTIVES

- To understand the concept of statistical inference
- To learn how to estimate a population mean or percentage
- To test a hypothesis about a population mean or percentage
- To compare two samples to see if their means or percentage findings are significantly different
- To comprehend the basics of analysis of variance

PRACTITIONER VIEWPOINT

The marketer has to base decisions on what you tell him or her. Those decisions will translate into actions, the consequences of which may be very far reaching. Take, for example, the results for a blind taste test of a number of different ketchups. If you know that, as a consequence of this test, one factory may close and another may prosper, you and your client will want to be as confident as possible that the differences you show are significant and that they would be replicable in another, identical test. The questions the marketer will be asking you are, "How can I be sure of your conclusion?," "How confident are you?," "Are the differences you show significant?"

This chapter lays out the methods you can use to give an informed and professional answer to these questions. It explains the concepts of statistical inference, parameter estimation, hypothesis testing, and significance testing; shows how to carry out such tests; and takes you through the most popular software program that you can use to help you in doing so.

— Simon Chadwick
Chairman & CEO, Research International

PAMPO'S SWIMWEAR

1. Establish the need for marketing research
2. Define the problem
3. Establish research objectives
4. Determine research design
5. Identify information types and sources
6. Determine methods of accessing data
7. Design data collection forms
8. Determine sample plan and size
9. Collect data
10. **Analyze data**
11. Prepare and present the final research report

Pampo's is a specialty retail store with two distinct product lines: swimwear and dancewear. The store is located in a large regional mall in the Southeast, and its owner, Mary Saver, was disappointed with sales growth in the swimwear line. Discussion with a marketing researcher revealed that much of Pampo's swimwear clientele might be what is called "walk-in" trade. That is, the mall attracts large numbers of shoppers, especially on the weekends, and Pampo's central location in the mall facilitates browsers' dropping in the store. Mary estimated that about one-half of the walk-ins made a swimwear purchase.

To stimulate more business, Pampo's invested in a $50,000 radio advertising campaign at the beginning of the swimwear buying season. The ads were placed during the morning and evening commute times and at noontime to reach the working lunchtime crowd. The ads emphasized Pampo's wide line, its convenient location, its competitive prices, and a layaway plan. A questionnaire was designed for self-administration, and every fifth visitor to Pampo's was asked to fill it out. At the end of a month, over 500 questionnaires had been completed and tabulation begun.

Early in the tabulations, it was discovered that two types of customers visited Pampo's: (1) those who had dropped in without originally intending to (walk-ins), and (2) those who came to the mall to visit Pampo's explicitly (loyal customers). The sample was divided into these two groups, and a comparison was made in the following fashion.

Questionnaire Questions	Walk-Ins (n = 357)	Loyal Customers (n = 158)
a. I heard a Pampo's ad on the radio in the past week.	30%	67%*
b. Pampo's has the best prices in town.	27%	49%*
c. Pampo's has a wide line of swimwear.	54%	92%*
d. Pampo's layaway is a good idea.	15%	17%
e. Pampo's is conveniently located.	67%	46%*
f. I made a special trip to visit Pampo's today.	5%	68%*
g. I would definitely come back to Pampo's.	33%	82%*

*Statistically significant difference.

These findings revealed that the advertising campaign was not attracting large amounts of new business. The loyal customers were hearing the ad more than were the walk-ins, because they had a favorable impression of Pampo's in the first place. The walk-ins appeared to be classic "browser" shoppers who had visited the mall without specifically intending to visit Pampo's. The implications of the findings were that Pampo's should invest more on in-store promotions and sales personnel tactics to convert more walk-ins to loyal customers.

As you learned in chapter 15, descriptive measures of central tendency and measures of dispersion adequately summarize the findings of a survey. However, whenever a probability sample is drawn from a population such as is the case with Pampo's, it is not enough to simply report the sample's descriptive statistics, for these measures contain a certain degree of error due to the sampling process. Every sample provides some information about its population, but there is always some sample error that must be taken into account. We begin the chapter by noting that the term "statistic" applies to a sample, whereas the term "parameter" pertains to the related population value. Next, we describe the concept of logical inference and show how it relates to statistical inference. There are three basic types of statistical inference, and we discuss all three. First, there is parameter estimation in which a value, such as the population mean, is estimated based on a sample's mean and its size. Second, there is hypothesis testing where an assessment is made as to how much of a sample's finding supports a manager's or researcher's *a priori* belief regarding the size of a population value. Finally, there are tests of significant differences between groups in which, for instance, the means of two groups in a sample are compared. We provide formulas and numerical examples, and also show you examples of SPSS for Windows procedures and output.

STATISTICS VERSUS PARAMETERS

Statistics are sample values, whereas parameters are corresponding population values.

We begin the chapter by defining the concepts of statistics and parameters. There is a fundamental distinction you should keep in mind. Values that are computed from information provided by a sample are referred to as the sample's **statistics,** whereas values that are computed from a complete census, which are considered to be precise and valid measures of the population, are referred to as **parameters.** Statisticians use Greek letters when referring to population parameters and Roman letters when referring to statistics. As you can see in Table 16.1, the notation used for a percentage is p for the statistic and π for the parameter, the notations for standard deviation are s (statistic) and σ (parameter), and the notations for the mean are $\bar{x}$ (statistic) and μ (parameter). Because a census is impractical, the sample statistic is used to estimate the population parameter. This chapter describes the procedures used when estimating various population parameters.

TABLE 16.1

Population Parameters and Their Companion Sample Statistics

STATISTICAL CONCEPT	POPULATION PARAMETER (GREEK LETTERS)	SAMPLE STATISTIC (ROMAN LETTERS)
Average	μ (mu)	$\bar{x}$
Standard deviation	σ (sigma)	s
Percentage	π (pi)	p
Slope	β (beta)	b

THE CONCEPTS OF INFERENCE AND STATISTICAL INFERENCE

We begin by defining inference because an understanding of this concept will help you understand what statistical inference is all about. **Inference** is a form of logic in which you make a generalization about an entire class based on what you have observed about a small set of members of that class. When you infer, you draw a conclusion from a small amount of evidence. For example, if two of your friends each bought a new Chevrolet and they both complained about their cars' performances, you might infer that all Chevrolets perform poorly. On the other hand, if one of your friends complained about his Chevy, whereas the other one did not, you might infer that your friend with the problem Chevy happened to buy a lemon.

Inference is drawing a conclusion based on some evidence.

Inferences are greatly influenced by the amount of evidence in support of the generalization. So, if 20 of your friends bought new Chevrolets, and they all complained about poor performance, your inference would naturally be stronger or more certain than it would be in the case of only two friends' complaining.

Statistical inference is based on sample size and variability, which then determines the amount of sampling error.

Statistical inference is a set of procedures in which the sample size and sample statistics are used to make estimates of population parameters. For now, let us concentrate on the percentage, p, as the sample statistic we are using to estimate the population percentage, π, and see how sample size enters into statistical inference. Suppose that Chevrolet suspected that there were some dissatisfied customers, and it commissioned two independent marketing research surveys to determine the amount of dissatisfaction that existed in its customer group. (Of course, our Chevrolet example is entirely fictitious. We don't mean to imply that Chevrolets perform in an unsatisfactory way.) In the first survey, 100 customers who had purchased a Chevy in the last six months were called on the telephone and asked, "In general, would you say that you are 'satisfied' or 'dissatisfied' with the performance of your Chevrolet since you bought it?" The survey found that 30 respondents (30%) are dissatisfied. This finding could be inferred to be the total population of Chevy owners who had bought one in the last six months, and we would say that there is 30 percent dissatisfaction. However, we know that our sample, which, by the way, was a probability sample, must contain some sample error, and in order to reflect this you would have to say that there was *about* 30 percent dissatisfaction in the population. In other words, it might actually be more or less than 30 percent if we did a census because the sample only provided us with an estimate.

Statistical inference takes into account that large random samples are more accurate than are small ones.

In the second survey, 1,000 respondents were called on the telephone and asked the same question. This survey found that 35 percent of the respondents are "dissatisfied." Again, we know that the 35 percent is an estimate containing sampling error, so now we would also say that the population dissatisfaction percentage was *about* 35 percent. This means that we have two estimates of the degree of dissatisfaction with Chevrolets. One is about 30 percent, whereas the other is about 35 percent.

How do we translate our answers (remember they include the word "about") into more accurate numerical representations? Let us say you could translate them into ballpark ranges. That is, you could translate them so we could say "30 percent plus or minus x percent" for the sample of 100 and "35 percent plus or minus y percent" for the sample of 1,000. How would x and y

compare? To answer this question, think back on how your logical inference was stronger with 20 friends than it was with 2 friends with Chevrolets. To state this in a different way, with a larger sample (or more evidence), we have agreed that you would be more certain that the sample statistic was accurate with respect to estimating the true population value. In other words, with a larger sample size you should expect the range used to estimate the true population value to be smaller. The range for *y* would be smaller than the range for *x* because you have a large sample and less sampling error.

As these examples reveal, when the statistician makes estimates of population parameters such as the percentage or mean, the sample statistic is used as the beginning point, and then a range is computed in which the population parameter is estimated to fall. The size of the sample, or *n*, plays a crucial role in this computation, as you will see in all of the statistical inference formulas we present in this chapter.

The three types of statistical inference are parameter estimation, hypothesis tests, and tests of significant differences.

Three types of statistical inferences are often used by marketing researchers: parameter estimation, hypothesis testing, and tests of significant differences. **Parameter estimation** is used to estimate the population value (parameter) through the use of confidence intervals. **Hypothesis testing** is used to compare the sample statistic with what is believed (hypothesized) to be the population value prior to undertaking the study. **Tests of significant differences** are used to compare the sample statistics of two (or more) subgroups in the sample to see whether or not there are statistically significant differences between their corresponding population values. (Although we distinguished between differences analysis and inference analysis in the previous chapter, strictly speaking, differences tests are a form of statistical inference.) We describe each of these types of statistical inference in order.

PARAMETER ESTIMATION

To estimate a population parameter you need a sample statistic (mean or percentage), the standard error of the statistic, and the desired level of confidence (95% or 99%).

Estimating population parameters is a common type of statistical inference used in marketing research survey analysis. As was indicated earlier, inference is largely a reflection of the amount of sampling error believed to exist in the sample statistic. When the *New York Times* conducts a survey and finds that readers spend an average of 45 minutes daily reading the *Times,* or when McDonald's determines through a nationwide sample that 78 percent of all Egg McMuffin Breakfast buyers buy a cup of coffee, both companies may want to determine more accurately how close these estimates are to what the actual population parameter is.

Parameter estimation is the process of using sample information to compute an interval that describes the range of a parameter such as the population mean (μ) or the population percentage (π). It involves the use of three values: the sample statistic (such as the mean or the percentage), the standard error of the statistic, and the desired level of confidence (usually 95% or 99%). A discussion of how each value is determined follows.

Sample Statistic

In parameter estimation, the sample statistic is usually a mean or a percentage.

The mean, you should recall from the formula provided in chapter 15, is the average of a set of interval- or ratio-scaled numbers. For example, you might be working with a sample of golfers and researching the average number of golf balls they buy per month. Or you might be investigating how much high school students spend, on average, on fast foods between meals. For a percentage, you could be examining what percentage of golfers buy only Maxfli golf balls, or you might be looking at what percentage of high school students buy from Taco Bell between meals. In either case, the mean or percentage is derived from a sample, so it is the sample statistic.

Standard Error

The standard error is a measure of the variability in a sampling distribution.

There usually is some degree of variability in the sample. That is, our golfers do not all buy the same number of golf balls per month and they do not all buy Maxfli. Not all of our high school students eat fast food between meals and not all of the ones who do go to Taco Bell. In chapter 15, we introduced you to variability with a mean by describing the standard deviation, and we used the percentage distribution as a way of describing variability when percentages are being used. Also, in chapter 13, we described how, if you theoretically took many, many samples and plotted the mean or percentage as a frequency distribution, it would approximate a bell-shaped curve called the sampling distribution. The **standard error** is a measure of the variability in the sampling distribution based on what is theoretically believed to occur were we to take a multitude of independent samples from the same population. We described the standard error formulas in chapter 13, but we repeat them here because they are vital to statistical inference, as they tie together the sample size and its variability.

The equation for the standard error of the mean is as follows:

$$s_{\bar{x}} = \frac{s}{\sqrt{n}}$$

where

$s_{\bar{x}}$ = standard error of the mean

s = standard deviation

n = sample size

The formula for mean standard error differs from a percentage standard error.

The equation for the standard error of the percentage is as follows:

$$s_p = \sqrt{\frac{p \times q}{n}}$$

where

s_p = standard error of the percentage

p = the sample percentage

$q = (100 - p)$

n = sample size

The standard error takes into account sample size and the variability in the sample.

In both equations, the sample size n is found in the denominator. This means that the standard error will be smaller with larger sample sizes and larger with smaller sample sizes. At the same time, both of these formulas for the standard error reveal the impact of the variation found in the sample. Variation is represented by the standard deviation s for a mean and by ($p \times$

q) for a percentage. In either equation, the variation is in the numerator, so the greater the variability, the greater the standard error. Thus, the standard error simultaneously takes into account both the sample size and the amount of variation found in the sample. The following examples illustrate this fact.

Suppose that the *New York Times* survey on the amount of daily time spent reading the *Times* had determined a standard deviation of 20 minutes and had used a sample of size 100. The resulting standard error of the mean would be as follows:

$$s_{\bar{x}} = \frac{s}{\sqrt{n}}$$

$$s_{\bar{x}} = \frac{20}{\sqrt{100}}$$

$$= \frac{20}{10}$$

$$= 2 \text{ minutes}$$

On the other hand, if the survey had determined a standard deviation of 40 minutes, the standard error would be as follows:

Notice how sample variability affects the standard error in these two examples.

$$s_{\bar{x}} = \frac{s}{\sqrt{n}}$$

$$s_{\bar{x}} = \frac{40}{\sqrt{100}}$$

$$= \frac{40}{10}$$

$$= 4 \text{ minutes}$$

As you can see, the standard error of the mean from a sample with little variability (20 minutes) is smaller than the standard error of the mean from a sample with much variability (40 minutes), as long as both samples have the same size. In fact, you should have noticed that when the variability was doubled from 20 to 40 minutes, the standard error also doubled, given identical sample sizes.

With a 50–50 percent split there is great variability.

The standard error of a percentage mirrors this logic, although the formula looks a bit different. In this case, as we indicated earlier, the degree of variability is inherent in the ($p \times q$) aspect of the equation. Very little variability is indicated if p and q are very different in size. For example, if a survey of 100 McDonald's breakfast buyers determined that 90 percent of the respondents ordered coffee with their Egg McMuffin and 10 percent did not, there would be very little variability because almost everybody orders coffee with breakfast. On the other hand, if the sample determined that there was a 50–50 split between those who had and those who had not ordered coffee, there would be a great deal more variability because any two customers would probably differ in their drink orders.

We can apply these two results to the standard error of percentage for a comparison. Using a 90–10 percent split, the standard error of percentage is as follows:

$$s_p = \sqrt{\frac{p \times q}{n}}$$

$$= \sqrt{\frac{(90)(10)}{100}}$$

$$= \sqrt{\frac{900}{100}}$$

$$= \sqrt{9}$$

$$= 3\%$$

Using 50–50 percent split, the standard error of the percentage is as follows:

$$s_p = \sqrt{\frac{p \times q}{n}}$$

$$= \frac{\sqrt{(50)(50)}}{100}$$

$$= \sqrt{\frac{2500}{100}}$$

$$= \sqrt{25}$$

$$= 5\%$$

A 50–50 percent split has a larger standard error than a 90–10 one when sample size is the same.

Again, these examples show that greater variability in responses results in a larger standard error of the percentage at a given sample size.

Confidence Intervals

Population parameters are estimated with the use of confidence intervals.

Confidence intervals are the degree of accuracy desired by the researcher and stipulated as a level of confidence in the form of a percentage. We also introduced confidence intervals in chapter 13, and we briefly review them here. Because there is always some sampling error when a sample is taken, it is necessary to estimate the population parameter with a range. We did this in the Chevrolet owners example earlier. One factor affecting the size of the range is how confident the researcher wants to be that the range includes the true population percentage. Normally, the researcher first decides on how confident he or she wants to be. The sample statistic is the beginning of the estimate, but because there is sample error present, a "plus" amount and an identical "minus" amount is added and subtracted from the sample statistic to determine the maximum and minimum, respectively, of the range.

The range of your estimate of the population mean or percentage depends largely on the sample size and the variability found in the sample.

Typically, marketing researchers rely only on the 90 percent, 95 percent, or 99 percent levels of confidence which correspond to ±1.64, ±1.96, and ±2.58 standard errors, respectively. They are designated z_α, so $z_{0.99}$ is ±2.58 standard errors. Now that the relationship between the standard error and the measure of sample variability—be it the standard deviation or the percentage—is apparent, it is a simple matter to determine the range in which the population parameter will be estimated. We use the sample statistic, $\bar{x}$ or p, compute the standard error, and then apply our desired level of confidence. In notation form these are as follows:

Confidence intervals are estimated using these formulas.

To estimate the population mean: $\bar{x} \pm z_{\alpha} s_{\bar{x}}$

To estimate the population percentage: $p \pm z_{\alpha} s_p$

If you wanted to be 99 percent confident that your range included the true population percentage, for instance, you would multiply the standard error of the percentage s_p by 2.58 and add that value to the percentage p to obtain the upper limit, and you would subtract it from the percentage to find the lower limit. Notice that you have now taken into consideration the sample statistic p, the variability which is in the formula for s_p, the sample size n which is also in the formula for s_p, and the degree of confidence in your estimate.

How do these formulas relate to inference? Recall that we are estimating a population parameter. That is, we are indicating a range into which it is believed that the true population parameter falls. The size of the range is determined by those three bits of information we have about the population on hand as a result of our sample. First, we have the sample statistic measure of central tendency. Second, we have an indication of the amount of variation in the sample. Third, we know the size of the sample. The final ingredient is our level of confidence or the degree to which we want to be correct in our estimate of the population parameter. If we are conservative and wish to assume the 99 percent level of confidence, then the range would be more encompassing than if we are less conservative and assume only the 95 percent level of confidence because 99 percent is associated with ±2.58 standard errors and 95 percent is associated with ±1.96 standard errors.

Marketing researchers typically use only 95 or 99 percent confidence intervals.

Using these formulas for the sample of 100 *New York Times* readers with a mean reading time of 45 minutes and a standard deviation of 20 minutes, the 95 percent and the 99 percent confidence interval estimates would be calculated as follows.

Here are two examples of confidence interval computations with a mean.

1. For a 95 percent confidence interval:

$$\bar{x} \pm 1.96 \times s_{\bar{x}}$$

$$45 \pm 1.96 \times \frac{20}{\sqrt{100}}$$

$$45 \pm 1.96 \times 2$$

$$45 \pm 3.9$$

41.1 – 48.9 minutes

2. For a 99 percent confidence interval:

$$\bar{x} \pm 2.58 \times s_{\bar{x}}$$

$$45 \pm 2.58 \times \frac{20}{\sqrt{100}}$$

$$45 \pm 2.58 \times 2$$

$$45 \pm 5.2$$

39.8 – 50.2 minutes

If 50 percent of the 100 Egg McMuffin eaters orders coffee, the 95 percent and 99 percent confidence intervals would be computed using the percentage formula.

1. For a 95 percent confidence interval:

$$p \pm 1.96 \times s_p$$

$$p \pm 1.96 \times \sqrt{\frac{p \times q}{n}}$$

$$50 \pm 1.96 \times \sqrt{\frac{50 \times 50}{100}}$$

$$50 \pm 1.96 \times 5$$

$$50 \pm 9.8$$

41.2% – 59.8%

2. For a 99 percent confidence interval:

$$p \pm 2.58 \times s_p$$

$$p \pm 2.58 \times \sqrt{\frac{p \times q}{n}}$$

$$50 \pm 2.58 \times \sqrt{\frac{50 \times 50}{100}}$$

$$50 \pm 2.58 \times 5$$

$$50 \pm 12.9$$

37.1% – 62.9%

Here are two examples of confidence interval computations with a percentage.

Notice that the only thing that differs when you compare the 95 percent confidence interval computations to the 99 percent confidence interval computations in each case is z_α. It is 1.96 for 95 percent and 2.58 for 99 percent of confidence. The confidence interval is always wider for 99 percent than it is for 95 percent when the sample size is the same and variability is equal.

A 99 percent confidence interval is always wider than a 95 percent confidence interval if all other factors are equal.

How to Interpret an Estimated Population Mean or Percentage Range

How are these ranges interpreted? The interpretation is quite simple when you remember that the sampling distribution notion is the underlying concept. If we were using a 99 percent level of confidence, and if we repeated the sampling process and computed the sample statistic many times, 99 percent of these repeated samples results would produce a range that includes the population parameter. The bell-shaped distribution assumption assures us that the sampling distribution is symmetric.

Obviously, a marketing researcher would take only one sample for a particular marketing research project, and this restriction explains why estimates must be used. Furthermore, it is the conscientious application of probability sampling techniques that allows us to make use of the sampling distribution

TABLE 16.2

How to Compute Confidence Intervals for a Mean or a Percentage

1. Find the sample statistic, either the mean, $\bar{x}$, or the percentage, p.
2. Determine the amount of variability found in the sample in the form of standard error of the mean, $s_{\bar{x}}$ or standard error of the percentage, s_p.
3. Identify the sample size, n.
4. Decide on the desired level of confidence, $z_{0.95}(1.96)$ or $z_{0.99}(2.58)$.
5. Compute your (95%) confidence interval as:
   $\bar{x} \pm 1.96s_{\bar{x}}$ or $p \pm 1.96s_p$

concept. So, statistical inference procedures are the direct linkages between probability sample design and data analysis. Do you remember that you had to grapple with confidence levels when we determined sample size? Now we are on the other side of the table, so to speak, and we must use the sample size for our inference procedures. Confidence intervals must be used when estimating population parameters, and the size of the random sample used is always reflected in these confidence intervals.

There are five steps to computing a confidence interval.

There are five steps involved in computing confidence intervals for a mean or a percentage (Table 16.2): (1) determine the sample statistic; (2) determine the variability in the sample for that statistic; (3) identify the sample size; (4) decide on the level of confidence; (5) perform the computations to determine the upper and lower boundary of the confidence interval range.

As a final note, we want to remind you that the logic of statistical inference is identical to the reasoning process you go through when you weigh evidence to make a generalization or conclusion of some sort. The more evidence you have, the more precise you will be in your generalization. The only difference is that with statistical inference we must follow certain rules that require the application of formulas so our inferences will be consistent with the assumptions of statistical theory. When you make a nonstatistical inference, your judgment can be swayed by subjective factors, so you may not be consistent with others who are making an inference with the same evidence. But in statistical inference, the formulas are completely objective and perfectly consistent. Plus, they are based on accepted statistical concepts.

PAMPO'S SWIMWEAR: HOW TO OBTAIN A CONFIDENCE INTERVAL FOR A MEAN WITH SPSS FOR WINDOWS

Your SPSS program will calculate the confidence interval for a mean. To illustrate this feature, we use part of the data from the Pampo's example described at the beginning of the chapter. As you will recall, the survey identified loyal customers and walk-ins. The data set has been input with the SPSS for Windows data editor, and closer inspection has found a group of about 90 walk-ins whose demographic profile is similar to the profile for loyal customers. Another question on the survey asked them to indicate how many stores they typically visit before they find the swimsuit they ultimately buy. To calculate the mean and to generate a confidence interval estimate of the population mean, the sequence of menu commands is: STATISTICS-COMPARE MEANS-ONE SAMPLE *t* TEST. From the dialog box, select numstore, the variable name provided for the number of stores they typically visit before finding their swimsuit for the season. Clicking on OK will generate a 95 percent confidence interval estimate, and the result is found in Table 16.3. You will see that the output provides the sample size (87), mean (4.89), standard deviation (3.62), and standard error of the mean (0.39). So everything is in place for estimating the parameter except the level of confidence. By default, SPSS will use the 95 percent level, which you see in the second table of the output. The lower value is 4.11, whereas the upper value is 5.66.

View: "Pampo's Swimwear: Testing Means"

In other words, assuming our sample is random and representative, the typical walk-in Pampo's shopper, whose demographic profile is similar to Pampo's loyal customer, is estimated to shop at between 4.1 and 5.7 different swimsuit stores, at the 95 percent level of confidence before she finds the swimsuit she wants. (For now, ignore other information in the table. We describe it in the next section.) If you want to use a different confidence level

TABLE 16.3

Output for an SPSS for Windows Mean Estimation

One-Sample Statistics

	N	Mean	Std. Deviation	Std. Error Mean
How many stores visit before actually purchase?	87	4.89	3.62	.39

One-Sample Test

	Test Value = 0					
					95% Confidence Interval of the Difference	
	t	df	Sig. (2-tailed)	Mean Difference	Lower	Upper
How many stores visit before actually purchase?	12.577	86	.000	4.89	4.11	5.66

such as 99 percent, you can specify it by selecting the Options button in the One-Sample *t* Test dialog box.

What about using SPSS for Windows to do percent estimation? Sorry, SPSS like most other statistical programs, does not include percentage estimation. You can use the STATISTICS-SUMMARIZE-FREQUENCIES command sequence to obtain the sample percentage and the sample size, but you will need to use the formulas in this chapter to perform the computations by hand.

HYPOTHESIS TESTING

A hypothesis is what the manager or researcher expects the population mean (or percentage) to be.

Sometimes, someone, such as the marketing researcher or marketing manager, makes a statement about the population parameter based on prior knowledge, assumptions, or intuition. This statement, called a **hypothesis,** most commonly takes the form of an exact specification as to what the population parameter value is.

Hypothesis testing is a statistical procedure used to "accept" or "reject" the hypothesis based on sample information. With all hypothesis tests, you should keep in mind that the sample is the only source of current information about the population. Because our sample is random and representative of the population, the sample results are used to determine whether or not the hypothesis about the population parameter has been supported.

People test and revise intuitive hypotheses often without thinking about it.

All of this might sound frightfully technical, but it is a form of inference that you do every day. You just do not use the words "hypothesis" or "parameter" when you do it. Here is an example to show how hypothesis testing occurs naturally. Your friend, Bill, does not wear his seat belt because he thinks only a few drivers actually wear them. But Bill's car breaks down, and he has to ride with his coworkers to and from work while it is being repaired. Over the course of a week, Bill rides with five different coworkers, and he notices that four out of the five buckle up. When Bill begins driving his car the next week, he begins fastening his seat belt.

This is intuitive hypothesis testing in action. Bill's initial belief that few people wear seat belts was his hypothesis. Obviously, if you had asked Bill before his car went into the repair shop, he might have said that only a small percentage, perhaps as low as 10 percent, of drivers wear seat belts. His week of car rides is analogous to a sample of five observations, and he observes that 80 percent of his coworkers buckle up. Now his initial hypothesis is not supported by the evidence. So Bill realizes that his hypothesis is in error, and it must be revised. If you asked Bill what percentage of drivers wear seat belts after his week of observations, he undoubtedly would have a much higher percentage in mind than his original estimate. The fact that Bill began to fasten his seat belt suggests he perceives his behavior to be out of the norm, so he has adjusted his belief and his behavior as well. In other words, his hypothesis was not supported, so Bill revised it to be consistent with what is actually the case.

The logic of hypothesis testing is very similar to this process Bill has just undergone. There are five basic steps involved in hypothesis testing:

Here are five steps in hypothesis testing.

1. Begin with a statement about what you believe exists in the population; that is, the population mean or percentage. (In our example, Bill believed only 10 percent of drivers buckle their seat belts.)
2. Draw a random sample and determine the sample statistic. (Bill found that 80 percent of his friends buckled up.)

3. Compare the statistic to the hypothesized parameter. (Bill noticed that 80 percent is different from 10 percent.)
4. Decide whether the sample supports the original hypothesis. (The observed 80 percent of drivers does not support the hypothesis that 10 percent buckle up.)
5. If the sample does not support the hypothesis, revise the hypothesis to be consistent with the sample's statistic. (The actual incidence of drivers who buckle their seat belts is about 80 percent.)

A hypothesis test gives you the probability of support for your hypothesis based on your sample evidence and sample size.

Due to the variation that we know will be caused by sampling, it is impossible to be absolutely certain that our assessment of the acceptance or rejection of the hypothesis will be correct if we simply compare our hypothesis arithmetically to the sample finding. Therefore, you must fall back on the sample size concepts discussed in chapter 13 and rely on the use of probabilities. The statistical concept underlying hypothesis testing permits us to say that if many, many samples were drawn, and a comparison made for each one, a true hypothesis would be accepted, for example, 99 percent of these times.

Statistical hypothesis testing involves the use of four ingredients: the sample statistic, the standard error of the statistic, the desired level of confidence, and the hypothesized population parameter value. The first three values were discussed in the section on parameter estimation. The final value is simply what the researcher believes the population parameter (π or μ) to be before the research is undertaken.

Statisticians often refer to the **alternative hypothesis** when performing statistical tests. This concept is important for you to know about. We have included Marketing Research Insight 16.1 (page 500) as a way to introduce you to the idea of an alternative hypothesis and to understand how it is used in statistical hypothesis tests.

There is always an alternative hypothesis.

Test of the Hypothesized Population Parameter Value

The hypothesized population parameter value can be determined using either a mean or a percentage. The equation used to test the hypothesis of a mean is as follows:

$$z = \frac{\bar{x} - \mu_H}{s_{\bar{x}}}$$

Here are formulas used to test a hypothesized population parameter.

where

$\bar{x}$ = the sample mean

μ_H = the hypothesized mean

$s_{\bar{x}}$ = standard error of the mean

The equation used to test the hypothesis of a population percentage is as follows:

$$z = \frac{p - \pi_H}{s_p}$$

where

p = the sample percentage

π_H = the hypothesized percentage

s_p = the standard error of the percentage

MARKETING RESEARCH INSIGHT 16.1

What Is an Alternative Hypothesis?

Whenever you test a stated hypothesis, you always automatically test its alternative. The alternative hypothesis takes in all possible cases that are not treated by the stated hypothesis. For example, if you hypothesize that 50 percent of all drivers fasten their seat belts, you are saying that the population percentage is equal to 50 percent (stated hypothesis), and the alternative hypothesis is that the population percent is not equal to 50 percent. To say this differently, the alternative hypothesis is that the population percentage can be any percentage other than 50 percent, the stated hypothesis. The alternative hypothesis is always implicit, but sometimes statisticians will state it along with the stated hypothesis.

To avoid confusion, we do not formally provide the alternative hypotheses in this textbook. But here are some stated hypotheses and their alternatives. You may want to refer back to this exhibit if the alternative hypothesis is important to your understanding of the concepts being described.

STATED HYPOTHESIS	ALTERNATIVE HYPOTHESIS
POPULATION PARAMETER HYPOTHESES	
The population mean is equal to $50.	The population mean is not equal to $50.
The population percentage is equal to 60 percent.	The population percentage is not equal to 60 percent.
DIRECTIONAL HYPOTHESES	
The population mean is greater than 100.	The population mean is less than or equal to 100.
The population percentage is less than 70 percent.	The population percentage is greater than or equal to 70 percent.
DIFFERENCES BETWEEN TWO MEANS HYPOTHESES	
No difference exists between means of two groups (populations).	A difference does exist between the means of two groups (populations).
The mean of one group (population) is greater than the mean of another group (population).	The mean of one group (population) is less than or equal to the mean of another group (population).
DIFFERENCES IN MEANS AMONG MORE THAN TWO GROUPS	
No difference exists between the means of all paired groups (populations).	A difference exists between the means of at least one pair of groups (populations).

The importance of knowing what the alternative hypothesis is stems from the fact that it is a certainty that the sample results must support either *the stated hypothesis* or *the alternative hypothesis. There is no other outcome possible. If the findings do not support the stated hypothesis, then they must support the alternative hypothesis because it covers all possible cases not specified in the stated hypothesis. Of course, if the stated hypothesis is supported by the findings, the alternative hypothesis cannot be supported.*

Tracking the logic of the equation for a mean, one can see that the sample mean ($\bar{x}$), is compared to the hypothesized population mean (μ_H). Similarly, the sample percentage (p) is compared to the hypothesized percentage (π_H). In this case, "compared" means "take the difference." This difference is divided by the standard error to determine how many standard errors away from the hypothesized parameter the sample statistic falls. The standard error, you should remember, takes into account the variability found in the sample as well as the sample size. A small sample with much variability yields a large standard error, so our sample statistic could be quite far away from the mean arithmetically but still less than one standard error away in certain circumstances. All the relevant information about the population as found by our sample is included in these computations. Knowledge of areas under the normal curve then come into play to translate this distance into a probability of support for the hypothesis.

To a statistician, "Compare means" amounts to "Take the difference."

Here is a simple illustration using Bill's seat belt hypothesis. Let us assume that instead of observing his friends buckling up, Bill reads that a Harris Poll finds that 80 percent of respondents in a national sample of 1,000 wear their seat belts. The hypothesis test would be computed as follows (notice we substituted the formula for s_p in the second step):

An example of no support for Bill's seat belt hypothesis.

$$
\begin{aligned}
z &= \frac{p - \pi_H}{s_p} \\
&= \frac{p - \pi_H}{\sqrt{\dfrac{p \times q}{n}}} \\
&= \frac{10 - 80}{\sqrt{\dfrac{80 \times 20}{1000}}} \\
&= \frac{-70}{\sqrt{\dfrac{1600}{1000}}} \\
&= \frac{-70}{\sqrt{1.6}} \\
&= -55.3
\end{aligned}
$$

The crux of statistical hypothesis testing is the sampling distribution concept. Our actual sample is one of the many, many theoretical samples comprising the assumed bell-shaped curve of possible sample results using the hypothesized value as the center of the bell-shaped distribution. There is a greater probability of finding a sample result close to the hypothesized mean, for example, than of finding one that is far away. But, there is a critical assumption working here. We have conditionally accepted from the outset that the person who stated the hypothesis is correct. So, if our sample mean turns out to be within ±2.58 standard errors of the hypothesized mean, it supports the hypothesis maker at the 99% level of confidence because it falls within 99 percent of the area under the curve. But, what if the sample result is found to be outside this range? Which is correct—the hypothesis or the researcher's sample results? The answer to this question is always the same: Sample information is invariably more accurate than a hypothesis. Of course, the sampling procedure must adhere strictly to probability sampling requirements and assure representativeness. As you can see, Bill was greatly mistaken because his hypothesis of 10 percent of drivers wearing seat belts was −55.3 standard errors away from the 80 percent finding of a national poll.

You always assume the sample information to be more accurate than any hypothesis.

The following example serves to describe the hypothesis testing process with a mean. Northwestern Mutual Life Insurance Company has a college student internship program. The program allows college students to participate in an intensive training program and to become field agents in one academic term. Arrangements are made with various universities in the United States whereby students will receive college credit if they qualify for and successfully complete this program. Rex Reigen, district agent for Idaho, believed, based on his knowledge of other programs in the country, that the typical college agent will be able to earn about $1,750 in his or her first semester of participation in the program. He hypothesizes that the population parameter, that is, the mean, will be $1,750. To check Rex's hypothesis, a survey was taken of current college agents, and 100 of these individuals were contacted through telephone calls. Among the questions posed was an estimate of the amount of money made in their first semester of work in the program. The sample mean is determined to be $1,800, and the standard deviation is $350.

Does the sample support Rex's hypothesis that student interns make $1,750?

In essence, the amount of $1,750 is the hypothesized mean of the sampling distribution of all possible samples of the same size that can be taken of the college agents in the country. The unknown factor, of course, is the size of the standard error in dollars. Consequently, although it is assumed that the sampling distribution will be a normal curve with the mean of the entire distribution at $1,750, we need a way to determine how many dollars are within ±1 standard error of the mean, or any other number of standard errors of the mean for that matter. The only information available that would help to determine the size of the standard error is the standard deviation obtained from the sample. This standard deviation can be used to determine a standard error with the application of the standard error formula.

How many standard errors is $1,800 away from $1,750?

The amount of $1,800 found by the sample differs from the hypothesized amount of $1,750 by $50. Is this amount a sufficient enough difference to cast doubt on Rex's estimate? Or, in other words, is it far enough from the hypothesized mean to reject the hypothesis? To answer these questions, we compute as follows (note that we have substituted the formula for the standard error of the mean in the second step):

$$z = \frac{\bar{x} - \mu_H}{S_{\bar{x}}}$$

$$= \frac{\bar{x} - \mu_H}{\frac{s}{\sqrt{n}}}$$

$$= \frac{1800 - 1750}{\frac{350}{\sqrt{100}}}$$

$$= \frac{50}{35}$$

$$= 1.43$$

The sample variability and the sample size have been used to determine the size of the standard error of the assumed sampling distribution. In this case, one standard error of the mean is equal to \$35. When the difference of \$50 is divided by \$35 to determine the number of standard errors away from which the hypothesized mean the sample statistic lies, the result is 1.43 standard errors. As is illustrated in Figure 16.1, 1.43 standard errors is within ±1.96 standard errors of Rex's hypothesized mean. It also reveals that the hypothesis is supported.

The z is calculated to be 1.43 standard errors. What does this mean?

A computed z of 1.43 is less than 1.96, so the hypothesis is supported.

Although the exact probability of support for the hypothesized parameter can be determined from the use of a table, it is often handy to just recall the two numbers, 1.96 and 2.58; as we have said, these two are directly associated to the confidence intervals of 95 percent and 99 percent, respectively. Anytime that the computed z value falls outside ±1.96, the probability that the hypothesis is supported is 0.05 or less, whereas anytime that the computed z value falls outside 2.58, the resulting probability of support for the hypothesis is 0.01 or less. Of course, computer statistical programs such as SPSS for Windows will provide the exact probability because they are programmed to look up the probability in the z table just as you would have to do if you did the test by hand calculations and you wanted the exact probability.

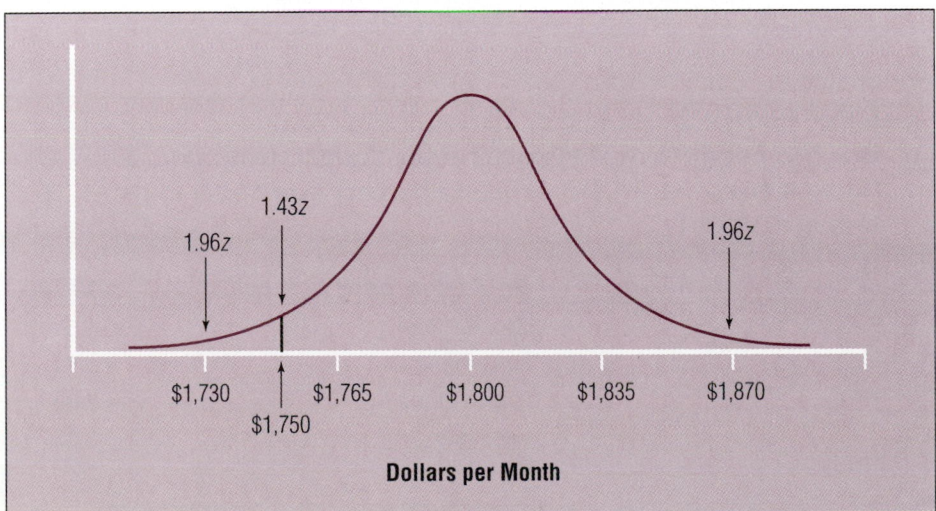

Figure 16.1

The sample findings support the hypothesis in this example.

Directional Hypotheses

A directional hypothesis is one in which you specify the hypothesized mean (or percentage) to be less than or greater than some amount.

It is sometimes appropriate to indicate a directional hypothesis. A **directional hypothesis** is one that indicates the direction in which you believe the population parameter falls relative to some target mean or percentage. That is, the owner of a toy store might not be able to state the exact number of dollars parents spend each time they buy a toy in that store, but the owner might say, "They spend under $100." A directional hypothesis is usually made with a "more than" or "less than" statement. For example, Rex Reigen might have hypothesized that the average college agent working for Northwestern Mutual Life earns *more than* $1,750. In both the "more than" case and the "less than" case, identical concepts are brought into play, but one must take into account that only one side (one tail) of the sampling distribution is being used.

When testing a directional hypothesis, you must look at the sign as well as the size of the computed z value.

There are only two differences to keep in mind for directional hypothesis tests. First, you must be concerned with the sign determined for the z value as well as its size. When you subtract the hypothesized mean from the sample mean, the sign will be positive with "greater than" hypotheses, whereas the sign will be negative for "less than" hypotheses if the hypothesis is true. To use Rex's example again, the hypothesized target of $1,750 would be subtracted from the sample mean of $1,800 yielding a +$50, so the positive sign does support the "greater than" hypothesis. But is the difference statistically significant?

To answer this question requires our second step: to divide the difference by the standard error of the mean to compute the z value. We did this earlier and determined the z value to be 1.43. Because we are working with only one side of the bell-shaped distribution, you need to adjust the critical z value to reflect this fact. As Table 16.4 shows, a z value of ±1.64 standard errors defines the endpoints for 95 percent of the normal curve, and a z value of ±2.33 standard errors defines the end points for 99 percent confidence levels. Now the directional hypothesis is supported at that level of confidence if the computed z value is *larger* than the critical cut point, *and*, of course, its sign is consistent with the direction of the hypothesis. Otherwise, the directional hypothesis is not supported at your chosen level of confidence. Although the computed z value is close (1.43), it is not equal to or greater than 1.64, so Rex's directional hypothesis is not supported.

Table 16.4: critical z values for directional hypotheses.

TABLE 16.4

With a Directional Hypothesis Test, the Critical Points for z Must Be Adjusted, and the Sign (+ or –) Is Important

LEVEL OF CONFIDENCE	DIRECTION OF HYPOTHESIS*	z Value
95%	Greater than	+ 1.64
	Less than	– 1.64
99%	Greater than	+ 2.33
	Less than	– 2.33

*Subtract the sample statistic (mean or percentage) *from* the hypothesized parameter (μ or π).

How to Interpret Hypothesis Testing

How do you interpret hypothesis tests? The interpretation of a hypothesis test is again directly linked to the sampling distribution concept. If the hypothesis about the population parameter is correct or true, then a high percentage of sample means must fall close to this value. In fact, if the hypothesis is true, then 99 percent of the sample results will fall between ±2.58 standard errors of the hypothesized mean. On the other hand, if the hypothesis is incorrect, there is a strong likelihood that the computed z value will fall outside ±2.58 standard errors. (Remember, you must adjust the number of standard errors to the levels indicated in Table 16.4 for directional hypothesis tests.) The further away the hypothesized value is from the actual case, the more likely the computed z value will not fall in the critical range. Failure to support the hypothesis essentially tells the hypothesizer that his or her assumptions about the population are in error, and that they must be revised in light of the evidence from the sample. This revision is achieved through estimates of the population parameter just discussed in the previous section. These estimates can be used to provide the manager or researcher with a new mental picture of the population through confidence interval estimates of the true population value.

If a hypothesis is not supported by a random sample finding, use the sample statistic and estimate the population parameter.

HOW TO USE SPSS FOR WINDOWS TO TEST A HYPOTHESIS FOR A MEAN

View: "Pampo's Swimwear: Testing Means"

Your SPSS software can be easily directed to make a mean estimation or to test a hypothesis for a mean. We again use part of the data from the Pampo's survey. Now, for the sake of illustration, let us suppose that the owner of Pampo's believed that the walk-ins whose demographic profiles matched those of very loyal customers were similar to the very loyal customers in their price sensitivity. She knows from past experience that the loyal Pampo's customer spends about $50 on her swimsuit. That is, the owner hypothesizes that walk-ins will want to spend about $50, too. To perform a mean hypothesis test, SPSS provides a Test Value box in which the hypothesized mean can be entered. You get to this box by using the STATISTICS-COMPARE MEANS-ONE SAMPLE t TEST command sequence. You then select the variable, willpay, which is the amount each respondent specified she would be willing to pay for a swimsuit that she likes. Next, enter in a "50" as the Test Value and click on the OK button.

The resulting output is contained in Table 16.5 (page 506). When you look at it, you will notice that the information layout for the output is identical to the previous output table. It indicates that 89 respondents answered this question, and the mean of their answers was calculated to be $37.9. The output indicates our test value equal to 50, and the bottom contains 95 percent confidence intervals for the estimated population parameter (the population parameter is the difference between the hypothesized mean and the sample mean, expected to be 0). There is a mean difference of −12.1, which was calculated by subtracting the hypothesized mean value (50) from the sample mean (37.9), and the standard error is provided in the upper half (1.46). A t value of −8.31 is determined by dividing −12.1 by 1.46. It is associated with a two-tailed significance level of 0.000. (For now, assume the t value is the z value we

Significance levels are discussed in Marketing Research Insight 16.2 on page 511.

TABLE 16.5

Output for an SPSS for Windows Mean Hypothesis Test

One-Sample Statistics

	N	Mean	Std. Deviation	Std. Error Mean
WILLPAY	89	37.8652	13.7735	1.4600

One-Sample Test

	Test Value = 50					
					95% Confidence Interval of the Difference	
	t	df	Sig. (2-tailed)	Mean Difference	Lower	Upper
WILLPAY	–8.312	88	.000	–12.1348	–15.0362	–9.2334

have used in our formulas and explanations. We describe use of the *t* value later in this chapter.) In other words, the walk-ins are not willing to pay the same amount that loyal customers are willing to pay. On the average, walk-ins whose demographic profiles match the loyal Pampo's customers are expecting to pay about $12 less for their swimsuits than the owner believed (hypothesized).

TESTING FOR SIGNIFICANT DIFFERENCES BETWEEN TWO GROUPS

There are statistical tests for when a researcher wants to compare the means or percentages of two different groups or samples.

Often, a researcher will want to compare means. There are two situations possible: (1) The researcher may have two independent groups such as walk-ins versus loyal customers, and he or she may want to compare their answers to the same question; or (2) the researcher may have two independent questions, and he or she may want to compare the responses to each question in the same sample. We describe each case. Then we describe the *t* value that substitutes for the *z* value.

Differences between Percentages or Means with Two Groups (Independent Samples)

Independent samples are treated as representing two potentially different populations.

Sometimes marketing researchers are interested in making comparisons between two groups of respondents to determine whether or not there are meaningful differences between them. They may perform two separate surveys or identify two subgroups within a particular survey and wish to compare the individuals who fall into each subgroup. In concept, marketing researchers are considering them as two potentially different populations, and they are interested in finding out whether their respective population parameters are different. But, as always, they can work only with the sample results. Therefore, they must fall back on statistical inference to determine whether the difference that they find between the two sample statistics is a true population difference.

Again, we refer to the intuitive approach you use every day when comparing two things to make an inference. Let us assume you have read a *Business Week* article about college recruiters that quotes a Louis Harris poll of 100 randomly selected companies, indicating that 60 percent of them will be visiting college campuses to interview business majors. The article goes on to say that a similar poll taken last year with 300 companies found that only 40 percent were going to make campus interview visits. Is this year's college recruiting environment different from last year's?

Although there is an arithmetic difference between 60 percent and 40 percent for the sample percentages, you cannot be completely confident of your conclusion about the populations they represent because of sampling error. If the difference between the percentages was very large, say 80 percent for this year and 20 percent for last year, you would be more inclined to believe that a true change had occurred. But if you found out that this large difference was based on small sample sizes, you would be less confident with your inference that last year's and this year's college recruiting are different. Intuitively, you have taken into account two critical factors in determining whether statistically significant differences exist between a percentage or a mean compared between two samples: the magnitude of the difference between the compared statistic and sample sizes.

The null hypothesis states there is no difference between the means being compared.

To test whether a true difference exists between two group percentages (or means), we test the **null hypothesis** or the hypothesis that the difference in their population parameters is equal to zero. The alternative hypothesis is that there is a true difference between them. To perform the test of significance of differences between two percentages (or means), the first step requires a comparison of the two percentages (means), and the second step requires that the difference be translated into a number of standard errors away from the hypothesized value of zero. Once the number of standard errors is known, knowledge of the area under the normal curve will yield an assessment of the probability of support for the null hypothesis.

With a differences test, you test the null hypothesis that no differences exist between the two group means (or percentages).

For a percentage, the equation looks like this:

$$z = \frac{p_1 - p_2}{s_{p_1 - p_2}}$$

where

p_1 = percentage found in sample 1

p_2 = percentage found in sample 2

$s_{p_1 - p_2}$ = standard error of the difference between two percentages

We define the standard error of the difference shortly. The equation for the test of difference between two sample means is as follows:

$$z = \frac{\bar{x}_1 - \bar{x}_2}{s_{\bar{x}_1 - \bar{x}_2}}$$

where

If the null hypothesis is true, when you subtract one group mean from the other, the result should be about zero.

$\bar{x}_1$ = mean found in sample 1

$\bar{x}_2$ = mean found in sample 2

$s_{\bar{x}_1 - \bar{x}_2}$ = standard error of the difference between two means

Divide the difference between the two group means (percentages) by the standard error of the difference to determine the number of standard errors (and significance).

If you compare these formulas to the ones we used in hypothesis testing, you will see two differences. First, in the numerator, we subtract one sample's statistic (p_2) from the other sample's statistic (p_1). You should have noticed that we use the subscripts, 1 and 2, to refer to the two different sample statistics. The second difference comes in the form of the sampling distribution that is expressed in the denominator. The sampling distribution under consideration now is the assumed sampling distribution of the differences between the percentages (or means). That is, the assumption has been made that the differences have been computed for comparisons of the two sample statistics for many repeated samplings. If the null hypothesis is true, this distribution of differences follows the normal curve with a mean equal to zero and a standard error equal to one. Stated somewhat differently, the procedure requires us, as before, to accept the (null) hypothesis as true until it lacks support from the statistical test. Consequently, the differences of a multitude of comparisons of the two sample means generated from many, many samplings would average zero. In other words, our sampling distribution is now the distribution of the difference between one sample and the other, taken over many, many times.

The standard error of the difference is very easy to calculate and again relies on the variability that has been found in the samples and their sizes. For example, the formula for the standard error of a difference between two means is:

$$s_{\bar{x}_1 - \bar{x}_2} = \sqrt{\frac{s_1^2}{n_1} + \frac{s_2^2}{n_2}}$$

where

Here are formulas for the standard errors of the difference between 2 means and between 2 percentages.

s_1 = standard deviation in sample 1

s_2 = standard deviation in sample 2

n_1 = size of sample 1

n_2 = size of sample 2

To compute the standard error of a difference between two percentages, the formula is:

$$s_{p_1 - p_2} = \sqrt{\frac{p_1 \times q_1}{n_1} + \frac{p_2 \times q_2}{n_2}}$$

where

p_1 = percentage found in sample 1

$q_1 = (100 - p_1)$

p_2 = percentage found in sample 2

$q_2 = (100 - p_2)$

n_1 = size of sample 1

n_2 = size of sample 2

To illustrate how significance of differences computations are made, we use the following example that answers the question, "Do male teens and female teens drink different amounts of soft drinks?" In a recent survey, teenagers were asked to indicate how many 12-ounce soft drinks in aluminum cans they consume in a typical week. The descriptive statistics revealed that males consume 9 cans of soft drinks on average and females consume 7.5 cans of soft drinks on average. The respective standard deviations were found to be 2 and 1.2. Both samples were of size 100. Applying this information to the formula for the test of statistically significant differences, we get the following:

$$z = \frac{x_1 - x_2}{\sqrt{\frac{s_1^2}{n_1} + \frac{s_2^2}{n_2}}}$$

$$= \frac{9.0 - 7.5}{\sqrt{\frac{2^2}{100} + \frac{1.2^2}{100}}}$$

$$= \frac{1.5}{\sqrt{.04 + 0.144}}$$

$$= \frac{1.5}{\sqrt{0.0544}}$$

$$= \frac{1.5}{0.233}$$

$$= 6.43$$

Here are the calculations for a test of the difference between the means of two groups.

Figure 16.2 (page 510) indicates how these two samples compare on the sampling distribution assumed to underlie this particular example. We have superimposed the standard error of the difference curve, and you know the probability of support for the null hypothesis of no difference between the two means is less than 0.001 because of the large number of standard errors calculated to exist for this example.

How do you interpret this test for significance of differences? As always, the sampling distribution concept underlies our interpretation. If the hypothesis were true, were we to draw many, many samples and do this explicit comparison each time, then 99 percent of differences would fall within ± 2.58 standard errors of zero. Of course, only one comparison can be made, and you have to rely on the sampling distribution concept and its attendant assumptions to determine whether this one particular instance of information supports or refutes the hypothesis of no significant differences found between the means (or percentages) of your two groups.

Directional hypotheses are also feasible in the case of tests of statistically significant differences. The procedure is identical to directional hypotheses that are stipulated in hypothesis tests. That is, you must first look at the sign of the computed z value to check that it is consistent with your hypothesized

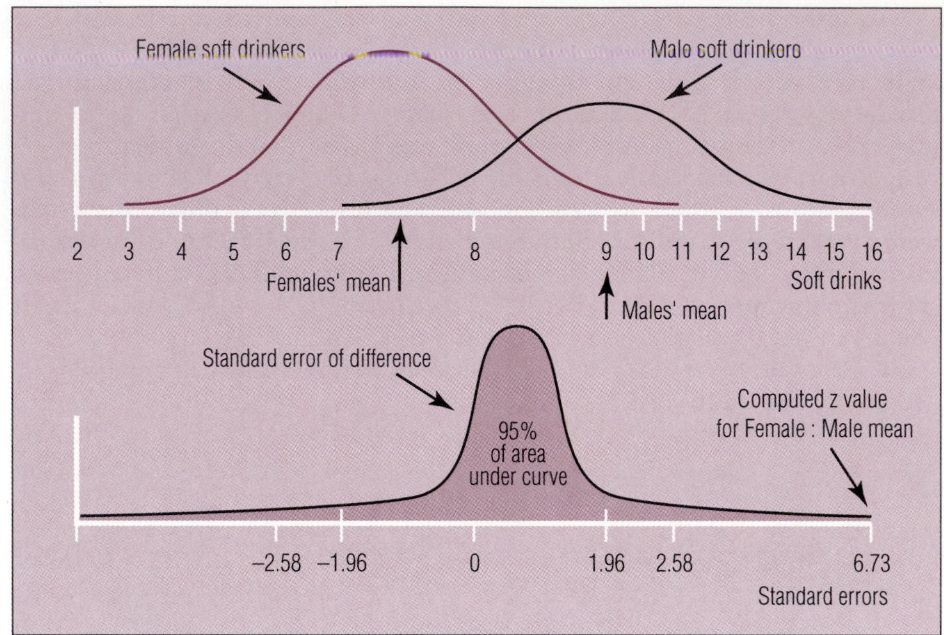

Figure 16.2

A significant difference exists between the two means because z is calculated greater than ± 1.96 (95 percent level of confidence).

direction. Then, you would use a cut-off *z* value such as 2.33 standard errors for 99 percent level of confidence because only one tail of the sampling distribution is being used.

Differences between Two Means within the Same Sample (Paired Sample)

Occasionally, a researcher will want to test for differences between the means for two variables within the same sample. For example, in the Pampo's survey, you might want to compare a five-point scale with disagree–agree responses to the question, "Pampo's has the best prices in town," with the question, "Pampo's has a wide line of swimwear." But the same respondents answered both questions, so you do not have two independent groups. Instead, you have two independent questions with one group. The logic and equations we have described still apply, but there must be an adjustment factor because there is only one sample involved. We do not provide the equations, but in the following SPSS section we describe how to perform and to interpret a paired samples *t* test with SPSS for Windows.

Small Sample Sizes: The Use of a *t* Test

The t test should be used when the sample size is 30 or less.

All of the equations related in this section have led to the computation of a *z* value. However, there are special instances in which the *z* test is not appropriate. We have pointed out that computation of the *z* value makes the assumption that the raw data for most statistics under scrutiny have normal or bell-shaped distributions. However, statisticians have shown that this normal curve assumption is invalid when the sample size is 30 observations or less. In this instance, a *t* value is computed instead of a *z* value. The ***t* test** is defined as the statistical inference test to be used with small samples sizes ($n \leq 30$). Instead of a constant normal distribution, the *t* test relies on Student's *t* distribution. The *t* distribution's shape is determined by the number of **degrees of freedom** defined as being equal to the sample size minus the number of population parameters estimated, which is $(n - 1)$ here because the population parameter is the difference between the two population means. The smaller the number of degrees of freedom, the more spread out the curve becomes. It still retains a bell shape, but it flattens out a little bit with each successive loss of a sample unit below 30.

Consequently, to determine the area under the curve, you must first determine the number of degrees of freedom for the case at hand, and then determine the number of standard errors expressed in *t* values. At this point you could turn to a *t* distribution table, found in any statistics textbook, to determine the cutoff or critical values for the computed *t*. Once the sample size exceeds 30 observations, the area under the curve for a *t* distribution is identical to that for the standard normal distribution, and you can simply fall back on the *z* test again. Again, virtually all statistical computer programs automatically adjust for small sample sizes in performing tests of significance of the difference between means. They are programmed to report not only the computed *t* and number of degrees of freedom, but they also provide the percent of the curve falling outside the computed *t* value. With a differences test, for example, they yield the probability of support for the null hypothesis of no differences between the means of the two groups compared in that analysis and adjusted for sample size. Because the *t* value is identical to *z* for large samples, statistical programs usually only report the *t* value.

Most computer statistical programs report only the t *value because it is identical to the* z *value with large samples.*

The great advantage to using statistical analysis routines on a computer is that they are programmed to compute the correct statistic. In other words, you do not need to decide whether you want the program to compute a *t* value, a *z* value, or some other value. You do, however, need to know when a statistically significant finding has occurred. To help you with this skill, we have included Marketing Research Insight 16.2.

MARKETING RESEARCH INSIGHT 16.2

Flag Waving and Significance in Statistical Analysis

The output from statistical procedures in all software programs can be envisioned as "flag-waving" devices. When the flag is waving briskly, statistical significance is present. Then, and only then, is it warranted to look at the findings more closely to determine the pattern of the findings; but if the flag is not waving, your time will be wasted by looking any further. To read statistical flags, you need to know two things. First, where is the flag located? Second, how much does it need to wave for you to pay attention to it and to delve further into the analysis in order to interpret it?

WHERE IS THE FLAG?

Virtually every statistical test or procedure involves the computation of some critical statistic, and that statistic is used to determine the statistical significance of the findings. The critical statistic's name changes depending on the procedure and its underlying assumptions, but usually the statistic is identified as a letter: z, t, F, or something similar. Statistical analysis computer programs will automatically identify and compute the correct statistic, so although it is helpful to know ahead of time what

(continued)

MARKETING RESEARCH INSIGHT 16.2 (continued)

statistic will be computed, it is not essential to know it. Moreover, the statistic is not the flag; rather it is just a computation necessary to raise the flag. You might think of the computed statistic as the flag pole.

The computer program will also raise the flag on the flag pole, but its name changes a bit depending on the procedure. The flags, called P *values by statisticians, are identified by the terms "significance" or "probability." Sometimes abbreviations such as "Sig" or "Prob" are used to economize on the output. To find the flag, locate the "Sig" or "Prob" designation in the analysis, and look at the number that is associated with it. The number will be a decimal perhaps as low as 0.000 but ranging to as high as 1.000. When you locate it, you have found the statistical significance flag.*

Statisticians determine statistical significance by calculating P *values.* P *values are sometimes reported by SPSS as either "Prob" or "Sig" values.*

HOW MUCH IS THE FLAG WAVING?

Perhaps an analogy about hurricane-force winds will help. Gentle winds blow all the time, and we are not concerned about them; but when hurricane-force winds build, we become concerned, and we pay a great deal of attention to the weather. Because hurricanes are very rare, the probability of their coming our way is very small, perhaps as small as 0.01 or even 0.001. So very small probabilities signal that hurricane-force winds are imminent, and we had better look into it to see where it is headed.

Similarly, statisticians have decided that they will not become interested unless the flag is waving very briskly. In fact, the standard 95 percent level of confidence rule says that the probability must be 0.05 or less, and the 99 percent level of confidence rule says that the probability must be 0.01 or less before we should worry about looking into the specific statistical findings. To say this differently, if the probability is 0.05 or less, it is something that has only 1 chance in 20 (5/100) of occurring, and if the probability is 0.01 or less, it is something that has only 1 chance in 100 of occurring; that is, a rare finding is present, and it is significant.

Statisticians set alpha levels to determine when a P *value is significant. If the* P *value is less than or equal to the alpha level, then there is statistical significance.*

Here is a table to help you interpret the flags waving in statistical analysis computer program output.

"PROB" OR "SIG" VALUE	DEGREE OF "FLAG WAVING"	STATISTICAL INTERPRETATION
Greater than 0.10	Fluttering every now and then	*Not significant:* Do not look any further at the findings
0.10 to greater than 0.05	Rippling the breeze	*Tentatively significant:* Look further at the findings if you are curious
0.05 to greater than 0.01	Flapping quite vigorously	*Significant:* Look at the findings to see what patterns are present
0.01 or less	About to rip off the flagpole	*Highly significant:* Absolutely look at the findings to see what is there

LIPTON PACKAGED DINNERS: HOW TO PERFORM AN INDEPENDENT SAMPLES SIGNIFICANCE OF DIFFERENCES BETWEEN MEANS TEST WITH SPSS FOR WINDOWS

View: "Lipton Prepared Dinners: Differences between Means"

We begin with some background on the example we will be using. Lipton not only markets tea, but it also has a line of packaged-dinner entrees such as rice or pasta dishes. In a telephone survey, Lipton has asked a sample of grocery purchasers who are responsible for the major grocery purchases in their households to respond to a series of statements involving how they go about buying grocery products. At this stage in the analysis, we are investigating possible differences between single and married respondents. If Lipton finds some differences, there may be important market segmentation implications on how they market their rice, pasta, and other packaged-dinner entrees to each demographic group. The responses to each statement are coded as follows: 1 for disagree strongly, 2 for disagree, 3 for neither agree nor disagree, 4 for agree, and 5 for agree strongly. We make the assumption that interval scaling is involved, and we want to compare the mean of the singles respondent group to the mean of the married respondent group. In our SPSS program, we have decided to use the variable name, mstatus, for marital status.

One important marketing variable often used by prepared food marketers is coupons, so we look at this statement's analysis. As you will see, this is the variable coupons. To obtain a statistical comparison of the means of two groups in a sample, select the STATISTICS-COMPARE MEANS-INDEPENDENT SAMPLES *t* TEST command sequence. The panel options for this procedure require you to indicate the Grouping Variable, which is mstatus, and to specify the values of the two groups you intend to have compared. In our coding scheme, "1" indicates single and "2" indicates the respondent is married.

The output provided in Table 16.6 on page 514 offers a good deal of information. First, we are informed that the variable, coupons, labeled USE COUPONS REGULARLY is being analyzed. Then, it indicates one group is where mstatus is labeled SINGLE, and the second group is the one labeled MARRIED. The Group Statistics output indicates the sample size of each group, its mean, standard deviation, and standard error.

The statistical test for the difference between the two means is given next. However, SPSS computes the results two different ways. One is identified as the "equal variances assumed," and the other is called the "equal variances not assumed." In our previous descriptions, we omitted a detail involved in tests for the significance of difference between two means. In some cases, the variances (standard deviations) of the two samples are about the same; that is, they are not significantly different. If so, you can use the formula pertaining to the equal variances (same variance for both samples), but if the standard deviations are statistically significant in their differences, you should use the unequal variances line on the output.

How do you know which one to use? The null hypothesis here is that there is no difference between the variances (standard deviations), and it is tested with an *F* value printed in the top row of the independent samples test table. (We describe what an *F* value is in more detail later in this chapter.) The *F* value is based on a procedure called "Levene's Test for Equality of Variances."

TABLE 16.6

Output for an SPSS *t* Test of the Difference in the Means of Two Groups

Group Statistics

	Marital Status	N	Mean	Std. Deviation	Std. Error Mean
Use coupons	Single	31	3.10	1.47	.26
	Married	57	2.44	1.35	.18

Independent Samples Test

		Levene's Test for Equality of Variances		t-test for Equality of Means						
									95% Confidence Interval of the Mean	
		F	Sig.	t	df	Sig. (2-tailed)	Mean Difference	Std. Error Difference	Lower	Upper
Use coupons regularly	Equal variances assumed	.751	.389	-2.118	86	.037	-.66	.31	-1.28	-4.04E-02
	Equal variances not assumed			-2.065	57.406	.043	-.66	.32	-1.30	-2.02E-02

In our output, the *F* value is identified as 0.751 (flag pole) with a Sig (probability) of 0.389 (flag waving). The probability reported here is the probability that the variances are equal, so anytime the probability is *greater than,* say 0.05, then you would use the equal variance line on the output. If the probability associated with the *F* value is *small, say 0.05 or less,* then the variances null hypothesis is not supported, and you should use the unequal variance line. If you forget this rule, then just look at the standard deviations, and try to remember that if they are about the same size, you would use the equal variances *t* value.

Using the equal variance estimate information, you will find that the computed *t* value is –2.12 with 86 degrees of freedom, and the associated probability of support for the null hypothesis of no difference between the single respondents mean and the married respondents is 0.037 (Sig: 2-tailed). In other words, they differ significantly. Married grocery shoppers use coupons more than do single individuals as their mean is 2.44, whereas the singles mean is 3.10 on the 1–5, disagree–agree scale. (Note: 1 is "disagree strongly.")

How to Perform a Paired Samples Significance of Differences between Means Test with SPSS for Windows

With the paired samples test, we can test the significance of the difference between the mean of any two questions by the same respondents in our sample. For illustration, we take the Lipton sample and compare the mean response

TABLE 16.7

Output for a Paired Samples *t* Test for the Significance of the Difference between Two Means Using Responses from the Respondents in the Same Sample

Paired Samples Statistics

		Mean	N	Std. Deviation	Std. Error Mean
Pair 1	LISRADIO	4.37	100	.68	6.77E-02
	READCOOK	3.08	100	1.40	.14

Paired Samples Test

		Paired Differences					t	df	Sig. (2-tailed)
					95% Confidence Interval of the Difference				
		Mean	Std. Deviation	Std. Error Mean	Lower	Upper			
Pair 1	LISRADIO READCOOK	1.29	1.45	.15	1.58	1.00	8.887	99	.000

for the statements, "I often read the cooking section of the newspaper," and "I usually listen to cooking programs on the radio." They are labeled, readcook and lisradio in the SPSS data file. The command sequence to perform the significance of differences test is STATISTICS-COMPARE MEANS-PAIRED SAMPLES *t* TEST, and the two variables were selected as the pair on which to perform the analysis. Table 16.7 is the output that was generated.

You should notice that the table is similar, but not identical, to the independent samples output. The relevant information includes: (1) 100 respondents gave answers to each statement and were analyzed; (2) the means for readcook and lisradio are 3.08 and 4.37, respectively; (3) the computed *t* value is 8.89; and (4) the two-tailed significance level is 0.000. In other words, the test gives almost no support for the null hypothesis that the means are equal. Reading the cooking section of the newspaper is more prevalent than is listening to cooking shows on the radio in the population represented by this sample. (Again, 1 is "agree strongly.")

TESTING FOR SIGNIFICANT DIFFERENCES IN MEANS AMONG MORE THAN TWO GROUPS: ANALYSIS OF VARIANCE

ANOVA is used when comparing the means of three or more groups.

Often, a researcher will want to compare the means of several different groups. Analysis of variance, sometimes called ANOVA, is used to accomplish multiple comparisons. The use of the word "variance" in the name "analysis of variance" is perhaps misleading—it is not an analysis of the standard deviations of the groups. To be sure, the standard deviations are taken into consideration, and so are the sample sizes just as you saw in all of our other statistical inference formulas. Fundamentally, **ANOVA** is an investigation of the differences between the group means to ascertain whether sampling errors or true population differences explain their failure to be equal. That is, the word "variance" signifies for our purposes differences between two or more groups' means—do they vary from one another significantly? Although a term like "ANOVA" sounds frightfully technical, it is nothing more than statistical procedures that embody inference when you are looking at the means of several groups. The following sections explain to you the basic concepts involved with analysis of variance, and also how it can be applied to marketing research situations.

Basic Logic in Analysis of Variance

The basis of analysis of variance is a desire on the part of a researcher to determine whether a statistically significant difference exists between the means for any two groups in his or her sample with a given variable regardless of the number of groups. The end result of analysis of variance is an indication to the marketing researcher as to whether a significant difference at some chosen level of statistical significance exists (*P* value) between *at least* two group means. Significant differences may exist between all of the group means, but analysis of variance results will not communicate how many pairs of means are statistically significant in their differences.

ANOVA will "flag" when at least one pair of means has a statistically significant difference, but it does not tell which pair.

ANOVA is a "flagging" device. If at least one pair of means has a statistically significant difference, ANOVA will signal this by indicating significance. Then, it is up to the researcher to conduct further tests to determine precisely how many statistically significant differences actually exist and which ones they are. Of course, if the flag does not pop up, the researcher knows that no significant differences exist.

The Three Types of Variation in ANOVA

The three types of variation in ANOVA are total, between groups, and within groups.

Everything in analysis of variance is based on differences from the mean, and there are three specific differences or "variations" between means that can be computed: total variation (TV), variation between groups (VB), and variation within groups (VW). Each one represents a unique way to assess the variation between means in our data set.

Total variation (TV) pertains to the summed squared differences of all individual observations, about the grand mean. The grand mean is the average of all observations across all groups. The formula for TV is:

$$TV = \sum_{j=1}^{k} \sum_{i=1}^{n_j} (x_{ij} - \bar{\bar{x}})^2$$

where

TV = total variation

$\bar{\bar{x}}$ = the grand mean

k = the number of groups

n_j = the size of each group

x_{ij} = individual value for observation i in group j

The squaring operation in this formula and the next two is necessary to avoid the cancellation of negative and positive differences during the summing step.

Variation between groups (VB) is the sum of the squared differences for each group's sample mean compared to the grand mean. The equation for VB is:

$$\text{VB} = \sum_{j=1}^{k} n_j \, (\bar{x}_j - \bar{\bar{x}})^2$$

where

VB = variation between groups

$\bar{\bar{x}}$ = the grand mean

k = the number of groups

n_j = the size of each group

$\bar{x}_j$ = mean of group j

Variation within groups (VW) is the sum of the squared differences of each individual compared to the respective group mean. The formula is:

$$\text{VW} = \sum_{j=1}^{k} \sum_{i=1}^{n_j} (x_{ij} - \bar{x}_j)^2$$

where

VW = variation within groups

k = the number of groups

n_j = the size of each group

x_{ij} = individual value for observation i in group j

$\bar{x}_j$ = mean for group j

Determining Statistical Significance in ANOVA

With ANOVA, degrees of freedom are adjustments associated with sums of squares that must be used to make them directly comparable. Degrees of freedom must be computed for each type of variation. Essentially, degrees of freedom are equal to the number of items whose squared deviations are being summed minus the number of sample statistics used in the analysis step. That is, for total variation, only the grand mean is used; hence, the degrees of freedom are equal to the total number of observations minus one. For the variation within groups, the number of degrees of freedom is equal to the number of observations minus the number of groups because a sample mean is computed for each group. Finally, the number of degrees of freedom for the between group mean variation is equal to the number of groups minus one because each group mean is considered an observation and the grand mean is the statistic against which they are compared. Thus,

$df_{\text{total}} = (n - 1)$

$\text{df}_{\text{between}} = (\# \text{ groups} - 1) \text{ or } (k - 1)$

$\text{df}_{\text{within}} = (n - \# \text{ groups}) \text{ or } (n - k)$

Mean square variation is the variation average, squared.

When the sum of squares between variation and within variation measures are divided by their respective degrees of freedom, the result is referred to as the **mean square.** The null hypothesis in an analysis of variance states that no difference exists between the population means for the various groups.[1] When the mean square variation between groups (between mean square) is found to be significantly greater than the mean square variance within groups (within mean square), the hypothesis is not supported. In other words, if the mean square number resulting from the comparisons between the group means is greater than the mean square for each group member compared to its respective mean, the discrepancy is attributed to real differences between the test groups, and the null hypothesis is rejected.

An Example of How ANOVA Works

This is a lot to remember, so let us slow down and walk through ANOVA and related concepts with an example. Suppose you were working for RCA Records, and you were in charge of the distribution of Metallica's newest CD, titled *Animal Lover.* A total of 1 million copies has been made, and your job is to decide how many are to be shipped to each of RCA's five regional warehouses located in New York, Chicago, Atlanta, Denver, and Los Angeles. Would you just send one-fifth (or 200,000) CDs to each center? If you did, your null hypothesis would be that there is no difference between the warehouse centers. But if you did this, and your hypothesis was wrong, you could be responsible for stock-outs in some centers and excess inventory in others.

Okay, how are you going to ship Metallica's Animal Lover *CD to your warehouses?*

You decide it might be a good idea to look at the sales of CDs in the past year. You tap into the RCA sales database and find that 10 heavy metal CDs were released last year. They include groups such as Megadeth, Alice in Chains, AC/DC, and Spinal Tap. The MIS indicates that the grand mean number of heavy metal CDs sold per region last year was 400,000. You next instruct the database software to compute the average sales by regional warehouse and to graph the averages for you. The resulting table and bar chart appear as Table 16.8 and Figure 16.3.

Now you can see that there are perhaps meaningful differences between some of the cities. Los Angeles tends to account for more heavy metal CD buyers than other cities, whereas Atlanta accounts for less. New York, Denver, and Chicago are the same. In fact, all three regions average the grand mean of 400,000 CDs. The important thing to remember is that you are using averages throughout. The average for Los Angeles is 600,000, for Atlanta it is 200,000, and 400,000 is the overall or grand average for heavy metal CDs across all five regional warehouse locations. Now the pattern of differences among the regions has become clear. New York, Chicago, and Denver tend to account for about the same, or 20 percent of the total each; Atlanta sells about one-half the average, or 10 percent of the total; and Los Angeles typically accounts for more than the average, at 30 percent of the total. As a result of these data, the 1 million Metallica CDs could be shipped as follows: 100,000 to Atlanta; 300,000 to Los Angeles; and 200,000 each to New York, Denver, and Chicago.

However, you have used only between groups analysis. That is, you have looked only at the average sales for each region. It is possible that the sales within the regions were very volatile. In other words, there might have been a great deal of variance across CDs in each city so the mean is not a good indication, and your shipment decision might be in error. ANOVA explicitly

TABLE 16.8

CD Sales of 10 Heavy Metal Groups by Region: Analysis of Variance Example (CD sales in thousands)

	Location of Regional Warehouse				
Heavy Metal Group	Atlanta	New York	Chicago	Denver	Los Angeles
AC/DC	400	500	300	400	300
Megadeth	500	400	500	100	800
Alice in Chains	200	600	600	300	600
Spinal Tap	600	200	700	200	500
Demonica	400	400	100	100	500
Great White	200	200	200	400	700
Blade Head	300	400	400	100	600
Ozzy Osborne	300	500	300	200	500
Terror on Wings	300	500	500	200	700
Steel Trap	800	300	400	100	600
Region average	200	400	400	400	600
Percent of total	10%	20%	20%	20%	30%

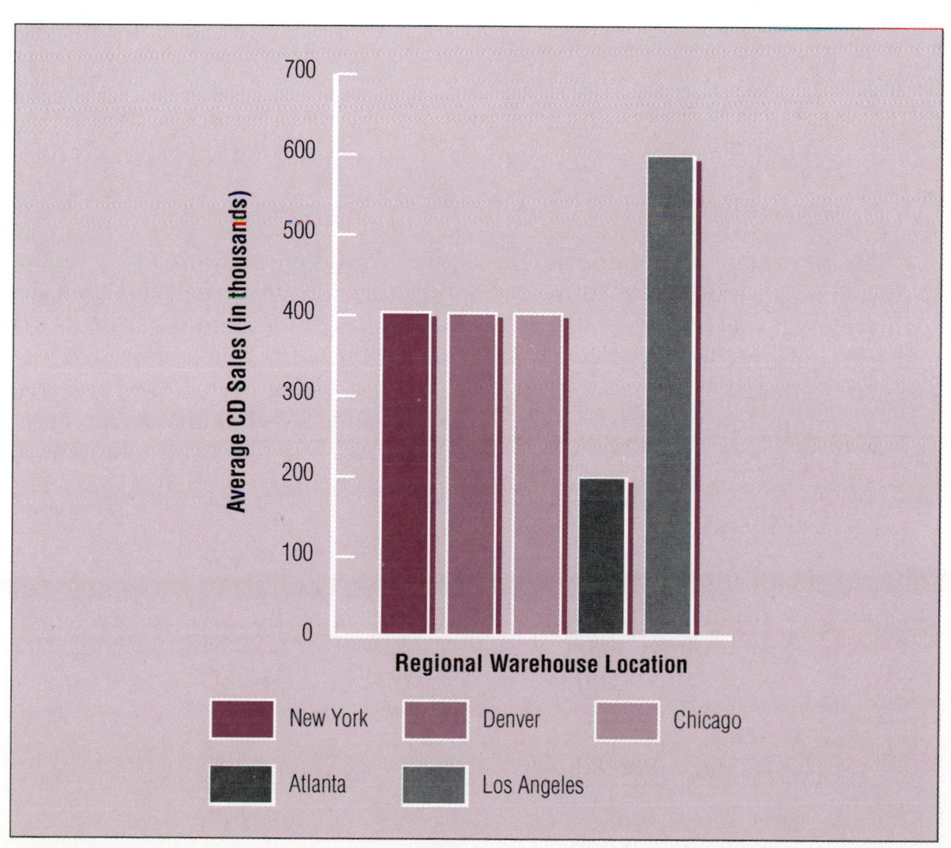

Figure 16.3

Where are the "heavy" heavy metal CD buyers?

compares the between groups variation to the within groups variation to avoid this error. Here are the computations for TV, VB, and VW.

For TV, each value in Table 16.8 is compared to the grand mean, the difference is squared, and all the squared values are summed.

$$\begin{aligned} TV &= \sum_{j=1}^{k} \sum_{i=1}^{n_j} (x_{ij} - \bar{\bar{x}})^2 \\ &= (400 - 400)^2 + (500 - 400)^2 + (200 - 400)^2 + \ldots + (600 - 400)^2 \\ &= 1,780,000 \end{aligned}$$

Note that for VB, the grand mean is subtracted from each region's average CD sales, and that difference is squared. Each squared value is multiplied by the number of CDs sold in that region, and these products are summed.

$$\begin{aligned} VB &= \sum_{j=1}^{k} n_j\ (\bar{x}_j - \bar{\bar{x}})^2 \\ &= 10 \times (200 - 400)^2 + 10 \times (400 - 400)^2 + 10 \times (400 - 400)^2 + 10 \times \\ &\quad (400 - 400)^2 + (600 - 400)^2 \\ &= 800,000 \end{aligned}$$

To calculate VW, each CD sales value in the table is compared to its region's mean, and the squared differences are summed. TV is a check for computation of VB and VW. VB (800,000) plus VW (980,000) equals TV (1,780,000).

$$\begin{aligned} VW &= \sum_{j=1}^{k} \sum_{i=1}^{n_j} (x_{ij} - \bar{x}_j)^2 \\ &= (400 - 200)^2 + (500 - 200)^2 + \ldots + (700 - 600)^2 + (600 - 600)^2 \\ &= 980,000 \end{aligned}$$

The next step is to compare the between groups variation (VB) to the within groups variation (VW) by calculating their mean squares and then dividing the VB mean square by the VW mean square. We cannot compare VB and VW directly, because they have not been adjusted for their respective degrees of freedom.

ANOVA requires a number of intermediate calculations. Aren't you glad that SPSS does them for you?

The mean square calculations for the variation between the region averages (VB) is as follows:

$$\begin{aligned} \text{Mean square}_{VB} &= \frac{VB}{df_{VB}} \\ &= \frac{VB}{\text{Number of groups} - 1} \\ &= \frac{800,000}{5 - 1} \\ &= \frac{800,000}{4} \\ &= 200,000 \end{aligned}$$

The mean square calculations of the variation within the regions (VW) is as follows:

$$\text{Mean square}_{\text{VW}} = \frac{\text{VW}}{df_{\text{VB}}}$$

$$= \frac{\text{VW}}{n - \text{Number of groups}}$$

$$= \frac{980{,}000}{50 - 5}$$

$$= \frac{980{,}000}{45}$$

$$= 21{,}777.8$$

The last step is to compute an F value by dividing the mean square for the variation between groups (VB) by the mean square of the variation within the groups (VW):

$$F = \frac{\text{Mean square}_{\text{VB}}}{\text{Mean square}_{\text{VW}}}$$

$$= \frac{200{,}000}{21{,}777.8}$$

$$= 9.18$$

The Computed *F* Value and *F* Distribution

The ***F* value** is a number that expresses the ratio of between groups mean square variance to within groups mean square variance. The computed F value is the acid test of the null hypothesis of no difference between the variances. If the average between groups variance is much larger than the average within groups variance, then the F value will, of course, be large. On the other hand, if the two are approximately equal, the F value will be close to 1. Finally, if the average between groups variances are much smaller than the average within groups variance, the F value approaches 0.

A large computed F value signifies that at least one pair of means is significantly different.

Just as with all other computed statistics, the computed F value must be compared with a table value. A table of critical F values for various levels of statistical significance is contained in practically all statistics textbooks. These books instruct you on how to use such a table to determine the significance level of a given F value with certain degrees of freedom. However, SPSS for Windows will do this task for you. SPSS output provides you with the computed F as well as its significance level.

SPSS will look up and indicate the significance level of the computed F value.

The ***F* distribution** is a statistical concept used to help assess the significance of differences between two variances. It is actually a family of curves based on an equation that uses the two degrees of freedom values to determine its exact shape. The F distribution is skewed as pictured in Figure 16.4 (page 522). As you can see, the beginning point on the horizontal axis is 0, or the case in which no differences are found between the groups' means. Values increase with movement to the right, designating cases of greater and greater dif-

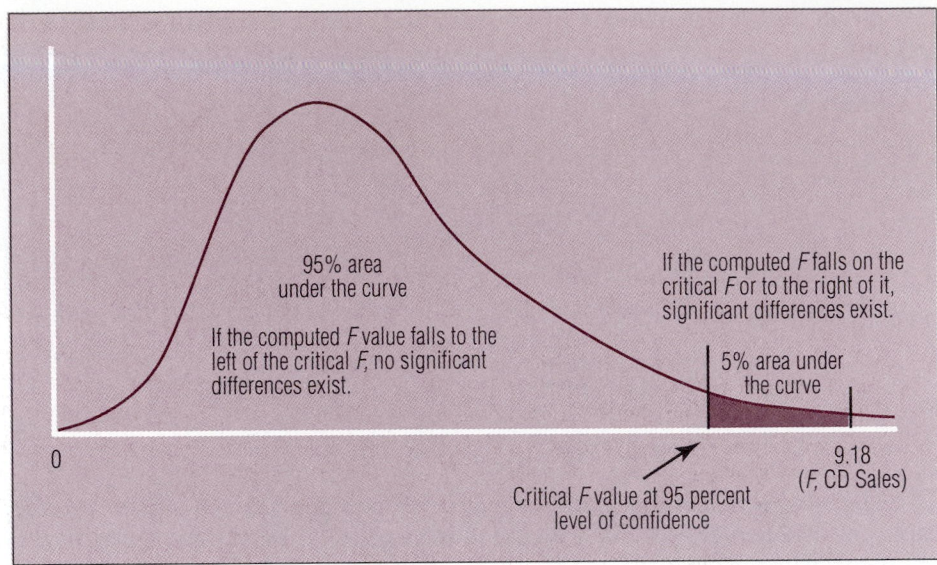

Figure 16.4

The F *distribution begins at zero and is skewed to the right.*

ferences between group means relative to differences within observations for each group. The rejection region is found at the right-hand tail, and if a computed *F* value is found to be greater than the critical value defining, say, the .05 level of statistical significance, there is assumed to be at least a 0.95 probability that a true difference exists between at least two of the compared group means. Stated differently, this means the probability of support for the null hypothesis is .05 or less.

Determining Specific Statistically Significant Differences between Group Means

When ANOVA signals that a significant difference exists, the researcher must go further to determine where the pairs of significant differences lie between the means.

The *F* test, as we indicated earlier, is a flag signaling the marketing researcher thac at least one statistically significant difference exists between the means. Once alerted, the researcher must now determine precisely where the statistical significant difference or differences lie. A number of custom-tailored procedures exist to determine where the pairs of statistically significant differences lie between the means. It is beyond the scope of this book to provide a complete delineation of the various types of tests. Consequently, only one test, **Duncan's multiple range test,** will be shown as an illustration of how the differences may be determined. There are other tests available on SPSS, including Scheffé's and Tukey's that you may recognize from statistics courses.

HOW TO RUN ANALYSIS OF VARIANCE ON SPSS FOR WINDOWS

Because you are familiar with ANOVA from our description of how it works, we use the RCA heavy metal CD sales data set to illustrate how to perform ANOVA with SPSS for Windows. The data editor has been used to create a data set that has two variables. The first is REGION with value codes of 1, 2, 3, 4, and 5 for Atlanta, New York, Chicago, Denver, and Los Angeles, respectively. The second is CDSALES, which is the sales, in thousands, for each heavy metal group's CD associated with the region value for that case. We describe the steps for SPSS for Windows next.

One-way ANOVA in this case is done under the STATISTICS-COMPARE MEANS-ONE-WAY ANOVA command sequence. The independent factor is REGION, and CDSALES is the dependent variable whose means will be compared across all five warehouse locations. Also, we have chosen the Duncan's Multiple Range option under the Post Hoc . . . Tests menu. ANOVA procedures on statistical computer programs generate a number of intermediate and additional computational results, but they customarily provide a summary table for the ANOVA results. A summary ANOVA table includes identification of the source of variation, the number of degrees of freedom, the sums of squares, the mean squares, and an *F* value. The ANOVA table in Table 16.9 contains the statistics we described earlier: the source (Between, Within, or Total), the degrees of freedom (*df*), Sum of Squares, and Mean Squares for each type of variation. You should notice that the summary table reports the level of statistical significance associated with the computed *F* value at the appropriate degrees of freedom. That is, SPSS is programmed to look into the *F* distribution table, to select the proper row and column, and to determine how much of the distribution falls to the right of the computed *F* value. The *F* value (*F*) and its associated *F* probability (Sig.) is also included in the SPSS for Windows one-way ANOVA output. As you can see, the flag is signaling significance, for the probability is found to be 0.000. (Recall, only three decimal places are given, so the probability might be .0001.)

SPSS®

View: "RCA Heavy Metal CD Sales: Analysis of Variance"

Table 16.10 (page 524) contains the Duncan's multiple range test results. The Duncan's option arranges the group means in ascending order and provides subsets whose means are significantly different. Each column represents

There are several "post hoc" tests with ANOVA, and we have used Duncan's multiple range test as an illustration.

Table 16.9

An ANOVA Table Indicating a Significant Difference Exists between the Means of at Least Two Groups

ANOVA

		Sum of Squares	df	Mean Square	F	Sig.
CDSALES	Between groups	800000.0	4	200000.0	8.491	.000
	Within groups	1060000	45	23555.56		
	Total	1860000	49			

TABLE 16.10

Duncan's Multiple Range Output Indicating Where Significant Differences between Means in Groups Are Found

CDSALES

Duncan[a]

REGION	N	Subset for alpha = .05		
		1	2	3
Atlanta	10	200.0000		
Denver	10		400.0000	
New York	10		400.0000	
Chicago	10		400.0000	
L. A.	10			600.0000
Sig.		1.000	1.000	1.000

Means for groups in homogeneous subsets are displayed.

a. Uses Harmonic Mean Sample Size = 10.000

a subset, and you can see that Atlanta's average heavy metal CD sales of 200 (thousand) is significantly different from all four other regions, and Los Angeles's average heavy metal CD sales of 600 (thousand) is significantly different from the other regions.

Study the Duncan's multiple range test output so you interpret it easily. Remember, the significance level of the ANOVA F is only a flag that indicates that at least one pair of means is statistically significant in its differences, and you must perform additional analysis such as the Duncan's test in order to identify which pair or pairs are involved.

n-Way ANOVA

n-way ANOVA allows you to test multiple grouping variables at the same time.

The RCA heavy metal CD example illustrates what is normally termed **one-way ANOVA** because there is only one independent factor used to set up the groups. However, it is not unusual to look at two or more grouping factors simultaneously, in which case one would use ***n*-way ANOVA.** For example, the Lipton managers might decide to use age groups and occupation classifications at the same time to test for coupon use differences. Or, with a test market experiment, the researcher might want to see the effect of a high versus a low price operating with a newspaper versus billboard advertising. The overlaying of various independent factors permits the marketing researcher to investigate "interaction effects." **Interaction effects** are cases in which the independent factors are operating in concert and simultaneously affecting the means of the groups. Conceptually, *n*-way ANOVA operates identically to the one-way ANOVA regardless of the number of treatment classification schemes being used. Of course, the formulas and computations are more complicated.

n-WAY ANOVA WITH SPSS FOR WINDOWS

n-way ANOVA is found in SPSS for Windows under the STATISTICS-GENERAL LINEAR MODEL-SIMPLE FACTORIAL command sequence, which leads to a Dialog Box where you can select the Factors, or independent grouping variables, and the dependent variable, or the one being used to calculate the group means. No *post hoc* test such as a Duncan's test can be performed with more than one grouping variable, so if you find a significant F value for a grouping variable with ANOVA, an option would be to revert to a one-way analysis using only that significant grouping variable. Finally, there are many features to *n*-way ANOVA on your SPSS program that we have not mentioned. We suggest that you refer to more advanced sources if you are interested in using *n*-way ANOVA.

SUMMARY

This chapter began by distinguishing a sample statistic from its associated population parameter. We then introduced you to the concept of statistical inference, which is a set of procedures for generalizing the findings from a sample to the population. A key factor in inference is the sample size, n. It appears in statistical inference formulas because it expresses the amount of sampling error: Large samples have less sampling error than do small samples given the same variability. We illustrated the three inference types commonly used by marketing researchers. First, we described how a population parameter, such as a mean, can be estimated by using confidence intervals computed by application of the standard error formula. Second, we related how a researcher can use the sample findings to test a hypothesis about a mean or a percentage. Third, we described how the t test procedure can be applied when the researcher is investigating whether significant differences exist between the means or percentages found between two subgroups in a sample or two samples.

Last, we introduced you to analysis of variance. ANOVA is used when more than two groups are being compared. With this procedure, the means of the various groups are compared systematically, and if at least one pair is statistically significant in its difference, ANOVA will "flag" it. When this happens, the researcher must use a second series of analysis, such as Duncan's multiple range test, to discover where the differences exist. If the researcher is interested in the simultaneous effects of two or more grouping variables, *n*-way ANOVA is used.

KEY TERMS

Statistics (p. 488)
Parameters (p. 488)
Inference (p. 489)
Statistical inference (p. 489)
Parameter estimation (p. 490)
Hypothesis testing (p. 490)
Tests of significant differences (p. 490)
Standard error (p. 491)
Confidence intervals (p. 493)
Hypothesis (p. 498)
Hypothesis testing (p. 498)
Alternative hypothesis (p. 499)
Directional hypothesis (p. 504)
Null hypothesis (p. 507)
t test (p. 510)
Degrees of freedom (p. 511)
ANOVA (p. 516)
Total variation (p. 516)
Variation between groups (p. 517)
Variation within groups (p. 517)
Mean square (p. 518)
F value (p. 521)
F distribution (p. 521)
Duncan's multiple range test (p. 522)
One-way ANOVA (p. 524)
n-way ANOVA (p. 524)
Interaction effects (p. 524)

REVIEW QUESTIONS/APPLICATIONS

1. What essential factors are taken into consideration when statistical inference takes place?
2. What is meant by "parameter estimation," and what function does it perform for a researcher?
3. How does parameter estimation for a mean differ from that for a percentage?
4. List the steps in statistical hypothesis testing.
5. When a researcher's sample evidence disagrees with a manager's hypothesis, who is right?
6. What does it mean when a researcher says that a hypothesis has been supported at the 95 percent confidence level?
7. Distinguish a directional from a nondirectional hypothesis, and provide an example of each one.
8. When should one-way ANOVA be used and why?
9. Describe the three types of variation that can be computed in ANOVA.
10. Describe the role of the computed *F* value in analysis of variance. Why can it be considered a "flagging" device?
11. When a researcher finds a significant *F* value in ANOVA, what is immediately known, and what is unknown at that time?
12. Here are several computation practice exercises to help you identify which formulas pertain and learn how to perform the necessary calculations. In each case, perform the necessary calculations and write your answers in the column identified by a "question mark."

DETERMINE CONFIDENCE INTERVALS FOR EACH OF THE FOLLOWING

SAMPLE STATISTIC	SAMPLE SIZE	CONFIDENCE LEVEL	YOUR CONFIDENCE INTERVALS?
Mean: 150 Std. dev: 30	200	95%	
Percent: 67%	300	99%	

Mean: 5.4	250	99%
Std. dev: 0.5		
Percent: 25.8%	500	99%

TEST THE FOLLOWING HYPOTHESES AND INTERPRET YOUR FINDINGS

HYPOTHESIS	SAMPLE FINDINGS	CONFIDENCE LEVEL	YOUR TEST RESULTS?
Mean = 7.5	Mean: 8.5 Std dev: 1.2 $n = 670$	95%	
Percent = 86%	$p = 95$ $n = 1{,}000$	99%	
Mean > 125	Mean: 135 Std dev: 15 $n = 500$	95%	
Percent < 33%	$p = 31$ $n = 120$	99%	

ARE THE FOLLOWING TWO SAMPLE RESULTS SIGNIFICANTLY DIFFERENT?

SAMPLE ONE	SAMPLE TWO	CONFIDENCE LEVEL	YOUR FINDING?
Mean: 10.6 Std. dev: 1.5 $n = 150$	Mean: 11.7 Std. dev: 2.5 $n = 300$	95%	
Percent: 45% $n = 350$	Percent: 54% $n = 250$	99%	
Mean: 1,500 Std. dev: 550 $n = 1{,}200$	Mean: 1,250 Std. dev: 500 $n = 500$	95%	

13. The manager of the aluminum recycling division of Environmental Services wants a survey that will tell him how many households in the city of Seattle, Washington, will voluntarily wash out, store, and then transport all of their aluminum cans to a central recycling center located in the downtown area and open only on Sunday mornings. A random survey of 500 households determines that 20 percent of households would do so, and that each participating household expects to recycle about 100 cans monthly with a standard deviation of 30 cans. What is the value of parameter estimation in this instance?

14. It is reported in the newspaper that a survey sponsored by *Forbes* magazine with *Fortune* 500 company top executives has found that 75 percent believe that the United States trails Japan and Germany in automobile engineering. The article notes that executives were interviewed at a recent "Bring the U.S. Back to Competitiveness" symposium held on the campus of the University of Southern California. Why would it be incorrect for the article to report confidence intervals?

15. Alamo Rent-A-Car executives believe that Alamo accounts for about 50 percent of all Cadillacs that are rented. To test this belief, a researcher randomly identifies 20 major airports with on-site rental car lots. Observers are sent to each location and instructed to record the number of rental company Cadillacs observed in a four-hour period. About 500 are observed, and 30 percent are observed being returned to Alamo Rent-A-Car. What are the implications of this finding for the Alamo executives' belief?

16. In a pilot study conducted for the Vermont Department of Transportation (VDT), a researcher finds that only 15 percent of automobile drivers are satisfied with the speed with which roads are cleared after a blizzard. The head of the VDT becomes enraged at hearing the results and claims that the findings are invalid because the sample size is only 300. Indicate who is correct—the researcher or the VDT head who believes that drivers are much more satisfied. Explain your answer.

CASE 16.1

General Hospital Importance–Performance Survey

General Hospital is a large regional hospital that employs over 2,000 full- and part-time workers, including custodial personnel, nurses, medical technicians, and doctors. On the ground floor of General Hospital there is a cafeteria that is operated by the hospital with Ms. Connie Wilson as its manager. Almost all employees use the cafeteria for lunch. There have been complaints about the cafeteria for many years, and Ms. Wilson has decided to look into these problems with a survey. She recruits the hospital's marketing research director to design a questionnaire that asks cafeteria patrons to rate the cafeteria on a 7-point satisfaction scale with 1 meaning "very dissatisfied" and 7 meaning "very satisfied." Based on a focus group, 17 different cafeteria attributes are rated. In addition, the importance of each attribute is also rated on an importance scale where 1 means "unimportant" and 7 means "very important" to a respondent's decision to eat at a particular location.

Using systematic sampling over a period of one week, cafeteria users who are General Hospital employees are identified during lunch and asked to fill out a questionnaire. A total of 340 usable questionnaires are gathered by the end of the data collection phase. The marketing research director prepares the following two tables. In each table, the researcher separated the 240 weekday from the 100 weekend cafeteria users with the rationale that weekend workers are generally part-time employees. They are also younger than full-time employees. Their mean responses follow.

TABLE A

IMPORTANCE OF SELECTED CAFETERIA ATTRIBUTES BY TYPE OF PATRON

Cafeteria Attribute	*Weekday*	*Weekend*	*Sig.*
Courteous employees	5.28	5.18	0.978
Helpful employees	5.20	5.15	0.876
Quality of service	5.07	4.98	0.540

Table A (continued)

Cafeteria Attribute	Weekday	Weekend	Sig.
Freshness of lunch items	5.07	4.50	0.034
High nutritional value of lunch items	5.03	4.44	0.045
Overall quality of lunch items	4.97	4.53	0.035
Comfortable seating	4.96	4.95	0.986
Discounts for employees	4.89	4.75	0.752
Appetizing look of lunch items	4.88	4.02	0.052
Speed of lunch service	4.83	4.97	0.650
Relaxed atmosphere	4.83	5.23	0.001
Good-tasting lunch items	4.80	4.02	0.012
Adequate lighting	4.71	4.80	0.659
Good variety of lunch menu	4.60	3.53	0.002
Low price of lunch items	4.52	4.20	0.102
Large portions	4.34	3.87	0.034
Clean surroundings	4.25	4.50	0.286

Table B

Evaluation of Cafeteria Performance on Selected Attributes by Type of Patron

Cafeteria Attribute	Weekday	Weekend	Sig.
Courteous employees	5.79	5.46	0.182
Helpful employees	5.83	5.51	0.044
Quality of service	5.54	5.60	0.276
Freshness of lunch items	5.80	4.46	0.001
High nutritional value of lunch items	5.29	5.23	0.197
Overall quality of lunch items	4.48	4.46	0.568
Comfortable seating	4.63	4.53	0.389
Discounts for employees	5.45	4.56	0.009
Appetizing look of lunch items	5.65	4.64	0.045
Speed of lunch service	5.52	4.22	0.010
Relaxed atmosphere	4.96	5.63	0.061
Good-tasting lunch items	5.31	4.37	0.048
Adequate lighting	4.52	4.62	0.369
Good variety of lunch menu	4.98	3.75	0.019
Low price of lunch items	5.35	6.86	0.045
Large portions	4.43	5.43	0.038
Clean surroundings	5.56	5.24	0.286

1. Interpret these findings for Ms. Wilson. What do they say about the two subpopulations of weekday and weekend workers?
2. What managerial implications are apparent from these findings?

CASE 16.2

Lipton's Prepared Dinners

We indicated in the SPSS for Windows section on *t* tests that, in addition to tea, Lipton makes other food products, including a line of prepared rice, pasta, and other prepackaged dinners. The survey addressed several aspects of cooking such as health consciousness and where people get meal ideas. For example, we noted earlier that a series of statements, such as "I often read the cooking section of the newspaper," were administered, and respondents used a scale of 1 for "agree strongly" to 5 for "disagree strongly." There were 26 of these statements in all, plus respondents indicated demographic characteristics such as working status, marital status, age category, and education level.

An SPSS for Windows data set called LIPTON.SAV is one of the data sets provided with this textbook. It contains 100 cases with descriptive variable labels and their associated value labels. Here is a series of questions about the means of the answers to the 26 statements. Use SPSS for Windows to read in the LIPTON.SAV file, perform the appropriate analysis, and interpret your findings.

You should be aware that you have an original, full data set with many variables given SPSS variable names of X1, X2, X3, etc. The Likert statement variables are X37 through X62. You will need to figure out other variables' names using the SPSS Utilities-Variables command, and you may want to recode the Likert scale codes to be consistent with your textbook's examples. Good luck.

1. A skeptical Lipton executive claims that most respondents will give a neutral or undecided answer to the agree–disagree questions such as those used in the Lipton prepared-dinner survey. The middle position on the 5-point scale was labeled "neither agree nor disagree," and it was coded with a 3. Test the executive's hypothesis for the answers of all 100 respondents to all 26 statements. Where the hypothesis is not supported, determine 95 percent confidence intervals.
2. Using the 26 statements, investigate whether significant differences exist at the .05 level or less between (a) working status (1 = yes, 2 = no), (b) singles (1) and marrieds (2), and (c) females (1) and males (2).
3. Perform the proper statistical test and interpret your findings for each of the following claims:
   a. People are more likely to use coupons than they are to look for bargains.

   b. No difference exists between agreement of enjoying cooking and cooking from scratch.

4. Determine if significant differences at the .05 level or less exist in the levels of agreement for each of the 26 statements among the following groups: (a) different age categories, (b) different income categories, and (c) different education categories.

CHAPTER 17

Determining and Interpreting Associations between Two Variables

LEARNING OBJECTIVES

- *To learn what is meant by an "association" between variables*
- *To examine various relationships that may be construed as associations*
- *To understand where and how chi-square analysis is applied*
- *To become familiar with the use of correlations*

PRACTITIONER VIEWPOINT

Marketers are constantly asking questions about the association between two variables. "Are sales related to increases in newspaper advertising?," "Is salespersons' morale associated with increases in recognition and awards programs?," "Will market share increase if we increase our network of retail dealers?" Such fundamental business questions are often the basis of our marketing research studies.

— Ronald L. Tatham, CEO
Burke Marketing Research

Is Joe Camel a Danger to Children?

1. Establish the need for marketing research
2. Define the problem
3. Establish research objectives
4. Determine research design
5. Identify information types and sources
6. Determine methods of accessing data
7. Design data collection forms
8. Determine sample plan and size
9. Collect data
10. **Analyze data**
11. Prepare and present the final research report

Research reveals that children readily identify Joe Camel, but do they want to smoke?

Controversy arose quickly when Camel cigarettes adopted "Old Joe" the camel as its trade character in the early 1990s. Early studies collectively pointed to the use of Joe Camel as a way to induce children to smoke and thereby become exposed to a significant health risk.[1] The Federal Trade Commission became involved immediately after these reports were published, and it recommended that ads featuring Joe Camel be banned because they encouraged minors to smoke. However, the FTC later dropped this recommendation due to a lack of sufficient evidence.[2]

In a study[3] aimed at determining the impact of the Joe Camel cartoon character on children aged three to eight, a researcher tested hypotheses about children's age and their identification of trade characters. Using cross-tabulations and correlations, the researcher's found the following: First, a child's recognition of advertising symbols increases with age; and second, his or her recognition of cigarette brand advertising increases with age. Older children are better able to identify Joe Camel than are younger children. However, the pattern was consistent for a number of adult product trade characters as well. These children were able to recognize symbols such as the Energizer Bunny and others identified with Budweiser Beer, Chevrolet, Folger's coffee, and even Bell Telephone.

When asked if they liked each of the brand symbol products, including cigarettes, 96 percent said they disliked cigarettes and 97 percent indicated that cigarettes were "bad for you." About 70 percent indicated that cigarettes were for adults, and this pattern was not associated with the child's age. The researcher concludes that Joe Camel, although recognizable to many children, is not associated with their intentions to smoke cigarettes.

This chapter illustrates the usefulness of statistical analyses beyond simple descriptive measures and statistical inference. Often, marketers are interested in relationships among variables. For example, Frito-Lay wants to know what kinds of people and under what circumstances these people choose to buy Doritos, Fritos, and any of the other items in the Frito-Lay line. The Pontiac Division of General Motors wants to know what types of individuals would respond favorably to the various style changes proposed for the Firebird. A newspaper wants to understand the life-style characteristics of its prospective readers so that it is able to modify or change sections in the newspaper to better suit its audience. Furthermore, the newspaper desires information about various types of subscribers so as to communicate this information to its advertisers, helping them in copy design and advertisement placement within the various newspaper sections. For all of these cases, there are statistical procedures available, termed **associative analyses,** which determine answers to these questions. Associative analyses determine whether stable relationships exist between two variables; they are the central topic of this chapter.

Associative analyses determine whether stable relationships exist between two variables.

We begin the chapter by describing the four different types of relationships possible between two variables. Then, we describe cross-tabulations and indicate how a cross-tabulation can be used to compute a chi-square value which, in turn, can be assessed to determine whether or not a statistically significant association exists between the two variables. For cross-tabulations, we move to a general discussion of correlation coefficients, and we illustrate the use of Pearson product moment correlations as well as rank correlations. As in our previous analysis chapters, we show you SPSS for Windows steps to perform these analyses and the resulting output.

TYPES OF RELATIONSHIPS BETWEEN TWO VARIABLES

A **relationship** is a consistent and systematic linkage between two variables. This linkage is *statistical,* not necessarily causal. A causal linkage is one in which you are certain one variable affected the other one, but with a statistical linkage you cannot be certain because some other variable might have had some influence. Associative analysis procedures are useful because they determine if there is a consistent and systematic relationship between the presence (or amount) of one variable and the presence (or amount) of another variable. There are four basic types of relationships between two variables: nonmonotonic, monotonic, linear, and curvilinear. A discussion of each follows.

Nonmonotonic Relationships

A nonmonotonic relationship means two variables are associated, but only in a very general sense.

A **nonmonotonic relationship** is one in which the presence (or absence) of one variable is systematically associated with the presence (or absence) of another variable. The term "nonmonotonic" means essentially that there is no discernible *direction* to the relationship, but a relationship exists. For example, McDonald's knows from experience that morning customers typically purchase coffee whereas noon customers typically purchase soft drinks. The relationship is in no way exclusive—there is no guarantee that a morning customer will always order a coffee or that an afternoon customer will always order a soft drink. In general, though, this relationship exists, as can be seen in Figure 17.1. The nonmonotonic relationship is simply that the morning customer tends to purchase breakfast foods such as eggs, biscuits, and coffee, and the afternoon customers tend to purchase lunch items such as burgers, fries, and soft drinks.

Here are some other examples of nonmonotonic relationships: (1) people who live in apartments do not buy lawn mowers but homeowners do; (2) tourists in Daytona Beach, Florida, during spring break are likely to be college students, not families; and (3) Nintendo game players are typically children, not adults. Again each example reports that the presence (absence) of one aspect of some object tends to be joined to the presence (absence) of an aspect of some other object. But the association is very general, and we must state each one by spelling it out verbally. In other words, we know only the general pattern of presence or nonpresence with a nonmonotonic relationship.

Monotonic Relationships

A monotonic relationship means you know the general direction of the relationship between two variables.

Monotonic relationships are ones in which the researcher can assign only a *general direction* to the association between the two variables. There are two types of monotonic relationships: increasing and decreasing. Monotonic increasing relationships are those in which one variable increases as the other variable increases. As you would guess, monotonic decreasing relationships are those in which one variable increases as the other variable decreases. You should note that in neither case is there any indication of the exact amount of

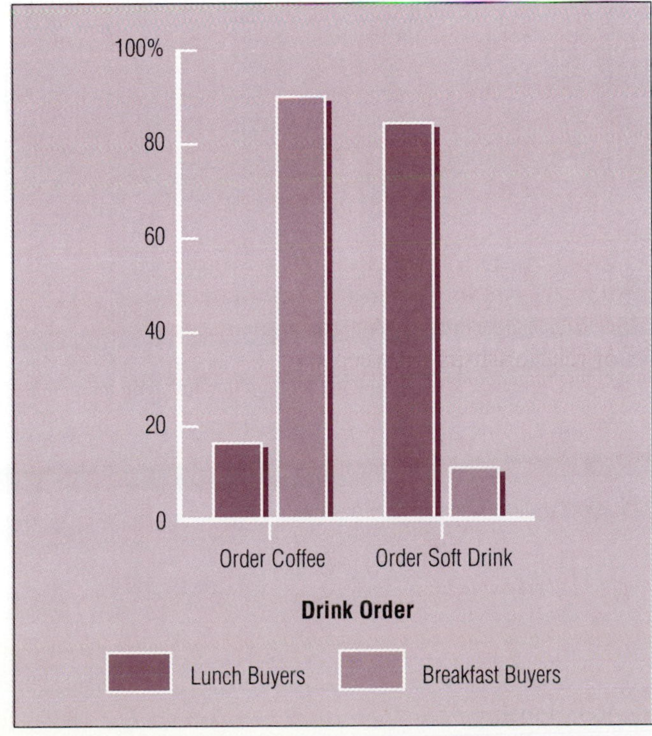

Figure 17.1

McDonald's Example of a Nonmonotonic Relationship

change in one variable as the other changes. "Monotonic" means that the relationship can be described only in a general directional sense. Beyond this, precision in the description is lacking. The following example should help to explain this concept.

Monotonic relationships can be increasing or decreasing.

The owner of a shoe store knows that older children tend to require larger shoe sizes than do younger children, but there is no way to equate a child's age with the right shoe size. No universal rule exists as to the rate of growth of a child's foot nor to the final shoe size he or she will attain. There is, however, a monotonic increasing relationship between a child's age and shoe size. At the same time, a monotonic decreasing relationship exists between a child's age and the amount of involvement of his or her parents in the purchase of his or her shoes. As Figure 17.2 illustrates, very young children often have virtually no input into the purchase decision, whereas older children tend to gain more and more control over the purchase decision process until they ultimately become adults and have complete control over the decision. Once again, no universal rule operates as to the amount of parental influence or the point in time at which the child becomes independent and gains complete control over the decision-making process. It is simply known that younger children have less influence in the decision-making process, and older children have more influence in the shoe purchase decision. The relationship is therefore monotonic.

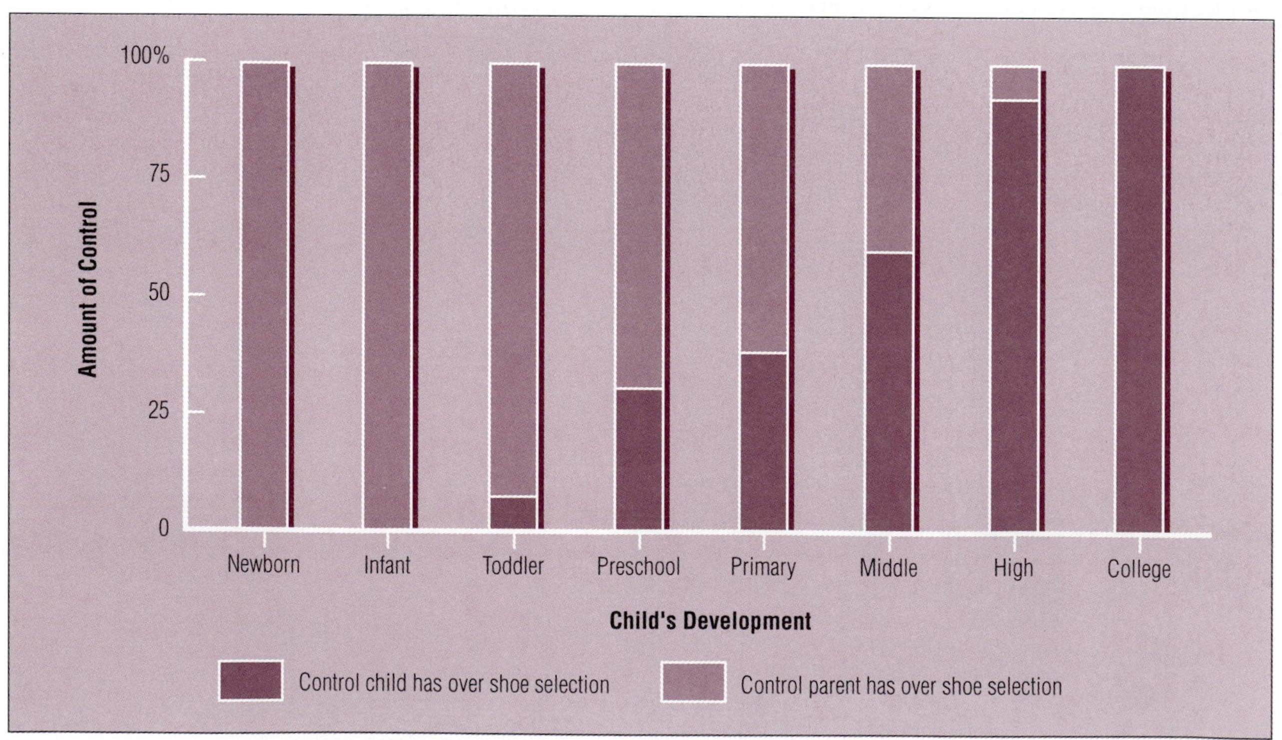

Figure 17.2

Child's Control of His/Her Shoe Purchases: Monotonic Relationship

Linear Relationships

A linear relationship means the two variables have a "straight-line" relationship.

Now, we will turn to a more precise relationship. Perhaps the most intuitive association between two variables is a linear relationship. A **linear relationship** is a "straight-line association" between two variables. Here, knowledge of the amount of one variable will automatically yield knowledge of the amount of the other variable as a consequence of applying the linear or straight-line formula that is known to exist between them. In its general form, a straight-line formula is as follows:

$$y = a + bx$$

where

y = the dependent variable being estimated or predicted

a = the intercept

b = the slope

x = the independent variable used to predict the dependent variable

The terms "intercept" and "slope" should be familiar to you, but if they are not, do not be concerned as we describe the straight-line formula in detail in the next chapter. We also clarify the terms "independent" and "dependent" in chapter 18.

Linear relationships are quite precise.

It should be apparent to you that a linear relationship is much more precise and contains a great deal more information than does a monotonic relationship. By simply substituting the values of a and b, an exact amount can be determined for y given any value of x. For example, South-Western Book Company hires college student representatives to work in the summer. These student representatives are put through an intensified sales training program and then they are divided into teams. Each team is given a specific territory, and each individual is assigned a particular district within that territory. The student representative then goes from house to house in the district making cold calls, attempting to sell children's books. Let us assume that the amount of sales is linearly related to the number of cold calls made. In this special case, no sales calls determines zero sales, or $a = 0$. If, on average, every 10th sales call resulted in a sale and the typical sale is \$62, then the average per call would be \$6.20. The linear relationship between total sales (y) and number of sales calls (x) is as follows:

$$y = 0 + 6.20x$$

Thus, if the college salesperson makes 100 cold calls in any given day, the expected total revenues would be \$620 (\$6.20 times 100 calls). Certainly, our student sales rep would not derive exactly \$620 for every 100 calls, but the linear relationship shows what is expected to happen, on average.

Curvilinear Relationships

A curvilinear relationship means some smooth curve pattern describes the association.

Now, we turn to the last type of relationship. **Curvilinear relationships** are those in which one variable is associated with another variable, but the relationship is described by a curve rather than a straight line. In other words, the formula for a curved relationship is used rather than the formula for a straight line. Many curvilinear patterns are possible. For example, the relationship may be an S-shape, a J-shape, or some other curved-shape pattern. An example of a curvilinear relationship with which you should be familiar is the product life-cycle curve that describes the sales pattern of a new product over time that grows slowly during its introduction and then spurts upward rapidly during its growth stage and finally plateaus or slows down considerably as the market becomes saturated. Curvilinear relationships are beyond the scope of this text; nonetheless, it is important to list them as a type of relationship that can be investigated through the use of special-purpose statistical procedures.

CHARACTERIZING RELATIONSHIPS BETWEEN VARIABLES

Depending on the type, a relationship can be characterized in three ways: by its presence, direction, and strength of association. We need to describe these before taking up specific statistical analyses of associations between two variables.

Presence

Presence means a relationship exists between two variables.

Presence refers to whether any systematic relationship exists between the two variables of interest. Presence is a statistical issue. By this statement, we mean that the marketing researcher relies on statistical significance tests to determine whether a particular association is present in the data. The previous chapter on statistical inference introduced the concept of a null hypothesis. With associative analysis, the null hypothesis states there is no association present and the appropriate statistical test is applied to test this hypothesis. If the test results reject the null hypothesis, then an association is present. We describe the statistical tests used in associative analysis later in this chapter.

Direction

Direction means that you know if the relationship is positive or negative.

In the case of monotonic and linear relationships, associations may also be described with regard to *direction.* As we described earlier, a monotonic relationship may be increasing or decreasing. In the case of the b or slope of a linear relationship, if b is positive, then the linear relationship is increasing; and if b is negative, then the linear relationship is decreasing. But positive or negative direction is inappropriate for nonmonotonic relationships, because we can only describe the pattern verbally. It will soon become clear to you that the scaling assumptions of variables having nonmonotonic association negate the directional aspects of the relationship. Nevertheless, we can verbally describe the association as we have in our examples, and that statement substitutes for direction.

Strength of Association

Strength means you know how consistent the relationship is.

Again, depending on the type of relationship being investigated, the *strength of association* between two variables can be envisioned as strong, moderate, weak, or nonexistent. The nonexistent case occurs when the marketing researcher finds no presence of a consistent and systematic linkage between two variables. When a consistent and systematic association is found to be present between two variables, it is then up to the marketing researcher to ascertain

Some associations are stronger than others.

the strength of association. Strong associations are those in which there is a high probability of the two variables' exhibiting a dependable relationship, regardless of the type of relationship being analyzed. A low degree of association, on the other hand, is one in which there is a low probability of the two variables' exhibiting a dependable relationship. The relationship exists between the variables, but it is less evident.

There is an orderly procedure for determining presence, direction, and strength of a relationship. First, you must decide what type of relationship can exist between the two variables of interest. The answer to this question depends on the scaling assumptions of the variables; as we illustrated earlier, low-level (nominal) scales can embody only imprecise relationships, but high-level (interval or ratio) scales can incorporate very precise relationships. Once you identify the appropriate relationship type as either monotonic, nonmonotonic, or linear, the next step is to determine whether that relationship actually exists in the population you are analyzing. This step requires a statistical test, and, again, we describe the proper test for each of these three relationship types beginning with the next section of this chapter.

Based on scaling assumptions, first determine the type of relationship, and then perform the appropriate statistical test.

Once you determine that a true relationship does exist in the population by means of the correct statistical test, you then establish its direction. Again, the type of relationship dictates how you describe its direction. You might have to inspect the relationship in a table or graph, or you might need only to look for a positive or negative sign before the computed statistic. Finally, the strength of the relationship remains to be judged. Some associative analysis statistics indicate the strength in a very straightforward manner—that is, just by their absolute size. With nominal-scaled variables, however, you must inspect the pattern to judge the strength. We describe this procedure next.

CROSS-TABULATIONS

Cross-tabulation and the associated chi-square value is used to assess whether a nonmonotonic relationship exists between two nominal-scaled variables.

Cross-tabulation and the associated chi-square value is used to assess whether a nonmonotonic relationship exists between two nominal-scaled variables. Remember that nonmonotonic relationships are those in which the presence of one variable coincides with the presence of another variable.

The Venn diagram in Figure 17.3 illustrates an appropriate example for chi-square analysis. In the figure, white-collar workers, who are identified by the circle on the right, and blue-collar workers, who are identified by the circle on the left, are encompassed by a larger circle, which identifies the beer mar-

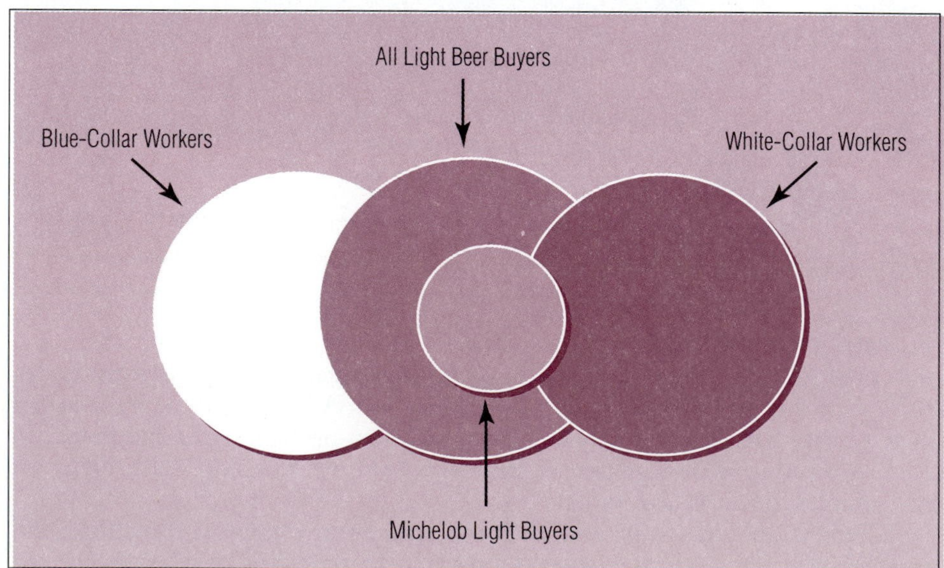

Figure 17.3

Michelob Light Preference and Occupational Category

ket as a whole. Within the larger circle is found a smaller circle, which identifies buyers of a particular brand. In this case, the brand is Michelob Light beer. The buyers' circle includes a much greater percentage of the white-collar consumers' circle than it does of the blue-collar workers. In other words, this diagram reveals that a greater percentage of white-collar workers buy Michelob Light than do blue-collar workers.

A cross-tabulation consists of rows and columns defined by the categories classifying each variable.

Venn diagrams provide a way of visualizing nonmonotonic relationships, but the most common method of presentation for these situations is through the use of a **cross-tabulation table,** defined as a table in which data is compared using a row and column format. A cross-tabulation table is sometimes referred to as an "$r \times c$" (r-by-c) table because it comprises rows and columns. The intersection of a row and a column is called a **cross-tabulation cell.** A cross-tabulation table for the Venn diagram is presented in Table 17.1 on page 542. Notice that we have identified the four cells with lines for the rows and columns. The columns are in vertical alignment and are indicated in this table as either "Buyer" or "Nonbuyer" of Michelob Light, whereas the rows are indicated as "White Collar" or "Blue Collar" for occupation.

Look at the Frequencies Table section in Table 17.1. The upper left-hand cell number identifies people in the sample who are both white-collar workers and buyers of Michelob Light (152), and the cell to its right identifies the number of individuals who are white-collar workers who do not buy Michelob Light (8). These cell numbers represent frequencies; that is, the number of respondents who possess the quality indicated by the row label as well as the quality indicated by the column label.

A cross-classification table can have four types of numbers in each cell: frequency, raw percentage, column percentage, and row percentage.

Table 17.1 illustrates how at least four different sets of numbers can be computed for cells in the table. These four sets are the frequencies table, the raw percentages table, the column percentages table, and the row percentages table. The **frequencies table** contains the raw numbers determined from the preliminary tabulation. The lower right-hand number of 200 refers to the total sample size, sometimes called the "grand total." Just above it are the totals for the number of white-collar (160) and blue-collar (40) occupation respondents in the sample. Going to the left of the grand total are the totals for Michelob Light nonbuyers (34) and buyers (166) in the sample. The four cells are the totals for the intersection points: 152 white-collar Michelob Light buyers, 8 white-collar nonbuyers, 14 blue-collar Michelob Light buyers, and 26 blue-collar nonbuyers.

Raw percentages are cell frequencies divided by the grand total.

These raw frequencies can be converted to raw percentages by dividing each by the grand total. The second cross-tabulation table, the **raw percentages table,** contains the percentages of the raw frequency numbers just discussed. The grand total location now has 100 percent (or 200/200) of the grand total. Above it are 80 percent and 20 percent for the raw percentages of white-collar occupational respondents and blue-collar occupational respondents, respectively, in the sample. Divide a couple of the cells just to verify that you understand how they are derived. For instance $152 \div 200 = 76\%$.

Two additional cross-tabulation tables can be presented, and these are more valuable in revealing underlying relationships. The **column percentages table** divides the raw frequencies by its column total raw frequency. That is, the formula is as follows:

$$\text{Column cell percent} = \frac{\text{Cell frequency}}{\text{Total of cells in that column}}$$

TABLE 17.1

Cross-Tabulation Tables for a Michelob Light Survey

FREQUENCIES TABLE

		BUYER	NONBUYER	TOTALS
Occupational Status	WHITE COLLAR	152	8	160
	BLUE COLLAR	14	26	40
	TOTALS	166	34	200

RAW PERCENTAGES TABLE

		BUYER	NONBUYER	TOTALS
Occupational Status	WHITE COLLAR	76% (152)	4% (8)	80% (160)
	BLUE COLLAR	7% (14)	13% (26)	20% (40)
	TOTALS	83% (166)	17% (34)	100% (200)

COLUMN PERCENTAGES TABLE

		BUYER	NONBUYER	TOTALS
Occupational Status	WHITE COLLAR	92% (152)	24% (8)	80% (160)
	BLUE COLLAR	8% (14)	76% (26)	20% (40)
	TOTALS	100% (166)	100% (34)	100% (200)

ROW PERCENTAGES TABLE

		BUYER	NONBUYER	TOTALS
Occupational Status	WHITE COLLAR	95% (152)	5% (8)	100% (160)
	BLUE COLLAR	35% (14)	65% (26)	100% (40)
TOTALS		83% (166)	17% (34)	100% (200)

For instance, it is apparent that of the nonbuyers, 24 percent were white-collar but 76 percent were blue-collar respondents. Note the reverse pattern for the buyers group: 92 percent of white-collar respondents were Michelob Light buyers and 8 percent were blue-collar buyers. You are beginning to see the nonmonotonic relationship.

The **row percentages table** presents the data with the row totals as the 100 percent base for each. That is, a row cell percentage is computed as follows:

Row (column) percentages are row (column) cell frequencies divided by the row (column) total.

$$\text{Row cell percent} = \frac{\text{Cell frequency}}{\text{Total of cells in that row}}$$

Now, it is possible to see that, of the white-collar respondents, 95 percent were buyers and 5 percent were nonbuyers. As you compare the Row Percentages Table to the Column Percentages Table, you should detect the relationship between Occupational Status and Michelob Light beer preference. Can you state it at this time?

An unequal percentage concentration of individuals in a few cells, as we have in this example, illustrates the possible presence of a nonmonotonic association. If we had found that approximately 25 percent of the sample had fallen in each of the four cells, *no relationship* would be found to exist—it would be equally probable for any person to be a Michelob Light buyer or nonbuyer and a white- or a blue-collar worker. However, the large concentrations of individuals in two particular cells here suggests that there is a high probability that a buyer of Michelob Light beer is also a white-collar worker, and there is also a tendency for nonbuyers to work in blue-collar occupations. In other words, there is probably an association between occupational status and the beer-buying behavior of individuals in this particular sample.

Cross-tabulations are useful whenever you want to compare two distributions. For example, suppose your sister, who is still in high school, has made good grades, but she is going to take the SAT next month. She has been worrying about it because she knows that colleges place much emphasis on the SAT. Marketing Research Insight 17.1 (page 544) will provide some insight as to how you might console her the next time you talk to her on the telephone.

CHI-SQUARE ANALYSIS

Chi-square (χ^2) analysis is the examination of frequencies for two nominal-scaled variables in a cross-tabulation table to determine whether the variables have a nonmonotonic relationship. The formal procedure for chi-square analysis begins when the researcher formulates a statistical null hypothesis that the two variables under investigation are *not* associated. Actually, it is not necessary for the researcher to state this hypothesis in a formal sense, for chi-square analysis always implicitly takes this hypothesis into account. Stated somewhat differently, chi-square analysis always begins with the assumption that no association exists between the two nominal-scaled variables under analysis.

Chi-square analysis assesses nonmonotonic associations in cross-tabulation tables.

Observed and Expected Frequencies

The statistical procedure is as follows. The first cross-tabulation table in Table 17.1 contains **observed frequencies,** which are the actual cell counts in the cross-tabulation table. These observed frequencies are compared to **expected frequencies,** which are defined as the theoretical frequencies that are derived from this hypothesis of no association between the two variables. The degree to which the observed frequencies depart from the expected frequencies is expressed in a single number called the chi-square statistic. The computed chi-

Observed frequencies are the counts for each cell found in the sample.

MARKETING RESEARCH INSIGHT 17.1

Why Did You Take the SAT?

Practically every university requires applicants to take the SAT (Scholastic Aptitude Test) or the ACT. About 1.7 million high school students take the SAT annually to determine their admission status. But was all that worry, anxiety, frustration, and, perhaps even panic you might have gone through justified? Are SAT scores associated with grades in college?

To answer these questions, two researchers looked at the SAT scores of 2,781 college students. They determined if there was an association between college freshman grade point average (GPA) and high school class ranking alone. They also determined if there was an association between GPA and high school class rankings plus SAT scores.

What did they find?

- *College GPAs were highly associated with high school class ranking.*
- *SAT scores were also highly associated with college GPAs.*

Performance in high school is highly associated with performance in college. The researchers, therefore, feel that the SAT is redundant and urge universities to rethink their requirement of applicants to take the SAT.

Adapted from *James Crouse, and Dale Trusheim, "How Colleges Can Correctly Determine Selection Benefits from the SAT,"* Harvard Educational Review, *vol. 61, no. 2 (1991), 125–147.*

square statistic is then compared to a table chi-square value (at a chosen level of significance) to determine whether the computed value is significantly different from zero.

Expected frequencies are calculated based on the null hypothesis of no association between the two variables under investigation.

Here's a simple example to help you understand what we just stated. Suppose you perform a blind taste test with 10 of your friends. You let each one try Diet Pepsi Cola served in a paper cup with no identification and ask him or her to guess whether it is Diet Pepsi or Diet Coke. If your friends had no idea of which brand was involved, they would guess randomly, so you would expect 5 to guess Diet Pepsi and 5 to guess Diet Coke. This is your null hypothesis: There is no relationship between the diet cola brand being tested and the guess. But you find that 8 of your friends correctly guess "Diet Pepsi," and 2 incorrectly guess "Diet Coke." In other words, you have found a departure in your observed frequencies from the expected frequencies. It looks like your friends can correctly identify Diet Pepsi about 80 percent of the time. There seems to be a relationship, but we are not certain of its statistical significance, because we have not done any significance tests. The chi-square statistic is used to perform such a test.

The expected frequencies are those that would be found if there were no association between the two variables. Remember, this is the null hypothesis. About the only "difficult" part of chi-square analysis is in the computation of the expected frequencies. The computation is accomplished using the following equation:

Here are calculations for expected cell frequencies.

$$\text{Expected cell frequency} = \frac{\text{Cell column total} \times \text{Cell row total}}{\text{Grand total}}$$

The application of this equation generates a number for each cell that would have occurred *if* the study had taken place and *no associations existed.* Returning to our Michelob Light beer example, you were told that 160 white-collar and 40 blue-collar consumers had been sampled, and it was found that there were 166 buyers and 34 nonbuyers of Michelob Light. The expected frequency for each cell, assuming no association, calculated with the expected cell frequency is as follows:

$$\text{White-collar buyer} = \frac{160 \times 166}{200} = 132.8$$

$$\text{White-collar nonbuyer} = \frac{160 \times 34}{200} = 27.2$$

$$\text{Blue-collar buyer} = \frac{40 \times 166}{200} = 33.2$$

$$\text{Blue-collar nonbuyer} = \frac{40 \times 34}{200} = 6.8$$

The Computed χ^2 Value

Next, compare the observed frequencies to these expected frequencies. The formula for this computation is as follows:

The computed chi-square value compares observed to expected frequencies.

$$\chi^2 = \sum_{i-1}^{n} \frac{(\text{Observed}_i - \text{Expected}_i)^2}{\text{Expected}_i}$$

where

Observed_i = observed frequency in cell i,

Expected_i = expected frequency in cell i,

n = number of cells

Applied to our Michelob beer example,

$$\chi^2 = \frac{(152 - 132.8)^2}{132.8} + \frac{(8 - 27.2)^2}{27.2} + \frac{(14 - 33.2)^2}{33.2} + \frac{(26 - 6.8)^2}{6.8}$$

$$= 81.64$$

You can see from the equation that each expected frequency is compared to the observed frequency and squared to adjust for any negative values and to avoid the cancellation effect. This value is divided by the expected frequency to adjust for cell size differences, and these amounts are summed across all of the cells. If there are many large deviations of observed frequencies from the expected frequencies, the computed chi-square value will increase; but if there are only a few slight deviations from the expected frequencies, the computed chi-square number will be small. In other words, the computed chi-square value is really a summary indication of how far away from the expected fre-

The chi-square statistic summarizes how far away from the expected frequencies the observed cell frequencies are found to be.

quencies the observed frequencies are found to be. As such, it expresses the departure of the sample findings from the null hypothesis of no association.

Let us apply this equation to the example of your 10 friends guessing about Diet Pepsi or Diet Coke. We already agreed that if they guessed randomly, you would find 5 guessing for each brand, on a 50–50 split. But if we found an 80–20 vote for Diet Pepsi, you would conclude that they could recognize Diet Pepsi. How did you decide that your friends could identify Diet Pepsi? You probably compared the observed 80 percent to the expected 50 percent and found a difference of 30 percent. If your friends were random guessers, the difference would be 0, so you decided that 30 percent was sufficiently far from 0 to justify your conclusion that your null hypothesis was not supported.

To determine the chi-square value, we calculate as follows:

$$\chi^2 = \sum_{i-1}^{n} \frac{(\text{Observed}_i - \text{Expected}_i)^2}{\text{Expected}_i}$$

$$= \frac{(8-5)^2}{5} + \frac{(2-5)^2}{5}$$

$$= 3.6$$

Remember, you need to use the frequencies, not the percentages.

Chi-square analysis is sometimes referred to as a "goodness of fit" test.

Some researchers think of a chi-square analysis as a "goodness-of-fit" test. It assesses how closely the actual frequencies fit the pattern of the expected frequencies. We have provided Marketing Research Insight 17.2 as an illustration of how chi-square analysis works.[4]

The Chi-Square Distribution

Now that you've learned how to calculate a chi-square value, you need to know if it is statistically significant. In the previous chapter, we described that the *F* distribution and Student's *t* distribution, both of which exist in tables, are used by a researcher or a computer statistical program to determine level of significance. Chi-square analysis requires the use of a different distribution. The **chi-square distribution** is skewed to the right and the rejection region is always at the right-hand tail of the distribution. It differs from the normal and *t* distributions in that it changes its shape depending on the situation at hand, but it is similar to the *F* distribution in that it does not have negative values. Figure 17.4 shows examples of two chi-square distributions.

The chi-square distribution's shape changes depending on the number of degrees of freedom.

The chi-square distribution's shape is determined by the number of degrees of freedom. The figure shows that the more the degrees of freedom, the more the curve's tail is pulled to the right. Or, in other words, the more the degrees of freedom, the larger the chi-square value must be to fall in the rejection region for the null hypothesis.

It is a simple matter to determine the number of degrees of freedom. In a cross-tabulation table, the degrees of freedom are found through the formula below:

$$\text{Degrees of freedom} = (r - 1)\ (c - 1)$$

where *r* is the number of *r*ows and *c* is the number of *c*olumns.

The computed chi-square value is compared to a table value to determine statistical significance.

A table of chi-square values contains critical points that determine the break between acceptance and rejection regions at various levels of significance. It also

MARKETING RESEARCH INSIGHT 17.2

"Zeroing in" on Goodness-of-Fit

Can you guess the next number based on the apparent pattern of 1,3,5? Okay, what about this series: 1,6,11,16?

In the first series, you realize that 2 was added to determine the next number (1,3,5,7,9, and so on). You looked at the series and noticed the equal intervals of 2. You then created a mental expectation of the series based on your suspected pattern.

Let us take the second series because it is a bit more difficult. Suppose your first inclination was to add a 3 to the previous number. Here is your expected series and the actual one compared:

Expected	1	4	7	10
Actual	1	6	11	16
Difference	0	2	4	6

Oops, not much of a match here. So let's try a 4.

Expected	1	5	9	13
Actual	1	6	11	16
Difference	0	1	2	3

Getting closer, but still not there. Now try a 5.

Expected	1	6	11	16
Actual	1	6	11	16
Difference	0	0	0	0

You have been performing "goodness-of-fit" tests. Notice that the differences became smaller as you zeroed in on the true pattern. (Catch the pun?) In other words, when the actual numbers are equal to the expected numbers, there is no difference, and the fit is perfect. This is the concept used in chi-square analysis. When the differences are small, you have a good fit to the expected values. When the differences are larger, you have a poor fit, and your hypothesis (the expected number sequence) is incorrect.

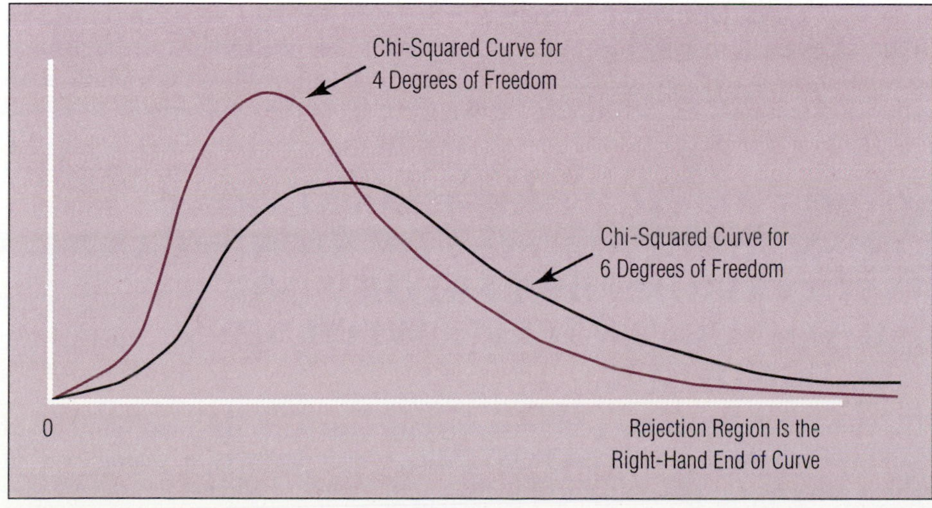

Figure 17.4

The chi-square curve's shape depends on the degrees of freedom.

takes into account the numbers of degrees of freedom associated with each curve. That is, a computed chi-square value says nothing by itself—you must consider the number of degrees of freedom in the cross-tabulation table because more degrees of freedom are indicative of higher critical chi-square table values for the same level of significance. The logic of this situation stems from the number of cells. With more cells, there is more opportunity for departure from the expected values. The higher table values adjust for potential inflation due to chance alone. After all, we want to detect real nonmonotonic relationships, not phantom ones.

Computer statistical programs look up table chi-square values and print out the probability of support for the null hypothesis.

Virtually all computer statistical analysis programs have chi-square tables in memory and print out the probability of the null hypothesis. Let us repeat this point: The program itself will take into account the number of degrees of freedom and determine the probability of support for the null hypothesis. This probability is the percentage of the area under the chi-square curve that lies to the right of the computed chi-square value. When rejection of the null hypothesis occurs, we have found a statistically significant nonmonotonic association existing between the two variables.

How to Interpret a Chi-Square Result

How does one interpret a chi-square result? The chi-square analysis yields the probability that the researcher would find evidence in support of the null hypothesis if he or she repeated the study many, many times with independent samples. For example, if the chi-square analysis yielded a 0.02 probability for the null hypothesis, the researcher would conclude that only 2 percent of the time he or she would find evidence to support the null hypothesis. This means there *is* a significant association.

A significant chi-square means the researcher should look at the cross-tabulation row and column percentages to "see" the association pattern.

It must be pointed out that chi-square analysis is simply a method to determine whether a nonmonotonic association exists between two variables. Chi-square does not indicate the nature of the association, and it indicates only roughly the strength of association by its size. It is best interpreted as a prerequisite to looking more closely at the two variables to discern the nature of the association that exists between them. When the computed chi-square value is small, then the null hypothesis or the hypothesis of independence between the two variables is generally assumed to be true. It is not worth the marketing researcher's time to focus on associations, because they are more a function of sampling error than they are of meaningful relationships between the two variables. However, when chi-square analysis identifies a relationship, the researcher can be assured that he or she is not wasting time and is actually pursuing a real association, a relationship that truly exists between the two variables in the population.

View: "Michelob Light: Using Crosstabulations"

MICHELOB LIGHT BEER: ANALYZING CROSS-TABULATIONS FOR SIGNIFICANT ASSOCIATIONS BY PERFORMING CHI-SQUARE ANALYSIS WITH SPSS FOR WINDOWS

The command sequence to perform a chi-square test with SPSS for Windows is STATISTICS-SUMMARIZE-CROSSTABS, which leads to a dialog box in which you can select the variables for chi-square analysis. We will use the Miche-

What demographic characteristics are associated with Michelob Light beer drinkers? Cross-tabulation analysis can be used to answer this question.

lob Light beer data that we have been describing so you can see how SPSS operates. In our example, we have selected occup (Occupation Classification) as the row variable, and mich (Buyer or Nonbuyer of Michelob Light) as the column variable. There are three options buttons at the bottom of the box. The Cells . . . option leads to the specification of observed frequencies, expected frequencies, row percentages, column percentages, and so forth. The Statistics . . . button opens up a menu of statistics that can be computed from cross-tabulation tables. Of course, the only one we want is the chi-square option.

The resulting output is found in Table 17.2 on page 550. In the Case Processing Summary table, it is apparent that 200 cases were processed, and there were no missing cases. In the middle table, you can see that we have variable and value labels, and the table contains the raw frequency as the first entry in each cell. Also, the row percentages are reported along with each row and column total. In the final table, there is information on the chi-square analysis result. For our purposes, the only relevant statistic is the "Pearson Chi-Square," which you can see has been computed to be 81.644. The *df* pertains to the number of degrees of freedom, which is 1; and the Asymp. Sig. corresponds to the probability of support for the null hypothesis. Significance in this example is .000, which means that there is practically no support for the hypothesis that occupation and Michelob Light preference are *not* associated. In other words, they *are* related. (Actually, the probability is not exactly equal to zero because SPSS reports only three decimal places. If it reported, say, 10 places, you would see a number somewhere past the third decimal place.)

So, SPSS has effected the first step in determining a nonmonotonic association. Through chi-square analysis it has signaled that a statistically significant association actually exists. The next step is to fathom the nature of the association. Remember that with a nonmonotonic relationship, you must inspect the pattern and describe it verbally. When we looked for the pattern in

TABLE 17.2

Cross-Tabulation and Chi-Square Output from SPSS for Windows

Case Processing Summary

	Cases					
	Valid		Missing		Total	
	N	Percent	N	Percent	N	Percent
OCCUPATION CLASSIFICATION * BUYER OR NONBUYER OF MICH	200	100.0%	0	.0%	200	100.0%

OCCUPATION CLASSIFICATION * BUYER OR NONBUYER OF MICH Crosstabulation

			BUYER OR NONBUYER OF MICH		Total
			BUYER	NONBUYER	
OCCUPATION CLASSIFICATION	WHITE COLLAR	Count	152	8	160
		% within OCCUPATION CLASSIFICATION	95.0%	5.0%	100.0%
	BLUE COLLAR	Count	14	26	40
		% within OCCUPATION CLASSIFICATION	35.0%	65.0%	100.0%
Total		Count	166	34	200
		% within OCCUPATION CLASSIFICATION	83.0%	17.0%	100.0%

Chi-Square Tests

	Value	df	Asymp. Sig. (2-sided)	Exact Sig. (2-sided)	Exact Sig. (1-sided)
Pearson Chi-Square	81.644[b]	1	.000		
Continuity Correction[a]	77.447	1	.000		
Likelihood Ratio	67.034	1	.000		
Fisher's Exact Test				.000	.000
Linear-by-Linear Association	81.236	1	.000		
N of Valid Cases	200				

a. Computed only for a 2x2 table

b. 0 cells (.0%) have expected count less than 5. The minimum expected count is 6.80.

our example, we converted the frequencies into row and column percentages. Now, you have a cross-tabulation table with row percentages in their respective cells. If you compare this output with our earlier examples, you will see that the percentages are the same, except that SPSS reports one decimal place, whereas we did not. The row percentages show that 95 percent of all white-collar respondents are Michelob Light buyers, but 65 percent of the blue-collar respondents are nonbuyers. So look at either the column percentages or the row percentages to identify the nonmonotonic relationship in the data. (Note Table 17.2 only shows row percentages. However, SPSS will easily provide you both row and column percentages by clicking the Cells . . . option.)

When you do so, you will have an appreciation of the pattern or nature of the association, and the percentages indicate its relative strength. More importantly, because the relationship was determined to be statistically significant, you can be assured that this association and the relationship you have observed will hold for the population that this sample represents.

CORRELATION COEFFICIENTS AND COVARIATION

Correlations range from −1.0 to +1.0.

The **correlation coefficient** is an index number, constrained to fall between the range of −1.0 and +1.0, that communicates both the strength and the direction of association between two variables. The amount of association between two variables is communicated by the absolute size of the correlation coefficient, whereas its sign communicates the direction of the association. Stated in a slightly different manner, a correlation coefficient indicates the degree of "covariation" between two variables. **Covariation** is defined as the amount of change in one variable systematically associated with a change in another variable. The greater the absolute size of the correlation coefficient, the greater is the covariation between the two variables, or the stronger is their association.

Your Student Assistant movie shows graphical representations of covariation.

Let us take up the statistical significance of a correlation coefficient first. Regardless of its absolute value, a correlation that is *not* statistically significant has no meaning at all. This is because of the null hypothesis, which states that the population correlation coefficient is equal to zero. If this null hypothesis is rejected (statistically significant correlation), then you can be assured that a correlation other than zero will be found in the population. But if the sample correlation is found to be not significant, the population correlation will be zero. Here is a question. If you can answer it correctly, you understand the statistical significance of a correlation. If you repeated a correlational survey many, many times and computed the average for a correlation that was *not* significant across all of these surveys, what would be the result? (The answer is zero because if the correlation is not significant, the null hypothesis is true, and the population correlation is zero.)

To use a correlation, you must first establish that it is statistically significant from zero.

How do you determine the statistical significance of a correlation coefficient? Tables exist that give the lowest value of the correlation coefficient significant for a given sample size. However, most computer statistical programs will indicate the statistical significance level of the computed correlation coefficient. Your SPSS program provides the significance in the form of the probability that the null hypothesis is supported. In addition, it will also allow you to indicate a directional hypothesis about the size of the expected correlation just as with a directional means hypothesis test.

Rules of thumb exist concerning the strength of a correlation based on its absolute size.

After we have established that a correlation coefficient is statistically significant, we can talk about some general rules of thumb concerning the strength of association. Correlation coefficients that fall between +1.00 and +.81 or between −1.00 and −.81 are generally considered to be "high." That is, the association between the two variables is strong. Those correlations that fall between +.80 and +.61 or −.80 and −.61 generally indicate a "moderate" association. Those that fall between +.60 and +.41 or −.60 and −.41 are typically considered to be "low," and they denote a weak association. Finally, any correlation that falls between the range of ±.21 and ±.40 is usually considered indicative of a very weak association between the variables. Next, any correlation that is equal to or less than ±.20 is typically uninteresting to marketing researchers because it rarely identifies a meaningful association between two variables. We have provided Table 17.3 as a reference on these rules of thumb. As you use these guidelines, remember two things: First, we are assuming that the statistical significance of the correlation has been established. Second, researchers make up their own rules of thumb, so you may encounter someone whose guidelines differ slightly from those in the table.

In any case, it is helpful to think in terms of the closeness of the correlation coefficient to zero or to ±1.00. Correlation coefficients that are close to zero show that there is no systematic association between the two variables, whereas those that are closer to +1.00 or −1.00 express that there is some systematic association between the variables.

A correlation indicates the strength association between two variables by its size. The sign indicates the direction of the association.

But what about the sign of the correlation coefficient? The sign indicates the direction of the association. A positive sign indicates a positive direction; a negative sign indicates a negative direction. For instance, if you found a significant correlation of 0.83 between years of education and hours spent reading *National Geographic,* it would mean that people with more education spend more hours reading this magazine. But if you found a significant negative correlation between education and cigarette smoking, it would mean that more educated people smoke less.

TABLE 17.3

Rules of Thumb about Correlation Coefficient Size*

COEFFICIENT RANGE	STRENGTH OF ASSOCIATION*
±.81 to ±1.00	Strong
±.61 to ±.80	Moderate
±.41 to ±.60	Weak
±.21 to ±.40	Very weak
±.00 to ±.20	None

*Assuming the correlation coefficient is statistically significant

Graphing Covariation Using Scatter Diagrams

We addressed the concept of covariation between two variables in our introductory comments on correlations. It is now time to present covariation in a slightly different manner. Here is an example: A marketing researcher is investigating the possible relationship between total company sales for Burroughs Business Machines Products Division in a particular territory and the number of salespeople assigned to that territory. At the researcher's fingertips are the sales figures and number of salespeople assigned for each of 20 different Burroughs territories in the United States. The researcher quickly computes the means and the standard deviations and finds sales to average about $200 million with a standard deviation of around $50 million. The number of salespeople assigned averages 12 with a standard deviation of 4. Because the two variables are expressed in numbers that are so vastly different (millions of dollars v. a handful of salespeople), standardizing the two variables can help us make a uniform comparison. To do this the researcher translates the number of sales in each district into the number of standard deviations away from the mean for all districts (subtracts district sales from the average district sales and divides that quantity by the standard deviation). He or she does the same for the number of salespeople for each district. The researcher then graphs two lines on a territory-by-territory basis: One for the sales figures that have been translated into the number of standard deviations away from their mean, and one for salespeople's figures that have been translated into the number of standard deviations away from their mean. The graph appears in Figure 17.5 on page 554.

By looking at the graph, you should see somewhat of a parallel pattern existing between the two lines. As the number of sales goes up in a district, so does the size of the salesforce; and the pattern, although not perfect, appears to be fairly consistent in terms of the number of standard deviations away from the mean. This pattern is essentially an illustration of the concept of covariation. That is, when two variables covary positively, not only do the two lines appear to rise and fall together, but they appear to be fairly consistent in terms of the number of their respective standard deviations away from their mean that they rise and fall.

Covariation can be examined with use of a scatter diagram.

It is also possible to depict the raw data for these two variables on a scatter diagram such as the one in Figure 17.6 on page 554. In this figure, the vertical axis is Burroughs sales for the territory and the horizontal axis contains the number of salespeople in that territory. The arrangement or scatter of points appears to fall in a long ellipse. Any two variables that exhibit systematic covariation will form an ellipse-like pattern on a scatter diagram. Of course, this particular scatter diagram portrays the information gathered by the marketing researcher on sales and the number of salespeople in each territory and only that information. In actuality, the scatter diagram could have taken any shape, depending on the relationship between the points plotted for the two variables concerned.

Covariation can be graphed and inspected in two different ways as shown on page 554.

A number of different types of scatter diagram results are portrayed in Figure 17.7 on page 555. Each of these scatter diagram results is indicative of a different degree of covariation. For instance, you can see that the scatter diagram depicted in Figure 17.7(a) is one in which there is no apparent association or relationship between the two variables; the points fail to create any identifiable pattern. Instead, they are clumped into a large, formless shape. Those points in Figure 17.7(b) indicate a negative relationship between variable x and variable y;

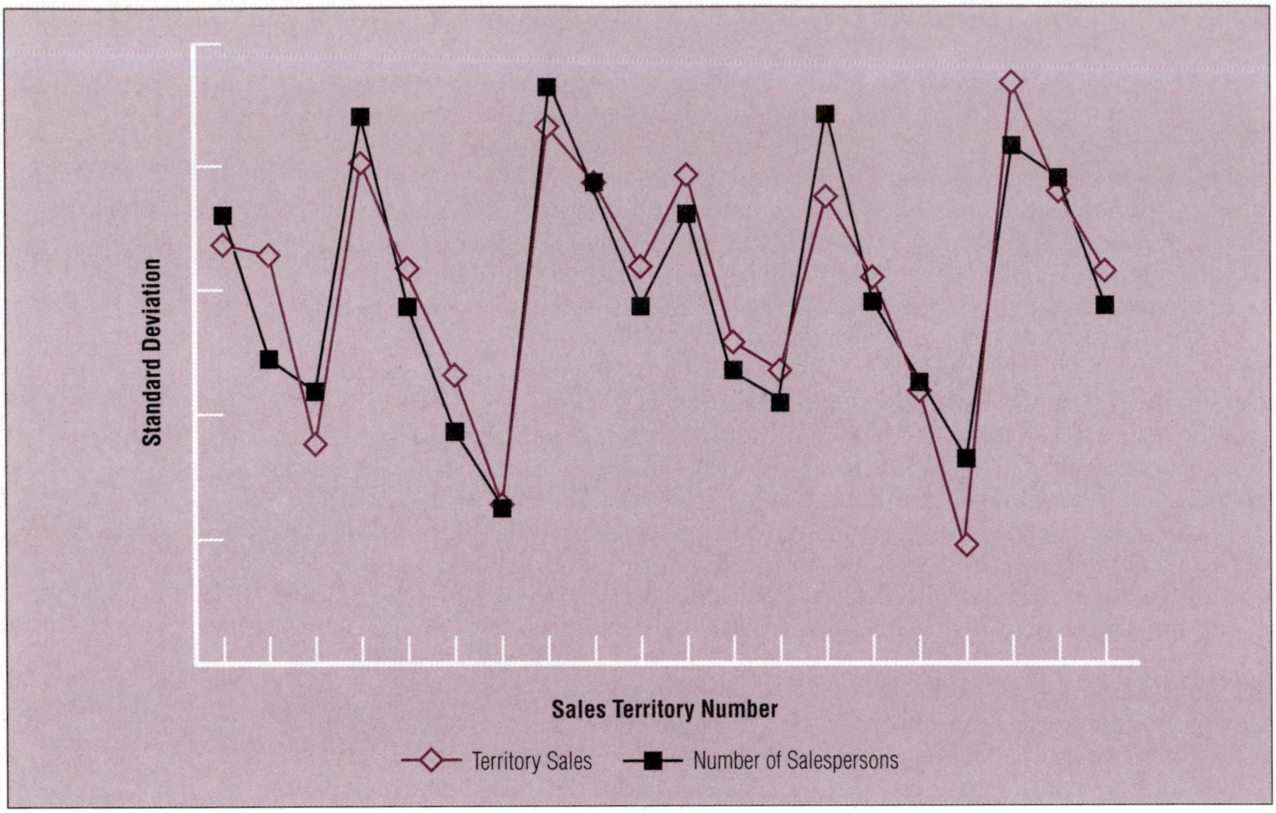

Standard Deviation
Sales Territory Number
Territory Sales
Number of Salespersons

Figure 17.5

Covariation Illustration Using Two Standardized Variables

300
250
200
150
100
Territory Sales
0
2
4
6
8
10
12
14
16
18
20
Number of Salespersons

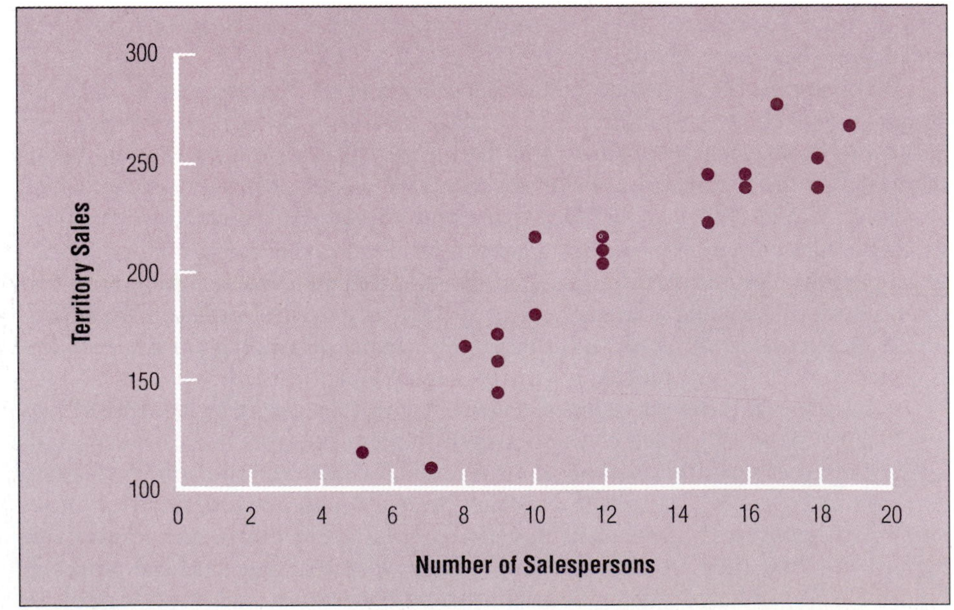

Figure 17.6

A Scatter Diagram Illustrating Covariation

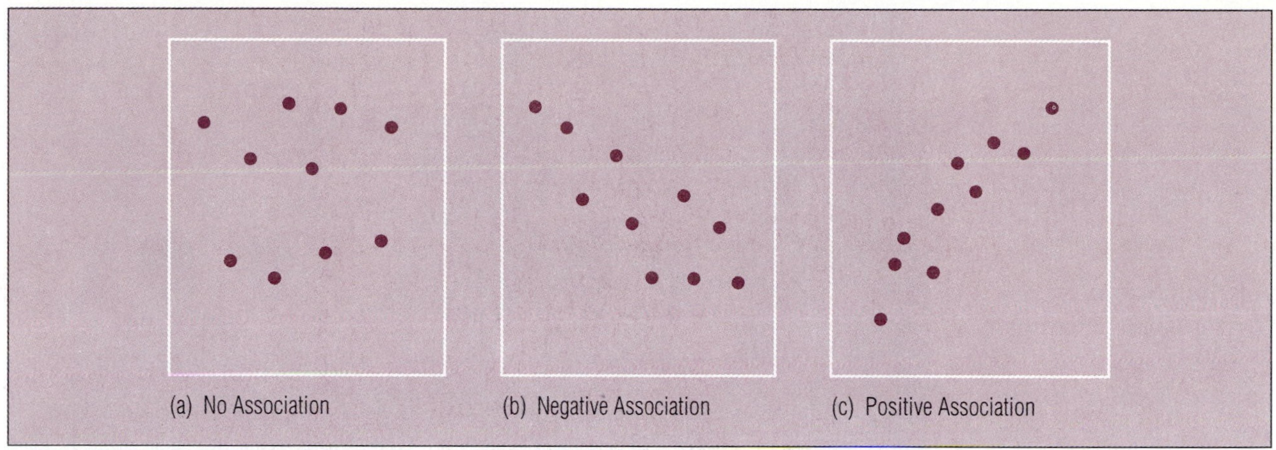

Figure 17.7

Scatter Diagram Illustrating Various Relationships

higher values of *x* tend to be associated with lower values of *y*. Those points in Figure 17.7(c) are fairly similar to those in Figure 17.7(b), but the angle or the slope of the ellipse is different. This slope indicates a positive relationship between *x* and *y*, for larger values of *x* tend to be associated with larger values of *y*.

Two highly correlated variables will yield a scatter diagram pattern of a tight ellipse.

What is the connection between scatter diagrams and correlation coefficients? The answer to these questions lies in the linear relationship described earlier in this chapter. Look at Figures 17.6 and 17.7(b) and 17.7(c). All form ellipses. Imagine taking an ellipse and pulling on both ends. It would stretch out and become thinner until all of its points fall on a straight line. If you happened to find some data that formed an ellipse with all of its points falling on the axis line and you computed a correlation, you would find it to be exactly 1.0 (*plus* 1.0 if the ellipse went up to the right and *minus* 1.0 if it went down to the right). Now imagine pushing the ends of the ellipse until it became the pattern in Figure 17.7(a). There would be no identifiable straight line. Similarly, there would be no systematic covariation. The correlation for a ball-shaped scatter diagram is zero because there is no discernable linear relationship. In other words, a correlation coefficient indicates the degree of covariation between two variables, and you can envision this relationship as a scatter diagram. The form and angle of the scatter pattern is revealed by the size and sign, respectively, of the correlation coefficient.

THE PEARSON PRODUCT MOMENT CORRELATION COEFFICIENT

The Pearson product moment correlation coefficient measures the degree of linear association between two variables.

The **Pearson product moment correlation** measures the linear relationship between two interval- and/or ratio-scaled variables such as those depicted conceptually by scatter diagrams. The correlation coefficient that can be computed between the two variables is a measure of the "tightness" of the scatter points to the straight line. You already know that in a case in which all of the points fall

Correlation analysis can determine the association between number of salespersons in a salesforce territory and the total sales for that territory.

exactly on the straight line, the correlation coefficient indicates this as a plus or minus 1. In the case in which it was impossible to discern an ellipse such as in scatter diagram Figure 17.7(a), the correlation coefficient approximates zero. Of course, it is extremely unlikely that you will find perfect 1.0 or 0.0 correlations. Usually, you will find some value in between that could be interpreted as "high," "moderate," or "low" correlation using the rules of thumb given earlier.

A positive correlation signals an increasing linear relationship, whereas a negative correlation signals a decreasing one.

Pearson product moment correlation and other linear association correlation coefficients indicate not only the degree of association but the direction as well. As we described in our introductory comments on correlations, the sign of the correlation coefficient indicates the direction of the relationship. Negative correlation coefficients reveal that the relationship is opposite: As one variable increases, the other variable decreases. Positive correlation coefficients reveal that the relationship is increasing: Larger quantities of one variable are associated with larger quantities of another variable. It is important to note that the angle or the slope of the ellipse has nothing to do with the size of correlation coefficient. Everything hinges on the width of the ellipse. (The slope will be considered in chapter 18 under regression analysis.)

Just to test your vizualization abilities, what would the *standardized covariation graph* look like for a *high negative correlation*? Remember, the standardized covariation graph is one in which the two lines represent the raw data divided by the respective standard deviations. For a negative correlation, the lines swing opposite to each other: One is a mirror image of its counterpart. It is very important to keep in mind that correlations deal with covariation, standardized by the standard deviation of each variable being examined. Do not make the error that was committed by Mark Reese of SmartCon described in Marketing Research Insight 17.3.

Basic Procedure in Pearson Product Moment Correlation Analysis

The computational formula for Pearson product moment correlations is as follows:

$$r_{xy} = \frac{\sum_{i-1}^{n} (x_i - \bar{x})(y_i - \bar{y})}{n\, s_x\, s_y}$$

MARKETING RESEARCH INSIGHT 17.3

Don't Confuse Correlation with Equality!

The Bedford Group had conducted a survey for its client, SmartCon of Indiana, to determine demand for video accelerator boards. SmartCon had developed a board to be used with Microsoft Windows that greatly increased the speed of the video display. Windows requires continual updating of the video display, and owners of personal computers with the old Pentium processors would benefit greatly from inserting the SmartCon board in their machines.

Mark Reese, SmartCon marketing manager, was briefed by the Bedford Group project manager on the findings of the survey. Mark then presented the findings to SmartCon's top management team. Mark felt he had good news for his management and he began with an eye opener.

"Ladies and gentlemen," Mark began, "I have what I believe is an important finding to report to you. As you know, in our survey, we asked respondents how many hours, on the average, they used their personal computers. We also asked them on a scale of 1 to 10, where 1 indicated 'not likely at all' and 10 indicated 'very likely,' their intentions to buy a SmartCon video board in the next six months. There is a strong positive correlation between how many hours Pentium 166 owners use their computers and their intentions to buy a SmartCon video board. Heavy users of these PCs will be buying a SmartCon video board soon."

Pamela Del Santiago, SmartCon's Comptroller, then interrupted with, "Mark, in the preliminary results you showed us last month, wasn't the intentions-to-buy average a 2.5 and the standard deviation a 1.0? That's pretty low on a 10-point intentions-to-purchase scale, and there is not much variability. So, I'm confused as to how all these sales are going to materialize."

Pamela was right to ask this question, and here is the reason: *Mark had mistaken a correlation for an equality. Correlation measures only the covariation or relative distance from the average for PC use and intentions. It does not compare the averages themselves. For illustration, take the standard deviation of 1 for intentions. A "heavy" Pentium 166 user would be 2 or more standard deviations from the average, and so would his or her intentions score. Adding (2 × 1) to the average of 2.5 yields 4.5. With a 10-point intentions-to-purchase scale, our heavy user is still near the neutral position. The correlation coefficient simply tells us the degree to which respondents' answers to the two questions tend to occupy the same* relative *positions on their respective scales.*

Source: *Adapted from Walter Branch, "On Interpreting Correlation Coefficients,"* American Psychologist, *vol. 45, no. 2 (February 1990), 296.*

where

x_i = each x value

$\bar{x}$ = mean of the x values

y_i = each y value

$\bar{y}$ = mean of the y values

n = number of paired cases

s_x, s_y = standard deviations of x and y, respectively

The Pearson product moment correlation standardizes the covariation between two variables into a correlation coefficient ranging from −1.0 to +1.0.

We briefly describe the components of this formula to help you see how the concepts we just discussed fit in. In the statistician's terminology, the numerator represents the cross-products sum and indicates the covariation or "covariance" between x and y. The cross-products sum is divided by n to scale it down to an average per pair of x and y values. This average covariation is then divided by both standard deviations to adjust for differences in units. The result constrains r_{xy} to fall between −1.0 and +1.0. Remember that in our initial diagram of Burroughs' salespeople and sales, we divided them by their respective standard deviations to make them comparable. The Pearson product moment correlation coefficient formula does the identical thing but with average covariation to derive the correlation's value.

Here is a simple computational example. You have some data on population and retail sales by county for 10 counties in your state. Is there a relationship between population and retail sales? You do a quick calculation and find the average number of people per county is 690,000, and the average retail sales is \$9.54 million. The standard deviations are 384.3 and 7.8, respectively, and the cross-products sum is 25,154. The computations to find the correlation are:

$$r_{xy} = \frac{\sum_{i-1}^{n} (x_i - \bar{x})(y_i - \bar{y})}{n\, s_x\, s_y}$$

$$= \frac{25{,}154}{10 \times 7.8 \times 384.4}$$

$$= \frac{25{,}154}{29{,}975.4}$$

$$= .84$$

A correlation of 0.84 is a high positive correlation coefficient for the relationship. This value reveals that the greater the number of citizens living in a county, the greater the county's retail sales.

View: "Burroughs Corporation: Interpreting Pearson Product Moment Correlation"

BURROUGHS CORPORATION: HOW TO OBTAIN PEARSON PRODUCT MOMENT CORRELATION(S) WITH SPSS FOR WINDOWS

With SPSS for Windows, it takes only a few clicks to compute correlation coefficients. Once again, we use data identical to that we have been describing in our Burroughs correlation example. We have defined the variables as sales and slsforce. The command sequence is STATISTICS-CORRELATE-BIVARIATE that leads to a selection box to specify which variables are to be correlated. Different types of correlations are optional, so we have selected Pearson's, and the two-tailed test of significance is the default. The output generated by this command is provided in Table 17.4.

TABLE 17.4

Correlation Output from SPSS for Windows

Correlations

		Territory Sales	Number of Salesmen
Pearson Correlation	Territory Sales	1.000	.941**
	Number of Salesmen	.941**	1.000
Sig. (2-tailed)	Territory Sales		.000
	Numer of Salesmen	.000	
N	Territory Sales	20	20
	Number of Salesmen	20	20

**. Correlation is significant at the 0.01 level (2-tailed).

A correlation matrix is symmetric with 1s on the diagonal.

As you can see, the correlation coefficient has been computed to be .941, and a Sig value of .000 signifies that it is significant at the .01 level because the Sig is less than .01. Again, this significance translates into a .001 or less probability that the null hypothesis of zero correlation is supported. If you look at our correlation printout, you will also notice that a correlation of 1.000 is reported where a variable is correlated with itself. This reporting may seem strange, but it serves the purpose of reminding you that the correlation matrix that is generated with this procedure is symmetric. In other words, the correlations in the matrix above the diagonal 1s are identical to those correlations below the diagonal. With only two variables, this fact is obvious; however, sometimes several variables are compared in a single run, and the 1s on the diagonal are handy reference points. As an example, we might have included some additional variables along with the territory sales and salesforce sizes such as advertising expenditures and number of customers' complaints for the time period. The sample size and level of significance for every correlation in the matrix will be indicated on the output.

Special Considerations in Linear Correlation Procedures

To begin, the scaling assumptions underlying linear correlation should be apparent to you, but it does not hurt to reiterate that the correlation coefficients discussed in this section assume that both variables share interval-scaling assumptions at minimum. Interpretation of the Pearson product moment correlation is not difficult, but there are three restrictions or assumptions within the interpretation you should understand.

First, the correlation coefficient takes into consideration only the relationship between two variables. It does not take into consideration interactions with any other variables. In fact, it explicitly assumes that they do not have any bearing on the relationship with the two variables of interest. All other factors are considered to be constant or "frozen" in their bearing on the two variables under analysis.

Correlation does not demonstrate cause and effect.

Second, the correlation coefficient assumes lack of causality. Although you might be tempted to believe that more company salespeople cause more company sales or that an increase in the competitor's sales force in a territory takes away sales, correlation should not be interpreted to demonstrate such cause-and-effect relationships. Just think of all of the other factors that affect sales: price, product quality, service policies, population, advertising, and more. It would be a mistake to assume that just one factor causes sales. Instead, a correlation coefficient merely investigates the presence, strength, and direction of a linear relationship between two variables.

Correlation will not detect nonlinear relationships between variables.

Third, the Pearson product moment correlation expresses only linear relationships. Consequently, a correlation coefficient result of approximately zero does not necessarily mean that the scatter diagram that could be drawn from the two variables defines a formless ball of points. Instead, it means that the points do not fall in a well-defined elliptical pattern. Any number of alternative, curvilinear patterns such as an S-shape or a J-shape pattern are possible, and the linear correlation coefficient would not be able to communicate the existence of these patterns to the marketing researcher. Any one of several other systematic but nonlinear patterns is entirely possible and would not be indicated by a linear correlation statistic. Only those cases of linear or straight-line relationships between two variables are identified by the Pearson product moment correlation. In fact, when a researcher does not find a significant or strong correlation, but still believes some relationship exists between two variables, he or she may resort to running a scatter plot. This procedure allows the researcher to visually inspect the plotted points and possibly to spot a systematic nonlinear relationship. You already know that your SPSS for Windows program has a scatter plot option that will provide a scatter diagram that you can use to obtain a sense of the relationship, if any, between two variables.

THE RANK ORDER CORRELATION COEFFICIENT

Rank correlation is used when rank order data is being analyzed.

The **rank order correlation** coefficient is used to determine the monotonic relationship that exists between two variables measured with rank order (ordinal) scales. Suppose, for example, that respondents were asked to rank toothpaste brands in two ways. Each respondent indicates a rank order of eight toothpaste brands for perceived decay prevention ability and a separate ranking for perceived whitening ability. We take only one respondent's ranks as an illustration of rank order correlation. Table 17.5 has the toothpaste brands and their ranks. As you can see, the brands are Crest, Gleem, Colgate, and so on. The number in the table under the rank headings are rank orders given by this person where 1 corresponds to the best and 8 designates the worst. That is, this person sees Colgate as best in whitening ability and Pepsodent as best in decay prevention. The question at issue is, "Does any relationship exist between the perceived whitening ability and the perceived decay prevention ability of these eight brands?" Furthermore, "If there is a relationship, what is the direction of that relationship, and how strong is it?"

When analyzing ordinal-scaled variables, the researcher uses a rank order correlation such as the **Spearman rank order correlation.** Here is the formula:

The Spearman rank order correlation indicates the strength and direction of the monotonic relationship between two rank (ordinal) variables.

$$r_s = 1 - \frac{6\left(\sum_{i-1}^{n} d_i^2\right)}{n\,(n^2 - 1)}$$

where

r_s = Spearman rank order correlation

d_i = the difference in ranks in the paired rankings

n = number of items ranked

The computation of the Spearman rank order correlation with our example rankings is as follows:

TABLE 17.5

Rankings of Toothpaste Brands as to Perceived Whitening Ability and Decay Prevention

BRAND	WHITENING ABILITY RANK	DECAY PREVENTION RANK	d	d^2
Crest	5	4	1	1
Gleem	2	8	–6	36
Colgate	1	6	–5	25
Aim	6	3	3	9
McCleans	3	5	–2	4
Pearl Drops	4	7	–3	9
Stripe	8	2	6	36
Pepsodent	7	1	6	36
				156

$$
\begin{aligned}
r_s &= 1 - \frac{6\left(\sum_{i=1}^{n} d_i^2\right)}{n\,(n^2-1)} \\
&= 1 - \frac{6 \times 156}{8 \times (8^2 - 1)} \\
&= 1 - \frac{936}{8 \times 63} \\
&= 1 - \frac{936}{504} \\
&= 1 - 1.86 \\
&= -.86
\end{aligned}
$$

Assuming it is statistically significant, a Spearman rank correlation of –.86 indicates a fairly strong monotonic relationship between the rank orders for whitening ability and decay prevention for these toothpaste brands. As the ranks are higher on whitening ability, they are lower on decay prevention, but they are not exact opposites. The interpretation of a rank order correlation is straightforward, except you should remember that the covariation pertains to rank orders given by respondents, plus the underlying relationship is monotonic.

View: "Crest Toothpaste: Rank Order Correlation"

SPEARMAN RANK ORDER CORRELATION AND KENDALL'S TAU RANK CORRELATION WITH SPSS FOR WINDOWS

The Spearman rank order correlation is provided on SPSS for Windows under the Correlate command. Kendall's tau rank correlation is also available in case there are ties allowed in the rank orderings. Either of these is a selection option in the Bivariate Correlations dialog box under STATISTICS-CORRELATE-BIVARIATE command sequence we indicated when we described how to obtain Pearson product moment correlations. The computed correlation coefficient, its significance level, and the effective sample size are provided as output as can be seen in your SPSS Student Assistant movie on this topic.

CONCLUDING COMMENTS ON ASSOCIATIVE ANALYSES

The scaling assumptions of the data being analyzed are the key to understanding associative analysis.[5] Sometimes a marketing researcher must use categorical measurements (nominal scale). As you know, nominal measurement provides the least amount of information about an object, whereas ratio measures provide the greatest amount of information. The amount of information in scales directly impact the amount of information yielded by their appropriate associative test. So the chi-square statistic that uses two nominal-scaled variables cannot have as much information as the Pearson product moment correlation that may be used for two interval or ratio-scaled variables. Similarly, the underlying relationships reflect the differences in information. Chi-square describes a nonmonotonic relationship, a Pearson product moment correlation describes a linear relationship, and a rank order correlation's relationship falls between these two with a monotonic relationship.

Researchers always test the null hypothesis of no association or no correlation, even though they hope to find a significant association or correlation to yield useful managerial implications.

Finally, throughout our descriptions of various statistical tests, we have referred to the "null hypothesis." For example, with chi-square analysis, there is the null hypothesis of no association between the two nominal-scaled variables, and with correlation analysis there is the null hypothesis of no correlation. But marketing managers really want to find strong evidence of an association that exists and can be used to their advantage. That is, they really want to find support for the "alternative hypothesis" that an association does exist. So why do we always test the null hypothesis? Here is an example that answers this question.

The Tree-Free Company of Medford, Massachusetts, makes paper products from 100 percent recycled paper. As a strategy to entice Kleenex to buy its tissue boxes, Tree-Free might conduct a survey asking, "If you learned that a company used recycled paper boxes, would that fact influence your decision to purchase a particular brand of tissue?," and "Do you typically buy Kleenex, or do you buy some other brand of facial tissue?" Of course, what Tree-Free management would love to discover is that buyers of some brand other than Kleenex are sensitive to the recycled paper issue. Then, they could make a persuasive argument that Kleenex should use Tree-Free tissue boxes, advertise how it is helping the environment, and increase its market share over tissue brands that do not use recycled paper boxes. The "hypothesis of interest" is a strong association between a "yes" answer to the first question and a "some other brand" answer to the second question.

In truth, marketing managers and researchers typically have hypotheses of interest in mind. But statistical tests do not exist that can assess these hypotheses conveniently. Instead, the researcher must use the two-step process we have described. First, the existence of an association must be demonstrated. If there is no association, there is no sense in looking for evidence of the hypothesis of interest. However, when the null hypothesis is rejected, an association does exist in the population, and the researcher is then justified to look at the direction of the association. When the second step takes place, the researcher is in pursuit of the hypothesis of interest. Now, the strength and direction aspects of the relationship are assessed to see if they correspond with the suspicions held by the marketing manager who wants to turn this association into managerial action.

When the null hypothesis is rejected, then the researcher may have a managerially important relationship to share with the manager.

Just think of the millions of boxes used by the facial tissue industry for packaging. Now do you see why Tree-Free has such a strong interest in a hypothesis other than the null? To do competent work, a researcher must ferret out all of the hypotheses of interest during the problem definition stage.

SUMMARY

This chapter dealt with instances in which a marketing researcher wants to see if there is a relationship between the responses to one question and the responses to another question in the same survey. Four different types of relationship are possible. First, there is a nonmonotonic relationship where the presence (or absence) of one variable is systematically associated with the presence (or absence) of another. Second, a monotonic relationship indicates the direction of one variable relative to the direction of the other variable. Third, a linear relationship is characterized by a straight-line appearance if the variables are plotted against one other on a graph. Fourth, curvilinear relationship means the pattern has a definite curved shape. Associative analyses are used to assess these relationships statistically.

Associations can be characterized by presence, direction, and strength, depending on the scaling assumptions of the questions being compared. With chi-square analysis, a cross-tabulation table is prepared for two nominal-scaled questions, and the chi-square statistic is computed to determine whether the observed frequencies (those found in the survey) differ significantly from what would be expected if there were no nonmonotonic relationship between the two. If the null hypothesis of no relationship is rejected, the researcher then looks at the cell percentages to identify the underlying pattern of association.

View: "Genie in a Bottle: SPSS Statistics Coach"

A correlation coefficient is an index number, constrained to fall between the range of –1.0 to +1.0, that communicates both the strength and the direction of association between two variables. The sign indicates the direction of the relationship and the absolute size indicates the strength of the association. Normally, correlations in excess of ±.8 are considered high. With two questions that are interval and/or ratio in their scaling assumptions, the Pearson product moment correlation coefficient is appropriate as the means of determining the underlying linear relationship. A scatter diagram can be used to inspect the pattern. A rank order correlation coefficient is used with rank order variables.

KEY TERMS

Associative analyses (p. 534)
Relationship (p. 534)
Nonmonotonic relationship (p. 534)
Monotonic relationships (p. 535)
Linear relationship (p. 537)
Curvilinear relationship (p. 537)
Cross-tabulation table (p. 541)
Cross-tabulation cell (p. 541)
Frequencies table (p. 541)
Raw percentages table (p. 541)
Column percentages table (p. 541)
Row percentages table (p. 543)
Chi-square analysis (p. 543)
Observed frequencies (p. 543)
Expected frequencies (p. 543)
Chi-square distribution (p. 546)
Correlation coefficient (p. 551)
Covariation (p. 551)
Pearson product moment correlation (p. 555)
Rank order correlation (p. 560)
Spearman rank order correlation (p. 561)

REVIEW QUESTIONS/APPLICATIONS

1. Explain the distinction between a statistical relationship and a causal relationship.
2. Define and provide an example for each of the following types of relationship: (a) nonmonotonic, (b) monotonic, (c) linear, and (d) curvilinear.
3. Relate the three different aspects of a relationship between two variables.
4. What is a cross-tabulation? Give an example.
5. With respect to chi-square analysis, describe or identify each of the following: (a) *r*-by-*c* table, (b) frequencies table, (c) observed frequencies, (d) expected frequencies, (e) chi-square distribution, (f) significant association, (g) scaling assumptions, (h) row percentages versus column percentages, and (i) degrees of freedom.
6. What is meant by the term "significant correlation"?
7. When should rank order correlation be used?
8. Briefly describe the connections among the following: covariation, scatter diagram, correlation, and linear relationship.
9. Indicate, with the use of a scatter diagram, the general shape of the scatter of data points in each of the following cases: (a) a strong positive correlation, (b) a weak negative correlation, (c) no correlation, (d) a correlation of +.98.
10. What are the scaling assumptions assumed by Pearson product moment correlation?
11. Listed below are various factors that may have relationships that are interesting to marketing managers. With each one, (1) identify the type of relationship, (2) indicate its nature or direction, and (3) specify how knowledge of the relationship could help a marketing manager in designing marketing strategy.
    - **a.** Readership of certain sections of the Sunday newspaper and age of the reader for a sporting goods retail store.
    - **b.** Ownership of a telephone answering machine and household income for a telemarketing service being used by a public television broadcasting station soliciting funds.
    - **c.** Number of miles driven in company cars and need for service such as oil changes, tune-ups, or filter changes for a quick auto service chain attempting to market fleet discounts to companies.
    - **d.** Plans to take a five-day vacation to Jamaica and the exchange rate of the Jamaican dollar to that of other countries for Sandals, an all-inclusive resort located in Montego Bay.
    - **e.** Amount of do-it-yourself home repairs and declining state of the economy (for example, a recession) for Ace Hardware stores.
12. Indicate the presence, nature, and strength of the relationship involving purchases of notebook personal computers and each of the following factors: (a) price (declining, stable, rising), (b) size (requires its own carry bag, can be placed in one's briefcase), (c) color display (12 inch, 13 inch), (d) hard disk size (2 GB, 3 GB, or 4 GB), and (e) CD-ROM speed (16X, 20X)."
13. With each of the following examples, compose a reasonable statement of an association you would expect to find existing between the factors involved, and construct a Venn diagram expressing that association.
    - **a.** Wearing of braces to straighten teeth by children attending expensive private schools versus those attending public schools.
    - **b.** Having a Doberman pinscher as a guard dog, use of a home security alarm system, and ownership of rare pieces of art.

c. Adherence to the "diet pyramid" recommended by the Surgeon General of the United States for healthful living and family history of heart disease.
d. Purchases of toys as gifts during the Christmas buying season versus other seasons of the year by parents of preschool-aged children.

14. Below is some information about 10 respondents to a mail survey concerning candy purchasing. Use SPSS for Windows to construct the four different types of cross-tabulation tables that are possible. Label each table, and indicate what you perceive to be the general relationship apparent in the data.

RESPONDENT	BUY PLAIN M&MS	BUY PEANUT M&MS
1	Yes	No
2	Yes	No
3	No	Yes
4	Yes	No
5	No	No
6	No	Yes
7	No	No
8	Yes	No
9	Yes	No
10	No	Yes

15. Morton O'Dell is the owner of Mort's Diner, which is located in downtown Atlanta, Georgia. Mort's opened up about 12 months ago, and it has experienced success, but Mort is always worried about what food items to order as inventory on a weekly basis. Mort's daughter, Mary, is an engineering student at Georgia Tech, and she offers to help her father. She asks him to provide sales data for the past 10 weeks in terms of pounds of food bought. With some difficulty, Mort comes up with the following list.

WEEK	MEAT	FISH	FOWL	VEGETABLES	DESSERTS
1	100	50	150	195	50
2	91	55	172	200	64
3	82	60	194	209	70
4	75	68	211	215	82
5	66	53	235	225	73
6	53	61	253	234	53
7	64	57	237	230	68
8	76	64	208	221	58
9	94	68	193	229	62
10	105	58	171	214	62

Mary uses these sales figures to construct scatter diagrams that illustrate the basic relationships among the various types of food items purchased at Mort's Diner over the past 10 weeks. She tells her father that the diagrams provide some help in his weekly inventory ordering problem. Construct Mary's scatter diagrams with your SPSS for Windows to indicate what assistance they are to Mort. Perform the appropriate associate analysis with SPSS for Windows and interpret your findings.

16. Perform associative analysis using your National Family Opinion panel data set (Nfo.sav) to answer the following questions.
    a. Do Visa card holders also hold a MasterCard?
    b. Do Visa card holders also hold a Discover card?
    c. Do MasterCard holders also hold a Discover card?
    d. Do dog owners also own cats?
    e. Do owners of IBM personal computers also subscribe to premium cable TV?

CASE 17.1

DATENET System

Telemedia, Incorporated, located in Beverly Hills, California, operates DATENET, which is a personal matchmaking system. To use DATENET, a person calls the 1-900 number using a touch-tone telephone. The service charge is $2.99 per minute, and a user can access any of several services while connected. Using the touch-tone buttons as a menu system, a user can listen to personal ads; hear a message left by another user; record a private message; or even order a variety of books, magazines, or other merchandise. Both men and women may use DATENET, and the only restriction is that users must be at least 18 years of age.

While DATENET has experienced success, Telemedia executives believe that increased advertising of DATENET is necessary. However, there are questions about who the target market should be, and how to reach this market. A marketing research effort is launched, and users are randomly selected while they are on DATENET. An interviewer intercepts the user and explains the survey. Then questions are administered if the user agrees to take part in the survey.

DATENET executives realize that the great majority of users are female, so they request a separate analysis of female respondents. One concern is relationships that might afford insights into the nature of the target market as well as magazines that might be good advertising vehicles for DATENET. Because several variables have interval- or ratio-scaling assumptions, the statistical analysis includes correlation coefficients. A primary factor is the amount of use of DATENET, measured in minutes per month, so it is correlated with several other variables. The results are listed below. All correlations are significant at the 0.01 level.

FACTOR		CORRELATION WITH AMOUNT OF DATENET USE
Demographics:	Age	–.25
	Income	–.65
	Education	–.78
	Number of years married	.13
	Number of children	.67
	Years at present address	–.90
	Years at present job	–.85
Reading of:	*Cosmopolitan*	.56
	Woman's Day	–.90

FACTOR		CORRELATION WITH AMOUNT OF DATENET USE
	Family Living	–.72
	National Enquirer	.76
	USA Today	–.84
Use of:	Make-up	.40
	Lipstick	.65
	Nail polish	.38
	Perfume	.77
Satisfaction with:	Spouse/significant other	–.56
	Job/career	–.86
	Personal appearance	–.72
	Life in general	–.50

1. Provide a thumbnail sketch that characterizes the typical DATENET female user with respect to demographic profile and relevant psychological traits.
2. Indicate the reading habits of the typical female DATENET user and indicate how these may be used in promotion decisions by an advertising agency hired by DATENET.

CASE 17.2

Friendly Market versus Circle K

Friendly Market is a convenience store located directly across the street from a Circle K convenience store. Circle K is a national chain, and its stores enjoy the benefits of national advertising campaigns, particularly the high visibility these campaigns bring. All Circle K stores have large red-and-white store signs, identical merchandise assortments, standardized floor plans, and they are open around the clock. Friendly Market, in contrast, is a one-of-a-kind "mom-and-pop" variety convenience store owned and managed by Cory James. Cory's parents came to the United States from Palestine when Cory was 15 years old. The family members became American citizens and adopted the last name of James. Cory had difficulty making the transition to U.S. schools, and he dropped out without finishing high school. For the next 10 years of his life, Cory worked in a variety of jobs, both full- and part-time, and for most of the past 10 years, Cory has been a Circle K store employee.

In 1992, Cory made a bold move to open his own convenience store. Don's Market, a mom-and-pop convenience store across the street from the Circle K where Cory was working at the time, had closed six months before, and Cory watched it month after month as it remained boarded up with a for sale sign on the front door with no apparent interested parties. Cory gathered up his life savings and borrowed as much money as he could from friends, relatives, and banks. He bought the old Don's Market building and equipment, renamed it Friendly Market, and opened its doors for business in November 1992. Cory's core business philosophy was to greet everyone who came in and to get to know them on a first-name basis. He also watched Circle K's prices closely and sought to have lower prices on at least 50 percent of merchandise sold by both stores.

To the surprise of the manager of the Circle K across the street, Friendly Market prospered. In 1996, Cory's younger sister, who had gone on to college and earned an MBA degree at Indiana University, conducted a survey of Cory's target market to gain a better understanding of why Friendly Market was successful. She drafted a simple questionnaire and did the telephone interviewing herself. She used the local telephone book, and called a random sample of over 150 respondents whose residences were listed within three miles of Friendly Market. She then created an SPSS for Windows data set with the following variables name and values.

Variable Name	Value Labels
FRIENDLY	0 = Do not use Friendly Market regularly; 1 = Use Friendly Market regularly
CIRCLE K	0 = Do not use Circle K regularly; 1 = Use Circle K regularly
DWELL	1 = Own home; 2 = Rent
SEX	1 = Male; 2 = Female
WORK	1 = Work full-time; 2 = Work part-time; 3 = Retired or Do not work
COMMUTE	0 = Do not pass by Friendly Market/Circle K corner on way to work; 1 = Do pass by Friendly Market/Circle K corner on way to work

In addition to these demographic questions, respondents were asked if they agreed (coded 3), disagreed (coded 1), or neither agreed nor disagreed (coded 2) to each of five different life-style questions. The variable names and questions are listed below:

Variable Name	Life-Style Statement
BARGAIN	I often shop for bargains.
CASH	I always pay cash.
QUICK	I like quick, easy shopping.
KNOW ME	I shop where they know my name.
HURRY	I am always in a hurry.

The data set is available to you as file friendly.sav, and it was copied to your c:\spsssa\data directory when you installed your SPSS Student Assistant. Use SPSS for Windows to perform the associative analyses necessary to answer the following questions.

1. Do Friendly Market and Circle K have the same customers?
2. What is the demographic profile associated with Friendly Market's customers?
3. What is the demographic profile associated with Circle K's customers?
4. What is the life-style profile associated with Friendly Market's customers?

CHAPTER 18

Predictive Analysis in Marketing Research

LEARNING OBJECTIVES

- *To understand the basic concept of prediction*
- *To learn how marketing researchers use regression analysis*
- *To see how time series analysis describes a historical pattern*
- *To discover how exponential smoothing works*

PRACTITIONER VIEWPOINT

Forecasting and control, two critical concepts for scientific approaches in modern times, should also be prerequisite key words for current marketing technology. Building a pertinent forecasting model through specifying various appropriate factors or variables, will enable you to predict not only what you want but also to attain the goals you have targeted by controlling whichever available variables you choose. To master state-of-the-art computerized forecasting techniques in modern society, students are initially asked to learn some basic approaches shown in this chapter. If you thoroughly master such fundamental ways of thinking, you will not feel anxious about learning more complex forecasting models or techniques, since they merely will be different kinds of extrapolation from the basic ones you will have already mastered in this chapter.

— Makoto Hori
Nikkei Research, Inc.

United Construction Company

1. Establish the need for marketing research
2. Define the problem
3. Establish research objectives
4. Determine research design
5. Identify information types and sources
6. Determine methods of accessing data
7. Design data collection forms
8. Determine sample plan and size
9. Collect data
10. **Analyze data**
11. Prepare and present the final research report

Construction companies need accurate ways to forecast their work in order to schedule equipment and personnel.

United Construction Company is a medium-sized general contractor operating in the Midwest. It takes on construction projects of all types, but its two primary business areas are residential homes and grocery store buildings. The residential homes are "spec" houses, or houses that have standard specifications and are not custom designed. The grocery buildings are also standardized to a large extent. United subcontracts electrical, plumbing, heating, air conditioning, and other work that requires skills beyond the basic construction skills of framing, light steel

fabrication, concrete work, carpentry, brick laying, countertop making, wall fabrication, and finishing.

United experienced difficulties in the 1980s when the Midwest economy sagged. Its sales dropped an average of 15 percent per year to bottom out at a low of $3 million in 1989 from a high of $20 million in the late 1970s. However, in the mid-1990s the economy began to recover. Construction, in particular, benefited from low interest rates, and construction loans became plentiful. United management first noticed a pickup in residential sales. Sales gained 10 percent in both 1993 and 1994, and 1995 accounted for a 20 percent increase. By 1996, the average residential sales increase was 18 percent.

The commercial division sales picked up in 1995, lagging about two years behind the residential division. United management reasoned that this lag was due to two factors: First, business owners are more conservative than homeowners, so the businesses waited until definite signals of economic recovery were evident. Second, grocery chains locate their stores where the population densities are increasing, and it took two years of residential housing construction recovery for the chains to identify viable high-growth areas. By 1996, the commercial side of United was experiencing an 11 percent annual increase. The 18 percent residential sales increase was used in establishing the 1997 sales forecast for the residential division. But a 15 percent figure was used for the commercial division because United management believed that other grocery chains would move quickly to expand now that others had announced their expansion plans.

This chapter is the last one in which we discuss statistical procedures frequently used by marketing researchers. A researcher will sometimes wish to offer the marketing manager a means of seeing into the future, or, alternatively, afford a means of predicting what might result if the manager were to implement a certain alternative. United Construction Company is a classic example of every company's need to forecast sales in order to plan its activities for the coming year. As can be seen with United, forecasting can be as simple as taking the percent change in sales over the past few years and applying it to next year's forecast. Or, as can also be seen in our United Construction Company description, forecasting can also involve attempting to understand the factors influencing sales and somehow factoring them into the prediction. In this chapter, we describe two broad categories of prediction analysis available to the marketing researcher: regression, both simple bivariate and multiple regression analysis, and time series analysis. But before we describe either one, we give some background on what prediction is and how you can assess the accuracy of a prediction.

DEFINING PREDICTION

Prediction is a statement of what is believed will happen in the future made on the basis of past experience or prior observation.

A **prediction** is a statement of what is believed will happen in the future made on the basis of past experience or prior observation. We are confronted with the need to make predictions on a daily basis. For example, you must predict whether it will rain to decide whether to carry an umbrella. You must predict how difficult an examination will be in order to properly study. You must predict how heavy the traffic will be in order to decide what time to start driving to make your dental appointment on time.

Marketing managers are also constantly faced with the need to make predictions, and the stakes are much higher than in the three examples just cited. That is, instead of getting wet, receiving a grade of C rather than a B, or being late for a dental appointment, the marketing manager has to worry about competitors' reactions, changes in sales, wasted resources, and whether profitability objectives will be achieved. Making accurate predictions is a vital part of the marketing manager's workaday world.

Two General Approaches to Prediction

The two approaches to prediction are extrapolation and predictive modeling.

There are two ways of making a prediction: extrapolation and predictive modeling. In **extrapolation,** you can use past experience as a means of predicting the future. This process identifies a pattern over time and projects that pattern into the future. For example, if the weather forecaster had predicted an 80 percent chance of rain every day for the past week and it had rained every day, you would expect it to rain if he or she predicted an 80 percent chance of rain today. Similarly, if the last two exams you took under a professor were quite easy, you would predict the next one would be easy as well. Of course, it might not rain or the professor might administer a hard exam, but the observed patterns argue for rain today and an easy next exam. In both cases, you have detected a consistent pattern over time and based your prediction on this pattern.

Extrapolation detects a pattern in the past and projects it into the future. Predictive modeling uses relationships found among variables to make a prediction.

In the other case, prediction relies on an observed relationship perceived to exist between the factor you are predicting and some condition you believe influences the factor. For example, how does the weather forecaster make his or her predictions? He or she inspects several pieces of evidence such as wind direction and velocity, barometric pressure changes, humidity, jet stream configuration, and temperature. That is, he or she goes far beyond taking what happened yesterday and forecasting that it will happen today. He or she builds a **predictive model,** using the relationships believed to exist among variables to make a prediction. A predictive model relates the conditions expected to be in place and influencing the factor you are predicting. It is not an extrapolation of a consistent pattern over time; rather, it is an observed relationship that exists across time.

How to Determine the "Goodness" of Your Predictions

All predictions should be judged as to their "goodness" (accuracy).

Regardless of the method of prediction, you will always want to judge the *"goodness" of your predictions,* which is how good your method is at making those predictions. But because predictions are for the future and we can never know the future until it occurs, how can you judge the accuracy of your predictions? Here is a simple example that will explain the basic approach. Imagine that you are away at college. Your little brother, who is a high school sophomore, works part-time at the movie theater in your hometown. He is rather cocky about himself. When you come home for the weekend, he claims that he can predict the theater's popcorn sales for each day in the week. It

The accuracy of a prediction method is based on how well it has performed in the past.

turns out that you also worked at the theater while in high school, and you know the theater manager very well. She agrees to keep a record of popcorn sales and to provide the daily amount to you for the next week. So you challenge your little brother to write down the sales for the next seven days. After the week passes, how would you determine the accuracy of your brother's predictions?

The goodness of a prediction is based on examination of the residuals.

The easiest way would be to compare the predictions for each day's popcorn sales to the actual amount sold. We have done this in Table 18.1. When you look at the table, you will see that we have calculated the difference between your brother's prediction and the actual sales for each evening. Notice that for some days, the predictions were high, whereas for others, the predictions were low. When you compare how far the predicted values are from the actual or observed values, you are performing **analysis of residuals.** Stated differently, assessment of the goodness of a prediction requires you to compare the pattern of errors in the predictions to the actual data. Analysis of residuals underlies all assessments of the accuracy of a forecasting method, and because researchers cannot wait a month, a quarter, or a year to compare a prediction with what actually happens, they fall back on past data. In other words, they select a predictive model and apply it to the past data. Then, they examine the residuals to assess the model's predictive accuracy.

Residuals are the errors: comparisons of predictions to actual values.

There are many ways to examine residuals. For example, in the case of your little brother's forecast, you could judge it either on a total basis or an individual basis. On a total basis, you might compute the average as we have done in the table, or you could sum all of the daily residuals. Of course, you would need to square the daily residuals or use the absolute values to avoid cancellation of the positive differences by the negative differences. (You have seen the necessary squaring operation before, for instance, in the formula for a standard deviation or the sums of squares formulas we described in chapter 16 for analysis of variance.) For the individual error, you might look for some pattern.[1] On an individual basis, you might notice a pattern: Your little

TABLE 18.1

Weekly Popcorn Sales: Using Residuals to Assess the Goodness of a Forecast

DAY OF WEEK	YOUR BROTHER'S FORECAST	ACTUAL SALES	RESIDUAL (DIFFERENCE)	TYPE OF ERROR
Monday	$100	$125	–25	Very low
Tuesday	$110	$130	–20	Low
Wednesday	$120	$135	–15	Low
Thursday	$125	$125	0	Exact
Friday	$260	$225	+35	Very high
Saturday	$300	$250	+50	Very high
Sunday	$275	$235	+40	Very high
Averages	$185	$175	+10	High

brother tends to underestimate how much popcorn will be bought on weekdays, which are low-sales days; whereas he overestimates it for Friday through Sunday, which are high-sales days. As you can see, the goodness of a prediction approach depends on how closely it predicts a set of representative values judged by examining the residuals (or errors).

Now that you have a basic understanding of prediction and how you determine the goodness of your predictions, we turn our attention to the first of our predictive methods: regression analysis.

BIVARIATE REGRESSION ANALYSIS

With bivariate regression, one variable is used to predict another variable.

We first define **bivariate regression analysis** as a predictive analysis technique in which one variable is used to predict the level of another by use of the straight-line formula. We review the equation for a straight line and introduce basic terms used in regression. We also describe basic computations and significance tests with bivariate regression. We show how a regression prediction is made, and we illustrate how to perform this analysis on SPSS for Windows.

The straight-line equation is the basis of regression analysis.

A straight-line relationship underlies regression, and it is a powerful predictive model. Figure 18.1 illustrates a straight-line relationship, and you should refer to it as we describe the elements in a general straight-line formula. The formula for a straight line is:

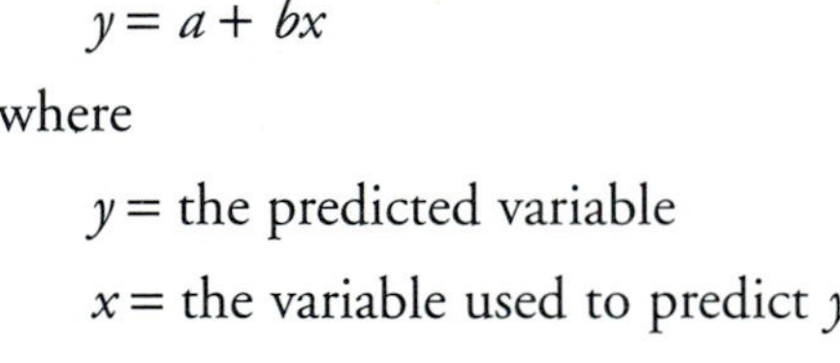

$$y = a + bx$$

where

$y =$ the predicted variable

$x =$ the variable used to predict y

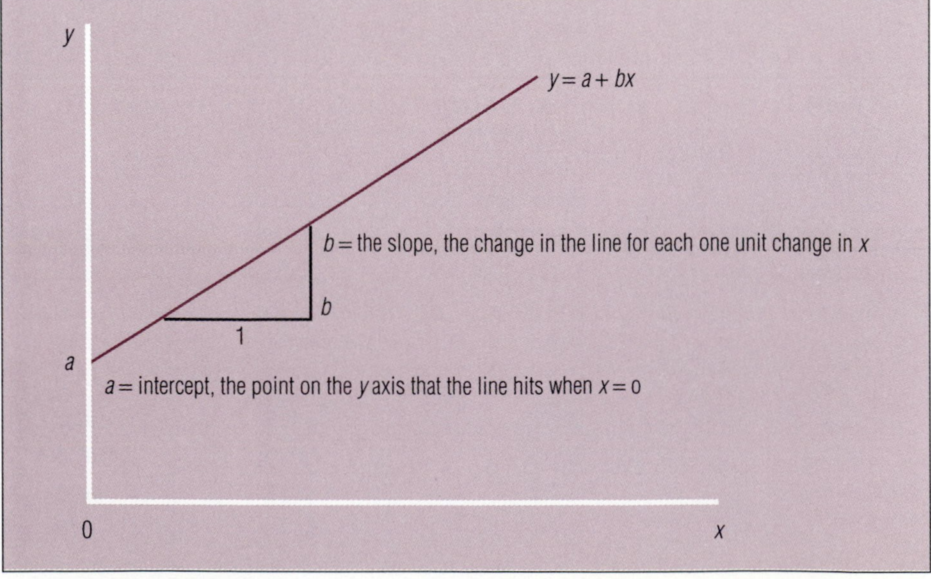

Figure 18.1

The General Equation for a Straight Line in Graph Form

a = the **intercept,** or point where the line cuts the y axis when $x = 0$

b = the **slope** or the change in y for any 1 unit change in x

You should recall the straight-line relationship we described underlying the correlation coefficient: When the scatter diagram for two variables appears as a thin ellipse, there is a high correlation between them. Regression is directly related to correlation. In fact, we use one of our correlation examples to illustrate the application of bivariate regression shortly.

Regression is directly related to correlation by the underlying straight-line relationship.

Basic Procedure in Bivariate Regression Analysis

We now describe independent and dependent variables and show how the intercept and slope are computed. Then we use SPSS for Windows output to show how tests of significance are interpreted.

Independent and Dependent Variables

In regression, the independent variable is used to predict the dependent variable.

As we indicated, bivariate regression analysis is a case in which only two variables are involved in the predictive model. When we use only two variables, one is termed dependent and the other is termed independent. The **dependent variable** is that which is predicted, and it is customarily termed y in the regression straight-line equation. The **independent variable** is that which is used to predict the dependent variable, and it is the x in the regression formula. We must quickly point out that the terms "dependent" and "independent" are arbitrary designations and are customary to regression analysis. There is no cause-and-effect relationship or true dependence between the dependent and the independent variable. It is strictly a statistical relationship, not causal, that may be found between these two variables.

Computing Slope and Intercept

To compute a and b, you need a number of observations of the various levels of the dependent variable paired with different levels of the independent variable, identical to the ones we illustrated previously when we were demonstrating how to perform correlation analysis. Refer to Table 18.2 on page 578, which has the Burroughs Corporation sales levels and number of sales people for 20 territories that we used for our Pearson product moment example in chapter 17. It also has the necessary intermediate computations for b and a.

The formula for computing the regression parameter b is:

Here is how to calculate the slope by hand.

$$b = \frac{n \sum_{i-1}^{n} x_i y_i - \left(\sum_{i-1}^{n} x_i\right)\left(\sum_{i-1}^{n} y_i\right)}{n \sum_{i-1}^{n} x_i^2 - \left(\sum_{i-1}^{n} x_i\right)^2}$$

where

x_i = an x variable value

y_i = a y value paired with each x_i value

n = the number of pairs

The calculations for b, the slop re as follows:

$$b = \frac{n \sum_{i-1}^{n} x_i y_i - (\sum_{i-1}^{n} x_i)(\sum_{i-1}^{n} y_i)}{n \sum_{i-1}^{n} x_i^2 - (\sum_{i-1}^{n} x_i)^2}$$

$$= \frac{20 \times 58603 - 251 \times 4325}{20 \times 3469 - 251^2}$$

$$= \frac{1172060 - 1085575}{69380 - 63001}$$

$$= \frac{86485}{6379}$$

$$= 13.56$$

TABLE 18.2

Bivariate Regression Analysis Data and Intermediate Calculations

TERRITORY (i)	SALES ($ MILLIONS) (y)	NUMBER OF SALESPERSONS (x)	xy	x^2
1	102	7	714	49
2	125	5	625	25
3	150	9	1350	81
4	155	9	1395	81
5	160	9	1440	81
6	168	8	1344	64
7	180	10	1800	100
8	220	10	2200	100
9	210	12	2520	144
10	205	12	2460	144
11	230	12	2760	144
12	255	15	3825	225
13	250	14	3500	196
14	260	15	3900	225
15	250	16	4320	256
16	275	16	4400	256
17	280	17	4760	289
18	240	18	4320	324
19	300	18	5400	324
20	310	19	5890	361
Sums	4325	251	58603	3469
	(Average = 216.25)	(Average = 12.55)		

The formula for computing the intercept is:

$a = \overline{y} - b\,\overline{x}$

Here is how to calculate the intercept by hand.

The computations for *a,* the intercept, are as follows:

$a = \overline{y} - b\,\overline{x}$

$= 216.25 - 13.56 \times 12.55$

$= 216.25 = 170.15$

$= 46.10$

In other words, the bivariate regression equation has been found to be:

$y = 46.10 + 13.56\,x$

One important connection between these equations and our straight-line diagram is that regression analysis computes the intercept and the slope on the basis of the "least squares criterion." The **least squares criterion** is a way of guaranteeing that the straight line that runs through the points on the scatter diagram is positioned so as to minimize the vertical distances away from the line of the various points. In other words, if you draw a line where the regression line is calculated and measure the vertical distances of all of the points away from that line, it would be impossible to draw any other line that would result in a lower total of all of those vertical distances. Or, to state the least squares criterion using residuals analysis, the line is the one with the lowest total squared residuals.

The least squares criterion used in regression analysis guarantees that the "best" straight-line slope and intercept will be calculated.

BURROUGHS CORPORATION: BIVARIATE REGRESSION OUTPUT WITH SPSS FOR WINDOWS

View: "Burroughs Corporation: Using Bivariate Regression"

Now let us illustrate bivariate regression with SPSS for Windows. We show you how to run a regression analysis with SPSS for Windows in the SPSS Student Assistant movie made for this purpose, and how we want to familiarize you with the SPSS output and various regression statistics found on it as presented in Table 18.3 on page 581. It contains some important statistical information, and we use it to describe bivariate regression analysis in more detail.

There are several pieces of information provided with a regression analysis such as this. First, there is information on "Variables Entered/Removed," which indicates that the number of salespeople was used in a method designated as "enter." This designation refers to the regression method we are using. (There are several methods, but most are beyond the scope of our textbook.) This part of the output also notes that the dependent variable is "Territory Sales."

In the Model Summary table, three types of "*Rs*" are indicated. For bivariate regression, *R Square* (.885 on the output) is the square of the correlation coefficient of 0.941 (which we found in our Burroughs correlation example in chapter 17). The Adjusted *R* Square (.878) reduces the R^2 by taking into ac-

A company can predict sales expected for next year with regression based on how many salespeople it will have in the field.

count the sample size and number of parameters estimated. This *R* Square value is very important, because it reveals how well the straight-line model fits the scatter of points. Because a correlation coefficient ranges from −1.0 to +1.0, its square will range from 0 to +1.0. The higher the *R* Square value, the better is the straight line's fit to the elliptical scatter of points. A standard error value is reported, and we explain its use later.

In regression analysis, a high R *Square suggests a good fit, and ANOVA tests it statistically.*

Next, an Analysis of Variance (ANOVA) section is provided. As you can see, regression is related to analysis of variance.[2] We must determine whether the straight-line model we are attempting to apply to describe these two variables is appropriate. The *F* value is significant (.000) so we reject the null hypothesis that a straight-line model does not fit the data we are analyzing. Just as in ANOVA, this test is a flag, and the flag has now been raised, making it justifiable to continue inspecting the output for more significant results. If the ANOVA *F* test is not significant, we would have to abandon our regression analysis attempts with these two variables. Finally, you can see in the Coefficients Table that the values of *b* and *a* are listed under "Unstandardized Coefficients." The constant (*a*) is 46.100, while *b*, identified as "B," is 13.558. In other words, rounding to hundredths, the regression equation has been found to be identical to the one we calculated before:

$$\text{Sales} = 46.10 + 13.56 \times \text{Number of salespeople}$$

(Remember, our values are in millions of dollars.)

Testing for Statistical Significance of the Intercept and the Slope

You must always test the regression model, intercept, and slope for statistical significance.

Simply computing the values for *a* and *b* is not sufficient for regression analysis, because the two values must be tested for statistical significance. The intercept and slope that are computed are sample estimates of population parame-

TABLE 18.3

Burroughs Territory Sales and Salesforce Size: Regression Output from SPSS for Windows

Variables Entered/Removed[b]

Model	Variable Entered	Variables Removed	Method
1	Number of Salesmen[a]		Enter

a. All requested variables entered.

b. Dependent Variable: Territory Sales

Model Summary

Model	R	R Square	Adjusted R Square	Std. Error of the Estimate
1	.941[a]	.885	.878	20.61

a. Predictors: (Constant), Number of Salesmen

ANOVA[b]

Model		Sum of Squares	df	Mean Square	F	Sig.
1	Regression	58627.177	1	58627.177	138.044	.000[a]
	Residual	7644.573	18	424.699		
	Total	66271.750	19			

a. Predictors: (Constant), Number of Salesmen

b. Dependent Variable: Territory Sales

Coefficients[a]

Model		Unstandardized Coefficients		Standardized Coefficients	t	Sig.
		B	Std. Error	Beta		
1	(Constant)	46.100	15.197		3.033	.007
	Number of Salesmen	13.558	1.154	.941	11.749	.000

a. Dependent Variable: Territory Sales

ters of the true intercept, α (alpha), and the true slope, β (beta). The tests for statistical significance are tests as to whether the computed intercept and computed slope are significantly different from zero (the null hypothesis). To determine statistical significance, regression analysis requires that a *t* test be undertaken for each parameter estimate. The interpretation of these *t* tests is identical to other significance tests you have seen. We describe what these *t* tests mean next.

The significance level of the intercept and the slope are provided on SPSS output.

In our example, you would look at the "Sig." column in the Coefficients table. This is where the slope and intercept *t* test results are reported. Both of our tests have significance levels less than .01, so our computed intercept and slope are valid estimates of the population intercept and slope. If *x* and *y* do not share a linear relationship, the population regression slope will equal zero and the *t* test result will support the null hypothesis. However, if a systematic linear relationship exists, the *t* test result will force rejection of the null hypothesis, and the researcher can be confident that the calculated slope estimates the true one that exists in the population. Remember, we are dealing with a statistical concept, and you must be assured that the straight-line parameters α and β really exist in the population before you can use your regression analysis findings as a prediction device.

Making a Prediction and Accounting for Error

Regression analysis pedictions are estimates that have some amount of error in them.

Now, there is one more step to relate, and it is the most important one. How do you make a prediction? The fact that the line is a best approximation representation of all the points means we must account for a certain amount of error when we use the line for our predictions. The true advantage of a significant bivariate regression analysis result lies in the ability of the marketing researcher to use that information gained about the regression line through the points on the scatter diagram and to estimate the value or amount of the dependent variable based on some level of the independent variable. For example, with our regression result calculated for the relationship between sales and salespeople, it is now possible to estimate the amount of sales predicted to be associated with a number of Burroughs salespeople in any average territory. However, the scatter of points does not describe a perfectly straight line. So our regression prediction can only be an estimate.

The standard error of the estimate is used to calculate a range of the prediction made with a regression equation.

Generating a regression prediction is conceptually identical to estimating a population mean. That is, it is necessary to express the amount of error by estimating a range rather than stipulating an exact estimate for your prediction. Regression analysis provides for a **standard error of the estimate,** which is a measure of the accuracy of the predictions of the regression equation. This standard error value is listed in the top half of the SPSS output and just beside the Adjusted *R* Square in Table 18.3. It is analogous to the standard error of the mean you used in estimating a population mean from a sample, but it is based on the residuals. In computing the standard error of the estimate, the estimated value for each independent variable value used in the computation of the regression result is used to generate a predicted dependent value, and this value is compared (with subtraction) to the actual amount of the dependent variable used in the original calculations. These residuals are squared simply as a means of controlling for the cancellation effect that would occur for negative values. Additional computations convert the squared differences into a standard error of estimate value. In our Burroughs example, the standard error of the estimate was found to be about \$20.61 (millions).

One of the assumptions of regression analysis is that the plots on the scatter diagram will be spread uniformly and in accord with the normal curve assumptions over the regression line. Figure 18.2 illustrates how this assumption might be depicted graphically. The points are congregated close to the line and then become more diffuse as they move away from the line. In other words, a greater percentage of the points is found on or close to the line than is found further away. The great advantage of this assumption is that it allows the marketing researcher to use his or her knowledge of the normal curve to specify the range in which the dependent variable is predicted to fall. For example, if the researcher used the predicted dependent value result ±1.96 times the standard error of the estimate, he or she would be stipulating a range with a 95 percent level of confidence; whereas if he or she uses ±2.58 times the standard error of the estimate, he or she would be stipulating a range with a 99 percent level of confidence. The interpretation of these confidence intervals is identical to interpretations for previous confidence intervals: Were the prediction made many times and an actual result determined each time, the actual results would fall within the range of the predicted value 95 percent or 99 percent of these times.

Your Student Assistant movie illustrates confidence intervals around a regression line.

The use of 95 percent or 99 percent confidence intervals is standard.

The numbers on the graph in Figure 18.3 (on page 584) illustrate how you can envision a regression prediction. Let us use the regression equation to make a prediction about the Burroughs sales volume that would be associated with 15 salespeople placed in a territory. Applying the regression formula, we have the following:

$$y = a + bx$$

$$\text{Territory sales} = 46.10 + 13.56(15)$$

$$= 46.10 + 203.40$$

$$= 249.50 \text{ (\$ millions)}$$

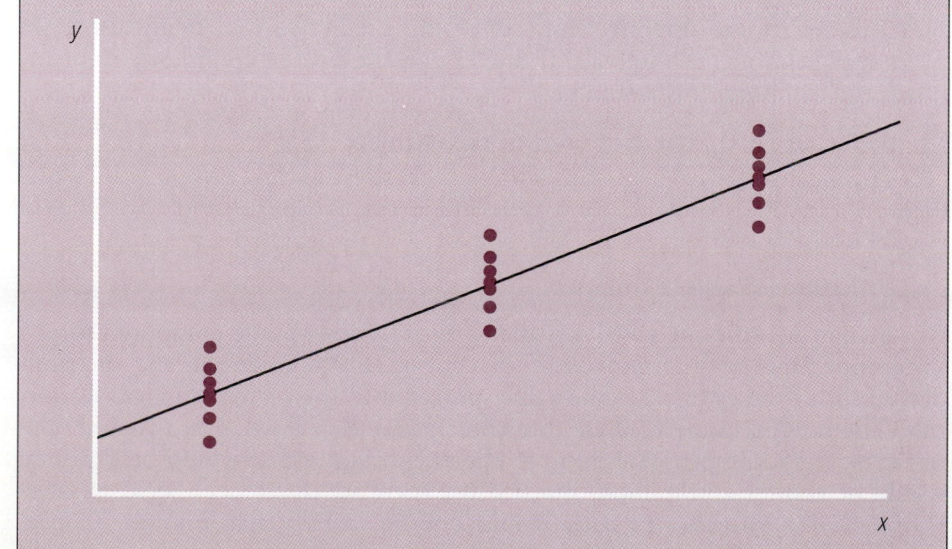

Figure 18.2

Regression assumes that data points are congregated closely next to the regression line and distributed out on both sides to form a bell-shaped curve.

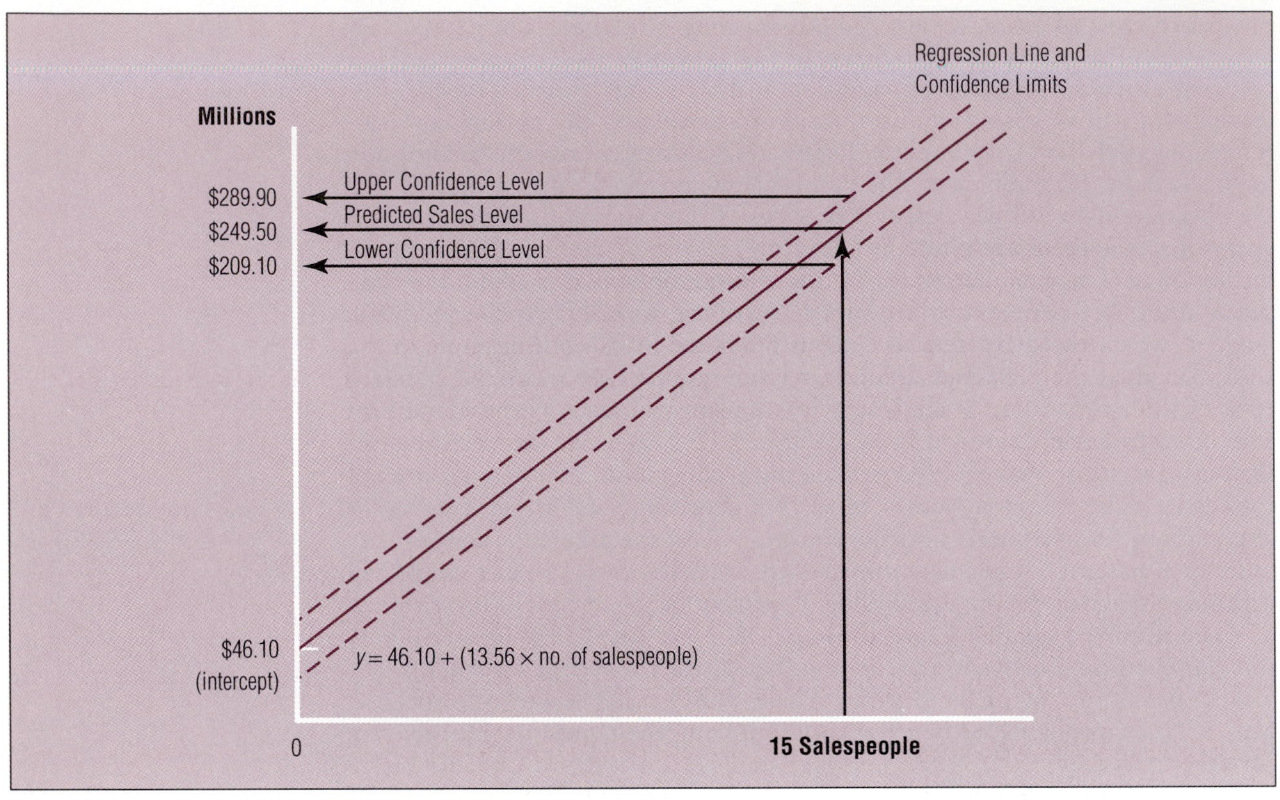

Figure 18.3

To predict with regression, apply levels of confidence around the regression line.

Regression predictions are made with confidence intervals.

Next, to reflect the imperfect aspects of the predictive tool being used, we must apply confidence intervals. If the 95 percent level of confidence were applied, the computations would be:

Predicted $y \pm z_{\alpha}$ Standard error of the estimate

$249.50 \pm (1.96)(20.61)$

249.50 ± 40.40

209.10 to 289.90 ($ millions)

As you can see, the predicted y is the territory sales we just computed for 15 salespeople, the 1.96 pertains to 95 percent level of confidence, and the standard error of the estimate is the value indicated in the regression analysis output. The interpretation of these three numbers is as follows. For a typical sales territory, if 15 salespeople were in it, the sales volume that would be expected would be about $250 million. But because there are differences between salespeople and territories, the sales would not be exactly that amount. Consequently, the 95 percent confidence interval reveals that the sales figure should fall between $209 million and $290 million. Finally, the prediction is valid only if conditions remain the same as they were for the time period from which the original data were collected.[3]

Two Warnings Regarding Regression Analysis

Before leaving this section, we must issue a warning about your interpretation of regression. We all have a natural tendency to think in terms of causes and effects, and regression analysis invites us to think in terms of a dependent variable's resulting or being caused by an independent variable's actions. This line of thinking is absolutely incorrect: Regression analysis is nothing more than a statistical tool that assumes a linear relationship between two variables. It springs from correlation analysis which is, as you will recall, a measure of the *linear association* and not the *causal relationship* between two variables. Consequently, even though two variables, such as sales and advertising, are logically

Regression is a statistical tool, not a cause-and-effect statement.

Using a regression equation based on U.S. consumers to predict Chinese consumers' behaviors is inappropriate.

connected, a regression analysis does not permit the marketing researcher to formulate cause-and-effect statements.

The second warning we have is that you should not apply regression analysis to predict outside of the boundaries of the data used to develop your regression model. That is, you may use the regression model to interpolate within the boundaries set by the range (lowest value to highest value) of your independent variable, but if you use it to predict for independent values outside those limits, you have moved into an area that is not accounted for by the raw data used to compute your regression line. For this reason, you are not assured that the regression equation findings are valid.

MULTIPLE REGRESSION ANALYSIS

Multiple regression means that you have more than one independent variable to predict a single dependent variable.

Multiple regression analysis is an expansion of bivariate regression analysis in that more than one independent variable is used in the regression equation. The addition of independent variables complicates the conceptualization by adding more dimensions or axes to the regression situation. But it makes the regression model more realistic because predictions normally depend on multiple factors, not just one.

Basic Assumptions in Multiple Regression

With multiple regression, you work with a regression plane rather than a line.

Consider our example with the number of salespeople as the independent variable and territory sales as the dependent variable. A second independent variable such as advertising levels can be added to the equation (Figure 18.4). You will note that the advertising dimension is included at a right angle to the axis representing the number of salespeople, which creates a three-dimensional display. At the same time, the addition of a second variable turns the regression line into a regression plane. A **regression plane** is the shape of the dependent variable in multiple regression analysis. If other independent variables are added to the regression analysis, it would be necessary to envision each one as a new and separate axis existing at right angles to all other axes. Obviously, it is impossible to draw more than three dimensions at right angles. In fact, it is difficult to even conceive of a multiple dimension diagram, but the assumptions of multiple regression analysis require this conceptualization.

Everything about multiple regression is essentially equivalent to bivariate regression except you are working with more than one independent variable. The terminology is slightly different in places, and some statistics are modified to take into account the multiple aspect, but for the most part, concepts in multiple regression are analogous to those in the simple bivariate case. We note these similarities in our description of multiple regression.

A multiple regression equation has two or more independent variables (x's).

The regression equation in multiple regression has the following form:

$$y = a + b_1x_1 + b_2x_2 + b_3x_3 + \ldots + b_mx_m$$

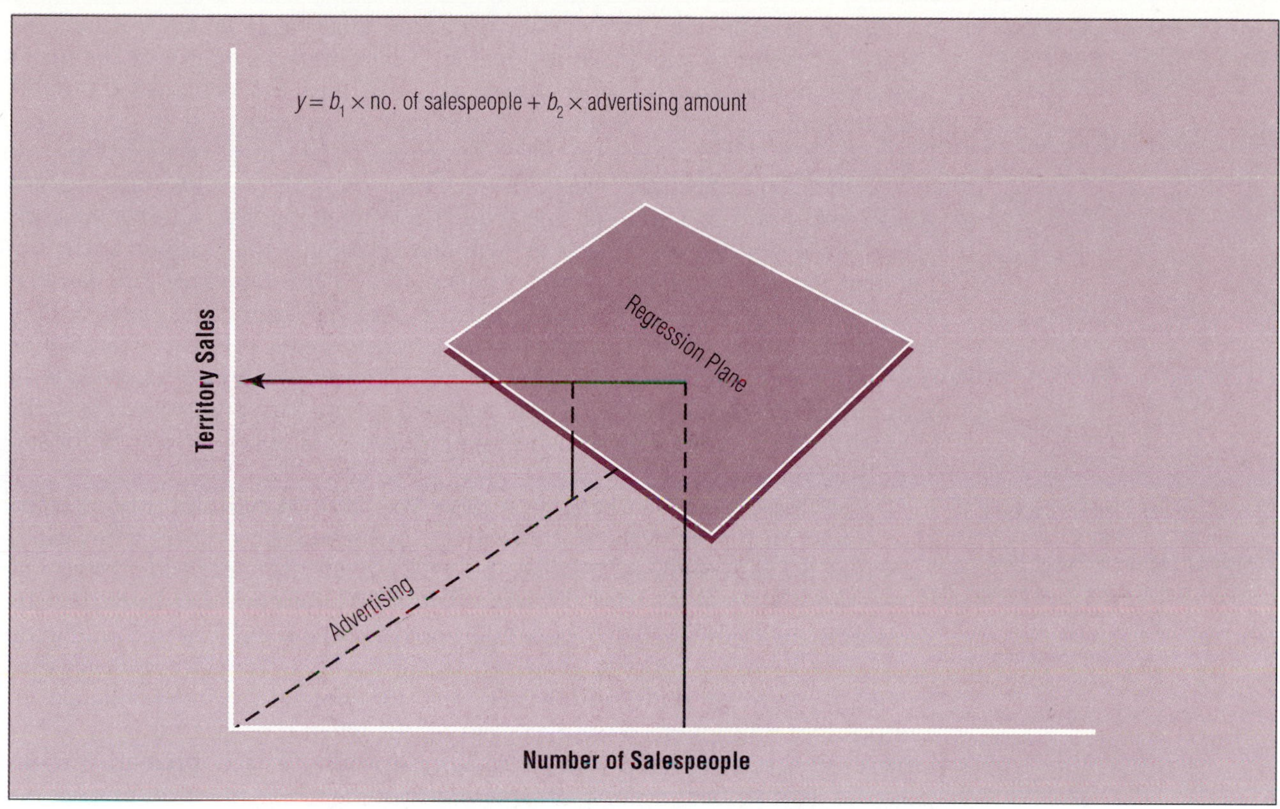

Figure 18.4

With multiple regression, the line becomes a plane.

where

y = the dependent, or predicted, variable

x_i = independent variable i

a = the intercept

b_i = the slope for independent variable i

m = the number of independent variables in the equation

As you can see, the addition of other independent variables has done nothing more than to add $b_i x_i$s to the equation. We still have retained the basic $y = a + bx$ straight-line formula, except now we have multiple x variables, and each one is added to the equation, changing y by its individual slope. The inclusion of each independent variable in this manner preserves the straight-line assumptions of multiple regression analysis. This is sometimes known as **additivity** because each new variable is added on.

Multiple R indicates how well the independent variables can predict the dependent variable in multiple regression.

Just as was the case in bivariate regression analysis in which we used the correlation between y and x, it is possible to inspect the strength of the linear relationship between the independent variables and the dependent variable with multiple regression. Multiple R, also called the coefficient of determination, is a handy measure of the strength of the overall linear relationship. Just as was the case in bivariate regression analysis, the multiple regression analysis model assumes that a straight-line (plane) relationship exists among the variables. Multiple R ranges from 0 to +1.0 and represents the amount of the dependent variable "explained," or accounted for, by the *combined* independent variables. High multiple R values indicate that the regression plane applies well to the scatter of points, whereas low values signal that the straight-line model does not apply well. At the same time, a multiple regression result is an estimate of the population multiple regression equation, and, just as was the case with other estimated population parameters, it is necessary to test for statistical significance.

With multiple regression, the independent variables should have low correlations with one another.

Let us issue a caution before we show you how to run a multiple regression analysis using SPSS for Windows. The **independence assumption** stipulates that the independent variables must be statistically independent and uncorrelated with one another. The independence assumption is portrayed by the right-angle alignment of each additional independent variable in Figure 18.4. The presence of even moderate correlations among the independent variables is termed **multicollinearity** and will violate the independence assumption of multiple regression analysis results when it occurs.[4] It is up to the researcher to test for and remove multicollinearity if it is present. Various methods exist to detect and overcome multicollinearity. One is examining the correlation matrix for the independent variables and selecting only those that have low correlations with one another. In other words, the researcher judges which independent variables are to be drawn from the original set based on the requirement that the independent variables have low correlations among themselves. Alternatively, statistical analysis programs, including SPSS, often have internal checks built into them, and they will signal that multicollinearity is a problem and identify the offending independent variables. The researcher may perform certain transformations such as taking the logarithm of one independent variable that is highly correlated with others, although this approach makes interpretation of your results difficult. This last method requires advanced knowledge of regression analysis.

VITALITY PHARMACEUTICALS: MULTIPLE REGRESSION WITH SPSS FOR WINDOWS

How to Run Multiple Regression Analysis on SPSS for Windows

Running multiple regression is almost identical to performing simple bivariate regression with SPSS for Windows. To illustrate a multiple regression run we need a data set. Just for variety, we use one that has not been described previously.

Vitality Pharmaceutical Company wants to market packets of reinforced vitamins for adults, and it wants to predict the types of people who would be likely users. It commissions a market research study in which telephone respondents indicate the number of high-energy vitamin packets bought per year. These are packets that contain six different vitamins you can buy at a drug or convenience store for a one-day energy booster. The market research company gathers information on several demographic factors that might reveal important segmentation relationships. Among the demographics are age, income, and family size. There is also a score from a fatalism scale that measures each respondent's belief that his or her fate is predetermined. Fatalism is included because one of Vitality's top managers thinks consumers who believe fate controls their lives do not take vitamins regardless of their demographic situation. These four factors, labeled age, income, family, and fatal are selected to be independent variables in the multiple regression analysis. That is, they are the x_is. Number of packets bought in the past six months is the dependent variable, and it is labeled packets.

The STATISTICS-REGRESSION-LINEAR command sequence is used to run a multiple regression analysis, and the variable, packets, is selected as the dependent variable, while the other four are specified as the independent variables.

View: "Microsoft Network: Using Multiple Regression"

As the computer printout in Table 18.4 (on page 590) shows, the Multiple *R* value (Model Summary table) indicating the strength of relationship between the independent variables and the dependent variable is 0.668, signifying that there is some linear relationship present. Next, the printout reveals that the ANOVA *F* is significant, signaling that the null hypothesis of no linear relationship is rejected, and it is justifiable to use a straight-line relationship to model the variables in this case.

The STATISTICS-REGRESSION-LINEAR command is used by multiple regression.

Just as we did with bivariate regression, it is necessary in multiple regression analysis to test for statistical significance of the b_is (betas) determined for the independent variables. Once again, you must determine whether sampling error is influencing the results and giving a false reading. You should recall that this test is a test for significance from zero (the null hypothesis) and is achieved through the use of separate *t* tests for each b_i. The computer printout indicates the calculated *t*s and their levels of statistical significance. In this particular example, it is apparent the age, income, and fatalism computed betas are statistically significant (all Sig. equal to .000) from zero whereas family size (Sig. of 0.818) is not. A regression coefficient that is not statistically significant from zero is playing no meaningful role in the prediction of the dependent variable. In other words, although a value has been calculated by the computer for this beta, it is more reflective of sampling error than of a true relationship in the population. Consequently, the use of that independent variable in this particular multiple regression result is meaningless. Also, the intercept (identified as the constant) is not significant, meaning it is actually equal to zero when all of the independent variables equal zero.

With multiple regression, look at the significance level of each calculated beta.

What do you do with the mixed significance results found in our vitamin-usage multiple regression example? It is customary to go back and to eliminate (trim) independent variables that are shown to be insignificant. You then rerun the trimmed model and inspect the *t* values again. This series of eliminations or iterations helps to achieve the simplest model by eliminating the nonsignificant independent variables. The rerun printout is shown in Table 18.5 on page 591.

A trimmed regression means that you eliminate the nonsignificant independent variables and rerun the regression.

TABLE 18.4

A Multiple Regression Analysis Printout

Model Summary

Model	R	R Square	Adjusted R Square	Std. Error of the Estimate
1	.668[a]	.446	.420	3.734940

a. Predictors: (Constant), FAMILY, FATAL, INCOME, AGE

ANOVA[b]

Model		Sum of Squares	df	Mean Square	F	Sig.
1	Regression	5569.867	4	1392.467	99.820	.000[a]
	Residual	6905.133	495	13.950		
	Total	12475.000	499			

a. Predictors: (Constant), FAMILY, FATAL, INCOME, AGE

b. Dependent Variable: PACKETS

Coefficients[a]

Model		Unstandardized Coefficients		Standardized Coefficients	t	Sig.
		B	Std. Error	Beta		
1	(Constant)	−.803	1.170		−.686	.493
	FATAL	−1.095	.188	−.216	−5.741	.000
	INCOME	1.095	.182	.438	6.006	.000
	AGE	.257	.019	.771	13.284	.000
	FAMILY	−.118	.119	−.071	−.997	.818

a. Dependent Variable: PACKETS

Run trimmed regressions iteratively until all betas are significant.

This additional run enables the marketing researcher to think in terms of fewer dimensions within which the dependent variable relationship operates. Generally, successive iterations cause the Multiple R to decrease somewhat, and it is advisable to scrutinize this value after each run. You can see that the new Multiple R is now 0.640. Iterations will also cause the beta values and the intercept value to shift slightly; consequently, it is necessary to inspect all t values to determine the statistical significance of the betas once again. Also, notice that the constant (alpha) of −3.349 is now statistically significant from zero. Through a series of iterations, the marketing researcher finally arrives at the final regression equation expressing the salient independent variables and their linear relationships with the dependent variable. A concise predictive model has been found.

TABLE 18.5

Output for the Second Run Using Multiple Regression

Model Summary

Model	R	R Square	Adjusted R Square	Std. Error of the Estimate
1	.640[a]	.410	.406	3.853370

a. Predictors: (Constant), FAMILY, FATAL, INCOME, AGE

ANOVA[b]

Model		Sum of Squares	df	Mean Square	F	Sig.
1	Regression	5110.155	3	1703.385	114.718	.000[a]
	Residual	7364.845	496	14.848		
	Total	12475.000	499			

a. Predictors: (Constant), FAMILY, FATAL, INCOME, AGE
b. Dependent Variable: PACKETS

Coefficients[a]

		Unstandardized Coefficients		Standardized Coefficients		
Model		B	Std. Error	Beta	t	Sig.
1	(Constant)	−3.349	1.117		−2.992	.003
	FATAL	−.153	.113	−.092	−1.355	.076
	INCOME	.737	.177	.295	4.170	.000
	AGE	.208	.018	.623	11.612	.000

a. Dependent Variable: PACKETS

Using Results to Make a Prediction

The use of a multiple regression result is identical in concept to the application of a bivariate regression result—that is, it relies on an analysis of residuals. Remember, we began this chapter with a description of residuals and indicated that residuals analysis is a way to determine the goodness of a prediction. Ultimately, the marketing researcher wishes to predict the dependent variable based on assumed or known values of the independent variables that are found to have significant relationships within the multiple regression equation. The standard error of the estimate is provided on all regression analysis programs, and it is possible to apply this value to forecast the ranges in which the dependent variable will fall, given levels of the independent variables.

Regression analysis can be applied to predict catalog sales of products sold by The Vermont Country Store.

Here is an example of a prediction using multiple regression.

Making a prediction with multiple regression is identical to making one with bivariate regression except you use the multiple regression equation. For a numerical example, let us assume that the marketing manager of Vitality Pharmaceutical Company is considering using The Vermont Country Store as a distribution outlet. Located in Weston, Vermont, The Vermont Country Store may seem an odd choice, but it mails out several thousand catalogs annually. The catalog lists nostalgic items and has many medicinal products such as Dr. Scholl's® Exercise Sandals or Bag Balm creme for chapped skin. Various types of vitamins are also sold through the catalog. The Vitality market research division does a survey of The Vermont Country Store catalog recipients, and it finds that the average age is 55 years, the average income is a "6" on a 10-point scale, and the average fatalism score is 3. These averages can be used to make a prediction as follows (notice that we have rounded the *b*s):

$$
\begin{aligned}
y &= a + b_1x_1 + b_2x_2 + b_3x_3 \\
&= -3.34 - 0.15 \times \text{fatalism} + 0.21 \times \text{age} + 0.74 \times \text{income} \\
&= -3.34 - 0.15 \times 3 + 0.21 \times 55 + 0.74 \times 6 \\
&= -3.34 - 0.45 + 11.55 + 4.44 \\
&= 12.20 \text{ vitamin packets}
\end{aligned}
$$

Now, we need to apply confidence intervals, so let us use 95 percent. The intervals are calculated as follows:

Predicted packets $\pm 1.96 \times$ Standard error of the estimate

$12.20 \pm 1.96 \times 3.85$

12.20 ± 7.55

4.65 to 19.75 high-energy vitamin packets per year

The interpretation would be that for those Vermont Country Store catalog receivers who are inclined to buy reinforced vitamin packets, their purchases will range from 5 to 20 packets per year. Of course, we must assume that all other factors are constant because the regression only takes into account fatalism, age, and income.

Special Uses of Multiple Regression Analysis

There are a number of special uses and considerations to keep in mind when running multiple regression analysis. These include using a "dummy" independent variable, using standardized betas to compare the importance of independent variables, and using multiple regression as a screening device.

Using a "Dummy" Independent Variable

The interval-at-minimum scaling assumption requirement of multiple regression may be relaxed by use of a dummy variable.

A **dummy independent variable** is defined as one that is scaled with a nominal 0-versus-1 coding scheme. The scaling assumptions that underlie multiple regression analysis require that the independent and dependent variables both be at least interval scaled. However, there are instances in which a marketing researcher may want to use an independent variable that does not embody interval-scaling assumptions. It is not unusual, for instance, for the marketing researcher to wish to use a dichotomous or two-level variable such as gender as an independent variable in a multiple regression problem. For instance, a researcher may want to use gender coded as 0 for male and 1 for female as an independent variable. Or you might have a buyer/nonbuyer dummy variable that you want to use as an independent variable. In these instances, it is usually permissible to go ahead and slightly violate the assumption of metric scaling for the independent variable to come up with a result that is in some degree interpretable.

Using Standardized Betas to Compare the Importance of Independent Variables

The researcher can compare standardized beta coefficients' sizes directly, but comparing unstandardized betas is like comparing apples and oranges.

Regardless of the application intentions of the marketing researcher, it is usually of interest to the marketing researcher to determine the relative importance of the independent variables in the multiple regression result. Because independent variables are often measured with different units, it is wrong to make direct comparisons between the calculated betas. For example, it is improper to directly compare the *b* coefficient for family size to another for money spent per month on personal grooming because the units of measurement are so different (people versus dollars). The most common approach is to standardize the independent variables through a quick operation that involves dividing the difference between each independent variable value and its mean by the standard deviation of that independent variable. This results in what is called the **standardized beta coefficient.** In other words, standardization translates each independent value into the number of standard deviations away from its own mean. Essentially, this procedure transforms these variables into a set of values with a mean of zero and a standard deviation equal to 1.0.

Once this procedure is effected, direct comparisons may be made between the resulting betas. The larger the absolute value of a standardized beta coefficient, the more relative importance it assumes in predicting the dependent variable. SPSS and most other statistical programs provide the standardized betas automatically. With SPSS the standardized values are found under the column designated as "Beta." It is important to note that this operation has no effect on the final multiple regression result. Its only function is to allow direct comparisons of the relative impact of the significant independent variables on the dependent variable. As an example, if you look at the "Betas" reported in our Vitality vitamins regression printout (Table 18.5), you will see that age is the most important variable (.623), whereas fatalism is the least important (−.092).

Using Multiple Regression as a Screening Device

Another application of multiple regression analysis is as a screening or identifying device. That is, the marketing researcher may be faced with a multitude of prospective independent variables, and he or she may use multiple regression as a way of spotting the salient (statistically significant) independent variables for the dependent variable at hand. In this instance, the intent is not to determine some sort of a prediction of the dependent variable; rather, it may be to search for clues as to what factors help the researcher understand the behavior of this particular variable. For instance, the researcher might be seeking market segmentation bases, and could use regression to spot which demographic variables are related to the consumer behavior variable under study.

Multiple regression is sometimes used to help a marketer apply market segmentation.

For example, referring again to our Vitality Pharmaceutical Company example, we initially stated that the pharmaceutical company marketing manager wanted market segmentation information. By inspecting the output, we can say that three segmentation variables are useful: age, income, and the person's fatalistic disposition. Also, it is apparent that older people with higher income and less fatalistic outlooks are a prime target market because the signs of these b_is are significant. The screening use of multiple regression can even offer insights between cultures. Marketing Research Insight 18.1 shows how multiple regression can be used on two samples, one from the United States and the other from Thailand, to reveal how important cultural differences operate in different cultures.

Stepwise regression is useful if a researcher has many independent variables and wants to narrow the set down to a smaller number.

Statistical programs are equipped with special regression routines to assist marketing researchers confronted with large numbers of independent variables. With **stepwise regression,** the computer program seeks out the one independent variable that explains the most variance in the dependent variable and enters it into the regression equation before others are entered. It then seeks out from the other independent variables the one independent variable that explains the greatest amount of the remaining variance and enters it as the second step. The procedure is continued until some cutoff point specified by the marketing researcher or when some default point in the program is reached. Stepwise regression has been sometimes referred to as a "brute strength" method of regression analysis. It is particularly helpful in the case of the use of multiple regression analysis as a screening device. In general, the use of stepwise regression or any of the several other types of regression analysis available that stray from the strict assumptions of multiple regression analysis requires additional reading on their assumptions, necessary conditions for their use, and cautions about their interpretation.[5]

Final Comments on Regression Analysis

As you will see when you work with the SPSS for Windows regression procedures, we have only scratched the surface of this topic. There are many more options, statistics, and considerations involved. For instance, there are

MARKETING RESEARCH INSIGHT 18.1

Using Multiple Regression to Find Differences across Cultures

Multiple regression analysis is a very versatile statistical technique, and it can be used to detect differences among countries because regression reveals three important pieces of knowledge. First, regression will determine whether a suspected independent variable is meaningfully related to a key dependent variable. Second, regression will identify the direction of the relationship existing between the independent variable and the dependent variable. Third, it will reveal the size of the relationship (size of the beta coefficient). For instance, if a researcher were investigating rice consumption across countries, he or she might gather information on selected demographics and the number of pounds of rice consumed per month by households.

Let us compare, for example, U.S. households to those in Thailand. The researcher can run two regressions, one for each country sample, and compare the results. The (significant) findings might look something like the following:

U.S. household sample: Rice consumption $(y_{USA}) = 0.3 - 1.5 \times \text{income} + 0.3 \times \text{education}$

Thailand sample: Rice consumption $(y_{Thailand}) = 2.4 - 0.2 \times \text{income}$

Here is what the comparison of the two regression results suggests about cross-cultural differences in rice consumption. First, there is more absolute eating of rice in Thailand because the intercept of 2.4 is greater than 0.3 for the U.S. That is, the starting point (where all significant independent variables = 0) on the y axis is higher with the Thailand regression than with the U.S. regression. Second, income is related to rice consumption in both cultures in that the negative sign in both cases reveals that as income goes down, rice eating goes up. But the negative relationship is greater for U.S. households than for Thai households (again, assuming that a comparable income measure is being used). Last, rice consumption is positively related to education in the United States, but it is not in Thailand. U.S. consumers with more education tend to eat more rice.

The regression comparisons plus some additional knowledge of eating habits in both countries lead to an understanding of cultural differences. The United States is a "meat and potatoes" country where rice is seen as a substitute good, and lower income consumers buy it because it is a less-expensive alternative to staple U.S. foods. At the same time, more educated U.S. consumers might be more health conscious, and rice is considered to be more healthy than heavy starches. Thailand, on the other hand, is part of the Asian "rice culture," and rice is a staple. It figures into religious ceremonies, and it is consumed at all three meals. Asian rice consumption tends to cut across demographic groups uniformly because of this cultural factor; but it is plentiful and inexpensive, so lower income Thai households tend to eat more rice than do higher income Thai households.

Source: *Based on "Rice, the Essential Harvest,"* National Geographic, *vol. 185, no. 5 (May 1994), 48–79.*

several ways to examine the residuals in regression analysis that we have not discussed. In fact, there is so much material that whole textbooks on regression exist. Our purpose has been to teach you basic concepts and to help you interpret the statistics associated with these concepts as you encounter them as statistical analysis program output. Our descriptions are merely an introduction to multiple regression analysis to help you comprehend the basic notions, common uses, and interpretations involved with this predictive technique.[6]

TIME SERIES ANALYSIS OF HISTORICAL DATA

A time series is data reported over time at regular intervals such as years, quarters, or months.

Much data handled by marketing researchers is reported over successive time intervals, such as on a year-by-year basis, a quarter-by-quarter basis, a month-by-month basis, a week-by-week basis, or even a day-by-day basis. Such historical data are referred to as **time series data.**

Time series patterns are trend, cycle, and seasonality.

Economists have worked with historical data for many years, and they have devised a family of procedures, collectively called **time series analysis,** which detect three patterns in business data: trend, cycle, and seasonality. Most of the following discussion is on the trend, which is the straight-line pattern assumed to underlie historical data of the type we have just described.

Trend

Trend is a long-term persistent pattern seen in time series data.

The **trend** is defined as the long-term persistent pattern in the data. There are various ways to identify a trend in historical time series data. We describe two popular methods: linear regression line and exponential smoothing. To illus-

TABLE 18.6

Regal Bicycle Company Sales Time Series Data

YEAR	ANNUAL SALES (1000S)
1	1340
2	1221
3	909
4	1501
5	1350
6	1253
7	1561
8	1435
9	1114
10	1239
11	1453
12	1890
13	2220
14	2450
15	2790
16	3450
17	3759
18	????

trate the use of both, we use the annual sales data for Regal Bicycle Company, which makes racing bicycles and children's bicycles. Its product line includes both off-road mountain bikes with wide, chubby tires and 14-speed racing bicycles with thin tires. Regal's sales over the past 17 years are reported in Table 18.6. Note that Regal's marketing manager is working to come up with a sales forecast for next year based on this time series.

Using a Linear Regression Line to Identify the Trend

Graphics and spreadsheet computer software usually provide simple linear trend analysis.

Let us suppose for the moment that you are helping Regal's marketing director with his forecasting problem. As just indicated, whenever you are confronted with time series of business data such as that in Table 18.6, you will probably attempt to make some sense of it by assessing its underlying straight-line tendency. Many graphics software programs and most spreadsheet programs will find the best-fitting straight line, and they typically rely on the least squares criterion to do so.

TIME SERIES ANALYSIS

Your SPSS for Windows has the ability to find the best-fitting straight line. The command sequence is GRAPHS-SCATTER. Next, identify the name of the time series variable. This procedure produces a scatter diagram without a trend line. From the chart window, the command sequence of CHART-OPTIONS opens the Scatterplot options where you can click on the "Fit Line" option. By default, SPSS for Windows draws in the linear regression trend line. We have done this with the Regal bicycle sales data in Figure 18.5. As you can see in the figure, if you project the trend line into the future you can make a prediction of what will result next year based on the straight-line trend apparent in the historical data.

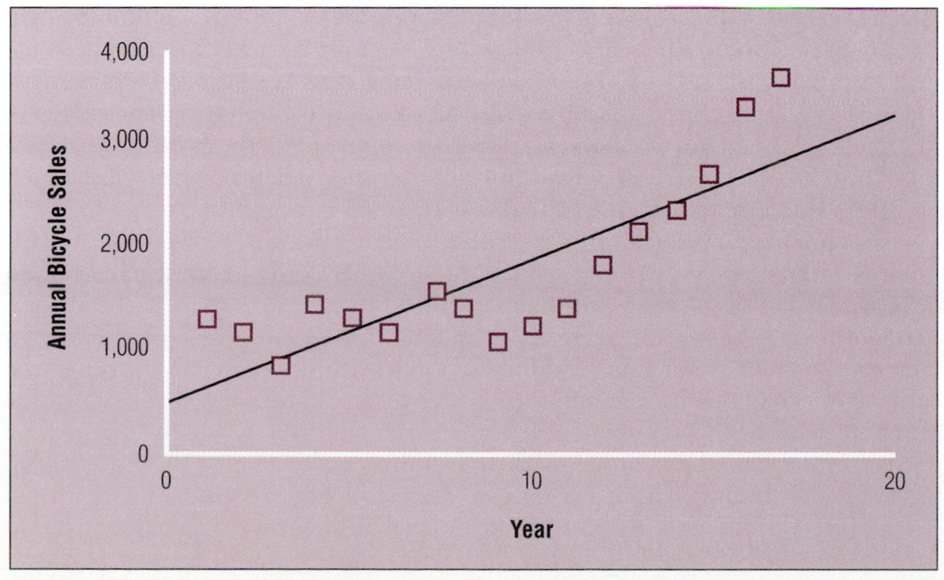

Figure 18.5

Scatter Plot of Regal Bicycle Sales with a Linear Trend Line

Time series analysis can be used to detect the steady change in a bicycle company's sales over a number of years.

Using Exponential Smoothing to Identify the Trend

When you look at Figure 18.5, you notice that the actual sales values fall above and below the line. Some are close to the line, whereas others are distant. This is a visual analysis of the residuals. That is, you are intuitively assessing how well the line mirrors the pattern described by the sales points over the 17-year time horizon. You should be concerned that the line does not describe the most recent years as well as you might like. In fact, it looks like a prediction for next year using the trend line will be much too low. Your concern arises because using a simple linear regression trend line produces what is called *naive forecasting* because it naively expects past patterns to extend into the future. For example, if time series data covers the years 1964 through 1997, the last five years are undoubtedly more relevant than 1964 to 1968 in predicting what will happen in 1998. But a trend line treats all years with equal importance.

Exponential smoothing applies weights so recent observations have more importance in computing the trend than do less recent observations.

Exponential smoothing is a technique that modifies a trend line by applying different weights to the years in the time series. The recent past is often a better indicator of what will happen in the near future than is the distant past, so it makes sense to weigh the data from the recent past more heavily in determining our trend line. A different way to think about how exponential smoothing works is to remember that every trend forecast will include some error because actual numbers practically never fall exactly on the trend line. Actual figures fall above or below the trend line, and if two or three actual figures fall consistently above (or below) the trend line, it probably signifies a trend line shift is coming into effect. However, because a linear regression trend line treats all numbers in the time series equally, it will be slow to detect the change in the trend. Exponential smoothing affords a simple means of detecting that change and incorporating it into the forecast.

A signal for the need for exponential smoothing is when the scatter diagram of the time series data does not reveal a smooth long-term linear growth pattern. You might detect an S-shape, a J-shape, or some other shape that does not lend itself well to the linear regression method of determining the straight-line trend. As long as there is some nonlinearity, discontinuity, or other break with a consistent trend pattern identifiable in the time series, it will make sense to consider using exponential smoothing to improve your predictions.

A signal to use exponential smoothing is a detectable, but nonlinear, pattern in time series data.

A general formula for exponential smoothing is:

$$F_{t+1} = \Gamma S_t + (1 - \Gamma)F_t$$

where

F_{t+1} = forecast for next period (t+1)

S_t = actual value for last period (t)

F_t = forecasted value for last period (t)

Γ = an exponential smoothing parameter (gamma)

We must comment that this exponential smoothing formula is a general approach to forecasting, and you will encounter variations of the formula if you work with this method to any degree. In our formula, the forecast is computed with a weighted average where the value of Γ (gamma) is the weighting mechanism. The term, Γ, may take any value from 0 to 1.0. If gamma is large, say .90 or .80, the forecast for next period will greatly reflect the recent past, particularly the last period's actual amount, S_t, and it will only take the past into account to the extent of $(1 - \Gamma)$. The forecasted value for the last period, F_t, represents the past because it would have been calculated to reflect all of the values from the previous periods. Actually, by selecting a Γ of 0.50, the equation will weight the last period's actual value and the forecast for that period equally, and with a Γ of, say, .2, the recent past will have less weight on the forecast than will the older past values.

Exponential smoothing uses a weighted average formula.

Here is a quick example with the Regal Bicycle time series data. We want to forecast next year's sales, given last year's sales of 3759 (year 17 in Table 18.6). Using the linear trend line in Figure 18.4, you can see that the line predicted last year to be roughly 3000. The prediction was quite low compared to the actual, so let's use a Γ of 0.80. The exponentially smoothed prediction for next year would be:

$$\begin{aligned} F_{t+1} &= \Gamma S_t + (1 - \Gamma)F_t \\ &= 0.80 \times S_t + 0.20 \times F_t \\ &= 0.80 \times 3759 + 0.20 \times 3000 \\ &= 3007 + 600 \\ &= 3607 \end{aligned}$$

Notice that our exponentially smoothed forecast is not on the linear trend line. It has been adjusted or pulled toward the recent string of years that suggests a shift in the trend has taken place.

Where appropriate, an exponentially smoothed prediction will be better than one using a straight trend line.

Again, there are many variations of weighting schemes used in an exponential smoothing forecast analysis. In fact, as you will see, other weighting parameters can be used in addition to gamma. We show you how SPSS for Windows performs exponential smoothing forecasting.

View: "Regal Bicycle Sales: Time Series Trend Analysis and Exponential Smoothing"

REGAL BICYCLE SALES: PERFORMING EXPONENTIAL SMOOTHING WITH SPSS FOR WINDOWS

The STATISTICS-TIME SERIES-EXPONENTIAL SMOOTHING command sequence leads to a dialog box from which you can select the time series variable and choose analyses from various options. In our example, we have the Regal Bicycle sales data identified as bikesls. There are four analysis options, and the "Holt" method is the one that treats a linear trend of time series data, plus we have directed SPSS for Windows to do a "grid" search to give us the best estimate of gamma.

Table 18.7 contains the results. When you inspect the table, you will see that the trend has been found to be 151.19 units per year. That is, the trend line has a slope of 151.19 per year. Note that two smoothing parameters, alpha and gamma, have been used. Alpha is a general smoothing parameter built into the SPSS for Windows program, and gamma is the trend smoothing parameter we described in our formula. (Remember, we said that our formula is just a general case, and variations are prevalent.) We directed SPSS to do the "grid" routine for an extensive search for the values of alpha and gamma, and the determination of the best values is based on analysis of the residuals. These are designated "SSE" (Summed Squared Error), and the Alpha–Gamma combination (.80 and .40, respectively) with the lowest total residuals is listed first. Two new variables have been created and added to the data set. These are specified as FIT_1 and ERR_1 in Table 18.7. FIT_1 is the data for the exponentially smoothed line, and ERR_1 is the difference between Regal's actual sales and the estimated FIT_1 sales for each year. That is, ERR_1 contains the residuals, and you could inspect them for any patterns they might exhibit by using SPSS Chart options. We have done this in your Student Assistant movie.

With SPSS using the "Holt" method, perform a "grid" search for alpha and gamma.

To inspect time series analyses, use SPSS Sequence charts.

Figure 18.6 on page 602 is a sequence chart generated by SPSS for Windows to compare Regal's actual sales, the exponentially smoothed trend line, and the linear regression trend line. As you can see, the exponentially smoothed line is not a straight line, but it does smooth out the ups and downs of the actual Regal sales values. It tracks the actual sales closely, because it takes recent past years more into account than distant past years. Figure 18.6 also contains a forecast based on our exponentially smoothed trend line. Year 18 has the trend line extended, whereas actual Regal sales stop in year 17. We instructed SPSS to make this prediction under the "Save . . . " button in the Exponential Smoothing dialog box. By using visual analysis of the residuals, you can see that the linear trend line has not detected the shifts in actual sales very well, but the exponentially smoothed trend has detected them, and the prediction for year 18 is more in tune with the recent change than is the linear trend line.

TABLE 18.7

Exponential Smoothing Linear Trend Output for Regal Bicycle Sales

```
Results of EXSMOOTH procedure for Variable BIKESLS
MODEL= HOLT (Linear trend, no seasonality)

Initial values:        Series            Trend
                   1264.40625        151.18750

DFE = 15.

The 10 smallest SSE's are:     Alpha      Gamma            SSE
                           .8000000   .4000000   1406358.0611
                           1.000000   .0000000   1408822.8525
                           .7000000   .4000000   1422836.7010
                           1.000000   .2000000   1426412.1874
                           .9000000   .4000000   1433005.0616
                           .7000000   .6000000   1437765.8639
                           .9000000   .2000000   1439330.8204
                           .6000000   .6000000   1440564.9512
                           .9000000   .0000000   1467322.8122
                           .8000000   .6000000   1484338.2077

The following new variables are being created:

  NAME     LABEL

  FIT#1    Fit for BIKESLS from EXSMOOTH, MOD_3 HO A .80 G .40
  ERR#1    Error for BIKESLS from EXSMOOTH, MOD_3 HO A .80 G .40

1 new cases have been added.
```

Cycle

Exponential smoothing can detect and adjust for a cyclical shift in a time series easily.

The **cycle** is a wave pattern over several years that often characterizes business data as it goes through upswings and downswings. Time series analysis will detect cycles as long as the time series covers an extended time horizon of, say, 30 or more years. Normally, marketing researchers do not concern themselves with business cycles because their historical data is relatively short. Granted, economists are vitally concerned with cycles, and marketing researchers may confer with economists for cycle detection to adjust their predictions, but beyond defining business cycles and noting their existence in time series data, we do not treat them here. Besides, as you just learned, exponential smoothing will sense cyclical swings quite satisfactorily. There is some evidence of a cycle in the Regal Bicycle Sales graph in Figure 18.6. When you look at the pattern

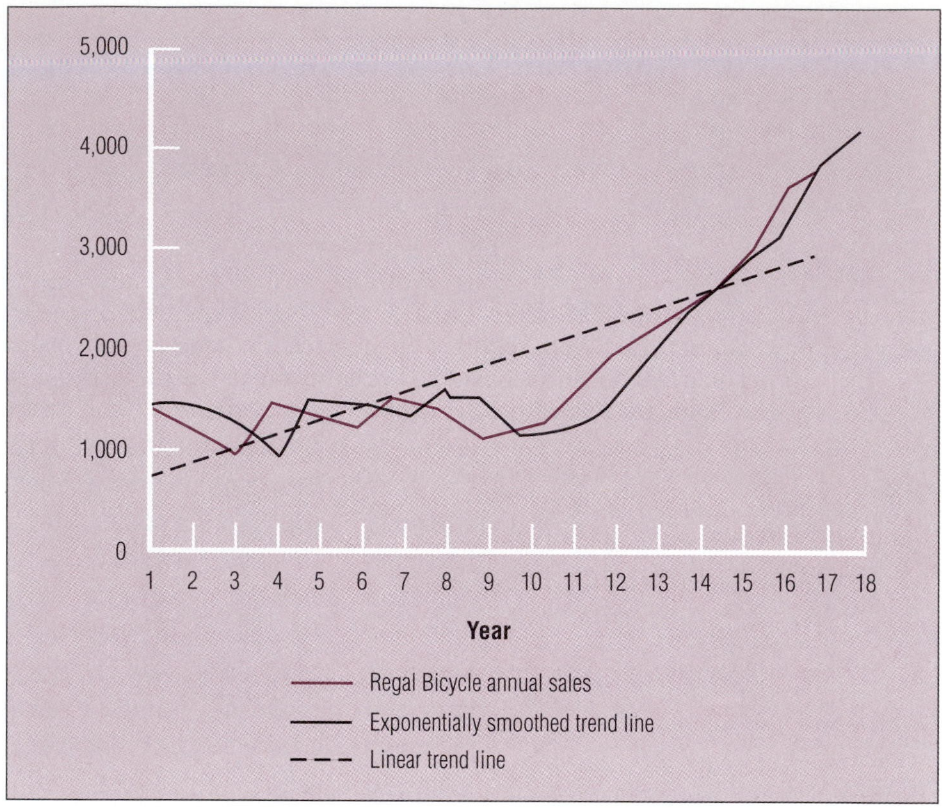

Figure 18.6

Comparison of Linear Trend, Exponentially Smoothed Trend, and Actual Regal Bicycle Company Sales

Many businesses experience regular seasonal ups and downs of sales.

of sales, you should notice that they fall on or above the trend line for the first few years, then they swing below the line during the middle years, and finally climb above the line in the last three years. This is a cyclical sales pattern.

Seasonality

Seasonality is the regular up and down fluctuation of business data each year when the data is reported on a quarterly or monthly basis. Seasonality is a very important aspect of the marketing manager's worries about the future, and detection of seasonal sales patterns is commonly performed by researchers. To identify seasonality, all you need do is think in terms of 100 percent of a year's sales. Suppose annual sales were reported in quarters. Whenever you realize that the various quarters do not account for equal percentages of yearly sales, and that pattern holds for several past years, you have evidence of seasonality. Because seasonality is a relatively constant pattern and readily identifiable because it is consistent within each year, you could easily apply these percentages to any annual sales prediction to yield the expected sales by quarter. Or you could use monthly seasonal indices if you desired.

Seasonality is a pattern in a time series seen consistently within each year.

ANALYZING SEASONALITY WITH SPSS FOR WINDOWS

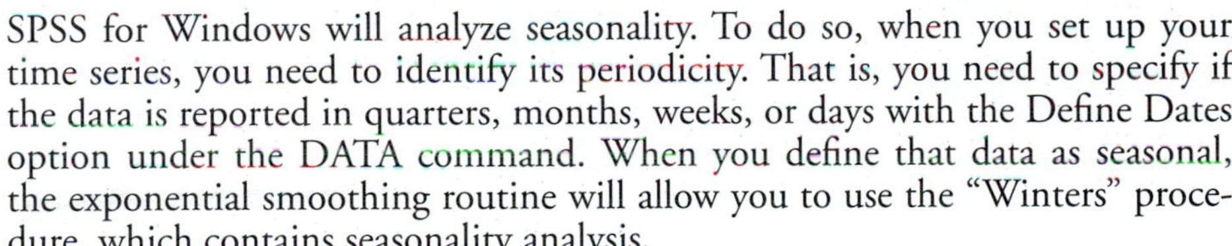

SPSS for Windows will analyze seasonality. To do so, when you set up your time series, you need to identify its periodicity. That is, you need to specify if the data is reported in quarters, months, weeks, or days with the Define Dates option under the DATA command. When you define that data as seasonal, the exponential smoothing routine will allow you to use the "Winters" procedure, which contains seasonality analysis.

SUMMARY

Predictive analyses are methods used to forecast the level of a variable such as sales. Model building and extrapolation are two general options available to market researchers. In either case, it is important to assess the goodness of the prediction. This assessment is typically performed by comparing the predictions against the actual data with procedures called residuals analyses.

Market researchers use regression analysis to make predictions. The basis of this technique is an assumed straight-line relationship existing between the variables. With bivariate regression, one independent variable, x, is used to predict the dependent variable, y, using the straight line formula of $y = a + bx$. A high R^2 and a statistically significant slope indicate that the linear model is a good fit. With multiple regression, several independent variables may be used, and it is necessary to determine which ones are significant. By systematically eliminating the nonsignificant independent variables in an iterative manner, a researcher will ultimately derive a set of significant independent variables that yield a good predictive model. The standard error of the estimate is used to compute a confidence interval range for a regression prediction.

Market researchers are also called on to make forecasts based on time series data. This chapter described two methods they use. The first is linear trend line analysis, in which a historical straight-line pattern that characterizes the complete time series is used to predict the future. However, sometimes a time series will exhibit breaks, swings, or other changes in its trend pattern. If this is the case, exponential smoothing, which is the second method for making forecasts based on time series data, should be used.

KEY TERMS

Prediction (p. 572)
Extrapolation (p. 573)
Predictive model (p. 573)
Analysis of residuals (p. 575)
Bivariate regression analysis (p. 576)
Intercept (p. 577)
Slope (p. 577)
Dependent variable (p. 577)
Independent variable (p. 577)
Least squares criterion (p. 579)
Standard error of the estimate (p. 582)
Multiple regression analysis (p. 586)
Regression plane (p. 586)
Additivity (p. 587)
Independence assumption (p. 588)
Multicollinearity (p. 588)
Dummy independent variable (p. 593)
Standardized beta coefficient (p. 593)
Stepwise regression (p. 594)
Time series data (p. 596)
Time series analysis (p. 596)
Trend (p. 596)
Exponential smoothing (p. 598)
Cycle (p. 601)
Seasonality (p. 603)

REVIEW QUESTIONS/APPLICATIONS

1. Construct and explain a reasonably simple predictive model for each of the following cases:
   a. What is the relationship between gasoline prices and distance traveled for family automobile touring vacations?
   b. How do hurricane-force warnings relate to purchases of flashlight batteries in the expected landfall area?
   c. What do florists do with regard to inventory of flowers for the weeks prior to and following Mother's Day?
2. Indicate what the scatter diagram and probable regression line would look like for two variables that are correlated in each of the following ways (in each instance, assume a negative intercept): (a) –0.89 (b) +0.48, and (c) –0.10.
3. Circle K runs a contest, inviting customers to fill out a registration card. In exchange, they are eligible for a grand prize drawing of a trip to Alaska. The card asks for the customer's age, education, gender, estimated weekly purchases (in dollars) at that Circle K, and approximate distance the Circle K is from his or her home. Identify each of the following if a multiple regression analysis were to be

performed: (a) independent variable, (b) dependent variable, and (c) dummy variable.

4. List the reasons a straight-line pattern is the one most commonly sought when one inspects business data reported over time.
5. What is a time series? Indicate the various time bases that can be used in reporting time series data.
6. Define the three basic patterns typically exhibited in a time series.
7. Describe the basic logic of exponential smoothing. Also, what are the conditions under which exponential smoothing will generally result in good predictions?
8. How can seasonality be demonstrated or illustrated?
9. In the table below is a time series for the sales of Rexall Brand Greaseless Sun Screen over a 20-year period.

20 Years of Rexall Greaseless Sun Screen Sales by Yearly Total

Year	Total	Year	Total
1978	6100	1988	8779
1979	6130	1989	9309
1980	6302	1990	10258
1981	6634	1991	10425
1982	7219	1992	11013
1983	8146	1993	12007
1984	8273	1994	12616
1985	8599	1995	13518
1986	8698	1996	14115
1987	8764	1997	14287

Note: Units are reported in 1000s and in 1.5-ounce package equivalents.

Use this time series to answer the following questions:

a. Make predictions for Rexall's sales in the year 1998 using SPSS for Windows scatter plot and time series routines.

b. Do you think exponential smoothing is needed? Why or why not?

10. The Maximum Amount is a company that specializes in making fashionable clothes in large sizes for large people. Among its customers are Al Hirt and Hulk Hogan. A survey was performed for The Maximum Amount, and a regression analysis was run on some of the data. Of interest in this analysis was the possible relationship between self-esteem (dependent variable) and number of Maximum Amount articles purchased last year (independent variable). Self-esteem was measured on a 7-point scale in which 1 signifies very low and 7 indicates very high self-esteem. Below are some items that have been taken from the output.

    Pearson product moment correlation = +0.63
    Intercept = 3.5
    Slope = +0.2
    Standard error = 1.5

    All statistical tests are significant at the 0.01 level or less. What is the correct interpretation of these findings?

11. Wayne LaTorte is a safety engineer who works for the U.S. Postal Service. For most of his life, Wayne has been fascinated by UFOs. He has kept records of UFO sightings in the desert areas of Arizona, California, and New Mexico over the past 15 years and he has correlated them with earthquake tremors. A fellow engineer suggests that Wayne use regression analysis as a means of determining the relationship. Wayne does this and finds a "constant" of 30 separate earth tremor events and a slope of 5 events per UFO sighting. Wayne then writes an article for the *UFO Observer*, claiming that earthquakes are largely caused by the subsonic vibrations emitted by UFOs as they enter the Earth's atmosphere. What is your reaction to Wayne's article?

CASE 18.1

Sales Training Associates, Inc.

Sales Training Associates, Inc. (STA) is a training company headquartered in Atlanta, Georgia. It specializes in training courses for sales, sales management, and marketing management. STA was founded by Harold "Bud" Simmons who began his sales career selling Rainbow vacuum cleaners door-to-door in 1960. Bud Simmons never attended college, and, in fact, he barely graduated from high school, but he demonstrated a strong aptitude for sales, and he took a job as a Rainbow sales rep immediately following graduation.

Bud was very successful from the start, and he moved through a succession of sales jobs in the 1960s and 1970s. In 1981, Bud joined the Equitable Life Insurance Company, and in two short years he was a member of the coveted million dollar round table. By the mid-1980s, Bud's annual sales were averaging over $5 million. Equitable realized that Bud had special selling talent, and it gradually shifted Bud's activities from selling to training of Equitable sales personnel. Bud developed a series of in-house training programs and special-purpose seminars that received high acclaim from all Equitable salespersons who participated in them. In 1992, Bud left Equitable to found Sales Training Associates, Inc, beginning at first with sales training in insurance sales only, but soon STA training programs covered practically all types of sales.

Bud's son, Harold Jr., joined STA in 1993 after struggling for 6 years to earn his undergraduate degree in marketing at the University of Alabama–Birmingham. Harold, or Hal, as he prefers to be called, took the position of administrative director, and his duties included home office management, human resources management, advertising, and long-range planning. One of Hal's early projects involved developing a predictive model of sales performance. Hal and Bud reasoned that if they could prove that STA training is a key success factor, it would be very valuable in future STA advertising and probably in long-range planning as well. From STA files, Hal selected 30 salespeople who had been enrolled in STA courses and programs over the past 3 years. He tallied the types of STA education each had received, and he pulled selected demographic factors from their files as well. Finally, to gauge sales success, he devised a 20-point overall sales performance index, and he called each salesperson, and asked him or her to rate last year's performance on that scale. These self-ratings and the other factors are listed in the following table:

SELECTED FACTORS AND SELF-EVALUATED SALES PERFORMANCE FOR LAST YEAR

Sales Performance Rating	Total STA Training Hours	Number of STA Certificates Earned	Sales-person's Age	Sales-person's Gender	Number of Years with Present Company
20	300	12	45	Male	25
2	60	2	22	Female	1
4	75	3	25	Male	5
12	200	7	37	Female	4
6	180	6	36	Male	12
3	30	5	23	Female	4
15	150	7	46	Male	20
18	200	8	59	Male	30
7	85	2	33	Male	7
10	100	3	43	Male	17
12	120	2	53	Female	18
7	90	3	35	Female	8
19	200	7	45	Male	15
13	150	5	25	Male	5
17	100	4	35	Female	4
12	100	4	45	Male	15
16	125	3	50	Female	10
20	175	7	65	Male	35
9	60	1	24	Male	4
16	150	5	48	Male	10

1. Using SPSS for Windows perform a series of bivariate regressions using the sales performance measure as the dependent variable, and each of the other factors in the table as independent measures. What did you find, and how do you interpret these findings?
2. Use multiple regression to determine the relationship of the various factors to self-evaluated sales performance for last year. What did you find, and what are the implications of the findings for STA?

CASE 18.2

Tunturi Exercise Equipment Company

Fitness was the rage of the 1980s, and moderation is the byword of the 1990s. Although running was in vogue in the previous decade, bicycling and swimming have come to be more popular exercise alternatives today. The Tunturi Exercise Equipment Company positioned itself to take advantage of the shift in exercise preferences as Baby Boomers moved into their 40s and 50s, and muscles and joints screamed for relief from the jarring and pounding exercise regimens of marathons, half-marathons, and 10-kilometer runs. Tunturi manufactures and sells several types of exercise equipment, but the three major items in Tunturi's product line are exercise bicycles, stairmasters, and rowing machines.

It is time for the 1998 annual plan, and Tunturi's marketing department has begun preliminary analyses for planning purposes. A primary ingredient in the annual plan is a sales forecast of Tunturi sales for each of the three major products. A time series of unit shipments (combined number of exercise bicycles, stairmasters, or rowing machines shipped to wholesalers, retailers, or direct to customers) has been established for each product for the years 1983–1997. The shipments data are contained in the following table:

ANNUAL SHIPMENTS OF TUNTURI EXERCISE EQUIPMENT COMPANY'S THREE MAJOR PRODUCTS 1983–1997 (10,000S)

Year	*Exercise Bicycles*	*Stairmasters*	*Rowing Machines*
1983	1.1	0.1	0.2
1984	3.2	0.1	0.3
1985	5.5	0.5	0.2
1986	3.2	0.3	0.4
1987	8.4	1.0	0.7
1988	6.3	1.5	1.0
1989	13.7	0.7	1.1
1990	13.5	1.5	1.3
1991	12.0	2.9	0.9
1992	16.4	4.5	1.3
1993	17.3	7.4	0.8
1994	19.0	10.7	1.4
1995	17.4	14.6	1.6
1996	22.6	18.3	2.0
1997	23.9	21.6	2.8

1. Construct time series scatter diagrams with linear trend lines fit to each of the three products. What is your assessment of the fit of the linear trend line to each time series?
2. Assess whether exponential smoothing is appropriate, and, if so, perform exponential smoothing, using SPSS for Windows for each time series to make a prediction of the sales in 1998.

CHAPTER 19

Presenting the Research Results

LEARNING OBJECTIVES

- *To appreciate the importance of the marketing research report*
- *To know what material should be included in each part of the marketing research report*
- *To learn the basic guidelines regarding the use of headings, style, and editing*
- *To know how to use visuals such as figures, tables, charts, and graphs*
- *To learn how to make visuals such as tables and figures using SPSS*
- *To learn how to transfer visuals you make using SPSS into your word processing program*
- *To understand the principles for making an oral presentation of your report*

PRACTITIONER VIEWPOINT

The tone, manner, and content of the presentation of research results makes a very important statement to the client about the professionalism of the company to whom they have entrusted their objectives. Clients will expect that you are able to implement the technical steps of the research process, but how well you communicate the results, recommendations, and conclusions will be essential to sustaining an ongoing relationship and developing future business. This chapter guides you through the critical elements of presentation and, for the benefit of your audience, mastering the preparation of the executive summary is worth particularly close attention.

— Patricia Botwinick
President, MPG International Ltd.

The Class Project

1. Establish the need for marketing research
2. Define the problem
3. Establish research objectives
4. Determine research design
5. Identify information types and sources
6. Determine methods of accessing data
7. Design data collection forms
8. Determine sample plan and size
9. Collect data
10. Analyze data
11. **Prepare and present the final research report**

The semester is finally drawing to a close. Only three more weeks and John Daniel, Joy Greer, and Mary Hall will finish their coursework and receive their B.S. degrees. They have worked hard all semester on their research project in their marketing research class. They met with their client, designed a research project, and developed a questionnaire. They devised a sampling plan and interviewed 300 local residents. Having spent three evenings in the university computing lab, they finally have the results.

"Gosh, this is a lot of information!" says John.

"Yes, now the challenging part really begins," replies Joy. "We've got to take these 125 pages of computer printouts and turn them into something that will suit our client's expectations."

The final stage of the marketing research process is the report; and Joy is right, the report is critical!

Knowing how to write the research report is challenging and critical.

The **marketing research report** is a factual message that transmits research results, vital recommendations, conclusions, and other important information to the client, who in turn bases his or her decision making on the contents of the report. This chapter deals with the essentials of writing the marketing research report.

The marketing research report communicates the marketing project's details to the client.

IMPORTANCE OF THE RESEARCH REPORT

The research report may be the only product of the research process that the client will ever see, and it is important for continuing relationships between clients and researchers.

As a marketer, you know the importance of packaging. If the product is not appropriately presented, regardless of how good it is, it will be discounted by the consumer. The same is true of your research. The marketing research report is the product that represents the efforts of the marketing research team, and it may be the only part of the project that the client will see. If the report is poorly written, riddled with grammatical errors, sloppy, or in any way inferior, the quality of the research, including its analysis and information, immediately becomes suspect. If organization and presentation are faulty, the reader may never reach the intended conclusions. The time and effort expended in the research process are wasted if the report does not communicate effectively. If, on the other hand, all aspects of the report are done well, the report will not only communicate properly, it will also serve to build credibility.

Marketing research users[1] as well as marketing research suppliers[2] agree that the research report is one of the most important aspects of the marketing research process. Many managers will not be involved in any aspect of the research process but will use the report to make business decisions. Effective reporting is essential, and all of the principles of organization, formatting, and good writing must be followed. Finally, as Patricia Botwinick stated at the beginning of this chapter, the research report is essential for a continuing business relationship between a research user and a research provider.

ORGANIZATION OF THE WRITTEN REPORT

Market research reports are tailored to specific audiences and purposes, and you must consider these in all phases of the research process, including preparing the report. If the organization for which you are conducting the research has specific guidelines for preparing the document, you should follow them. However, if no specific guidelines are provided, there are certain elements that must be considered when preparing the report. These elements can be grouped in three sections: front matter, body, and end matter.[3] See Table 19.1 for details.

Front Matter

Front matter includes all those items before the body of the report.

The **front matter** consists of the title fly page, title page, letter of authorization (optional), letter/memo of transmittal, table of contents, list of illustrations, and abstract/executive summary.

Title Fly Page

Figure 19.1 (page 614) is an example of the **title fly page.** It contains only the title of the report, centered horizontally and vertically on the page. It immediately precedes the title page. Title flies are optional and generally appear only in formal reports. If a title fly is used, it is counted as page i; however, no number is printed on the page.

Title Page

The title should be as informative as possible.

The title page gives: (1) title, (2) for whom, (3) by whom, and (4) when.

The **title page** (Figure 19.2 on page 615) contains four major items of information: (1) the title of the document, (2) the organization/person(s) for whom the report has been prepared, (3) the organization/person(s) who prepared the report, and (4) the date of submission. If names of individuals appear on the ti-

Table 19.1

The Elements of a Marketing Research Report

- **A.** Front Matter
  - **1.** Title Fly Page (optional)
  - **2.** Title Page
  - **3.** Letter of Authorization
  - **4.** Letter/Memo of Transmittal
  - **5.** Table of Contents
  - **6.** List of Illustrations
  - **7.** Abstract/Executive Summary
- **B.** Body
  - **8.** Introduction
  - **9.** Research Objectives
  - **10.** Methodology
  - **11.** Results
  - **12.** Limitations
  - **13.** Conclusions or Conclusions & Recommendations
- **C.** End Matter
  - **14.** Appendices

tle page, they may be in either alphabetical order or some other agreed-on order. Persons' names should also be given a designation or some descriptive title.

The title should be as informative as possible. It should include the purpose and content of the report, such as "An Analysis of the Demand for a Branch Office of the CPA Firm of Saltmarsh, Cleveland & Gund," or "Alternative Advertising Copy to Introduce the New M&M/Mars Low-Fat Candy Bar." The title should be centered and printed in all uppercase (capital) letters. Other items of information on the title page should be centered and printed in upper- and lowercase letters. Although the title page is counted as page i of the front matter (if a title fly is not used), a page number is not printed on it.

Letter of Authorization

The letter of authorization is optional.

The **letter of authorization** is the marketing research firm's certification to do the project and is also optional. If you allude to the conditions of your authorization in the letter/memo of transmittal (see following discussion), the letter of authorization is not necessary in the report. However, if your reader does not know the conditions of authorization, inclusion of this document is helpful. The letter of authorization includes the name and title of the persons authorizing the research to be performed. It may also include a general description of the nature of the research project, completion date, terms of payment, and any special conditions of the research project requested by the client or research user.

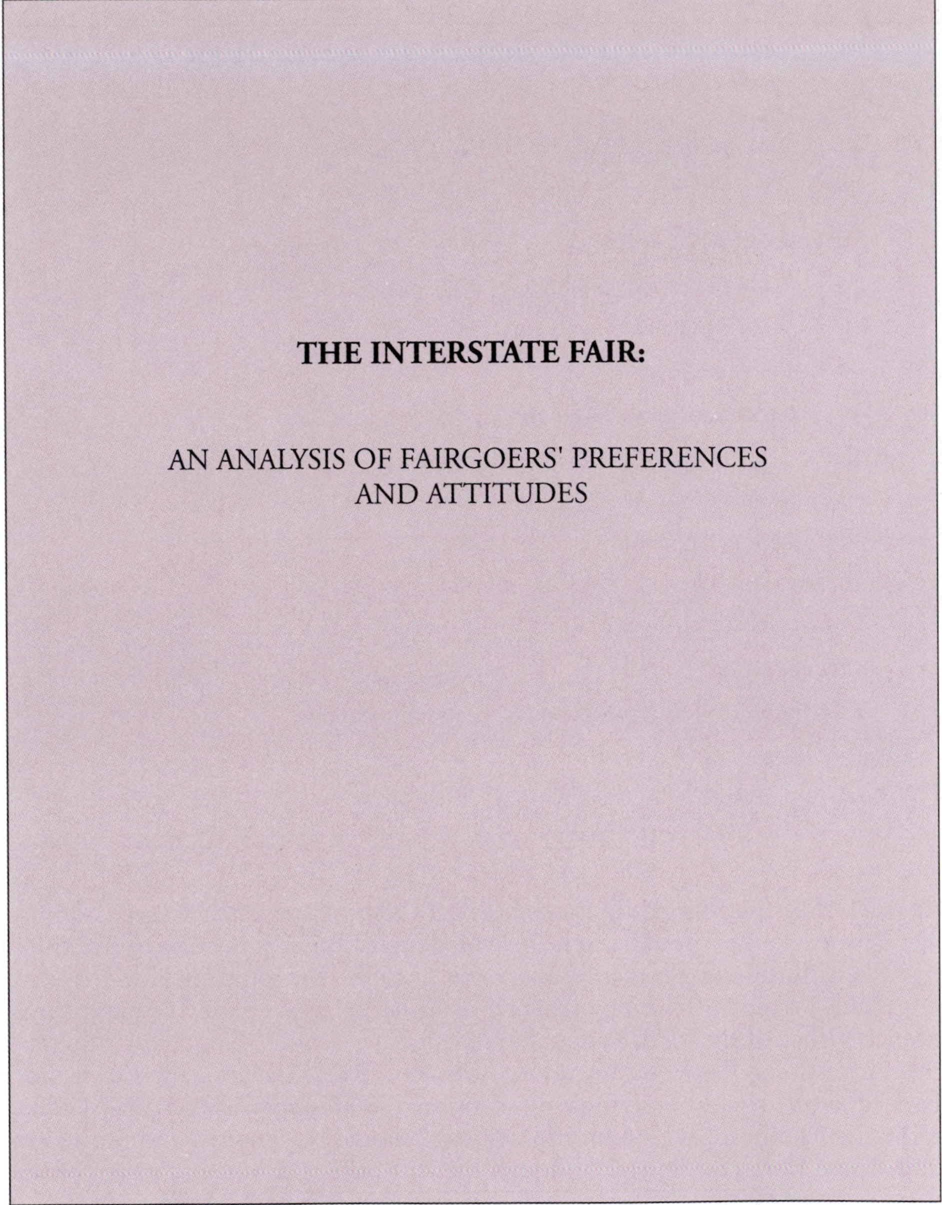
THE INTERSTATE FAIR:

AN ANALYSIS OF FAIRGOERS' PREFERENCES AND ATTITUDES

Figure 19.1

A Title Fly Page

Letter/Memo of Transmittal

The letter (memo) of transmittal orients the reader to the report.

Use a **letter of transmittal** to release or deliver the document to an organization for which you are not a regular employee. Use a **memo of transmittal** to deliver the document within your own organization. The letter/memo of transmittal describes the general nature of the research in a sentence or two and identifies the individual who is releasing the report. The primary purpose of the letter/memo of transmittal is to orient the reader to the report and to build a positive image of the report. It should establish rapport between the writer and receiver. It gives the receiver a person to contact should there be questions concerning any aspect of the report.

THE INTERSTATE FAIR:

AN ANALYSIS OF FAIRGOERS' PREFERENCES
AND ATTITUDES

Prepared for
The Board of Directors
The Interstate Fair
Tulsa, Oklahoma

by
MarkSearch Consulting Group, Inc.
Suite 6
122 South Palafox Street
Indianapolis, Indiana

November 1998

Figure 19.2

A Title Page

Writing style in the letter/memo of transmittal should be personal and slightly informal. Some general ingredients in the letter/memo of transmittal are a brief identification of the nature of the research, a review of the conditions of the authorization to do the research (if there is no letter of authorization, see previous discussion), comments on findings, suggestions for further research, and an expression of interest in the project and further research. Personal observations, unsupported by data, are appropriate. Figure 19.3 (page 616) presents an example of a letter of transmittal.

November 8, 1998

Ms. Courtney Struble
Chairperson
Board of Directors
The Interstate Fair
2268 S. Harvard Boulevard
Tulsa, OK

Dear Ms. Struble:

As you requested in your letter of authorization dated August 5, 1998, I have now completed the analysis of fairgoers attending the The Interstate Fair during October, 1998. The results of my research are contained in the report entitled "The Interstate Fair: An Analysis of Fairgoers' Attitudes and Preferences." The report is based on personal interviews of 668 persons attending The Interstate Fair between October 8th and 19th, 1998. The complete methodology is described in the report. Standard marketing research practices were used in the conduct of the study, and I believe the results to be valid and reliable within the constraints as identified in the report.

I believe you will find the results to be interesting and certainly of use to you and other board members in making your recommendations for operating the fair during the 1999 season. Please do not hesitate to call me should you have any questions.

Sincerely,

Laura Holladay

Laura Holladay
President
MarkSearch Consulting Group, Inc.

Figure 19.3

A Letter of Transmittal

Table of Contents

A table of contents lists each report heading exactly and gives its page number.

The **table of contents** helps the reader locate information in the research report. The table of contents (Figure 19.4) should list each heading exactly as it appears and the number of the page on which it appears. If a section is longer than one page, list the page on which it begins. Indent subheadings under headings. All items except the title page and the table of contents are listed with page numbers in the table of contents. Front matter pages are numbered with lowercase Roman numerals: i, ii, iii. Arabic numerals are used beginning with the introduction section of the body of the report.

CONTENTS

Figure 19.4

An Example of a Table of Contents

List of Illustrations

If the report contains tables and/or figures, you need to include a **list of illustrations** in the table of contents. As you can see from Figure 19.5 on page 618, these lists help the reader find specific illustrations that serve to graphically portray the information. In the example shown, all of the illustrations are figures, hence the title, "Figures." **Tables** are words or numbers that are arranged in rows and columns; **figures** are graphs, charts, maps, pictures, and so on. Because tables and figures are numbered independently, you may have both a Figure 1 and a Table 1 in your list of illustrations. Give each a name, and list each in the order in which it appears in the report.

Tables and figures have their own separate tables of contents sections.

FIGURES

Figure 19.5

A Table of Figures

Abstract/Executive Summary

The executive summary is provided for readers who have only a general "need to know."

Your report may have many readers. Some of them will need to know the details of your report such as the supporting data on which you base the conclusions and recommendations. Others will not need as many details but will only want to read the conclusions and recommendations. Still others with only a general need to know may read only the executive summary. For this reason, the **abstract** or **executive summary** is a "skeleton" of your report. It serves as a summary for the busy executive or a preview for the in-depth reader. It provides an overview of the most useful information, including the conclusions and recommendations. The abstract or executive summary should be very carefully written, conveying the information as concisely as possible. It should be single spaced and, preferably, confined to only a few paragraphs and less than one page. The abstract or executive summary should cover (a) the general subject of the research, (b) the scope of the research (what the research covers/does not cover), (c) identification of the type of methodology used (that is, a mail survey of 1,000 homeowners), (d) conclusions, and (e) recommendations.[4]

Body

The **body** is the bulk of the report. It contains an introduction to the report, an explanation of your methodology, a discussion of your results, a statement of limitations, and a list of conclusions and recommendations. Don't be alarmed by the repetition that may appear in your report. Only a few people will read the entire report. Most will read the executive summary, conclusions and recommendations. Therefore, formal reports are repetitious. For example, you may specify the research objectives in the executive summary and refer to them again in the findings section as well as in the conclusions section. Also, do not be concerned that you use the same terminology to introduce the several tables and/or figures that may appear in your report. In many lengthy reports, repetition actually enhances reader comprehension. The first page of the body is counted as page 1, but no page number is printed on it. All other pages throughout the document are numbered consecutively.

Use liberal repetition in the report as most readers will not read it cover to cover.

Introduction

The **introduction** to the marketing research report orients the reader. It should contain a statement of the general purpose of the report and also the specific objectives for the research, a description of what it intended to discover, and any essential background information to explain why the research was undertaken. The list of specific objectives often serves as a good basis for organizing the results section of the report.

The introduction provides: (1) a problem statement, (2) research objectives, and (3) essential background facts.

Methodology

The **methodology** describes, in as much detail as necessary, how you conducted the research, who (or what) your subjects were, and what methods were used to achieve your objectives. Supplementary information should be placed in the appendix. If you used secondary information, you will need to document your sources (provide enough information so that your sources can be located).[5] You do not need to document facts that are common knowledge or can be easily verified. But, if you are in doubt, document! Marketing Research Insight 19.1 (page 620) illustrates plagiarism and suggests how you can avoid the "world's dumbest crime."

The methodology section does not need to be long but it should provide the reader with enough information to understand how the study was conducted.

In most cases, the methodology section (sometimes called the "method" section) does not need to be long. It should, however, provide the essential information your reader needs to understand how the data were collected and the results achieved. In some cases, the needs of the research user may dictate a very extensive methodology section. A client may, for example, want the researcher to not only thoroughly describe the methodology that was used but also discuss why other methodologies were not selected. In situations in which research information will be provided in litigation, where you are certain to have an adversary, a researcher may be asked to provide an exhaustive description of the methods used in the conduct of the study.

MARKETING RESEARCH INSIGHT 19.1

Plagiarism: The World's Dumbest Crime

Let's not beat around the bush: plagiarism is theft. It is the act of stealing the words of another writer without crediting the source and, where appropriate, asking for permission. Although it is against the law, plagiarism remains common wherever words are written. Plagiarism is also a problem in public speaking.

Journalist Gregg Easterbrook uncovered nearly three pages of his own words in a book authored by Richard Pascal, a Stanford University business school lecturer. Easterbrook had written these words four years before Pascal's book was published. Compare two sentences taken from each version:

- ***Easterbrook Version,*** *from an article in a 1986 issue of* The Washington Monthly: *On a very dark day in 1980, Donald Petermen, newly chosen president of Ford Motors, visited the company design studios. Ford was in the process of losing $2.2 billion, the largest single-year loss in U.S. history.*
- ***Pascal Version,*** *from his 1990 book,* Managing on the Edge: *On a dark day in 1980, Donald Petermen, the newly chosen President of Ford Motor Company, visited the company's Detroit design studio. That year, Ford would lose $2.2 billion, the largest loss in a single year in U.S. corporate history.*

Knowing how to avoid plagiarism like this is as crucial as knowing the rules of grammar. Here are some guidelines that will help you avoid the problem.

1. *Develop the habit of documenting the ideas and words that you obtain from other sources. When citing the exact words of a source, set off the citation in quotation marks and use a footnote for documentation.*
2. *Develop effective note-taking habits and be very careful in your use of quotation marks. Plagiarism often occurs when, during the research stage, sources are copied verbatim without quotation marks.*
3. *You are still responsible for documenting your sources even if you rephrase someone else's thoughts in your own words and with your own sentence structure (the essence of paraphrasing and summarizing).*
4. *Finally, learn when documentation is not necessary. First, personal ideas and knowledge require no documentation. Footnotes, for example, are not needed if you are presenting an original new product marketing strategy. Second, "common knowledge"—information known and readily available to most people—is not subject to plagiarism. Thus, when writing a report on a major corporation, there is no need to document the source that gave you the name of the CEO or the location of the corporate headquarters.*

Plagiarism is a breach of ethics as well as a theft of property. It is also the "world's dumbest crime," says Gregg Easterbrook. "If you are caught, there is absolutely nothing you can say in your own defense."

Source: *This excellent piece on plagiarism was taken, almost verbatim, from Louis E. Boone and David L. Kurtz,* Contemporary Business Communication, *Upper Saddle River, NJ: Prentice Hall (1994), 378. Reprinted by permission. Sources cited in the original article are James Atlas, "When an Original Idea Sounds Really Familiar,"* New York Times *(July 28, 1991), E2; Gregg Easterbrook, "The Sincerest Flattery,"* Newsweek *(July 29, 1991), 45–46; and Lynn Quitman Troyka,* Simon & Schuster Handbook for Writers, *2d ed. (Upper Saddle River, NJ: Prentice Hall, 1990), 580–83.*

Results

The **results** section is the major portion of your report. It logically presents the findings of your research and should be organized around your objectives for the study. The results should be presented in narrative form and accompanied by tables, charts, figures, and other appropriate visuals that support and enhance the explanation.

You should outline your results section carefully before you begin writing the report.

You should outline your results section before you write the report. Sometimes the survey questionnaire itself serves as a useful aid in organizing your results because the questions themselves are often grouped in some logical format. Another useful method for organizing your results is to individually print out all of your tables and figures and arrange them in some logical sequence. Once you have the results outlined properly, you are ready to write in the introductory sentences, definitions (if necessary), review of the findings (often referring to tables and figures), and transition sentences to lead into the next topic.

Arrange your results logically, perhaps based on your objectives.

Limitations

Do not attempt to hide or disguise problems in your research; no research is faultless. Suggest what the **limitations** are or may be and how they impact the results. Typical limitations in research reports note factors such as time, money, and personnel, as well as other limitations. Consider the following example: ". . . the reader should be cautioned that the findings in this study were based on a survey of supermarket managers in the Northeastern United States. Time and budget constraints limited the sample to this region of the country. Care should be exercised in generalizing these findings to other geographical regions."

Conclusions and Recommendations

Conclusions and recommendations may be listed separately or together, depending on how much you have to report. In any case, you should note that conclusions are not the same thing as recommendations. **Conclusions** are the outcomes and decisions you have reached based on your research results. **Recommendations** are suggestions for how to proceed based on the conclusions. Unlike conclusions, recommendations may require knowledge beyond the scope of the research findings themselves—that is, information on conditions within the company, the industry, and so on. Therefore, researchers should exercise caution in making recommendations. The researcher and the client should determine *prior* to the study whether the report is to contain recommendations. Although a research user may desire the researcher to provide recommendations, both parties must realize that the researcher's recommendations are being made based solely on the knowledge gained from the research project. Other information, if made known to the researcher, may totally change the researcher's recommendations.

Recommendations are stated cautiously as the researcher does not have intimate knowledge of the manager's situation.

End Matter

The **end matter** comprises the **appendices,** which contain additional information to which the reader may refer for further reading but that is not essential to reporting the data. Tables, figures, additional reading, technical descriptions, data collection forms, appropriate computer printouts, and a bibliography (if appropriate) are some elements that may appear in an appendix. Each appendix should be labeled with both a letter and a title, and each should be listed in the table of contents.

The appendix should contain additional information to which the reader may refer for further reading but is not essential to reporting the data.

GUIDELINES AND PRINCIPLES FOR THE WRITTEN REPORT

The parts of the research report have already been described. However, you should also consider its form and format and its style.

Form and Format

Form and format concerns include headings and subheadings and visuals.

Headings and Subheadings

Headings and subheadings provide visual signposts that serve as a map for your reader.

In a long report, your reader needs signals and signposts to serve as a map. Headings and subheadings perform this function. **Headings** indicate the topic of each section. All information under a specific heading should relate to that heading. A new heading should introduce a change of topic. Choose the kind of heading that fits your purpose—single word, phrase, sentence, question—and consistently use that form throughout the report. If you use **subheadings** within the divisions, they must be similar to one another but not similar to the headings so as to clearly differentiate subheads from headings.[6]

Visuals

Visuals have the potential to dramatically present information.

Visuals are tables, figures, charts, diagrams, graphs, and other graphic aids. Used properly, they can dramatically and compactly present information that might otherwise be difficult to follow. Tables systematically present numerical data or words in columns and rows. Figures translate numbers into visual displays so that relationships and trends become comprehensible. Examples of figures are graphs, pie charts, and bar charts.

Visuals should be uncluttered and self-explanatory. Even though they are self-explanatory, the key points of all visuals should be explained in the text. Refer to visuals by number: for example, " . . . as shown in Figure 1." Place the visual immediately below the paragraph in which its first reference appears. Or, if sufficient space is not available, continue the text and place the visual on the next page. Visuals can also be placed in an appendix. Additional information on preparing visuals is presented later in this chapter.

Style

There are a number of stylistic devices you need to consider when you are actually writing the sentences and paragraphs in your report. These may best be presented as "tips" for the writer.

Before you begin writing, carefully consider your audience.

1. Before you begin writing, carefully consider your audience. Who is your audience? How much information can you assume your audience knows? How much detail do you need to provide so that the audience can act on your information and recommendations? What specific considerations do you need to make to communicate effectively with your audience?
2. As a rule, begin paragraphs with topic sentences. A good paragraph has one main idea. Topic sentences alert your reader and let him or her know what to expect. Topic sentences can also appear in the middle or at the end of a paragraph. Examples of good topic sentences are: "The Southern California market is not receptive to 'Good

Cookings' new apple-flavored soda" and "This research concludes that the corner of 181st St. and Zazinski Ave. is an excellent site location for a new Subway, Inc. franchise."

3. Use jargon sparingly. Some of your audience may understand technical terms; others may not. When in doubt, properly define the terms for your readers. If many technical terms are required in the report, you might consider including a glossary of terms in an appendix to assist the less-informed members of your audience.

Good writing style guides: topic sentences, minimal use of jargon, strong verbs, and active voice.

4. Use strong verbs to carry the intent of your sentences, and cut out all unnecessary words. Instead of "making a recommendation," "recommend." Or, instead of "performing an investigation," "investigate."
5. Generally, you want to write in the active voice. Voice indicates whether the subject or the verb is doing the action (active voice) or being acted on (passive voice). For example, "The report was written by John" uses the passive voice. "John wrote the report" uses the active voice. Active voice is direct and forceful, and the active voice uses fewer words.
6. Avoid unnecessary changes in tense. Tense tells if the action of the verb occurred in the past (past tense), is happening right now (present tense), or will happen in the future (future tense). Changing tenses within a document is an error writers frequently make. Be aware of moving from tense to tense within your paper.
7. Eliminate extra words. Write your message clearly and concisely. Combine and reword sentences to eliminate unnecessary words.
8. In sentences, keep the subject and verb close together. The farther apart they become, the more difficulty the reader has understanding the message and the greater the chance there is for errors in subject/verb agreement.
9. Vary the length and structure of sentences.
10. Edit carefully. Your first draft is not a finished product, nor is your second. Edit your work carefully, rearranging and rewriting until you communicate the intent of your research as efficiently and effectively as possible.

Your first draft is not a finished product . . . edit, edit, edit!

11. Proofread carefully. After you have a finished product, check it carefully to make sure everything is correct. Double check names and numbers, grammar, spelling, and punctuation. Although spell checks and grammar checks are helpful, you cannot rely on them to catch all errors. One of the best ways to proofread is to read the document aloud, preferably with a reader following along on the original document. An alternative is to read the document twice—once quickly for content and meaning and once slowly for mechanical errors.

Proofread your report aloud with a reader following along on the written document.

GUIDELINES FOR THE USE OF VISUALS: TABLES AND FIGURES

Visuals assist in the effective presentation of numerical data. The key to a successful visual is a clear and concise presentation that conveys the message of the report. The selection of the visual should match the presentation purpose for the data. Common visuals include the following:[7]

Here are several types of visuals and their appropriate uses.

- *Tables,* which identify exact values.
- *Charts* and *graphs,* which illustrate relationships among items.
- *Pie charts,* which compare a specific part to the whole.
- *Bar charts* and *line graphs,* which compare items over time, or show correlations among items.
- *Flow diagrams,* which introduce a set of topics and illustrate their *relationships* (Figure 19.6).
- *Stratum charts,* which show *relative* emphasis by area and change over time (Figure 19.7).
- *Maps,* which define locations.
- *Photographs,* which present an aura of legitimacy because they are not "created" in the sense that other visuals are created. Photos depict factual content.
- *Drawings,* which focus on visual details.

A discussion of some of these visuals follows.

Tables

Here are guidelines for creating tables.

Tables allow the reader to compare numerical data (see Table 19.2). Effective table guidelines are as follows:

1. Do not allow computer analysis to imply a level of accuracy that is not achieved. Limit your use of decimal places (that is, 12% instead of 12.22%).
2. Place items you want the reader to compare in the same column, not the same row.
3. If you have many rows, darken alternate entries or double space after every five entries to assist the reader to accurately line up items.
4. Total columns and rows when relevant.

Marketing Research Insight 19.2 (pages 626–627) gives you the necessary keystroke instructions to create tables using SPSS and to import these tables into your word processing program.

Pie Charts

Pie charts are particularly useful for illustrating relative size or static comparisons. The pie chart is a perfect circle divided into sections. Each section represents a percentage of the total area of the circle associated with one compo-

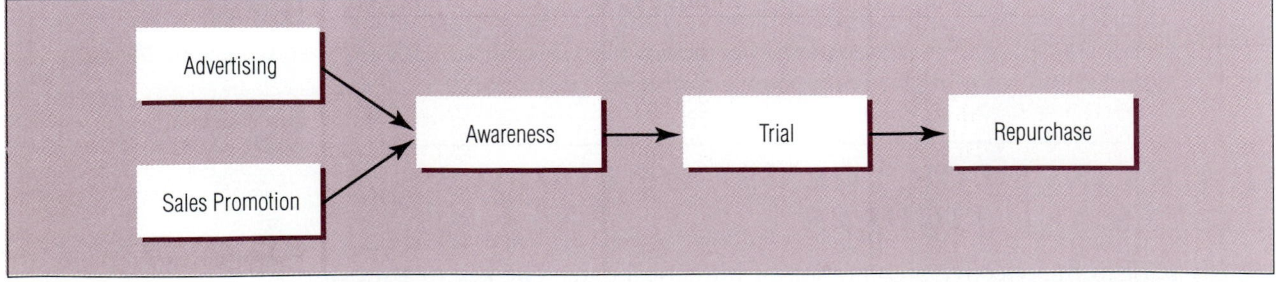

Figure 19.6

A Flow Diagram

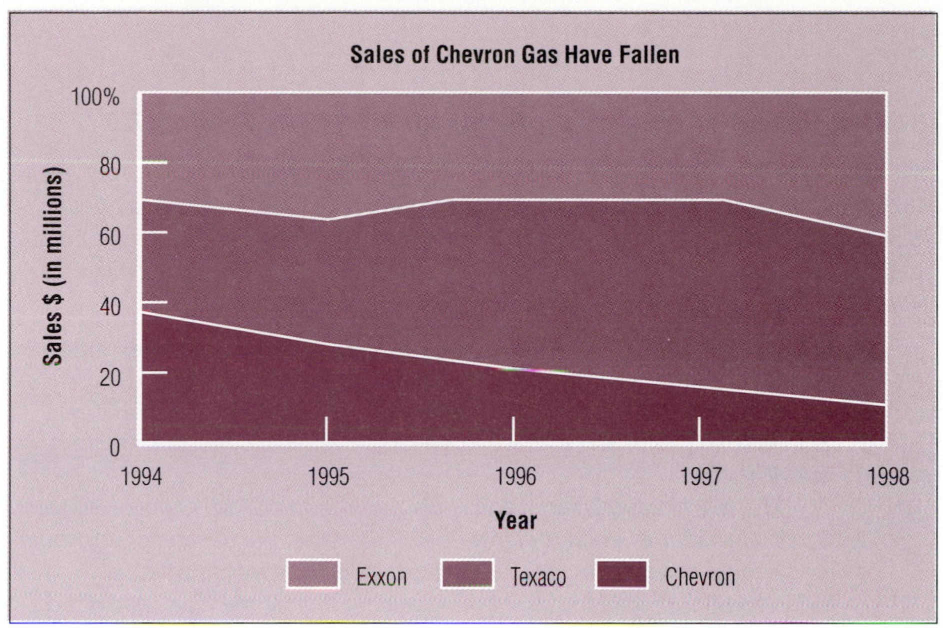

Figure 19.7
A Stratum Chart

nent. Today's data analysis programs easily and quickly make pie charts. Your SPSS for Windows program, for example, allows you to build customized pie charts.

The pie chart should have a limited number of segments (five or six). If your data has many small segments, you may consider combining the smallest or the least important into an "other" or "miscellaneous" category. Because in-

Table 19.2

Main Attraction Drawing You to the Fair

		Frequency	Percent
Attraction	Livestock	36	5.3
	Exhibits	82	12.0
	Music	105	15.4
	Rides	273	39.9
	Games	28	4.1
	Food	61	8.9
	Other	85	12.4
	Missing	14	2.0
Total		684	100.0

View: "Interstate Fair: Making Presentation Tables and Graphs"

MARKETING RESEARCH INSIGHT 19.2

How to Create a Table Using SPSS for Windows Version 7.5

We will use the Interstate Fair data set (Fair.sav) described to you in Case 15.2 (page 481) to demonstrate the creation of tables using SPSS. Say we wish to find out the relative popularity of the various attractions at the fair. To do this, we create a simple frequency table for responses to question 10a on the questionnaire: "What main *attractions drew you to the fair this year?"*

1. *Create a frequency table for responses to question 10a on the questionnaire: "What* main *attractions drew you to the fair this year?"*

   After opening the data file, use the Command Options STATISTICS-SUMMARIZE-FREQUENCIES and select the variable corresponding to question 10a.

   The resulting frequency table is displayed in the SPSS Output Navigator.
2. *Scroll down to the frequency table. To edit the table, put the cursor anywhere on the table and double-click. This activates the table editor, which is indicated by a shaded highlight box appearing around the table, and a red arrow pointing to the selected table. You may also see a toolbar appearing on your screen.*
3. *To change the format of the table, use command options FORMAT-TABLELOOKS.*
4. *To select a particular table format,* browse *through the directory and select one that suits your need. In this case, we used the* Boxed (VGA) *format. However, we wanted to change the fonts. Therefore, we needed to edit the format we had selected.*
5. *To edit an already available format, click Edit Look while in TABLELOOKS. To change the fonts, alignment, margins, etc., click on Cell Formats. Change the fonts, size, style, etc. to suit your needs. To change borders, click on Borders and select appropriate borders.*
6. *After adjusting the table properties for the attributes you want, save your customized table format by clicking on Save As and saving it under a new file name. Keep reading. We show you how you can recall this new table format for all the tables you make without having to re-edit each new table. You can use this customized table look for any future tables that you might create.*

   After you Save As and name the table format to be saved, click OK.
7. *You are now back in the table edit mode. The next step is to change the text in specific cells. To do this, double-click on the cell in which you want to change the text. The selected text will be highlighted. Simply type over and press Enter when you are done.*
8. *To hide the "Valid Percent" and "Cumulative Percent" columns, place the cursor on the selected column and Ctrl-Alt-click the category label of the column. The column will now be highlighted.*

   Right click (use right mouse button) the highlighted column to get the pop-up menu. From the pop-up menu, choose Hide Category.

   Similarly, hide any other rows or columns that you do not want in the final output.
9. *The table is now ready to be transferred to a word processing document. Click outside the table so that the shaded highlight box disappears. The red arrow should still be there. Now select Edit, Copy.*

In your word processing document, select Edit, Paste Special, and paste it as an SPSS Pivot Table. The table will appear on your screen.

10. *In this example, the word processing software used was WordPerfect for Windows 95.*

    Right click on the table. The pop-up menu gives you a set of tools to further edit the chart.

11. *From the pop-up menu, select Image Tools and use the arrow icon to move the table around in your document.*
12. *From the pop-up menu, select Wrap to format the way in which your running text wraps around the table. For instance, in this case, we selected Neither Side because we wanted the table to stand alone.*
13. *From the same pop-up menu, you can select Caption and enter the appropriate caption. You can also change the font, alignment, placing, and appearance of the caption.*

The table that we have created is shown in Table 19.2 on page 625.

ternal labels are difficult to read for small sections, labels for these sections should be placed outside the circle. Figure 19.8 is a pie chart from the Interstate Fair study.

Marketing Research Insight 19.3 (pages 628–629) gives you the keystroke instructions for creating pie charts using SPSS 7.5. It also shows you how to import your pie charts into a word processing program.

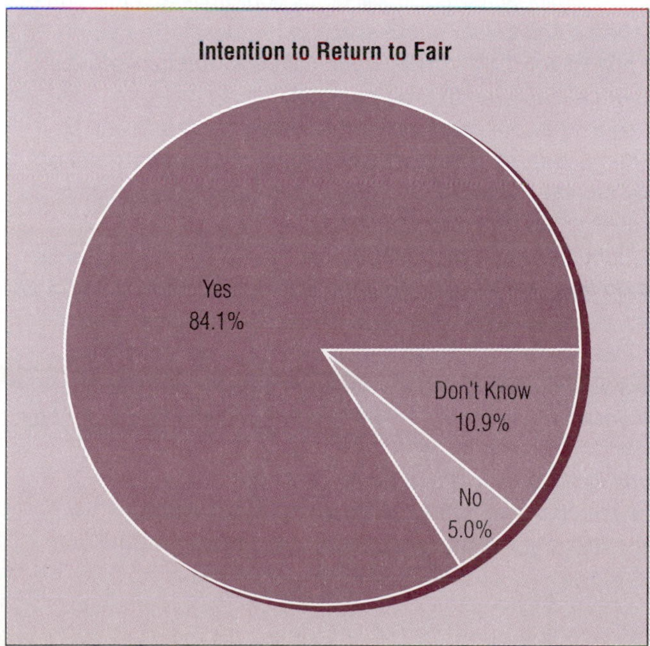

Figure 19.8

Example of a Pie Chart

Review: "NFO Panel Data: Making Simple Graphs"

MARKETING RESEARCH INSIGHT 19.3

How to Create a Pie Chart Using SPSS for Windows Version 7.5

We use data from the Interstate Fair to demonstrate the creation of a simple pie graph using SPSS. Say we want to show responses to question 5: "Do you plan on coming back to the fair next year?" in the form of a pie chart.

1. *Create a pie chart for responses to question 5 on the questionnaire: "Do you plan on coming back to the fair next year?"*

   After opening the data file, use the Command Options GRAPH and PIE. Click Summaries for Groups of Cases and then Define.

   The next screen allows you to choose the variable which you want to graph. Select the variable corresponding to question 5 on the questionnaire, click ▶ for Define Slices By, and the variable will be entered.

   You can choose what you want your slices to represent. In this case, we selected the pies to represent % of.

2. *At this stage, you can also enter the titles and footnotes for the chart by clicking on Titles and entering the appropriate labels.*

   Using the command OPTIONS, you can decide how you want missing values to be treated. Here, we have not included missing values in the chart by clicking off the check mark (✓) on the Display Groups Defined by Missing Values.

   Click OK and the resulting pie chart will appear in the SPSS Output Navigator. You are now ready to edit the chart.

   If you have an existing template of a pie graph, you can request the output to be formatted according to template specifications by clicking on Use Chart Specifications From and selecting the saved file name.

3. *Scroll down to the pie chart. To edit the chart, double-click the chart. This takes you to the SPSS Chart Editor screen. You will do all your editing in this screen.*
4. *To edit the filled patterns and colors of the slices of the pie chart, use command options FORMAT-FILL PATTERN and COLOR. You can see the final pie chart presented in Figure 19.8 on page 627.*
5. *To edit the textual content of the chart, select the text you want to edit by clicking once with the mouse. When your text is selected, a box or a set of markers will appear around the text. Now, double-click and you will get a box that allows you to change the text and justification of the text.*

   To change the font and size of the text, select the text by clicking once on the text with the mouse. Now, use command options FORMAT-TEXT and select the fonts and sizes you want. To edit and position the labels, use command options CHART-OPTIONS. This takes you to a box titled Pie Options. This allows you to change the format and positioning of the labels. It also gives you the option of collapsing slices that are less than 5 percent by summing them.

   You can choose to have your labels presented with values and percentages. In the pie chart presented in Figure 19.8 on page 627, we have opted to present the text and the percentages by clicking on the Text and Percents boxes.

Click on Edit Text to change the text of the labels. This takes you to a box titled Pie Options:Label Format. Here, you can decide the position of the labels, number of decimal places for the values and percentages, and the type of connecting lines if labels are outside the slices. We chose the labels to be inside the slices, and one decimal place to be displayed.

6. *To fit the entire chart with a frame, use command options CHART-OUTER FRAME.*
7. *After making all the changes, you can save your customized chart by using command options FILE-SAVE CHART TEMPLATE. For future charts, you can call up the customized template, saving you the need to edit every pie chart you create.*
8. *The chart is now ready to be transferred to a word processing document. Use command options EDIT-COPY CHART.*

   In your word processing document, select Edit. The chart will appear on your screen.
9. *In this example, the word processing software used was WordPerfect for Windows 95.*

   Right click on the chart. The pop-up menu gives you a set of tools to further edit the chart.
11. *From the pop-up menu, select Image Tools and use the arrow icon to move the chart around in your document.*
12. *From the pop-up menu, select Wrap to format the way in which your running text wraps around the chart. For instance, in this case, we selected Neither Side because we wanted the chart to stand alone.*
13. *From the same pop-up menu, you can select Caption and enter the appropriate caption. You can also change the font, alignment, placing, and appearance of the caption.*

The chart that we have created is shown in Figure 19.8 on page 627.

Bar Charts

There are several types of **bar charts** that can be used. Figure 19.9 (page 630) is a simple bar chart created by SPSS. Marketing Research Insight 19.4 (pages 630–631) gives you the keystroke instructions for creating bar charts of various types using SPSS. It also shows you how to import your bar charts into your word processing program. Study the types of bar charts available to you in SPSS. Your selection of the type of bar chart will depend on what you are trying to communciate to your reader.

Line Graphs

Line graphs are easy to interpret if designed appropriately. Line graphs may be drawn in SPSS using the GRAPHS option. You will see there are several options for different types of line graphs.

Flow diagrams introduce a set of topics and illustrate their relationships. Flow diagrams are particularly useful to illustrate topics that are sequential, e.g., step 1, step 2, etc.

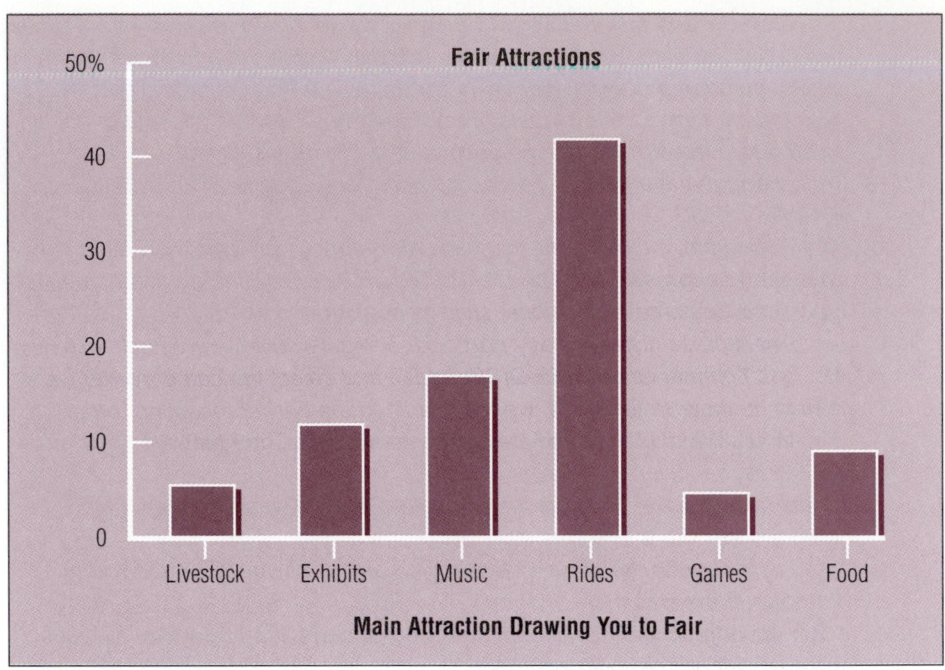

Figure 19.9

Example of a Simple Bar Chart

***Review*: "NFO Panel Data: Making Simple Graphs"**

MARKETING RESEARCH INSIGHT 19.4

How to Create a Bar Chart Using SPSS for Windows Version 7.5

We use data from the Interstate Fair to demonstrate the creation of a simple bar graph using SPSS. Say we want to show graphically the frequency distribution presented in Table 19.2 (see page 625). This frequency distribution shows the relative popularity of various attractions at the fair.

1. *Create a bar chart for responses to question 10a on the questionnaire: "What* main *attractions drew you to the fair this year?"*

   After opening the data file, use the Command Options GRAPH and BAR. You have the option of choosing from three different styles of bar charts. In this case, we used the simple chart. Click Summaries for Groups of Cases and then Define.

   The next screen allows you to choose the variable which you want to graph. Select the variable corresponding to question 10a on the questionnaire, click ▶ and the variable will be entered as the Category Axis.

   You can choose what you want your bars to represent. In this case, we selected the bars to represent % of Cases, because we are interested in the relative popularity of attractions at the fair.

2. *At this stage, you can also enter the titles and footnotes for the chart by clicking on Titles and entering the appropriate labels.*

   Using the command OPTIONS, you can decide how you want missing values to be treated. Here, we have not included missing values in the chart by clicking off the check mark (✓) on the Display Groups Defined by Missing Values.

Click OK and the resulting bar chart will appear in the SPSS Output Navigator. You are now ready to edit the chart.

If you have an existing template of a bar graph, you can request the output to be formatted according to template specifications by clicking on Use Chart Specifications From, and selecting the saved file name.

3. *Scroll down to the bar chart. To edit the chart, double-click the chart. This takes you to the SPSS Chart Editor screen. You will do all your editing in this screen.*

4. *To edit the bars, use command options FORMAT-BAR STYLE and Bar Label Style. As you can see from the final bar chart presented in Figure 19.9, we have used the three-dimensional style for the bars.*

To suppress display of any particular category such as livestock, exhibits, etc., use commands SERIES-DISPLAYED, and select the category you want to hide or show. In this case, we have omitted the bar representing "other" attractions. We did this to reduce the number of bars, and because it did not provide any additional information.

5. *To edit the textual content of the chart, select the text you want to edit by clicking once with the mouse. When your text is selected, a box or a set of markers will appear around the text. Now, use commands FORMAT-TEXT and change the fonts and sizes accordingly.*

To change the contents and alignment of the text, double-click on the text to be edited. You can now make the appropriate changes.

To change the orientation of the axis labels, double-click on the labels. This takes you to a box titled Category Axis. In that box, select Labels. This takes you to another box titled Category Axis: Labels. In this box, make your Orientation selection.

6. *To fit the entire chart with a frame, use command options CHART-OUTER FRAME. You can also edit the axis, legends, annotations, etc. under CHART.*

7. *After making all the changes, you can save your customized chart by using command options FILE-SAVE CHART TEMPLATE. For future charts, you can call up the customized template, saving you the need to edit every bar chart you create.*

8. *The chart is now ready to be transferred to a word processing document. Use command options EDIT-COPY CHART.*

In your word processing document, select Edit. The chart will appear on your screen.

9. *In this example, the word processing software used was WordPerfect for Windows 95.*

Right click on the chart. The pop-up menu gives you a set of tools to further edit the chart.

11. *From the pop-up menu, select Image Tools and use the arrow icon to move the chart around in your document.*

12. *From the pop-up menu, select Wrap to format the way in which your running text wraps around the chart. For instance, in this case, we selected Neither Side because we wanted the chart to stand alone.*

13. *From the same pop-up menu, you can select Caption and enter the appropriate caption. You can also change the font, alignment, placing, and appearance of the caption.*

The chart that we have created is shown in Figure 19.9.

Stratum charts show relative emphasis by area and change over time. Stratum charts are useful to display changes in comparative data over time, e.g., as company A's market share goes up, what happens to the market shares of companies B and C?

AN ACCURATE AND ETHICAL VISUAL

Graphs have the capacity to misrepresent information.

A marketing researcher should always follow the doctrine of "full disclosure." An **ethical visual** is one that is totally objective in terms of how information is presented in the research report. Sometimes misrepresenting information is intentional (as when a client asks a researcher to misrepresent the data in order to promote his or her "pet project") or it may be unintentional. In the latter case, those preparing a visual are sometimes so familiar with the material being presented that they falsely assume that the graphic message is apparent to all who view it.

Consider a report to top management written by the R&D department of a large chemical firm. The report was written to allow the R&D department to make the argument that their funding has decreased in the past and they now

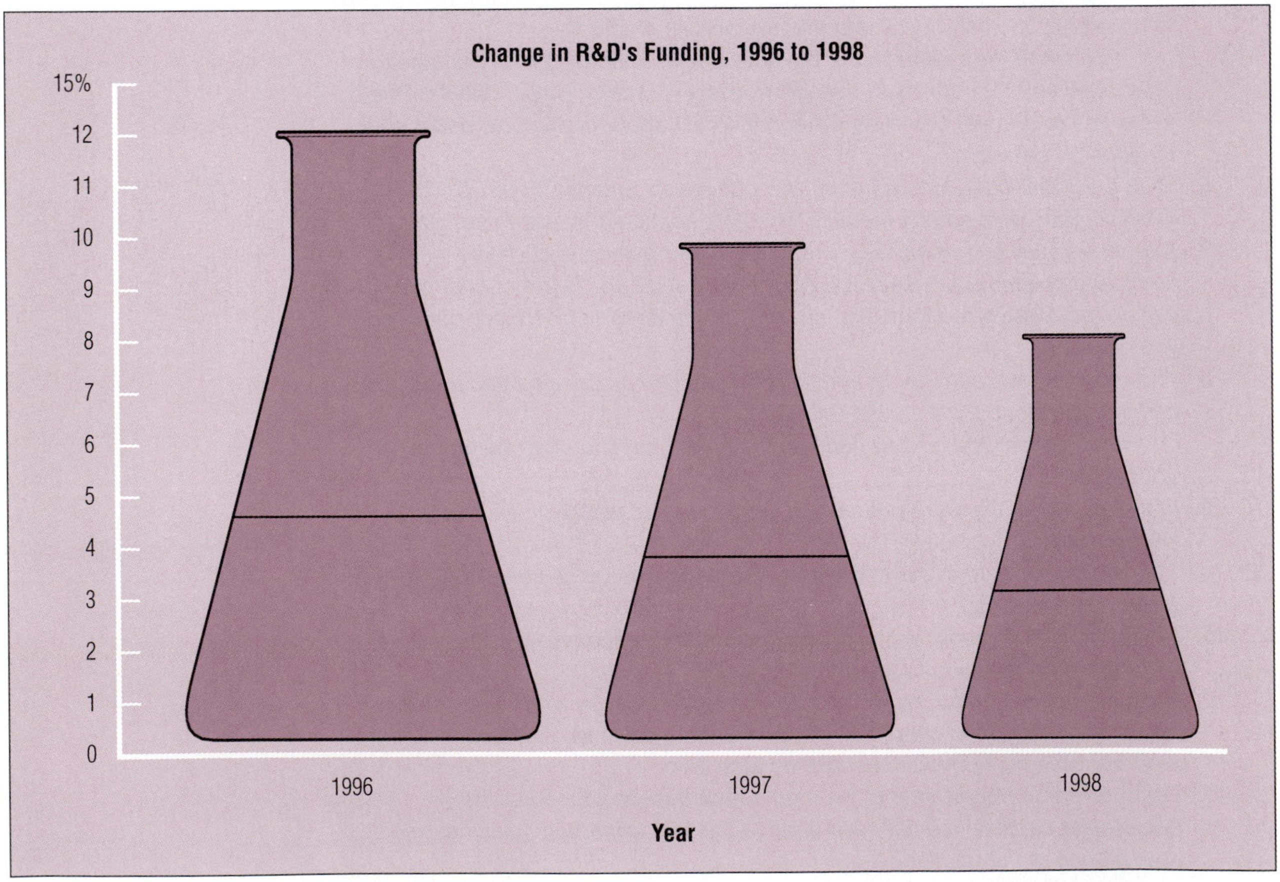

Change in R&D's Funding, 1996 to 1998

15%
12
11
10
9
8
7
6
5
4
3
2
1
0

1996 1997 1998

Year

Figure 19.10

A Misleading Figure

need additional funds. In support of their argument, they present Figure 19.10, which is supposed to show how funding to the R&D department has decreased as a percentage of sales from 1996 to 1998. However, by showing flasks of various sizes, the point being made has been biased. As a result, the 13 percent funding of 1996 looks to be at least three or four times larger than the funding in 1998. A line chart showing the actual decline, from 13 percent to 8 percent would have been a much fairer presentation of what actually transpired.[8]

To ensure that you have objectively and ethically prepared your visuals you should do the following:

Here are guidelines for preparing ethical visual presentations.

1. Double check and triple check all labels, numbers, and visual shapes. A faulty or misleading visual discredits your report and work.
2. Exercise caution if you use three-dimensional figures. They may distort the data by multiplying the value by the width and the height.
3. Make sure all parts of the scales are presented. Truncated graphs (having breaks in the scaled values on either axis) are acceptable only if the audience is familiar with the data.

ORAL PRESENTATIONS

You may be asked to present an oral summary of the recommendations and conclusions of your research. The purpose of the **oral presentation** is to succinctly present the information and to provide an opportunity for questions and discussion. The presentation may be accomplished through a simple conference with the client, or it may be a formal presentation to a room full of people. To be adequately prepared, follow these steps:

Marketing researchers often make oral presentations.

1. Identify and understand your audience.
2. Determine the key points your audience needs to hear.
3. Outline the key points, preferably on 3-by-5 cards to which you can easily refer. Present your points succinctly and clearly. The written report will serve as a reference for further reading.

Oral presentations provide an opportunity to discuss the research.

It is a good idea to practice your oral presentation at least three times.

4. Prepare visuals to graphically portray your key points.
5. Practice your presentation. A good "rule of thumb" is to rehearse your presentation a minimum of three times. Be comfortable with what you are going to say.
6. Check out the room and media equipment prior to the presentation.
7. Be positive. You know more about your subject than anyone else does.

Today, you have a choice of several computerized presentation packages. Some brand names are PowerPoint, Aldus Persuasion, and Presentations. These programs allow you to make up your own slides in various formats and project them on a screen either from your laptop computer or from any multimedia presentation platform.

SUMMARY

The final stage of the marketing research process is the preparation and presentation of the marketing research report. This stage is as important, if not more important, than any other stage in the research process. This importance is attributed to the fact that, regardless of the care in the design and execution of the research project itself, if the report does not adequately communicate the project to the client, all is lost. Properly "packaging" the final report can be just as important as the report itself.

Marketing research reports should be tailored to their audiences. They are typically organized into the categories of front matter, body, and end matter. Each of these categories has subparts, with each subpart having a different purpose. Conclusions are based on the results of the research, and recommendations are suggestions based on conclusions.

Guidelines for writing the market research report include using proper headings and subheadings, which serve as signposts and signals to the reader, and proper use of visuals such as tables and figures. Style considerations include beginning paragraphs with topic sentences, spare use of jargon, use of strong verbs, writing in the active voice, avoiding changes in tense, being concise, keeping the subject and verb close together, and varying sentence structure and length. Editing and proofreading, preferably by reading the report aloud, are important steps in writing the research report. Care should be taken to ensure that all presentations are clear and objective to the reader. Many visual aids may be distorted so that they have a different meaning to the reader. Yes, this means that ethical considerations must be made in the preparation of the research report.

In some cases, marketing researchers are required to orally present the findings of their research project to their client. Guidelines for making an oral presentation include knowing the audience and the key points you wish to make, correctly preparing the visuals, practicing, checking out the presentation room and equipment prior to the presentation, and being positive.

Reports rely on tables, figures, and graphical displays of various types. SPSS for Windows includes routines for creating report tables and graphs. We describe step-by-step commands on how to use SPSS for Windows Version 7.5 to make professional-appearing tables and graphs and to move them into a word processor program report file.

KEY TERMS

Marketing research report (p. 611)
Front matter (p. 612)
Title fly page (p. 612)
Title page (p. 612)
Letter of authorization (p. 613)
Letter of transmittal (p. 614)
Memo of transmittal (p. 614)
Table of contents (p. 616)
List of illustrations (p. 617)
Tables (p. 617)
Figures (p. 617)
Abstract/executive summary (p. 618)
Body (p. 619)
Introduction (p. 619)
Methodology (p. 619)
Results (p. 621)
Limitations (p. 621)
Conclusions (p. 621)
Recommendations (p. 621)
End matter (p. 621)
Appendix (p. 621)
Headings (p. 622)
Subheadings (p. 622)
Visuals (p. 622)
Pie charts (p. 624)
Bar charts (p. 629)
Line graphs (p. 629)
Flow diagrams (p. 629)
Stratum charts (p. 632)
Ethical visuals (p. 632)
Oral presentation (p. 633)

REVIEW QUESTIONS/APPLICATIONS

1. Discuss the relative importance of the marketing research report to other stages in the marketing research process.
2. What are the components of the marketing research report?
3. When should you include or not include a letter of authorization?
4. Distinguish between results, conclusions, and recommendations.
5. When should you use a subheading?
6. What is the most important consideration in aiding you to determine the style in which you will write your report?
7. What is the preferred method of proofreading?
8. What visual would be the best at displaying the relative changes in spending between four promotion mix variables over time?
9. What kind of visual would you use if you wanted to use images of people to illustrate the differences in employment levels among three different industries?
10. Why do you think we included a discussion of ethics in preparing visuals? Can you illustrate how a visual could present data in an unethical fashion?
11. Visit your library and ask your reference librarian if he or she is aware of any marketing research reports that have been placed in the library. Chances are good that you will be able to find several reports of various kinds. Examine the reports. What commonalities do they have in terms of the sections that the authors have created? Look at the sections carefully. What types of issues were addressed in the introduction section? The methodology section? How did the authors organize all of the information reported in the results section? Are recommendations different from the conclusions?

CASE 19.1

The Mean World of Marketing Research[9]

Bob Johnson, a rising young product manager with a manufacturer of upscale consumer products, was vying with an associate for recognition and possible promotion. Each had been assigned the task of developing a new product concept that would appeal to high-income consumers not presently purchasing from the company. Depending on the outcome of marketing research, one of the concepts would be selected for full development and nationwide marketing.

At the conclusion of several months of hard work, both managers were ready to submit their product concepts for testing. Bob was asked to contract with an outside marketing research firm for an appropriate study. He selected a small firm that had depended on him for a substantial portion of their billing. Bob and his associate met with the research firm and agreed on a methodology involving a mail survey, randomly selected, of 1,000 potential consumers. It was understood that the product concept selected by respondents with the "best" demographics would be recommended for development.

The survey mailings resulted in 131 usable questionnaires being returned. Income, the most important of the demographic variables, was reported as shown:

	RESPONDENTS PREFERRING	
RESPONDENT'S INCOME	PRODUCT *X*	PRODUCT *Y*
Mean	$62,500	$43,000
Median	$34,800	$51,000
Mode	$22,000	$47,200

In their report, the research firm reported the "average income of respondents preferring product *X* was $62,500 compared to $43,000 for those preferring product *Y*." Bob, delighted with the results (product *X* was his product concept), congratulated the research firm on an excellent study as he sat back and anticipated his upcoming promotion.

1. What ethical problems do you see in the research process from its inception through the analysis and preparation of the research report?

CASE 19.2
Interstate Fair Tables and Graphs

You have had an opportunity to work with the Interstate Fair data set (Fair.sav) with basic descriptive analysis in Case 15.2. Here is some practice with various tables and graphs using that data set. Construct a professional-appearing final report table or graph for each of the following items.

Construct tables for:

1. Number of people in the party
2. Times at the fair in the past five years
3. Second reason why came to the fair
4. Overall rating of the fair
5. Age of the respondent

Construct appropriate graphs for:

1. Days at the fair this year
2. Radio station listened to most
3. Second reason why came to the fair
4. Rating of fair security
5. Money spent on oneself at the fair this year

Endnotes

Chapter 1

1. "GM to Market Electric Car" (September 21, 1996, http://www.autorevista.com/articles/ar/ev1.htm), and author's interview with Mr. Shawn McNamara, General Motors, September 20, 1996.
2. Vincent P. Barabba, *Meeting of the Minds* (Boston: Harvard Business School Press, 1995) and Vincent P. Barabba and Gerald Zaltman, *Hearing the Voice of the Market: Competitive Advantage through Creative Use of Market Information* (Boston: Harvard Business School Press, 1991).
3. Philip Kotler, *Marketing Management: Analysis, Planning, Implementation, 21 and Control,* 9th ed. (Upper Saddle River, N.J.: Prentice Hall, 1997), 19.
4. *Ibid.*
5. William L. Huth, David R. Eppright, and Paul M. Taube, "The Indexes of Consumer Sentiment and Confidence: Leading or Misleading Guides to Future Buyer Behavior," *Journal of Business Research* (March 1994), 199–206.
6. "Electric Cars," *Business Week* (May 30, 1994), 104–114.
7. Peter D. Bennett, ed., *Glossary of Marketing Terms* (Chicago: American Marketing Association, 1988), 117–118.
8. Nancy J. Merritt and William H. Redmond, "Defining Marketing Research: Perceptions vs. Practice," *Proceedings: American Marketing Association* (1990), 146–150.
9. Bennett, *op. cit.;* also see Michael Y. Hu, "An Experimental Study of Managers' and Researchers' Use of Consumer Market Research," *Journal of the Academy of Marketing Science* (Fall 1986), 44–51.
10. "Food Marketers Won't Lighten Up," *Advertising Age* (October 7, 1996), 2.
11. Donna De La Cruz, "Campbell's New Meals in the Mail," *Pensacola News Journal* (September 21, 1996), 8D.
12. "Edison Environmental Awards," *Marketing News* (April 25, 1994), E8.
13. "Drill Bits, Paint Thinner, Eyeliner," *Business Week* (September 25, 1995), 83; and Susan Chandler, "An Endangered Species Makes a Comeback," *Business Week* (November 27, 1995), 96.
14. "Data Is Power. Just Ask Fingerhut," *Business Week* (June 3, 1996), 69.
15. Chad Rubel, "Uphill Battle for Marketer of Shelf-Stable Milk," *Marketing News* (May 20, 1996), 19.
16. Chad Rubel, "Pizza Hut Explores Customer Satisfaction," *Marketing News* (March 25, 1996), 15.
17. Jeffrey Heilbrunn, "Legal Lessons from the Delicare Affair—1. United States," *Marketing and Research Today,* vol. 17, no. 3 (August 1989), 151–155; Claude Benazeth, "Legal Lessons from the Delicare Affair—2. Europe," *Marketing and Research Today,* vol. 17, no. 3 (August 1989), 156–160. Also see Paul D. Frederickson and Jeff W. Totten, "Marketing Research Projects in the Academic Setting: Legal Liability after Beecham vs. Yankelovich," in Louis M. Capello, et al., eds., "Progress in Marketing Thought," *Proceedings of the Southern Marketing Association* (1990), 250–253.
18. Ronald Alsop, "Coke's Flip-Flop Underscores Risks of Consumer Taste Tests," *The Wall Street Journal* (July 18, 1985), 27.
19. Willard I. Zangwill, "When Customer Research Is a Lousy Idea," *The Wall Street Journal* (March 8, 1993), A-12.
20. Thomas C. Kinnear and Ann R. Root, eds., *1994 Survey of Marketing Research* (Chicago: American Marketing Association, 1994), 43–50.
21. The description of the MIS is adapted from Philip Kotler, *Marketing Management: Analysis, Planning, Implementation, and Control,* 9th ed. (Upper Saddle River, N.J.: Prentice Hall, 1997), 110ff.
22. "Lotus: Working Together," *Sales & Marketing Management Magazine* (September 1996), 7.
23. David J. Curry, *The New Marketing Research Systems* (New York: John Wiley & Sons, Inc., 1993).
24. Verne B. Churchill, "The Role of Ad Hoc Survey Research in a Single Source World," *Marketing Research* (December 1990), 22–26; Gale D. Metzger, "Single Source: Yes and No (The Backward View)," *Marketing Research* (December 1990), 27–33.
25. This is an actual case.
26. Owen Alexander Jr., "Facing the Future: How Utilities Will Market a Product Never Marketed Before," *Services Marketing Today* (August 1995), 1, 3.

Chapter 2

1. Mr. Honomichl is president of Marketing Aid Center Inc. of Barrington, Illinois, and publisher of *Inside Research,* a newsletter for marketing research executives.
2. Robert Bartels, *The History of Marketing Thought,* 3rd ed. (Columbus, Ohio: Publishing Horizons, Inc., 1988), 125. Also, this entire historical section parallels the work of Professor Bartels.

3. For a discussion of how statistical theory was introduced in sampling plans for surveys see Hugh S. Hardy, ed., *The Politz Papers: Science and Truth in Marketing Research* (Chicago: American Marketing Association, 1990).
4. Bartels, *op. cit.,* 125.
5. Naresh K. Malhotra, *Marketing Research: An Applied Orientation.* (Upper Saddle River, N.J.: Prentice Hall, 1996.)
6. Thomas C. Kinnear and Ann R. Root, *1994 Survey of Marketing Research: Organization, Function, Budget, and Compensation* (Chicago: American Marketing Association, 1995), 38.
7. William R. BonDurant, "Research: The 'HP Way'," *Marketing Research,* vol. 4, no. 2 (June 1992), 28–33.
8. Kinnear and Root, *op. cit.,* 7.
9. *Ibid.,* 12.
10. *Ibid.,* 44.
11. Jack Honomichl, "Top 50 Research Revenue up 9.4% in '95," *Marketing News* (June 3, 1996), H2.
12. Claes Fornell, Michael D. Johnson, Eugene W. Anderson, Jaesung Cha, and Barbara Everitt Bryant, "The American Customer Satisfaction Index: Nature, Purpose, and Findings," *Journal of Marketing,* vol. 60 (October 1996), 7–18.
13. Richard W. Pollay, S. Siddarth, Michael Siegel, Anne Haddix, Robert K. Merritt, Gary A. Giovino, and Michael P. Eriksen, "The Last Straw? Cigarette Advertising and Realized Market Shares among Youth and Adults, 1979–1993," *Journal of Marketing,* vol. 60 (April 1996), 1–16.
14. James R. Krum, "B for Marketing Research Departments," *Journal of Marketing,* vol. 42 (October 1978), 8–12; James R. Krum, Pradeep A. Rau, and Stephen K. Keiser, "The Marketing Research Process: Role Perceptions of Researchers and Users," *Journal of Advertising Research,* vol. 27 (December–January 1987/1988), 9–21; and Scott Dawson, Ronald F. Bush, and Bruce Stern, "An Evaluation of Services Provided by the Market Research Industry," *Service Industries Journal,* vol. 14, no. 4 (October 1994), 515–526; also see John R. Austin, "An Exploratory Examination of the Development of Marketing Research Service Relationships: An Assessment of Exchange Evaluation Dimensions," in Mary C. Gilly, et al., eds.,"Enhancing Knowledge Development in Marketing," *1991 AMA Educators' Conference Proceedings* (1991), 133–141; also see John E. Swan, I. Frederick Trawick, and Maxwell G. Carroll, "Effect of Participation in Marketing Research on Consumer Attitudes toward Research and Satisfaction with a Service," *Journal of Marketing Research* (August 1981), 356–363.
15. Scott Dawson, Ronald F. Bush, and Bruce Stern, "An Evaluation of Services Provided by the Market Research Industry," *Service Industries Journal,* vol. 144 (October 1994), 515–526.
16. "Consensus Eludes Certification Issue," *Marketing News* (September 11, 1989), 125, 127; Bruce Stern and Terry Crawford, "It's Time to Consider Certification of Researchers," *Marketing News* (September 12, 1986), 20–21; Bruce L. Stern and Edward L. Grubb, "Alternative Solutions to the Marketing Research Industry's 'Quality Control' Problem," in Robert L. King, ed., "Marketing: Toward the Twenty-First Century," *Proceedings of the Southern Marketing Association* (1991), 225–229; and Michael A. Jones and Roger McKinney, "The Need for Certification in Marketing Research," in Donald Thompson, ed., "Marketing and Education: Partners in Progress," *Proceedings of the Atlantic Marketing Association* (1993), 224–229. Also, for an excellent review of the pros and cons of certification, see Terri L. Rittenburg and Gene W. Murdock, "Highly Sensitive Issue Still Sparks Controversy within the Industry," *Marketing Research,* vol. 6, no. 2 (Spring 1994), 5–10. Also see Ralph W. Giacobbe and Madhav N. Segal, "Credentialing of Marketing Research Professionals: An Industry Perspective," in Ravi Achroll and Andrew Mitchell, eds., "Enhancing Knowledge Development in Marketing," *A.M.A. Educators' Conference Proceedings* (1994), 229–301.
17. Alvin A. Achenbaum, "Can We Tolerate a Double Standard in Marketing Research?" *Journal of Advertising Research,* vol. 25 (June–July 1985), RC3-7.
18. Patrick E. Murphy and Gene R. Laczniak, "Emerging Ethical Issues Facing Marketing Researchers," *Marketing Research,* vol. 4, no. 2 (June 1992), 6–11.
19. See Margery S. Steinberg, "The 'Professionalization' of Marketing," *Marketing Research,* vol. 4, no. 2 (June 1992), 56.
20. Steve Bernstein, "A Call to Audit Market Research Providers," *Marketing Research,* vol. 2, no. 3 (September 1990), 11–16.
21. Stephen McDaniel, Perry Verille, and Charles S. Madden, "The Threats to Marketing Research: An Empirical Reappraisal," *Journal of Marketing Research* (February 1985), 74–80; I. P. Akaah and Edward A. Riordan, "Judgments of Marketing Professionals about Ethical Issues in Marketing Research," *Journal of Marketing Research* (February 1989), 112–120; Gene R. Laczniak and Patrick E. Murphy, *Marketing Ethics* (Lexington, Mass.: Lexington Books, 1985) and O. C. Ferrell and L. G. Gresham, "A Contingency Framework for Understanding Ethical Decision Making in Marketing," *Journal of Marketing Research* (Summer 1985), 87–96; R. Eric Reidenbach and Donald P. Robin, "A Partial Testing of the Contingency Framework for Ethical Decision Making: A Path Analytical Approach," in Louis M. Capella, Henry W. Nash, Jack M. Starling, and Ronald D. Taylor, eds., "Progress in Marketing Thought," *Proceedings of the Southern Marketing Association* (1990), 121–128; Elizabeth K. LaFleur and R. Eric Reidenbach, "A Taxonomic Construction of Ethics Decision Rules: An Agenda for Research," in Tom K. Massey Jr., ed., "Marketing: Satisfying a Diverse Customerplace," *Proceedings of the Southern Marketing Association* (1993), 158–161; R. Eric Reidenbach, Elizabeth K. LaFleur, Donald P. Robin, and P. J. Forest, "Exploring the Dimensionality of Ethical Judgements Made by Advertising Professionals Concerning Selected Child-Oriented Television Advertising Practices," in Tom K. Massey Jr., ed., "Marketing: Satisfying a Diverse Customerplace," *Proceedings of the Southern Marketing Association* (1993), 166–170; Jill G. Klein and N. Craig Smith, "Teaching Marketing Research Ethics in the Business School Classroom," in Ravi Achrol and Andrew Mitchell,

eds., "Enhancing Knowledge Development in Marketing," *A.M.A. Educators' Conference Proceedings* (1994), 92–99.

22. Shelby D. Hunt, Lawrence B. Chonko, and James B. Wilcox, "Ethical Problems of Marketing Researcher," *Journal of Marketing Research,* vol. 21 (August 1984), 309–324.
23. *Ibid.,* 309–324.
24. Cyndee Miller, "ESOMAR Sets Guidelines to Prevent 'Sugging'," *Marketing News* (November 21, 1988), 16. Also see O. C. Ferrell and S. J. Skinner, "Ethical Behavior and Bureaucratic Structure in Marketing Research Organizations," *Journal of Marketing Research* (February 1988), 103–109.
25. Hunt, Chonko, and Wilcox, *op. cit.,* 313.
26. Pamela L. Kiecker and James E. Nelson, "Cheating Behavior by Telephone Interviewers: A View from the Trenches," in Paul Bloom, et al., eds., "Enhancing Knowledge Development in Marketing," *A.M.A. Educators' Conference Proceedings* (Chicago: American Marketing Association, 1989), 182–188.
27. Shelby D. Hunt, Lawrence B. Chonko, and James B. Wilcox, "Ethical Problems of Marketing Researcher," *Journal of Marketing Research,* vol. 21 (August 1984), 309–324.
28. *Ibid.,* 314.
29. D. Toy, J. Olsen, and L. Wright, "Effects of Debriefing in Marketing Research Involving 'Mild' Deceptions," *Psychology and Marketing* (Spring 1989), 69–85.
30. Diane K. Bowers, "Sugging: A Federal Offense," *Marketing Research,* vol. 6, no. 4 (Fall 1994), 54–55.
31. Diane K. Bowers, "Confidentiality Challenges," *Marketing Research,* vol. 7, no. 3 (Summer 1995), 34–35.
32. Diane K. Bowers, "Privacy Concerns and the Research Industry," *Marketing Research,* vol. 6, no. 2 (1994), 48–49.
33. *Ibid.,* 48–49.
34. Diane K. Bowers, "The Privacy Challenge—Part 2," *Marketing Research,* vol. 3, no. 3 (September 1991), 61–64.
35. Donald S. Tull and Deli Hawkins, *Marketing Research: Measurement and Method* (New York: Macmillan Publishing Company, 1990); Patrick E. Murphy and Gene R. Laczniak, "Emerging Ethical Issues Facing Marketing Researchers," *Marketing Research,* vol. 4, no. 2 (June 1992), 6–11.
36. *Newsweek,* "The Science of Polling" (September 28, 1992), 38, 39.
37. *Advertising Age,* "Have It Your Way with Research" (April 4, 1983), 16.
38. This case was drawn from information in Cynthia Crossen, *Tainted Truth: The Manipulation of Fact in America* (New York: Simon & Schuster, 1994).
39. The material for this case was modified to suit chapter material from Robert M. Smith, "Research Provider Partnerships: Do They Consider the Client's Real Needs?" *Marketing Research,* vol. 4, no. 2 (June 1992), 24–26.
40. *Marketing and Sales Career Directory* (4th ed., 1993), Detroit, Mich.: Gale Research Inc., 81–95.
41. Graduate degree programs in marketing research are available at The University of Georgia, Department of Marketing, Athens, GA, 30602; and The University of Texas, Arlington, Department of Marketing, Arlington, TX 76019.
42. Kinnear and Root, *op. cit.,* 85–86.
43. *Marketing and Sales Career Directory* (4th ed., 1993), Detroit, Mich.: Gale Research Inc., 81–95.

Chapter 3

1. Mr. Glitman is the founder and principal of The Fletcher Mountain Group, Burlington, Vermont.
2. Lois Therrien, "The Hunger Pangs Let Up a Little," *Business Week* (January 11, 1993), 97.
3. See Howard Schlossberg, "Cost Allocation Can Show True Value of Research," *Marketing News,* vol. 24 (January 8, 1990), 2; also see John Martin and John Chadwick, "Factors Associated with Executive Decisions to Conduct Marketing Research: An Exploratory Study," in David L. Moore, ed., "Marketing: Forward Motion," *Proceedings of the Atlantic Marketing Association* (1988), 698–709.
4. R. Kenneth Wade, "The When/What Research Decision Guide," *Marketing Research,* vol. 5, no. 3 (Summer 1993), 24–27.
5. William D. Perreault Jr., "The Shifting Paradigm in Marketing Research," *Journal of the Academy of Marketing Science,* vol. 20, no. 4 (Fall 1992), 369.
6. Richard F. Tomasino, "Integrate Market Research with Strategic Plan to Get Budget Okay," *Marketing News* (January 4, 1985), 8.
7. Maria Cone, "GM and the Juicemobile," *Los Angeles Times* (June 21, 1992), 8.
8. Gary Levin, "Data Bases Loom Large for the '90s," *Advertising Age,* vol. 62, no. 45 (October 21, 1991), 22.
9. Cyndee Miller, "China Emerges as Latest Battleground for Marketing Researchers," *Marketing News* (February 14, 1994), 1–2.
10. This case was provided by permission of PepsiCo Restaurants International.

Chapter 4

1. Michael J. Weiss, "Pudding People," *The Demographic Detective,* http://pathfinder.com/twep/detective/pudding/pudding-mediaalt.html
2. Pamela L. Alreck and Robert B. Settle, *The Survey Research Handbook* (Homewood, Ill.: Richard D. Irwin, 1985), 9–11.
3. Christine Moorman, Gerald Zaltman, and Rohit Despande, "Relationships between Providers and Users of Marketing Research: The Dynamics of Trust within and between Organizations," *Journal of Marketing Research,* vol. 24, no. 3 (August 1992), 314–328.
4. Adapted from Lee Adler, "Secrets of When, and When Not to Embark on a Marketing Research Project," *Sales and Marketing Management,* vol. 123 (September 17, 1979), 108; vol. 124 (March 17, 1980), 108; and vol. 124 (May 19, 1980), 77.
5. Adapted from Lee Adler, "Secrets of When, and When Not to Embark on a Marketing Research Project," *Sales and Marketing Management,* vol. 123 (September 17, 1979), 108; vol. 124 (March 17, 1980), 108; and vol. 124 (May 19, 1980), 77.
6. Randall G. Chapman, "False Economies in Survey Research," *Applied Marketing Research,* vol. 28, no. 1 (Spring 1988), 16–20.

7. Randall G. Chapman, "Problem-Definition in Marketing Research Studies," *Journal of Consumer Marketing,* vol. 6, no. 2 (Spring 1989), 51–59.
8. For more information on proposals and reports see N. Carroll, M. Mohn, and Thomas H. Land, "A Guide to Quality Marketing Research Proposals and Reports," *Business,* vol. 39, no. 1 (January/February/March 1989), 38–40.
9. Jack Honomichl, "Satisfaction Measurement Jump-Starts Industry Research, *Marketing News,* vol. 25, no. 14 (July 8, 1991), 15.

Chapter 5

1. See David W. Stewart, *Secondary Research: Information Sources and Methods* (Newbury Park, Calif.: Sage Publications, 1984) and Jeffrey P. Davidson, "Low Cost Research Sources," *Journal of Small Business Management,* vol. 23 (April 1985), 73–77.
2. Thomas V. Bonoma, "Case Research in Marketing: Opportunities, Problems, and a Process," *Journal of Marketing Research,* vol. 22 (May 1985), 199–208.
3. Jason Meyers, "Wireless for the 21st Century," *Telephony,* vol. 231, no. 6 (August 6, 1996), S24(2).
4. Thomas L. Greenbaum, *The Practical Handbook and Guide to Focus Group Research* (Lexington, Mass.: D.C. Heath, 1988).
5. Jeffrey J. Stoltman and James W. Gentry, "Using Focus Groups to Study Household Decision Processes and Choices," in Robert P. Leone and V. Kumar, eds., Enhancing Knowledge Development in Marketing, *AMA Educator's Conference Proceedings,* vol. 3 (Chicago: American Marketing Association, 1992), 257–263.
6. Thomas C. Kinnear and James R. Taylor, *Marketing Research: An Applied Approach* (New York: McGraw-Hill, 1991), 142.
7. Laura Klepacki, "Stores Urged to Use Consumer Panels," *Supermarket News,* vol. 44, no. 19 (May 9, 1994), 38.
8. See Fred N. Kerlinger, *Foundations of Behavioral Research,* 3rd ed. (New York: Holt, Rinehart and Winston, 1986).
9. Donald T. Campbell and Julian C. Stanley, *Experimental and Quasi-Experimental Designs for Research* (Chicago: Rand McNally, 1963).
10. Bobby J. Calder, Lynn W. Phillips, and Alice M. Tybout, "The Concept of External Validity," *Journal of Consumer Research,* vol. 9 (December 1992), 240–244.
11. L. R. Gray and P. L. Diehl, *Research Methods for Business and Management* (New York: Macmillan Publishing Company, 1992), 387–390.
12. Jim Doyle, "In With the New, Out With the Old," *Beverage World,* vol. 113, no. 1576 (October 1994), 204–205.
13. Leslie Brennan, "Test Marketing," *Sales & Marketing Management Magazine,* vol. 140 (March 1988), 50–62.
14. This classification is based upon Gilbert A. Churchill, *Basic Marketing Research* (Fort Worth, Tex: The Dryden Press, 1991), 151–152; see also Charles R. Duke and Susan L. Holak, "Concept Tests: A Review and Research Taxonomy," in Robert L. King, ed., "Marketing: Toward the Twenty-First Century," *Proceedings of the Southern Marketing Association* (1991), 236–240; see also Madhav N. Segal and J. S. Johar, "City Selection for Test Marketing," in Robert L. King, ed., "Marketing: Toward the Twenty-First Century," *Proceedings of the Southern Marketing Association* (1991), 516–518.
15. Betsy Spethmann, "Test Market USA," *Brandweek,* vol. 36, no. 19 (May 8, 1985), 40–43.
16. Kevin J. Clancy and Robert S. Shulman, "Test for Success," *Sales & Marketing Management Magazine,* vol. 147, no. 10 (October 1995), 111–115.
17. Melvin Prince, "Choosing Simulated Test Marketing Systems," *Marketing Research,* vol. 4, no. 3 (September 1992), 14–16.
18. *Ibid.* Also see J. Turner and J. Brandt, "Development and Validation of a Simulated Market to Test Children for Selected Consumer Skills," *Journal of Consumer Affairs* (Winter 1978), 266–276.
19. Steve Blount, "It's Just a Matter of Time," *Sales & Marketing Management,* vol. 144, no. 3 (March 1992), 32–43.
20. Christopher Power, "Will It Sell in Podunk? Hard to Say," *Business Week* (August 10, 1992), 46–47.
21. Sam Greene, "Chattanooga Chosen as Test Market for Smokeless Cigarette," *Knight-Ridder/Tribune Business News* (May 4, 1996), 5040084.
22. Jack Hayes, "McD Extends Breakfast Buffet Test in Southeast Markets," *Nation's Restaurant News,* vol. 29, no. 4 (January 23, 1995), 3.
23. Philip Kotler, *Marketing Management: Analysis, Planning, Implementation, & Control* (Upper Saddle River, N.J.: Prentice Hall, 1991), 335.
24. Christopher Power, "Will It Sell in Podunk? Hard to Say," *Business Week* (August 10, 1992), 46–47.
25. Mark Tosh, "Unfurling New Format, Kmart Aims to Build Rapid-Repeat Business," *WWD,* vol. 172, no. 41 (August 28, 1996), 1–2.
26. Michelle Dorfman, "Vending Offers a Hot Selection," *ID: The Voice of Foodservice Distribution,* vol. 32, no. 5 (May 1996), 39–40.

Chapter 6

1. *Books in Print, 1986–87: Authors,* vol. 1 (New York: R. R. Bowker, 1986), xi.
2. *Books in Print, 1996–97* (New Providence, N.J.: R. R. Bowker, 1996), 134.
3. *Books in Print, 1991–92, Titles A–F,* vol. 4 (New Providence, N.J.: R. R. Bowker, 1991), v.
4. Allen B. Veaner, "Into the Fourth Century," *Drexel Library Quarterly,* vol. 21, no. 1 (Winter 1985), 9.
5. William F. Schoell and Joseph P. Guiltinan, *Marketing,* 6th ed. (Upper Saddle River, N.J.: Prentice Hall, 1995), 507.
6. Martha E. Williams, "The State of Databases Today: 1996," *Gale Directory of Databases* (Detroit, Mich: Gale Research, 1996), xvii–xxix.
7. Salvatore M. Meringolo, "Secondary Information: The Major Access Tools" in William R. Dillon, Thomas J. Madden, and Neil H. Firtle, *Marketing Research in a Marketing Environment,* 2nd ed. (Homewood, Ill.: Richard D. Irwin, Inc., 1987), 118–119; also see K. A. Anderson, "Using SIC Codes to Improve Market Position," *Industrial Marketing* (June 1979), 60.

8. See, for example, *U.S. Industrial Outlook 1992,* U.S. Industrial Outlook H1211 (Washington, D.C.: International Trade Administration, U.S. Department of Commerce).
9. Gordon L. Patzer, *Using Secondary Data in Marketing Research: United States and Worldwide* (Westport, Conn.: Quorum Books, 1995), 24.
10. *Market Statistics* is a division of Bill Communications, Corporate Headquarters: 355 Park Avenue South, New York, NY 10010.
11. Patzer, *op. cit.,* 21.
12. These questions and much of the following discussion is taken from David W. Stewart, *Secondary Research: Information Sources and Methods* (Newbury Park, Calif: Sage Publications, 1984).
13. Cynthia Crossen, *Tainted Truth: The Manipulation of Fact in America* (New York: Simon & Schuster, 1994), 140.
14. John Chapman, "Cast a Critical Eye: Small Area Estimates and Projections Sometimes Can Be Dramatically Different," *American Demographics,* 9 (February 1987), 30.
15. These steps are updated and adapted from David W. Stewart, *Secondary Research: Information Sources and Methods* (Newbury Park, Calif: Sage Publications, 1984), 20–22, by Ms. Peggy Toifel, MSLS, MBA, University Librarian, University of West Florida, 1996.
16. Researchers wishing to use SIC codes should refer to the *Standard Industrial Classification Manual 1987,* rev. ed. (Executive Office of the President, U.S. Office of Management and Budget, Washington, D.C.: U.S. Government Printing Office).
17. Jennifer Boettcher, "NAFTA Prompts a New Code System for Industry—The Death of SIC and Birth of NAICS," *Database* (April/May 1996), 42–45.

Chapter 7

1. Documents supplied by Claritas, Inc., Alexandria, Virginia, 1996.
2. Information regarding the Yankelovich monitor may be obtained from Yankelovich Partners, Inc., 101 Merritt 7 Corporate Park, Norwalk, CT 06851. voice: (203) 846-0100, fax: (203) 845-8200, or http://www.yankelovich.com
3. Information regarding the Harris Poll may be obtained from Gordon S. Black Corporation, 135 Corporate Woods, Rochester, NY 14623.
4. *What Does America Think About?* (Wilmington, Del.: Scholarly Resources, Inc., undated publication).
5. William D. Wells, "Attitudes and Behavior: Lessons from the Needham Life Style Study," *Journal of Advertising Research,* vol. 25 (February–March 1985), 40–44.
6. Rebecca Holman, "A Value and Life Styles Perspective on Human Behavior," in Robert E. Pitts Jr. and Arch G. Woodside, eds., *Personal Values and Consumer Psychology* (Lexington, Mass.: Lexington Books, 1984); Lynn R. Kahle, Sharon E. Beatty, and Pamela M. Homer, "Alternative Measurement Approaches to Consumer Values: The List of Values (LOV) and Lifestyle Segmentation (VALS)," *Journal of Consumer Research,* vol. 13 (December 1986), 405–409.
7. James Rothman, "Editorial: Special Issue on Geodemographics," *Journal of the Market Research Society,* vol. 31, no. 1 (January 1989), 1–5.
8. Gilbert A. Churchill Jr., *Basic Marketing Research,* 2nd ed. (Fort Worth, Tex.: The Dryden Press, 1992), 222.
9. Based, in part, on Bob Kimball, "The Nielsen Report," unpublished paper, 1997; also see Richard Mizerski, Kathryn Straugh, and Bill Jolley, "The Adoption and Application of Scanner Data," in Robert L. King, ed., "Marketing: Positioning for the 1990s," *Proceedings of the Southern Marketing Association,* 1989, 313–17; James M. Sinukula, "Some Factors Affecting the Adoption of Scanner-Based Research in Organizations," *Journal of Advertising Research* (April/May 1991), 50–55.
10. Information supplied by ACNielsen.
11. *NFO Household Sample, 1992–93* (Greenwich, Conn.: NFO Research, Inc.).
12. A. S. C. Ehrenberg and J. Wakshlag, "Repeat-Viewing with People Meters," *Journal of Advertising Research* (February 1987), 9–13; L. R. Stoddard Jr., "The History of People Meters," *Journal of Advertising Research* (October 1987), 10–12.
13. *Arbitron Radio Market Report Reference Guide: A Guide to Understanding and Using Radio Audience Estimates* (New York: The Arbitron Company, 1992).
14. Information provided by Mr. Bob Pares and Ms. Edith Weinberg, Starch INRA Hooper.
15. Phil Gullen and Hugh Johnson, "Relating Product Purchasing and TV Viewing," *Journal of Advertising Research* (December 1986/January 1987), 9–19.
16. Blair Peters, "The 'Brave New World' of Single Source Information," *Marketing Research,* vol. 2, no. 4 (December 1990), 16.
17. *Ibid.,* 16–18.
18. Verne B. Churchill, "The Role of Ad Hoc Survey Research in a Single Source World," *Marketing Research,* vol. 12, no. 4 (December 1990), 22–26.
19. Gale D. Metzger, "Single Source: Yes and No (The Backward View)," *Marketing Research,* vol. 2, no. 4 (December 1990), 29. Also see Melvin Prince, "Some Uses and Abuses of Single-Source Data for Promotional Decision Making," *Marketing Research,* vol. 1, no. 4 (December 1989), 18–22.
20. Information provided by ACNielsen and Information Resources, Inc., by permission.
21. The authors wish to thank Dr. Bob Kimball, Associate Professor of Marketing, University of West Florida, for preparing this case.
22. The authors wish to thank Ms. Diane Sadler-Diaz for preparing this case. The case is an actual case, although the company, Designer Interiors, Ltd., is used here for illustration only.

Chapter 8

1. Mary Beth Solomon, "Targeting Trendsetters," *Marketing Research: A Magazine of Management and Applications,* vol. 8, no. 2 (Summer 1996), 9.
2. Sarah Newton and David Iddiols, "From Hearses to Horses: Launching the Volvo 850," *Journal of the Market Research Society,* vol. 35, no. 2 (April 1993), 145.

3. Rebecca Piirto, "Socks, Ties and Videotape," *American Demographics* (September 1991), 6.
4. Modified from Donald S. Tull and Dell I. Hawkins, *Marketing Research,* 4th ed. (New York: Macmillan, 1987), 331.
5. Langbourne Rust, "How to Reach Children in Stores: Marketing Tactics Grounded in Observational Research," *Journal of Advertising Research,* vol. 33, no. 6 (November–December 1993), 6772; and Langbourne Rust, "Parents and Children Shopping Together: A New Approach to the Qualitative Analysis of Observational Data," *Journal of Advertising Research,* vol. 33, no. 4 (July–August 1993), 6570.
6. Rebecca Piirto, "Socks, Ties and Videotape," *American Demographics* (September 1991), 6.
7. Peter Viles, "Company Measures Listenership in Cars," *Broadcasting,* vol. 122, no. 35 (August 24, 1992), 28.
8. Paula Kephart, "The Spy in Aisle 3," *American Demographics Marketing Tools* (May 1996), http://www.marketingtools.com/Publications/MT/96_mt/9605MD04.htm
9. Eugene Del Vecchio, "Generating Marketing Ideas when Formal Research Is Not Available," *Journal of Services Marketing,* vol. 2, no. 2 (Spring 1988), 71–74.
10. Hy Mariampolski, "Ethnography Makes Comeback as Research Tool," *Marketing News,* vol. 22, no. 1 (January 4, 1988), 32, 44.
11. Sonia Yuspeh, "Dracula and Frankenstein Revisited: Two Research Ogres in Need of Restraint," *Journal of Advertising Research,* vol. 29, no. 1 (February/March 1989), 53–59.
12. Daniel Seymour, "Soft Data-Hard Data: The Painful Art of Fence-Sitting," *Journal of Consumer Marketing,* vol. 6, no. 2 (Spring 1989), 25–32.
13. Aron Kahn, "Focus Groups Alter Decisions Made in Business, Politics," *Knight-Ridder/Tribune Business News* (September 6, 1996), 916.
14. Cheri Berlamino, "Designing the Qualitative Research Project: Addressing the Process Isues," *Journal of Advertising Research,* vol. 29, no. 6 (December 1989/January 1990), S7–S9.
15. William J. McDonald, "Provider Perceptions of Focus Group Research Use: A Multicountry Perspective," *Journal of the Academy of Marketing Science,* vol. 22, no. 3 (Summer 1994), 265–273.
16. Thomas L. Greenbaum, "Focus Group Research Is Not a Commodity Business," *Marketing News,* vol. 27, no. 5 (March 1, 1993), 4.
17. Thomas L. Greenbaum, "Answer to Moderator Problems Starts with Asking Right Questions," *Marketing News,* vol. 25, no. 11 (May 27, 1991), 8–9; Edward F. Fern, "The Use of Focus Groups for Idea Generation: The Effects of Group Size, Acquaintanceship, and Moderator on Response Quantity and Quality," *Journal of Marketing Research* (February 1982), 1–13.
18. Patrice M. Wooldridge, "Focus Group Respondents Deserve a Little Empathy," *Marketing News,* vol. 25, no. 11 (May 27, 1991), 6–7.
19. Richard Grinchunas and Tony Siciliano, "Focus Groups Produce Verbatims, Not Facts," *Marketing News,* vol. 27, no. 1 (January 4, 1993), FG-19.
20. Thomas L. Greenbaum, "Focus Groups Can Play a Part in Evaluating Ad Copy," *Marketing News,* vol. 27, no. 19 (September 13, 1993), 24–25.
21. Michael R. Czinkota and Likka A. Ronkainen, "Conducting Primary Market Research: Market Research for Your Export Operations, Part 2," *International Trade Forum,* section no. 1 (January 1995), 16.
22. Kelly Shermach, "Research Firms Take Unusual Approach to Kids," *Marketing News,* vol. 30, no. 8 (April 8, 1996), 26.
23. Marcy M. Rowan, "Bankers Beware! Focus Groups Can Steer You Wrong,"*Bottom Line,* vol. 8, no. 4 (July/August 1991), 37–41.
24. Deborah Potts, "Bias Lurks in All Phases of Qualitative Research," *Marketing News,* vol. 24, no. 18 (September 3, 1990), 12–13.
25. Alice Rodgers, "Better, Faster, Cheaper Doesn't Always Mean 'Best'," *Marketing News,* vol. 27, no. 1 (January 4, 1993), FG-19.
26. Karen Fletcher, "Not Just a Room with a View," *Marketing* (March 23, 1995), 27–28.
27. Cyndee Miller, "Anybody Ever Hear of Global Focus Groups?," *Marketing News,* vol. 25, no. 11 (May 27, 1991), 14.
28. Thomas L. Greenbaum, "Focus Group by Video Next Trend of 90s," *Marketing News,* vol. 30, no. 16 (July 26, 1996), 4.
29. Thomas L. Greenbaum, "Focus Group Spurt Predicted for the 90s," *Marketing News,* vol. 24, no. 1 (January 8, 1990), 21–22.
30. Hazel Kahan, "One-on-Ones Should Sparkle Like the Gems They Are," *Marketing News,* vol. 24, no. 18 (September 3, 1990), 8–9.
31. Margaret R. Roller, "A Real In-Depth Interview Wades into the Stream of Consciousness," *Marketing News,* vol. 21, no. 18 (August 28, 1987), 14; Matt Elbeck, "The Effects of Participant Knowledge, Group Size, Elapsed Time and Supplementary Questionnaires on Focus Group Information Quantity," in Robert L. King, ed., "Marketing: Positioning for the 1990s," *Proceedings of the Southern Marketing Association* (1989), 303–307.
32. Hazel Kahan, "One-on-Ones Should Sparkle Like the Gems They Are," *Marketing News,* vol. 24, no. 18 (September 3, 1990), 8–9.
33. Vincent-Wayne Mitchell, "Getting the Most from In-Depth Interviews," *Business Marketing Digest,* vol. 18, no. 1 (First quarter 1993), 63–70.
34. An example is Rebecca Piirto, "Measuring Minds in the 1990s," *American Demographics,* vol. 12, no. 12 (December 1990), 30–35.
35. Dean E. Allmon, "Voice Stress and Likert Scales: A Paired Comparison," in David L. Moore, ed., "Marketing: Forward Motion," *Proceedings of the Atlantic Marketing Association,* 1988, 710–714.

Chapter 9

1. John Chisholm, "Surveys by E-Mail and Internet," *Unix Review,* vol. 13, no. 13 (December 1995), 11–16.

2. Kim Cleland, "Online Research Costs about One-Half That of Traditional Methods," *Business Marketing,* vol. 81, no. 4 (May 1996), B8-B9.
3. See Helen Jacobs, "Entering the 1990s—The State of Data Collection—From a Mall Perspective," *Applied Marketing Research,* vol. 30, no. 2 (Second quarter 1989), 24–26; Richard L. Lysaker, "Data Collection Methods in the U.S.," *Journal of the Market Research Society,* vol. 31, no. 4 (October 1989), 477–488; Roger Gates and Paul J. Solomon, "Research Using the Mall Intercept: State of the Art," *Journal of Advertising Research* (August–September 1982), 43–50; Alan J. Bush, Ronald F. Bush, and Henry C. K. Chen, "Method of Administration Effects in Mall Intercept Interviews," *Journal of the Market Research Society,* vol. 33, no. 4 (1991), 309–319.
4. Jacob Hornik and Shmuel Ellis, "Strategies to Secure Compliance for a Mall Intercept Interview," *Public Opinion Quarterly,* vol. 52, no. 4 (Winter 1989), 539–551.
5. At least one study refutes the concern about shopping frequency. See Thomas D. DuPont, "Do Frequent Mall Shoppers Distort Mall-Intercept Results?" *Journal of Advertising Research,* vol. 27, no. 4 (August/September 1987), 45–51.
6. Alan J. Bush and E. Stephen Grant, "The Potential Impact of Recreational Shoppers on Mall Intercept Interviewing: An Exploratory Study," *The Journal of Marketing Theory and Practice,* vol. 3, no. 4 (Fall 1995), 73–83.
7. Alan J. Bush and Joseph F. Hair, "An Assessment of the Mall Intercept as a Data Collection Method," *Journal of Marketing Research,* vol. 22 (May 1983), 158–167.
8. See, for example, Minghua Xu, Benjamin J. Bates, and John C. Schweitzer, "The Impact of Messages on Survey Participation in Answering Machine Households," *Public Opinion Quarterly,* vol. 57 (1993), 232–237; David B. Meinert, Troy A. Festervand, and James R. Lumpkin, "Computerized Questionnaires: Pros and Cons," in Robert L. King, ed., "Marketing: Perspectives for the 1990s," *Proceedings of the Southern Marketing Association* (1992), 201–206.
9. Todd D. Remington, "Telemarketing and Declining Survey Response Rates," *Journal of Advertising Research,* vol. 32, no. 3 (1993), RC-6, RC-7.
10. Karen Fletcher, "Jump on the Omnibus," *Marketing* (June 15, 1995), 25–28.
11. Roger H. Gates, and Glen R. Jarboe, "Changing Trends in Data Acquisition for Marketing Research," *Journal of Data Collection,* vol. 27, no. 1 (Spring), 25–29; also see Nicolaos E. Synodinos and Jerry M. Brennan, "Computer Interactive Interviewing in Survey Research," *Psychology and Marketing* (Summer 1988), 117–138.
12. William L. Nicholls II, "Highest Response," *Marketing Research: A Magazine of Management and Applications,* vol. 8, no. 1 (Spring 1996), 5–7.
13. Howard Gershowitz, "Entering the 1990s—The State of Data Collection—Telephone Data Collection," *Applied Marketing Research,* vol. 30, no. 2 (Second quarter 1990); also see Elizabeth Ferrell and James B. Wilcox, "Response Error: Conceptual and Methodological Issues," in Louis M. Capella, Henry W. Nash, Jack M. Starling, and Ronald D. Taylor, eds., "Progress in Marketing Thought," *Proceedings of the Southern Marketing Association* (1990), 324–329; F. Kelly Shuptrine, "Survey Research: Respondent Attitudes Response and Bias," in Robert L. King, ed., "Marketing Perspectives for the 1990s," *Proceedings of the Southern Marketing Association* (1992), 197–200.
14. Peter J. DePaulo and Rick Weitzer, "Interactive Phone Technology Delivers Survey Data Quickly," *Marketing News,* vol. 28, no. 1 (January 3, 1994), 15.
15. Cyndee Miller, "Wand Replaces Pencil for Research at Product Clinics," *Marketing News,* vol. 25, no. 22 (1991), 18.
16. Laurence N. Gold, "Do-It-Yourself Interviewing," *Marketing Research,* vol. 8, no. 2 (Summer 1996), 40–41.
17. Peter Jones and John Palk, "Computer-Based Personal Interviewing: State-of-the-Art and Future Prospects," *Journal of the Market Research Society,* vol. 35, no. 3 (1993), 221–233.
18. Scott G. Dacko, "Data Collection Should Not Be Manual Labor," *Marketing News,* vol. 29, no. 18 (August 28, 1995), 31.
19. Barbara A. Schuldt and Jeff W. Totten, "Electronic Mail vs. Mail Survey Response Rates," *Marketing Research,* vol. 6, no. 1 (Winter 1994), 36–39.
20. Kim Cleland, "Online Research Costs about Half That of Traditional Methods," *Advertising Age's Business Marketing,* vol. 81, no. 4 (May 1996), B8–B9.
21. Stephen Brown, "Drop and Collect Surveys: A Neglected Research Technique?" *Journal of the Market Research Society,* vol. 5, no. 1 (1987), 19–23.
22. Nonresponse is a concern with any survey, and our understanding of refusals is minimal. See, for example, Robert M. Groves, Robert B. Cialdini, and Mick P. Couper, "Understanding the Decision to Participate in a Survey," *Public Opinion Quarterly,* vol. 56 (1992), 475–495.
23. See, for example, Stephen W. McDaniel and Perry Verille, "Do Topic Differences Affect Survey Non-Response?," *Journal of the Market Research Society,* vol. 29, no. 1 (January 1987), 55–66; or John C. Whitehead, "Environmental Interest Group Behavior and Self-Selection Bias in Contingent Valuation Mail Surveys," *Growth & Change,* vol. 22, no. 1 (Winter 1991), 10–21.
24. A large number of studies have sought to determine response rates for a wide variety of inducement strategies. Review articles include R. J. Fox, M. Crask, and J. Kim, "Mail Questionnaires in Survey Research: A Review of Response Inducement Techniques," *Public Opinion Quarterly,* vol. 52, no. 4 (Winter), 467–91; Srinivasan Ratneshwar and David W. Stewart (1989), 37–46; and the source noted in Marketing Research Insight 9.1.
25. Francis Yammarino, Steven Skinner, and Terry Childers, "Understanding Mail Survey Response Behavior," *Public Opinion Quarterly,* vol. 55 (1991), 613–639.
26. Jeffery Conant, Denise Smart, and Bruce Walker, "Mail Survey Facilitation Techniques: An Assessment and Proposal Regarding Reporting Practices," *Journal of the Market Research Society,* vol. 32, no. 4 (1990), 369–380.

27. Raymond A. Jassaume Jr. and Yoshiharu Yamada, "A Comparison of the Viability of Mail Surveys in Japan and the United States," *Public Opinion Quarterly,* vol. 54, no. 2 (Summer 1990), 219–228.
28. Robert Arnett, "Mail Panel Research in the 1990s," *Applied Marketing Research,* vol. 30, no. 2 (Second quarter 1990), 8–10.
29. Del Hawkins, Kenneth A. Coney, and Donald W. Jackson Jr., "The Impact of Monetary Inducement on Uninformed Response Error," *Journal of the Academy of Marketing Science,* vol. 16, no. 2 (Summer 1998), 30–35.
30. Melvin F. Hall, "Patient Satisfaction or Acquiescence? Comparing Mail and Telephone Survey Results," *Journal of Health Care Marketing,* vol. 15, no. 1 (Spring 1995), 54–61.

Chapter 10

1. Annual Soft Drink Report, "Knowing Your Target Consumer Is Key to Brand Development," *Beverage Industry,* vol. 86, no. 3 (March 1995), SD4(1).
2. Jack Honomichl, "Satisfaction Measurement Jump-Starts Survey Research," *Marketing News,* vol. 25, no. 14 (1994), 15.
3. Some researchers claim the use of a 0–10 scale over the telephone is actually better than a 3-, 4-, or 5-point scale. See Barbara Loken, et al., "The Use of 0–10 Scales in Telephone Surveys," *Journal of the Market Research Society,* vol. 29, no. 3 (July 1987), 353–362.
4. See, for example, James H. Leigh and Claude R. Martin Jr., " 'Don't Know' Item Nonresponse in a Telephone Survey: Effects of Question Form and Respondent Characteristics," *Journal of Marketing Research,* vol. 29, no. 3 (1987), 317–339.
5. Ideally, respondents should respond to the scale as having equal intervals. See, for example, Melvin R. Crask and Richard J. Fox, "An Exploration of the Interval Properties of Three Commonly Used Marketing Research Studies: A Magnitude Estimation Approach," *Journal of the Market Research Society,* vol. 29, no. 3 (1987), 317–339.
6. Statements are taken from W. D. Wells and D. J. Tigert, "Activities, Interests, and Opinions," *Journal of the Advertising Research* (1971), reported in H. H. Kassarjain and T. S. Robertson, *Perspectives in Consumer Behavior* (Glenview, Ill.: Scott Foresman, 1973), 175–176.
7. Another way to avoid the halo effect is to have subjects rate each stimulus on the same attribute and then move to the next attribute. See Bob T. W. Wu and Susan Petroshius, "The Halo Effect in Store Image Management," *Journal of the Academy of Marketing Science,* vol. 15, no. 1 (1987), 44–51.
8. Rajendar K. Garg, "The Influence of Positive and Negative Wording and Issue Involvement on Responses to Likert Scales in Marketing Research," *Journal of the Marketing Research Society,* vol. 38, no. 3 (July 1996), 235–246.
9. Scale development is a rigorous process involving a number of steps to establish the reliability and validity of the scale. Interested readers are directed to William Bearden, Richard Netemeyer, and Mary Ann Mobley, *Handbook of Marketing Scales* (Newbury Park, Calif.: Sage Publications, 1993).
10. See, for example, George F. Bishop, "Experiments with the Middle Response Alternative in Survey Questions," *Public Opinion Quarterly,* vol. 51 (Summer 1985), 220–232; or Clinton B. Schertizer and Jerome B. Kernan, "More on the Robustness of Response Scales," *Journal of the Marketing Research Society,* vol. 27 (October 1985), 262–282.
11. See also Otis Dudley Duncan and Magnus Stenbeck, "No Opinion or Not Sure?," *Public Opinion Quarterly,* vol. 52 (Winter 1988), 513–525; and Richard M. Durand and Zarrell V. Lambert, "Don't Know Responses in Survey: Analyses and Interpretational Consequences," *Journal of Business Research,* vol. 16 (March 1988), 533–543.
12. Scale development requires rigorous research. See, for example, Gilbert A. Churchill, "A Paradigm for Developing Better Measures of Marketing Constructs," *Journal of Marketing Research,* vol. 16 (February 1979), 64–73, for method; or S. Ram and Hyung-Shik Jung, "The Conceptualization and Measurement of Product Usage," *Journal of the Academy of Marketing Science,* vol. 18, no. 1 (1990), 67–76, for an example; Hugh M. Cannon, Kim Petit, and Cheryl Boglarsky, "Towards a Scale for Assessing the Nature of Advertising Knowledge," in Louis M. Capella, Henry W. Nash, Jack M. Starling, and Ronald D. Taylor, eds., "Progress in Marketing Thought," *Proceedings of the Southern Marketing Association* (1990), 320–323; Marsha L. Richins and Scott Dawson, "A Consumer Values Orientation for Materialism and Its Measurement: Scale Development and Validation," *Journal of Consumer Research,* vol. 19 (December 1992), 303–316.
13. Pam Humbaugh, "Duplicate Number Validation—The Value of the Extra Step," *Applied Marketing Research,* vol. 30, no. 2 (Second quarter 1990), 59–64.
14. For example, bogus recall was found negatively related to education, income, and age, but positively related to "yea-saying" and attitude toward the slogan. See Myron Glassman and John B. Ford, "An Empirical Investigation of Bogus Recall," *Journal of the Academy of Marketing Science,* vol. 16, nos. 3, 4 (Fall 1988), 38–41; Raghav Singh, "Reliability and Validity of Survey Research in Marketing: The State of the Art," in Robert L. King, ed., "Marketing: Toward the Twenty-First Century," *Proceedings of the Southern Marketing Association* (1991), 210–213; Milton M. Pressley, H. David Strutton, and Mark G. Dunn, "Demographic Sample Reliability among Selected Telephone Sampling Replacement Techniques," in Robert L. King, ed., "Marketing: Toward the Twenty-First Century," *Proceedings of the Southern Marketing Association* (1991), 214–219; Barry J. Babin, William R. Darden, and Mitch Griffin, "A Note on Demand Artifacts in Marketing Research," in Robert L. King, ed., "Marketing: Perspectives for the 1990s," *Proceedings of the Southern Marketing Association* (1992), 227–230; Richard A. Dunipace, Rita A. Mix, and Rob R. Poole, "Overcoming the Failure to Replicate Research in Marketing: A Chaotic Explanation," in Tom K. Massey, Jr., ed., "Marketing: Satisfying a Diverse Customerplace," *Proceedings of the Southern Marketing Association* (1993), 194–197; K. Patrick Malawian and Daniel D.

Butler, "The Semantic Differential: Is It Being Misused in Marketing Research?," in Ravi Achrol and Andrew Mitchell, eds., "Enhancing Knowledge Development in Marketing," *A.M.A. Educators' Conference Proceedings* (1994), 19.

Chapter 11

1. Humberto Valencia, "Hispanic Values and Subcultural Research," *Journal of the Academy of Marketing Science,* vol. 17, no. 1 (1990), 23–28.
2. Contributed by Mr. Joel Axelrod of BRX/Global, Inc. Personal communication with the authors.
3. Susan Carroll, "Questionnaire Design Affects Response Rate," *Marketing News,* vol. 28 (1994), H25; and Maria Elena Sanchez, "Effects of Questionnaire Design on the Quality of Survey Data," *Public Opinion Quarterly,* vol. 56 (1992), 206–217.
4. Earl Babbie, *Survey Research Methods,* 2nd ed. (Belmont, Calif.: Wadsworth Publishing Co., 1990), 131–132.
5. Shelby D. Hunt, Richard D. Sparkman Jr., and James Wilcox, "The Pretest in Survey Research: Issues and Preliminary Findings," *Journal of Marketing Research* (May 1982), 269–273.
6. Even simple words may be interpreted differently by respondents from what the researcher intends. See James H. Barnes and Michael J. Dotson, "The Effect of Mixed Grammar Chains on Response to Survey Questions," *Journal of Marketing Research,* vol. 26, no. 4 (November 1989), 468–472.
7. These guidelines are adapted from Pamela L. Alreck and Robert B. Settle, *The Survey Research Handbook* (Homewood, Ill.: Richard D. Irwin, 1995), 88–99; also see James H. Barnes and Michael J. Dotson, "The Effect of Mixed Grammar Chains on Response to Survey Questions," *Journal of Marketing Research* (November 1989), 468–472.
8. For memory questions, it is advisable to have respondents reconstruct specific events. See, for example, William A. Cook, "Telescoping and Memory's Other Tricks," *Journal of Advertising Research,* vol. 27, no. 1 (February/March 1987), RC5–RC8.
9. Alreck and Settle, *op. cit.,* 98.
10. Screens can be used to quickly identify respondents who will not answer honestly. See Kevin M. Waters, "Designing Screening Questionnaires to Minimize Dishonest Answers," *Applied Marketing Research,* vol. 31, no. 1 (Spring/Summer 1991), 51–53.
11. Based on Seymour Sudman and Norman Bradburn, *Asking Questions* (San Francisco: Jossey-Bass, 1982), 219–221.
12. Neils J. Blunch, "Position Bias in Multiple Choice Questions," *Journal of Marketing Research,* vol. 21 (November 1984), 216–220; Joe L. Welch and Cathy Owens Swift, "Question Order Effects in Taste Testing of Beverages," *Journal of the Academy of Marketing Science* (Summer 1992), 265–268; and Barbara A. Bickart, "Carryover and Backfire Effects in Marketing Research," *Journal of Marketing Research* (February 1993), 52–62.
13. Don A. Dillman, Michael D. Sinclair, and Jon R. Clark, "Effects of Questionnaire Length, Respondent-Friendly Design, and a Difficult Question on Response Rates for Occupant-Addressed Census Mail Surveys," *Public Opinion Quarterly,* vol. 57 (1993), 289–304.
14. Question order may also affect responses. See, for example, Stephen A. Ayidiya and McKee J. McClendon, "Response Effects in Mail Surveys," *Public Opinion Quarterly,* vol. 54, no. 2 (Summer 1990), 229–247.
15. Susan Carroll, "Questionnaire Design Affects Response Rate," *Marketing News,* vol. 28, no. 2 (1994), 14, 23.
16. Normally pretests are done individually, but a focus group could be used. See Steven A. Long, "Pretesting Questionnaires Minimizes Measurement Error," *Marketing News,* vol. 25, no. 11 (May 27, 1991), 12.
17. Response latency or subtle hesitations in respondents can be used as a pretest aid. See, for instance, John N. Bassili and Joseph F. Fletcher, "Response-Time Measurement in Survey Research," *Public Opinion Quarterly,* vol. 55 (1991), 331–346.

Chapter 12

1. Terrence F. Coen is vice president and director of sales and marketing at Survey Sampling, Inc. Mr. Coen has been a professional in information products for over 20 years. He has been involved in the design of sampling plan for over 50,000 marketing research studies.
2. This case is loosely based on Alfred J. Funk and Edward J. Neumann, "Future Banker: Lessons in Virtual Banking," *American Banker,* vol. 161, no. 221 (November 18, 1996), A7–10.
3. Susan Garland, "Money, Power and Numbers: A Firestorm Over the Census," *Business Week* (September 19, 1990), 45.
4. See, for example, Elizabeth Hervey Stephen and Beth J. Soldo, "How to Judge the Quality of a Survey," *American Demographics,* vol. 12, no. 4 (April 1990), 42–43.
5. Jane Foreman and Martin Collins, "The Viability of Random Digit Dialing in the UK," *Journal of the Market Research Society,* vol. 33, no. 3 (July 1991), 219–227; Firooz Hekmat and Madhav Segal, "Random Digit Dialing: Some Additional Empirical Observations," in David M. Klein and Allen E. Smith, eds., "Marketing Comes of Age," *Proceedings of the Southern Marketing Association* (1984), 176–180.
6. The option of random telephone number dialing may become expensive in the future. At least one state is considering a mandatory payment to consumers who are contacted by telemarketers. See Howard Schlossberg, "Marketing Researchers Face 'Increasingly Hostile' Legislation," *Marketing News,* vol. 27, no. 17 (August 16, 1993), 1, 8.
7. See John Latham, "Bias Due to Group Size in Visitor Surveys," *Journal of Travel Research,* vol. 29, no. 4 (Spring 1991), 32–35; Seymour Sudman, "Improving the Quality of Shopping Center Sampling," *Journal of Marketing Research,* vol. 17 (November 1980), 423–431; Johan de W. Bruwer, Norbert E. Haydam, and Binshan Lin, "Bias Reduction in Shopping Mall-Intercept Sureys: The Time-Based Systematic Sampling Method," in Ravi Achroll and Andrew Mitchell, eds., "Enhancing Knowledge Development in Marketing," *A.M.A. Educators' Conference Proceedings* (1994), 206–207.

8. See also Seymour Sudman, "Efficient Screening Methods for the Sampling of Geographically Clustered Special Populations," *Journal of Marketing Research,* vol. 22 (February 1985), 20–29.
9. Pym Cronish, "Geodemographic Sampling in Readership Surveys," *Journal of the Market Research Society,* vol. 31, no. 1 (January 1989), 45–51.
10. Adapted from Susan Ellerin, "Lies, Damn Lies and (Some) Readership Research," *Business Marketing,* vol. 74, no. 4 (1989), 56, 58.
11. For an application of referral sampling see Rowland T. Moriarity Jr. and Robert E. Spekman, "An Empirical Investigation of the Information Sources Used During the Industrial Buying Process," *Journal of Marketing Research,* vol. 21 (May 1984), 137–147.
12. James Rothman and Dawn Mitchell, "Statisticians Can Be Creative Too," *Journal of the Market Research Society,* vol. 31, no. 4 (October 1989), 456–466.
13. The need for substitutions can be affected by the respondent selection procedure. See, for example, Dan E. Hagen and Charlotte Meier Collier, "Must Respondent Selection Procedures for Telephone Surveys Be So Invasive?," *Public Opinion Quarterly,* vol. 47 (Winter 1982), 547–556; or Diane O'Rourke and Johnny Blair, "Improving Random Respondent Selection in Telephone Survey," *Journal of Marketing Research,* vol. 20 (November 1983), 428–432.
14. Cooperation is known to vary across demographic groups. See Bernard Guggenheim, "All Research Is Not Created Equal!," *Journal of Advertising Research,* vol. 29, no. 1 (February/March 1989), RC7–RC11.
15. "Meatless Alternatives at Every Meal," *Frozen Food Digest,* vol. 9, no. 4 (July 1994), 36–38.

Chapter 13

1. A different statistical analysis determination of sample size is through use of estimated effect sizes. See, for example, Thomas T. Semon, "Save a Few Bucks on Sample Size, Risk Millions in Opportunity Cost," *Marketing News,* vol. 28, no. 1 (1994), 19.
2. W. G. Eaton, "South Africa's Research Outlook Optimistic," *Marketing News,* vol. 22, no. 18 (August 29, 1988), 49, 51; Michael D. Geurts, Howard Christensen, and Del Scott, "The Trend to Using the Coefficient of Variation to Estimate Sample Sizes," in Terry L. Childers, et al., eds., "Marketing Theory Applications," *1991 A.M.A. Winter Educators' Conference Proceedings* (1991), 284–285.
3. Ronald E. Shiffler and Arthur J. Adams, "A Correction for Biasing Effects of Pilot Sample Size on Sample Size Determination," *Journal of Marketing Research,* vol. 24, no. 3 (August 1987), 319–321.

Chapter 14

1. Susan Krafft, "Who Slams the Door on Research?," *American Demographics,* vol. 13, no. 9 (1991), 14; also see Curt J. Dommeyer, Terry McGraw, and Karen Nestlerode, "Comparing Eager Respondents to Reluctant Respondents on Attitudes toward Survey Participation," in Donald Thompson, ed., "Marketing and Education: Partners in Progress," *Proceedings of the Atlantic Marketing Association* (1993), 219–223.
2. For a breakdown of the types of nonsampling errors encountered in business-to-business marketing research studies, see Gary Lilien, Rex Brown, and Kate Searls, "Cut Errors, Improve Estimates to Bridge Biz-to-Biz Info Gap," *Marketing News,* vol. 25, no. 1 (January 7, 1991), 20–22.
3. Intentional errors are especially likely when data is supplied by competitors. See Robin Croft, "How to Minimize the Problem of Untruthful Response," *Business Marketing Digest,* vol. 17, no. 3 (Third quarter 1992), 17–23.
4. To better understand this area, see Raymond A. Barker, "A Demographic Profile of Marketing Research Interviewers," *Journal of the Market Research Society,* vol. 29 (July 1987), 279–292.
5. These problems are international in scope. See Leon Kreitzman, "Market Research: Virgins and Groupies," *Marketing* (February 22, 1990), 35–38, for the United Kingdom.
6. Louis G. Pol and Thomas G. Ponzurick, "Gender of Interviewer/Gender of Respondent Bias in Telephone Surveys," *Applied Marketing Research,* vol. 29, no. 2 (Spring 1989), 9–13.
7. Jack Honomichl, "Legislation Threatens Research by Phone," *Marketing News,* vol. 25, no. 13 (June 24, 1991), 4; Cynthia Webster, "Consumers' Attitudes toward Data Collection Methods," in Robert L. King, ed., "Marketing: Toward the Twenty-First Century," *Proceedings of the Southern Marketing Association* (1991), 220–224.
8. See, for example, Jack Honomichl, "Making a Point—Again—For an 'Industry Identifier'," *Marketing News,* vol. 25, no. 11 (May 27, 1991), H35; or Betsy Spethmann, "Cautious Consumers Have Surveyors Wary," *Advertising Age,* vol. 62, no. 24 (June 10, 1991), 34.
9. Robert Arnett, "Mail Panel Research in the 1990s," *Applied Marketing Research,* vol. 30, no. 2 (Second quarter 1990), 8–10.
10. Not all observers share this view. See Howard Schlossberg, "Research's Image Better Than Many Think," *Marketing News,* vol. 25, no. 1 (January 7, 1991), 24–25.
11. Of course, eliminating the interviewer entirely may be an option. See Ken Horton, "Disk-based Surveys: New Way to Pick Your Brain,"' *Software Magazine,* vol. 10, no. 2 (February 1990), 76–77.
12. See Terry Childers and Steven Skinner, "Theoretical and Empirical Issues in the Identification Survey Respondents," *Journal of the Market Research Society,* vol. 27 (January 1985), 39–53; Jim L. Finlay and Fazal J. Seyyed, "The Impact of Sponsorship and Respondent Attitudes on Response Rate to Telephone Surveys: An Exploratory Investigation," in David L. Moore, ed., "Marketing: Forward Motion," *Proceedings of the Atlantic Marketing Association* (1988), 715–721; Ronald E. Goldsmith, "Spurious Response Error in a New Product Survey," in J. Joseph Cronin Jr. and Melvin T. Stith, eds., "Marketing: Meeting the Challenges of the 1990s," *Proceedings of the Southern Marketing Association* (1987), 172–175; Phillip E. Downs and John R. Kerr, "Recent Evidence on the Relationship between Anonymity and Response Variables," in

John H. Summey, Blaise J. Bergiel, and Carol H. Anderson, eds., "A Spectrum of Contemporary Marketing Ideas," *Proceedings of the Southern Marketing Association* (1982), 258–264; George Glisan and Jim L. Grimm, "Improving Response Rates in an Industrial Setting: Will Traditional Variables Work?," in John H. Summey, Blaise J. Bergiel, and Carol H. Anderson, eds., "A Spectrum of Contemporary Marketing Ideas," *Proceedings of the Southern Marketing Association* (1982), 265–268; Ronald D. Taylor, John Beisel, and Vicki Blakney, "The Effect of Advanced Notification by Mail of a Forthcoming Mail Survey on the Response Rates, Item Omission Rates, and Response Speed," in David M. Klein and Allen E. Smith, eds., "Marketing Comes of Age," *Proceedings of the Southern Marketing Association* (1984), 184–187; H. H. Friedman, "The Effects of a Monetary Incentive and the Ethnicity of the Sponsor's Signature on the Rate and Quality of Response to a Mall Survey," *Journal of the Academy of Marketing Science* (Spring 1979), 95–100; L. Goldstein and H. H. Friedman, "A Case for Double Postcards in Surveys," *Journal of Advertising Research* (April 1975), 43–49; Raymond Hubbard and Eldon L. Little, "Cash Prizes and Mail Response Rates: A Threshold Analysis," *Journal of the Academy of Marketing Science* (Fall 1988), 42–44; Terry L. Childers and O. C. Ferrell, "Response Rates and Perceived Questionnaire Length in Mail Surveys," *Journal of Marketing Research* (August 1979), 429–431; Terry L. Childers, William M. Pride, and O. C. Ferrell, "A Reassessment of the Effects of Appeals on Response to Mail Surveys," *Journal of Marketing Research* (August 1980), 365–370; T. Steele, W. Schwendig, and J. Kilpatrick, "Duplicate Responses to Multiple Survey Mailings: A Problem?," *Journal of Advertising Research* (March/April 1992), 26–33; James B. Wilcox, "The Interaction of Refusal and Not-at-Home Sources of Nonresponse Bias," *Journal of Marketing Research* (November 1977), 592–597.

13. A comparison on nonresponse errors under different incentives is Jonathan K. Barsky and Stephen J. Huxley, "A Customer-Survey Tool: Using the 'Quality Sample'," *The Cornell Hotel and Restaurant Administration Quarterly,* vol. 33, no. 6 (December 1992), 18–25.
14. Screening questionnaires can also be used. See Kevin M. Waters, "Designing Screening Questionnaires to Minimize Dishonest Answers," *Applied Marketing Research,* vol. 31, no. 1 (Spring/Summer 1991), 51–53.
15. For examples, see Dom Del Prete, "Clients Want More Specific Research—and Faster," *Marketing News,* vol. 25, no. 18 (September 2, 1991), 18; Keith Hawk, "More Marketers Going Online for Decision Support," *Marketing News,* vol. 24, no. 23 (November 12, 1992), 14; Martha Farnsworth Riche, "Look before Leaping," *American Demographics,* vol. 12, no. 2 (1990), 18–20; or Michael J. Wolfe, "New Way to Use Scanner Data and Demographics Aids Local Marketers," *Marketing News,* vol. 23, no. 19 (September 11, 1989), 8–9.
16. Lynn G. Coleman, "Researchers Say Nonresponse Is Single Biggest Problem," *Marketing News,* vol. 25, no. 1 (January 7, 1991), 32–33.
17. Mark Landler, "The 'Bloodbath' in Market Research," *Business Week* (February 11, 1991), 72, 74.
18. Julian Baim, "Response Rates: A Multinational Perspective," *Marketing & Research Today,* vol. 19, no. 2 (June 1991), 114–119.
19. Bill Farrell and Tom Elken, "Adjust Five Variables for Better Mail Surveys," *Marketing News* (August 29, 1994), 20.
20. Pradeep K. Tyagi, "The Effects of Appeals, Anonymity, and Feedback on Mail Survey Response Patterns from Salespeople," *Journal of the Academy of Marketing Science,* vol. 17, no. 3 (Summer 1989), 235–241.
21. *Marketing News,* "The Researchers' Response: Four Industry Leaders Tell How to Improve Cooperation" (August 16, 1993), A12.
22. Lester R. Frankel, "On the Definition of Response Rates," *A Special Task Force Report Published by the Council of American Survey Research Organizations,* 3 Upper Devon, Belle Terre, Port Jefferson, NY 11777.
23. For a comparison of response rates by mail versus fax, see John P. Dickson and Douglas L. MacLachlan, "Fax Surveys: Return Patterns and Comparison with Mail Surveys," *Journal of Marketing Research,* vol. 33, no. 1 (February 1996), 108–113.
24. For more complex procedures see J. Scott Armstrong and Terry S. Overton, "Estimating Nonresponse Bias in Mail Surveys," *Journal of Marketing Research,* vol. 14 (August 1977), 396–402; Dennis K. Pearl and David Fairley, "Testing for the Potential of Nonresponse Bias in Sample Surveys," *Public Opinion Quarterly,* vol. 49 (Winter 1985), 553–560; or Trevor Sharlot, "Weighting the Survey Results," *Journal of the Market Research Society,* vol. 28 (July 1986), 363–366.
25. For yea-saying and nay-saying, see Jerald G. Bachman and Patrick M. O'Malley, "Yea-Saying, Nay-Saying, and Going to Extremes: Black–White Differences in Response Styles," *Public Opinion Quarterly,* vol. 48 (Summer 1985), 491– 509.

Chapter 15

1. Laura Reina, "Who's Reading Newspapers?," *Editor & Publisher,* vol. 128, no. 45 (November 11, 1995), 24–25.
2. Information on Apian products may be found on the Apian homepage, http://www.apian.com. At the time of this writing, Merator's homepage was not operating; interested parties can contact Mercator at (508)-463-4093. An Internet reference for questionnaire development software is http://www.mercatorCorp.com

Chapter 16

1. For illumination, see Richard K. Burdick, "Statement of Hypotheses in the Analysis of Variance," *Journal of Marketing Research,* vol. 20 (August 1983), 320–324.

Chapter 17

1. Examples are Joseph R. DiFranza, et al., "RJR Nabisco's Cartoon Camel Promotes Camel Cigarettes to Children," *Journal of the American Medical Association,* vol. 266, no. 22 (1991), 3149–3153; Paul M. Fischer, et al., "Brand Logo Recognition

by Children Aged 3 to 6 Years," *Journal of the American Medical Association,* vol. 266, no. 22 (1991), 3145–3148; and John P. Pierce, et al., "Does Tobacco Advertising Target Young People to Start Smoking?," *Journal of the American Medical Association,* vol. 266, no. 22 (1991), 3154–3158.
2. Steven W. Colford and Ira Teinowitz, "Joe Camel Gets Reprieve, For Now," *Advertising Age* (June 6, 1994), 52.
3. Lucy L. Henke, "Young Children's Perceptions of Cigarette Brand Advertising Symbols: Awareness, Affect, and Target Market Identification," *Journal of Advertising,* vol. 24, no. 4 (Winter 1995), 13–28.
4. Here are some articles that use cross-tabulation analysis: Scot Burton and George M. Zinkhan, "Changes in Consumer Choice: Further Investigation of Similarity and Attraction Effects," *Psychology in Marketing,* vol. 4 (Fall 1987), 255–266; Alan J. Bush and James H. Leigh, "Advertising on Cable versus Traditional Television Networks," *Journal of Advertising Research,* vol. 24 (April/May 1984), 33–38; and Frederick W. Langrehr, "Consumer Images of Two Types of Competing Financial Institutions," *Journal of the Academy of Marketing Science,* vol. 13 (Summer 1985), 248–264.
5. Refer, also, to Emin Babakus and Carl E. Ferguson Jr., "On Choosing the Appropriate Measure of Association When Analyzing Rating Scale Data," *Journal of the Academy of Marketing Science,* vol. 16 (Spring 1988), 95–102.

Chapter 18

1. Residual analysis can take many forms. See, for example, A. P. Dempster and M. Gasko-Green, "New Tools for Residual Analysis," *Annals of Statistics,* vol. 9 (1981), 945–959.
2. See E. L. Melnick and F. R. Shoaf, "Regression Equals Analysis of Variance," *Journal of Advertising Research,* vol. 17 (June 1977), 27–31.
3. We admit that our description of regression is introductory. Two books that expand our description are Michael S. Lewis-Beck, *Applied Regression: An Introduction* (1980); Larry D. Schroeder, David L. Sjoffquist, and Paula E. Stephan, *Understanding Regression Analysis: An Introductory Guide* (1986), both published by Sage Publications, Inc., Newbury Park, California.
4. For more information, see, for example, Robert L. Mason, R. F. Gunst, and J. T. Webster, "Regression Analysis and Problems of Multicollinearity in Marketing Models: Diagnostics and Remedial Measures," *International Journal of Research in Marketing,* vol. 3, no. 3 (1986), 181–205.
5. See, for example, Shelby H. McIntyre, et al., "Evaluating the Statistical Significance of Models Developed by Stepwise Regression," *Journal of Marketing Research,* vol. 20 (February 1983), 1–11.
6. Regression analysis is commonly used in academic marketing research. Here are some examples: Francis X. Callahan, "Advertising and Profits 1969–1978," *Journal of Advertising Research,* vol. 22 (April/May 1982), 17–22; Alan J. Dubinsky and Michael Levy, "Influence of Organizational Fairness on Work Outcomes of Retail Salespeople," *Journal of Retailing,* vol. 65 (Summer 1989), 221–252; Jon B. Frieden and Phillip E. Downs, "Testing the Social Involvement Model in an Energy Conservation Context," *Journal of the Academy of Marketing Science,* vol. 14 (Fall 1986), 13–20; and Gerald J. Tellis and Claes Fornell, "The Relationship between Advertising and Product Quality Over the Product Life Cycle: A Contingency Theory," *Journal of Marketing Research,* vol. 25 (February 1988), 64–71. For an alternative to regression analysis, see Barbara S. Quaintance and George R. Franke, "Neural Networks for Marketing Research," in Robert L. King, ed., "Marketing: Toward the Twenty-First Century," *Proceedings of the Southern Marketing Association* (1991), 230–235.

Chapter 19

1. R. Deshpande and G. Zaltman, "Factors Affecting the Use of Market Research Information: A Path Analysis," *Journal of Marketing Research,* vol. 19 (February 1982), 14–31.
2. R. Deshpande and G. Zaltman, "A Comparison of Factors Affecting Researcher and Manager Perceptions of Market Research Use," *Journal of Marketing Research,* vol. 21 (February 1984), 32–38.
3. William Obee, *Contemporary Business Communications* (Boston: Houghton Mifflin, 1990), 416–425.
4. David Morris and Satish Chandra, *Guidelines for Writing a Research Report* (Chicago: American Marketing Association, 1993), 6.
5. To properly cite your sources see Kate L. Turabian, *A Manual for Writers of Term Papers, Theses, and Dissertations,* 6th ed. (Chicago: The University of Chicago Press, 1996); Joseph Gibaldi, *MLA Handbook for Writers of Research Papers,* 4th ed. (New York: The Modern Language Association of America, 1995); *Publication Manual of the American Psychological Association,* 4th ed. (Washington, D.C.: The American Psychological Association, 1994); *The Chicago Manual of Style,* 14th ed. (Chicago: The University of Chicago Press), 1993.
6. Kitty O. Locker, *Business and Administrative Communications* (Hillsdale, Ill.: Richard D. Irwin, 1990), 390.
7. Edward R. Tufte, *The Visual Display of Quantitative Information* (Cheshire, Conn.: Graphics Press, 1983).
8. Ronald E. Dulek and John S. Fielden, *Principles of Business Communication* (New York: Macmillan, 1990), 114–115.
9. The authors wish to thank Dr. Gerald U. Skelly, Professor of Business Administration, North Georgia College, for preparing this case.

Credits

Chapter 1

page xxii: General Motors Corporation, by permission. page 6: D. Young-Wolff/PhotoEdit. page 7: Courtesy of Sears, Roebuck and Co. page 13: Bacon's Clipping Bureau, by permission.

Chapter 2

page 18: Photo by permission. Fig. 2.1, page 22: Socratic Software, by permission. page 26: (left) New York AMA, by permission. (right) Quirk Enterprises, by permission. Fig. 2.4, page 31: NFO, by permission. Fig. 2.5, page 32: Quick Test, Inc., by permission. Fig. 2.6, page 33: Kidfacts Research, by permission. Fig. 2.7, page 34: Pulse Train Technology, LTD, by permission. Fig. 2.8, page 35: Genesys Sampling Systems, by permission. Fig. 2.9, page 36: NameQuest, by permission. Fig. 2.10, pages 40–41: Marketing Research Association, by permission.

Chapter 3

page 56: Brian Phillips/The Image Works. Photo © Brian Phillips. All rights reserved.

Chapter 4

page 82: John Coletti.

Chapter 5

page 108: Ariel Skelley/The Stock Market.

Chapter 6

page 138: U.S. Census Bureau. page 143: Text and artwork copyright © 1996 by Yahoo! Inc. All rights reserved. Yahoo! and the Yahoo! logo are trademarks of Yahoo! Inc. page 146: Jean-Claude LeJeune/Stock Boston. Fig. 6.2, page 157: U.S. Census Bureau.

Chapter 7

page 170: Information Resources, Inc., by permission. pages 178–180: Claritas Inc. page 187: Information Resources, Inc., by permission. page 189: NFO, by permission. pages 194–195: Copyright 1997 The Arbitron Company. Used with permission. May not be reproduced without the prior written permission from Arbitron.

Chapter 8

page 207: Will & Deni McIntyre/Photo Researchers, Inc. page 210: Volvo Cars of North America, Inc. page 212: C. W. McKeen/The Image Works. Photo © C. W. McKeen. All rights reserved. page 215: Daniel Grogan/ Uniphoto Picture Agency. page 216: D. Young-Wolff/PhotoEdit. page 221: Michael Newman/PhotoEdit. page 224: Frank Siteman/Stock Boston. page 226: Uniphoto Picture Agency. page 232: Tony Freeman/PhotoEdit.

Chapter 9

page 243: Decisive Technology, by permission. page 246: John Coletti. page 248: Robert Harbison. page 252: Tom McCarthy/PhotoEdit. page 254: R. Sidney/The Image Works. page 260: Richard Shock/Gamma-Liaison, Inc. page 265: Bard Wrisley/Gamma-Liaison, Inc.

Chapter 10

page 283: Barbara Alper/Stock Boston. page 285: Henry Sims/The Image Bank. page 291: Carroll Seghers/Photo Researchers, Inc. page 299: (top left) Michael Weisbrot/Stock Boston. (top right) Judy Gelles/Stock Boston. (center right) The Image Works. (bottom) John Running/Stock Boston. page 302: David Simson/Das Photo. page 307: Jim Coyners/Stock Boston. page 311: Antony Edwards/The Image Bank.

Chapter 11

page 320: Wal-Mart Stores, Inc., by permission. page 321: Hispanic Market Connections, by permission. Cartoon, page 334: By permission. Fig. 11.2, page 345: Mercator Corporation, by permission. Fig. 11.3, page 346: Mercator Corporation, by permission. Fig. 11.4, page 346: Mercator Corporation, by permission. Fig. 11.5, page 346: By permission.

Chapter 12

page 357: Uniphoto Picture Agency. page 361: Ronald F. Bush. page 364: Dave Jennings/AP/Wide World Photos. page 367: Tim Barnwell/Stock Boston. page 371: Kathleen Campbell/Gamma-Liaison, Inc. page 373: Steve Dunwell/The Image Bank. page 377: Michael Dwyer/Stock Boston. page 383: The Image Works.

Chapter 13

page 391: Michael Heron/Simon & Schuster/PH College. page 395: Andrew Klapatiuk/Gamma-Liaison, Inc. page 398: Rick Maiman/AP/Wide World Photos. page 410: Skjold/The Image Works.

Chapter 14

page 421: Mary Kate Denny/PhotoEdit. Fig. 14.2, page 441: Survey Sampling, Inc., by permission.

Chapter 15

page 451: Michael Newman/PhotoEdit. page 453: Uniphoto Picture Agency. page 455: Software Publishing Corp. page 457: David De Lossy/The Image Bank. page 473: L. D. Gordon/The Image Bank.

Chapter 17

page 533: D. Young-Wolff/PhotoEdit. page 539: AP/Wide World Photos. page 549: Anheuser-Busch Companies, Inc. page 556: Frank Herholdt/ Tony Stone Images.

Chapter 18

page 571: Zigy Kaluzny/Tony Stone Images. page 574: Corbis-Bettmann. page 580: John Coletti. page 585: Owen Franken/Stock Boston. page 592: Paul E. Johnson/Gamma-Liaison, Inc. page 598: Frank Siteman/Stock Boston. page 602: Peter Menzel/Stock Boston.

Chapter 19

page 611: Ronald F. Bush. page 633: Len Kaltman.

Index

NAMES

SUBJECTS

SPSS® 7.5 for Windows® Student Version Installation Instructions

What You Need to Run SPSS 7.5 for Windows Student Version

The minimum hardware and software requirements for SPSS 7.5 for Windows are:

- Windows 95 or Windows NT 3.51 or higher.
- An 80486 processor or higher, with a floating-point processor.
- 8MB or more of random-access memory (RAM) for Windows 95; 12MB of RAM for Windows NT.
- A hard disk with at least 25MB of available disk space (for the Base system). An additional 24 MB of hard disk space is required to run SPSS (virtual memory for temporary files).
- A high density 3 1/2-inch floppy disk drive or CD-ROM drive.
- A graphics adaptor with 640 x 480 resolution (VGA) or higher.

> Important: Before installing the software, please read the license agreement on the reverse side.

Installing SPSS 7.5 for Windows 95 or Windows NT 4.0

CD-ROM

To install SPSS, insert the CD-ROM into the CD-ROM drive. The first time you do this, the AutoPlay feature will present a dialog box, prompting you to choose one of the following options: Install SPSS, Browse the CD-ROM, or Exit. To run the Setup program, choose Install, and then follow the instructions that appear on the screen.

To update or modify your installation, you must invoke the Setup program manually:

1. Insert the CD-ROM into the CD-ROM drive.
2. From the Start menu, choose Run.
3. In the Run dialog box, type `d:\setup`. (If you are not using the ***D*** drive, type the appropriate drive location.)
4. Then follow the instructions that appear on the screen.

Diskettes

1. Insert the ***Installation Disk*** into the disk drive.
2. From the Start menu, choose Run.
3. In the Run dialog box, type `a:\setup`. (If you are not using the ***A*** drive, type the appropriate drive location.)
4. Then follow the instructions that appear on the screen.

Installing SPSS 7.5 for Windows NT 3.51

1. Insert the ***Installation Disk*** or the CD-ROM into the appropriate drive.
2. From the Program Manager or File Manager menus, choose:
   File
     Run
3. In the Run dialog box, type d:\setup. (If you are not using the ***D*** drive, type the appropriate drive location.)
4. Then follow the instructions that appear on the screen.

THIS LICENSE AGREEMENT IS YOUR PROOF OF LICENSE

THIS IS A LEGAL AGREEMENT BETWEEN YOU AND SPSS INC. (hereinafter "SPSS") TO USE A SINGLE-USER VERSION OF THE SPSS SOFTWARE (hereinafter "SOFTWARE"). If you do not agree to the terms of this License Agreement, immediately return the package. To license this SOFTWARE, you must be a student or an instructor using this SOFTWARE for educational purposes only. If you are not, immediately return the SOFTWARE to the place of purchase.

This SOFTWARE is protected by both United States copyright law and international copyright treaty provisions.

LICENSE
SPSS grants you a non-exclusive license to use the SOFTWARE in accordance with the following terms. SPSS retains title and all ownership rights to the SOFTWARE.

SPSS grants you a single-user license which allows one (1) designated individual, and only one (1) individual, the right to install and use the SOFTWARE on a home, work, and portable computer for educational purposes only.

SPSS grants you the right to make one (1) archival copy of the SOFTWARE for the sole purpose of backing up the SOFTWARE and protecting your investment from loss.

SPSS further grants you the right to transfer this license and the SOFTWARE to another party provided: 1) the other party accepts all terms of this agreement; 2) all copies of the SOFTWARE are transferred and you discontinue use of the SOFTWARE after transferring; 3) SPSS is promptly notified of the name and address of the other party and the serial number of the SOFTWARE; and 4) SPSS is not required to supply new media.

TERM AND TERMINATION
Failure to comply with any of these terms will terminate this agreement and your right to use the SOFTWARE. You may also choose to terminate the agreement at any time. Upon termination of this agreement, you must immediately destroy the SOFTWARE and all copies of it.

LIMITED WARRANTY
The media on which the SOFTWARE is furnished is warranted to be free of defects in workmanship and material under normal use for a period of sixty (60) days from the date of purchase by you. SPSS and its suppliers' sole responsibility and your exclusive remedy under this warranty will be to receive a replacement of the media or a full refund if SPSS or its suppliers are unable to deliver media free from defects in workmanship and materials.

You alone are responsible for determining which SOFTWARE best meets your particular needs for installing SOFTWARE and for the results obtained.

THIS SOFTWARE IS LICENSED "AS IS" WITHOUT WARRANTY AS TO ITS PERFORMANCE. EXCEPT FOR THE MEDIA WARRANTY PROVIDED ABOVE, THERE ARE NO WARRANTIES EXPRESSED OR IMPLIED, INCLUDING BUT NOT LIMITED TO IMPLIED WARRANTIES OF MERCHANTABILITY OR FITNESS FOR A PARTICULAR PURPOSE, AND ALL SUCH WARRANTIES ARE EXPRESSLY DISCLAIMED. IN NO EVENT SHALL SPSS OR ITS SUPPLIERS BE RESPONSIBLE FOR ANY INDIRECT OR CONSEQUENTIAL DAM-